Historical *Volume 2*
THEOLOGY
IN - DEPTH

· Themes and Contexts of Doctrinal Development since the First Century ·

David Beale

BOB JONES
UNIVERSITY PRESS

Greenville, South Carolina

Library of Congress Cataloging-in-Publication Data

Beale, David, 1944–
  Historical theology in-depth : themes and contexts of doctrinal development
since the first century / David Beale.
    pages cm
  Includes bibliographical references and index.
  Summary: "A closer look at the major theological developments in Christian
history"—Provided by publisher.
  ISBN 978-1-60682-468-9 (hardcover : alk. paper) — ISBN 978-1-60682-
469-6 (hardcover. : alk. paper) 1. Theology, Doctrinal—History. I. Title.
  BT21.3.B43 2013
  230.09—dc23

                          2012050567

BWHEBB [Hebrew] and BWGRKL [Greek] Postscript® Type 1 and TrueTypeT fonts
Copyright © 1994–2006 BibleWorks, LLC. All rights reserved. These Biblical Greek and
Hebrew fonts are used with permission and are from BibleWorks, software for Biblical
exegesis and research.

Design by Chris Taylor
Page layout by Michael Boone

© 2013 BJU Press
Greenville, South Carolina 29614
Bob Jones University Press is a division of BJU Press

Printed in the United States of America
All rights reserved

ISBN 978-1-60682-469-6

15   14   13   12   11   10   9   8   7   6   5   4   3   2   1

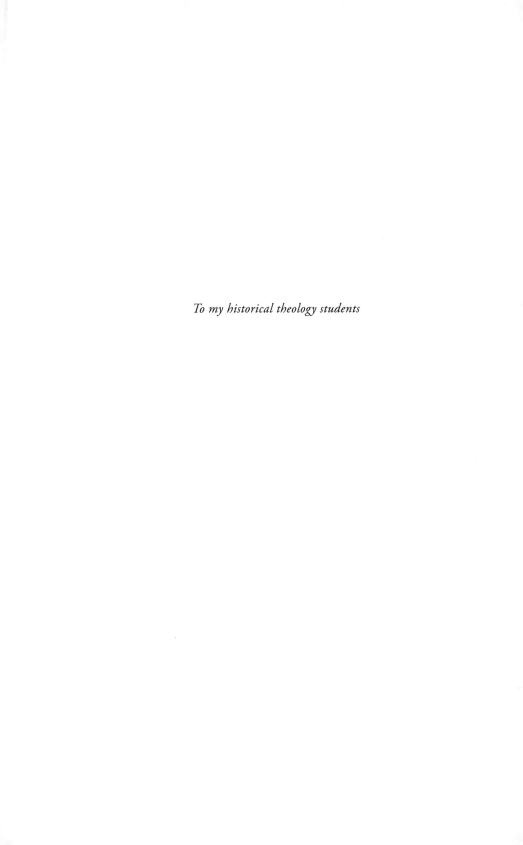

To my historical theology students

Contents

Abbreviations

AA   *Anno Adam* (Year of Adam) from creation; same as AM

ACO   Schwartz, E., et al., eds. *Acta Conciliorum Oecumenicorum* (Acts of Ecumenical Councils). Berlin: Walter de Gruyter, 1924–40.

AD   *Anno Domini* (or *Domine*) (Year of our Lord)—birth of Christ

AM   *Anno Mundi* (Year of the World) from creation; same as AA

ANF   Roberts, Alexander, and James Donaldson, eds. *The Ante-Nicene Fathers, Translations of the Fathers Down to A.D. 325.* 10 vols. Edinburgh: T. & T. Clark, 1866–72.

ASV   American Standard Version (1901)

BC   Before Christ's birth

CCEL   *Christian Classics Ethereal Library.* http://www.ccel.org/.

CCSL   Simonetti, Manlius, ed. *Corpus Christianorum, Series Latina.* Turnholt, Belgium: Brepols, 1961.

CSEL   *Corpus Scriptorum Ecclesiasticorum Latinorum,* an ongoing project by a group of Austrian scholars. The set is now approaching a hundred volumes. http://www.oeaw.ac.at/kvk/kv01.htm.

CT   *Codex Theodosianus* (Code of Theodosius)

ESV   English Standard Version (Crossway, 2001)

KJV   King James Version

LXX   Septuagint

NASB   New American Standard Bible (Lockman Foundation, 1973)

NIV   New International Version (Zondervan, 1984)

NKJV	New King James Version (Thomas Nelson, 1982)
NPNF 1	Schaff, Philip, ed. *A Select Library of Nicene and Post-Nicene Fathers of the Christian Church*. First series. 14 vols. New York: Christian Literature, 1886–90.
NPNF 2	Schaff, Philip, and Henry Wace, eds. *A Select Library of Nicene and Post-Nicene Fathers of the Christian Church*. Second series. 14 vols. New York: Christian Literature, 1890–1900.
NT	New Testament
OT	Old Testament
PG	Migne, J. P., ed. *Patrologiae Cursus Completus, Series Graeca*. 162 vols. Paris: J. P. Migne, 1857–66.
PL	Migne, J. P., ed. *Patrologiae Cursus Completus, Series Latina*. 221 vols. Paris: J. P. Migne, 1844–80.

*"Look carefully into the Scriptures, which are
the true utterances of the Holy Spirit."*
—*Clement of Rome,* Epistle to the Corinthians *(45)*

1

Martin Luther:
Progenitor of Lutheran Theology

As Augustinianism unfolds in the life of Augustine, Lutheranism germinates and blossoms in the life of Martin Luther. While its systematic and dogmatic expressions would derive primarily from Philip Melanchthon, Lutheranism is inseparable from the pilgrimage of its progenitor. The subsequent chapter will set forth the system of Lutheranism and how it differs from Reformed theology. The present chapter will establish the immediate setting of the German Reformation.[1]

Martin Luther was born shortly before midnight on November 10, 1483 to Hans and Margaret Luther in Eisleben, Saxony, Germany. Luther would die in the same city in 1546 at the age of sixty-two. Hans and Margaret named the firstborn after St. Martin of Tours and baptized him about eleven o'clock the next morning, St. Martin's Day, in the Church of St. Peter and St. Paul, just around the corner from their home.

---

[1] Helpful biographies include Roland H. Bainton, *Here I Stand: A Life of Martin Luther* (New York: Abingdon-Cokesbury, 1950); Heiko A. Oberman, *Luther: Man between God and the Devil*, trans. Eileen Walliser-Schwarzbart (New Haven, CT: Yale University Press, 1989); and Oskar Thulin, ed., *A Life of Luther*, trans. Martin O. Dietrich (Philadelphia: Fortress, 1966).

The Pathway to Luther's Conversion

Humble Origins

Eventually, Martin would have probably seven or eight siblings, yet only four (his brother Jacob and three sisters) lived to adulthood. Hans worked in the local copper mines. He and his ancestors came from the town of Möhra, a little half-timbered cluster in the Thuringian Forest. Hans's father owned a farm there, and if primogeniture had been the custom (as it was in England), Hans, as the eldest son, would have inherited that farm, and later his firstborn son, Martin, would have inherited that farm. But since the German system at that time was ultimogeniture, where the youngest son inherits the land, Luther's father headed north to Eisleben, became a copper miner, and a few months after Martin's birth, moved to Mansfeld. One is tempted to wonder, "What if Hans and Martin had inherited the farm in Möhra, where Martin would have had to stay home and help work the land as a boy?"

Pre-College Training

Before Martin was a year old, the family moved to Mansfeld, where, at the age of seven, he entered the Latin grammar school. When Martin was nine, Christopher Columbus set sail on his 1492 voyage.

At thirteen, Luther traveled forty miles north, to the bustling city of Magdeburg, on the Elbe River, where he entered the School of Common Brethren, which emphasized Renaissance humanism, with its Latin and strict discipline. Here, Luther learned that he could serve God in a secular sense. He learned not only to read music but Latin selections of classical works, along with a few portions of Scripture. Luther helped to support himself by singing in the streets—door-to-door—for handouts. Indeed, Luther's favorite subject was music, and he became proficient at playing the lute.

When fifteen, he moved to the town of Eisenach to complete his elementary education in St. George's Parish School. Here, he continued to sing and to pray in the streets to supplement his parents' support. A wealthy merchant's wife, Frau Ursala Cotta, would often open her home to him "on account of his hearty singing and praying." The hardships of youth, along with lack of refinement, would later reflect themselves in his appeal to the common people.

Meanwhile, back in Mansfeld, Hans Luther, "by sweat and labor," had managed to emerge from the copper mines in the bowels of the earth and to become an entrepreneur in mining and smelting; he now owned six foundries and had become a member of the town council. Hans could now afford to send Martin to the University of Erfurt—one of Germany's oldest and best. It had been founded in 1392, being Germany's third university after Heidelberg and Cologne. It would finally close its doors and go out of business in 1816. It reopened in modern facilities in 1994, on its 602nd anniversary and Erfurt's 1252nd anniversary.

University of Erfurt

The university, along with multiple churches and monasteries, prompted many to describe the city as "many-towered" Erfurt. Here, "*Martinus Ludher ex Mansfeld*" matriculated in May 1501, at the age of seventeen. The bachelor's degree in liberal arts consisted of the *trivium* (grammar, dialectic, and rhetoric) along with a little physics and philosophy. The program normally took about eighteen months to complete. It was designed to teach the student how to express himself. The BA was conferred upon Luther in September 1502, when he was eighteen years old.

Upon receiving his bachelor's degree, Luther began working on the master's degree in liberal arts, consisting of the *quadrivium* (geometry, mathematics, music, and astronomy), designed to teach the student to think logically and to qualify him for further training in one of three branches of law, theology, or medicine. While pursuing his master's degree, he taught grammar and logic in the university. In modern terms, the demands for earning the MA were relatively equivalent to those of the PhD. In fact, the MA would provide Luther the right and recognition to lecture publicly on moral philosophy.

He received his MA in January 1505, when he was twenty-one years of age, in a magnificent ceremony in which torches were carried before him in public procession. Proud father Hans came and presented his son with a huge, expensive copy of the *Corpus Juris Civilis* (*Body of Civil Law*). He expected Martin to study law for his life's work. Martin remained at the university as professor of moral philosophy and began his study of law in May 1505. However, he had lost interest in studying law. Deep in his heart, Luther's academic interest was theology. He had developed an awareness of the Bible during his undergraduate training and had read classical works that provided mental tools for developing logical and independent thinking. He was hungry for more of the Scriptures, and an opportunity was about to reveal itself.

Lightning Experience near Stotternheim

On July 2, 1505, as Luther was returning to Erfurt from a visit with his parents, a violent thunderstorm terrified him at Stotternheim, just a mile north of Erfurt. Falling to the ground, he cried out, "Help, beloved Saint Anne! I will become a monk." It was only natural that Luther would spontaneously call out to Saint Anne since to the Catholic Church she was the mother of the Virgin Mary and the patron saint of mine workers. The Luther family would have often invoked her name.

Inside Erfurt's Augustinian Monastery

On July 17, 1505, just two weeks after the lightning experience, and over his father's strong objections, twenty-one-year-old Martin Luther presented himself at the gate of Erfurt's Augustinian monastery of the Mendicant Friars—the hermit Eremites, called Observantines—the strictest of Erfurt's fourteen monasteries. The inmates' familiar black cowl (long, hooded gown or cloak) gave the place the name "black monastery." Luther would wear his black cowl until three years after his eventual excommunication. The cowl was held secure with an outer leather band (called a girdle). A frock or robe, called a habit, was placed over the shoulders. Underneath this black gown the monks wore a long white woolen shirt, symbolizing (and in honor of) the pure Virgin Mary. Meanwhile, his father, Hans, would object to Martin's new life until the deaths of two sons convinced him otherwise.

As required, upon entering the monastery, Luther gave away all of his possessions—books, clothing, eating utensils, the prized lute—everything! The first year was considered a probation period to see if the novice was really serious about becoming a monk. Luther far exceeded the monastery's severest demands. His rosary contained twenty-one beads, representing twenty-one saints he had chosen as his helpers, three for each day of the week. His tiny 6 x 9 foot cell had a bed, a chair, a prayer book on a table with a crucifix above it, and a whip nearby. The cell had one small window. It was on the door and above eye level. There was no privacy. The door opened from the outside. That cell, along with its meager articles of furniture, was destroyed by fire in 1872. It was later reconstructed and is now part of an orphanage.

In addition to whipping himself regularly, Luther forced himself to go without sleep for long periods of time, even exposing himself to freezing temperatures without a blanket. There was only one meal a day—at noonday—with one item on the menu, plus beer or wine. This was continuous controlled hunger, just short of starvation. One hundred days a year were fast days. At the end of his probation, he solemnly vowed to live in poverty, chastity, and obedience for the rest of his life. Meanwhile, the tormenting question of his heart was "What must I do to be saved?" The monastery offered no answer except for the counsel of Luther's best friend, Johann Von Staupitz, vicar general of the Augustinian Order.

Influence of Johann Von Staupitz

During his visits, Staupitz had learned of Luther's unrest. During their numerous talks, Luther confided to Staupitz that he could not rid himself of guilt for insubordination. He explained that while God commanded complete and unreserved love, He seemed to manifest Himself only in judgment, even terrorizing man for not loving Him enough. Out of fear of punishment, Luther wanted to love God but, as much as he tried, he could not. Staupitz gave the young monk some shocking advice. He told him to stop struggling with love and simply trust Christ's words, even if he could not love Him. Luther had never before heard this. He would eventually discover that to trust is to love and to love is to obey. When Luther was converted, some thirteen years later, he wrote a letter to Staupitz to say that it had been he who "first caused the light of the gospel to shine in the darkness" of his heart. Luther referred to Staupitz as his "first evangelical." Staupitz began to encourage Luther to enter the priesthood.

Meanwhile, the monastery had a theological seminary (an extension of the University of Erfurt), enabling him to earn several degrees in theology, including the *Formatus* (Licentiate) and the *Sententiarius* (Master of Sentences). These two degrees would be prerequisites for his later doctorate.

Ordination to the Priesthood

Luther received ordination on April 3, 1507, and said his first mass on May 2. He was twenty-three years old. He was amazed at his own unworthiness in "sacrificing" Christ. His father came with some friends to witness the solemn occasion. Hans brought a gift of twenty guilders, but he could still express no heartfelt sympathy with his son's work. Much later, when Martin had started to raise a family outside the church, the elderly father would voice more confidence in his son.

Transfer to University of Wittenberg

Under Staupitz's direction, Luther transferred to the University of Wittenberg in October 1508, where he was entrusted with the professorial chair of his monastic order in the faculty of the arts. He was twenty-four years old. He lectured for a semester on Aristotelian philosophy and ethics. While there he earned another theology degree, the *Baccalaureus Biblicus* (Bachelor of Bible), which was conferred in 1509 and which qualified him to lecture on the Bible. He was now beginning to study the Hebrew and Greek languages. Prince Frederick the Wise had founded the University of Wittenberg in 1502, in electoral Saxony, as a rival of the University of Leipzig. He had gone to Staupitz for recommendations for prospective faculty members. Frederick especially wanted to emphasize ancient sources rather than church traditions alone. From the fall of 1509 until spring of 1510, Luther was back at the University of Erfurt filling a temporary position of teaching theology. While his lectures focused on Peter Lombard's *Sentences* and Augustine's works, his personal time was spent studying Greek and Hebrew.

Trip to Rome

During 1510–11, Luther went on a business trip to Rome in behalf of seven Augustinian monasteries. He traveled with another monk and a lay brother. Journeying by foot for some forty days, Luther longed to see the "holy city." Years later, in his "Table Talks," he would describe details of this journey of some eight hundred miles across the Alps. Luther never speaks, however, of the wonderful natural beauties along the way. His only interest was religion. Childlike faith in Roman Catholic legends drove him on a frenzied round of Rome's holy places and relics. He wished his parents were already dead so that he might help them out of purgatory by reading mass in the Church of St. John of the Lateran. On bended knees, he ascended the twenty-eight steps of the Scala Santa. According to Roman Catholic myth, this is the staircase that Christ climbed to enter Pilate's Judgment Hall.

Years later, Luther would testify to his son, Paul, that at every step of the Scala Santa, the words of Romans 1:17, "The just shall live by faith," filled his heart in silent protest. In addition, he saw firsthand the shocking worldliness and unbelief of the Roman clergy, including Pope Julius II himself. The twenty-seven-year-old Martin Luther returned to Erfurt with profound doubts regarding the leadership of the Roman church.

Doctoral Oath and Chair of Theology

In 1511, Staupitz had transferred Luther back to the monastery at Wittenberg, where he would preach regularly, both in the monastery and in the town church. Here Luther resumed his work as lecturer in the university. The following year, on October 18, 1512, at the age of twenty-eight, he took his doctoral oath, "I wish to defend the evangelical truth with all my might" (*Juro me veritatem evangelicam pro virili defensurum*) and consequently, the chair of Biblical Theology. There was no special curriculum for the doctoral degree. This degree was awarded in acknowledgment of theological accomplishment and academic achievement, including public debate. Luther would remain in Wittenberg until his death in 1546. Altogether, he would spend thirty-six years of his life in Wittenberg.

The Influence of Scripture

Beginning in 1513, during his preparations for daily expositional lectures at the University of Wittenberg, the Bible made a powerful impact on Martin Luther. He lectured on these books of Scripture and in this order:

(1) Psalms (1513–15)
(2) Romans (1515–16)
(3) Galatians (1516–17)
(4) Hebrews (1517–18)
(5) Second series on the Psalms (1518–21)

Gradually, Luther was coming to reject the scholastic methods of interpretation. He now began applying the grammatical-historical approach to the Bible. He studied Greek under Melanchthon, while teaching theology to Melanchthon, who joined the faculty in 1518.

Luther was converted when he was about thirty-five years of age, in Wittenberg's Augustinian monastery, probably near the beginning of his second series on Psalms (1518–19). In their immediate context, the following words from Luther, "during that year," seem to point to 1518:[2] "I had already during that year returned to interpret the Psalter anew." Although "I lived as a monk without reproach, I felt that I was a sinner before God with an extremely disturbed conscience. I could not believe that [God] was placated by my satisfaction." As Luther's eyes were suddenly opened to the truth of Romans 1:17, he experienced saving grace and conversion: "Here I felt that I was altogether born again and had entered paradise itself through open gates. There[,] a totally other face of the entire Scripture showed itself to me." Although Luther had previously "hated" the term "righteousness of God," and even "the righteous God," when he experienced forgiveness, he found himself loving and extolling "God's righteousness" as the "sweetest" of phrases. Romans 1:17 had opened the "gate of paradise" to him: "For therein is the righteousness of God revealed from faith to faith: as it is written, The just shall live by faith." Luther now knew the experience of loving the only righteous and merciful God of heaven. A "joyous exchange" had occurred in his soul,[3] and the Augsburg Confession (1530) would explain it in terms of "imputed" righteousness:

---

[2] The immediate context of Luther's remark could also place his conversion in 1519, but prior to Johann Tetzel's death in July.

[3] The above citations of Luther's conversion are from Martin Luther, *Preface to the Complete Edition of Luther's Latin Writings* (Wittenberg, 1545), trans. Lewis

Men cannot be justified before God by their own powers, merits, or works; but are justified freely for Christ's sake through faith, when they believe that they are received into favor, and their sins forgiven for Christ's sake, who by his death hath satisfied for our sins. This faith doth God impute for righteousness before him. Rom. 3 and 4.[4]

The Pathway to Luther's Separation and Doctrinal Maturity

Beginning with 1517 the path to separation is easily traceable to the January 1521 excommunication from the Church and from there to the May 1521 secular edict of Worms, which declared him a public outlaw. As for his doctrinal growth, Luther explained, "I did not learn my theology at once, but had to seek ever deeper and deeper after it."[5]

The Ninety-Five Theses

Luther's Ninety-Five Theses reached the doors of Wittenberg's Castle Church on October 31, 1517, as a public invitation for scholarly debate on the subject of indulgences. The doors served as a bulletin board, and it was probably Luther who nailed them there. He had chosen the eve of All Saints Day (November 1) because this was a popular feast day that attracted professors, students, and all classes of people to a church with five thousand precious relics, owned and displayed in eight halls by Prince Frederick the Wise, just for this occasion.[6] The Castle Church, with the famous wooden doors, was

---

W. Spitz Sr., in *Career of the Reformer IV*, ed. Lewis W. Spitz, vol. 34 of Luther's *Works*, ed. Helmut T. Lehmann (Philadelphia: Muhlenberg Press, 1960), 336–37.

[4] Philip Schaff, *The Creeds of Christendom, with a History and Critical Notes* (New York: Harper and Brothers, 1877), 3:10. Even in 1517, Luther had at least started articulating hints of justification by faith, as shown by Julius Köstlin, *Theology of Luther in Its Historical Development and Inner Harmony*, trans. Charles E. Hay (Philadelphia: Lutheran Publication Society, 1897), 1:72–78. Luther's mature view is discussed in Köstlin, 2:435–53.

[5] See Heiko A. Oberman, *Luther: Man between God and the Devil*, 185.

[6] "'Official Catalogue' of Relics in the Wittenberg Castle Church," in *The European Reformations Sourcebook*, ed. Carter Lindberg (Malden, MA: Blackwell, 2000), 29.

destroyed by fire in 1760 during the Seven Years' War. The present doors, cast in bronze, were dedicated in 1858.

The Dominican friar Johann Tetzel had recently enraged Luther by selling indulgence notes that falsely promised to insure purchasers against purgatorial sufferings, or to release souls already there. Even though Frederick the Wise forbade Tetzel from selling indulgences in Saxony, Tetzel came to the bordering province of Magdeburg, only eighteen miles from Wittenberg (Saxony), and many people were crossing the border to make purchases. Tetzel traveled with great pomp and circumstance. Luther was concerned for the people of Wittenberg. Pope Leo X had called for indulgence sales in 1514 to help complete the rebuilding of St. Peter's Church in Rome[7] and in 1515 to benefit Albrecht of Hohenzollern (Brandenburg). In 1513, Albrecht had obtained the office of archbishop of Magdeburg before reaching the required minimal age. The following year, while still underage, he had acquired the archbishopric of Mainz, which made him one of the seven electors of the Holy Roman Empire. It did not seem to matter to anyone that he was guilty of simony (purchasing church offices) and pluralism (multiple office-holding). Albrecht had purchased these offices from the Roman Curia. The Fugger banking family of Augsburg had agreed to lend him the money when the pope agreed to arrange for indulgence sales for the repayment. As prescribed, a Fugger representative traveled along with Tetzel. Within weeks, Luther's Latin Theses were appearing in public places in German translation.

Luther unwittingly stepped into a hornet's nest when he naively sent a copy to Albrecht, asking him to stop Tetzel and his false teaching. He was completely unaware that the indulgence sales were for Albrecht's benefit and that Albrecht was a part of a scandal. Albrecht sent a copy of the Theses to Pope Leo X in Rome, urging the Curia to quash "the rash monk of Wittenberg." Leo X, dismissing the uproar as a "monkish squabble," replied, "It is a drunken German who wrote the Theses; when sober he will change his mind."

---

[7] For a helpful discussion, see R. A. Scotti, *Basilica: The Splendor and the Scandal: Building St. Peter's* (New York: Viking Penguin, 2006).

Popular Appeals, Papal Concerns, and Political Changes

Approval of the theses among the common people prompted a papal summons, in August 1518, for Luther to appear in Rome within sixty days to recant. When the papal legate, Cardinal Cajetan, demanded of Elector Frederick the Wise that he deliver up this "child of the devil," Frederick managed to protect Luther by arranging a meeting in Augsburg between Luther and Cajetan.[8] Frederick determined to keep the Reformer's hearings on German soil. Inside the Fugger Mansion in Augsburg, October 12–14, 1518, Luther and Cajetan held three talks that ended with the cardinal's threatening Luther with excommunication if he did not retract the Theses.[9] During January 4–6, 1519, a meeting in Lochau between Luther and papal secretary Karl von Miltitz failed to bring any permanent results. Both sides agreed not to attack one another until either side broke the agreement. Both sides would break the agreement at the Leipzig debate in July. For the moment though, all attention would turn to the major struggle over a successor to Emperor Maximilian I, who died January 10, 1519. Luther's Germany was a quilt-like maze of territories nominally under the Holy Roman Emperor. The seven most powerful magnates—four secular princes and three archbishops—served as the German electorate for replacing emperors. Periodically, the emperor would call the seven electors together, where he could hear grievances and appeal for money for building projects and for fighting the Turks. When Maximilian died, no German leader had the wealth, power, or will to seek such a powerful position.

The two leading candidates for emperor were Maximilian's grandson Charles I of Spain and Francis I of France.[10] And popes always kept constant Machiavellian eyes on the political scene. Seeking to maintain a delicate balance of ecclesiastical power between France and Spain, Pope Leo X extended his support to the German elector, Frederick the Wise. This could help to silence Luther! After all, the imperial coronation oath at Aachen would include a pledge to

---

[8] For more discussion, see Scott H. Hendrix, *Luther and the Papacy: Stages in a Reformation Conflict* (Philadelphia: Fortress, 1981).

[9] Carter Lindberg, ed., *The European Reformations Sourcebook*, 34–35.

[10] Henry VIII of England was a candidate but with little support.

protect the pope and his church. Frederick declined. On June 28, 1519, the electors unanimously selected Charles to be crowned as Emperor Charles V of the Holy Roman Empire. Facing multiple conflicts regarding Italy, Spain, France, and the ever-threatening Turks, the new emperor would be long-delayed before he could give sufficient attention to halting the Reformation. Meanwhile, Frederick the Wise would abandon his relics and defend Luther and the Reformation until his death, which would occur during the troublous time of the Peasant War in 1525.

Leipzig Debate with John Eck

During the years that Magellan's ships were groping their way around the globe, 1519–22, Martin Luther was boldly moving towards an inevitable break with Rome. Had he foreseen the break, he would have shrunk back in fear. "It was the love of truth that drove me to enter this labyrinth," said Luther. Led on by Providence, he confessed, "I do not control my life. I am driven into the middle of the storm." For eleven grueling days, beginning July 4, 1519, Luther debated Johann Eck, Dominican theology professor from Ingolstadt, Bavaria, on issues of papal authority. The faculty of the University of Leipzig had invited the Reformer Andreas von Carlstadt to debate Johann Eck. Luther and Melanchthon were present. After the Carlstadt-Eck debate, Luther himself was invited to debate Eck one-on-one. Luther welcomed the opportunity. This would be Luther's first opportunity to present his views publicly.[11] These debates took place in a large hall of Leipzig's Pleissenburg Castle, a site now occupied by the Town Hall. Topics focused on papal and conciliar authority.

While Eck appealed primarily to church councils and tradition, Luther appealed primarily to Scripture. Luther contended that "this rock" of Matthew 16:18 is Peter's confession of faith and that, in Matthew 18:18–19, Christ gave the authority of binding and loosing to the whole church.[12] When Eck resorted to calling Luther a Hussite, Luther at first felt offended. During a break-time, he visited

---

[11] For more discussion, see Donald J. Ziegler, ed., *Great Debates of the Reformation* (New York: Random House, 1969).

[12] For more, see Köstlin, *Theology of Luther*, 1:294–98.

the library to learn more about John Huss's teachings. Here he was assured that Huss had indeed taught scriptural truths for which the Council of Constance had unjustly condemned and burned him. From this point forward, Martin Luther lost all confidence both in the popes and in the councils of the Roman Catholic Church.

Papal Bull of Condemnation

On June 15, 1520, the pope issued the Bull of Condemnation, *Exsurge Domine* (Arise Lord), from its two opening words from Psalm 74:22, "Arise, O God, plead thine own cause: remember how the foolish man reproacheth thee daily." The papal bull denounced forty-one propositions selected from Luther's writings as erroneous or heretical. It was called a bull because it contained the pope's official seal, the *bulla*, from which we get the English word *bulletin*. Since, however, *bulla* (*bullio*) literally means "water bubble," some of Luther's students threw printed copies into the river, saying, "It is only a water bubble; let it float on the water!" The document forbade all reading, printing, or publishing of any of Luther's works and ordered all of his works burned. It ordered all secular authorities, on threat of excommunication, to exclude Luther and his followers from their territories and to turn the heretic over to Rome at once. It threatened the interdict on any place harboring Luther or his followers. It threatened Luther with excommunication if he did not recant within sixty days. In Rome's Piazza Navona, Luther was burned in effigy and his books thrown to the flames. Officials in Cologne also burned Luther's books.

Luther's Reformation Treatises

In the crucible of confrontation, Luther forged the Reformation's creed: *Sola Scriptura*, *Sola Fide*, and *Sola Gratia* ("Scripture Alone, Faith Alone, and Grace Alone"). That message reached its climax in three Reformation manifestos that Luther wrote and published between June and October of 1520. In his *Address to the Christian Nobility of the German Nation*, he emphasized the absolute authority of *sola scriptura*; in *Babylonian Captivity of the Church*, he emphasized justification by *sola fide*; and in *The Freedom of the Christian Man*, he emphasized the priesthood of every believer by *sola gratia*.[13]

Luther's Bonfire and Excommunication

On the morning of December 10, 1520, the expiration date for the grace period of the papal *Exsurge Domine*, Luther invited the faculty and students of the university to assemble outside Wittenberg's Elster Gate for a bonfire. They too could burn books. Into the flames they committed books written by the papal hierarchy, the papal constitutions, and a copy of the canon law, which Luther described as "the abomination of desolation." For good measure, Luther tossed in a copy of the *Exsurge Domine*. Excommunication would be emancipation. Students paraded through the town in celebration of this monumental break from the "Romish Antichrist." Papal reaction, especially to Luther's three treatises, was the Bull of Excommunication, *Decet Romanun Pontificem* (January 3, 1521). The ecclesiastical break was complete. A secular break was inevitable.

Worms (1521)

On March 6, 1521, Luther was summoned to appear at an official diet, or court, in Worms. Granted safe conduct, with an imperial herald in coat-of-arms leading the way, Luther made his way to the city. He arrived on the 16th of April. Warfare has since destroyed the gateway through which Luther's wagon, surrounded by supporters, entered Worms in triumphant procession. The house where he stayed has since given way to a shopping mall. The imperial palace in which the diet met was destroyed in 1689, and the exact site is now occupied by a garden near the cathedral. In the late afternoon of the 17th of April, a thirty-seven-year-old Martin Luther stood before a hall filled with an august assembly. Here sat the twenty-one-year-old Emperor Charles V, with princes, prelates, bishops, archbishops, nobles, gentry, burghers, foreign ambassadors, and doctors of the law. Luther's books had been placed on a table. The appointed official asked Luther two questions. Were these books his? And was he

---

[13] For valuable discussion, see "The Three Principal Reformatory Publications," in Julius Köstlin, *Theology of Luther*, 1:368–438; see also Lindberg, ed., *The European Reformations Sourcebook*, 36–40.

ready to retract them? To the first, he acknowledged that they were his. The second question would require time for reflection. He was given twenty-four hours, and he prayed all that night. Close friends kept vigilant watch outside Luther's door and wrote down parts of the Reformer's outpouring prayers:

O Almighty and Everlasting God! How terrible is this world! Behold, it opens its mouth to swallow me up, and I have so little trust in Thee! . . . How weak is the flesh, and Satan how strong! If it is only in the strength of this world that I must put my trust, all is over! . . . My last hour is come, my condemnation has been pronounced! . . . O God! O God! . . . O God! Help me against all the wisdom of the world! Do this; Thou shouldst do this . . . Thou alone . . . for this in not my work, but Thine. I have nothing to do here, nothing to contend for with these great ones of the world! I should desire to see my days flow on peaceful and happy. But the cause is Thine . . . and it is a righteous and eternal cause. O Lord! Help me! Faithful and unchangeable God! In no man do I place my trust. It would be vain! All that is of man is uncertain; all that cometh of man fails. . . .Thou hast chosen me for this work. I know it well! . . . Act, then, O God! Stand at my side, for the sake of thy well-beloved Jesus Christ, who is my defense, my shield, and my strong tower.

After a moment of silent struggle, Luther continues:

I will never separate myself from Thee, neither now nor through eternity! . . . And though the world should be filled with devils— though my body, which is still the work of Thy hands, should be slain, be stretched upon the pavement, be cut to pieces . . . reduced to ashes—my soul is Thine! . . . Yes! Thy Word is my assurance of it. My soul belongs to Thee! It shall abide forever with Thee . . . Amen! O God! Help me! . . . Amen![14]

The following evening, Luther was led into a larger, torch-lit room packed to suffocation with secular and ecclesiastical notables. To the second question, he then replied:

Since your most serene majesty and your high mightinesses require from me a clear, simple, and precise answer, I will give you

---

[14] J. H. Merle d'Aubigné, *History of the Reformation of the Sixteenth Century*, trans. H. White (New York: American Tract Society, n.d.), 2:242–43; see also Philip S. Watson, *Let God Be God: An Interpretation of Martin Luther* (Philadelphia: Muhlenberg Press, 1947).

one, and it is this: I cannot submit my faith either to the pope or to the councils, because it is clear as the day that they have frequently erred and contradicted each other. Unless therefore I am convinced by the testimony of Scriptures, or by the clearest reasoning—unless I am persuaded by means of the passages I have quoted—and unless they thus render my conscience bound by the Word of God, I cannot and I will not retract, for it is unsafe for a Christian to speak against his conscience.

After a momentary pause as he glanced across his audience, Luther concluded in German (at least in substance), "Here I stand. I can do no other; God help me! Amen!"[15] (*Hier steh' ich. Ich kann nicht anders. Gott helfe mir! Amen.*) Those words reflect the Reformer's true sentiments during that momentous occasion and for the rest of his life.

Luther departed from Worms on the 26th of April. Within days the emperor placed him under imperial ban. The official edict was issued on May 26, 1521. The secular break was complete. The edict proclaimed Martin Luther a public outlaw banned from the empire and wanted for execution as a dangerous heretic.[16] But Luther would live another twenty-five years and die of natural causes in his German homeland. Until it had run the course of Providence, no human power could halt the Reformation.

Wartburg Castle and the Luther Bible

On May 4, during Luther's journey from Worms, horsemen suddenly surrounded his wagon in the Thüringen forest. Luther was not surprised. In a planned mock abduction, they spirited him off to a castle commanding a ridge over Eisenach. It is called the Wartburg. Disguising himself as a bearded squire, "Junker Georg," with tonsure growing into unruly dark hair, Luther would live here for the next ten months under the protective custody of Frederick the Wise. Rumors abounded that Luther was dead. One supporter, the famous German artist, Albrecht Dürer, exclaimed, "O God, if Luther is dead, who will from now on present the Gospel to us so clearly?"[17]

---

[15] J. H. Merle d'Aubigné, 2:248–49.

[16] Lindberg, ed., *The European Reformations Sourcebook*, 44–45.

[17] "Albrecht Dürer (1471–1528): Rumors of Luther's Capture," in Lindberg, ed., *The European Reformations Sourcebook*, 45.

Providentially, Erasmus had published the first edition of his Greek New Testament in 1516, just a year before the nailing of Luther's Theses. Now, working at a feverish pace in his castle study, Luther translated the entire New Testament into German from Erasmus's text in eleven weeks. Beautifully illustrated with woodcuts from Lucas Cranach's workshop and selections from Albrecht Dürer's own Apocalypse series, Luther's *Das Newe Testament Deutzsch* would be published in September 1522. An estimated five thousand copies would be sold in the first two months. Luther's complete Bible translation would appear in 1534. Luther had replaced the authority of the Roman Catholic Church with the authority of the written Word of God for doctrine and practice. Unlike leaders of the Reformed branches of Protestantism, however, Luther assumed that the Roman Catholic Church had determined the biblical canon.

To Luther the only essential principle of canonicity is justification by faith, and that makes the book of James a "right strawy epistle."[18] Indeed, in terms of canonicity, Luther assigned four New Testament books to a questionable status: Hebrews, James, Jude, and Revelation. He never considered himself as sitting in judgment on the Word of God. In his view, the true canon lies within the traditional canon and becomes its own judge. Thus, under the spotlight of Paul's epistles, the book of James appears to Luther as something contradictory and unprofitable. Luther seems oblivious to the fact that, in James, deeds of love are the inevitable expressions, or evidences, of saving faith. Even the Anabaptists Menno Simons[19] and Melchior Hofmann expressed concern that Luther's view was latent with antinomian tendencies. Hofmann writes of Lutherans who cry, "Believe, believe; grace, grace," but whose faith evidences no fruit.[20]

Luther's German translation, however, included all sixty-six books of the Protestant Bible. While at the Wartburg Castle, he wrote

---

[18] *Luther's Works*, gen. ed., Helmut T. Lehmann (St. Louis: Concordia Publishing House, 1960), 35:362. For more discussion, see Timothy George, "'A Right Strawy Epistle': Reformation Perspectives on James," *The Southern Baptist Journal of Theology* 4, no. 3 (Fall 2000): 20–31.

[19] *The Complete Writings of Menno Simons*, trans. Leonard Verduin and ed. John Wenger (Scottdale, PA: Herald Press, 1956), 333–34.

[20] "The Ordinance of God," in *Spiritual and Anabaptist Writers*, ed. G. H. Williams (London: SCM Press, 1957), 201.

fourteen additional treatises, along with some fifty letters. He left the Wartburg on March 1, 1522, and arrived back in Wittenberg five days later. It was during and soon after his seclusion in the Wartburg that external circumstances, such as revolts among the peasants and challenges from theologians, prompted Luther to formulate and express some of his key doctrines in a mature manner. These include the Reformer's teaching on baptism and the Eucharist.

Luther on Baptism

In Luther's view, "baptism is not simply common water, but it is the water comprehended in God's command, and connected with God's Word." It is efficacious since "it worketh forgiveness of sins, delivers from death and the devil, and gives everlasting salvation to all who believe, as the Word and promise of God declare." Luther explains,

> It is not water, indeed, that does it, but the Word of God which is with and in the water, and faith, which trusts in the Word of God in the water. For without the Word of God the water is nothing but water, and no baptism; but with the Word of God it is a baptism—that is, a gracious water of life and a washing of regeneration in the Holy Ghost.

Luther immediately adds Titus 3:5*b*–7: "By the washing of regeneration, and renewing of the Holy Ghost; which he shed on us abundantly through Jesus Christ our Savior; that being justified by his grace, we should be made heirs according to the hope of eternal life." Baptism "signifies that the old Adam in us is to be drowned by daily sorrow and repentance, and perish with all sins and evil lusts; and that the new man should daily come forth again and rise, who shall live before God in righteousness and purity forever."[21]

While clearly rejecting the notion that baptism removes original sin, Luther defended infant baptism on the premise that baptism is analogous to Old Testament circumcision, which he viewed as an efficacious sacrament in which the infant's faith was provided

---

[21] Luther, *Small Catechism* (1529), in Schaff, *The Creeds of Christendom*, 3:85–87. The catechism at times reflects Luther's tendency to keep the status quo. For instance, as he had been taught from boyhood, Luther omits Moses' second commandment ("Thou shalt not make unto thee any graven image. . . .") and splits the last commandment into two in order to have a total of ten. Schaff, 3:74–77.

vicariously and miraculously by the faith of the Old Testament church. Luther added that if such teaching is false, there has been no church on earth since the earliest New Testament times. He insisted that the spiritual condition of the administrator has no relevance to the efficacy of the baptism. For illustration, he appealed to the fourth-century tradition of the Alexandrian bishop, Alexander, who happened to be watching from his upper window when he saw the boy Athanasius at play performing baptism on the other children playing at the seashore with him. According to the story, Alexander accepted the baptisms as valid and efficacious.[22]

While we discuss this more fully in the next chapter, concerning Christ's presence in the Eucharist, Luther essentially adhered to a real and literal presence: "It is the true body and blood of our Lord Jesus Christ, under the bread and wine, given unto us Christians to eat and to drink, as it was instituted by Christ himself. . . . The remission of sins, life and salvation are given us in the sacrament."[23]

Marriage and Family Life

On June 13, 1525, Martin Luther married Katherine von Bora, the daughter of an impoverished Saxon nobleman. Two years before her marriage, Katherine, with eleven other nuns, had fled from a Nimbschen convent to Wittenberg and found shelter in a home. The newlyweds would turn the old Wittenberg monastery into the Luther House (*Lutherhalle*) and raise a family here. Sixteen years younger than Luther, Katie proved herself more than a good house-wife and gardener. She even administered the household expenses. It was said that Dr. Luther did not have a clue about how to run a household, especially one that would eventually include six children, numerous relatives, and a large number of students. In the evenings, the household would delight in Luther's entertaining conversation, much of which was transcribed and later published as *Table Talk*.

---

[22] For the substance of this paragraph, I am indebted to the valuable discussion from a Lutheran perspective and with primary sources in Köstlin, *Theology of Luther*, 2:45–58, 502–11.

[23] Luther, *Small Catechism* (1529), in Schaff, *The Creeds of Christendom*, 3:90–92.

Final Years and Lasting Legacy

Luther spent his last twenty years completing and editing his Bible translations, and writing commentaries, numerous essays, letters, and hymns. Besides the Bible translation, his other works fill 102 volumes in the famous Weimar edition. To the end of his life, he continued teaching in the University of Wittenberg, preaching regularly in the City Church, and resolving multiple conflicts. In early 1546, Luther returned to Eisleben to settle a family quarrel between the princes of Mansfeld.

Accomplishing his mission, he fell sick there in the town of his birth. He seemed to know that he was dying. A little past one o'clock on the morning of February 18, he was heard repeating Psalm 31:5, "Into thine hand I commit my spirit: thou hast redeemed me, O Lord God of truth." A while later, he prayed,

> I thank you, God and Father of our Lord Jesus Christ, that you have revealed your dear son to me, in whom I have believed, whom I have loved, and whom I have preached, confessed, and trusted. My Lord Jesus Christ, I commend my little soul to you. O heavenly father, I know that even though I am separated from this body, I shall live with you eternally. "For God so loved the world that he gave his only Son, that whosoever believes in him shall not perish but have eternal life" (John 3:16).

As Luther seemed to be slipping away, his doctor and an old friend, Michael Coelius, started shouting, "Reverend father, are you ready to die trusting in your Lord Jesus Christ, and to confess the doctrine which you have taught in his name?"[24] Everyone in the room heard the Reformer's quick "Ja!" A few minutes before three o'clock in the morning, he passed into eternity. His body was returned to Wittenberg and laid to rest in front of the pulpit of the Castle Church. Friends later found a note scribbled on a paper lying on Luther's bedside desk. It contained his last known written words. Half in German, half in Latin, it reads, *Wir sein Pettler, Hoc est Verum* ("We are beggars, that is true.").[25]

---

[24] Michael Coelius's eye-witness account, *The Death of the Reformer*, in Oskar Thulin, ed., *A Life of Luther*, trans. Martin O. Dietrich (Philadelphia: Fortress, 1966), 128–29.

[25] For more details see Timothy George, "Yearning for Grace: Martin Luther," in *Theology of the Reformers* (Nashville: B&H Publishing Group, 1999), 104.

Martin Luther's Ninety-Five Theses

Disputation of Doctor Martin Luther on the Power and Efficacy of Indulgences October 31, 1517[26]

Out of love for the truth and the desire to bring it to light, the following propositions will be discussed at Wittenberg, under the presidency of the Reverend Father Martin Luther, Master of Arts and of Sacred Theology, and Lecturer in Ordinary on the same at that place. Wherefore he requests that those who are unable to be present and debate orally with us, may do so by letter.

In the Name our Lord Jesus Christ. Amen.

1. Our Lord and Master Jesus Christ, when He said Poenitentiam agite, willed that the whole life of believers should be repentance.

2. This word cannot be understood to mean sacramental penance, i.e., confession and satisfaction, which is administered by the priests.

3. Yet it means not inward repentance only; nay, there is no inward repentance which does not outwardly work divers mortifications of the flesh.

4. The penalty [of sin], therefore, continues so long as hatred of self continues; for this is the true inward repentance, and continues until our entrance into the kingdom of heaven.

5. The pope does not intend to remit, and cannot remit any penalties other than those which he has imposed either by his own authority or by that of the Canons.

6. The pope cannot remit any guilt, except by declaring that it has been remitted by God and by assenting to God's remission; though, to be sure, he may grant remission in cases reserved to his judgment. If his right to grant remission in such cases were despised, the guilt would remain entirely unforgiven.

7. God remits guilt to no one whom He does not, at the same time, humble in all things and bring into subjection to His vicar, the priest.

8. The penitential canons are imposed only on the living, and, according to them, nothing should be imposed on the dying.

---

[26] The source of the document is Martin Luther, "Disputation of Doctor Martin Luther on the Power and Efficacy of Indulgences," in *Works of Martin Luther*, trans. and ed. Adolph Spaeth, et al. (Philadelphia: A. J. Holman, 1915), 1:29–38.

9. Therefore the Holy Spirit in the pope is kind to us, because in his decrees he always makes exception of the article of death and of necessity.

10. Ignorant and wicked are the doings of those priests who, in the case of the dying, reserve canonical penances for purgatory.

11. This changing of the canonical penalty to the penalty of purgatory is quite evidently one of the tares that were sown while the bishops slept.

12. In former times the canonical penalties were imposed not after, but before absolution, as tests of true contrition.

13. The dying are freed by death from all penalties; they are already dead to canonical rules, and have a right to be released from them.

14. The imperfect health [of soul], that is to say, the imperfect love, of the dying brings with it, of necessity, great fear; and the smaller the love, the greater is the fear.

15. This fear and horror is sufficient of itself alone (to say nothing of other things) to constitute the penalty of purgatory, since it is very near to the horror of despair.

16. Hell, purgatory, and heaven seem to differ as do despair, almost-despair, and the assurance of safety.

17. With souls in purgatory it seems necessary that horror should grow less and love increase.

18. It seems unproved, either by reason or Scripture, that they are outside the state of merit, that is to say, of increasing love.

19. Again, it seems unproved that they, or at least that all of them, are certain or assured of their own blessedness, though we may be quite certain of it.

20. Therefore by "full remission of all penalties" the pope means not actually "of all," but only of those imposed by himself.

21. Therefore those preachers of indulgences are in error, who say that by the pope's indulgences a man is freed from every penalty, and saved;

22. Whereas he remits to souls in purgatory no penalty which, according to the canons, they would have had to pay in this life.

23. If it is at all possible to grant to any one the remission of all penalties whatsoever, it is certain that this remission can be granted only to the most perfect, i.e., to the very fewest.

24. It must needs be, therefore, that the greater part of the people are deceived by that indiscriminate and high-sounding promise of release from penalty.

25. The power which the pope has, in a general way, over purgatory, is just like the power which any bishop or curate has, in a special way, within his own diocese or parish.

26. The pope does well when he grants remission to souls [in purgatory], not by the power of the keys (which he does not possess), but by way of intercession.

27. They preach man who say that so soon as the penny jingles into the money-box, the soul flies out [of purgatory].

28. It is certain that when the penny jingles into the money-box, gain and avarice can be increased, but the result of the intercession of the Church is in the power of God alone.

29. Who knows whether all the souls in purgatory wish to be bought out of it, as in the legend of Sts. Severinus and Paschal.

30. No one is sure that his own contrition is sincere; much less that he has attained full remission.

31. Rare as is the man that is truly penitent, so rare is also the man who truly buys indulgences, i.e., such men are most rare.

32. They will be condemned eternally, together with their teachers, who believe themselves sure of their salvation because they have letters of pardon.

33. Men must be on their guard against those who say that the pope's pardons are that inestimable gift of God by which man is reconciled to Him;

34. For these "graces of pardon" concern only the penalties of sacramental satisfaction, and these are appointed by man.

35. They preach no Christian doctrine who teach that contrition is not necessary in those who intend to buy souls out of purgatory or to buy confessionalia.

36. Every truly repentant Christian has a right to full remission of penalty and guilt, even without letters of pardon.

37. Every true Christian, whether living or dead, has part in all the blessings of Christ and the Church; and this is granted him by God, even without letters of pardon.

38. Nevertheless, the remission and participation [in the blessings of the Church] which are granted by the pope are in no way to be despised, for they are, as I have said, the declaration of divine remission.

39. It is most difficult, even for the very keenest theologians, at one and the same time to commend to the people the abundance of pardons and [the need of] true contrition.

40. True contrition seeks and loves penalties, but liberal pardons only relax penalties and cause them to be hated, or at least, furnish an occasion [for hating them].

41. Apostolic pardons are to be preached with caution, lest the people may falsely think them preferable to other good works of love.

42. Christians are to be taught that the pope does not intend the buying of pardons to be compared in any way to works of mercy.

43. Christians are to be taught that he who gives to the poor or lends to the needy does a better work than buying pardons;

44. Because love grows by works of love, and man becomes better; but by pardons man does not grow better, only more free from penalty.

45. Christians are to be taught that he who sees a man in need, and passes him by, and gives [his money] for pardons, purchases not the indulgences of the pope, but the indignation of God.

46. Christians are to be taught that unless they have more than they need, they are bound to keep back what is necessary for their own families, and by no means to squander it on pardons.

47. Christians are to be taught that the buying of pardons is a matter of free will, and not of commandment.

48. Christians are to be taught that the pope, in granting pardons, needs, and therefore desires, their devout prayer for him more than the money they bring.

49. Christians are to be taught that the pope's pardons are useful, if they do not put their trust in them; but altogether harmful, if through them they lose their fear of God.

50. Christians are to be taught that if the pope knew the exactions of the pardon-preachers, he would rather that St. Peter's church should go to ashes, than that it should be built up with the skin, flesh and bones of his sheep.

51. Christians are to be taught that it would be the pope's wish, as it is his duty, to give of his own money to very many of those from whom certain hawkers of pardons cajole money, even though the church of St. Peter might have to be sold.

52. The assurance of salvation by letters of pardon is vain, even though the commissary, nay, even though the pope himself, were to stake his soul upon it.

53. They are enemies of Christ and of the pope, who bid the Word of God be altogether silent in some Churches, in order that pardons may be preached in others.

54. Injury is done the Word of God when, in the same sermon, an equal or a longer time is spent on pardons than on this Word.

55. It must be the intention of the pope that if pardons, which are a very small thing, are celebrated with one bell, with single processions and ceremonies, then the Gospel, which is the very greatest thing, should be preached with a hundred bells, a hundred processions, a hundred ceremonies.

56. The "treasures of the Church," out of which the pope grants indulgences, are not sufficiently named or known among the people of Christ.

57. That they are not temporal treasures is certainly evident, for many of the vendors do not pour out such treasures so easily, but only gather them.

58. Nor are they the merits of Christ and the Saints, for even without the pope, these always work grace for the inner man, and the cross, death, and hell for the outward man.

59. St. Lawrence said that the treasures of the Church were the Church's poor, but he spoke according to the usage of the word in his own time.

60. Without rashness we say that the keys of the Church, given by Christ's merit, are that treasure;

61. For it is clear that for the remission of penalties and of reserved cases, the power of the pope is of itself sufficient.

62. The true treasure of the Church is the Most Holy Gospel of the glory and the grace of God.

63. But this treasure is naturally most odious, for it makes the first to be last.

64. On the other hand, the treasure of indulgences is naturally most acceptable, for it makes the last to be first.

65. Therefore the treasures of the Gospel are nets with which they formerly were wont to fish for men of riches.

66. The treasures of the indulgences are nets with which they now fish for the riches of men.

67. The indulgences which the preachers cry as the "greatest graces" are known to be truly such, in so far as they promote gain.

68. Yet they are in truth the very smallest graces compared with the grace of God and the piety of the Cross.

69. Bishops and curates are bound to admit the commissaries of apostolic pardons, with all reverence.

70. But still more are they bound to strain all their eyes and attend with all their ears, lest these men preach their own dreams instead of the commission of the pope.

71. He who speaks against the truth of apostolic pardons, let him be anathema and accursed!

72. But he who guards against the lust and license of the pardon-preachers, let him be blessed!

73. The pope justly thunders against those who, by any art, contrive the injury of the traffic in pardons.

74. But much more does he intend to thunder against those who use the pretext of pardons to contrive the injury of holy love and truth.

75. To think the papal pardons so great that they could absolve a man even if he had committed an impossible sin and violated the Mother of God—this is madness.

76. We say, on the contrary, that the papal pardons are not able to remove the very least of venial sins, so far as its guilt is concerned.

77. It is said that even St. Peter, if he were now Pope, could not bestow greater graces; this is blasphemy against St. Peter and against the pope.

78. We say, on the contrary, that even the present pope, and any pope at all, has greater graces at his disposal; to wit, the Gospel, powers, gifts of healing, etc., as it is written in 1 Cor. 12.

79. To say that the cross, emblazoned with the papal arms, which is set up [by the preachers of indulgences], is of equal worth with the Cross of Christ, is blasphemy.

80. The bishops, curates and theologians who allow such talk to be spread among the people, will have an account to render.

81. This unbridled preaching of pardons makes it no easy matter, even for learned men, to rescue the reverence due to the pope from slander, or even from the shrewd questionings of the laity.

82. To wit:—"Why does not the pope empty purgatory, for the sake of holy love and of the dire need of the souls that are there, if he redeems an infinite number of souls for the sake of miserable money with which to build a Church? The former reasons would be most just; the latter is most trivial."

83. Again:—"Why are mortuary and anniversary masses for the dead continued, and why does he not return or permit the

withdrawal of the endowments founded on their behalf, since it is wrong to pray for the redeemed?"

84. Again:—"What is this new piety of God and the pope, that for money they allow a man who is impious and their enemy to buy out of purgatory the pious soul of a friend of God, and do not rather, because of that pious and beloved soul's own need, free it for pure love's sake?"

85. Again:—"Why are the penitential canons long since in actual fact and through disuse abrogated and dead, now satisfied by the granting of indulgences, as though they were still alive and in force?"

86. Again:—"Why does not the pope, whose wealth is to-day greater than the riches of the richest, build just this one church of St. Peter with his own money, rather than with the money of poor believers?"

87. Again:—"What is it that the pope remits, and what participation does he grant to those who, by perfect contrition, have a right to full remission and participation?"

88. Again:—"What greater blessing could come to the Church than if the pope were to do a hundred times a day what he now does once, and bestow on every believer these remissions and participations?"

89. "Since the pope, by his pardons, seeks the salvation of souls rather than money, why does he suspend the indulgences and pardons granted heretofore, since these have equal efficacy?"

90. To repress these arguments and scruples of the laity by force alone, and not to resolve them by giving reasons, is to expose the Church and the pope to the ridicule of their enemies, and to make Christians unhappy.

91. If, therefore, pardons were preached according to the spirit and mind of the pope, all these doubts would be readily resolved; nay, they would not exist.

92. Away, then, with all those prophets who say to the people of Christ, "Peace, peace," and there is no peace!

93. Blessed be all those prophets who say to the people of Christ, "Cross, cross," and there is no cross!

94. Christians are to be exhorted that they be diligent in following Christ, their Head, through penalties, deaths, and hell;

95. And thus be confident of entering into heaven rather through many tribulations, than through the assurance of peace.

Select Bibliography for Further Reading

Bainton, Roland H. *Here I Stand: A Life of Martin Luther*. New York: Abingdon-Cokesbury, 1950.

Bayer, Oswald. "Martin Luther." In *The Reformation Theologians: An Introduction to Theology in the Modern Period*, edited by Carter Lindberg, 51–66. Malden, MA: Blackwell, 2002.

George, Timothy. "'A Right Strawy Epistle': Reformation Perspectives on James." *The Southern Baptist Journal of Theology* 4, no. 3 (Fall 2000): 20–31.

———. "Yearning for Grace: Martin Luther." In *Theology of the Reformers*, 51–107. Nashville: B&H Publishing Group, 1999.

Kidd, B. J., ed. *Documents Illustrative of the Continental Reformation*. Oxford: Clarendon Press, 1911.

Köstlin, Julius. *Theology of Luther in Its Historical Development and Inner Harmony*. Translated by Charles E. Hay. 2 vols. Philadelphia: Lutheran Publication Society, 1897.

Lindberg, Carter. *The European Reformations*. Malden, MA: Blackwell, 1996.

Luther, Martin. *Luther's Works*. General editors are Jaroslav Pelikan for volumes 1–30 and Helmut T. Lehmann for volumes 31–55. St. Louis: Concordia Publishing House, 1955–76.

———. *Works of Martin Luther*. Translated and edited by Adolph Spaeth, et al. 6 vols. Philadelphia: A. J. Holman, 1915.

MacCulloch, Diarmaid. *The Reformation: A History*. New York: Penguin, 2003.

Nichols, Stephen J. *Martin Luther*. Phillipsburg, NJ: P&R Publishing, 2002.

Oberman, Heiko A. *Luther: Man between God and the Devil*. Translated by Eileen Walliser-Schwarzbart. New Haven, CT: Yale University Press, 1989.

Schramm, Brooks, and Kirsi I. Stjerna, eds. *Martin Luther, the Bible, and the Jewish People: A Reader*. Minneapolis: Fortress, 2012.

Thulin, Oskar, ed. *A Life of Luther*. Translated by Martin O. Dietrich. Philadelphia: Fortress, 1966.

2

Philip Melanchthon: Nine Lutheran Controversies

Melanchthon as Christian Humanist

Melanchthon (1497–1560) was born Philip Schwarzerd in Bretten (now in Baden).[1] He was educated at the Universities of Heidelberg and Tübingen. When he entered Heidelberg at the age of twelve, he changed his surname to Melanchthon, meaning "black earth" (the Greek equivalent of his real surname). This was done at the advice of his great-uncle Johann Reuchlin, German humanist and Hebraist, who sponsored his education. Through his uncle's influence, Philip was elected to the chair of Greek at the University of Wittenberg in 1518. His inaugural address, *Discourse on Reforming the Studies of Youth*, attracted the interest of Martin Luther, by whom Philip was so profoundly influenced that he turned to the study of theology and obtained a bachelor's degree in that field the following year.

---

[1] Among the most helpful biographies are Francis Augustus Cox, *The Life of Philip Melanchthon: Comprising an Account of the Most Important Transactions of the Reformation*, 2nd ed. (London: Gale and Fenner, 1817); Robert Stupperich, *Melanchthon: The Enigma of the Reformation*, trans. Robert H. Fischer (Philadelphia: Westminster, 1965); and Harold Herbert Lentz, *Reformation Crossroads: A Comparison of the Theology of Luther and Melanchthon* (Minneapolis: Augsburg, 1958).

In 1521, Melanchthon's *Loci Communes Rerum Theologicarum* ("Commonplaces of Theology")[2] contributed logical, argumentative force to the German Reformation, and after Luther's confinement in the Castle of Wartburg the same year, he replaced Luther as leader in Wittenberg. In 1526, Melanchthon became professor of Theology and was appointed one of twenty-eight commissioners who made the Constitutions of the German Lutheran churches uniform. At the German Diet of Augsburg in 1530, Melanchthon's Augsburg Confession, consisting of twenty-one articles, was read aloud. The general tone of the confession was so conciliatory that it surprised even Catholics. Luther's only complaint was that the confession was not sufficiently militant. He thought it should have denounced the pope along with his doctrine of purgatory. Melanchthon's *Apology*, published a year later, was an attempt to vindicate the Confession. As we will see below, however, by 1540 he would divide Lutheranism by altering specific doctrinal statements of the Confession into generalizations.

With the death of Luther in 1546, Melanchthon's propensity to weakness and compromise increased. In 1548, he worked as special peacemaker, seeking ecclesiastical harmony between the Protestant and Roman Catholic churches. His views were regarded as heretical by strict Lutherans. This breach with the old Lutherans could only increase, with his insistence on peace at almost any price. Melanchthon would go to his grave praying that Protestant and Roman Catholic churches might be "one in Christ."

Sketch of Melanchthon's Life

- Feb. 16, 1497: Born at Bretten in Baden-Württemberg.
- 1509: To Heidelberg where he earns the BA degree upon completion of a program consisting of philosophy, rhetoric, astronomy.
- 1512: To Tübingen where he earns the MA degree upon completion of a program of humanistic philosophical studies.

---

[2] See B. J. Kidd, ed., *Documents Illustrative of the Continental Reformation* (Oxford: Clarendon Press, 1911), 90–94.

- 1518: Reuchlin relays a call from the elector of Saxony for Melanchthon to teach Greek at Wittenberg.

- 1518: On August 29, Melanchthon delivers his inaugural address, *Discourse on Reforming the Studies of Youth* (or *Improvement of Studies*).

- 1519: Accepts a BD degree at Wittenberg. Melanchthon became so much a part of Luther and the evangelical movement that late in this year he would openly break with Reuchlin. He would soon help Luther translate the Scriptures.

- 1519: At the Leipzig Disputation (June 27–July 8), Melanchthon gives scholarly aid to Luther and Carlstadt during the debates with Rome's "Dr. Eck."

- 1520: Marries Katherine Krapp of Wittenberg. They would have four children.

- 1521: During Luther's confinement in Wartburg Castle, Melanchthon is leader of the Reformation at Wittenberg. He publishes his *Loci Communes Rerum Theologicarum*, the first systematized presentation of the Lutheran theology.

- 1526: Appointed as one of the twenty-eight commissioners to visit the Lutheran states and regulate the constitution of the churches.

- 1528: Publishes *Unterricht der Visitatoren*, a set of instructions for the church visitors.

- 1529: Present at Speyer, where the protest of freedom of conscience is lodged against the Roman Catholics.

- 1530: At the Diet of Augsburg, he is the leading Lutheran representative, writing the major Lutheran creedal statement, the Augsburg Confession.

- 1546: Death of Martin Luther, his most beloved friend.

- 1548: Melanchthon demonstrates his desire for peace, even at the price of doctrinal purity. He works to promote the Leipzig Interim, an attempt to reunite Catholics and Protestants.

- April 19, 1560: Melanchthon dies; his body is placed beside Luther's at Schlosskirche, in Wittenberg.

Nine Important Lutheran Controversies

The Formula of Concord,[3] completed in 1577 and published in 1580, contains twelve articles born out of controversy. It is from the publication of the Formula and no earlier that we begin to see the labels *Lutheran* and *Reformed* being adopted by these groups. Since 1520, Rome had referred to adherents of the Reformation as Lutherans, but it was soon after 1585 that advocates of Luther's teachings began to call themselves Lutherans. Advocates of Calvin's teachings preferred the title *Reformed* to indicate their aim to reform Protestant churches of "Romish leaven." Viewed in terms of their relationship with the traditional Roman Church, Lutheranism would be conservative in matters such as the eucharistic presence, traditionalism, and ceremonies, while the Reformed would be far more progressive. The regulatory principle for Lutheranism was to retain what the Bible does not forbid. The regulatory principle for the Reformed was to abolish what the Bible does not command. The word *normative* is frequently used synonymously with *regulatory*.

The following two controversies occurred before the sharp distinctions between strict Lutherans and Melanchthonians (or Philippists):

1. Antinomian Controversy

John Agricola (1492–1566), the Lutheran reformist who recorded the minutes at the Leipzig debate, attacked Melanchthon's *Instructions for Visitors*, (written at Luther's request), especially the "second use of biblical law." Melanchthon (with Luther and Calvin) taught three uses of the law: (1) to maintain outward discipline in society; (2) to lead individuals to repentance; and (3) to regulate the lives of the regenerate. Agricola held that only the gospel, not the

---

[3] The text is in Philip Schaff, *The Creeds of Christendom, with a History and Critical Notes* (New York: Harper and Brothers, 1877), 3:93–180; for Schaff's analysis, see 1:258–340.

preaching of the law, could produce repentance. Article V of the Formula of Concord would confirm the second use of the law and explain that preaching the law is necessary to lead to a knowledge of sin, that sinners might not merely feel secure in their sins. Agricola renewed his attacks on Melanchthon and Luther. Finally, Luther defeated him so badly in a debate that Agricola recanted. Fellowship was never restored. Meanwhile, Andrew Poach (1516–85) led a group of his followers to attack the third use of the law, that is, the regulation of believers' lives. Article VI of the Formula of Concord would condemn Antinomianism and affirm the third use of the law.

2. Osiandrian Controversy: Mystical Justification vs. Forensic Justification

Andreas Osiander (1498–1552), a Lutheran reformist in Nuremberg, wrote *Disputation on Justification* (1550), in which he promoted a doctrine of mysticism that identified justification with regeneration. Osiander objected to forensic justification, insisting that righteousness cannot be imputed. He asserted that justification is a process of being made righteous by the indwelling Christ and by the indwelling divine nature, which are received by faith. The atonement was not essentially necessary for justification. In effect, Osiander's was an internal justification rather than an external forensic justification. It was an *infused* righteousness (divine nature) rather than an *imputed* righteousness. To Osiander, one is justified inwardly by virtue of the indwelling Christ. That is the essence of his doctrine of justification. It ran totally against the biblical doctrine as taught by the apostle Paul and by the major Reformation spokesmen. The most influential opponent of Osiander was the strict Lutheran, Matthias Flacius (1520–75). Article III of the Formula of Concord would condemn mysticism and affirm forensic justification.

Here are the three controversies between strict Lutherans and Melanchthonians:

1. Adiaphoristic (Interimistic) Controversy

In 1540, Melanchthon produced a modified version of the Augsburg Confession called the *Variata* ("Altered") edition. It included John Calvin's view of a spiritual-yet-real presence of Christ in the Lord's Supper. This was now Melanchthon's position, and many Lutheran churches would specify that they subscribed to the Unaltered Augsburg Confession, as opposed to the *Variata*. Melanchthon and his followers, sometimes called Philippists, were also called secret Calvinists, or Crypto-Calvinists, for their view on the Lord's Supper.

Luther died in 1546. That same year Emperor Charles V crushed the Smalcald League at Muehlberg and imprisoned its founders, Elector John Frederick of Saxony and Philip of Hesse, Protestantism's two most powerful continental civil rulers at the time. The league had served since 1531 as a defensive Protestant alliance of five princes and eleven cities for mutual protection against the war that Charles V had threatened at Augsburg in 1530. In 1548, Charles ordered the creation of a doctrinal agreement called the Augsburg Interim. Its purpose was to settle the disputes between Lutherans and Roman Catholics. Its primary authors were Roman Catholics and Protestants such as John Agricola the Antinomian. The committee was stacked against the Protestants, and the only concessions that the Interim made towards Lutherans were that the communion cup could be available to the laity and that clergy could be permitted to marry. German Lutheran pastors were required to submit to German Catholic bishops. The Interim restored the use of images, Roman Catholic ceremonies, the mass, and all seven sacraments. The Augsburg Interim was not binding on the Roman Catholics. It was binding on the Protestants, and Charles V enforced it by the atrocities of his troops. For refusing to accept the Interim, many Protestants pastors were exiled, and some were killed.

Meanwhile, Melanchthon and the Wittenberg theologians agreed to accept a modified version of the Augsburg Interim on the one condition that it include the words "justification by faith." As long as it had this one fundamental, other matters could be regarded as *adiaphora* (ἀδιάφορα), or "non-essentials," things indifferent. This new confession was called the Leipzig Interim (1548), and under its conditions Protestant preachers were to submit to Roman Catholic bishops. *Adiaphora* included not only confirmation, candles, vestments, and holy days, but the Romish mass as well. Several hundred Protestant clergy were exiled or murdered for noncompliance. Even the "justification by faith" of the Leipzig Interim was impregnated with infused sacramental righteousness. These things prompted the strict Lutheran opponent, Matthias Flacius, to write his work *Against the Interim* (1548). His message declares, "Nothing is unimportant in the case of confession and scandal" (*Nihil est adiaphoron in casu confessionis et scandal*). Forensic justification is a "case of confession." Article X of the Formula of Concord, in essence, makes the weak statement that in times of persecution the statement of Flacius is important, but in other times such things should be left up to the individual. The regulative Lutheran principle would be to retain whatever the Bible does not expressly forbid.

Grieved at the extent to which Melanchthon had carried the *adiaphora*, John Calvin sent him a passionate letter of rebuke mingled with love. Calvin says to his friend,

> My present grief . . . renders me almost speechless. . . . You are too facile in making concessions . . . to the Papists. . . . You have loosed what the Lord has bound in his Word, and . . . have afforded occasion for bringing insult upon the Gospel. . . . Seeing that the Lord led us forth into the arena, it became us on that account to strive the more manfully. . . . The trepidation of a general or leader is more dishonorable than the flight of a whole herd of private [common] soldiers. . . . I had rather die with you a hundred times, than to see you survive the doctrines surrendered by you.[4]

2. Majoristic (Works) Controversy

George Major (1502–74), rector of the University of Wittenberg and friend of Melanchthon, taught that good works are necessary for salvation. In opposition, Matthias Flacius and Nicholas von Amsdorf took the strict Lutheran view. The controversy was another expression of the adiaphoristic controversy. Article IV of the Formula of Concord states that good works are necessary, not as the ground of salvation, but as the fruit of salvation.

3. Two Intertwined Controversies—Synergistic and Flacian

The Leipzig Interim (1548) had expressed the notion that salvation is grounded largely upon the human will. Melanchthon had accepted this idea, affirming that in conversion three things work

---

[4] John Calvin, "To Melanchthon," in *Letters of John Calvin*, trans. Jules Bonnet (Edinburgh: Thomas Constable, 1857), 2:256–61.

together: the Word, the Holy Spirit, and the will of man. To strict Lutherans, this was semi-Pelagian "synergism" (συνεργητικός, from συνεργεῖν, "to work together"; σύν, "with" + ἔργον, "work"). The term *Arminianism* would have fit better than semi-Pelagianism, but Arminianism was not yet on the playing field so it still cannot be applied here. Following Melanchthon's death in 1560, Melanchthonian theologians John Pfeffinger and Victorin Strigel defended synergism against the Calvinistic monergism of such strict Lutherans as Matthias Flacius and Nicholas von Amsdorf. Pfeffinger's published series of *Propositions on Free Will* were strongly synergistic and Melanchthonians were also applying synergism to regeneration.

In his opposition to synergism and defense of monergism, Flacius slipped into the serious error of equating original sin with the essence of human nature. In other words, Flacius seemed to identify the Adamic or inherent "sin nature" with the very substance of human nature itself. With their doctrine of traducianism, some strict Lutherans were prone to this error. It originated from the old philosophical distinctions between the "substance" of which a thing is and the outer "form" that it takes. While the term *nature* must generally apply to essential attributes rather than to any substantive entity, Flacius readily applied it to the latter. Articles I and II of the Formula of Concord condemn Flacius's view of the sin nature as a "Manichaean error." The articles also condemn synergism and affirm Luther's view of the "bondage of the will."

The Two Parties Contrasted

Strict Lutherans	Melanchthonians
Gnesio (Genuine) Lutherans	Secret (Crypto) Calvinists on Eucharist
Consubstantiation	Spiritual-yet-real
Monergists	Synergists
Universities of Jena & Magdeburg	Universities of Leipzig & Wittenberg

Leaders:
  Nicholas von Amsdorf
  Matthias Flacius
  Joachim Westphal
	Leaders:
	  George Major
	  John Pfeffinger
	  Victorin Strigel

Gradual Emergence of a Central Party

Johann Brenz
Jacob Andreae
Martin Chemnitz
Andreae and Chemnitz would be the
main authors of the Formula of Concord.

Below are the four controversies between Lutheranism and Calvinism (Reformed):

1. **Interrelated Issues over Depravity, Election, Grace, and Atonement**

   The Calvinistic or Reformed views are total depravity, unconditional election, and limited atonement. For the Lutherans, Article XI and related articles of the Formula of Concord uphold Luther's view of total depravity, reject election to reprobation, and teach universal grace and atonement.

2. **Eucharistic (Crypto-Calvinistic or Westphal) Controversy**

   In 1552, Joachim Westphal, a concerned strict Lutheran pastor at Hamburg, published the differences between the Crypto-Calvinist Melanchthonians and the Gnesio (Genuine) strict Lutherans. The German Palatinate had become Calvinist and Reformed, as expressed in their Heidelberg Catechism (1563), written by Calvinist theologians Zacharius Ursinus and Caspar Olevianus. The catechism expresses Calvin's own inexplicable view of a spiritual-yet-real partaking of Christ's body and blood in the mystery of the Lord's Supper.[5] Article VII of the Formula of Concord affirms the strict Lutheran view of consubstantiation, that "in, with, and under" the literal bread and wine are the literal body and blood of Christ. This is likened to the fire in red-hot iron. The fire and the iron are both present and both are literally real. To strict Lutherans, Christ's literal body and blood are inexplicably received by virtue of the "sacramental" words, "This is my body. This is my blood."[6]

---

[5] Heidelberg Catechism, Questions 75–82.

[6] For more on Luther's view of eucharistic presence, see Luther's "Expositions of the Lord's Supper and the Sacrifice of the Mass in A.D. 1520," in Julius Köstlin, *Theology of Luther in Its Historical Development and Inner Harmony*, trans. Charles E.

The Heidelberg Catechism (1563) on the Imputed Righteousness of Christ

Question 60: How art thou righteous before God?

Answer: "Only by true faith in Jesus Christ; that is, although my conscience accuse me that I have grievously sinned against all the commandments of God, and have never kept any of them, and that I am still prone always to all evil, yet God, without any merit of mine, of mere grace, grants and imputes to me the perfect satisfaction, righteousness, and holiness of Christ, as if I had never committed nor had any sin, and had myself accomplished all the obedience which Christ has fulfilled for me, if only I accept such benefit with a believing heart."

3. Personal (Hypostatic) Union vs. Communication of Attributes

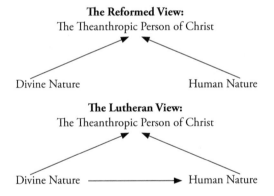

The Reformed View:
The Theanthropic Person of Christ

Divine Nature   Human Nature

The Lutheran View:
The Theanthropic Person of Christ

Divine Nature   Human Nature

Martin Chemnitz, of the central Lutheran party, defined the official Lutheran view, and Article VIII of the Formula of Concord affirms it. To describe Christ's presence, they use the term *multivolipresence*, a blend of *multiple, volitional,* and *presence*. It is a consubstantiation in which Christ wills His literal body and blood to be present in multiple places of Eucharistic observance. Christ's omnipresence, at least His ubiquity, is communicated to His humanity (as

---

Hay (Philadelphia: Lutheran Publication Society, 1897), 1:346–54. See 2:58–83 for Luther's debates with Andreas von Carlstadt on the Eucharist. See 2:502–06 and 511–21 for an excellent systematic overview of Luther's position.

the arrows on the diagram indicate). As noted, the Reformed view is that there is no communication of attributes between natures since the natures are bonded with the person of Christ. Some Lutherans now hold to an actual "exchange" of attributes between deity and humanity. They contend that if there is to be any real *communicatio idiomatum* there must be mutual communication.

4. Controversy over the Nature of Christ's Descent into Hades

The idea of a descent into Hades emerged from the Apostles' Creed. Primary texts used for a literal interpretation are Ephesians 4:9 and 1 Peter 3:19. The Reformed view[7] was that Christ's descent was into death and the grave. The Lutheran view,[8] as expressed in Article IX of the Formula of Concord, was that Christ's descent was into the literal hell in order to announce His triumph over death and hell in behalf of believers. The Formula does urge that questions of curiosity be set aside for eternity.

Martin Luther on Purgatory and Prayers for the Dead

❡ If you do not believe in a purgatory, you are not therefore a heretic. The Scriptures know nothing of it. It is better that you disbelieve what is not taught in the Scriptures, than that you reject what is found in the Scriptures. Let the pope and papists be as angry as they will. They have made an article of faith of purgatory because it has brought them the world's riches, and sent innumerable souls into hell, since they placed their reliance on works and consoled themselves with the thought that works would bring them release. God has given no command concerning purgatory; he has commanded you not to consult the dead nor to believe

---

[7] On the Reformed view, see Daniel R. Hyde, *In Defense of the Descent: A Response to Contemporary Critics* (Grand Rapids: Reformation Heritage Books, 2010). Hyde defends the idea of keeping the descent into Hades in the Apostles' Creed but interpreting it as *death* and *grave*. Cf. Wayne Grudem, "He Did Not Descend into Hell: A Plea for Following Scripture Instead of the Apostles' Creed," *Journal of the Evangelical Theological Society* 34, no. 1 (March 1991): 103–13.

[8] On the Lutheran view, see Robert Kolb, "Christ's Descent into Hell as Christological Locus in the Era of the Formula of Concord," *Lutherjahrbuch* 69 (2002): 101–18.

what they say. Accept God as more reliable and truthful than all angels, and let the pope and his papists keep silence, the more so since their doctrines are lies and deceit which do little to inspire faith in purgatory. I will not stop you if you desire to offer prayers for the dead. In my opinion purgatory is not our common lot, as they teach; I think very few souls get there. Nevertheless, as I said, there is no danger at all for your soul if you do not believe in purgatory. You are not obliged to believe more than what is taught in the Scriptures. If here, too, they should cite Gregory, Augustine, and other saints and their pronouncements, glosses, and examples concerning purgatory, I remind you of what you heard earlier, namely, to what extent we should follow those dear saints and believe what they say. Who can convince us that they were not deceived in this matter or did not err as in many other matters? Our faith must have a foundation which is God's word, and not sand or moss, which are the delusions and works of men.[9]

Select Bibliography for Further Reading

Cox, Francis Augustus. *The Life of Philip Melanchthon: Comprising an Account of the Most Important Transactions of the Reformation*. 2nd ed. London: Gale and Fenner, 1817.

Fuerbringer, L., Th. Engelder, and P. E. Kretzmann, eds. *The Concordia Cyclopedia: A Handbook of Religious Information, with Special Reference to the History, Doctrine, Work, and Usages of the Lutheran Church*. St. Louis: Concordia, 1927.

Klotsche, E. H. *Christian Symbolics: Exposition of the Distinctive Characteristics of the Catholic, Lutheran and Reformed Churches as Well as the Modern Denominations and Sects Represented in This Country*. Burlington, IA: Lutheran Literary Board, 1929.

———. "Controversies in the Lutheran Church after Luther's Death Settled by the Formula of Concord." In *The History of Christian Doctrine*, 205–19. Burlington, IA: Lutheran Literary Board, 1945. The last chapter was authored by J. Theodore Mueller.

Kolb, Robert. "Christ's Descent into Hell as Christological Locus in the Era of the Formula of Concord." *Lutherjahrbuch* 69 (2002): 101–18.

Köstlin, Julius. *Theology of Luther in Its Historical Development and Inner Harmony*. Translated by Charles E. Hay. 2 vols. Philadelphia: Lutheran Publication Society, 1897.

---

[9] In *Sermons* II, vol. 52 of *Luther's Works*, ed. Helmut T. Lehmann (St. Louis: Concordia, 1974), 52:180.

Lentz, Harold Herbert. *Reformation Crossroads: A Comparison of the Theology of Luther and Melanchthon.* Minneapolis: Augsburg Publishing House, 1958.

Lindberg, Carter, ed. *The Reformation Theologians: An Introduction to Theology in the Modern Period.* Malden, MA: Blackwell, 2002.

Oberman, Heiko A. *The Two Reformations: The Journey from the Last Days to the New World.* Edited by Donald Weinstein. New Haven, CT: Yale University Press, 2003.

Seeberg, Reinhold. "Lutheran Doctrine to the Adoption of the Formula of Concord." In *Text-Book of the History of Doctrines,* translated by Charles E. Hay, 2:347–89. Philadelphia: Lutheran Publication Society, 1905.

Stupperich, Robert. *Melanchthon: The Enigma of the Reformation.* Translated by Robert H. Fischer. Philadelphia: Westminster Press, 1965.

Watson, Philip S. *Let God Be God: An Interpretation of Martin Luther.* Philadelphia: Muhlenberg Press, 1947.

Wengert, Timothy J. *Martin Luther's Catechisms: Forming the Faith.* Minneapolis: Fortress, 2009.

3

Ulrich Zwingli:
Bold Reformer of
German Switzerland

Ulrich (Huldrych or Huldreich) Zwingli,[1] son of a free peasant who became village magistrate, was born on January 1, 1484, in Wildhaus, some forty miles from Zurich, Switzerland. Ulrich's uncle, Bartholomew Zwingli, was priest of Wildhaus. In 1494, Ulrich entered high school at Kleinbazel, where he studied Latin, dialectic, and music. He completed high school at Berne, where his musical abilities were discovered. He could play any instrument given him. The schoolmaster inspired him with an enthusiasm for the classics. In 1498, the Dominicans were so interested in his musical gifts that they almost enticed him to enter the services of a monastery. Afraid that he might become a monk, Zwingli's father and uncle moved him to Vienna, and he enrolled in the university there.

In 1502, he matriculated at the University of Basel, receiving his BA in 1504 and his MA in 1506 and supporting himself by teaching in the school of St. Martin's Church. During these years, Zwingli's theological reading, along with his attendance at the lectures of humanist Thomas Wyttenbach on Peter Lombard's *Sentences*, sowed the seeds of the young man's later beliefs in the supremacy of Scripture and justification by faith.

---

[1] The best biographies include Samuel Macauley Jackson, *Huldreich Zwingli: The Reformer of German Switzerland 1484–1531* (New York: G. P. Putnam's Sons, 1901); and G. R. Potter, *Zwingli* (Cambridge: Cambridge University Press, 1976).

Ordained to the priesthood in 1506, Zwingli immediately accepted a parish at Glarus, which included three villages. During the next few years, he proved successful as a priest, encouraging education, teaching himself Greek, studying Hebrew, and reading widely in the church fathers. Humanistic studies made him highly sympathetic toward Renaissance thinking, and he especially treasured his correspondence with Dutch humanist, Desiderius Erasmus. With his early humanist influences, even Zwingli the Reformer would insist that among ancient pagan philosophers, some were virtuous and are in heaven, even though they never heard the gospel.[2] His service as chaplain with the Swiss army led him to oppose the mercenary system as contributing to moral deterioration. With this stand provoking hostility at Glarus, Zwingli moved on to a new parish at Einsiedeln in 1516, where he enjoyed more opportunities for preaching and better library facilities.

It was here in Einsiedeln that Zwingli would become the pioneer Reformer in German-speaking Switzerland. He would later date the beginnings of his evangelical convictions to these years. While there is no record of a deep conversion experience, in 1516 Zwingli began reading Erasmus's Greek New Testament transcribing Paul's epistles into notebooks and memorizing large portions. Convinced that the Bible was above the Church and that Christ was above the Virgin Mary, Zwingli began preaching that Roman Catholic churches had seriously departed from the simplicity of the gospel. Attracting large crowds of supporters, he warned against vain superstitions such as indulgences and relics. When the Franciscan preacher Bernhardin Samson began promoting local sales of indulgences, Zwingli's witty reprimands brought chuckles even from his enemies. His vivid contrast between the regenerate man's appetite for God's Word and the unregenerate man's rejection of it illustrates his robust manner:

> Take some good and strong wine; he who is in good health enjoys it, for it renders him merry, strengthens him, and warms his blood; but he who is suffering from pestilence or from fever may not even taste it, and still less drink it, and he wonders how people in health can drink it. But that is not on account of the wine, but

---

[2] George P. Fisher, *History of Christian Doctrine* (Edinburgh: T. & T. Clark, 1896), 288.

on account of his disease. In the same manner the Word of God is perfect in itself, and revealed for the welfare of man; but he who neither loves it, nor understands it, nor will receive it, is sick. Thus much in reply to those who daringly assert, that God does not mean his Word to be understood, as if he desired to exclude us from its light.[3]

On January 1, 1519, despite great opposition, Zwingli was appointed peoples' (preaching) priest at the Grossmünster, Zurich's "Great Minster" cathedral. Here he commenced a series of expositions of the New Testament expounding the original Greek chapter by chapter, one book after another, beginning with the Gospels. The Catholic priests had based their sermons on the Vulgate and patristic literature. In 1519, a friend made a printing press available, and with it Zwingli's bold messages spread rapidly.

During the same year, Zwingli began reading the works of his contemporary, Martin Luther, and was encouraged by Luther's stand against the Roman hierarchy. Zwingli supported the authority of Zurich's civil council in ecclesiastical matters, but only with the understanding that the council itself is subject to the Word of God. He insisted that as Christ is over the church, the Bible is over the state. In 1520, Zwingli secured official permission from the city's governing council to preach the "true divine scriptures." He persuaded Zurich's city council to forbid all religious teachings that lacked a scriptural basis. At every level of society, he poured himself into his ministry. Even a serious plague found Zwingli steadfastly caring for the sick and the dying. He fell sick and looked death in the face but he recovered. Then his brother died. Each of these experiences helped to deepen the spiritual and theological character of his thinking.

When some of Zwingli's supporters ate their normal meals during the Roman Catholic Fast of Lent, they were arrested. Zwingli so vigorously defended the accused that they were released with only a token punishment. He published his arguments in a tract *On Meats* (1522). The resulting series of sermons stirred opposition against all forms of extra-biblical asceticism. The sermons essentially established the Swiss Reformation upon the Scriptures and

---

[3] Trans. K. R. Hagenbach in, *A Text-Book of the History of Doctrines* (New York: Sheldon, 1866–67), 2:242.

even appeared in print under the title *The Clarity and Certainty of the Word of God* (1522). The papacy, angered by Zwingli's influence, requested Zurich's city council to repudiate him as a heretic. When the Catholic bishop of Constance sent an investigative committee, Zurich's citizens supported the Reformer.

In 1523, he wrote and published his Sixty-Seven Articles[4] in preparation for a disputation with the vicar-general of Constance. Unlike Luther's Ninety-Five Theses, which are concerned with indulgences and are addressed to academics, Zwingli's articles address a popular audience with a clear "sum of the gospel," as he calls them (Art. 2). During the disputation, Zwingli clearly asserted the supremacy of Scripture over ecclesiastical tradition. With the authority of Scripture, he repudiated the doctrine of transubstantiation, the Catholic Church's enforced clerical celibacy, and veneration to images, relics, and saints. After deliberation, the city council upheld Zwingli by withdrawing the Zurich canton from the jurisdiction of the bishop of Constance. The council officially banned any preaching not based upon Scripture. With these steps the city council had officially adopted the Reformation.

Zwingli immediately drafted his plan of reform for the Grossmünster.[5] A key part of his program was the reconstitution of the cathedral school into both a grammar school and a theological seminary to train Reformed pastors. The question of removing the images from the churches provoked a second disputation in October, when Zwingli and his friend and fellow Reformer Leo Jud carried the day in favor of removing the images. Before the end of 1523, Zwingli was preaching the doctrine of the bondage of the human will as powerfully as Luther. This distanced him from Desiderius Erasmus. Zwingli publicly married Anna Reinhard on April 2, 1524,

---

[4] There is an English translation of Zwingli's Sixty-Seven Articles in Mark A. Noll, ed., *Confessions and Catechisms of the Reformation* (Grand Rapids: Baker, 1991), 37–46.

[5] Frank Hugh Foster, "Zwingli's Theology, Philosophy, and Ethics," in Jackson, *Huldreich Zwingli*, 365–401; and Timothy George, "Something Bold for God: Huldrych Zwingli," in *Theology of the Reformers* (Nashville: B&H Publishing Group, 1999), 108–62. The most comprehensive study of Zwingli's theology is W. P. Stephens, *Theology of Huldrych Zwingli* (Oxford: Oxford University Press, 1986).

and it was no secret that they had been living together since the spring of 1522. Such practice was common among Roman Catholic priests, but unheard-of among Reformers. Between 1526 and 1530 Anna bore him four children. There are no descendents.

The sweeping reforms that came to Zurich in 1524 included the conversion of monasteries into hospitals and the elimination of music from the churches. With his great love for music, it now appears strange that Zwingli had interpreted Paul's expressions of singing with the mind and in the heart (1 Cor. 14:15; Col. 3:16) as mandates against audible singing in church. It was not until 1598 that the German-Swiss restored music to their Reformed churches.

Abolition of the mass officially came on April 13, 1525, when the Grossmünster observed the Lord's Supper for the first time, using Zwingli's liturgy, with men and women sitting on opposite sides of a long table situated in the center aisle of the church. They received the bread and wine from wooden platters and cups. The introduction of Bible readings and special studies also began in Zurich at this time. Zwingli would later provide still another major advancement for the Swiss Reformation with the completion of his Zurich Bible (1525–29).

Meanwhile, it was also during 1524–25 that the Anabaptists challenged Zwingli's views concerning the biblical nature of the church, the biblical qualifications for baptism, and the biblical relationship between church and state. The Anabaptists held to a regenerated membership, the baptism of believers only, and the separation of church and state. Following a disputation in January 1525, Zwingli and the city council banished the Anabaptist leaders from Zurich. As a theological refutation of the Anabaptists,[6] Zwingli wrote *On Baptism* (1525), with emphasis on the significance of water baptism as a badge and sign of the covenant. He did agree with the Anabaptists that "no element or external thing in this world can purify the soul, but the purification of the soul is only of the grace of God. So it follows, that baptism cannot wash away any sin. As it cannot wash sin away, and yet has been appointed of God, it must

---

[6] See Abraham Friesen, *Erasmus, the Anabaptists, and the Great Commission* (Grand Rapids: Eerdmans, 1988).

be a *sign of dedication* of the people of God, and *nothing at all else.*"[7] During the next few years, he devoted many other tracts to the subject, culminating in his *Refutation of the Tricks of the Catabaptists* (1527).

Zwingli greatly fostered the Swiss Reformation with his comprehensive *Commentary on True and False Religion* (1525). His work *On the Lord's Supper*, though, would help spawn a serious break with Martin Luther. The two agreed in rejecting the idea of the Eucharist as a sacrifice. They also agreed in rejecting the medieval notion of a change of substance in the sacrament. Luther, however, felt bound by the words "This is my body" to teach a real, essential, and substantive presence of Christ's body and blood, not in place of, but in, with, and under the bread and wine. Conversely, Zwingli was convinced (with Erasmus) that the word translated "is" (*est*) has the force of "symbolizes," or "signifies" (*significat*). Philip of Hesse arranged a Colloquy in Marburg in 1529 for the purpose of reconciliation. The participants reached cordial agreement on most issues, but Luther and Zwingli clashed over the question of consubstantiation versus symbolism. Luther finally pulled back the velvet tablecloth and wrote on the table, *Hoc est corpus meum* ("This is my body"). He refused the hand of fellowship that Zwingli extended. The conference failed to reconcile the two leaders and Luther, and his followers would refuse to acknowledge the Swiss movement as a true Reformation.

Meanwhile, Zwingli carried his crusade to cantons beyond Zurich. Six cantons converted to the Reformation. The remaining five, known as the Forest Cantons, remained staunchly Catholic. The antagonism between Catholic and Protestant cantons created a serious split within the Swiss confederation. In 1529, the hostility between the cantons flared into open civil war. On October 11, 1531, Zwingli was dressed in armor and on the battlefield at Kappel. As the senior pastor of Zurich, he was chaplain to its troops. A vastly outnumbered Protestant defense fell to the Catholic army. Zwingli was among the many that died. When they recognized the fallen Reformer, the Catholics assaulted his corpse with the punishment of a traitor and a heretic. Their hangman quartered his body, mixed the

---

[7] Hagenbach, 2:366.

sections with dung, and burned them. Zwingli was only forty-seven years of age.

Often called the "third man" of the Reformation,[8] after Luther and Calvin, Zwingli was a bold and courageous pioneer for the cause of the Reformation. His Trinitarian and Christological doctrines were sound. Foundational to his doctrine of sin was his insistence that in the Garden of Eden, Adam plunged the whole human race into sin: "There he and all his race in him died as dead as stone."[9] His Sixty-Seven Articles, the earliest Protestant confession, laid the groundwork for notable Swiss Reformed confessions that would follow: the First Helvetic Confession (1536) and the Second Helvetic Confession (1566).[10] Zwingli's work continued in Zurich through the work of his successor, Heinrich Bullinger (1504–75). Building upon the groundwork that Zwingli had established, John Calvin, with his widespread influence from Geneva, Switzerland, would systematize and define the Swiss Reformation.

Select Bibliography for Further Reading

Bainton, Roland H. "The Reformed Church: in German Switzerland." In *The Reformation of the Sixteenth Century*, 77–94. Boston: Beacon Press, 1952.

Collinson, Patrick. *The Reformation: A History*. New York: Random House, 2004.

Cunningham, William. "Zwingli and the Doctrine of the Sacraments." In *The Reformers and the Theology of the Reformation*, 212–91. Edinburgh: T. & T. Clark, 1862.

George, Timothy. "Something Bold for God: Huldrych Zwingli." In *Theology of the Reformers*, 108–62. Nashville: B&H Publishing Group, 1999.

Grimm, Harold J. *The Reformation Era: 1500–1650*. Toronto: Collier-Macmillan, 1971.

Jackson, Samuel Macauley. *Huldreich Zwingli: The Reformer of German Switzerland 1484–1531*. New York: G. P. Putnam's Sons, 1901.

Lindberg, Carter. *The European Reformations*. Malden, MA: Blackwell, 1996.

———. *The European Reformations Sourcebook*. Malden, MA: Blackwell, 2000.

MacCulloch, Diarmaid. *The Reformation: A History*. New York: Penguin, 2003.

Miller, Gregory J. "Huldrych Zwingli." In *The Reformation Theologians: An Introduction to Theology in the Modern Period*, edited by Carter Lindberg, 157–69. Malden, MA: Blackwell, 2002.

---

[8] For example, see Jean Rilliet, *Zwingli: Third Man of the Reformation*, trans. Harold Knight (London: Lutterworth, 1964).

[9] Reinhold Seeberg, *Text-Book of the History of Doctrines*, trans. Charles E. Hay (Philadelphia: Lutheran Publication Society, 1905), 2:309.

[10] *Helvetic* is from the Latin *Helveticus*, meaning "Swiss."

Noll, Mark A., ed. *Confessions and Catechisms of the Reformation*. Grand Rapids: Baker, 1991.

Potter, G. R. *Zwingli*. Cambridge: Cambridge University Press, 1976.

Rilliet, Jean. *Zwingli: Third Man of the Reformation*. Translated by Harold Knight. London: Lutterworth Press, 1964.

Stephens, W. P. *Theology of Huldrych Zwingli*. Oxford: Oxford University Press, 1986. This is the first comprehensive study of Zwingli's theology in the English language.

Zwingli, Huldreich. *Selected Writings of Huldreich Zwingli: The Reformer of German Switzerland 1484–1531*. Edited by Samuel Macauley Jackson. Philadelphia: University of Pennsylvania, 1901.

———. *Writings*. Translated by H. Wayne Pipkin. 2 vols. Allison Park, PA: Pickwick, 1984.

4

John Calvin: Quiet Theologian and Apologist of Geneva

John Calvin (1509–64) was born in Noyon, northeast of Paris. He died in Geneva, Switzerland. He is perhaps the most misunderstood among the Reformers. Rather than being the cold scholastic, as some have described him, Calvin was a warm and loving husband, father, pastor, and theologian. He never sought public attention. He ran from it. Calvin was a quiet student of the Scriptures. He was one of the most brilliant men in the history of church, but this alone did not make him the greatest of the sixteenth-century Reformers. His practical life of devotion and commitment to God and to the Word of God did more to qualify him for that, but Calvin seems never to have been aware of his own qualities. His desire was to glorify the Lord. Like everyone, he made mistakes, but he was a mighty and humble instrument in the hand of the Lord.

Born on July 10, 1509, John Calvin was the second of five sons. Only one of his brothers survived childhood. During John's youth his mother died, and his father married a widow who bore him two daughters. John's early upbringing was characterized by devout and strict faithfulness to the Catholic Church. At the age of twelve he received a benefice (minor orders) from the bishop of Noyon. John's father was able to provide for him the best education, and his high expectation was for his son to become a priest. When John had just turned fourteen, his father enrolled him at the University of Paris to study scholastic theology and to begin preparation for the priesthood. He consistently excelled in his studies and demonstrated rare ability for his age. By 1528, when he was nineteen years old, he had completed what in modern terms we would call his undergraduate studies. Surprisingly, however, plans concerning his advanced studies were not at all what he expected.

Calvin's father suddenly ordered him to abandon theological studies, enroll at the University of Orleans, and pursue a degree in civil law. He humbly submitted to his father's wishes. After he became a Reformer, he would refer to the transition as "God's secret providence." The University of Orleans was a famous center of law at the time. Calvin enjoyed his studies there, but he later transferred to the University at Bourges to study under a famous Italian jurist. Upon the death of his father in 1531, John transferred back to the University of Paris, resumed his theological studies, took up the study of Hebrew, and soon discontinued his formal interest in law. Throughout his training, he had met noble individuals who had been willing quietly to raise questions concerning doctrinal inconsistencies and practical abuses in the Roman Catholic Church. Calvin was probably still in the Catholic fold in 1532, when he published at Paris his own edition, with commentary, of Seneca's treatise *On Clemency* (*De Clementia*).

While the precise date in unknown, it could have been between 1532 and 1534, when he was between twenty-two and twenty-five years old, that Calvin experienced his "sudden conversion" to Christ. He testifies of it in the autobiographic preface to his *Commentary on the Book of Psalms* (1557):

> And first, since I was too obstinately devoted to the superstitions of Popery to be easily extricated from so profound an abyss of mire, God by a sudden conversion subdued and brought my mind to a teachable frame, which was more hardened in such matters than might have been expected from one at my early period of life. Having thus received some taste and knowledge of true godliness, I was immediately inflamed with so intense a desire to make progress therein, that although I did not altogether leave off other studies, I yet pursued them with less ardor. I was quite surprised to find that before a year had elapsed, all who had any desire after purer doctrine were continually coming to me to learn, although

I myself was as yet but a mere novice and tyro. Being of a disposition somewhat unpolished and bashful, which led me always to the shade and retirement, I then began to seek some secluded corner where I might be withdrawn from the public view, but so far from being able to accomplish the object of my desire, all my retreats were like public schools. In short, whilst my one great object was to live in seclusion without being known, God so led me about through different turnings and changes, that he never permitted me to rest in any place, until, in spite of my natural disposition, he brought me forth to public notice.[1]

In 1533, Calvin's close and scholarly friend Nicholas Cop (1501–40) was appointed to the office of rector at the University of Paris. It was customary for the annual incumbent to deliver an inaugural oration before the academic world. The event would take place on All Saints Day (November 1) in the Church of Mathurins. Cop's oration constituted a carefully prepared commendation of the Reformation. He titled it "Christian Philosophy." His message was a bold presentation of the pure gospel of Jesus Christ. His audience was shocked. Many among the general audience were no doubt sympathetic, but when he criticized Sorbonne theologians as "sophists," both ecclesiastical and governmental leaders became infuriated. Cop had to flee the city. Calvin fled with him, and, for the next two years, the precise order of Calvin's whereabouts is uncertain.

By 1535, he was in secret lodging in Basel, Switzerland, for safety and for quiet time to study and write. Here he wrote two commendatory prefaces for the French New Testament translated by Pierre Robert Olivétan for the persecuted Waldenses living among the valleys of the southern Alps. It was also in Basel that twenty-seven-year-old Calvin published the first edition of his *Institutes of the Christian Religion* (*Christianae Religionis Institutio*, Basileae, 1536). This edition is six chapters in length.

In 1536, Calvin, with his younger brother Antoine and his half-sister Marie, was traveling from Paris to Strasbourg, where he had planned to settle down for a private life of study. War between

---

[1] John Calvin, "Preface," in *Commentary on the Book of Psalms*, trans. James Anderson (Edinburgh: Calvin Translation Society, 1845), 1:xl–xli. The final phrase cited above, that God "brought me forth to public notice," can be translated, He "has thrust me onto the stage."

Francis I of France and Emperor Charles V necessitated an extended detour that brought them to Geneva, Switzerland. Calvin "had resolved to pass quickly by Geneva, without staying longer than a single night." As he explains, however, the Genevan Reformer William Farel, "detained me at Geneva, not so much by counsel and exhortation, as by a dreadful imprecation, which I felt to be as if God had from heaven laid his mighty hand upon me to arrest me." Calvin describes Farel's response at hearing of his desire to retire to writing:

> [He] proceeded to utter an imprecation that God would curse my retirement, and the tranquility of the studies which I sought, if I should withdraw and refuse to give assistance, when the necessity was so urgent. By this imprecation I was so stricken with terror, that I desisted from the journey which I had undertaken.[2]

Remaining in Geneva, Calvin began his "verse-by-verse" pastoral ministry in the Church of Saint Peter (*Cathedrale Saint Pierre*), which had been erected during the twelfth and thirteenth centuries over the ruins of a fifth-century church. Calvin found it a struggling Protestant church in much need of leadership and instruction in God's Word. In 1538, less than two years after Calvin's arrival, the General Assembly ordered him and Farel to leave the city within three days. Neither one expressed any thought of ever returning.

Calvin went to Basel, then on to Strasbourg, where he ministered to French refugees among three churches, including the Saint-Nicholas Church. This period would include some of the most joyous and some of the most painful years of his life. He published the second edition of his *Institutes* (1539) expanding it to seventeen chapters. He also published his *Commentary on Romans* (1540), with his own Latin translation from the Greek. Later that year, Calvin, at age thirty-one, married Idelette de Bure, the widow of a former Anabaptist. In 1542, she bore him a son who died when only a few days old. Seven years later Idelette also died. Calvin never remarried.

In 1541, the city of Geneva appealed to Calvin to return and restore order in the midst of turmoil. Calvin returned to his pulpit, and on the first Sunday he resumed at the text where he had been forced to stop three years earlier. With his effective *Ecclesiastical Ordinances*, Calvin continued here for the remainder of his life as faithful pastor,

---

[2] Ibid., 1:xlii–xliii.

brilliant scholar, prolific author, and effective church administrator. He wrote commentaries on most of the books of the Bible.

The city council called upon Calvin to testify at the trial of the zealous Michael Servetus, a Spanish unitarian who arrived while being hunted for heresy by the Catholic Inquisition. Indicative of the fact that the Reformation would not find completion for another two centuries, Geneva executed Servetus for heresy in 1553 by burning him at the stake. Calvin had sought for a milder form of execution, but to no avail. At the time Calvin held no civil office, and he would not be a Genevan citizen for six more years.

In 1559, with his future successor Theodore Beza, Calvin established an important theological institution, the Geneva Academy (*Schola Genevensis*), which after the Enlightenment era became the secular University of Geneva. Having established Geneva as the center for international Reformed Protestantism, John Calvin died on May 27, 1564. He was buried without pomp, at his own request, in an unmarked grave somewhere in the city's Plainpalais cemetery. Calvin's personal life symbol had been a hand offering up to God the sacrifice of a bleeding heart. In 1909 (four-hundredth anniversary of Calvin's birth), the first stone was laid for the International Monument to the Reformation in Geneva. Better known as the Reformation Wall, it stretches for some 325 feet. In its center are four sculpted statues depicting famous Reformers who were present in Geneva in 1559: William Farel (seventy years of age in 1559), John Calvin (fifty years of age in 1559), Theodore Beza, and Scotsman John Knox.

The same year also witnessed the debut of the final edition of the *Institutes of the Christian Religion* (Geneva: Robert Estienne, 1559), a massive four-book treatise. Except for translations of the Bible, it stands as the most significant theological work from the sixteenth-century Reformation.

A Book-and-Chapter Outline of Calvin's *Institutes*

Book 1: The Knowledge of God the Creator
    A. Natural revelation (1–5)
    B. Special revelation (6)

    C. Creation, government, and providence of the trinitarian God (7–18)

Book 2: Hamartiology and Christology

    A. Fall of man and the human condition (1–11)

    B. Christology (12–17):

        1. Hypostatic union (12–14)

        2. Three offices—Prophet, Priest, King (15)

        3. Redeemer and His finished work—the gospel(16–17)

Book 3: Soteriology and the Christian Walk

    A. Secret operation of the Holy Spirit (1)

    B. Faith (2)

    C. Repentance (3–5)

    D. Self-denial and focus on eternity—sum of the Christian life (6–10)

    E. Justification by faith and imputation of Christ's righteousness (11–18)

    F. Christian liberty (19)

    G. Prayer (20)

    H. Election (21–24)

    I. Final resurrection (25)

Book 4: Ecclesiology and Civil Government

    A. The church visible and its government (1–4)

    B. Repudiation of papal corruption in church government (5–11)

    C. Keys of the church: discipline, censures, and excommunication (12)

    D. Vows: warnings and advice (13)

    E. Sacraments: Baptism and the Lord's Supper (14–17)

    F. Repudiation of papal corruption of the sacraments (18–19)

    G. Civil government and the relationship between church and state (20)

The Theology of the Four Books

Since Calvin's theology can be best understood by grasping the content and argumentation of the *Institutes*, the following paragraphs offer a synopsis of the Reformer's systematic approach.

Summation of Book 1

Nearly all human knowledge can be divided into two kinds: the knowledge of God and the knowledge of self.

> In the first place, no man can survey himself without forthwith turning his thoughts towards the God in whom he lives and moves; because it is perfectly obvious, that the endowments which we possess cannot possibly be from ourselves; nay, that our very being is nothing else than subsistence in God alone. In the second place, those blessings which unceasingly distil to us from heaven, are like streams conducting us to the fountain. . . . The miserable ruin into which the revolt of the first man has plunged us, compels us to turn our eyes upwards. (1.1.1)[3]

"A seed of religion is divinely sown in all" (1.4.1). This awareness is sufficient only to make all men inexcusable:

> That there exists in the human minds and indeed by natural instinct, some sense of Deity, we hold to be beyond dispute, since God himself, to prevent any man from pretending ignorance, has endued all men with some idea of his Godhead, the memory of which he constantly renews and occasionally enlarges, that all to a man being aware that there is a God, and that he is their Maker, may be condemned by their own conscience when they neither worship him nor consecrate their lives to his service. (1.3.1)

> We cannot open our eyes without being compelled to behold him. His essence, indeed, is incomprehensible, utterly transcending all human thought; but on each of his works his glory is engraved in characters so bright, so distinct, and so illustrious, that none, however dull and illiterate, can plead ignorance as their excuse. (5.1.1)

The sole cause of the failure of the natural revelation is the corruption of the human heart. It is not a question of the extinction of the knowledge of God, but of its corruption in the heart of man.

---

[3] All citations from the *Institutes* are from John Calvin, *Institutes of the Christian Religion*, 3 vols., trans. Henry Beveridge (Edinburgh: Edinburgh Printing Company for the Calvin Translation Society, 1845).

While general revelation presents itself to all eyes and is more than sufficient to deprive men of every excuse, God's supernatural revelation is a special kind of revelation intended only for the elect. Only God's chosen ones are illuminated to the true comprehension of supernatural revelation (1.6.1–3). In this section, among others, Calvin is truly a theologian of the Holy Spirit. The Scriptures proceeded from the Spirit of God. Scripture is the "School of the Holy Spirit," and God alone can properly bear witness to His own words. The "internal testimony of the Holy Spirit" is superior to all human reason and is necessary for the confirmation of all evidences. He secures the efficacy, antiquity, and preservation of all Scripture, and the certainty of its prophecies. Although Calvin sometimes uses the word *dictation* in reference to the Scriptures, he never uses it in terms of their mode of inspiration. Assured that every word of Scripture is the very word of God, Calvin simply exalts its majesty, beauty, and absolute authority over both church and state. "The authority of the scriptures is derived not from men but from the Spirit of God" (1.7.1–4).

Calvin describes God as infinite, invisible, eternal, and almighty. In one essence there are three distinct persons: the Father, the Son, and the Holy Spirit. God manifests Himself in His governance and regulation of all things by His will and by His wisdom. He takes care of the whole human race, but especially of His church. He has abundant power for doing good, for in His hand are heaven and earth, and all creatures are subject to His sway. The godly rest on His protection, and the power of hell is restrained by His authority. Nothing happens by chance, though the causes may be concealed. Our holy God turns the works of evil men into the fulfillment of His own eternal decrees. Unable to explore His secret will, we can only adore it with reverence. His law and gospel convey His revealed will (1.8–18).

Summation of Book 2

Adam, our first parent, is the fountainhead of sin. Infidelity, ambition, pride, and ingratitude were all at the root of Adam's fall. Since that time, sin has been universally and perpetually transmitted from parent to child. Sin essentially obliterated the image of God in man. Not by imitation but in Adam, all mankind is conceived in guilt and depravity. Adam was not merely a progenitor, but the corrupt root, and by his corruption the whole human race is deservedly accursed. "Wherefore, as by one man sin entered into the world, and death by sin; and so death passed upon all men, for that all have sinned, . . . even so might grace reign through righteousness unto eternal life by Jesus Christ our Lord" (Rom. 5:12, 21). The only explanation for the axiom "all" died in Adam (1 Cor. 15:22), is that Adam's corruption infected his whole seed, making them guilty and "by nature the children of wrath" (Eph. 2:3). Sin is not a physical essence, but a spiritual intruder into God's perfect material creation. God's dealings with Israel, especially His law and covenants, were schoolmasters pointing to Christ as Redeemer. The law was threefold: ceremonial, judicial, and moral. The ceremonial and judicial (political) laws were specific to the Jews and have been set aside. The moral law remains as the law of universal justice. The purpose of the moral law is threefold (2.1–11): (1) to reveal to man his weakness, unrighteousness, and condemnation, that he might flee to Christ, (2) to restrain sinners for the good of society at large, and (3) to guide and strengthen believers in the will of God regarding every sphere of life.

By the hypostatic union of His two natures, our perfect Mediator is very God and very man (2.12–14). He fulfills the three offices of Prophet, Priest, and King (2.15). God's justice has been perfectly satisfied by His own mercy in Christ. Christ fulfilled the office of Redeemer in His death, burial, resurrection, and ascension to heaven, where He sits at the right hand of the Father (2.16–17).

Summation of Book 3

The gift of faith is the hand of the soul. By the efficacy and secret operation of the Holy Spirit, faith reaches out and receives the Christ who is offered to us in the gospel. The Spirit of sanctification and adoption is also the earnest and seal of our salvation. He unites us into Christ. The single duty of faith is to assent to God's truth. The four effects of faith are (1) repentance, (2) a Christian life of service and death to self, (3) justification by faith alone through the imputation of Christ's righteousness, and (4) prayer to God (not to saints).

These four effects of faith will ultimately result in the certainty of one's election and resurrection to life. In the midst of such practical matters, the doctrine of election becomes most applicable. The elect are called by the preaching of the word, illuminated by the Holy Spirit, justified, sanctified, and at last glorified. The *efficient* cause of election is the free mercy of God. The *material* cause of election is Jesus Christ, the well-beloved Son of God. The *final* cause of election is the eternal glorification of God (3.1–25).

Summation of Book 4

There are two aspects of the church: (1) invisible or catholic (universal) and (2) visible or particular. The invisible church consists of all the elect since creation. Only God's eye can behold them. The visible church was Old Testament Israel, whose covenant promises were in some cases forfeited and in other cases given over to the church as the new Israel. The visible church is discerned by the pure preaching of the Word and the lawful administration of the sacraments of baptism and the Lord's Supper, which replaced Old Testament purifications and sacrifices, especially the sacraments of circumcision and Passover. Old Testament females, by virtue of the covenant, would have been counted as "associates in circumcision" (4.16.16; 4.1.3–4; 4.14.18–26).

The offices of pastor and teacher are indispensable and of perpetual duration. The word *pastor* is synonymous with the words *minister*, *bishop*, and *presbyter*. The New Testament office of apostle/evangelist was one in nature, and it was temporary. The work of pastors now corresponds with that of the New Testament apostle/evangelist. The New Testament office of prophet was temporary. The work of teachers now corresponds with that of the New Testament prophets. The primary duties of the pastor are to preach the Word, to administer the sacraments, and to exercise discipline. There are two functions for deacons: distributing alms and taking care of the poor. The work of elders is in some ways similar to that of deacons but it also includes a major involvement in church order and discipline (4.1–7).

A sacrament is "a visible form of an invisible grace" (4.14.1). The Spirit of God makes the sacraments efficacious. As the Lord calls His promises "covenants" (Gen. 6:18; 9:9; 17:2), He calls His sacraments "signs" of the covenants (4.14.6). "Baptism is the initiatory sign by which we are admitted to the fellowship of the Church, that being engrafted into Christ we may be accounted children of God" (4.15.1). There is a distinction between the "substance" (essential matter) of a sacrament and the "accidents" (outward mode) of a sacrament. As to substance, there are three "essential" elements necessary for the proper administration of baptism: (1) a proper *consecration*, which includes prayer and thanksgiving, the words of the Confession of Faith, and the covenant promises associated with the sacrament; (2) a proper *distribution*, which involves the application of water in the name of the Trinity; and (3) a proper *reception*, which consists of faith on the part of the recipient (or the parents in the case of infants). Concerning the "accidents," even though the term *baptize* does mean "to immerse," and though the early churches did baptize by immersion, there is nothing of significance or importance attached to mode (4.14; 4.15.19).

Calvin thinks that Paul is describing the sacrament of water baptism when he says, "Christ also loved the church, and gave himself for it; that he might sanctify and cleanse it with the washing of water by the word" (Eph. 5:25–26). And again, "Not by works of righteousness which we have done, but according to his mercy he saved us, by the washing of regeneration, and renewing of the Holy Ghost" (Titus 3:5). Peter speaks of the sacrament when he says that "baptism doth also now save us" (1 Pet. 3:21).[4] Calvin explains, "For he did not mean to intimate that our ablution and salvation are perfected by water, or that water possesses in itself the virtue of purifying, regenerating, and renewing; nor does he mean that it is the cause of salvation, but only that the knowledge and certainty of such gifts are perceived in this sacrament" (4.15.2). Calvin says that the sign of baptism "promises that a full and entire remission has been made, both of the guilt which was imputed to us, and the penalty incurred by the guilt" (4.15.10). Passively, "infants are renewed by the Spirit of God, according to the capacity of their age, till that power which was concealed within them grows by degrees, and becomes fully manifest at the proper time."[5]

Baptism is efficacious *ex opere operato* ("by virtue of the work that is worked"). It is never to be repeated since it is not affected by the

---

[4] Calvin, *Institutes* 4.15.2; cf. 4.16.25, where he adds John 3:5.
[5] Calvin, *Commentary on a Harmony of the Evangelists: Matthew, Mark, and Luke*, trans., Wm. Pringle (Edinburgh: Calvin Translation Society, 1845), 2:390, on Matt. 19:14.

worthiness or unworthiness of the administrator and since circumcision was never repeated (4.15.16). In his Gallican Confession (1559), Calvin summarizes his thoughts "On the Sacrament of Baptism" (Art. 28): "We condemn the papal assemblies. . . . Nevertheless, as some trace of the Church is left in the papacy, and the virtue and substance of baptism remain, and as the efficacy of baptism does not depend upon the person who administers it, we confess that those baptized in it do not need a second baptism." This issue has often surfaced in Reformed historical theology. (See the excursus that follows these summations.)

Concerning the Lord's Supper (4.17), Calvin agrees with other Reformers in rejecting Roman Catholic transubstantiation. Parallel to this section of the *Institutes* are Calvin's pivotal commentary explanations of 1 Corinthians 11:24. His distinctive view begins with the Lord's Supper as "a heavenly action," whereby the faithful are elevated to heaven, where Christ dwells in glory. It is here that He nourishes the souls of believers:

> That participation in the body of Christ, which, I affirm, is presented to us in the Supper, does not require a local presence, nor the descent of Christ, nor infinite extension, nor anything of that nature, for the Supper being a heavenly action, there is no absurdity in saying, that Christ, while remaining in heaven, is received by us. For as to his communicating himself to us, that is effected through the secret virtue of his Holy Spirit, which can not merely bring together, but join in one, things that are separated by distance of place, and far remote. But, in order that we may be capable of this participation, we must rise heavenward. Here, therefore, faith must be our resource, when all the bodily senses have failed.[6]

Calvin's was a mediating view between what he considered the two extremes within Protestant circles. On the one hand, there was Luther's literal view of a consubstantial real presence of Christ's body and blood in, with, and under the elements of bread and wine. On the other hand, there was the spiritual or symbolic position of Zwingli and the Anabaptists, who rested their memorial view upon

---

[6] Calvin, *Commentary on the Epistles of Paul the Apostle to the Corinthians*, trans. John Pringle (Edinburgh: Calvin Translation Society, 1848), 1:380.

the words of Christ at the Last Supper: "This do in remembrance of me" (Luke 22:19; 1 Cor. 11:24–25). To them, the saying, "This is my body," is as the expression, "Behold the Lamb" (John 1:29). Jesus was brought "as a lamb" and "as a sheep" (Isa. 53:7). Calvin declares a *spiritual-yet-real presence* of Christ's body and blood within the sacramental elements for the nourishment of the elect unto eternal life.

First, Calvin finds the "spiritual" aspect in Ephesians 5. Arguing against the Romish view of marriage as "a great *sacramentum*," Calvin contends that Ephesians 5:31*b*, "they two shall be one flesh," is the "mystery" of the Lord's Supper. Paul's declaration that we are members "of his flesh, and of his bones" (Eph. 5:30) means that Christ "holds out his body to be enjoyed by us, and to nourish us unto eternal life." Therefore, verse 32*a*, "This is a great mystery [μυστήριον]," explains that Christ mysteriously feeds us with His body and blood. To Protestant critics of this exegesis, Calvin responds, "I am overwhelmed by the depth of this mystery."[7] In the *Institutes*, Calvin reiterates, "It is too high a mystery either for my mind to comprehend or my words to express; and to speak more plainly, I rather feel than understand it" (4.17.32).

Second, Calvin finds the "real" aspect in Christ's Bread of Life sermon of John 6:48–59, especially in verse 53, "Verily, verily, I say unto you, Except ye eat the flesh of the Son of man, and drink his blood, ye have no life in you" (4.17.1, 5, 33, 34). Many Reformed spokesmen believe that it is time to reclaim Calvin's view.[8] Conversely, William Cunningham, of the Free Church of Scotland, described Calvin's argument as "altogether unsuccessful" and "about as unintelligible as Luther's consubstantiation." Cunningham thought that it was "perhaps, the greatest blot in the history of Calvin's labors as a public instructor."[9] Southern Presbyterian theologian Robert Lewis

---

[7] On Eph. 5:28–33, see John Calvin, *Commentaries on the Epistles of Paul to the Galatians and Ephesians*, trans. William Pringle (Edinburgh: Thomas Clarke, 1841), 305–8. There are valuable discussions in Randall C. Zachman, ed., *John Calvin and Roman Catholicism: Critique and Engagement, Then and Now* (Grand Rapids: Baker, 2008), 177, passim.

[8] Keith A. Mathison, *Given For You: Reclaiming Calvin's Doctrine of the Lord's Supper* (Phillipsburg, NJ: P&R Publishing, 2002). The forward is by R. C. Sproul.

[9] *The Reformers and the Theology of the Reformation* (Edinburgh: T. & T. Clark, 1862), 240.

Dabney described Calvin's view as "strange," "curious," and so "impossible" that the framers of the Westminster Confession "had to modify all that was untenable and unscriptural in it."[10] Reformed theologian Robert L. Reymond speaks of Calvin's "inappropriateness" in using the language of John 6. Reymond explains, "By urging that Christians feed by faith upon the *literal* flesh and blood of Christ," Calvin "comes perilously close to suggesting the Godhead's apotheosizing [deifying] of Christ's humanity and to transferring, at least in the Lord's Supper, the saving benefits of Christ's atoning death directly to his human nature now localized in heaven."[11] Reformed evaluations of Calvin's usage of John 6:48–59 consist essentially in four critical points:

(1) Jesus spoke those words to a largely unsaved and hostile audience inside a Jewish synagogue in Capernaum.

(2) It is inconceivable that such an audience would have connected the Lord's Supper to this message.

(3) Jesus did not reveal this ordinance until just before His crucifixion.

(4) The view compromises the veracity of the orthodox doctrine of the theanthropic person of Christ.

Calvin's Gallican Confession (1559) summarizes his position "On the Sacrament of Lord's Supper":

> We believe that by the secret and incomprehensible power of his Spirit he feeds and strengthens us with the substance of his body and of his blood. We hold that this is done spiritually . . . because the greatness of *this mystery exceeds the measure of our senses and the laws of nature*. In short, because it is heavenly, it can only be apprehended by faith. (Art. 36)

Calvin closes the *Institutes* with a section on civil government. Here we are enjoined to obey not only good magistrates but all who

---

[10] *Syllabus and Notes of the Course of Systematic and Polemic Theology Taught in Union Theological Seminary, Virginia*, 2nd ed. (St. Louis: Presbyterian Publishing Co. of St. Louis, 1878), 810–14.

[11] *A New Systematic Theology of the Christian Faith* (Nashville: Thomas Nelson, 1998), 963. On the other hand, "Mercersburg Theology," as crafted by John W. Nevin (1803–86), would defend Calvin's view; see Nevin, *The Mystical Presence: A Vindication of the Reformed or Calvinistic Doctrine of the Holy Eucharist* (Philadelphia: S. R. Fisher, 1867).

possess authority, even those who exercise tyranny since they too were appointed on God's authority. When tyrants reign, let us first remember our faults. This produces a humility that helps to restrain our impatience. It is not in our own power to remedy the evil of civil tyranny. We can only implore the assistance of the Lord, whose hands hold the hearts of men and the revolutions of kingdoms. God restrains the fury of tyrants in two ways: (1) by raising up avengers to overturn one tyranny by means of another tyranny; (2) or at other times, by setting up popular magistrates whose office it is to restrain tyrants and to protect the liberty of the people. We must pray for our civil leaders. Our obedience to magistrates must never replace or hamper the obedience that we owe to the King of Kings. He is our ultimate ruler (4.20).

Excursus on the Validity of Roman Catholic Baptism: A Controversy between Charles Hodge and James Henley Thornwell

In 1845, the Old School General Assembly of the Presbyterian Church U.S.A. ruled by an overwhelming majority that Roman Catholic baptism is invalid. The ruling was contrary to the teachings of Augustine and Calvin (*Institutes* 4.15). While conservatives have always appreciated the Old Princeton theologian Charles Hodge (1797–1878), many have disagreed with his criticism of the Assembly's decision to reject Roman Catholic baptism. The episode continues to be cited in similar controversies.[12] Hodge argued that, even if the institution of the papacy is the antichrist, the baptism of the Romish Church is still valid.[13] Appealing to Calvin and the

---

[12] There is a helpful discussion by Charles's son, A. A. Hodge, *The Life of Charles Hodge* (New York: Charles Scribner's Sons, 1880), 340–41.

[13] Charles Hodge, *Systematic Theology* (New York: Scribner, Armstrong, 1877), 3:812ff.

Westminster Standards,[14] Hodge published an important article called "Romish Baptism."[15] Here are his key points:

¶ Romish baptism fulfills all the conditions of valid baptism, as given in our standards. It is a washing with water in the name of the Trinity, with the ostensible and professed design of making the recipient a member of the visible Church, and a partaker of its benefits. (452)

¶ We maintain that as the Romish priests are appointed and recognized as presbyters in a community professing to believe the Scriptures, the early creeds, and the decisions of the first four general councils, they are ordained ministers in the sense above stated; and consequently baptism administered by them is valid. It has accordingly been received as valid by all Protestant Churches from the Reformation to the present day. (457–58)

¶ The illustration[, as] used by Calvin, derived from the fact that those circumcised by apostate priests under the old dispensation, were never re-circumcised. (458)

¶ According to our standards, there is no salvation out of the visible Church. It is a common saying of Protestant theologians, "No man has God for his father, who has not the Church for his mother." This is only saying, with the Scriptures, that there is no salvation out of Christ. (463)

¶ Does the Church of Rome retain truth enough to save the soul? We do not understand how it is possible for any Christian man to answer this question in the negative. They retain the doctrine of the Incarnation, which we know from the infallible word of God, is a life-giving doctrine. They retain the whole doctrine of the Trinity. They teach the doctrine of atonement far more fully and

---

[14] Westminster Confession of Faith 27.3–4 and 28.6–7; the confession does not explicitly support Hodge's view. In 27.4, it states that the sacraments must be dispensed only "by a minister of the word, lawfully ordained." Perhaps more helpful to Hodge is the Larger Catechism, where the answer to Question 161 states, "The sacraments become effectual means of salvation, not by any power in themselves, or any virtue derived from the piety or intention of him by whom they are administered, but only by the working of the Holy Ghost, and the blessing of Christ, by whom they are instituted."

[15] Charles Hodge, "The General Assembly: Romish Baptism," *The Biblical Repertory and Princeton Review* 17, no. 3 (July 1845): 444–71. Hodge says, "Calvin, in his *Institutes*, Lib. iv. c. 15 and 16, after saying that baptism does not owe its value to the character of the administrator, adds: 'By this consideration, the error of the Donatists is effectually refuted'" (458).

accurately than multitudes of professedly orthodox Protestants. They hold a much higher doctrine, as to the necessity of divine influence, than prevails among many whom we recognize as Christians. They believe in the forgiveness of sins, the resurrection of the body, and in eternal life and judgment. These doctrines are in their creeds, and however they may be perverted and overlaid, still as general propositions they are affirmed. (463)

Citing from the Roman Catholic Council of Trent article "On Justification" and Thomistic apologist Jacques Bossuet's *Exposition of the Doctrines of the Catholic Church in Matters of Controversy*, Hodge concludes, "Romanists teach that Christ is the meritorious ground of our justification." In Hodge's opinion, in spite of the "unhappy blending of justification and sanctification," Roman Catholic dogma constitutes a "far better statement of the truth" than Arminianism.[16] Appealing to Calvin's *Institutes*,[17] Hodge asserts that, since the church is the new Israel, the Church of Rome is a true church, "just as the apostate Israelites were still the covenant people of God."[18] Hodge continues:

¶ Baptism, therefore, not being an ordinance of any particular Church, but of the Church catholic, and every man who professes saving truth being a member of that Church, Romish baptism, if administered by a man professing such truth, is Christian baptism. (469)

¶ We maintain, therefore, Romish baptism to be valid; that is, that it avails to make the recipient a member of the Church catholic, because it is a washing with water, in the name of the Trinity, with the design to signify, seal and apply the benefits of the covenant of grace. It is administered by ordained ministers; for a Romish priest is a man publicly called to the office of a presbyter. (469)

In a one-hundred-and-thirty-page rebuttal,[19] fellow Presbyterian conservative James Henley Thornwell (1812–62) answered Hodge

---

[16] Ibid., 464.

[17] Calvin, *Institutes* 4.15.15–16; cf. 4.2.10–12.

[18] Hodge, "The General Assembly: Romish Baptism," 466.

[19] James Henley Thornwell, "The Validity of the Baptism of the Church of Rome," in *The Collected Writings of James Henley Thornwell, D.D., LL.D., Late Professor of Theology in the Theological Seminary at Columbia, South Carolina*, ed. John B. Adger and John L. Girardeau (Richmond: Presbyterian Committee of Publication, 1871–73), 3:283–412.

on every point. To Thornwell, any church that views God as essentially unknowable and unapproachable without the aid of saints and iconic mediators is a church that falsifies biblical and historic Trinitarianism. Any church that appeals to the aid of the Virgin Mary and human works is presenting a Christ who is insufficient unto salvation. Such a Christ is not the person depicted in the patristic and Protestant creeds of Christendom. One cannot separate the person of Christ from the soteriological work of Christ. Arguing from Scripture, creeds, historical theology, and fundamental logic, Thornwell argues that "the one baptism of Paul is inseparably connected with the one Lord and the one faith." Thornwell concludes that since the Church of Rome has introduced "another Gospel and another scheme of salvation, she must necessarily have introduced another baptism"—a baptism that is "worth nothing."[20]

Select Bibliography for Further Reading

Calvin, John. *Commentaries on the Catholic Epistles*. Vol. 45 of *Calvin's Commentaries*, translated by John King. Edinburgh: Calvin Translation Society, 1847–50.

———. *Commentary on the Epistles of Paul the Apostle to the Corinthians*. 2 vols. Translated by John Pringle. Edinburgh: Calvin Translation Society, 1848–49.

———. *A Defense of the Secret Providence of God*. Vol. 2 of *Calvin's Calvinism*. Translated by Henry Cole. London: Wertheim and Macintosh, 1857.

———. *Institutes of the Christian Religion*. 2 vols. Edited by John T. McNeill and translated by Ford Lewis Battles. Volumes 20–21 in The Library of Christian Classics. Philadelphia: Westminster, 1960.

———. *A Treatise on the Eternal Predestination of God*. Vol. 1 of *Calvin's Calvinism*. Translated by Henry Cole. London: Wertheim and Macintosh, 1856.

George, Timothy. "Given Unto God: John Calvin." In *Theology of the Reformers*, 163–251. Nashville: B&H Publishing, 1999.

Hodge, Charles. "Validity of Romish Baptism." In *Discussions in Church Polity*, compiled by William Durant from the works of Charles Hodge, 191–215. New York: Charles Scribner's Sons, 1878.

McGrath, Alister E. *A Life of John Calvin: A Study in the Shaping of Western Culture*. Oxford: Basil Blackwell, 1990.

---

[20] Ibid., 412. Hodge continued his same arguments in 1846, in his article, "Is the Church of Rome a Part of the Visible Church," in *Essays and Reviews: Selected from the Princeton Review* (New York: Robert Carter and Brothers, 1857), 221–44.

Murray, Iain H. *Spurgeon v. Hyper-Calvinism: The Battle for Gospel Preaching.* Edinburgh: Banner of Truth Trust, 1995.

Reymond, Robert L. *John Calvin: His Life and Influence.* Geanies House, Fearn, Ross-shire, Scotland: Christian Focus Publications, 2004.

Roney, John B., and Martin I. Klauber, eds. *The Identity of Geneva: The Christian Commonwealth, 1564–1864.* Westport, CT: Greenwood, 1998.

Selderhuis, Herman J. *John Calvin: A Pilgrim's Life.* Translated by Albert Gootjes. Downers Grove, IL: InterVarsity, 2009.

Stauffer, Richard. *The Humanness of John Calvin.* Translated by George Shriver. Nashville: Abingdon, 1971.

Walker, Williston. *John Calvin: The Organizer of Reformed Protestantism 1509–1564.* New York: G. P. Putnam's Sons, 1906.

Zachman, Randall C. "John Calvin." In *The Reformation Theologians: An Introduction to Theology in the Modern Period,* edited by Carter Lindberg, 184–97. Malden, MA: Blackwell, 2002.

5

Classical Arminianism versus Dortian Calvinism and Beyond

Jacobus Arminius (ca. 1559–1609)[1] was born in Oudewater, in South Holland. Upon completing his studies at the University of Leiden (1576–81), he enrolled in the Academy in Geneva, where he studied under Calvin's successor, Theodore Beza. Arminius studied in Basel in 1583–84, but then returned to Geneva, where he completed his degree in 1587. He served a Reformed pastorate in Amsterdam from 1587 to 1603, when he became professor of Theology at the University of Leiden, where he remained until his death. Becoming alarmed at "high Calvinism," Arminius began to raise questions for debate over issues that included unconditional election and perseverance. When he died his body was laid to rest in dignity beneath the floor inside Pieterskerk, the magnificent Dutch Reformed church in Leiden. Following his death, Arminius's views were championed and propagated by two Reformed leaders: Simon Episcopius (1583–1643) and Jan Uytenbogaert (1557–1644).[2]

In 1610, these men and their supporters sent a petition, called the "Remonstrance" (Reproof), to the States of Holland and West Friesland. The petition set forth their views in "Five Articles," called

---

[1] Arminius's year of birth was fifty years after Calvin's and in the publication year of the final edition of the *Institutes* and in the year of the founding of the Genevan Academy.

[2] Carl Bangs, "Arminius's Theology Reviewed," in *Arminius: A Study in the Dutch Reformation* (Eugene, OR: Wipf and Stock, 1998), 332–49.

the Articles of Remonstrance. These define the original or classical Arminianism, and in summary they teach the following:

1. Conditional Election: All men have fallen in Adam. Election is based upon God's foreknowledge of personal faith. The non-elect are left to condemnation for their own sins.

2. Unlimited Atonement: In Christ's penal satisfaction, God desires the salvation of every person, on the condition of personal faith and repentance.

3. Total Depravity: All humanity is the offspring of Adam, and every child is born in total depravity. The human will is in bondage to sin. Left to himself, no man can or will accept the gospel. Saving faith is the product of divine grace. God must take the initiative in salvation. This includes common, or prevenient, grace.

4. Resistible Grace: God's grace has been resisted many times.

5. Uncertainty of Perseverance: "It has not yet been proved from the Scriptures that grace, once given, can never be lost." If any Christian does apostatize, he is lost forever.

While classical Arminianism is an immense contrast to Calvinism,[3] it should never have been confused with the heresy of Pelagianism, which denies original sin, sovereign grace, and justification by faith alone. Neither should it be confused with the heresy of Open Theism, which denies God's sovereign and total omniscience. Even the various notions of perfectionism, or entire sanctification, are absent in classical Arminianism. Diverse views such as Wesleyan sanctification, the Oberlin Perfectionism of Charles Finney, Pentecostalism, and the Keswick doctrine would come much later.[4] Although John Wesley allowed for the possibility of a "Christian perfection" that he defined as the absence of all known, or voluntary, sin, it is the older, classical Arminianism that appears in many of the sermons and hymns of John and Charles Wesley and in

---

[3] Currently, the best book on classical Arminianism is Robert Picirilli, *Grace, Faith, Free Will: Contrasting Views of Salvation; Calvinism and Arminianism* (Nashville: Randall House, 2002).

[4] See Donald L. Alexander, ed., *Christian Spirituality: Five Views of Sanctification* (Downers Grove, IL: InterVarsity, 1988).

England's eighteenth-century revivals. It also appears in some of the nineteenth-century American camp meetings and in the continued witness of fundamentalist Methodists and Free Will Baptists. In the Arminian system, God's order of decrees is as follows:

(1) To create the world
(2) To permit the fall
(3) To make atonement for all men
(4) To give all men the grace to believe if they will
(5) To elect to eternal life those whom He foresaw would believe

The Arminian order of salvation (*Ordo Salutis*) is as follows:

(1) Prevenient grace
(2) General (resistible) gospel call
(3) Faith and repentance
(4) Justification
(5) Regeneration
(6) Sanctification

The Five Arminian Articles (1610)

The following Articles of Remonstrance constitute the original system of classical or Reformed Arminianism.[5]

Article One

That God, by an eternal, unchangeable purpose in Jesus Christ his Son, before the foundation of the world, hath determined, out of the fallen, sinful race of men, to save in Christ, for Christ's sake, and through Christ, those who, through the grace of the Holy Ghost, shall believe on this his Son Jesus, and shall persevere in this faith and obedience of faith, through this grace, even to the end; and, on the other hand, to leave the incorrigible and unbelieving in sin and under wrath, and to condemn them as alienate from Christ, according to the word of the gospel in John 3:36: "He that believeth on the Son hath everlasting life: and he that believeth not the Son shall not see life; but the wrath of God abideth on him," and according to other passages of Scripture also.

---

[5] Source: Philip Schaff, "The Five Arminian Articles A.D. 1610," in *The Creeds of Christendom, with a History and Critical Notes* (New York: Harper and Brothers, 1877), 3:545–49.

Article Two

That, agreeably thereto, Jesus Christ, the Savior of the world, died for all men and for every man, so that he has obtained for them all, by his death on the cross, redemption and the forgiveness of sins; yet that no one actually enjoys this forgiveness of sins except the believer, according to the word of the Gospel of John 3:16: "God so loved the world that he gave his only-begotten Son, that whosoever believeth in him should not perish, but have everlasting life." And in the First Epistle of John 2:2: "And he is the propitiation for our sins; and not for ours only, but also for the sins of the whole world."

Article Three

That man has not saving grace of himself, nor of the energy of his free will, inasmuch as he, in the state of apostasy and sin, can of and by himself neither think, will, nor do anything that is truly good (such as saving Faith eminently is); but that it is needful that he be born again of God in Christ, through his Holy Spirit, and renewed in understanding, inclination, or will, and all his powers, in order that he may rightly understand, think, will, and effect what is truly good, according to the Word of Christ, John 15:5: "Without me ye can do nothing."

Article Four

That this grace of God is the beginning, continuance, and accomplishment of all good, even to this extent, that the regenerate man himself, without prevenient or assisting, awakening, following and cooperative grace, can neither think, will, nor do good, nor withstand any temptations to evil; so that all good deeds or movements, that can be conceived, must be ascribed to the grace of God in Christ. But as respects the mode of the operation of this grace, it is not irresistible, inasmuch as it is written concerning many, that they have resisted the Holy Ghost (Acts 7 and elsewhere in many places).

Article Five

That those who are incorporated into Christ by a true faith, and have thereby become partakers of his life-giving Spirit, have thereby full power to strive against Satan, sin, the world, and their own flesh, and to win the victory; it being well understood that it is ever through the assisting grace of the Holy Ghost; and that Jesus Christ assists them through his Spirit in all temptations, extends to them his hand, and if only they are ready for the conflict, and desire his help, and are not inactive, keeps them from falling, so that they, by no craft or power of Satan, can be misled nor plucked out of Christ's hands, according to the Word of Christ, John 10:28: "Neither shall any man pluck them out of my hand." But whether they are capable, through negligence, of forsaking again the first beginnings of their life in Christ, of again returning to this present evil world, of turning away from the holy doctrine which was delivered them, of losing a good conscience, of becoming devoid of grace, that must be more particularly determined out of the Holy Scripture, before we ourselves can teach it with the full persuasion of our minds.

The Synod of Dort (1618–19)

The main apologist for the Contra-Remonstrants was Franciscus Gomarus (1563–1641), professor of Theology and former colleague of Arminius at the University of Leiden. When all attempts at reconciliation between the two parties failed, a National Synod convened in the city of Dort (Dordrecht), November 13, 1618, to May 9, 1619, with delegates representing each of the Dutch provinces, along with twenty-six invited attendees from several countries including England, Scotland, the southern provinces of Germany, and Switzerland. Leader of the powerful merchants of Amsterdam, Johan van Oldenbarnevelt, the highest official in the Dutch Republic, shared the Remonstrants' Arminian views. Supporting the Counter-Remonstrants' party was Prince Maurice, who had succeeded his father William of Orange as stadholder of the northern provinces. As the largest and most daunting of all previous synods of the Reformed churches, the Synod of Dort would be one of the most consequential international topics of discussion for many years to come.

The pastor of the Mayflower Pilgrims, John Robinson, honorary member of the University of Leiden since 1615, and known for his impressive debates against the Arminians, probably attended some of the sessions, which ended with the condemnation of the Remonstrants as heretics and their doctrine as heresy. Two hundred Arminian ministers were deposed from their pulpits, eighty of whom were sent into exile. There were hundreds of imprisonments, including that of the theologian Hugo Grotius (1583–1645), who was sentenced for life. He later escaped, but Johan van Oldenbarnevelt was beheaded.

The violent atrocities that occurred in the political climate surrounding Dordrecht are among the disastrous results of a hermeneutic that since the fourth century had applied to the church God's methods for Israel. It was handed down from the time of Cyprian by the priesthood of the traditional church. Such atrocities distort Christ's perfections and saving work, so beautifully described in the Reformed creeds, including the Canons of Dort, the Heidelberg Catechism, the Belgic Confession, the True Confession of the Separatist Ancient Church (used by the Mayflower Pilgrims), the Westminster Confession, the London Baptist Confessions, the Philadelphia Baptist Confession, and lives and ministries of Puritans, Presbyterians, and Particular Baptists from Charles Spurgeon to William Carey. The Great Awakenings in America would originate with faithful Dutch Reformed ministers such as Theodore Frelinghuysen and later with the Fulton Street Dutch Reformed Church in New York City.

In classic Calvinism the *Ordo Salutis* is as follows:

(1) Election

(2) Regeneration

(3) Effectual call

(4) Faith and repentance

(5) Justification

(6) Sanctification

The familiar outline of the "tulip" acrostic, whose origin remains unknown, differs slightly from the Synod's own fivefold division of classical Dortian Calvinism. The following summation of the five "canons," or "heads," will follow the Synod's own arrangement:

1. Unconditional Election: All men have fallen in Adam and God is obliged to save none. Election is an act of God's will, a fruit of His love and mercy. Election is absolute and unconditional. It is the fountain out of which flows faith, eternal life, and holiness. Election is a source of gratefulness and humility. The non-elect are left to condemnation for their own sins.

2. Limited Atonement: The saving efficacy of Christ's atonement will infallibly bring only the elect to salvation. The atonement is sufficient for the whole world. The gospel is offered universally.

3. Total Depravity: Every child is conceived in sin, born in total depravity, and by nature a child of wrath—spiritually dead. The human will is in bondage to a fallen nature.

4. Irresistible Grace: Besides hearing the outward call of the gospel, each one of God's elect will exercise saving faith through the inward, efficacious call of the Holy Spirit, who infuses life into the innermost recesses of the dead sinner.

5. Perseverance of the Saints: God preserves His people to the end. This is no cause for laxity in the Christian life. Perseverance is an exhortation to holiness, humility, and good works, out of gratefulness to God.

The Synod's replacement of the Five Articles of the Remonstrance was presented under five Canons, or Heads, each subdivided into several articles. The full Dortian explanation of Calvinism is as follows:

The Canons of the Synod of Dort (1618–19)[6]

First Head of Doctrine: Of Divine Predestination

Art. 1. As all men have sinned in Adam, lie under the curse, and are obnoxious to eternal death, God would have done no injustice by leaving them all to perish, and delivering them over to condemnation on account of sin, according to the words of the Apostle (Rom. 3:19), "that every mouth may be stopped, and all the world may become guilty before God." And verse 23, "for all have sinned, and come short of the glory of God." And Rom. 6:23, "for the wages of sin is death."

Art. 2. But "in this the love of God was manifested, that he sent his only begotten Son into the world" (1 John 4:9), "that

---

[6] Source: "Canons Ratified in the National Synod of the Reformed Church, Held at Dordrecht, in the Years 1618 and 1619," in *The Constitution of the Reformed Dutch Church in the United States of America* (New York: George Forman, 1815), 149–70. I slightly modernized a few spellings and punctuations.

whosoever believeth on him should not perish, but have everlasting life" (John 3:16).

Art. 3. And that men may be brought to believe, God mercifully sends the messengers of these most joyful tidings to whom he will, and at what time he pleaseth; by whose ministry men are called to repentance and faith in Christ crucified. "How then shall they call on him in whom they have not believed? And how shall they believe in him of whom they have not heard? And how shall they hear without a preacher? And how shall they preach, except they be sent?" (Rom. 10:14, 15).

Art. 4. The wrath of God abideth upon those who believe not this gospel. But such as receive it, and embrace Jesus the Savior by a true and living faith, are by him delivered from the wrath of God, and from destruction, and have the gift of eternal life conferred upon them.

Art. 5. The cause or guilt of this unbelief, as well as of all other sins, is nowise in God, but in man himself: whereas faith in Jesus Christ, and salvation through him is the free gift of God, as it is written, "By grace ye are saved through faith, and that not of yourselves: it is the gift of God" (Eph. 2:8). "And unto you it is given in the behalf of Christ, not only to believe on him," etc. (Phil. 1:29).

Art. 6. That some receive the gift of faith from God, and others do not receive it, proceeds from God's eternal decree. "For known unto God are all his works from the beginning of the world" (Acts 15:18; Eph. 1:11). According to which decree he graciously softens the hearts of the elect, however obstinate, and inclines them to believe; while he leaves the non-elect in his just judgment to their own wickedness and obduracy. And herein is especially displayed the profound, the merciful, and at the same time the righteous discrimination between men, equally involved in ruin; or that decree of election and reprobation, revealed in the Word of God, which, though men of perverse, impure, and unstable minds wrest it to their own destruction, yet to holy and pious souls affords unspeakable consolation.

Art. 7. Election is the unchangeable purpose of God, whereby, before the foundation of the world, he hath, out of mere grace, according to the sovereign good pleasure of his own will, chosen, from the whole human race, which had fallen through their own fault, from their primitive state of rectitude, into sin and destruction, a certain number of persons to redemption in Christ, whom he from eternity appointed the Mediator and head of the elect, and the foundation of salvation.

This elect number, though by nature neither better nor more deserving than others, but with them involved in one common misery, God hath decreed to give to Christ to be saved by him, and effectually to call and draw them to his communion by his Word and Spirit; to bestow upon them true faith, justification, and sanctification; and having powerfully preserved them in the fellowship of his Son, finally to glorify them for the demonstration of his mercy, and for the praise of the riches of his glorious grace: as it is written, "According as he hath chosen us in him before the foundation of the world, that we should be holy and without blame before him in love; having predestinated us unto the adoption of children by Jesus Christ to himself, according to the good pleasure of his will, to the praise of the glory of his grace wherein he hath made us accepted in the Beloved" (Eph. 1:4–6). And elsewhere, "Whom he did predestinate, them he also called; and whom he called, them he also justified; and whom he justified, them he also glorified" (Rom. 8:30).

Art. 8. There are not various decrees of election, but one and the same decree respecting all those who shall be saved, both under the Old and New Testament: since the scripture declares the good pleasure, purpose, and counsel of the divine will to be one, according to which he hath chosen us from eternity, both to grace and to glory, to salvation and the way of salvation, which he hath ordained that we should walk therein.

Art. 9. This election was not founded upon foreseen faith, and the obedience of faith, holiness, or any other good quality or disposition in man, as the prerequisite, cause, or condition on which it depended; but men are chosen to faith and to the obedience of faith, holiness, etc. Therefore election is the fountain of every saving good; from which proceed faith, holiness, and the other gifts of salvation, and finally eternal life itself, as its fruits and effects, according to that of the Apostle. "He hath chosen us (not because we were), but that we should be holy and without blame, before him in love" (Eph. 1:4).

Art. 10. The good pleasure of God is the sole cause of this gracious election; which doth not consist herein, that God foreseeing all possible qualities of human actions, elected certain of these as a condition of salvation, but that he was pleased out of the common mass of sinners to adopt some certain persons as a peculiar people to himself, as it is written, "For the children being not yet born, neither having done any good or evil," etc. "It was said (namely, to Rebecca) the elder shall serve the younger; as it is written, Jacob have I loved, but Esau have I hated" (Rom. 9:11–13). "And as many as were ordained to eternal life believed" (Acts 13:48).

Art. 11. And as God himself is most wise, unchangeable, omniscient, and omnipotent, so the election made by him can neither be interrupted nor changed, recalled nor annulled; neither can the elect be cast away, nor their number diminished.

Art. 12. The elect in due time, though in various degrees and in different measures, attain the assurance of this their eternal and unchangeable election, not by inquisitively prying into the secret and deep things of God, but by observing in themselves, with a spiritual joy and holy pleasure, the infallible fruits of election pointed out in the Word of God—such as a true faith in Christ, filial fear, a godly sorrow for sin, a hungering and thirsting after righteousness, etc.

Art. 13. The sense and certainty of this election afford to the children of God additional matter for daily humiliation before him, for adoring the depth of his mercies, and rendering grateful returns of ardent love to him who first manifested so great love towards them. The consideration of this doctrine of election is so far from encouraging remissness in the observance of the divine commands or from sinking men into carnal security, that these, in the just judgment of God, are the usual effects of rash presumption, or of idle and wanton trifling with the grace of election, in those who refuse to walk in the ways of the elect.

Art. 14. As the doctrine of divine election by the most wise counsel of God was declared by the Prophets, by Christ himself, and by the Apostles, and is clearly revealed in the scriptures both of the Old and New Testament; so it is still to be published in due time and place in the church of God, for which it was peculiarly designed, provided it be done with reverence, in the spirit of discretion and piety, for the glory of God's most holy name, and for enlivening and comforting his people, without vainly attempting to investigate the secret ways of the Most High.

Art. 15. What peculiarly tends to illustrate and recommend to us the eternal and unmerited grace of election is the express testimony of sacred Scripture, that not all, but some only, are elected, while others are passed by in the eternal decree; whom God, out of his sovereign, most just, irreprehensible and unchangeable good pleasure, hath decreed to leave in the common misery into which they have willfully plunged themselves, and not to bestow upon them saving faith and the grace of conversion; but permitting them in his just judgment to follow their own way; at last for the declaration of his justice, to condemn and punish them forever, not only on account of their unbelief, but also for all their other sins. And this is the decree of reprobation which by no means makes God the author of sin (the very thought of which is blasphemy), but declares him to be an awful, irreprehensible, and righteous judge and avenger.

Art. 16. Those who do not yet experience a lively faith in Christ, an assured confidence of soul, peace of conscience, an earnest endeavor after filial obedience, and glorying in God through Christ, efficaciously wrought in them, and do nevertheless persist in the use of the means which God hath appointed for working these graces in us, ought not to be alarmed at the mention of reprobation, nor to rank themselves among the reprobate, but diligently to persevere in the use of means, and with ardent desires devoutly and humbly to wait for a season of richer grace. Much less cause have they to be terrified by the doctrine of reprobation, who, though they seriously desire to be turned to God, to please him only, and to be delivered from the body of death, cannot yet reach that measure of holiness and faith to which they aspire; since a merciful God has promised that he will not quench the smoking flax, nor break the bruised reed. But this doctrine is justly terrible to those who, regardless of God and of the Savior Jesus Christ, have wholly given themselves up to the cares of the world and the pleasures of the flesh, so long as they are not seriously converted to God.

Art. 17. Since we are to judge of the will of God from his Word, which testifies that the children of believers are holy, not by nature, but in virtue of the covenant of grace, in which they together with the parents are comprehended, godly parents have no reason to doubt of the election and salvation of their children whom it pleaseth God to call out of this life in their infancy.

Art. 18. To those who murmur at the free grace of election, and just severity of reprobation, we answer with the Apostle: "Nay but, O man, who art thou that repliest against God?" (Rom. 9:20).

And quote the language of our Savior: "Is it not lawful for me to do what I will with mine own?" (Matt. 20:15). And therefore with holy adoration of these mysteries, we exclaim, in the words of the Apostle: "O the depth of the riches both of the wisdom and knowledge of God! how unsearchable are his judgments, and his ways past finding out! For who hath known the mind of the Lord, or who hath been his counselor? or who hath first given to him, and it shall be recompensed unto him again? For of him, and through him, and to him are all things: to whom be glory forever. Amen." (Rom. 11:33–36).

Second Head of Doctrine: Of the Death of Christ and the Redemption of Men thereby

Art. 1. God is not only supremely merciful, but also supremely just. And his justice requires (as he hath revealed himself in his Word) that our sins committed against his infinite majesty should be punished, not only with temporal, but with eternal punishments, both in body and soul; which we cannot escape, unless satisfaction be made to the justice of God.

Art. 2. Since, therefore, we are unable to make that satisfaction in our own persons, or to deliver ourselves from the wrath of God, he hath been pleased of his infinite mercy to give his only begotten Son for our surety, who was made sin, and became a curse for us and in our stead, that he might make satisfaction to divine justice on our behalf.

Art. 3. The death of the Son of God is the only and most perfect sacrifice and satisfaction for sin; is of infinite worth and value, abundantly sufficient to expiate the sins of the whole world.

Art. 4. This death derives its infinite value and dignity from these considerations; because the person who submitted to it was not only really man and perfectly holy, but also the only begotten Son of God, of the same eternal and infinite essence with the Father and Holy Spirit, which qualifications were necessary to constitute him a Savior for us; and because it was attended with a sense of the wrath and curse of God due to us for sin.

Art. 5. Moreover the promise of the gospel is, that whosoever believeth in Christ crucified shall not perish, but have everlasting life. This promise, together with the command to repent and believe, ought to be declared and published to all nations, and to all persons promiscuously and without distinction, to whom God out of his good pleasure sends the gospel.

Art. 6. And, whereas many who are called by the gospel do not repent nor believe in Christ, but perish in unbelief; this is not owing to any defect or insufficiency in the sacrifice offered by Christ upon the cross, but is wholly to be imputed to themselves.

Art. 7. But as many as truly believe, and are delivered and saved from sin and destruction through the death of Christ, are indebted for this benefit solely to the grace of God given them in Christ from everlasting, and not to any merit of their own.

Art. 8. For this was the sovereign counsel, and most gracious will and purpose of God the Father, that the quickening and saving efficacy of the most precious death of his Son should extend to all the elect, for bestowing upon them alone the gift of justifying faith, thereby to bring them infallibly to salvation: that is, it was the will of God, that Christ by the blood of the cross, whereby he confirmed the new covenant, should effectually redeem out of every people, tribe, nation, and language, all those, and those only, who were from eternity chosen to salvation, and given to him by the Father; that he should confer upon them faith, which, together with all the other saving gifts of the Holy Spirit, he purchased for them by his death; should purge them from all sin, both original and actual, whether committed before or after believing; and having faithfully preserved them even to the end, should at last bring them free from every spot and blemish to the enjoyment of glory in his own presence forever.

Art. 9. This purpose proceeding from everlasting love towards the elect, has, from the beginning of the world to this day, been powerfully accomplished, and will, henceforward, still continue to be accomplished, notwithstanding all the ineffectual opposition of the gates of hell; so that the elect in due time may be gathered together into one, and that there never may be wanting a Church composed of believers, the foundation of which is laid in the blood of Christ, which may steadfastly love and faithfully serve him as their Savior, who, as a bridegroom for his bride, laid down his life for them upon the cross; and which may celebrate his praises here and through all eternity.

Third and Fourth Heads of Doctrine: Of the Corruption of Man, His Conversion to God, and the Manner thereof

Art. 1. Man was originally formed after the image of God. His understanding was adorned with a true and saving knowledge of his Creator, and of spiritual things; his heart and will were upright, all his affections pure, and the whole Man was holy; but revolting from God by the instigation of the devil, and abusing the freedom of his own will, he forfeited these excellent gifts, and on the contrary entailed on himself blindness of mind, horrible darkness, vanity, and perverseness of judgment; became wicked, rebellious, and obdurate in heart and will, and impure in his affections.

Art. 2. Man after the fall begat children in his own likeness. A corrupt stock produced a corrupt offspring. Hence all the posterity of Adam, Christ only excepted, have derived corruption from their original parent, not by imitation, as the Pelagians of old asserted, but by the propagation of a vicious nature.

Art. 3. Therefore all men are conceived in sin, and are by nature children of wrath, incapable of any saving good, prone to evil, dead in sin, and in bondage thereto; and, without the regenerating grace of the Holy Spirit, they are neither able nor willing to return to God, to reform the depravity of their nature, nor to dispose themselves to reformation.

Art. 4. There remain, however, in man since the fall, the glimmerings of natural light, whereby he retains some knowledge of God, of natural things, and of the difference between good and evil, and discovers some regard for virtue, good order in society, and for maintaining an orderly external deportment. But so far is this light of nature from being sufficient to bring him to a saving knowledge of God, and to true conversion, that he is incapable of using it aright even in things natural and civil. Nay farther, this light, such as it is, man in various ways renders wholly polluted, and holds it [back] in unrighteousness; by doing which he becomes inexcusable before God.

Art. 5. In the same light are we to consider the law of the Decalogue, delivered by God to his peculiar people the Jews, by the hands of Moses. For though it discovers the greatness of sin, and more and more convinces man thereof, yet as it neither points out a remedy nor imparts strength to extricate him from misery, and thus being weak through the flesh, leaves the transgressor under the curse, man cannot by this law obtain saving grace.

Art. 6. What, therefore, neither the light of nature nor the law could do, that God performs by the operation of his Holy Spirit through the word or ministry of reconciliation: which is the glad tidings concerning the Messiah, by means whereof it hath pleased

God to save such as believe, as well under the Old as under the New Testament.

Art. 7. This mystery of his will God discovered to but a small number under the Old Testament; under the New, he reveals himself to many, without any distinction of people. The cause of this dispensation is not to be ascribed to the superior worth of one nation above another, nor to their making a better use of the light of nature, but results wholly from the sovereign good pleasure and unmerited love of God. Hence they to whom so great and so gracious a blessing is communicated, above their desert, or rather notwithstanding their demerits, are bound to acknowledge it with humble and grateful hearts, and with the Apostle to adore, not curiously to pry into the severity and justice of God's judgments displayed in others, to whom this grace is not given.

Art. 8. As many as are called by the gospel are unfeignedly called; for God hath most earnestly and truly declared in his Word what will be acceptable to him, namely, that all who are called should comply with the invitation. He, moreover, seriously promises eternal life and rest to as many as shall come to him, and believe on him.

Art. 9. It is not the fault of the gospel, nor of Christ offered therein, nor of God, who calls men by the gospel, and confers upon them various gifts, that those who are called by the ministry of the Word refuse to come and be converted. The fault lies in themselves; some of whom when called, regardless of their danger, reject the Word of life; others, though they receive it, suffer it not to make a lasting impression on their heart; therefore, their joy, arising only from a temporary faith, soon vanishes, and they fall away; while others choke the seed of the Word by perplexing cares and the pleasures of this world, and produce no fruit. This our Savior teaches in the parable of the sower (Matt. 13).

Art. 10. But that others who are called by the gospel, obey the call, and are converted, is not to be ascribed to the proper exercise of freewill, whereby one distinguishes himself above others, equally furnished with grace sufficient for faith and conversion (as the proud heresy of Pelagius maintains); but it must be wholly ascribed to God, who, as he hath chosen his own from eternity in Christ, so he confers upon them faith and repentance, rescues them from the power of darkness, and translates them into the kingdom of his own Son, that they may show forth the praises of him who hath called them out of darkness into his marvelous light; and may glory not in themselves but in the Lord, according to the testimony of the apostles in various places.

Art. 11. But when God accomplishes his good pleasure in the elect, or works in them true conversion, he not only causes the gospel to be externally preached to them, and powerfully illuminates their minds by his Holy Spirit, that they may rightly understand and discern the things of the Spirit of God, but by the efficacy of the same regenerating Spirit he pervades the inmost recesses of the man; he opens the closed and softens the hardened heart, and circumcises that which was uncircumcised; infuses new qualities into the will, which, though heretofore dead, he quickens; from being evil, disobedient, and refractory, he renders it good, obedient, and pliable; actuates and strengthens it, that, like a good tree, it may bring forth the fruits of good actions.

Art. 12. And this is the regeneration so highly celebrated in scripture, and denominated a new creation; a resurrection from the dead; a making alive, which God works in us without our aid. But this is nowise effected merely by the external preaching of the gospel, by moral suasion, or such a mode of operation that, after God has performed his part, it still remains in the power of man to be regenerated or not, to be converted or to continue unconverted; but it is evidently a supernatural work, most powerful, and at the same time most delightful, astonishing, mysterious, and ineffable; not inferior in efficacy to creation or the resurrection from the dead, as the Scripture inspired by the author of this work declares; so that all in whose hearts God works in this marvelous manner are certainly, infallibly, and effectually regenerated, and do actually believe. Whereupon the will thus renewed is not only actuated and influenced by God, but, in consequence of this influence, becomes itself active. Wherefore, also, man is himself rightly said to believe and repent, by virtue of that grace received.

Art. 13. The manner of this operation cannot be fully comprehended by believers in this life. Notwithstanding which, they rest satisfied with knowing and experiencing that by this grace of God they are enabled to believe with the heart and to love their Savior.

Art. 14. Faith is therefore to be considered as the gift of God, not on account of its being offered by God to man, to be accepted or rejected at his pleasure, but because it is in reality conferred, breathed, and infused into him; nor even because God bestows the power or ability to believe, and then expects that man should, by the exercise of his own free will, consent to the terms of salvation, and actually believe in Christ; but because he who works in man both to will and to do, and indeed all things in all, produces both the will to believe and the act of believing also.

Art. 15. God is under no obligation to confer this grace upon any; for how can he be indebted to man, who had no previous gift to bestow as a foundation for such recompense? Nay, who has nothing of his own but sin and falsehood? He therefore who becomes the subject of this grace owes eternal gratitude to God, and gives him thanks forever. Whoever is not made partaker thereof is either altogether regardless of these spiritual gifts and satisfied with his own condition, or is in no apprehension of danger, and vainly boasts the possession of that which he has not. With respect to those who make an external profession of faith and live regular lives, we are bound, after the example of the Apostle, to judge and speak of them in the most favorable manner; for the secret recesses of the heart are unknown to us. And as to others, who have not yet been called, it is our duty to pray for them to God, who calleth those things which be not as though they were. But we are in no wise to conduct ourselves towards them with haughtiness, as if we had made ourselves to differ.

Art. 16. But as man by the fall did not cease to be a creature endowed with understanding and will, nor did sin, which pervaded the whole race of mankind, deprive him of the human nature, but brought upon him depravity and spiritual death; so also this grace of regeneration does not treat men as senseless stocks and blocks, nor take away their will and its properties, neither does violence thereto; but spiritually quickens, heals, corrects, and at the same time sweetly and powerfully bends it, that where carnal rebellion and resistance formerly prevailed a ready and sincere spiritual obedience begins to reign; in which the true and spiritual restoration and freedom of our will consist. Wherefore, unless the admirable Author of every good work wrought in us, man could have no hope of recovering from his fall by his own free will, by the abuse of which, in a state of innocence, he plunged himself into ruin.

Art. 17. As the almighty operation of God, whereby he prolongs and supports this our natural life, does not exclude, but requires the use of means, by which God of his infinite mercy and goodness hath chosen to exert his influence; so also the before-mentioned supernatural operation of God, by which we are regenerated, in nowise excludes or subverts the use of the gospel, which the most wise God has ordained to be the seed of regeneration and food of the soul. Wherefore as the apostles, and the teachers who succeeded them, piously instructed the people concerning this grace of God, to his glory and the abasement of all pride, and in the mean time, however, neglected not to keep them by the sacred precepts of the gospel, in the exercise of the Word, the sacraments and discipline; so, even to this day, be it far from either instructors or instructed to presume to tempt God in the church by separating what he of his good pleasure hath most intimately joined together. For grace is conferred by means of admonitions; and the more readily we perform our duty, the more eminent usually is this blessing of God working in us, and the more directly is his work advanced; to whom alone all the glory, both of means and their saving fruit and efficacy, is forever due. *Amen.*

Fifth Head of Doctrine: Of the Perseverance of the Saints

Art. 1. Whom God calls, according to his purpose, to the communion of his Son our Lord Jesus Christ, and regenerates by the Holy Spirit, he delivers also from the dominion and slavery of sin in this life; though not altogether from the body of sin and from the infirmities of the flesh, so long as they continue in this world.

Art. 2. Hence spring daily sins of infirmity, and hence spots adhere to the best works of the saints, which furnish them with constant matter for humiliation before God, and flying for refuge to Christ crucified; for mortifying the flesh more and more by the spirit of prayer and by holy exercises of piety; and for pressing forward to the goal of perfection, till being at length delivered from this body of death, they are brought to reign with the Lamb of God in heaven.

Art. 3. By reason of these remains of indwelling sin, and the temptations of sin and of the world, those who are converted could not persevere in a state of grace if left to their own strength. But God is faithful, who having conferred grace, mercifully confirms and powerfully preserves them therein, even to the end.

Art. 4. Although the weakness of the flesh cannot prevail against the power of God, who confirms and preserves true believers in a state of grace, yet converts are not always so influenced and actuated by the Spirit of God as not in some particular instances sinfully to deviate from the guidance of divine grace, so as to be seduced by, and to comply with, the lusts of the flesh; they must therefore be constant in watching and prayer, that they be not led into temptation. When these are neglected, they are not only liable to be drawn into great and heinous sins by Satan, the world, and the flesh, but sometimes by the righteous permission of God actually fall into these evils. This the lamentable fall of David, Peter, and other saints described in Holy Scriptures, demonstrates.

Art. 5. By such enormous sins, however, they very highly offend God, incur a deadly guilt, grieve the Holy Spirit, interrupt the exercise of faith, very grievously wound their consciences, and sometimes lose the sense of God's favor, for a time, until on their returning into the right way by serious repentance, the light of God's fatherly countenance again shines upon them.

Art. 6. But God, who is rich in mercy, according to his unchangeable purpose of election, does not wholly withdraw the Holy Spirit from his own people, even in their melancholy falls; nor suffer them to proceed so far as to lose the grace of adoption and forfeit the state of justification, or to commit the sin unto death; nor does he permit them to be totally deserted, and to plunge themselves into everlasting destruction.

Art. 7. For in the first place, in these falls he preserves in them the incorruptible seed of regeneration from perishing or being totally lost; and again, by his Word and Spirit, he certainly and effectually renews them to repentance, to a sincere and godly sorrow for their sins, that they may seek and obtain remission in the blood of the Mediator, may again experience the favor of a reconciled God, through faith adore his mercies, and henceforward more diligently work out their own salvation with fear and trembling.

Art. 8. Thus, it is not in consequence of their own merits or strength, but of God's free mercy, that they do not totally fall from faith and grace, nor continue and perish finally in their backslidings; which, with respect to themselves is not only possible, but would undoubtedly happen; but with respect to God, it is utterly impossible, since his counsel cannot be changed, nor his promise fail, neither can the call according to his purpose be revoked, nor the merit, intercession, and preservation of Christ be rendered ineffectual, nor the sealing of the Holy Spirit be frustrated or obliterated.

Art. 9. Of this preservation of the elect to salvation, and of their perseverance in the faith, true believers for themselves may and do obtain assurance according to the measure of their faith, whereby they arrive at the certain persuasion that they ever will continue true and living members of the church; and that they experience forgiveness of sins, and will at last inherit eternal life.

Art. 10. This assurance, however, is not produced by any peculiar revelation contrary to, or independent of the Word of God, but springs from faith in God's promises, which he has most abundantly revealed in his Word for our comfort; from the testimony of the Holy Spirit, witnessing with our spirit, that we are children and heirs of God (Rom. 8:16); and, lastly, from a serious and holy desire to preserve a good conscience, and to perform good works. And if the elect of God were deprived of this solid comfort, that they shall finally obtain the victory, and of this infallible pledge or earnest of eternal glory, they would be of all men the most miserable.

Art. 11. The scripture moreover testifies that believers in this life have to struggle with various carnal doubts, and that under grievous temptations they are not always sensible of this full assurance of faith and certainty of persevering. But God, who is the Father of all consolation, does not suffer them to be tempted above that they are able, but will with the temptation also make a way to escape, that they may be able to bear it (1 Cor. 10:13); and by the Holy Spirit again inspires them with the comfortable assurance of persevering.

Art. 12. This certainty of perseverance, however, is so far from exciting in believers a spirit of pride, or of rendering them carnally secure, that, on the contrary, it is the real source of humility, filial reverence, true piety, patience in every tribulation, fervent prayers, constancy in suffering, and in confessing the truth, and of solid rejoicing in God; so that the consideration of this benefit should serve as an incentive to the serious and constant practice of gratitude and good works, as appears from the testimonies of scripture and the examples of the saints.

Art. 13. Neither does renewed confidence of persevering produce licentiousness or a disregard to piety in those who are recovered from backsliding; but it renders them much more careful and solicitous to continue in the ways of the Lord, which he hath ordained, that they who walk therein may maintain an assurance of persevering; lest by abusing his fatherly kindness, God should turn away his gracious countenance from them, to behold which is to the godly dearer than life, the withdrawing whereof is more bitter than death; and they in consequence thereof should fall into more grievous torments of conscience.

Art. 14. And as it hath pleased God, by the preaching of the gospel, to begin this work of grace in us, so he preserves, continues, and perfects it by the hearing and reading of his Word, by meditation thereon, and by the exhortations, threatenings, and promises thereof, as well as by the use of the sacraments.

Art. 15. The carnal mind is unable to comprehend this doctrine of the perseverance of the saints, and the certainty thereof, which God hath most abundantly revealed in his Word, for the glory of his name and the consolation of pious souls, and which he impresses upon the hearts of the faithful. Satan abhors it; the world ridicules it; the ignorant and hypocrite abuse, and heretics oppose it. But the spouse of Christ hath always most tenderly loved and constantly defended it, as an inestimable treasure; and God, against whom neither counsel nor strength can prevail, will dispose her to continue this conduct to the end. Now to this one God, Father, Son, and Holy Spirit be honor and glory forever. *Amen.*

While Dortian Calvinism is an immense contrast to Arminianism, it should not be confused with "hyper-Calvinism," or with anti-missions movements. There is no denial of common grace. There is a free offer of the gospel. There is no antinomianism and no teaching of a supra-temporal justification. On the question of the order of divine decrees, Reformed theologians agree with Louis Berkhof that with our eternal and omniscient God there is only one decree.[7] Most seem to agree, though, that a logical arrangement might be helpful for finite man. The Canons of Dort (as is Calvin)[8] are consistent with

---

[7] Louis Berkhof, *Systematic Theology* (1938; repr., Grand Rapids: Eerdmans, 1972), 102.

[8] I do not concur with those who claim that a clear system of supralapsarianism is found in the following works by John Calvin, *A Treatise on the Eternal Predestination of God*, vol. 1 of *Calvin's Calvinism*, trans. Henry Cole (London: Wertheim and Macintosh, 1856); and *A Defense of the Secret Providence of God*, vol. 2 of *Calvin's Calvinism*, trans. Henry Cole (London: Wertheim and Macintosh, 1857). The *Treatise* of volume 1 originated in Geneva in 1552, and the *Defense* of volume 2 originated in Geneva in 1558. In addition, J. V. Fesko

infralapsarianism, which places God's decree of election immediately after or below (*infra*) His decree to permit the fall of humanity. The Dortian order of decrees is as follows:

(1) Create the world and the human race
(2) Permit all humanity to fall
(3) Elect some to eternal life and pass by all others
(4) Provide Christ's atoning work of redemption
(5) Apply salvation to each of the elect by the Word and the Holy Spirit

The Dortian *Ordo Salutis*:

(1) Regeneration
(2) Conversion (faith and repentance)
(3) Forensic justification based on faith
(4) Sanctification

Conversely, supralapsarianism places God's decree of personal election before or above (*supra*) His decree to permit the fall. This makes the fall necessary; therefore, it appears to make God the author of sin:

(1) Election of some to eternal life and reprobation of all others
(2) Creation of the world and the human race
(3) Fall of all humanity
(4) Redemption provided for the elect by Christ's atonement
(5) Application of redemptive benefits to the elect

Anti-missionary movements have characteristically been supralapsarian. Calvin's successor, Theodore Beza, was supralapsarian, and so were key representatives at the Synod of Dort. Nevertheless, the Canons of Dort are infralapsarian, in that the elect are "chosen, from the whole human race, which had fallen through their own fault, from their primitive state of rectitude, into sin and destruction" (1.7).

Those who are reprobate "are passed by in the eternal decree." God "decreed to leave (them) in the common misery into which they have willfully plunged themselves" (1.15). Thus, a precise distinction

---

falls short of his aim at demonstrating that Calvin was a supralapsarian. See his *Diversity within the Reformed Tradition: Supra- and Infralapsarianism in Calvin, Dort, and Westminster* (Greenville, SC: Reformed Academic Press, 2001). Fesko repeatedly reads supralapsarianism into neutral passages.

is made between the two expressions "chosen" and "passed by." The Scriptures do not provide a reason for the "passing by" except the sovereign will of God. This "by no means makes God the author of sin (the very thought of which is blasphemy)" (1.15). Far from being anti-missionary, the soteriology of Dort is expressed as follows:

> That men may be brought to believe, God mercifully sends the messengers of these most joyful tidings to whom he will, and at what time he pleaseth; by whose ministry men are called to repentance and faith in Christ crucified. "How then shall they call on him in whom they have not believed? And how shall they believe in him of whom they have not heard? And how shall they hear without a preacher? And how shall they preach, except they be sent?" (Rom. 10:14, 15). (1.3)

Supralapsarians among English Puritans included William Perkins (1558–1602) and, a little later, William Twisse, the chairman of the Westminster Assembly (1647). The Westminster Confession, though, stands non-committal on the debate between the supralapsarians and infralapsarians. Supralapsarianism received no confessional endorsement and no confessional condemnation. The point of view is generally considered as being within confessional boundaries, but the usual conviction among Calvinists has generally been Calvin's infralapsarianism.

Amyraldianism

In the wake of the Synod of Dort, a French Protestant theologian, Moses (or Moïse) Amyraldus (1596–1664), of the School of Saumur, developed his own system of four-point Calvinism. Amyraldus, whose name also appears as Moyses Amyraut,[9] devised his new system for four reasons: (1) to eliminate insinuations that

---

[9] The most helpful sources are in this order: Roger Nicole, "Moyse Amyraut (1596–1664) and the Controversy on Universal Grace: First Phase (1634–1637)" (PhD diss., Harvard University, 1966); Roger Nicole, *Moyse Amyraut: A Bibliography with Special Reference to the Controversy on Universal Grace* (New York: Garland, 1981); Lawrence Proctor, "The Theology of Moïse Amyraut Considered as a Reaction against Seventeenth-Century Calvinism" (PhD diss., University of Leeds, 1952); and Brian G. Armstrong, *Calvinism and the Amyraut Heresy: Protestant Scholasticism and Humanism in Seventeenth-Century France* (Madison: University of Wisconsin Press, 1969).

God is the author of sin; (2) to eliminate difficult questions over limited atonement; (3) to bring Calvinists and Lutherans closer together on soteriological issues; and (4) to argue that his system agreed with John Calvin's teachings.

A former lawyer, Amyraut had become a theologian through reading Calvin's *Institutes*. Known as the School of Saumur, Amyraldism, Amyraldianism, "hypothetical universalism," or "four-point Calvinism," the system presupposes a twofold will of God. It begins by changing the covenant of grace (discussed below) into two covenants—one of common grace and one of saving grace. We will consider them in that order.

First, God provided an ideal, conditional, hypothetical covenant of objective and universal grace (*gratia universalis*), which offers salvation to all men on condition of repentance and faith. Theoretically, all possess a "natural ability" to believe. Second, God provided a particular, unconditional, guaranteed covenant of subjective grace that saves only the elect. The elect receive a "moral ability" to be willing to believe. All men possess natural ability but only the elect possess moral ability. While maintaining the standard Reformed doctrine of a double decree of election and reprobation, Amyraldianism asserts that God also decreed an atonement that was "sufficient for all, but efficient only for the elect." John Calvin, commenting on 1 John 2:2, says that he agrees with that old adage, "yet I deny that it is suitable to this passage." The Amyraldian arrangement of God's eternal decrees is as follows:

(1) Create the world and the human race
(2) Permit the fall of all humanity
(3) Provide an atonement that is universal in its extent but particular in its effect
(4) Elect some to eternal life and pass by all others
(5) Apply salvation to each of the elect by the Word and Holy Spirit

Molinism: Another Four-Point Soteriology Revived

Prior to the Synod of Dort, a theology called "Molinism," after its founder Luis Molina (1535–1600), a Spanish Jesuit priest, presented a view of unlimited atonement that caused great controversy even in Protestant circles. It finds current support in a work by Kenneth Keathley, *Salvation and Sovereignty: A Molinist Approach*.[10] Keathley, a professor of Theology at Southeastern Baptist Theological Seminary, seeks to promote Molinism in a more palatable way by packaging it into a five-fold acrostic of "Roses":

(1) Radical depravity (includes volition)
(2) Overcoming grace (euphemism for "irresistible" grace)
(3) Sovereign election (unconditional election with conditional reprobation)
(4) Eternal life (euphemism for "eternal security")
(5) Singular redemption (provided for all, but applied only to the elect)

Covenant Theology

The most formidable Reformed weapon against both Molinism and Amyraldianism would be covenant theology. While its seed thoughts had appeared in the works of John Calvin, English Puritan William Ames (1576–1633), and in the Westminster Confession (1647), the development of covenant theology into a system would largely be the work of two men. The first was Johannes Cocceius (1603–69), who was born and educated in Bremen, Germany, then moved to the Netherlands for a teaching ministry, first at the University of Franeker and then at the University of Leiden, where he spent the rest of his public life as professor of Dogmatic Theology. Cocceius's chief literary work was his *Doctrinal Summary of the Covenant and Testament of God* (*Summa Doctrina de Foedere et Testamento Dei*), published in 1648. The second figure was Francis Turretin (François Turrettini) 1623–87, a Genevan scholar with Swiss-Italian roots, who became the more significant of the two progenitors of the system. His massive set of *Institutes of Elenctic Theology* (*Institutio Theologiae Elencticae*) was published 1679–85.[11] Due to its embedded doctrine of federal headship imputation, covenant theol-

---

[10] Kenneth Keathley, *Salvation and Sovereignty: A Molinist Approach* (Nashville: B&H Publishing Group, 2010).

[11] Francis Turretin, *Institutes of Elenctic Theology*, trans. George Musgrave Giger and ed. James T. Dennison Jr. (Phillipsburg, NJ: P&R Publishing, 1992–97), 1:574–78; 2:169–269.

ogy is often called federal theology. The system teaches that the logical order of God's eternal decrees is as follows:

(1) Create the world and the human race
(2) Permit Adam to sin as federal head of humanity
(3) Elect some to eternal life and pass by all others
(4) Send Christ, as the second Adam, the new representative, to provide His atoning work of redemption
(5) Apply salvation to each of the elect by the Word and Holy Spirit

In federal theology, the fourth decree came to be called the "covenant of redemption" (*pactum salutis*), whereby Christ would make atonement and impute His own righteousness to the elect. On the basis of the decrees, and prior to Adam's fall, God revealed a "covenant of works" (*foedus operum*) with Adam and with all humanity "in Adam." The covenant promised eternal life for perfect obedience. Because Adam, before the fall, possessed the natural ability to perform his part of this covenant, Cocceius and Turretin sometimes refer to it as the "covenant of nature" (*foedus naturae*). Its contract was written upon man's conscience (Rom. 2:14). After the fall, God revealed a "covenant of grace" (*foedus gratiae*) with His elect. The promise of Genesis 3:15 is a sort of dividing line between the two covenants of works and grace.

Cocceius and Turretin distinguished three dispensations, or economies of grace, essentially differing only in the manner in which grace is dispensed: (1) the patriarchal period of grace administered through human conscience; (2) the national period of grace administered through the law and the prophets; and (3) the present era of grace administered through the completed work of Christ. The church totally replaced the dispersed Israel at the beginning of this era and redemptive grace is now administered to God's elect among many nationalities being gathered into His kingdom.

Turretin's Latin work would become the standard expression of covenant theology, and its legacy would continue with Charles Hodge's three-volume *Systematic Theology* (1871–73), a modern restatement of this theology. While covenant theology makes no essential distinction between Israel and the church, dispensationalists believe that the church is presently a separate entity from Israel and that Israel will be restored in the last days. In terms of imputation, however, dispensationalists generally agree with the federal headship view, which is as follows:

(1) Adam was the representative head of the human race.

(2) Therefore, all sinned through Adam, their central spokesman. We mentioned in the previous volume that when a head of state declares war, every citizen is at war. The federal head has spoken in behalf of his country. The consequences fall upon every citizen. Similarly, in the case of Adam and the first sin, the imputation of sin and guilt falls upon every person conceived into the world.

(3) Accordingly, all are born in sin, depraved, guilty, and under the sentence of death. We are not sinners because we sin, but rather we sin because we are sinners. When Adam sinned, he disqualified himself from continuing as the federal head of humanity; thus, only the first sin was imputed to the human race. God extends saving, efficacious grace to His elect, enabling them to respond to the call to salvation. The federal headship view maintains the vital connection between Adam and his race, while avoiding Augustine's maneuver of changing "because" (ἐφ' ᾧ) to "in whom" (*in quo*) in Romans 5:12.

By the late nineteenth century and early twentieth century, Calvinism would be well explained by the Old Princeton theologians such as Benjamin Breckinridge Warfield (1851–1921). This reading is from Warfield's article called "Calvinism":[12]

¶ Since the eternal plan, decree, or purpose of God includes all things that come to pass, none of which comes to pass without His prevision and provision, it includes also the destinies of all creatures. Predestination, in its restricted sense, is the term employed to express the purpose of God in relation to the salvation of individual men. . . . It thus includes both the selection of one portion of the race to be saved and the leaving of the rest to perish in sin. This act of discrimination is necessarily absolutely sovereign. . . .

---

[12] B. B. Warfield, "Calvinism," in *Johnson's Universal Cyclopedia* (New York: D. Appleton, 1897), 2:17–25.

¶ The great majority of Calvinists have always been what has come to be known as Infra- or Sublapsarians—that is, they hold that God's predestinating decree contemplates man as already fallen and resting under the curse of the broken law. God is conceived of as, moved by ineffable love for man, selecting out of the mass of guilty sinners a people in whom to show forth the glory of His grace, and then as providing redemption for them in order to carry out His loving purposes in election. The "order of decrees," as it is technically called, stands in this view thus: Creation, fall, election, redemption by Christ, and application of redemption by the Holy Spirit. A few Calvinists, whose inconsiderable number is balanced by their considerable learning and logical power, have always contended that on logical grounds it would be better to place the decree of election in the order of thought before that of the fall; they are therefore called Supralapsarians, and give the "order of decrees" thus: Creation, election (or even election, creation), fall, redemption, and application. This question did not come into discussion until the close of the sixteenth century, so that the position upon it of Calvinistic writers before that date is usually in dispute. There seems no good reason to doubt, however, that Augustine and Calvin were essentially Infralapsarian in their fundamental conceptions. On the other hand, the Supralapsarian scheme was adopted by men of such mark and influence as Beza, successor to Calvin in Geneva; Gomarus and Voetius, the great opponents to the Remonstrants in Holland; and Twisse, the prolocutor of the Westminster Assembly. . . .

¶ On the other hand, a departure from typical Calvinism was proposed by the school of Saumur [Amyraldism] in the first half of the seventeenth century, in the opposite direction. In the effort to conceive of the work of Christ as having equal reference to all men indiscriminately, they proposed to place the decree of election subsequent in the order of thought to that of redemption, making the "order of decrees" the following: Creation, fall, redemption by Christ, election, and application of redemption by the Holy Spirit to the elect. This change is of greater theological importance, as it involves an entirely different view of the nature of the atonement from that taught by typical Calvinism. It has exercised far more influence than Supralapsarianism; but has left the great majority of Calvinists unaffected, chiefly on account of its inability to coalesce with a truly substitutionary doctrine of the atonement.

¶ In all its forms alike Calvinism makes God the sole arbiter of the destiny of His creatures. But in no form does it make Him the author of sin, or the condemner of man irrespective of his sin. In all forms alike man is made the author of his own sin, and sin is made the ground of his condemnation. God positively decrees grace, and thus produces all that is good. He only determines the permission of sin, and punishes it because He forbids and in every way morally discountenances it. He elects of free grace all those He purposes to save, and actually saves them, while those whom He does not elect are simply left under the operation of the law of exact justice, whatever that may be in their case.

Conclusion: Five Guidelines for Studying the Great Doctrines of Grace

These guidelines harmonize with the "Seven Principles of Historical Theology" listed in the General Introduction preceding our study of the earliest church fathers.

First, never jeopardize your ministry or your testimony by trying to defend unnecessary systems. Labels are often necessary and theological labels are absolutely necessary to avoid confusion, but, in any circle of churches, there are certain labels that can do nothing more than to confuse and to limit your ministry. Often, people will assume that your label means that you believe everything that has been historically associated it. Preach whatever is clearly scriptural within any system, but be leery of defending systems *per se*, merely for the sake of a popular system, even if all your friends are tagging themselves as being "of Cephas" or "of Apollos" (1 Cor. 1:12). We must be of Christ alone. We must preach Christ alone.

We can come to our own strong convictions and still graciously acknowledge that good men differ over such things as limited or unlimited atonement. From the moment that you commit to a system, you will have a proneness to make the Bible conformable to your system. That can become eisegesis rather than exegesis. God does not expect you to know everything or to be able to explain everything in neat and popular clichés. Your faithful and careful handling of God's Word will be your most effective tool in revealing to others who you are and what you believe.

Second, a sure mark of Christian maturity is the willingness to accept both of what may seem to be two opposing biblical affirmations, without emphasizing one at the expense of the other. We overcome the difficulty of combining truly militant opposites by keeping both as true, and by keeping them militantly. Each truth is part of the whole truth. The very essence of truth reflects the nature of the Triune God, who is the source of all truth. God Himself is Three in One—One in Three (plurality in unity and unity in plurality). And God's absolute truth, in its oneness, is properly perceived only through the plurality of its nature. This explains the reality of theological perspective and mystery. Truth is one, with multiple sides. We must be aware of our limitations. There is the ongoing necessity of distinguishing between the divine and human elements of doctrine and practice. Into systems of theology, men import human baggage. The one absolute and infallible standard is God's Word.

Third, any emphasis that places the ground or basis of salvation in man is wrong. John 1:12–13 says, "As many as received him, to them gave he power to become the sons of God, even to them that believe on his name: which were born, not of . . . the will of man, but of God." Jesus prayed in John 17:24, "Father, I will that they also, whom thou hast given me, be with me where I am; that they may behold my glory, which thou hast given me: for thou lovedst me before the foundation of the world." Paul adds then, "According as he hath chosen us in him before the foundation of the world, that we should be holy and without blame before him in love" (Eph. 1:4). "When the Gentiles heard this, they were glad, and glorified the word of the Lord: and as many as were ordained to eternal life believed" (Acts 13:48). We are elected to bring forth fruit, and bringing forth fruit results in answered prayer. Jesus says in John 15:16, "Ye have not chosen me, but I have chosen you, and ordained you, that ye should go and bring forth fruit, and that your fruit should remain: that whatsoever ye shall ask of the Father in my name, he may give it you."

Fourth, any emphasis that quenches one's enthusiasm for reaching the lost with the gospel is seriously wrong. God's omniscience means "that He knows Himself and all other things, whether they be actual or merely possible, whether they be past, present, or future, and that He knows them perfectly and from all eternity."[13] Prayer changes things, and God knows our prayers from eternity. "Even before there is a word on my tongue, behold, O Lord, You know it all" (Ps. 139:4, NASB). This means that God has already considered all of our prayers in His eternal decrees. By the authority of God's Word, we can without reservation tell any lost sinner that God loves him, Christ died for him, and that God desires for him to repent and turn to Christ. First John 2:2 says, "He is the propitiation for our sins: and not for ours only, but also for the sins of the whole world." Paul says in 2 Timothy 2:10, "Therefore I endure all things for the elect's sakes, that they may also obtain the salvation which is in Christ Jesus with eternal glory." In 1 Timothy 2:1, he says, "I exhort therefore, that, first of all, supplications, prayers, intercessions, and giving of thanks, be made for all men." Jesus commands in Matthew 28:19, "Go ye therefore, and teach all nations." Paul encourages us in 1 Corinthians 1:21 that although "the world by wisdom knew not God, it pleased God by the foolishness of preaching to save them that believe."

Fifth, no person can possibly understand completely the mind of God in these matters. Job 37:16 asks, "Dost thou know . . . the wondrous works of him which is perfect in knowledge?" Deuteronomy 29:29 says, "The secret things belong unto the Lord our God: but those things which are revealed belong unto us and to our children for ever, that we may do all the words of this law." God says in Isaiah 55:8–9, "For my thoughts are not your thoughts, neither are your ways my ways, saith the Lord. For as the heavens are higher than the earth, so are my ways higher than your ways, and my thoughts than your thoughts." Isaiah 46:9–11: "I am God, and there is none like me, declaring the end from the beginning, and from ancient times the things that are not yet done, saying, My counsel shall stand, and I will do all my pleasure: . . . yea, I have spoken it, I will also bring it to pass; I have purposed it, I will also do it."

---

[13] Henry Clarence Thiessen, *Introductory Lectures in Systematic Theology* (Grand Rapids: Eerdmans, 1949), 124.

Select Bibliography for Further Reading

Arminius and Classical Arminianism

Arminius, James. *The Writings of James Arminius*. Translated by James Nichols, 3 vols. Buffalo, NY: Derby, Miller, and Orton, 1853.

Bangs, Carl. *Arminius: A Study in the Dutch Reformation*. Eugene, OR: Wipf and Stock, 1998.

Burrows, Roland. *John Wesley in the Reformation Tradition: The Protestant and Puritan Nature of Methodism Rediscovered*. Stoke-on-Trent, Staffordshire, UK: Tentmaker Publications, 2008.

Burtner, Robert W., and Robert E. Chiles, eds. *John Wesley's Theology: A Collection from His Works*. Previously published as *A Compend of Wesley's Theology*. Nashville: Abingdon, 1982.

Buzzell, John. *The Life of Elder Benjamin Randall*. Limerick, ME: Hobbs, Woodman, 1827.

Miley, John. *Systematic Theology*. 2 vols. 1893. Reprint, Peabody, MA: Hendrickson, 1989.

Murray, Iain H. *Wesley and Men Who Followed*. Edinburgh: Banner of Truth Trust, 2003.

Panosian, Edward M. "John Wesley's Doctrine of Christian Perfection." *Biblical Viewpoint* 6, no. 2 (November 1972): 120–29.

Picirilli, Robert E. *Grace, Faith, Free Will: Contrasting Views of Salvation; Calvinism and Arminianism*. Nashville: Randall House, 2002.

Wheeler, Henry. *History and Exposition of the Twenty-Five Articles of Religion of the Methodist Episcopal Church*. New York: Eaton & Mains, 1908. These articles were used by John Wesley.

Wiley, Frederick. *Life and Influence of the Rev. Benjamin Randall: Founder of the Free Baptist Denomination*. Philadelphia, PA: American Baptist Publication Society, 1915.

Wiley, H. Orton. *Christian Theology*. 3 vols. Kansas City, MO: Beacon Hill, 1952.

Classical Calvinism, Dortian Calvinism, and Covenant (Federal) Theology

Allen, David L., and Steve W. Lemke, eds. *Whosoever Will: A Biblical-Theological Critique of Five-Point Calvinism*. Nashville: B&H Publishing Group, 2010.

Beeke, Joel, and Sinclair Ferguson, eds. *Reformed Confessions Harmonized*. Grand Rapids: Baker, 1999.

"Canons Ratified in the National Synod of the Reformed Church, Held at Dordrecht, in the Years 1618 and 1619." In *The Constitution of the Reformed Dutch Church in the United States of America*, 149–70. New York: George Forman, 1815.

Daniel, Curt. *The History and Theology of Calvinism*. Springfield, IL: Good Books; Reformed Bible Church, 2003.

Fisher, George P. "The Augustinian and the Federal Doctrines of Original Sin." In *Discussions in History and Theology*, 355–409. New York: Charles Scribner's Sons, 1880.

Hoeksema, Homer A. *The Voice of Our Fathers: An Exposition of the Canons of Dordrecht.* Grand Rapids: Reformed Free Publishing Association, 1980.

Hyde, Daniel R. *With Heart and Mouth: An Exposition of the Belgic Confession.* Grandville, MI: Reformed Fellowship, 2008.

McNeill, John T. *The History and Character of Calvinism.* Oxford: Oxford University Press, 1967.

Maze, Scott. *Theodorus Frelinghuysen's Evangelism: Catalyst to the First Great Awakening.* Grand Rapids: Reformation Heritage Books, 2011.

Steele, David N., and Curtis C. Thomas. *The Five Points of Calvinism Defined, Defended, Documented.* Philadelphia: Presbyterian and Reformed, 1963.

Turretin, Francis. *Institutes of Elenctic Theology.* Translated by George Musgrave Giger. Edited by James T. Dennison Jr. 3 vols. Phillipsburg, NJ: P&R Publishing, 1992–97.

Warfield, Benjamin Breckinridge. *The Plan of Salvation.* Philadelphia: Presbyterian Board of Publication, 1915. The book consists of five lectures delivered at Princeton Seminary in June 1914.

Wells, David F., ed. *Dutch Reformed Theology.* Grand Rapids: Baker, 1989.

The [Westminster] Confession of Faith [and] the Larger and Shorter Catechisms: With Scripture Proofs at Large; Together with the Sum of Saving Knowledge. London: Thomas Nelson, 1877.

Molinism and Amyraldianism

Armstrong, Brian G. *Calvinism and the Amyraut Heresy: Protestant Scholasticism and Humanism in Seventeenth-Century France.* Madison: University of Wisconsin Press, 1969.

Keathley, Kenneth. *Salvation and Sovereignty: A Molinist Approach.* Nashville: B&H Publishing Group, 2010.

Nicole, Roger. *Moyse Amyraut: A Bibliography with Special Reference to the Controversy on Universal Grace.* New York: Garland, 1981.

———. "Moyse Amyraut (1596–1664) and the Controversy on Universal Grace: First Phase (1634–1637)." PhD diss., Harvard University, 1966.

Proctor, Lawrence. "The Theology of Moïse Amyraut Considered as a Reaction against Seventeenth-Century Calvinism." PhD diss., University of Leeds, 1952.

Strehle, Stephen. "Universal Grace and Amyraldianism." *Westminster Theological Journal* 51 (1989): 345–57.

6

The Sabbath Day: Christian Views from New Testament Times to the Present

New Testament Times

To the Jewish rabbis, it was a shocking violation of their interpretation of the law for Jesus to heal the cripple on a Sabbath Day (John 5:9–18). When questioned, Jesus answered with a radical departure from rabbinical teachings:[1] "My Father is working even until now, and I work." To the rabbis, this "Sabbath breaker" was claiming that God was His Father, that they were both equal, and that they both worked on the Sabbath. Ultimately, those would be the charges presented at His religious trial. From the start, the Jewish leaders wanted Him dead for being a blasphemer and a Sabbath breaker.

Following Christ's resurrection, there is no mention in the Scriptures of Saturday being the primary day for Christian worship. Christ had earlier visited the synagogues to present Himself as Messiah, and the apostle Paul visited synagogues for the purpose of presenting the gospel of Christ. Paul did not visit the synagogues for the breaking of bread or for fellowship. He made his final synagogue

---

[1] The rabbis of that day insisted that God Himself observes all the statutes of the Sabbath. See Ferdinand Weber, *Jüdische Theologie* (Leipzig: Dörffling and Franke, 1897), 17–18.

visit in Acts 18:4–7 where, due to the group's blasphemies, he announced that he would turn to the Gentiles.

The New Testament does not reveal any explicit divine command for Christians to assemble for worship on a specific day of the week. The following ten factors, however, indicate that there was a biblical *terminus a quo* for the Sunday paradigm, that it finds its provenance in the time of Christ's post-resurrection ministry, and that this became the standard that His disciples would consistently practice:

1. Jesus' resurrection from the dead was on the first day of the week (John 20:1).

2. Jesus' first post-resurrection appearance was to ten disciples on the first day of the week (John 20:19).

3. Jesus' next appearance was to all eleven disciples, eight days later (John 20:26), on the first day of the week. In standard Jewish reckoning, "the starting day was also included in counting the number of days" (*ESV Study Bible*). Lange, in his commentary on John, not only concurs that this appearance was "on the first Sunday after the resurrection-day"; he also points to its historical significance: "That the disciples already attribute a particular importance to Sunday is evidenced by the numeric completeness of their assembly." Philip Schaff is even more assertive:

   > This is the beginning of the history of the Lord's day, which to this day has never suffered a single interruption in Christian lands, except for a brief period of madness in France during the reign of terror. Sunday is here pointed out by our Lord Himself and honored by His special presence as *the day of religion, and public worship*, and so it will remain to the end of time. God's Word and God's Day are inseparable companions, and the pillars of God's church.[2]

4. The church was inaugurated on the Day of Pentecost (Acts 2), which always fell on the first day of the week as in the Old Testament (Lev. 23:16). It was here in Jerusalem on

---

[2] John Peter Lange, *The Gospel According to John*, in Commentary on the Holy Scriptures, trans. and ed. Philip Schaff (Grand Rapids: Zondervan, n.d.), 9:620–21.

the first day of the week that the church assembled and received the promised baptism of the Holy Spirit.

5. On that Day of Pentecost, Peter preached the first gospel message (Acts 2:14ff.).

6. On that same day, three thousand converts were added to the first church (Acts 2:41).

7. On the same day, Christians administered Trinitarian water baptism to new converts for the first time (Acts 2:41).

8. The Christians at Troas were observing their worship on the first day of the week when Paul arrived, preached until midnight, and restored the young Eutychus to life (Acts 20:6–12).

9. Paul instructed the Corinthian Christians to make their contributions on the first day of the week (1 Cor. 16:2).

10. The apostle John, in Revelation 1:10, says that on the Isle of Patmos he was in the Spirit on the Lord's (κυριακῇ) day, that is, the day "belonging to the Lord." The term appears in only one other place, 1 Corinthians 11:20, where Paul tells the disorderly Corinthians that when they come together it is certainly not to eat the Lord's (κυριακὸν) Supper, that is, the supper "belonging to the Lord." The term is different from the familiar eschatological expression, "the day of the Lord," as in the book of Joel, which refers to a coming day of judgment. During the post-apostolic church period, Christians would continue to ascribe to Sunday the designation "the Lord's Day."

We turn now to documents composed only a few years after John received his Revelation on the Isle of Patmos. In the early second century, Pliny the Younger, governor of Pontus and Bithynia, sent a letter to Emperor Trajan reporting a common practice that had been observed among Christians: "On an appointed day they had been accustomed to meet before daybreak, and to recite a hymn antiphonally to Christ, as to a god."[3] Pliny knew that when followers of Christ described their day of worship as their "Lord's" day, they

---

[3] Pliny the Younger, *Epistle* 10 (To Trajan), in *Documents of the Christian Church*, ed. Henry Bettenson (London: Oxford University Press, 1943), 3–6.

were ascribing deity to Christ. During times of imperial worship, emperors often forbade the use of the word *Lord* as denoting anyone but themselves.

Initially, Christians met daily for prayer and Bible study, and from the earliest times they set aside Sunday, which they called the Lord's Day, as the special day for their weekly assemblies for edification, for rejoicing, and for worshiping Christ as Lord. There are rare instances of some church members who wished to honor Saturday, then make Sunday their main day of worship, but any such thought of Sabbath observance always met with swift and successful pastoral rebuke. Except for rare, isolated, obscure, or mystical references from Alexandria, patristic writers do not refer to Sunday as a "Christian Sabbath."

Nor do patristic authors teach that God's cessation from His six-day creative work obligated man to rest on one day of the week. In the few places where patristic writers mention the creation week in conjunction with Sabbath rest, the application is eschatological. To them the seventh day of the creation week is symbolic of the future seventh millennium of Sabbath rest, which will be followed by a new beginning, the "eighth day" of the new heavens and new earth. They likewise speak of Sunday as the "eighth day" since the first day of the week follows the seventh day. It is possible, as is sometimes suggested, that some of the church fathers could have found partial support for their use of the term *eighth day* by combining John 20:1, 19, and 26, but their interpretive focus is always eschatological, as revealed in writers such as Barnabas, who wrote his epistle during the middle of the second century.

Christian Authors through the Centuries

Barnabas (mid-2nd c.)

The Sabbath is mentioned at the beginning of the creation [thus]: "And God made in six days the works of His hands, and made an end on the seventh day, and rested on it, and sanctified it." Attend, my children, to the meaning of this expression, "He finished in six days." This implies that the Lord will finish all things in six thousand years, for a day is with Him a thousand years. And He Himself testifies, saying, "Behold, today will be as a thousand years." Therefore, my children, in six days, that is, in six thousand years, all things will be finished. "And He rested on the seventh day." This means: when His Son, coming [again], shall destroy the time of the wicked man, and judge the ungodly, and change the-sun, and the moon, and the stars, then shall He truly rest on the seventh day. . . . Ye perceive how He speaks: Your present Sabbaths are not acceptable to Me, but that is which I have made, [namely this,] when, giving rest to all things, I shall make a beginning of the eighth day, that is, a beginning of another world [age]. Wherefore, also, we keep the eighth day with joyfulness, the day also on which Jesus rose again from the dead.[4]

Ignatius of Antioch (early 2nd c.)

Arguing against "Judaizing," or legalistic, Christians who insisted on keeping the old Sabbath, Ignatius of Antioch writes that Christians are those who "have come to the possession of a new hope, no longer observing the Sabbath, but living in the observance of the Lord's Day."[5]

Didache (ca. 100–150)

"But every Lord's day do ye gather yourselves together, and break bread, and give thanksgiving after having confessed your transgressions, that your sacrifice may be pure."[6]

Justin Martyr (ca. 100–167)

In his *Dialogue with Trypho* the Jew, Justin explains that although the pre-Mosaic patriarchs "kept no Sabbaths," they were still "righteous" and "pleasing to God." There was "no need" of "the observance of Sabbaths" (19–27). Irenaeus echoes the same sentiment in *Against Heresies* (4.16.2). Justin Martyr describes the weekly Sunday worship of Christians:

> And we afterwards continually remind each other of these things. And the wealthy among us help the needy; and we always keep together; and for all things wherewith we are supplied, we bless the Maker of all through His Son Jesus Christ, and through the Holy

---

[4] *Epistle of Barnabas* 15, in ANF (1:146–47). Except where otherwise noted, patristic citations and references are from ANF, NPNF 1, and NPNF 2.

[5] Ignatius, *Epistle to the Magnesians* 9.

[6] *Didache* 14.

Ghost. And on the day called Sunday, all who live in cities or in the country gather together to one place, and the memoirs of the apostles or the writings of the prophets are read, as long as time permits; then, when the reader has ceased, the president verbally instructs, and exhorts to the imitation of these good things. Then we all rise together and pray, and, as we before said, when our prayer is ended, bread and wine and water are brought, and the president in like manner offers prayers and thanksgivings, according to his ability, and the people assent, saying Amen; and there is a distribution to each, and a participation of that over which thanks have been given, and to those who are absent a portion is sent by the deacons. And they who are well to do, and willing, give what each thinks fit; and what is collected is deposited with the president, who succors the orphans and widows and those who, through sickness or any other cause, are in want, and those who are in bonds and the strangers sojourning among us, and in a word takes care of all who are in need. But Sunday is the day on which we all hold our common assembly, because it is the first day on which God, having wrought a change in the darkness and matter, made the world; and Jesus Christ our Savior on the same day rose from the dead. For He was crucified on the day before that of Saturn (Saturday); and on the day after that of Saturn, which is the day of the Sun, having appeared to His apostles and disciples, He taught them these things, which we have submitted to you also for your consideration.[7]

Irenaeus of Lyon (fl. late 2nd c.)

Irenaeus, in his *Demonstration (Proof) of Apostolic Preaching*, says that since believers are "not under the Mosaic Law," they are not commanded to leave idle one day of rest since we "constantly keep Sabbath" in our bodies.[8]

Origen of Alexandria (ca. 185–254)

Besides a couple of mystical and obscure comments,[9] Origen's normal pattern is clearly to emphasize the importance of perpetual

---

[7] *First Apology* 67.

[8] *Proof of the Apostolic Preaching*, trans. Joseph P. Smith, vol. 16 of Ancient Christian Writers (Westminster, MD: Newman Press, 1952), 96.

[9] Origen, *Homilies on Numbers* (*Homily* 23, in Migne *PG* 12.749). Origen's comments are on Numbers 28–29 and are extant only in a Latin translation. Their

days of worship, that is, "every day is the Lord's Day." He explains that, while Christians observe the "Lord's Day," the "perfect Christian . . . is always keeping the Lord's Day."[10] The commandment concerning the Sabbath day is just "impossible" to be taken literally.[11] Origen's advice is that it is best to consider the Sabbath as the eternal rest to come and that we can begin to enjoy it now through "contemplation of celestial things" and of "the assembly of righteous and blessed beings."[12]

Tertullian of Carthage (ca. 160–220)

"It follows, accordingly," says Tertullian, "that, in so far as the abolition of carnal circumcision and of the old law is demonstrated as having been consummated at its specific times, so also the observance of the Sabbath is demonstrated to have been temporary."[13] Tertullian taught that the Old Testament Sabbath was abolished but that there will be a future spiritual Sabbath.[14] He explains, "We devote Sun-day to rejoicing," but "from a far different reason than Sun-worship."[15] Tertullian is explaining that Christ's resurrection has so wonderfully sanctified the first day of the week, which the pagans had already named Sunday, that we Christians can rejoice even on a day whose name had originated in honor of sun-worship. Pagans had named all of the calendar days for their own gods.[16]

---

allegorical and numerical mysticism renders them almost meaningless for any contribution to the matter at hand. The same applies to the seventh of Origen's Homilies on Exodus. The most complete and valuable of all analyses of Origen's remarks on this topic is Robert Cox, *The Literature of the Sabbath Question* (London: Maclachlan and Stewart, 1865), 1:345–54.

[10] *Contra Celsum* 8.22; Origen's sentiment echoes Clement's *Stromata* 7.7.

[11] *De Principiis* 4.1.17.

[12] *Contra Celsum* 6.61. Likewise, Clement of Alexandria viewed the seventh day of the fourth commandment as figurative of the "Primal Day," or First Day, of eternal rest of all believers (*Stromata* 6.16).

[13] *An Answer to the Jews* 4.

[14] Ibid., 6.

[15] *Apology* 16.

[16] The names of the calendar days are of pagan derivation and were intended to honor pagan gods: *Sunday* was for the Sun. *Monday* was for the Moon. *Tuesday* was for Zeus, the same as the Latin god Jupiter. *Wednesday* derives from the Middle English word *wodnesdi*, for Woden (Wodan from Odin), the highest god of the ancient Teutonic people and identical with the Roman god Mercury. *Wodnesdi* is actually the Middle English translation of the Latin *dies Mercurii*, or

Cyprian of Carthage (200–258)

Cyprian says that Christians observe the "day after the Sabbath," the "eighth day," as the "Lord's Day."[17]

Victorinus of Pettau (d. ca. 300)

In his treatise, *On the Creation of the World*, Victorinus warns churches to take care, "lest we should appear to observe any Sabbath" that Christ has already "abolished." Emphasizing the premillennial return of Christ at the end of the tribulation period, at which time the saints will be resurrected to enter the kingdom, Victorinus says that the six days of creation are representative of six thousand years of world history. The seventh day speaks of the literal one-thousand-year reign of Christ on earth. According to this divine "sevenfold arrangement," the "true Sabbath will be in the seventh millenary of years, when Christ with His elect shall reign."[18]

Contrary to modern seventh-day Sabbatarians who claim that Sunday worship was not instituted until Constantine in the fourth century, the ante-Nicene fathers from Barnabas to Victorinus taught that the Old Testament Sabbath had been abolished and that Sunday is the day when Christians should meet for regular public worship.

Emperor Constantine I (272–337)

The first day of the week fell under a degree of state regulation when, in the spring of 321 Constantine, who would not have had the Jewish Sabbath in mind, decreed that Sunday, commemorated by pagans as "the venerable Day of the Sun," would be observed as the Roman day of rest, with only farmers exempt:

> On the venerable Day of the Sun let the magistrates and people residing in cities rest, and let all workshops be closed. In the country, however, persons engaged in agriculture may freely and lawfully continue their pursuits; because it often happens that another day is not so suitable for grain-sowing or vine-planting; lest by

---

day of Mercury. *Thursday* was for Thor, the Teutonic god of thunder. *Friday* derives from *Frigg* (a goddess) + *daeg* ("day"). Frigg was the wife of Woden. *Saturday* was for Saturn (*Saturnus*), the Roman god of agriculture.

[17] *Epistle* 58.

[18] *On the Creation of the World*, in ANF (7:341–43).

neglecting the proper moment for such operations the bounty of heaven should be lost.[19]

Eusebius of Caesarea (ca. 260–340)

Eusebius, in his *Commentary on the Psalms*,[20] comments on the Sabbath and Sunday. His specific remarks pertain to Psalm 21:30 (22:29 in our modern Bibles); 45:6 (46:5); 58:17 (59:16); and especially Psalm 91 (92). In this work, like most of his commentaries, Eusebius's interpretive approach is hopelessly vague. If he were teaching a Sabbatarian Lord's Day, he would be contradicting the clear affirmations of his historical works, such as *The Demonstratio Evangelica* (*The Proof of the Gospel*), where he expresses his view that the Old Testament Sabbath was a part of the law that was set aside after the resurrection of Christ:

> The day of His [Christ's] light . . . was the day of His Resurrection from the dead, which they say, as being the one and only truly Holy Day and the Lord's Day, is better than any number of days as we ordinarily understand them, and better than the days set apart by the Mosaic Law for Feasts, New Moons and Sabbaths, which the Apostle [Paul] teaches are the shadow of days and not days in reality. And this Lord's Day of our Savior is alone said to show its light not in every place but only in the courts of the Lord. And these must mean the Churches of Christ throughout the world.[21]

Likewise, in his *Ecclesiastical History*, Eusebius demonstrates in a literal and straightforward style his clear belief that the Sabbath belonged solely to the Mosaic law, that it was not known by the Old Testament patriarchs, and that it constitutes no part of the church:

> They [Old Testament patriarchs before Moses] did not care about circumcision of the body, neither do we. They did not care about

---

[19] Philip Schaff, *History of the Christian Church* (New York: Charles Scribner's Sons, 1882–1910), 3:380. See also the comments by Eusebius of Caesarea, *Life of Constantine* 4.18.

[20] For Eusebius's most elaborate discussion on the Sabbath and the Lord's Day, see Eusebius Caesariensis, *Commentaria in Psalmos* (Migne *PG* 23.1165–83), on Psalm 91 (92 in modern Bibles). Any in-depth study of Eusebius on the Sabbath should also include the valuable and neglected Robert Cox, *The Literature of the Sabbath Question*, 1:345–54.

[21] Eusebius of Caesarea, *The Proof of the Gospel: Being the Demonstratio Evangelica*, trans. W. J. Ferrar (London: Society for Promoting Christian Knowledge, 1920), 1:207–08.

observing Sabbaths, nor do we. They did not avoid certain kinds of food, neither did they regard the other distinctions which Moses first delivered to their posterity to be observed as symbols; nor do Christians of the present day do such things. But they also clearly knew the very Christ of God. (1.4.8.)

Athanasius of Alexandria (ca. 298–373)

In his work *On Sabbath and Circumcision*, Athanasius separates the Sabbath from the Lord's Day:

> The Sabbath was the end of the first creation, the Lord's day was the beginning of the second, in which he renewed and restored the old in the same way as he prescribed that they should formerly observe the Sabbath as a memorial of the end of the first things, so we honor the Lord's day as being the memorial of the new creation. (3)[22]

Cyril of Jerusalem (315–86)

Cyril, in his *Catechetical Lectures*, offers a warning:

> Fall not away either into the sect of the Samaritans or into Judaism, for Jesus Christ has henceforth ransomed you. Stand aloof from all observance of Sabbaths and from calling any indifferent meats common or unclean. (4.37)

Chrysostom of Constantinople (ca. 344/354–407)

In his *Homilies on the Statues*, Chrysostom teaches the "abolishing" of the Sabbath observance. He explains that God inserted a reason for the fourth commandment since it was not engraved upon man's conscience from the beginning, and, unlike the moral laws, this one would be temporary:

> For what purpose then I ask did He add a reason respecting the Sabbath, but did no such thing in regard to murder? Because this commandment was not one of the leading ones. It was not one of those which were accurately defined of our conscience, but a kind of partial and temporary one; and for this reason it was abolished afterwards. But those which are necessary and uphold our life are the following; "Thou shalt not kill; Thou shalt not commit

---

[22] While its authorship is questioned on occasion, the text is from the fourth century, and Migne ascribes its authorship to Athanasius, in *PG* 28.133–44, *De Sabbatis et Circumcisione*. Migne describes the entire volume as being the works of Athanasius.

adultery; Thou shalt not steal." On this account then He adds no reason in this case, nor enters into any instruction on the matter, but is content with the bare prohibition. (Homily 12.9)

In his *Homilies on Galatians*, Chrysostom encourages believers that in Christ they are free from the bondage of the law:

Thou hast put on Christ, thou hast become a member of the Lord, and been enrolled in the heavenly city, and dost thou still grovel in the Law? How is it possible for thee to obtain the kingdom? Listen to Paul's words, that the observance of the Law overthrows the Gospel, and learn, if thou wilt, how this comes to pass, and tremble, and shun this pitfall. Wherefore dost thou keep the Sabbath, and fast with the Jews? . . . If thou keep the Sabbath, why not also be circumcised? And if circumcised, why not also offer sacrifices? (NPNF 1 [13:21])

In his *Homilies on Philippians*, Chrysostom urges that under the law circumcision was more important than the Sabbath. If circumcision is abolished, even more is the Sabbath:

"Beware," he says, "of the concision." The rite of circumcision was venerable in the Jews' account, forasmuch as the Law itself gave way thereto, and the Sabbath was less esteemed than circumcision. For that circumcision might be performed the Sabbath was broken; but that the Sabbath might be kept, circumcision was never broken; and mark, I pray, the dispensation of God. This is found to be even more solemn than the Sabbath, as not being omitted at certain times. When then it is done away, much more is the Sabbath. (Homily 10)

In his *Homilies on the Gospel according to St. Matthew*, Chrysostom exhorts believers to faithfulness in their weekly worship:

For we ought not as soon as we retire from the Communion,[23] to plunge into business unsuited to the Communion, but as soon as ever we get home, to take our Bible into our hands, and call our wife and children to join us in putting together what we have heard, and then, not before, engage in the business of life. . . . When you retire from the Communion, you must account nothing more necessary than that you should put together the things that have been said to you. Yes, for it were the utmost folly for us,

---

[23] The term Chrysostom uses here is τῆς συνάξεως, which is not likely referring to the Lord's Supper since he and other writers normally used this word in the more general way of describing a regular preaching service.

while we give up five and even six days to the business of this life, not to bestow on things spiritual so much as one day, or rather not so much as a small part of one day. . . . Let us write it down an unalterable law for ourselves, for our wives, and for our children, to give up this one day of the week entire to hearing, and to the recollection of the things we have heard. (Homily 5, Section 1, on Matt. 1:22–23)

Synod of Laodicea (ca. 360)

"Christians must not Judaize by resting on the Sabbath, but must work on that day, rather honoring the Lord's Day; and, if they can, resting then as Christians. But if any shall be found to be Judaizers, let them be anathema from Christ" (Canon 29).[24]

Ambrose of Milan (ca. 339–97)

Ambrose closes his nine homilies on the six days of creation, the *Hexaemeron*, with this single interpretation of the Sabbath:[25] God needed no rest. Foreseeing man's fall, however, He spoke of the Sabbath as anticipating the future passion of Christ when He would say, "It is finished." "God's rest" would be the repose of Christ's body in the grave, signifying the complete work of redemption when He sat down at the right hand of God.

Augustine of Hippo (354–430)

Building upon Ambrose's teaching, Augustine says that the Jews received the Sabbath to keep *secundum carnem* ("according to the flesh"), while Christians received the Lord's Day to observe *secundum Spiritus* ("according the Spirit"). God used codes to hide from the Jews the "true" meaning of the Sabbath, in order later to reveal its mystery to His true people, the New Testament church.[26] The foremost mystery was that the Sabbath pointed to Christ and was meant to make way for the "eighth day," which is the Lord's Day,

---

[24] NPNF 2 (14:148).

[25] *Hexaemeron*, Ninth Homily 6.76, trans. John J. Savage, in vol. 42 of *The Fathers of the Church* (New York: Fathers of the Church, 1961), 282–83.

[26] *Literal Meaning of Genesis*, book 4, passim, especially the section on the seventh day. For a moderating view, see Paula Fredriksen, *Augustine and the Jews: A Christian Defense of Jews and Judaism* (New York: Doubleday, 2008). This work has no specific section on the Sabbath, but there are relevant *principia* throughout.

the day of new beginnings—the day of salvation and eternal rest for believers. In his treatise, *On the Spirit and the Letter*, Augustine agrees with Chrysostom that Sabbath observance was abolished with circumcision and other such laws:

> Well, now, I should like to be told what there is in these ten commandments, except the observance of the Sabbath, which ought not to be kept by a Christian,—whether it prohibit the making and worshipping of idols and of any other gods than the one true God, or the taking of God's name in vain; or prescribe honor to parents; or give warning against fornication, murder, theft, false witness, adultery, or coveting other men's property? Which of these commandments would anyone say that the Christian ought not to keep? Is it possible to contend that it is not the law which was written on those two tables that the apostle [Paul] describes as "the letter that killeth," [2 Cor. 3:6] but the law of circumcision and the other sacred rites which are now abolished? (23)[27]

The following is from Augustine's *Expositions on the Book of Psalms*. This selection on Psalm 92 (Latin 91) is a sermon that he preached to the people on a Saturday (Sabbath Day):

> This Psalm is entitled, a Psalm to be sung on the Sabbath day. Lo, this day is the Sabbath, which the Jews at this period observe by a kind of bodily rest, languid and luxurious. They abstain from labors, and give themselves up to trifles; and though God ordained the Sabbath, they spend it in actions which God forbids. Our rest is from evil works, theirs from good; for it is better to plough than to dance. They abstain from good, but not from trifling, works. God proclaims to us a Sabbath. What sort of Sabbath? First, consider where it is. It is in the heart, within us; for many are idle with their limbs, while they are disturbed in conscience. . . . That very joy in the tranquility of our hope is our Sabbath. This is the subject of praise and of song in this Psalm, how a Christian man is in the Sabbath of his own heart, that is, in the quiet, tranquility, and serenity of his conscience, undisturbed; hence he tells us here, whence men are wont to be disturbed, and he teaches thee to keep Sabbath in thine own heart. (Section 2)

---

[27] See also *On the Spirit and the Letter* 27 and 36.

Gregory I of Rome (ca. 540–604)

Included in the *Register of the Epistles* of Gregory "the Great" is a letter addressed "to the Roman citizens." In this letter Gregory equates Sabbath laws and Sunday regulations with the teachings of the antichrist. To Gregory, Sabbath keeping is no more important than circumcision. He closes, however, with an exhortation for believers to take the day off from earthly labors and to honor the Lord's Day as the day of Christ's resurrection:

¶ It has come to my ears that certain men of perverse spirit have sown among you some things that are wrong and opposed to the holy faith, so as to forbid any work being done on the Sabbath day. What else can I call these but preachers of Antichrist, who, when he comes, will cause the Sabbath day as well as the Lord's Day to be kept free from all work. For, because he pretends to die and rise again, he wishes the Lord's Day to be had in reverence; and, because he compels the people to Judaize that he may bring back the outward rite of the law, and subject the perfidy of the Jews to himself, he wishes the Sabbath to be observed.

¶ For this which is said by the prophet, *Ye shall bring in no burden through your gates on the Sabbath day* (Jeremiah 17:24), could be held to as long as it was lawful for the law to be observed according to the letter. But after that the grace of Almighty God, our Lord Jesus Christ has appeared, the commandments of the law which were spoken figuratively cannot be kept according to the letter. For, if any one says that this about the Sabbath is to be kept, he must needs say that carnal sacrifices are to be offered: he must say too that the commandment about the circumcision of the body is still to be retained. But let him hear the Apostle Paul saying in opposition to him, *If ye be circumcised, Christ profiteth you nothing* (Galatians 5:2).

¶ We therefore accept spiritually, and hold spiritually, this which is written about the Sabbath. For the Sabbath means rest. But we have the true Sabbath in our Redeemer Himself, the Lord Jesus Christ. And whoso acknowledges the light of faith in Him, if he draws the sins of concupiscence through his eyes into his soul, he introduces burdens through the gates on the Sabbath day. . . .

¶ On the Lord's Day, however, there should be a cessation of earthly labor, and attention given in every way to prayers, so that if anything is done negligently during the six days, it may be expiated by supplications on the day of the Lord's resurrection.[28]

John of Damascus (ca. 665–749)

John of Damascus, the last of the Greek fathers, monastic defender of the "holy icons," is still hailed by many for his brilliance as a philosopher, scientist, theologian, and even as a writer of hymns composed in a monastery near the Dead Sea. In his *Exposition of the Orthodox Faith*, John expresses his conviction that the Sabbath was restricted to the Jewish people under the law of Moses. Christians worship on the Lord's Day and each believer is free from the law in order to devote each day of his life towards the spiritual and mystical fulfillment of the deeper purposes of the Sabbath:

> The observance of the Sabbath was devised for the carnal that were still childish and *in the bonds of the elements of the world* [Gal. 4:3], and unable to conceive of anything beyond the body and the letter. *But when the fullness of the time was come, God sent forth His Only-begotten Son, made of a woman, made under the law, to redeem them that were under the law that we might receive the adoption of sons* [Gal. 4:4–5]. *For to as many of us as received Him, He gave power to become sons of God, even to them that believe on Him* [John 1:12]. *So that we are no longer servants but sons* [Gal. 4:7:] no longer under the law but under grace: no longer do we serve God in part from fear, but we are bound to dedicate to Him the whole span of our life.[29]

Thomas Aquinas (1224–74) and the Roman Catholic Church

During the Middle Ages, the Roman Catholic Church controlled Sunday worship by means of relics, saints' days, and other superstitions, along with the usual Church calendars and liturgies. Thomas Aquinas, an expert in equivocation, tempered such ecclesiastical rulings by arguing that the precept of the Jewish Sabbath had been both ceremonial and moral, but only relatively binding since God allowed exceptions in many special cases. As a replacement of the Jewish Sabbath, the Lord's Day is relatively binding as well due

---

[28] Gregory I of Rome, *Register of the Epistles*, book 13, *Epistle* 1, in NPNF 2 (13:92–93).
[29] *Exposition of the Orthodox Faith* 4.23, in NPNF 2 (9:95–96).

to special exceptions. In fact, during the present age there is room for even greater flexibility for special situations:

> The precept of the Sabbath observance is moral in one respect, in so far as it commands man to give some time to the things of God, according to Ps. xlv.11: *Be still and see that I am God*. In this respect it is placed among the precepts of the Decalogue: but not as to the fixing of the time, in which respect it is a ceremonial precept.[30]

In addition, Thomas believed that God created man with the principle of regulated rest as an integral part of his rational nature in the image of God. There "is a natural inclination in man," says Thomas, "to appoint a certain time for his spiritual refreshing, whereby his soul is refreshed in God." Seventeenth-century Puritans would appeal to this argument in defense of the Sabbath Lord's Day:

> ¶ The precept about hallowing the Sabbath, understood literally, is partly moral and partly ceremonial. It is a moral precept in the point of commanding man to set aside a certain time to be given to Divine things. For there is in man a natural inclination to set aside a certain time for each necessary thing, such as refreshment of the body, sleep, and so forth. Hence according to the dictate of reason, man sets aside a certain time for spiritual refreshment, by which man's mind is refreshed in God. And thus to have a certain time set aside for occupying oneself with Divine things is the matter of a moral precept. But, in so far as this precept specializes the time as a sign representing the Creation of the world, it is a ceremonial precept. Again, it is a ceremonial precept in its allegorical signification, as representative of Christ's rest in the tomb on the seventh day: also in its moral signification, as representing cessation from all sinful acts, and the mind's rest in God, in which sense, too, it is a general precept. Again, it is a ceremonial precept in its analogical signification, as foreshadowing the enjoyment of God in heaven. Hence the precept about hallowing the Sabbath is

---

[30] Thomas Aquinas, *Summa Theologica*, Prima Secundae Partis, Question 100 (Moral Precepts of the Old Law), Article 3, reply to objection 2. "Ps. xlv.11" (45:11) in our modern Bibles is Ps. 46:10. All *Summa* references are from *The "Summa Theologica" of St. Thomas Aquinas*, trans. Fathers of the English Dominican Province, 22 vols. 2nd rev. ed. (London: Burns Oates & Washbourne, 1912–36).

placed among the precepts of the Decalogue, as a moral, but not as a ceremonial precept.[31]

¶ The other ceremonies of the Law are signs of certain particular Divine works: but the observance of the Sabbath is representative of a general boon, namely, the production of all creatures. Hence it was fitting that it should be placed among the general precepts of the Decalogue, rather than any other ceremonial precept of the Law.[32]

The theology of Thomas Aquinas remains among the official teachings of the Roman Catholic Church. Soon after the publication of its latest catechism, Pope John Paul II issued an "Apostolic Letter" titled *Dies Domini* to the whole church, "On Keeping the Lord's Day Holy"(1998). Breaking no new ground, the document reviews the Church's records on the Lord's Day with special attention to worship, encyclicals, and liturgies. Along with the *Catechism*,[33] the apparent purpose of the pope's letter was to generate more interest among the laity.

Martin Luther (1483–1546)

The Lutheran position, essentially a revivification and simplification of the traditional ante-Nicene position, was set forth at the beginning of the Reformation in Luther's Larger Catechism. Here he teaches that the Sabbath commandment was abrogated with other externals and does not concern the New Testament church. Christians should be as faithful as they can on the Lord's Day:

> This commandment, therefore, according to its gross sense, does not concern us Christians; for it is altogether an external matter, like other ordinances of the Old Testament. . . . No one day is better than another. . . . But since . . . of old, Sunday has been appointed for this purpose, we also should continue the same, in order that everything be done in harmonious order, and no one create disorder by unnecessary innovation. . . . Yet that the resting

---

[31] Ibid., Secunda Secundae Partis, Question 122 (of the Precepts of Justice), Article 4, reply to objection 1.

[32] Ibid., Secunda Secundae Partis (second), Question 122 (of the Precepts of Justice), Article 4, reply to objection 2.

[33] *Catechism of the Catholic Church* (New York: Doubleday, 1995), sections 345–48; 2168–73; 2175; 2189–90.

be not so strictly interpreted as to forbid any other incidental work that cannot be avoided.[34]

The Augsburg Confession (1530)

Written by Philip Melanchthon (1497–1560), the Augsburg Confession remains the primary symbolic statement of Lutheran doctrine and practice. It teaches that the Lord's Day has replaced the Sabbath, which was abrogated as a ceremonial law:

> The Scripture, which teacheth that all the Mosaical ceremonies can be omitted after the Gospel is revealed, has abrogated the Sabbath. And yet, because it was requisite to appoint a certain day, that the people might know when they ought to come together, it appears that the Church did for that purpose appoint the Lord's Day: which for this cause also seemed to have been pleasing, that men might have an example of Christian liberty, and might know that the observation, neither of the Sabbath, nor of another day, was of necessity. (Part II, Article 7)

The traditional Lutheran position on the Sabbath is the same that Luther had taught: that God presented no Sabbath-keeping commandment at creation, and that the Sabbath is not mentioned again until Exodus 16:23–29, when God gave His initial instructions for the Israelites to keep the Sabbath as a ceremonial observance as they were leaving Egypt. After citing Genesis 2:2–3, the Lutheran *Concordia Cyclopedia* explains the denomination's historic view:

> There is not the slightest intimation in this [passage] that God commanded Adam and Eve to observe the seventh day as a day of rest. . . . We nowhere read that Adam and Eve or Noah, or Abraham, or Isaac, or Jacob, or any of the other Patriarchs ever observed the seventh day as the Sabbath. . . . The Sabbath law was part of the Ceremonial Law of the Jews and not part of the Moral Law, which concerns all men and which for all times sets down what is right and wrong in the sight of God. At least at one time Jesus did not only overlook, but even defended, a breach, by His apostles, of the Sabbath commandment. That incident is recorded in Mark [2:23–28]. . . . He defends the disciples by three distinct arguments: first, by what David did [1 Sam. 21:1–6] in

---

[34] Martin Luther, *The Large Catechism*, in *Triglot Concordia: The Symbolical Books of the Evangelical Lutheran Church*, trans. F. Bente and W. H. T. Dau (St. Louis: Concordia, 1921), 603-09.

eating the show-bread, consequently in breaking a Ceremonial Law; secondly, by announcing the general and incontrovertible principle: "The Sabbath was made for man, and not man for the Sabbath"; and thirdly, in drawing the conclusion: "So the Son of Man is Lord also of the Sabbath." When our Lord compares these two "trespasses," He has conclusively shown that as far as that part of the commandment about a specific day is concerned, it is of a ceremonial and transient character, which in itself should be respected as long as that Ceremonial Law is in force, but may as readily be omitted when the law should be abolished. If the Sabbath was "made for man," on account of man's needs and for his benefit, then, the conditions being changed, the law will change. And this very thing is about to happen. For, as indicated in the third argument, the Son of Man has the power to abolish even the Sabbath.[35]

The Concordia Cyclopedia further instructs (below) that God left the specific day of rest or worship to the discretion of His people. In order to maintain ecclesiastical regularity and efficiency, New Testament Christians chose Christ's resurrection day as the ideal time for their special weekly assemblies:

> There can be no doubt, then, that there is in the New Testament no divinely appointed day of rest or worship. Why, then, do we observe Sunday? It is man's duty to worship, to honor, to praise his Maker. In the New Testament the law fixing particular days has been revoked, and only the command to worship God remains. Neither can man worship God as he pleases, but God has told us how to worship Him. His Word shall be preached. The Sacraments are to be administered. Public prayer and praise shall be in vogue. If this is to be done, it is evident that a certain time and place must be fixed for public worship. While, in the Old Testament God prescribed time and place of public worship, He has in the New Testament left these details entirely to the discretion and the choice of His people. And so from the early times of

---

[35] L. Fuerbringer, Th. Engelder, and P. E. Kretzmann, eds., *The Concordia Cyclopedia: A Handbook of Religious Information, with Special Reference to the History, Doctrine, Work, and Usages of the Lutheran Church* (St. Louis: Concordia, 1927), 669–72.

the apostles the Christians have chosen Sunday, the day of Christ's resurrection, as the day which they would use for public worship.[36]

John Calvin (1509–64)

Like Luther and Melanchthon, John Calvin continues the traditional view that the Sabbath was part of the Jewish ceremonial law and is in no way perpetually binding upon humanity. The English Puritans would fault him severely at times for this view. Nevertheless, while Calvin emphatically taught the abrogation of the Jewish Sabbath, he in no way reduced the Lord's Day to an adiaphoristic status. He sought to avoid any sharp tone, and he euphemistically suggested that Christians avoid harsh criticism of fellow believers who believed that the Sabbath is decisively and forever nonbinding, but still a type of the Lord's Day.

Calvin's overall view became the dominant one in first-generation Reformed churches. Scotland's Presbyterians, for example, would use the Geneva Catechism until the publishing of the Westminster Standards.[37] Here in Calvin's *Institutes* is the summary of his views on the fourth commandment:

> It was not, however, without a reason that the early Christians substituted what we call the Lord's Day for the Sabbath. The resurrection of our Lord being the end and accomplishment of that true rest which the ancient Sabbath typified, this day, by which types were abolished serves to warn Christians against adhering to a shadowy ceremony. I do not cling so to the number seven as to bring the Church under bondage to it, nor do I condemn churches for holding their meetings on other solemn days, provided they guard against superstition. This they will do if they employ those days merely for the observance of discipline and regular order. The whole may be thus summed up: As the truth was delivered typically to the Jews, so it is imparted to us without figure; first, that during our whole lives we may aim at a constant rest from our own works, in order that the Lord may work in us by his Spirit; secondly that every individual, as he has opportunity, may diligently exercise himself in private, in pious meditation on

---

[36] Ibid.

[37] The Geneva Catechism was included in the popular edition of *The Psalms of David in Metre, etc.*, printed at Edinburgh in 1611.

the works of God, and, at the same time, that all may observe the legitimate order appointed by the Church, for the hearing of the word, the administration of the sacraments, and public prayer: And, thirdly, that we may avoid oppressing those who are subject to us. In this way, we get quit of the trifling of the false prophets, who in later times instilled Jewish ideas into the people, alleging that nothing was abrogated but what was ceremonial in the commandment, (this they term in their language the taxation of the seventh day), while the moral part remains—viz. the observance of one day in seven. But this is nothing else than to insult the Jews, by changing the day, and yet mentally attributing to it the same sanctity; thus retaining the same typical distinction of days as had place among the Jews. And of a truth, we see what profit they have made by such a doctrine. Those who cling to their constitutions go thrice as far as the Jews in the gross and carnal superstition of sabbatism; so that the rebukes which we read in Isaiah (1:13; 58:13) apply as much to those of the present day, as to those to whom the Prophet addressed them. We must be careful, however, to observe the general doctrine—viz. in order that religion may neither be lost nor languish among us, we must diligently attend on our religious assemblies, and duly avail ourselves of those external aids which tend to promote the worship of God.[38]

The following selection on the fourth commandment vividly reveals Calvin's contempt for any hypocrisy related to the Lord's Day. This is a sermon that he preached on Thursday, June 20, 1555 on Deuteronomy 5:12–14. It was his fifth sermon on chapter 5, and it was published as Sermon 34 in John Calvin's *Sermons upon the Fifth Booke of Moses, called Deuteronomie*:

¶ Yea[,] and we have to mark also, that it is not enough for us to think upon God and his works upon the Lord's day every man alone by himself: but that we must meet together upon some day certain, to make open confession of our faith. Indeed this ought to be done every day[,] as I have said afore. But yet in respect of men's rawness, and by reason of their slothfulness: it is necessary to have one special day dedicated wholly thereunto. It is true that we be not bound to the seventh day: neither do we (in deed) keep the same day that was appointed to the Jews: for that was the

---

[38] John Calvin, *The Institutes of the Christian Religion*, trans. Henry Beveridge (Edinburgh: Calvin Translation Society, 1845), 2.8.34.

Saturday. But to the intent to show the liberty of Christians, the day was changed because Jesus Christ in his resurrection did set us free from the bondage of the law, and cancelled the obligation thereof. That was the cause why the day was shifted. But yet must we observe the same order of having some day in the week, be it one or be it two, for that is left to the free choice of Christians.

¶ Nevertheless, if a people assemble to have the Sacraments ministered, and to make common prayer unto God, and to show one agreement and union of faith: it is convenient to have some one day certain for that purpose.

¶ Then it is not enough for every man to withdraw himself into his own house, whether it be to read the holy Scripture or to pray unto God: but it is meet that we should come into the company of the faithful, and there show the agreement which we have with all the whole body of the Church, by keeping this order which our Lord hath so commanded.

¶ But what? There a man may see too apparent unhallowing of God's service. For (as I have touched afore) are there not a great sort which could well find in their hearts to show that they do but mock God, and that they would fain be exempted from the common law? It is true that they will come to a sermon five or six times a year. And what to do there? Forsooth even to mock at God and all his doctrine. Indeed they be very swine, which come to defile God's temple, and are worthier to be in stables than there, and they were better to keep themselves at home in their stinking cabins. To be short, it were better that such rascals and filthy villains were quite cut off from the Church of God, than that they should come and intermingle themselves after that sort in company with the faithful. But yet how many times come they thither? The bell may ring well enough: for look where a man left them, there shall he find them. So then we ought to be the more diligent and careful, in quickening up ourselves, to make such confession of our faith as God may be honored with one common consent among us.

¶ And besides that, all superstitions must be banished. For we see how it is an opinion in popery, that God is served with idleness. It is not after that sort that we must keep holy the Sabbath day. But to the intent it may be applied to the right and lawful use, we must consider (as I said afore) how our Lord requireth to have this day bestowed in nothing else, but in hearing of his word, in making common prayer, in making confession of our faith, and in having the use of the Sacraments. These are the things that we be called to. Howbeit, we see how all things have been corrupted and confounded in the popedom. For like as they have allotted days to honoring of their he Saints and she Saints, and set up images of them, so have they surmised that they were to be worshipped with idleness.

¶ But seeing that the world is so given to corruption: it stands us so much the more in hand to mark well this discourse concerning the Sabbath day, as it is set down here by Moses. And let us consider to what end our Lord commanded the people of old time, to have one day in the week to rest in: to the intent that we[,] knowing how the same is abolished by the coming of our Lord Jesus Christ, may take ourselves to the spiritual rest, that is to say, dedicate ourselves wholly unto God, forsaking all our own reason and affections. Again let us retain still the outward order, so far as is meet for us, that is to wit, of forbearing our own affairs and worldly businesses, that we may intend wholly to the minding of God's works, and occupy ourselves in the consideration of the good things that he hath done for us. And above all things[,] let us strain ourselves to acknowledge the grace that he offereth us daily in his Gospel that we may be strengthened in it still more and more. And when we have bestowed the Lord his day in praising and magnifying God's name, and in minding his works: let us show all the week after that we have profited in the same.[39]

The Heidelberg Catechism (1563)

Composed by two German Reformed scholars Zacharias Ursinus and Caspar Olevianus, the Heidelberg Catechism is similar to the works of Luther and Calvin in its advancement of the traditional view of Sunday as the important and practical day of worshipful rest. God's people are "diligently" to attend church and partake of its

---

[39] John Calvin, *The Sermons of M. John Calvin upon the Fifth Booke of Moses, Called Deuteronomie*, trans. Arthur Golding (London: Henry Middleton for Thomas Woodcocke, 1583), 204–5 (200–205). I have modernized some of the spelling. Golding (1536–1606) was a man of high culture who sacrificially supported Puritan causes. He dated his dedicatory page December 21, 1582. The work is folio size and nearly fourteen hundred pages long. In separate publications, Golding also translated Calvin's commentaries on Galatians, Ephesians, Job, and Psalms.

benefits, especially on "the day of rest," for the maintenance of the ministry. For the Christian, every day is a "Sabbath" of rest from evil works. Thus, "all the days of [his] life" he should participate in the "everlasting Sabbath":

> Question 103: What does God require in the fourth commandment? Answer: In the first place, that the ministry of the Gospel and schools [should] be maintained; and that I, especially on the day of rest, diligently attend church, to learn the Word of God, to use the holy Sacraments, to call publicly upon the Lord, and to give Christian alms. In the second place . . . all the days of my life I [will] rest from my evil works, [and] allow the Lord to work in me by his Spirit, and thus begin in this life the everlasting Sabbath.

Thomas Cranmer (1489–1556)

Thomas Cranmer's position on the Sabbath clearly foreshadows the full-blown Lord's Day Sabbath of the Puritans. Contrary to the traditional Lord's Day concept of the early church and of men such as Luther and Calvin, the English Puritans would develop their own position based upon the premise that the Old Testament Sabbath is an essential part of God's moral law—integrally, solemnly, and perpetually binding upon all. The Puritans' view was to enforce the fourth commandment by replacing the seventh day with the first day. To those who hold this view, the one-in-seven principle of rest began at the creation, is obligatory for all mankind, and points to the eternal rest of believers.

Many English Reformers struggled long and hard over these issues. Some did not live long enough to see the Puritan concept played out in everyday life. Others sympathized with the position in a time when England's political climate would prevent its full expression. Finding much that was attractive to him in the Sabbath Lord's Day concept, Archbishop Thomas Cranmer, with his chaplain, Thomas Becon, wrote of it with extreme care as they struggled for political correctness on such a sensitive question. Published the same year as his *Book of Common Prayer*, Cranmer's 1548 catechism reveals the future martyr's typically careful manner:

> But we, Christian men, in the New Testament are not bound to such commandments of Moses' law concerning differences of times, days, and meats, but have liberty and freedom to use other

days for our Sabbath-days, therein to hear the word of God, and to keep a holy rest. And therefore that this Christian liberty may be kept and maintained, we now no more keep the Sabbath on Saturday as the Jews do, but we observe the Sunday, and certain other days, as the magistrates do judge it convenient, whom in this thing we ought to obey.[40]

In a changing political climate, by 1563 the Church of England had officially sanctioned a series of Puritan-type sermons, or *Homilies*, appointed to be read in churches, especially during the absence of regular ministers. Prepared by bishops of the Edwardian era, they provided an immense early boost towards the development and propagation of the Puritan view of the Sabbath. Most influential was the homily "Of the Place and Time for Prayer." While these messages did not represent a full-blown Sabbath-Lord's Day, they sounded forth in no uncertain terms that the Sabbath precept of one-day-in-seven was a divine imperative for all people. Such voices began echoing across the continent to the sympathetic ears of others who had already begun to speak of these ideas in private.

Theodore Beza (1519–1605)

Beza was successor to John Calvin upon the latter's death in Geneva, Switzerland, in 1564. In his Confession of Faith, published in 1560, Beza had essentially echoed Calvin's traditionalist stance on the Lord's Day observance:

> We declare it superstitious to believe that one day is more holy than another, and that resting from daily labors is in itself pleasing to God. Nevertheless we keep holy one day in seven, as the Lord has commanded; that is, we devote it entirely to the holding of assemblies and hearing the word of God, but without any Jewish ceremony or foolish superstition; on which account also we follow the custom of the ancient Church, in choosing for that purpose, not the Sabbath, but the Lord's-day.[41]

---

[40] Thomas Cranmer, *Catechismus*, in *Writings of the Rev. Dr. Thomas Cranmer: Archbishop of Canterbury and Martyr, 1556*, ed. William M. Engles (Philadelphia: Presbyterian Board of Publication, 1842), 127–28.

[41] Chapter 5 of Theodore Beza, "Confession of Faith" (1560), in Robert Cox, *The Literature of the Sabbath Question* (London: Maclachlan and Stewart, 1865), 1:134.

In 1612, however, a posthumously-published collection of Beza's *Annotations* on various passages of Scripture seems to reveal an approach to the Sabbath that is fundamentally different from Calvin's. Beza's "Note" on Revelation 1:10, for instance, asserts that a "perpetual" Sabbath obligation originated at the time of creation and continues as a precept of God's "unchanging moral law."[42] Beza had become another forerunner of the Puritan idea.

Henry Bullinger (1504–75)

The view of Henry Bullinger largely parallels that of Beza. Bullinger was successor to Swiss Reformer Ulrich Zwingli, as pastor of the Grossmünster Church in Zurich. In the Second Helvetic Confession[43] of Faith, published in 1566, Bullinger had essentially echoed Calvin's and Zwingli's traditionalist stance on the Lord's Day observance: "Neither do we believe that one day is in itself holier than another" (chapter 24).

In 1587, however, in a posthumously published collection of Bullinger's sermons, a message titled "Of the Fourth Precept of the First Table, that is, of the Order and Keeping of the Sabbath-Day," reveals an approach to the Sabbath that is fundamentally different from Calvin's and Zwingli's. Clearly departing from the position of first-generation Reformers, Bullinger now taught that the Lord's Day is a continuation of the Old Testament Sabbath, morally and legally binding on all humanity, and enforceable and punishable by civil law. Bullinger had become yet another forerunner of the Puritan view. The following is from Bullinger's sermon on the Christian duties of keeping the Sabbath:

> These are the duties, wherein the Lord's Sabbath is kept holy even in the church of Christians; and so much the rather, if to these be added an earnest good will to do no evil all the day long. This discipline now must be brought in and established by every householder in all our several houses, with as great diligence as it was with the Jews. Touching which thing I have nothing to say here,

---

[42] In his "Note" on Rev. 1:10, Beza also bases his perpetual Sabbath argument on 1 Cor. 16:2 and Acts 20:7. For detailed discussion, see Cox, 1:134.

[43] *Helvetic* is Latin for "Switzerland" or "Swiss" and originates from the ancient Helvetii tribes who settled in the region. Their roots were believed to trace back to the first century.

since I have before so plainly handled this point, as that ye perceive that it agreeth even to the church of us that are Christians. This one thing I add more; that it is the duty of a Christian magistrate, or at leastwise of a good householder, to compel to amendment the breakers and condemners of God's Sabbath and worship. The peers of Israel, and all the people of God, did stone to death (as the Lord commanded them) the man that disobediently did gather sticks on the Sabbath-day [Num. 15:32–36]. Why then should it not be lawful for a Christian magistrate to punish by bodily imprisonment, by loss of goods, or by death, the despisers of religion, of the true and lawful worship done to God, and of the Sabbath-day? Verily, though the foolish and indiscreet magistrate in this corrupted age do slackly look to his office and duty; yet notwithstanding, let every householder do his endeavor to keep his several family from that ungodly naughtiness; let him punish them of his household by such means as he lawfully may.[44]

Nicolas Bownd (d. 1613)

The earliest full defense of the English Puritan position comes from Nicolas Bownd (Bownde or Bound) of Norton in the county of Suffolk. His father, Richard, a physician to the Duke of Norfolk, helped to provide him with a quality education at Cambridge. Nicolas later obtained a doctorate at Oxford. In 1585, Bownd became minister of St. Andrews Church in Norton and in 1611, became minister in Norwich at the Church of St. Andrew the Apostle. He served there for the remainder of his life[45] but returned to Norton to preach on occasion, according to local records.

In 1592, Bownd published a series of his sermons titled *The Doctrine of the Sabbath*. This collection was expanded in 1606 into a two-part edition titled *Sabbathum Veteris et Novi Testamenti* (*Sabbath in Old and New Testaments*), sometimes referenced under its subtitle *The True Doctrine of the Sabbath*. Reviving an idea once expressed by Thomas Aquinas and other scholastics, Bownd appeals to natural

---

[44] Henry Bullinger, "Of the Fourth Precept of the First Table, that is, of the Order and Keeping of the Sabbath-Day," Sermon IV of the Second Decade, in *The Decades of Henry Bullinger, Minister of the Church at Zurich*, trans. H. I. and ed. Thomas Harding (Cambridge: University Press, 1849), 1:261–62; the whole sermon covers 1:253–67. Vol. 1 includes the first two of five decades.

[45] *The Dictionary of National Biography*, s.v. "Bownde or Bound, Nicholas."

law, that is, "that the law of the Sabbath was so deeply graven in the heart of man at the first by God himself, that" even after the fall of Adam and his race, "it was not so wholly raced out. . . . There is a natural inclination in man . . . to appoint a certain time for his spiritual refreshing, whereby his soul is refreshed in God."[46] Bownd argues that an ancient pagan practice of Sabbath keeping is proof that man had once universally observed God's true Sabbath. Such a notion is absent in the works of Calvin and other Reformers, who argued that since pagan Sabbaths included nature worship, they simply displayed man's own desire to worship the creation rather the Creator. Bownd also initiates, or advances, the idea that the Sabbath is moral but in no way ceremonial.[47] Prior to this time, Puritans had generally held that the Sabbath law was both ceremonial and moral. Bownd insists that the "morality" of keeping the Lord's Day "Sabbath" remains as binding as the Old Testament Sabbath.

Doubting that anyone could be a true Christian and a Sabbath breaker any more than one could have been a true Jew and a Sabbath breaker, Bownd warns that the curses of God continue to be upon those who violate this law.[48] For Bownd, the Lord's Day Sabbath is a full twenty-four-hour day, beginning early on Sunday morning.[49] Civil magistrates must be required to enforce the Sabbath, to punish Sabbath breakers, and to forbid all false religions from having their own places of worship or any opportunity to speak their doctrines in public.[50] Bownd quotes church fathers such as Augustine and Reformers such as Calvin as if to give the impression that they held to his point of view. In context, however, such quotes typically pertain strictly to the nation of Israel.[51] Many of the individuals cited for support by Bownd did not teach the Lord's Day Sabbath legislation

---

[46] Nicolas Bownd, *Sabbathum Veteris et Novi Testamenti: or The True Doctrine of the Sabbath, held and practiced of the Church of God, both before, and under the Law; and in the time of the Gospell* (London: Felix Kyngston for Thomas Man and Iohn Porter, 1606), 22–23 (bk. 1).

[47] Ibid., 37ff. (bk. 1).

[48] Ibid., 281ff. (bk. 1).

[49] Ibid., 366–76 (bk. 2).

[50] Ibid., 465–75 (bk. 2).

[51] All of these individuals and their words on the subject have been provided earlier in this chapter. Peter Heylyn's *History of the Sabbath*, discussed below, refutes Nicolas Bownd point-by-point on his historical inaccuracy.

that he is promoting, and some of them were openly antagonistic to such a view. The Puritans, as a movement, enthusiastically accepted Bownd's position. His book seemed to be a crucial tool at a critical time; although, in many ways, it produced more heat than light.

The Irish Articles (1615)

Through the indubitable influence of Nicolas Bownd's *Sabbathum Veteris et Novi Testamenti*, the doctrine of the Christian Sabbath received its first symbolic endorsement in the Irish Articles: "The first day of the week, which is the *Lord's Day*, is wholly to be dedicated unto the service of God; and therefore we are bound therein to rest from our common and daily business, and to bestow that leisure upon holy exercises, both public and private" (Article 56).

The Book of Sports (1617)

Some Puritans measured the duration of their Sabbath as running from sundown on Saturday to sundown on Sunday. Others measured it, like Nicolas Bownd, as beginning early Sunday morning, the time of Christ's resurrection, and ending twenty-four hours later. Whichever way, the practice would not escape opposition from fellow countrymen—the most frequent charges being leveled against its alleged draconian moralism. The heat intensified when King James I in 1617 issued for the county of Lancashire a Declaration of Sports (Book of Sports) to settle a local dispute over the issue and to encourage Sunday sports and festivities for all those who would first attend their parish churches. The declaration attacks the "Papists" for neglecting church attendance and the Puritans for insisting on setting aside the entire Christian Sabbath day as a government-enforced national holy day of worship and rest. The following year, James felt compelled to reissue his Declaration as applicable to the whole realm of England. Charles I would reissue it in 1633:

> As for our good people's lawful recreation, our pleasure likewise is, that after the end of divine service our good people be not disturbed, letted [hindered] or discouraged from any lawful recreation, such as dancing, either men or women; archery for men, leaping, vaulting, or any other such harmless recreation, nor from having of May-games, Whitsun-ales, and Morris-dances; and the setting up of May-poles and other sports therewith used. . . . And likewise we bar from this benefit and liberty all such known

Recusants, either men or women, as will abstain from coming to church or divine service.[52]

Peter Heylyn (1600–1662)

At this juncture, two groups—Puritans on the one side and high church prelates on the other—became polarized to an unprecedented degree, with the 1635 publishing of an impressive, scholarly, sharp-witted rebuttal of Nicolas Bownd's *Sabbathum Veteris et Novi Testamenti* and the whole concept of a "Christian" Sabbath. The new book came from the pen of an Oxford prelate, a prominent historian of Welsh descent, Peter Heylyn (Heylin), chaplain to King Charles I and later to Charles II. Heylyn's two-part book, *History of the Sabbath*,[53] is dedicated to Charles I in the following terms: "Most dread Sovereign, Your Majesty's most Christian care, to suppress those rigors, which some, in the maintenance of their Sabbath doctrines, had pressed upon this church in these latter days."

The politico-religious tension surrounding Heylyn's book was incredibly high. As prebendary and sub-dean of Westminster Abbey, he ardently supported Archbishop William Laud and later became Laud's biographer. On bended knees in Westminster Abbey, Heylyn would present the royal scepter to King Charles II at his coronation, and Heylyn would be buried with honor in Westminster. The books of Heylyn and Bownd resembled two great armies facing off. Any truth contained in either book did not really matter to the other side. The whole controversy was engulfed in state-church politics and woven into an intricate web that constantly blurred the simplicity of the gospel and the true meaning of worship. Each side made mistakes. On each side there were many good men.

---

[52] Samuel Rawson Gardiner, ed., *The Constitutional Documents of the Puritan Revolution 1625–1660*, 3rd ed. rev. (Oxford: Clarendon Press, 1906), 101–2.

[53] Peter Heylyn, *History of the Sabbath*, 2nd ed. (London: Henry Seile, 1636). For additional biographical information on Heylyn, see *The Dictionary of National Biography*, s.v. "Heylyn, Peter," and the biased but helpful biography by Heylyn's son-in-law, John Barnard, *Theologo-Historicus: or the True Life of the Most Reverend Divine, and Excellent Historian Peter Heylyn D.D.* (London: Printed for J. S. and to be sold by Ed. Eckelston, 1683).

In point of fact, Peter Heylyn stoutly opposed the Roman Church,[54] and his *History of the Sabbath* demonstrates indefatigable and preponderant research. If the biblical and historical content alone in his work had been published in a different era, without the vitriolic verbiage, it would have received wide acceptance. The atmosphere of Heylyn's day bred contempt on both sides, and the tone of this book excited nerves all the more. Like Bound, Heylyn had produced more heat than light.

Almost seventeen hundred years earlier, Julius Caesar and his army had reached a point of no return when they crossed the River Rubicon into northern Italy. Civil war was inevitable from that point. So it did seem at this juncture in the Sabbath controversy, which represented a small part of a complexity of tension pent up until this critical moment. The Sabbath contenders had crossed the Rubicon—the die was cast!

Relentlessly determined to enforce the controversial Declaration (Book) of Sports, Charles I immediately ordered in threatening words that all bishops compel parish priests to read the Declaration of Sports to their congregations. But as the Puritans rapidly gained power in the Long Parliament, hostility increased against the Book of Sports until all attempts at enforcement suddenly ended in 1640. The following year, Parliament ordered a public burning of the Book of Sports. A new and better era had begun.

With the exception of the Lutherans, who held tenaciously to the view of their progenitor, numerous groups gravitated to the English Puritans' Christian Sabbath doctrine as a spiritual antidote to the increasing and troubling lures of secularism. Future skirmishes would appear, such as the "Sabbath War" of 1865–66[55] among Scotland's confessional churches. For now, however, Reformed Christians savored the moment. The major and long-term victory belonged to them. Particular (Reformed) Baptists, Dutch Reformed,

---

[54] This is seen, for example, in Peter Heylyn's *Ecclesia Restaurata, or the History of the Reformation of the Church of England* (London: Printed for H. Twyford, 1661); see also 2nd ed. 1670; 3rd ed. 1674.

[55] Ian Hamilton, *The Erosion of Calvinist Orthodoxy: Drifting from the Truth in Confessional Scottish Churches* (Geanies House, Fearn, Ross-shire, Scotland: Mentor, 2010), 170ff.

and others immediately embraced the doctrine and practice of the Sabbath Lord's Day. It would become a symbol of orthopraxy for most Reformed groups and beyond, not only among the American Puritans,[56] but also among the Free Will Baptists.

The Westminster Standards (1647)

Their long-awaited Lord's Day concept was finally embedded with Reformed dogma, as English Puritans inscribed the Christian Sabbath into its most precise and definitive expression—the Westminster Confession:

> As it is of the law of nature, that, in general, a due proportion of time be set apart for the worship of God; so, in his Word, by a positive, moral, and perpetual commandment, binding all men in all ages, he has particularly appointed one day in seven for a Sabbath, to be kept holy unto him: which, from the beginning of the world to the resurrection of Christ, was the last day of the week; and, from the resurrection of Christ, was changed into the first day of the week, which in Scripture is called the Lord's Day, and is to be continued to the end of the world as the Christian Sabbath. This Sabbath is to be kept holy unto the Lord when men, after a due preparing of their hearts, and ordering of their common affairs beforehand, do not only observe an holy rest all the day from their own works, words, and thoughts, about their worldly employments and recreations; but also are taken up the whole time in the public and private exercises of this worship, and in the duties of necessity and mercy. (21. 7–8)

A poignant illustration of the widespread Presbyterian transition from John Calvin's concept to the Puritans' Christian Sabbath position appears in the 1843 disclaimer made by the Executive Committee of the Presbyterian Board of Publication, "in introducing to the public a new edition of the inimitable" *Institutes of the Christian Religion*:

> The most decidedly objectionable feature in the "Christian Institutes," is to be found in the explanation of the Fourth

---

[56] New England Puritans embraced the Christian Sabbath wholeheartedly, as typified by Thomas Shepard (1605–49), pastor of the church in Cambridge, Massachusetts, who wrote the popular defense called *Theses Sabbaticae* (London: T. R. and E. M. for John Rothwell, 1650). In Massachusetts and Connecticut, the government-enforced Puritan Sabbath began at sundown on Saturday.

Commandment, where the author asserts the abrogation of the Sabbath. In Calvin's view, this ordinance was a mere type of better blessings, and, with the types and ceremonies of the old dispensation, was done away by the introduction of a new and better dispensation. In this opinion there can be no doubt that he greatly erred; and so universal is the conviction of the Church on the perpetual obligation of the Sabbath as a moral institution, that no danger is to be apprehended from a contrary view, even under the sanction of so great a name as that of Calvin. In justice to his opinion on this subject, however, it should be stated, that he distinctly recognized not only the propriety but the necessity of a consecration of stated days for public religious service, without which regulation, he declares that "it is so far from being possible to preserve order and decorum, that if it were abolished, the Church would be in imminent danger of immediate convulsion and ruin." It is much to be lamented that so great a mind should have been led astray on so important a point by attempting to avoid an opposite extreme.[57]

The earliest English Baptists, both Calvinists and Arminians, on both sides of the Atlantic, wholeheartedly endorsed the doctrine of the Christian Sabbath. The major exception is the Southern Baptist Convention's confession of faith, called "The Baptist Faith and Message," which never uses the term *Sabbath* as a descriptive of the Lord's Day. (This is true of all three editions: 1925, 1963, and 2000.) From the seventeenth century on, though, many Baptists have echoed the Presbyterians' Westminster Confession on this doctrine.

The Assembly or Second London Confession— Particular Baptist (1677, 1688)

Chapter 22: Of Religious Worship, and the Sabbath Day

7. As it is of the Law of nature, that in general a proportion of time by Gods appointment, be set apart for the Worship of God; so by his Word, in a positive moral, and perpetual commandment, binding all men, in all Ages, he hath particularly appointed one day in seven for a *Sabbath* to be kept holy unto him, which from the

---

[57] John Calvin, *Institutes of the Christian Religion*, 4th American ed., trans. John Allen (Philadelphia: Presbyterian Board of Publication, 1843), publisher's editorial introduction, 1:4.

beginning of the World to the Resurrection of Christ, was the last day of the week; and from the resurrection of Christ, was changed into the first day of the week which is called the Lords day; and is to be continued to the end of the World, as the *Christian Sabbath*; the observation of the last day of the week being abolished.

8. The *Sabbath* is then kept holy unto the Lord, when men after a due preparing of their hearts, and ordering their common affairs a forehand, do not only observe an holy rest all the day, from their own works, words, and thoughts, about their worldly employment, and recreations, but also are taken up the whole time in the publick and private exercises of his worship, and in the duties of necessity and mercy.

The Orthodox Creed—General Baptist (1678)

Article 40: Of religious Worship, and the Sabbath-day

God hath instituted one day in seven, for his Sabbath to be kept holy unto him, which from the resurrection of Christ, is the first day of the week, which is called the Lord's day, and is to be observed and continued to the end of the world, as a Christian Sabbath, the last day of the week being abolished. And this Christian Sabbath is to be kept after a due and reverent manner, in preparing of our hearts, and ordering of affairs so beforehand, that we may rest that day from worldly and carnal employments, and frequent the solemn assemblies of the church, and in all public and private duties of religion, as hearing, meditating, and conferring, and reading in, or of the holy scriptures, together with prayer, public and private, and in the duties of necessity, charity, and mercy, and not in any vain or worldly discourse, or idle recreations whatsoever.

The New Connection of General Baptists (1770)

Article 2: On the Nature and Perpetual Obligation of the Moral Law

We believe, that the moral law not only extends to the outward actions of the life, but to all the powers and faculties of the mind, to every desire, temper and thought; that it demands the entire devotion of all the powers and faculties of both body and soul to God: or, in our Lord's words, to love the Lord with all our heart, mind, soul and strength:—that this law is of perpetual duration and obligation, to all men, at all times, and in all places or parts of the world. And, we suppose that this law was obligatory to Adam in his perfect state—was more clearly revealed in the Ten

135

Commandments—and more fully explained in many other parts of the bible.

The Philadelphia Baptist Confession (1742)

Article 22 is the same as the Particular Baptist Second London Confession above.

The New Hampshire Confession of Faith (1833)

Like the previous confession, this clearly reflects the Puritan's Christian Sabbath:

15. Of the Christian Sabbath

We believe that the first day of the week is the Lord's Day, or Christian Sabbath; and is to be kept sacred to religious purposes, by abstaining from all secular labor and sinful recreations; by the devout observance of all the means of grace, both private and public; and by preparation for that rest that remaineth for the people of God.

Treatise on the Faith of the Free Will Baptists— Benjamin Randall (1834)

Chapter 12: The Sabbath

This is a seventh part of time, which from the creation of the world, God has set apart for a day of sacred rest and holy service. It was included in the Ten Commandments written on tables of stone, and given to Moses on Mount Sinai. . . . Nature itself teaches the necessity of its observance. Its obligation is taught both in the Old and New Testaments, and is to continue with that of the other commandments till the end of time. As the law of the Sabbath was at first given to the whole world, it requires all men, on this day, to refrain from all servile labor, and devote themselves entirely to the service of the God that made them.

This section was revised in the 1948 edition:

Chapter 14: The Sabbath

This is one day in seven, which from the creation of the world God has set apart for sacred rest and holy service. Under the former dispensation, the seventh day of the week as commemorative of the work of creation, was set apart for the Sabbath. Under the Gospel, the first day of the week, in commemoration of the resurrection of Christ, and by authority of Christ and the apostles, is observed as the Christian Sabbath. On this day all men are required to refrain from secular labor, and devote themselves to the worship and service of God.

The Baptist Faith and Message— Southern Baptist Convention (2000)

Article 8: The Lord's Day

The first day of the week is the Lord's Day. It is a Christian institution for regular observance. It commemorates the resurrection of Christ from the dead and should include exercises of worship and spiritual devotion, both public and private. Activities on the Lord's Day should be commensurate with the Christian's conscience under the Lordship of Jesus Christ.

Current Status, Summary, and Conclusion

Contrary to nearly all the early church fathers and sixteenth-century Reformers, many today teach that a Christian Sabbath is binding. They believe that Genesis 2:2–3 proves the Sabbath to be part of God's moral law, a "creation ordinance," instilled in man's nature from the beginning and perpetually binding upon all humanity. They believe that its inclusion in the Ten Commandments (Exod. 20:8–11) makes Sabbath observance a vital part of the eternal moral law of God. Arthur W. Pink, a defender of this view, writes, "It should thus be quite evident that this law for the regulation of man's time was not a temporary one, designed for any particular dispensation, but is continuous and perpetual in the purpose of God."[58]

Traditionalists, on the other hand, celebrate the sacredness of the Lord's Day, but they do not refer to it as the "Sabbath" Lord's Day. They understand Genesis 1:31 and 2:1–3 to mean that, upon completion of His work, God took pleasure in all that He had made. He blessed and sanctified that day in anticipation of the eternal rest that His whole creation will ultimately enjoy. The passage is not about what man is to do, but about what God has done. Even as they receive specific instructions (Gen. 2:16–17), Adam and Eve do not

---

[58] *The Ten Commandments* (n.p.: Jay P. Green Sr., 2003), 29.

receive so much as an implied command (or ordinance) to observe the Sabbath.

Along with the consensus of patristic and first-generation Reformation representatives, traditionalists teach that the Sabbath observance of the fourth commandment (Exod. 20:8–11) is part of the distinct covenant document that God made exclusively with Israel at Sinai (Exod. 34:27–28). It is part of the ceremonial law. It is often asked, "Why was the ceremonial Sabbath observance included with the moral commandments if it were not a part of the moral law?" John Reisinger, a Reformed Baptist, answers that since "the Tablets of Stone were a distinct covenant," the tablets "were accompanied with a specific 'covenant sign.'" The Sabbath was the "*sign of the covenant and therefore it had to be* part of the covenant of which it *was the sign.*"[59] Harold H. P. Dressler further explains: "As a sign of the covenant, the Sabbath can only be meant for Israel, with whom the covenant was made. It has a 'perpetual' function, i.e., for the duration of the covenant, and derives its importance and significance from the covenant itself."[60]

Thus, traditionalists believe that the Old Testament regulations governing Sabbath observances are ceremonial rather than moral aspects of the law. As such, those regulations passed away with the sacrificial system, the Levitical priesthood, and all other ceremonial laws prefiguring Christ. Paul, in Colossians 2:16–17, refers to the Sabbath as a "shadow" of Christ. Since the substance (Christ) has come, the shadow is no longer binding or necessary. In the Colossians passage, expressions such as "festivals" and "Sabbath days" refer to the annual, monthly, and weekly holy days of the Jewish calendar.[61] The early churches followed the pattern of designating the first day of the week as the Lord's Day on which His people gathered in worship. To them it was the day of light and glory, with each obedient believer enjoying Christ's own presence.

---

[59] *Tablets of Stone* (Southbridge, MA: Crowne, 1989), 43.

[60] "The Sabbath in the Old Testament," in *From Sabbath to Lord's Day: A Biblical, Historical, and Theological Investigation*, ed. D. A. Carson (Grand Rapids: Zondervan, 1982.), 30.

[61] See, e.g., 1 Chron. 23:31; 2 Chron. 2:4; 31:3; Ezek. 45:17; and Hosea 2:11.

Traditionalists insist that, prior to the time of Moses the lawgiver, there are no commands in the Bible to keep the Sabbath and that there is no evidence of anyone keeping the Sabbath before the time of Moses. Nowhere in the Bible are Gentile nations commanded to keep the Sabbath; nor are they condemned for not keeping it. The Sabbath was Israel's sign of the Mosaic Covenant (Exod. 31:16–17; Ezek. 20:12).

God does not instruct the church to observe the sign of the Mosaic Covenant. The command to observe the Sabbath was to those who were under the Mosaic Covenant that God made with the people of Israel at Mount Sinai. When the apostles met at the Jerusalem council, they did not impose Sabbath keeping upon Gentile believers or upon anyone else (Acts 15). The apostle Paul clearly corrected the Galatians who thought that God expected them to observe special days such as the Sabbath (Gal. 4:10–11). Each day, for the believer, is a day of resting in the assurance of salvation and progressive purification granted by the Spirit of God through the Word of God (Heb. 4:9–11). In the New Testament, there is an emphasis that centers upon the eternal serenity that results from the redemptive work of Christ. The redeemed will fully realize their rest when the last battle is won, and the church militant becomes the church triumphant.

Even in the Genesis account, our blessed Creator and Redeemer, who needed no rest, provides for His redeemed a gracious reminder of His promise of eternal rest. Like the church fathers, such as Justin Martyr, and like the Reformers, such as John Calvin, every Christian with his conscience submitted to the Lordship of Christ embraces God's gracious benefit of calmness and celebration. To committed believers, the Lord's Day is the most important day of every week. Locally, every true and obedient body of Christ delights in gathering in peaceful celebration of Christ's glorious resurrection and in fulfillment of the inspired scriptural instructions concerning His church— its edification, its proclamation, its offices, and its ordinances. These functions are of foremost importance in God's design for each local body belonging to Christ and for each member of that body.

The Lord's Day reminds us of the pedagogical rest that followed the completion of God's perfect creation. The Lord's Day directs us to the perpetual rest that will follow the completion of God's redeemed creation. In spiritual gifts, the church is already receiving New Covenant blessings (Heb. 8) that Israel will enjoy when she accepts her Messiah at His glorious appearing to establish His millennial and eternal kingdom. The Scriptures speak of a future time when all of God's elect since the beginning of creation will sit down together as one at the Marriage Supper of the Lamb (Rev. 19:6–9; Luke 13:29). There is a beautifully designed confluence, where the perfect oneness of God's people flows into eternal rest in the New Heavens and New Earth (Heb. 3:18–4:11; Rev. 21–22).

> Let us therefore fear, lest, a promise being left us of entering into his rest, any of you should seem to come short of it. For unto us was the gospel preached, as well as unto them: but the word preached did not profit them, not being mixed with faith in them that heard it. For we which have believed do enter into rest, as he said, As I have sworn in my wrath, if they shall enter into my rest: although the works were finished from the foundation of the world. *For He spake in a certain place of the seventh day on this wise, And God did rest the seventh day from all his works.* And in this place again, If they shall enter into my rest. (Heb. 4:1–5; italics added)

Select Bibliography for Further Reading

Beckwith, Robert T., and Wilfrid Stott. *The Christian Sunday: A Biblical and Historical Study.* Grand Rapids: Baker, 1980. This is a reprint of an earlier title, *This Is the Day: The Biblical Doctrine of the Christian Sunday in Its Jewish and Early Church Setting.* London: Marshall, Morgan and Scott, 1978.

Bownd, Nicolas. *Sabbathum Veteris et Novi Testamenti: or The True Doctrine of the Sabbath, held and practiced of the Church of God, both before, and under the Law; and in the time of the Gospell.* 2 vols. London: Felix Kyngston, for Thomas Man and Iohn Porter, 1606.

Bullinger, Henry. "Of the Fourth Precept of the First Table, that is, of the Order and Keeping of the Sabbath-Day." Sermon IV of the Second Decade. In *The Decades of Henry Bullinger, Minister of the Church at Zurich*, 4 vols. translated by H. I. and edited by Thomas Harding, 1:253–67. Cambridge: University Press, 1849–52.

Calvin, John. *The Sermons of M. John Calvin upon the Fifth Booke of Moses, Called Deuteronomie.* Translated from the French by Arthur Golding. London: Printed by Henry Middleton for Thomas Woodcocke, 1583.

Carson, D. A., ed. *From Sabbath to Lord's Day: A Biblical, Historical, and Theological Investigation.* Grand Rapids: Zondervan, 1982.

Cox, Robert. *The Literature of the Sabbath Question.* 2 vols. London: Maclachlan and Stewart, 1865.

————, ed. *The Whole Doctrine of Calvin about the Sabbath and the Lord's Day; extracted from his Commentaries, Catechism, and Institutes of the Christian Religion.* Edinburgh: Robert Cox, 1860. This is a collection of the passages in which Calvin discusses the Sabbath.

Cranmer, Thomas. *Writings of the Rev. Dr. Thomas Cranmer: Archbishop of Canterbury and Martyr*, 1556. Edited by William M. Engles. Philadelphia: Presbyterian Board of Publication, 1842.

Donato, Christopher John, ed. *Perspectives on the Sabbath: Four Views.* Nashville: B&H Publishing Group, 2011.

Heylyn, Peter. *History of the Sabbath.* 2nd ed. London: Henry Seile, 1636.

Houghton, Myron. *Law and Grace.* Schaumburg, IL: Regular Baptist Books, 2011.

MacArthur, John, Jr. "Are the Sabbath Laws Binding on Christians Today?" Available at http://www.gty.org/resources/questions/QA135.

Reisinger, John G. *Tablets of Stone.* Southbridge, MA: Crowne, 1989.

7

The Doctrinal Development of the Eternal Generation of Christ

The doctrine of the "eternal generation" of Christ originated from the metaphysical blending of the meanings of the two New Testament words *begotten* and *monogenēs*. Standard lexicons concur that the word *begotten* (γεννηθέντα) derives from *gennao* (γεννάω) and primarily means "to be born or conceived." Christ was "conceived" (γεννηθὲν) of the Holy Spirit in Mary, "of whom was born [ἐγεννήθη] Jesus, who is called Christ" (Matt. 1:20, 16). Standard lexicons also agree that the word *monogenēs* (μονογενής) derives from two words: *monos* (μόνος), meaning "one" or "only," and *genos* (γένος), meaning "one of a kind" or "unique."[1] On the dubious assumption that the word *monogenēs* derived from *gennao* ("to beget"), fourth-century patristic writers depicted *monogenēs* as "only-begotten." But *monogenēs* consistently denotes "uniqueness," even in post-apostolic literature. Clement of Rome, in his first-century

---

[1] Samples include James H. Moulton and George Milligan, *The Vocabulary of the Greek Testament*; Joseph Henry Thayer, *Greek-English Lexicon of the New Testament*; George Abbott-Smith, *A Manual Greek Lexicon of the New Testament*; Henry George Liddell and Robert Scott, *A Greek-English Lexicon*; and Johannes P. Louw and Eugene A. Nida, *Greek-English Lexicon of the New Testament Based on Semantic Domains* (New York: United Bible Societies, 1989). The word *genos* can refer to a people, a stock, a generation, or a family, such as Joseph's "kindred" (*genos*, Acts 7:13); see Walter Bauer, *A Greek-English Lexicon of the New Testament and Other Early Christian Literature*, 3rd ed., rev. and ed. Frederick W. Danker (Chicago: University of Chicago Press, 2000), 194–95, 658. Even in such instances, *genos* retains the element of uniqueness.

Epistle to the Corinthians, describes the legendary phoenix as a one-of-its-kind (*monogenēs*) bird rising up out of her own ashes:

ὄρνεον γάρ ἐστιν ὃ προσονομάζεται φοίνιξ.

"There is a bird which is called the phoenix."

τοῦτο μονογενὲς ὑπάρχον ζῇ ἔτη πεντακόσια.

"It is the only one of its kind [*monogenēs*] and lives five hundred years."[2]

The phoenix story is a legitimate example of uniqueness. The uniqueness of the bird is her self-existence. She is the only bird inhabiting the eternal forest and she resurrects herself after a self-inflicted death. Each time she prepares to die, she must enter another world where death reigns. After her death and resurrection, she returns once again to the blissful forest where the trees always produce fruit. The fable states, "She is an offspring to herself, her own father and heir, her own nurse, and always a foster-child to herself. She is herself indeed, but not the same since she is herself, and not herself, having gained eternal life by the blessing of death."[3] The point of the story that illustrates Christ is the bird's unique self-existence.

An essential attribute of deity is self-existence. Christ's deity inherently includes the perfection of *autotheos* (αὐτόθεος), meaning "God in Himself." The same is true of the Father and of the Holy Spirit. The Trinity is one divine essence in three distinct persons. "Oneness" and "distinctiveness" are fundamentally equal in importance. The ontological Trinity is not asymmetrical. Each distinct person is an *autotheos* element of the eternal Trinity. Three distinct

---

[2] Clement of Rome, *Epistle to the Corinthians* 25, in Migne *PG* 1.261-65. Unless otherwise noted, patristic citations and references are from ANF, NPNF 1, or NPNF 2.

[3] The phoenix story was popular in the earliest periods of church history. There are many versions, as seen, for example, in Herodotus (*History* 2.73), Pliny the Elder (*Natural History* 10.2), and Pomponius Mela, *De Situ Orbis* 3.8, the latter two being closest to the version used by Clement of Rome. Among other Christian writers, Tertullian rightly uses it to illustrate the resurrection (*On the Resurrection of the Flesh* 13), while Origen correctly scorns anyone who would take the story literally (*Against Celsus* 4.98). A full version that comes close to Clement's is in ANF (7:324–26). A few details differ, such as the number of years for each life-cycle. The fable is at times mistakenly attributed to Lactantius of Nicomedia. It could have originated in Arabia or quite possibly India and was no doubt one of many such tales made popular by Oriental travelers on the ancient trade routes. It is short and entertaining.

persons are substantially one God. They can be neither confused nor divided. This is established not upon fable, but upon Scripture alone, as emphasized by the sixteenth-century Reformers.

"From the moment it is seen, that from eternity there were three persons in one God," from that moment, says John Calvin, "this idea of continual generation becomes an absurd fiction."[4] In like manner, Benjamin B. Warfield argues that the Bible has nothing whatsoever to say about "begetting" as an eternal *act*. It speaks simply of the *fact* of the unique and eternal Son of God.[5] Warfield argues against using either the term *eternal generation* or the term *eternal procession*. To him, such terms risk the suggestion of an eternal subordination of the Son and the Holy Spirit. It is the contextual study of Scripture, not philosophical speculation, that must provide the foundational basis for biblical exegesis.[6]

George Bull (1634–1710) produced an ambitious *Defensio Fidei Nicaenae*[7] to defend the Niceno-Constantinopolitan doctrine of eternal generation, and it is drawn entirely from ante-Nicene statements, including extreme examples, to prove an eternal subordination of Christ and the Holy Spirit. The one thing that Bull does prove is that the teaching of eternal generation depends essentially upon eternal subordinationism. Bull's work has many helpful sections, but he repeatedly utilizes Bible proof texts that are applicable only to Christ's earthly humiliation, and he wrongly applies such texts to our Lord's present state. To his credit, Bull defends the deity of Christ and of the Holy Spirit, but the author's inappropriate proof texts, both biblical and patristic, for eternal subordination, are often the same ones used and abused by modern Unitarians.

---

[4] *Institutes of the Christian Religion* 1.13.29.

[5] Benjamin Breckinridge Warfield, *Biblical and Theological Studies*, ed. Samuel G. Craig (Philadelphia: Presbyterian and Reformed Publishing, 1968), 58–59, and passim.

[6] D. A. Carson, *Exegetical Fallacies* (Grand Rapids: Baker, 1984), 29–30. Carson discusses *monogenēs* and the book is filled with helpful cautions and examples.

[7] George Bull, *Defensio Fidei Nicaenae: A Defense of the Nicene Creed out of the Extant Writings of the Catholic Doctors who Flourished during the Three First Centuries of the Christian Church; in which also Is Incidentally Vindicated the Creed of Constantinople Concerning the Holy Ghost*, 2 vols. (1685; repr., Oxford: John Henry Parker, 1851–52).

Monogenēs occurs five times in Scripture in reference to Christ, and the apostle John penned them all: John 1:14, 18; 3:16, 18; and 1 John 4:9. Many conservative scholars believe that in all five verses the word clearly depicts the idea of *one-and-only* and nothing more, as seen in a growing number of translations.[8] The ESV, for example, translates John 3:16, "he gave his *only* son," and the NIV (1984) has it, "he gave his *one and only* son." The NASB adds this marginal note: "Or, *unique*, only one of His kind." Such renderings avoid any blending of the words *begotten* and *monogenēs*. The doctrine of eternal generation does not derive explicitly, nor perhaps even implicitly, from Scripture. That does not mean *per se* that the concept is heretical. The 381 Council dogmatized it into orthodox doctrine. That does not mean *per se* that the concept is biblical. We will focus on its historical provenance and development and draw some additional conclusions.

Niceno-Constantinopolitan Creed

The 150 who assembled in Constantinople's Church of Saint Irene in the early summer of 381 brought to the table two conjectures that influenced their usage of *begotten* and *monogenēs*. One presumption was etymological, and the other was philosophical. The etymological presumption was that the last part of the word μονογενής (*monogenēs*) derived from γεννάω (*gennao*, "to beget"). Etymology is a weak basis for dogma. The philosophical presumption was that they could properly apply a metaphysical interpretation to *gennao* and *monogenēs*. The outcome of those two conjectures was the transfer of *begotten* from a literal-historical event into an eternal

---

[8] The 1952 RSV and the 1989 NRSV surprisingly render *monogenēs* (μονογενή) as "only," which is consistent with the doctrine of Christ's virgin conception. See Dale Moody, "God's Only Son: The Translation of John 3:16 in the Revised Standard Version," *Journal of Biblical Literature* 72, no. 4 (December 1953): 213–19. The RSV and the NRSV were published by the National Council of the Churches. For years conservatives have rightly criticized their liberal stance, illustrated for instance at Isa. 7:14, where their translators render the word *'almah* (עַלְמָה) as "young woman" and relegate "virgin" to a footnote. For more on the translation of *'almah*, see the valuable discussion by Allan A. MacRae, in *Theological Wordbook of the Old Testament*, ed. R. Laird Harris, Gleason L. Archer Jr., and Bruce K. Waltke (Chicago: Moody Press, 1980), 2:672.

concept. These church fathers believed vehemently in Christ's literal virgin birth. They were not "liberals." In fact, they were great men contributing immeasurably to the proper expression of our fundamental views on the Trinity. We have the advantage of hindsight and of those who have gone before us.[9] The Fathers were virtually inimitable in their extraordinary labors. It is with profound respect for these patristic writers, therefore, that we point out a couple of significant handicaps. Their classical education in the pagan schools made it only natural for them to approach the Scriptures with the standard hermeneutical methods used in every classical school of their day, specifically allegorical, analogical, and philosophical. Even the major Jewish scholars revered these methods. The church fathers employed a Platonic concept in order to answer an immediate heresy.

Platonic philosophy had combined and elevated the words *begotten* and *monogenēs* to a non-historical concept of an eternal generation of Christ. In terms of Platonic philosophy, *monogenēs* can sometimes include the idea of uniqueness, but it always reflects the idea of eternal generation as a higher truth than any literal-historical event. By definition, the concept of eternal generation highlights derivation and subordination. It obfuscates Christ's *self-existence*, which is an essential attribute of deity. It blurs His uniqueness. It is impossible even to express the concept of eternal generation without the use of terms indicative of eternal derivation and subordination. Theological dictionaries, with no explanation or caution, define *monogenēs* in such terms as the "eternal and changeless activity in the Godhead by which the Father *produces* the Son without division of essence and by which the *Second* Person of the Trinity is identified as an individual subsistence . . . of the divine essence."[10] Scripture speaks of "Father, Son, and Holy Spirit," but Scripture never depicts the persons of the Trinity in terms of "First," "Second," and "Third."

---

[9] For a brief defense of the patristic view, see the article, "Eternal Generation," in John Henry Blunt, ed., *Dictionary of Doctrinal and Historical Theology* (London: Longmans, Green, 1891), 243-44.

[10] Richard A. Muller, *Dictionary of Latin and Greek Theological Terms: Drawn Principally from Protestant Scholastic Theology* (Grand Rapids: Baker, 1985), 127. Italics are added to highlight terms of subordination often found in reference works. Muller's is still a good basic dictionary that I can recommend. Its subtitle qualifies its limitations.

Such terminology has potential for being misleading. In ordinary language, especially in a sports-oriented society, anyone who is second or third is immediately considered inferior to first. Even in the family unit, such numerical ranking would be considered crude. To use an ancient term now in cinematic vocabulary, we might wonder how the *morphing* (μορφή) of eternal generation emerged in 381 inside Constantinople's opulent Church of Holy Peace. We will take a closer look.

The Niceno-Constantinopolitan Creed begins this section by expressing the patristic belief "in one Lord Jesus Christ" (εἰς ἕνα κύριον Ἰησοῦν Χριστόν). Then, as the church fathers proceeded to blend *begotten* with *monogenēs*, the "one-and-only" became the "only-begotten" (τὸν υἱὸν τοῦ Θεοῦ τὸν μονογενῆ, τὸν ἐκ τοῦ πατρὸς γεννηθέντα). And by adding the phrase, "before all ages" (πρὸ πάντων τῶν αἰώνων),[11] they conceptualized *monogenēs* into an "eternal generation" elevated above the temporal realm. Over time, it became a normal assumption that the word *monogenēs* itself comes fully-packed with the whole idea of eternal generation. While this was the first conciliar creed to teach the eternal generation of Christ, the concept was really not a brainstorm of the framers of the Niceno-Constantinopolitan Creed. Beginning with Justin Martyr we can trace its roots. Beginning with Origen we can trace its development. We will bring it to Jerome who passed it on to the Nicene fathers who gave it creedal status. The journey will show how the terms *begotten* and *monogenēs* were gradually modified from the grammatical and historical into the conceptual and speculative.

Justin Martyr and Eternal Generation

Justin (ca. 100–167), the Greek apologist, sets a far-reaching precedent by interpreting Proverbs 8:22 in a way that depicts Christ, the Logos, as the created Creator. In a good English rendering of the verse, Wisdom, poetically personified, is exclaiming, "The Lord possessed me in the beginning of his way, before his works of old" (KJV). Justin's error is rooted in the mistaken LXX translation of the

---

[11] The Greek text is from *ACO* 2, 1, 2, 80 [276].

Hebrew word *qanah* (קָנָה) as ἔκτισε ("created" or "made"),[12] rather than the correct word ἐκτήσατο ("possessed"), as in the ancient text of Aquila. Even the Vulgate has it *possedit me*. Besides the KJV, other English translations, such as the ASV, NASB, and ESV, also render it "possessed." The idea of *created* finds no support from the context. The passage is a poetic declaration that wisdom is an eternal attribute of God, and as such it would never have been created.

By applying the Logos to the LXX rendering, Justin equates the "created" wisdom of Proverbs 8:22 with Christ, who was "begotten as a Beginning before all His creatures and as Offspring by God."[13] Justin adds that God the Father "created and arranged all things by Him."[14] The Arians as well, however, would later appeal to the LXX rendering to teach that Christ was the created Creator. Clearly attempting to connect Christianity with Middle Platonism, Justin tends at times to depict the Logos more as a cosmic concept than as a person of the Trinity. "*Next to God*," explains Justin, "we worship and love the Word (Λόγος) who is from the unbegotten and ineffable God."[15]

In his *Dialogue with Trypho*, Justin twice uses the word *monogenēs* within a quotation from the LXX version of Psalm 22:20.[16] In the first occurrence, he makes no attempt to discuss the meaning of the word—only to preach the message of Christ's crucifixion to Trypho, an unconverted Jew.[17] In the other occurrence, Justin emphasizes the idea of uniqueness and postulates that the application of *monogenēs* is pre-incarnate, in the sense that Christ was the unique Son of God prior to His virgin birth and sacrificial death.[18] It would take many more years for the word *monogenēs* to be used in the sense of *only-*

---

[12] The Targums are also mistaken in making the "wisdom" of this passage a creature.

[13] *Dialogue with Trypho* 61–62.

[14] *Second Apology* 6.

[15] Ibid., 13. Italics added.

[16] The chapter number in the LXX is Psalm 21 rather than our familiar 22.

[17] *Dialogue with Trypho* 98.

[18] *Dialogue with Trypho* 105: Μονογενὴς γὰρ ὅτι ἦν τῷ πατρὶ τῶν ὅλων οὗτος, ιδίως ἐξ αὐτοῦ Λόγος καὶ δύναμις γεγενημένος, καὶ ὕστερον ἄνθρωπος διὰ τῆς Παρθένου γενόμενος. A couple of accent marks and breathing marks are difficult to decipher in the worn manuscript, but not enough to compromise accuracy of the essential meaning in the translation process. *Justini Philosophi et*

begotten, but the historical development of the concept of eternal generation would continue unfolding.

Tatian of Assyria and Eternal Generation

As a young man, Tatian (ca. 110–72) had become enamored with Gnosticism and other philosophical schemes, but for a time he seemed to turn against all pagan philosophy. It was probably in Rome that he met Justin Martyr, who introduced him to Christianity and instructed him in the faith. Irenaeus reports that after Justin's death, Tatian apostatized from the faith, left the church, composed his own strange doctrines, including a system of Gnostic aeons, and cast off cardinal Christian doctrines. He established an ascetic group that required abstinence from marriage, wine, and meats.[19] Because of their inward power of self-control, the group's adherents were called Encratites (ἐνκρατής; from ἐν, "in" + κράτος, "strength"). Even while still professing to be a Christian apologist, Tatian wrote an *Address to the Greeks*, his only extant work,[20] in which he postulates that the souls of the wicked are dissolved at death, to be reunited with the body at the resurrection.[21] In the following discussion, Tatian offers his philosophical and candid concept of eternal generation.[22] "Begotten in the beginning," the Logos was brought "into being" by the Father in order to create the world:

> Him (the Logos) we know to be the beginning of the world. But He came into being by participation, not by abscission; for what is cut off is separated from the original substance, but that which comes by participation, making its choice of function, does not render him deficient from whom it is taken. For just as from one torch many fires are lighted, but the light of the first torch is not

Martyris, Dialogus cum Tryphone Judaeo (Migne *PG* 6.720–21). In *PG* 6.707-08 Justin uses the word μονογενῆ.

[19] Irenaeus, *Against Heresies* 1.28; Eusebius, *Ecclesiastical History* 4.28–29; and Epiphanius, *Panarion* 46.

[20] Tatian compiled his *Diatesseron* in Syriac. This combined the four Gospels into a single consecutive narrative. The original was lost, and it survives in a late Arabic recension. Its value lies in its being yet another witness to the four canonical Gospels being preserved as one unit as early as the second century.

[21] Tatian, *Address to the Greeks* 13.

[22] The text is quite legible in Tatianus Syriacus, *Oratio Adversus Graecos* 5 (Migne *PG* 6.813–18).

lessened by the kindling of many torches, so the Logos, coming forth from the Logos-power of the Father, has not divested of the Logos-power Him who begat Him. I myself, for instance, talk, and you hear; yet, certainly, I who converse do not become destitute of speech (λόγος) by the transmission of speech, but by the utterance of my voice I endeavor to reduce to order the unarranged matter in your minds. And as the Logos, begotten in the beginning, begat in turn our world, having first created for Himself the necessary matter. (*Address to the Greeks* 5)

Theophilus of Antioch and Eternal Generation

Little is known of the life of the apologist Theophilus (ca. 115–80). Eusebius describes him as an early bishop of Antioch in Syria. His only extant work is an apology written in answer to an antagonist named Autolycus. Many of his interpretations are so fanciful that they are of little or no theological value. Their value is in their historical significance. Using Proverbs 8:22ff. (like Justin) for his support, Theophilus sets forth his crude notion of an eternal generation of Christ:

God, then, having His own Word internal within His own bowels, begat Him, emitting Him along with His own wisdom before all things. He had this Word as a helper in the things that were created by Him, and by Him He made all things. He is called "governing principle" [ἀρχή], because He rules, and is Lord of all things fashioned by Him. (*To Autolycus* 2.10)

Irenaeus of Lyon and Eternal Generation

While correctly maintaining the eternality of the Lord Jesus Christ and His work in the creation of the universe, Irenaeus (fl. late 2nd c.) erroneously takes the word *bara'* in Genesis 1:1 for "son" (*bar*) rather than "created." Thus, he interprets the words *Bereshith bara* as "the Son in the beginning"[23] rather than "in the beginning created."

---

[23] *Demonstration (Proof) of the Apostolic Preaching* 43: "Now that there was a Son of God, and that He existed not only before He appeared in the world, but also before the world was made, Moses, who was the first that prophesied, says in Hebrew: *Baresith bara Elowin basan benuam samenthares.* And this, translated into our language, is: 'The Son in the beginning: God established then the heaven and the earth.'" Irenaeus, *The Demonstration of the Apostolic Preaching*, trans.

He does lament that Gnostics were beginning "presumptuously" to transfer the theory of eternal emissions to the "only-begotten" Word of God. Paraphrasing from Isaiah 53:8, he asks, "Who shall describe His generation?" The Gnostics "pretend to set forth His generation from the Father." Those who "have excogitated [the theory of] emissions have not discovered anything great, or revealed any abstruse mystery, when they have simply transferred what all understand to the only-begotten Word of God."[24] The Gnostics had "transferred" (*transtulerunt*) the idea of "emissions" (*emissiones*) to the "only-begotten Word of God" (*unigenitum Dei Verbum*).[25]

In the midst of minuscule descriptions of Gnostic speculation concerning emissions (aeons) generating and proceeding from the Pleroma (Πλήρωμα), Irenaeus makes it clear that he believes that there is a *true* eternal generation of the Logos from the Father. He cautiously warns that since Christ's "generation is unspeakable, those who strive to set forth generations and productions cannot be in their right mind, inasmuch as they undertake to describe things which are indescribable."[26] He argues that the apostle John's purpose in writing his Gospel was to refute similar errors. Such was John's reason for beginning his Gospel with "In the beginning was the Word [Λόγος]. . . ." To Irenaeus, the doctrine of the eternal generation of Christ is one of the true and "unspeakable mysteries" of Christianity—"altogether indescribable."

Typically, the Fathers were quick to categorize the idea of eternal generation as a sort of hidden "mystery" of eternal derivation, subordination, or limitation as belonging to Christ. Even Irenaeus

---

J. Armitage Robinson (London: Society for Promoting Christian Knowledge, 1920), 108.

[24] Irenaeus, *Against Heresies* 2.28.6; see text in *Contra Haeresis* (Migne *PG* 7.809).

[25] The Greek manuscript does not exist. The word *unigenitum* appears to be anachronistic, being from the fourth century, when parts of the manuscript were edited. The phrase "only Word of God" in typical Old Latin is *unicum Dei Verbum*. In John 3:16, God gave "His *monogenēs* Son," rendered in Old Latin as *Filium suum unicum*—"His only Son." When Jerome later translated it as *Filium suum unigenitum*—"His only-begotten Son"—he formally equated *monogenēs* with "only-begotten" and standardized the equation by embedding it into a major Bible translation, the Vulgate.

[26] *Against Heresies* 2.28.5–6; cf. 3.11.1.

instantly focuses the reader on the words of Christ, "that the Father alone knows the very day and hour of judgment." This raises a question that apparently Irenaeus did not wish to answer. He withholds even the modest explanation that Jesus' statement refers only to His own voluntary and temporary setting aside of the knowledge of the "very day and hour" during the time of His earthly humiliation. Irenaeus simply describes "eternal generation" as a mystery as inexplicable as the origin of sin.

Origen of Alexandria and Eternal Generation

It was Origen of Alexandria (ca. 185–254), in *De Principiis*, who firmly established the idea of eternal generation as a Christian doctrine.[27] There is no extant Greek for some sections of the work, but in the fourth-century Latin translation, Origen contends that Christ was "born of the Father before all creation" (*Ante omnem creaturum natus ex Patre est*). Origen made two serious mistakes that became the basis for his own notion of eternal generation, and they quickly become apparent: (1) he interprets the personification of wisdom in Proverbs 8:22–25 as the person of Christ; (2) he injects into the Proverbs passage Paul's description of Christ as the "firstborn (πρωτότοκος) of all creation." Origen does not deny Christ's deity or distinct personality, but the eternal subordination of Christ becomes inevitable, especially when Origen interweaves faulty reasoning into a faulty exegesis of Scripture:

> In the first place, we must note that the nature of that deity which is in Christ in respect of His being the only-begotten Son of God is one thing, and that human nature which He assumed in these last times for the purposes of the dispensation (of grace) is another. And therefore we have first to ascertain what the only-begotten Son of God is, seeing He is called by many different names, according to the circumstances and views of individuals. For He is termed Wisdom, according to the expression of Solomon: "The Lord created me—the beginning of His ways, and among His works, before He made any other thing; He founded

---

[27] Origen, *De Principiis*, preface, section 4; see also Philip Schaff, *The Creeds of Christendom, with a History and Critical Notes* (New York: Harper and Brothers, 1877), 2:23.

me before the ages. In the beginning, before He formed the earth, before He brought forth the fountains of waters, before the mountains were made strong, before all the hills, He brought me forth" [Prov. 8:22–25]. He is also styled First-born, as the apostle has declared: "who is the first-born of every creature" [Col. 1:15]. The first-born, however, is not by nature a different person from the Wisdom, but one and the same. Finally, the Apostle Paul says that "Christ (is) the power of God and the wisdom of God" [1 Cor. 1:24]. (*De Principiis* 1.2.1)[28]

Although never denying Christ's eternal sonship, Origen's Christology is false, and, by biblical and post-Nicene standards, it is heretical. Origen was using the LXX version of Proverbs 8:22–25, but here is a better rendering, from the ESV, of God's wisdom speaking forth:

> (22) The Lord possessed me at the beginning of his work, the first of his acts of old. (23) Ages ago I was set up, at the first, before the beginning of the earth. (24) When there were no depths I was brought forth, when there were no springs abounding with water. (25) Before the mountains had been shaped, before the hills, I was brought forth.

Utilizing an inflammatory term, Origen repeatedly calls Christ the "demiurge" (δημιουργός), which the Gnostics had applied to the Old Testament Jehovah (or Logos) as creator of evil (matter). Philo had earlier used *demiurge* in a somewhat neutral way simply to indicate *creator*, or fashioner of the world. It was Plato who had first used the term, however, and he applied it figuratively to an *idea*, or ultimate good.

Origen's explanation of the eternal generation of the Son constitutes a connecting link with Plotinus, the founder of Neo-Platonism and this is the first clear instance of pagan Logos philosophy affecting the Christian theology of God's transcendence. Origen's philosophy of the Son's procession from the Father is strikingly similar to Plotinus's philosophy of Mind proceeding from the One. Such

---

[28] See also Origen, *Homilies on Jeremiah* (Homily 9), in vol. 97 of *The Fathers of the Church*, trans. John Clark Smith (Washington, DC: Catholic University of America Press, 1998), 92–93 (Jer. 11:1–11). The volume also includes Origen's *Homily on 1 Kings 28*.

parallels are especially significant when we recall that Origen and Plotinus both studied under the same teacher, Ammonius Saccas, and they were well aware of each other. In Neo-Platonism, the highest concept imaginable is *the* One, and the One is essentially "True Being" (ὀυσία). True Being is eternal, incomprehensible, and unknowable—the One who is larger than Reason and higher than Goodness. The One does not condescend to create. The universe originated with Mind or Reason (Logos), which proceeded from the One as a necessary emanation.

While insisting that Christ is the eternal, divine, and sinless Creator, it is in the clearest Neo-Platonic language that Origen concludes that Christ remains perpetually inferior to the Father who eternally "created" Him. He never hesitates to use the term *created* for Christ. He explains, "Let no one imagine that we mean anything impersonal when we call Him the wisdom of God." The Son of God is "wisdom hypostatically existing." [29] Origen builds on that clarification: "The Father is the beginning of the Son; and the demiurge the beginning of the works of the demiurge, and that God in a word is the beginning of all that exists."[30] As the created demiurge, Christ became the *arche* (ἀρχή), that is, the first principle of all else that followed:

> For Christ is, in a manner, the demiurge, to whom the Father says, "Let there be light," and, "Let there be a firmament." But Christ is demiurge as a beginning (arche), inasmuch as He is wisdom. It is in virtue of His being wisdom that He is called arche. For Wisdom says in Solomon: "God created me the beginning of His ways, for His works," so that the Word might be in an arche, namely, in wisdom. [It is] Christ we have taken to be the demiurge, and the Father the greater than He.[31]

To Origen, Christ's generation makes Him an eternally derived deity: "Wherefore we have always held that God is the Father of His only-begotten Son, who was born indeed of Him, and derives from Him what He is, but without any beginning."[32] Christ's own existence continues to depend constantly upon the will of His Father.

---

[29] *De Principiis* 1.2.2.

[30] *Commentary on John* book 1, section 17.

[31] *Commentary on John* book 1, sections 22 and 40.

[32] *De Principiis* 1.2.2.

When Origen speaks of eternal generation, his language is conceptual rather than historical. He describes it as an act. This act of begetting is only in the mind and will of God the Father. Origen supposes that since everything is eternally in God, the generating (begetting) act *must* be eternal. The Son proceeds from the Father indivisibly, just as *will* proceeds from reason and *acts* proceed from will:

> For if the Son do, in like manner, all those things which the Father doth, then, in virtue of the Son doing all things like the Father, is the image of the Father formed in the Son, who is born of Him, like an act of His will proceeding from the mind. And I am therefore of opinion that the will of the Father ought alone to be sufficient for the existence of that which He wishes to exist. For in the exercise of His will He employs no other way than that which is made known by the counsel of His will. And thus also the existence [*subsistentia*] of the Son is generated by Him. For this point must above all others be maintained by those who allow nothing to be unbegotten, i.e., unborn, save God the Father only. . . . As an act of the will proceeds from the understanding, and neither cuts off any part nor is separated or divided from it, so after some such fashion is the Father to be supposed as having begotten the Son, His own image; namely, so that, as He is Himself invisible by nature, He also begat an image that was invisible. For the Son is the Word, therefore, we are not to understand that anything in Him is cognizable by the senses. He is wisdom, and in wisdom there can be no suspicion of anything corporeal. He is the true light, which enlightens every man that cometh into this world; but He has nothing in common with the light of this sun. Our Savior, therefore, is the image of the invisible God, inasmuch as compared with the Father Himself He is the truth: and as compared with us, to whom He reveals the Father, He is the image by which we come to the knowledge of the Father, whom no one knows save the Son, and he to whom the Son is pleased to reveal Him. (*De Principiis* 1.2.6)

By sheer speculation, Origen states that *the Son was created as inferior to the Father who, through the Son, created the Holy Spirit as inferior both to the Father and the Son*, but of the highest order among the rest of creation:

> We consider, therefore, that there are three hypostaseis, the Father and the Son and the Holy Spirit; and at the same time we believe

nothing to be uncreated but the Father. We therefore, as the more pious and the truer course, admit that all things were made by the Logos, and that the Holy Spirit is the most excellent and the first in order of all that was made by the Father through Christ. And this, perhaps, is the reason why the Spirit is not said to be God's own Son. The Only-begotten only is by nature and from the beginning a Son, and the Holy Spirit seems to have need of the Son, to minister to Him His essence, so as to enable Him not only to exist, but to be wise and reasonable and just, and all that we must think of Him as being.[33]

Confessing both the eternality and deity of Christ, Origen continues without qualification to speak of Christ as inferior to the Father. His extreme subordinationism is seen in these remarks: "The Son of God, divesting Himself of His equality with the Father, and showing to us the way to the knowledge of Him, is made the express image of His person."[34] To Origen, "If this be fully understood, it clearly shows that the existence of the Son is derived from the Father but not in time, nor from any other beginning, except, as we have said, from God Himself."[35] Origen applies Christ's words in John 14:28 to the *present* state of Christ and seeks to convince even Celsus that the Father *remains* the greater: "Grant that there may be some individuals among the multitudes of believers who are not in entire agreement with us, and who incautiously assert that the Savior is the Most High God; however, we do not hold with them, but rather believe Him when He says, 'The Father who sent Me is greater than I.'"[36]

---

[33] *Commentary on John* book 2, section 6, in Origen's words: Ἡμεῖς μέντοι γε τρεῖς ὑποστάσεις πειθόμενοι τυγχάνειν, τὸν Πατέρα, καὶ τὸν Υἱὸν, καὶ τὸ ἅγιον Πνεῦμα, καὶ ἀγέννητον μηδὲν ἕτερον τοῦ Πατρὸς εἶναι πιστεύοντες, ὡς εὐσεβέστερον καὶ ἀληθὲς, προσιέμεθα τὸ, πάντων διὰ τοῦ λόγου γενομένων, τὸ ἅγιον Πνεῦμα πάντων εἶναι τιμιώτερον, καὶ τάξει πάντων τῶν ὑπὸ τοῦ πατρὸς διὰ Χριστοῦ γεγενημένων. Origenis, *Commentaria in Euangelium Joannis* (Migne *PG* 14.128–29).

[34] *De Principiis* 1.2.8.

[35] Ibid., 1.2.11.

[36] *Contra Celsum* 8.14.

Gregory Thaumaturgus and Eternal Generation

Gregory Thaumaturgus, bishop of Neocaesarea[37] in Pontus (ca. 240–70; b. ca. 213), was hailed as "Wonderworker" for his purported miraculous powers. For five years, Gregory attended Origen's lectures in Caesarea of Palestine and became so mesmerized by his teacher that, upon leaving the school, he delivered an *Oration and Panegyric Addressed to Origen* expressing his profound appreciation and commitment to his philosophical training and, above all, to Origen, his beloved teacher. Gregory expresses it this way: "One thing only was dear and affected by me: philosophy and its teacher—this divine man" (6).[38] Gregory said that his departure from Origen's school made him feel as a "second Adam," departing from the "Garden of Eden" (16). Upon his return to Neocaesarea, Gregory received his ordination as bishop and brought many lost people into Christendom during his lifetime. One who was impacted, at least indirectly, by his ministry was the matron Macrina, who would become a powerful spiritual influence on her grandchildren, Basil of Caesarea, Gregory of Nyssa, Peter of Sebaste, and their sister, who was also called Macrina. Ancient tradition has it that when Gregory came to Neocaesarea to begin his ministry, he found only seventeen Christians, and when he came to die, there were found only seventeen pagans.

According to a less reliable but more popular legend, near the end of Gregory's life (ca. 270), the Virgin Mary brought the apostle John to him in a dream in which John dictated to Gregory a Trinitarian creed. Whatever the source of its inspiration, the creed that Gregory wrote is one of the most complete overall ante-Nicene expressions of the Trinity and the earliest creed to use the term *monogenēs* in its conceptual rather than historical meaning. In Origenistic style, the creed affirms that the Father originated His Son. Precisely, the Father is τέλειος τελείου γεννήτωρ, πατὴρ υἱοῦ μονογενοῦς (*monogenēs*), which Philip Schaff translates as "the perfect origin (begetter) of the perfect (begotten): the Father of the only-begotten Son."[39] Basil of

---

[37] Neocaesarea in Pontus corresponds to the present-day Niksar area in Turkey.

[38] The translation is from W. Metcalfe, *Gregory Thaumaturgus Address to Origen* (New York: Macmillan, 1920), 60.

[39] *Creeds of Christendom*, 2:24.

Caesarea would later describe Gregory Thaumaturgus as a "second Moses" and liken him to prophets and apostles.[40]

Eusebius of Caesarea and Eternal Generation

The following is from the creed that Eusebius of Caesarea (ca. 260–340) placed before Constantine in Nicea in 325. It echoes Gregory's usage of *monogenēs*. The council rejected the creed, but only because the term ὁμοούσιον ("consubstantial") is missing: "We believe in . . . One Lord Jesus Christ . . . υἱὸν μονογενῆ, . . . πρὸ πάντων τῶν αἰώνων ἐκ τοῦ Θεοῦ πατρὸς γεγννημένον," that is, "the only-begotten Son . . . begotten of God the Father before all ages." Schaff translates υἱὸν μονογενῆ as "the only-begotten Son,"[41] which is likely what Eusebius intended to convey.

Hilary of Poitiers and Eternal Generation

Situated on the Clain River in west central France, Poitiers was home to one who in his day was known as the "Hammer" against the Arians. Hilary (d. 367) wrote in Latin but knew a little Greek as well. Now regarded by eastern and western Christendom as an orthodox father, saint, and doctor of the church, Hilary went to great lengths in his work *On the Trinity* to defend the doctrine of the Father's eternal generation of His Son. Realizing that he must explain it in terms of an eternal subordination, he repeatedly presses his conviction that Christ "does not share in the supreme majesty of being unbegotten" since He has "received from the Unbegotten God the nature of divinity." The real importance of Christ's unique and historic birth continued to be elevated from the literal realm to the conceptual. Regarding Christmas, "We believe His birth," says Hilary, "though we know it never had a beginning."[42] While frequently and strongly exalting Christ's deity, Hilary often works from an exegetical method not unlike that of Origen. While subordinating Christ as deriving deity in eternity past, Hilary elevates man as destined to derive deity

---

[40] Basil the Great, *On the Holy Spirit* 29.74.

[41] *Creeds of Christendom*, 2:30.

[42] *On the Trinity* 9.57; Hilary's heaviest concentration on eternal subordination seems to be in 12.5–50.

in eternity future. Emphatically he states that God became man so that man may become God:

> When God was born to be man the purpose was not that the Godhead should be lost, but that, the Godhead remaining, man should be born to be God. Thus Emmanuel is His name, which is God with us, that God might not be lowered to the level of man, but man raised to that of God.[43]

Cyril of Jerusalem and Eternal Generation

Like Eusebius's creed, that of Cyril (315–86; creed, ca. 350) includes *monogenēs*, but excludes ὁμοούσιον ("consubstantial"), a term that was needed for widespread orthodox acceptance at that time: "We believe in . . . One Lord Jesus Christ, τὸν υἱὸν τοῦ Θεοῦ τὸν μονογενῆ, τὸν ἐκ τοῦ πατρός γεννηθέντα, πρὸ πάντων αἰώνων," that is, "the only-begotten Son of God, begotten of the Father before all ages."[44] Again, Schaff renders τὸν υἱὸν τοῦ Θεοῦ τὸν μονογενῆ as Cyril likely[45] intended: "the only-begotten Son" (2:31).

Gregory of Nazianzus and Eternal Generation

In the works of Gregory of Nazianzus (ca. 326–90), we discover an unusually natural and generous use of the term *monogenēs* in its new conceptual application: "He is called Only-Begotten,[46] not

---

[43] Ibid., 10.7.

[44] There is a similar and interesting creed of unknown authorship, originating ca. 300 and sometimes attributed to Lucian, "the Martyr," of Antioch (d. 312). It clearly expresses an eternal generation of the Son of God: "We believe in . . . One Lord Jesus Christ . . . τὸν μονογενῆ Θεόν . . . τὸν γεννηθέντα πρὸ τῶν αἰώνων ἐκ τοῦ πατρός," i.e., "the only-begotten God . . . who was begotten of the Father before all ages." Schaff's *Creeds of Christendom* also translates τὸν μονογενῆ Θεόν as "the only-begotten God" (2:26), which is the concept that the author or redactors probably intended. Schaff attributes this creed to Lucian, but that seems doubtful considering (1) that Epiphanius, in his *Panarion* (section on the Arians), refers to Lucian as an "Arian martyr" and (2) that the creed appears replete with interpolation in places. It is, of course, possible that Lucian wrote it prior to his becoming Arian in his doctrine. The creed was found after his death.

[45] This application of *monogenēs* is clearly evident, for example, in Cyril of Jerusalem, *Catechetical Lectures* 11 and 12.

[46] Arthur James Mason, ed., *The Five Theological Orations of Gregory of Nazianzus* (Cambridge: Cambridge University Press, 1899), 162. The book includes the complete Greek text.

because He is the only Son and of the Father alone, and only a Son; but also because the manner of His Sonship is peculiar to Himself and not shared by bodies."[47] Gregory attempts to explain this in terms that can best preserve the doctrine of Christ's consubstantiality with the Father:

> The Father is Father, and is Unoriginate, for He is of no one; the Son is Son, and is not unoriginate, for He is of the Father. But if you take the word Origin in a temporal sense, He too is Unoriginate, for He is the Maker of Time, and is not subject to Time. The Holy Ghost is truly Spirit, coming forth from the Father indeed, but not after the manner of the Son, for it is not by Generation but by Procession (since I must coin a word for the sake of clearness; for neither did the Father cease to be Unbegotten because of His begetting something, nor the Son to be begotten because He is of the Unbegotten (how could that be?), nor is the Spirit changed into Father or Son because He proceeds, or because He is God— though the ungodly do not believe it. For Personality is unchangeable; else how could Personality remain, if it were changeable, and could be removed from one to another? But they who make "Unbegotten" and "Begotten" natures of equivocal gods would perhaps make Adam and Seth differ in nature, since the former was not born of flesh (for he was created), but the latter was born of Adam and Eve. There is then One God in Three, and these Three are One, as we have said. (*Oration on Holy Lights* 39.12)

Jerome, the Latin Vulgate, and Eternal Generation

Sophronius Eusebius Hieronymus, better known as Jerome (ca. 347–420), would be named in 1298 as one of the four original *Doctores Ecclesiae* of the western Church.[48] He was born to wealthy parents in Stridon. While Stridon was overrun and destroyed by Goths even during Jerome's lifetime,[49] its location was somewhere

---

[47] Gregory of Nazianzus, *Oration* 30, *Fourth Theological Oration: the Second Concerning the Son* 20; to compare this with the thought of Athanasius, see Panachiotis Christou, "Uncreated and Created, Unbegotten and Begotten in the Theology of Athanasius of Alexandria," *Augustinianum* 13 (1973): 399–409.

[48] The other three were Ambrose, Augustine, and Pope Gregory I.

[49] Jerome, *On Illustrious Men* 135.

near Ljubljana, the capital of modern Slovenia. Receiving a classical education in Rome, Jerome identified with Christianity and eventually received baptism. Of the ensuing years we have little more than sketches of his life. He traveled widely, acquired an enduring love for the ascetic life, and began studying Greek. As a newly ordained man in his early or mid-thirties, Jerome traveled to Constantinople to study under the private instruction of Gregory of Nazianzus, whose primary exegetical method was deeply Origenistic. Through Gregory's influence, Jerome immersed himself in the teachings of Origen and totally embraced the Alexandrian's doctrine of eternal generation.[50] He became so enamored with the whole corpus of Origenistic literature that he set out to Latinize Origen by translating scores of his homilies. It was during his time with Gregory of Nazianzus that the Council of Constantinople (381) took place.

Following the Council, Jerome traveled directly to Rome in 382 where, at the request of Bishop Damasus, he undertook a revision of the text of the Old Latin copies of the Scriptures. The expression "Old Latin (*Vetus Latina*) Bible" is an umbrella term referring to the numerous pre-Vulgate translations of the Bible or sections of it. Within a year, Jerome had completed his revision of the four Gospels and had started on the Psalms. Damasus died in 384, and the following year Jerome traveled to the Holy Land to acquire more knowledge of Israel's geography, culture, and Hebrew language. Among the Jewish scholars who provided assistance, there was at least one who was a convert to Christianity. Jerome would live the remainder of his life writing his works in a monastic cell near Bethlehem. Usually surrounded by a select group of well-educated male and female friends,[51] he finally (ca. 404) completed the massive revision of the entire Latin Bible. Known as the Latin Vulgate, from its descriptive phrase *versio vulgata* (commonly used version), this was the only Latin version that the Roman Catholic Church would consider authentic. The Vulgate became its official Bible and the most

---

[50] See the valuable study by Alexander Souter, *The Earliest Latin Commentaries on the Epistles of St. Paul: A Study* (Oxford: Clarendon Press, 1927), 96–137.

[51] Jerome's friend Paula, who ran a nearby nunnery, and her daughter, Eustochium, assisted him in writing his commentaries on Paul's epistles to Philemon, Galatians, Ephesians, and Titus.

commonly used version of the scholastics. The first of its three major editions would appear in the late sixteenth century.[52]

The Old Latin (*Vetus Latina*) remains important, however, especially for comparative studies in textual scholarship. Although there has never been an actual *Vetus Latina* Bible, one is now in preparation[53] since numerous manuscript collections bear witness to a massive number of Old Latin translations that precede Jerome's Vulgate. In the Old Latin, the original meaning of *monogenēs* was *unicus* ("one" or "only").[54] For the word *begotten*, the Old Latin sometimes uses *natus* but usually *genuit* ("to be born" or "begotten"). In all five Johannine Christological passages containing *monogenēs*,[55] Jerome opted to use the word *unigenitus* ("only-begotten"), a blend of *unicus* and *genuit*, thereby introducing the concept of *only-begotten* into the corpus of Scripture. *One-and-only* became *only-begotten*, which was conceptualized into an *eternal generation*. As we have seen, the Greek words translated "begotten" (γεννηθέντα) and "only" (*monogenēs*, μονογενής) received identical morphing, and this would influence later Bible translations. Indeed, the same translational influence of Jerome's Latin Vulgate would pass virtually unnoticed into modern English translations.

Jerome, having recently become infatuated with Origenistic philosophy, had traveled directly from Constantinople to Rome with

---

[52] The three major editions of the Vulgate: (1) The Clementine Vulgate, first published in the 1590s, is often preferred by conservative Catholics who lived prior to the liturgical reforms of Vatican II (1962–65). (2) The Stuttgart edition was first published in 1969. (3) The *Nova Vulgata*, published in 1979 and 1986, is now the usual edition published by the Roman See. The popular *Novum Testamentum Latine*, published in 1984 and 1992, is actually the *Nova Vulgata*, but with critical apparatus containing variant readings from the major earlier editions.

[53] The Vetus Latina Institute, founded in Beuron, Germany, in 1945, is still preparing for the publication of a critical edition of the Old Latin Bible. The institute has the complete listing and description of all the manuscripts of this Bible. http://www.vetus-latina.de/en/index.html. http://www.itsee.bham.ac.uk/vetuslatina/index2.htm.

[54] E.g., cf. the Vetus Latin form of the Old Roman Creed, "Jesus Christ His 'only' [*unicum*] Son," with its later revision, "Jesus Christ His 'only-begotten' [*unigenitum*] Son," which in Greek quickly became, "Jesus Christ His 'only-begotten'" (*monogenēs*, μονογενής); see Schaff, 2:47.

[55] John 1:14, 18; John 3:16, 18; and 1 John 4:9. Jerome also changed Heb. 11:17.

incredible devotion to Damasus,[56] who commissioned him to revise the Old Latin versions. Jerome's first project was to revise the four Gospels, and this brings us directly into the magnificent cathedral of an ancient city situated in the Piedmont region of Northern Italy.

In the Cathedral of Vercelli is Codex Vercellensis,[57] one of the earliest and best-preserved Old Latin manuscripts of the four Gospels (codex a). It is calculated to have been written circa 365–70 by Bishop Eusebius of Vercelli (ca. 283–371). Codex Vercellensis provides for us one of the best opportunities for comparing typical Old Latin with Jerome's Vulgate:[58]

- Codex Vercellensis renders John 1:14 as *unici filii a Patre* ("only son of the Father"). Jerome's Vulgate has it *unigeniti a Patre* ("only-begotten of the Father").

- Codex Vercellensis renders John 1:18 as *unicus filius solus* ("one and only son"). The Vulgate has it *unigenitus Filius* ("only-begotten Son").

- Codex Vercellensis renders John 3:16 as *Filium suum unicum* ("His only Son"). The Vulgate has it *Filium suum unigenitum* ("His only-begotten Son").

- Codex Vercellensis renders John 3:18 as *unici Filii Dei* ("only Son of God"). The Vulgate has it *unigeniti Filii* ("only-begotten Son").

Other Old Latin manuscripts reveal that the same thing occurred in 1 John 4:9 and Hebrews 11:17. Is it possible that doctrinal bias rather than linguistic analysis might have prompted such changes? Jerome left the older Latin *unicus* ("only") as the rendering of *monogenēs* in Luke 7:12 (*filius unicus matri*), 8:42 (*filia unica*), and

---

[56] E.g., see Jerome, *Letter* 15.1–5 (To Pope Damasus of Rome), in NPNF 2 (6:18–20) and Migne *PL* 22.355–58.

[57] This codex must not be confused with the Vercelli Book of Middle English homilies, also located in this cathedral.

[58] *Codex Vercellensis: Quatuor Evangelia Ante Hieronymum Latine Translata ex Reliquiis Codicis Vercellensis Saeculo ut Videtur Quarto Scripti et ex Editione Iriciana Principe*, denuo ededit, J. Belsheim (Christianiae: Libraria Mallingiana, 1894). The Gospels are listed in the order of Matthew, John, Luke, and Mark. There are a few lacunae, including Mark 16:1–6, but the work as a whole remains a rich source.

9:38 (*filium . . . unicus*), where no Christological issue is involved.[59] Jerome's changes would appear later in English versions. Translators had their Greek texts in hand, but they would have often consulted the Latin Vulgate as well. In all five Johannine Christological passages containing *monogenēs*, the "only-begotten" (*unigenitus*) passed from the Latin Vulgate into every English translation, with one exception, until the turn of the twentieth century. Prior to that time, William Tyndale was the only English translator to render *monogenēs* with the simple *only*, and this occurs in John 3:16 and 18. Tyndale was the first to translate the Bible directly from Greek and Hebrew. While he failed to amend the Latin Vulgate in John 1:14 and 18 and 1 John 4:9 (also Heb. 11:17), Tyndale's rendering of John 3:16–18 is typical of his delightful work. Here is the 1534 edition:

> 16 For God so loveth the worlde, that he hath geven his only sonne, that none that beleve in him, shuld perisshe: but shuld have everlastinge lyfe. 17 For God sent not his sonne into the

---

[59] An excellent analytical tool for comparing Jerome's New Testament Latin with Old Latin manuscripts is this one, edited by John Wordsworth and Henry Julian White: *Nouum Testamentum Domini Nostri Iesu Christi Latine*, secundum editionem, Sancti Hieronymi, ad Codicum Manuscriptorum Fidem Recensuit, Iohannes Wordsworth, in Operis Societatem Adsumto, Henrico Iuliano White (Oxonii: E Typographeo Clarendoniano, 1889–1954), 1:507–24 for chapters 1 and 3 of *Evangelium Secundum Iohannem*; and 1:347–76 for chapters 7–9 of *Evangelium Secundum Lucam*. There are three volumes, with additional editors contributing to volumes 2 and 3. Contents of the three volumes are as follows: vol. 1: Gospels; vol. 2: Pauline Epistles; and vol. 3: Acts, Catholic Epistles, and Revelation. This recension is a valuable attempt at restoring Jerome's original New Testament by means of a careful collation of ancient manuscripts. At the bottom of each page is the critical apparatus. The Vulgate is printed in the upper part of each page, in double columns, and divided into sections and lines of varying length according to the arrangement found in Codex Amiatinus. Beautifully illuminated, Codex Amiatinus is the earliest surviving and probably the most accurate copy of Jerome's Vulgate. Below this, in the Gospels, is placed the Old Latin text of Codex Brixianus. The reader will notice that Codex Brixianus contains both *unicus* and *unigenitus* in the Johannine passages under discussion, and this is to be expected since the manuscript is a sixth-century edition, well past the Christological controversies. There are other Old Latin text collections that contain both *unicus* and *unigenitus*, but they too were edited after the ecumenical councils. Codex Corbeiensis, for example, uses both words, but it was produced between the eighth and tenth centuries. This later editing explains why *unigenitus* appears to replace *unicus* in a few Old Latin patristic texts, including a few places in Irenaeus's *Against Heresies* that were edited in the fourth century and later.

worlde, to condempne the worlde: but that the worlde through him, might be saved. 18 He that beleveth on him, shall not be condempned. But he that beleveth not, is condempned all redy, be cause he beleveth not in the name of the only sonne of God.[60]

The Twentieth Century New Testament[61] was the first English translation to amend the "only-begotten" (*unigenitus*) of all five Johannine occurrences of *monogenēs*. Released around the turn of the twentieth century, it was a work of some twenty translators using the Greek text of Westcott[62] and Hort,[63] both of whom had published their research on *monogenēs*. Meanwhile, Jerome's *unigenitus* had also passed into the Latin edition of the Westminster Confession, whose 1647 English edition renders it "only-begotten."[64] The Westminster Confession says, "The Father is none, neither begotten nor proceeding; the Son is eternally begotten of the Father; and the Holy Ghost eternally proceeding from the Father and the Son."[65] This passed

---

[60] From David Beale, *A Pictorial History of Our English Bible* (Greenville, SC: Bob Jones University Press, 1982), 16. This provides the *English Hexapla*, depicting the Greek text of John 3:16–18, underneath which, in parallel columns, are juxtaposed the translations from the Wyclif Bible (1380), the Tyndale Bible (1534); and the Cranmer Bible (1539). See also Philip Burton, *The Old Latin Gospels: A Study of Their Texts and Language* (New York: Oxford University Press, 2000), 62–73.

[61] As with other translations, this reference is not intended as an endorsement of *The Twentieth Century New Testament*, which was initially released in two parts, first in 1898 by Horace Marshall in London and then in 1901 by Fleming H. Revell in New York. The 1904 revised edition by Revell became its final.

[62] Westcott emphasizes that the meaning of *monogenēs* is "unique," or "one-and-only." In his discussion of *monogenēs* in 1 John 4:9, he explains: "The earliest Latin forms of the Creed uniformly represent the word by *unicus*, the *only son*, and not by *unigenitus* the *only-begotten son*. . . . But towards the close of the fourth century in translations from the Greek *unigenitus* came to be substituted for *unicus*, and this interpretation has passed into our version of the Constantinopolitan Creed (*only-begotten*)." Brooke Foss Westcott, *The Epistles of St. John* (London: Macmillan, 1883), 162–65; and 141; see also Westcott's commentary *The Gospel according to St. John* (London: John Murray, 1896), 12, 54–55.

[63] Hort also emphasizes that the meaning of *monogenēs* is "unique," or "one-and-only." See Fenton John Anthony Hort, "On ΜΟΝΟΓΕΝΗΣ ΘΕΟΣ in Scripture and Tradition," in *Two Dissertations* (Cambridge: Macmillan, 1876), 1–72; and by the same author, "On the 'Constantinopolitan' Creed and Other Eastern Creeds of the Fourth Century," in *Two Dissertations* (Cambridge: Macmillan, 1876), 73–150.

[64] Westminster Confession, chapter 8 section 1.

[65] Ibid., chapter 2 section 3.

verbatim into the Particular Baptists' Second London Confession.[66] It all began when the Niceno-Constantinopolitan Creed of 381 became the first ecumenical conciliar creed to express the doctrine of eternal generation. All previous creeds that included it were private or local.

These are all remarkably wonderful documents that have defended the faith for centuries. One can understand how those great conciliar creeds developed, ever so slowly, phrase-by-phrase, controversy-by-controversy, over years of battle. Creeds are not inspired and never complete. At best they can only express man's humble attempt at striving scripturally to answer new diabolical assaults against Christ's church in every generation. Creeds are born to be progressively improved and expanded.

These things are reminders never to obfuscate the most vital dimension of the biblical account of Christ's birth. An excellent way to meditate on the incarnation of Christ is to view it as a concrete, once-for-all, historical *fact*: in the fullness of the time (Gal. 4:4), God sent forth His only Son—unique, eternal, and precious—to be conceived of the Holy Spirit in the womb of a virgin, in a pivotal moment of time, to take human flesh, to live and to die vicariously, as the perfect and unique God-Man, in order to reconcile sinful man to Himself.

Application and Conclusion

Today many Christians often have as many occasions to speak with Muslims as with Unitarians. Muslims think that since there are many "sons" of God, Christ came into existence at His birth, just like all others. Properly prepared, the Christian must present the powerful message of the uniqueness of Christ as *the* Son of God. He is the one and only Son to whom the title belongs. Most Muslims do not know that Christ was divinely conceived by the Holy Spirit. Many Christians have discovered that it empowers their effectiveness when they use the word *only* (*monogenēs*) to convey the uniqueness

---

[66] Second London Confession, chapter 8 section 1; and chapter 2 section 3.

of the consubstantiality of God's precious Son.[67] Believers also find that when they use the word *begotten* (γεννηθέντα) to convey the historical fact of the Son's miraculous conception, it transforms their efficiency. Indeed, many Muslims have been taught all of their lives that the Christians' God begot a son, and that Christians worship the Father, the Son, and His Mother.

Nineteenth-century liberals expressed dismay that conservatives would be willing to accept eternal generation, with its eternal derivation and subordination of Christ. Liberals had rejected the biblical Trinity because they were convinced that any consistent belief in that doctrine must include the belief that "Trinity" has more than a numerical significance, and that "Oneness" and "distinctiveness" must rank as fundamentally equal. They knew that the doctrine of the Trinity must include "self-existence" (*autotheos*, αὐτόθεος) as an essential attribute of deity and that each person of the Trinity must be *autotheos*, "God in Himself."[68]

Unfortunately, many have equated the term *eternal generation* with a separate and fundamental doctrine of Christianity, the *eternal sonship* of Christ. Christ's eternal sonship is *clearly* a Bible truth. "For unto us a child is born, unto us a son is given" (Isa.

---

[67] See Francis Marion Warden, "Monogenes in the Johannine Literature" (PhD diss., Southern Baptist Theological Seminary, 1938). Warden concluded, "The evidence hitherto presented leads to the necessity of regarding μονογενής as expressing basically uniqueness of being, rather than any remarkableness of manner of coming into being, or yet uniqueness resulting from any manner of coming into being" (35–36). Here are the contents of his study: chap. 1, "The Historical Setting of the Johannine Literature" (1–17); chap. 2, "The Preparatory Development of Μονογενής" (18–36); chap. 3, "Related Terms Compared with Μονογενής" (37–52); chap. 4, "Μονογενής Θεός the Revealer of God" (53–81); and chap. 5, "Ὁ Μονογενής Υἱός the Redeemer of Man" (82–109); bibliography (110–17). The "related terms" covered in chap. 3 are Ἀγαπητός, Ἑαυτοῦ, Ἴδιος, Μόνος, Πρωτότοκος, and Υἱός.

[68] E.g., Moses Stuart, *Letters on the Eternal Generation of the Son of God, Addressed to the Rev. Samuel Miller* (Andover, MA: Flagg and Gould, 1822); and Frederic Schleiermacher, "On the Discrepancy between the Sabellian and Athanasian Method of Representing the Doctrine of a Trinity in the Godhead," trans. with notes and illustrations by Moses Stuart, in the *Biblical Repository and Quarterly Observer* 5, no. 18 (April 1835): 265–353; and 6, no. 19 (July 1835): 1–116. The liberal Stuart was less radical than Schleiermacher, but he described Schleiermacher as a genuine Christian and eagerly introduced his work to conservatives.

9:6*a*). At His appointed time, "God sent forth His Son" (Gal. 4:4). J. Oliver Buswell agrees and cautions that, since the Bible is wonderfully clear in its doctrine of Christ's eternal sonship, one must always avoid the risk of confusing that with the similar-sounding "eternal generation."[69] In the biblical, historic, and miraculous incarnation, the eternal Son of God, acquired a human nature and human flesh. The notions of eternal derivation and eternal subordination are outside the bounds of Scripture.

In His incarnation, Jesus came from His mother's womb as the God-Man, in perfect humiliation, to suffer, to die, and to come forth from the grave for our sins. When Jesus says, "My father is greater than I" (John 14:28), He is referring to His earthly humiliation. "As a man, he humbled himself, and became obedient unto death, even the death of the cross" (Phil. 2:8*b*). "Wherefore God also hath highly exalted him, and given him a name which is above every name: that at the name of Jesus every knee should bow, of things in heaven, and things in earth, and things under the earth; and that every tongue should confess that Jesus Christ is Lord, to the glory of God the Father" (Phil. 2:9–11).

Israel's ancient and clarion creed is as pertinent now as it was in the Old Testament: "Hear, O Israel: the Lord our God is one Lord" (Deut. 6:4). Christ refers to that creed in His high-priestly prayer (John 17:11), and Paul affirms for the Christian that "there is none other God but one" (1 Cor. 8:4). The New Testament presupposes the unity of the Godhead, and it makes the eternal deity, equality, and uniqueness of the Father, the Son, and the Holy Spirit to be distinctive and fundamental articles of the Christian faith. It is a mystery incomprehensible, but God reveals Himself in Scripture in a way that, by the Holy Spirit, we can fundamentally know what He is saying. This is why Scripture speaks in such clear terms as God's

---

[69] J. Oliver Buswell, *Systematic Theology of the Christian Religion* (Grand Rapids: Zondervan, 1962), 1:106–12. On the other hand, Buswell believes that the term *eternal procession* is actually "a hindrance rather than a help"; see 1:119–20. Interestingly, the Westminster Confession says that "the Son is eternally begotten of the Father; and the Holy Ghost eternally proceeding from the Father and the Son" (Schaff, 3:608).

"only (*monogenēs*) son." This is clear and literal truth with no anomalies and no additions.

Gregory of Nyssa describes the theological cacophony that filled the city of Constantinople during the Council: "If you ask someone to give you change, he philosophizes about the Begotten and the Unbegotten; if you inquire about the price of a loaf, you are told by way of reply that the Father is greater and the Son inferior; if you ask 'Is my bath ready?' the attendant answers that the Son was made out of nothing."[70] The lessons from Gregory should be obvious to each of us as we handle the pure Word of God and, in the mystery of godliness, proclaim the incarnation of His Son (1 Tim. 3:16).

Some of the Fathers thought that they could find the concept of eternal generation in the words of Psalm 2:7, "Thou art my Son; this day have I begotten thee." The apostle Paul, in his synagogue sermon at Pisidian Antioch (Acts 13:33), finds its fulfillment in Christ's resurrection.[71] The writer of Hebrews expands its application to the total sphere of Christ's unique preeminence (Heb. 1:5; 5:5).

Hebrews 11:17 says that Abraham was ready to "offer up his only (*monogenēs*) son." Abraham had an older son, Ishmael, but Isaac was Abraham's one-of-a-kind son. Israel's King David and the Messiah would descend through the line of promise in Isaac. God's promises to Israel will find their ultimate fulfillment when Christ rules the world for a thousand years upon the throne of His father David (2 Sam. 7:8–16; Rev. 20:1–7). In Genesis 22, verses 2, 12, and 16, Isaac is called Abraham's "only (*yachid*) son." In Psalm 22:20, the Septuagint translates *yachid* (יָחִיד) as *monogenēs* (μονογενῆ) where some English versions render it "darling." Indeed, God so loved the world that He gave His darling Son to atone for our sin.

Select Bibliography for Further Reading

Burton, Philip. *The Old Latin Gospels: A Study of Their Texts and Language*. New York: Oxford University Press, 2000.

Carson, D. A. *Exegetical Fallacies*. Grand Rapids: Baker, 1984.

---

[70] Gregory of Nyssa, *Oration on the Deity of the Son and Holy Spirit* (Migne *PG* 46.557*b*); and Timothy Ware, *The Orthodox Church*, rev. ed. (New York: Penguin, 1997), 35.

[71] Cf. Rom. 1:3–4.

Christou, Panachiotis. "Uncreated and Created, Unbegotten and Begotten in the Theology of Athanasius of Alexandria." *Augustinianum* 13 (1973): 399–409.

Codex Vercellensis: Quatuor Evangelia Ante Hieronymum Latine Translata ex Reliquiis Codicis Vercellensis Saeculo ut Videtur Quarto Scripti et ex Editione Iriciana Principe. Denuo ededit J. Belsheim. Christianiae: Libraria Mallingiana, 1894.

Hort, Fenton John Anthony. "On ΜΟΝΟΓΕΝΗΣ ΘΕΟΣ in Scripture and Tradition." In *Two Dissertations*, 1–72. Cambridge: Macmillan, 1876.

Irenaeus. *Demonstration (Proof) of the Apostolic Preaching.* Translated from the Armenian with introduction and notes by J. Armitage Robinson. London: Society for Promoting Christian Knowledge, 1920.

Jerome. *On Illustrious Men.* Translated by Thomas P. Halton. Vol. 100 of *The Fathers of the Church*, edited by Thomas P. Halton. Washington, DC: Catholic University of America Press, 1999.

Kelly, J. N. D. *Jerome: His Life, Writings, and Controversies.* Peabody, MA: Hendrickson, 1998.

Metcalfe, W., trans. *Gregory Thaumaturgus Address to Origen.* New York: Macmillan, 1920.

Moody, Dale. "God's Only Son: The Translation of John 3:16 in the Revised Standard Version." *Journal of Biblical Literature* 72, no. 4 (December 1953): 213–19.

Siecienski, A. Edward. *The Filioque: History of a Doctrinal Controversy.* Oxford: Oxford University Press, 2010.

Warden, Francis Marion. "Monogenes in the Johannine Literature." PhD diss., Southern Baptist Theological Seminary, 1938.

8

First-Generation Evangelical Anabaptists

The term *Anabaptist* (ἀνά, "again" + βαπτίζω, "I baptize") means "rebaptizer." It describes those who rejected their infant baptism and were rebaptized as professing Christians. While there were heretical and violent groups called Anabaptists, such as those in Muenster, Germany, during the sixteenth century, this study is limited to the group characterized as peaceful and evangelical.[1] This group emerged in and around Zurich, Switzerland. The earliest key leaders of the Zurich Anabaptists included Conrad Grebel and Michael Sattler. Their movement would become a major component in the early history of the Mennonite movement,[2] whose name would derive from the Dutch Anabaptist, Menno Simons.

Conrad Grebel

Conrad Grebel (1498–1526) was born into a patrician family in or near Zurich. During the years 1514–19, he attended the Universities

---

[1] One of the more recent contributions is the valuable work by Dennis E. Bollinger, *First-Generation Anabaptist Ecclesiology, 1525–1561: A Study of Swiss, German, and Dutch Sources* (Lewiston, NY: Edwin Mellen, 2009).

[2] Other Anabaptist leaders, often relocating as hunted refugees, included Dirk Philips (1504–68); Balthasar Hubmaier (ca. 1480–1528), who was burned by Roman Catholics in Vienna, Austria; and Pilgram Marpeck (ca. 1495–1556). During 1528–56, Marpeck helped to solidify Anabaptist doctrine, especially among Mennonites. He achieved a degree of consensus among divided elements of the Anabaptist movement.

of Basel, Vienna, and Paris. Without completing an academic degree, he returned to Zurich and joined a circle of scholars around Ulrich Zwingli, the German-Swiss pastor of Zurich's Grossmünster Church. Although, in practical matters, the Reformation had not yet begun in the Grossmünster, Zwingli's exegetical sermons had begun to establish a strong foundation and the sermons were buttressed by his strong work on *The Clarity and Certainty of the Word of God* (1522). Conrad Grebel studied Greek with the small group led by Zwingli, and a friendship was established between the two men. While there is no known record of his conversion, the changed tone of Grebel's letters indicates that it likely occurred in 1522, probably under Zwingli's influence.

Early in the following year, Grebel participated in one of the home Bible-study groups that were starting up in the region. People were noticing differences between the teachings of the New Testament and those of the state church. A strong reformist element emerged from within these study groups and began to pressure Zurich's city council for reform. Such insistence provided the momentum that led to a public disputation, set for January 29, 1523, when civil authorities cautiously prepared the way for some basic reform. They allowed evangelical preaching, but major features of Roman Catholicism, such as graven images and the celebration of the Mass, remained in place. Under continuing pressure, the city council called for a second disputation, set for October 26–29, 1523. Gradually, some of Zwingli's supporters, including Conrad Grebel, sensed a need for immediate and thorough reform, with or without approval or support from Zwingli or the council. Grebel had become an Anabaptist.

Since baptism into the Grossmünster Church constituted citizenship, the city council, as the church's supreme governing body, kept the records of all infant baptisms. Thus, in 1524, the issue of infant baptism entered the reform controversy, and Zwingli supported the council's demand for infant baptism. Zwingli responded to the Anabaptists with his *Treatise on Rebels and Rebellion* (1524). Zurich's council then issued the *Council Mandate for Infant Baptism* (January 18, 1525), a declaration requiring immediate obedience or permanent banishment. The council decreed that the Anabaptists had three choices: (1) conform to the official practice of Zurich;

(2) leave the city at once; or (3) face the impending consequences of the decree. The Anabaptists chose the latter. Three days later, on January 21, 1525, at a secret cottage prayer meeting held in the home of Felix Mantz, the Anabaptists organized their first church. At the meeting Conrad Grebel rebaptized George Blaurock, a former Roman Catholic priest, who then administered believer's baptism to the rest of the group.

Over the next few months, Grebel traveled widely and preached to great crowds. In Grüningen, a city east of Zurich, Grebel, Blaurock, and Felix Mantz were preaching before a large group in October, 1525, when Grebel and Blaurock were arrested by local officials. Felix Mantz evaded capture but only for a short time. At the trials, the judges sentenced Grebel, Blaurock, and Mantz to imprisonment in the Zurich tower, and this was followed by a sentence of life in prison. Two weeks later the men made a rope that enabled them to escape through an unlocked window. Blaurock was eventually beaten and burned to death by Roman Catholics in the Italian town of Clausen. Grebel died in 1526, probably from a plague that was spreading through the region. Grebel is recognized by many today as the founder of the Anabaptist movement, particularly among Mennonites.

Michael Sattler

Michael Sattler (ca. 1490–1527) was born near Freiburg, Germany. As a youth he entered a Benedictine monastery and eventually attained to the office of prior. While in the monastery, his private reading of Scripture led to his conversion. In early 1525, Sattler renounced his vows and left the monastery. The resulting hostility from Roman Catholic priests and civil authorities forced him to flee to Switzerland, where he met Grebel and other Anabaptists. In late 1525, the city authorities at Zurich cast Sattler into prison with Grebel, Mantz, and Blaurock. With the banishment of Anabaptists from Zurich, Sattler soon traveled as a refugee, and his faithful witness resulted in conversions and more house churches. On January 5, 1527, Zurich's city council executed a decree to drown Felix Mantz in the Limmat River that flows through the city.

In February, Sattler accepted an invitation to preach at a conference of Anabaptists in Schleitheim, Switzerland, where he is believed to have written the earliest Anabaptist statement of faith, the Schleitheim Confession. Participants at the meeting signed the Confession on February 24, 1527. Roman Catholic authorities learned of the conference and arrested Sattler. On May 17, Michael Sattler was tried on the following nine charges:

> 1. That he and his adherents acted contrary to the decree of the emperor. 2. He taught, maintained, and believed, that the body and blood of Christ were not present in his sacraments. 3. He taught and believed, that infant-baptism was not promotive of salvation. 4. They rejected the sacraments of unction. 5. They despised and reviled the Mother of God, and condemned the saints. 6. He declared that men should not swear before a magistrate. 7. He has commenced a new and unheard of custom in regard to the Lord's Supper, placing the bread and wine on a plate, eating and drinking the same. 8. Contrary to the rule, he has married a wife. 9. He said if the Turks invaded the country, we ought not to resist them, and if he approved of war, he would rather take the field against the Christians than against the Turks, notwithstanding, it is an important matter to set the greatest enemies of our faith against us.[3]

The judges soon returned to the courtroom and read their sentence:

> It was as follows: "In the case of the Governor of his Imperial Majesty versus Michael Sattler, judgment is passed, that Michael Sattler shall be delivered to the executioner, who shall lead him to the place of execution, and cut out his tongue; then throw him upon a wagon, and there tear his body twice with red hot tongs; and after he has been brought without the gate, he shall be pinched five times in the same manner." After this had been done in the manner prescribed, he was burned to ashes as a heretic. His fellow brethren were executed with the sword, and the sisters drowned. His wife, also, after being subjected to many entreaties, admonitions and threats, under which she remained very

---

[3] Gustav Bossert Jr., "Michael Sattler's Trial and Martyrdom in 1527," trans. Elizabeth Bender, *Mennonite Quarterly Review* 25 (July 1951): 209–10; see also 201–18.

steadfast, was drowned a few days afterwards. Done the 21st day of May, A.D. 1527.[4]

With his confession of seven basic principles, Sattler had made a major contribution towards stability among the Swiss Brethren.

Menno Simons

Menno Simons (ca. 1496–1561) was a Dutchman who, under the influence of Reformation literature, left the Roman Catholic priesthood in 1536. Following his ordination in 1537, he became a leader of the Anabaptist movement in the Netherlands. While moving frequently to avoid capture, he also found time to produce several works, two of which constituted major contributions to the Anabaptist movement: (1) an apology for the Anabaptist movement, establishing the *Foundation of Christian Doctrine* (1540), and (2) a treatise of ten "case studies" from Scripture, illustrating *The True Christian Faith* (ca. 1541). Menno taught that water baptism follows faith and that the Lord's Supper is a memorial of Christ's love. The mode of baptism was not an issue. In most cases Anabaptists baptized by pouring.

Menno's acceptance of the apocryphal writings as canonical illustrates the doctrinal imprecision of some first-generation Anabaptists. In seeking to emphasize Christ's sinlessness, Menno insisted that Christ brought His own celestial body with Him from heaven. In his view, Jesus passed through Mary as sunlight passes through a glass. She contributed nothing.[5] While asserting that Adam's original sin passed upon the whole human race, Menno also insisted that Christ's crucifixion immediately removed the guilt of original sin from all mankind. Each person still becomes guilty, but only when he actually sins. Like some other early Anabaptists, Menno rejected the Protestant doctrine of justification by faith alone. To Menno, the

---

[4] Thieleman J. van Braght, *The Bloody Theater or Martyrs Mirror* (Scottdale, PA: Herald Press, 1950), 418. The book was first published in 1660.
[5] See Irvin E. Burkhart, "Menno Simons on the Incarnation," *Mennonite Quarterly Review* 4 (1930): 113–39, 178–207; and Timothy George, "No Other Foundation: Menno Simons," in *Theology of the Reformers* (Nashville: B&H Publishing Group, 1999), 280–85.

Reformers' presentations often sounded antinomian.[6] Many of the Swiss and German Anabaptists were never in full agreement with Menno's view that when one is excommunicated from the church, his own family members—parents, children, wives, and husbands—must observe the ban against him.[7]

While the Mennonites would inherit Menno's name, they would also refine their own doctrinal nuances and cast off any remaining doctrinal aberrations of the progenitors of the movement. The earliest evangelical Anabaptist churches made significant contributions to future generations: (1) their doctrine of the nature of the church, that is, a pure church with proper leadership and discipline; (2) their insistence on strict qualifications for church membership, including believers' baptism; and (3) their doctrine of the proper relationship between church and state. Indeed, they constituted the first "free-church" movement in early-modern history, that is, they kept themselves separated or "free" from state or government alliances.

Michael Sattler's Schleitheim Confession, the earliest Anabaptist statement of faith, reveals the earliest concerns of their movement:

The Schleitheim Confession (1527)

Letter of the brotherly union of certain believing baptized children of God, who have assembled at Schleitheim, to the congregation of believing baptized Christians:

¶ Joy, peace, and mercy from our Father, through the union of the blood of Christ Jesus, together with the gifts of the Spirit (who is sent by the Father to all believers for strength and comfort and constancy in all distress unto the end, Amen) be with all who love God, and with the children of the light everywhere scattered abroad, wherever they are appointed by God our Father, wherever they are assembled with one accord in one God and Father of us all. Grace and peace in heart be with you all. Amen.

---

[6] See Timothy George, 265–72; and J. A. Oosterban, "The Theology of Menno Simons," *Mennonite Quarterly Review* 35 (1961): 187–96.

[7] See Frank C. Peters, "The Ban in the Writings of Menno Simons," *Mennonite Quarterly Review* 29 (1955): 16–33.

❡ Beloved in the Lord, brothers and sisters, we are first and specially concerned for the comfort and assurance of your minds, which have perhaps been disturbed; that ye should not always, like foreigners, be separated from us and almost cut off, justly, but that ye may again turn to the true implanted members of Christ who are armed by longsuffering and knowledge of himself and so be united again with us in the power of one divine Spirit of Christ and zeal toward God.

❡ It is also plain that with a thousand wiles the devil has turned us away, in order that he may disturb and destroy the work of God, which has been mercifully and graciously begun in us. But the true Shepherd of our souls, Christ, who has begun this in us, will direct and guide the same to the end, to His honor and our salvation. Amen.

❡ Beloved brethren and sisters, we, who are assembled together in the Lord at Schlaitten [Schleitheim] Am [on] Randen [the Border], make known to all who love God that we have agreed in certain points and articles, which we should hold in the Lord, as the obedient children of God, and sons and daughters who are and should be separated from the world in all things we do or forbear. And, to God be everlasting praise and glory, we were perfectly at peace, without opposition from any brother. By this we have perceived that the harmony of the Father and our common Christ, with their Spirit, was with us; for the Lord is the Lord of peace and not of contention, as Paul shows.

❡ But that ye may understand what these articles were, mark and understand. Scandal has been brought in among us by certain false brethren, so that some have turned from the faith, because they have presumed to use for themselves the freedom of the Spirit and of Christ. But such have erred from the truth and are given over (to their condemnation) to the wantonness and freedom of the flesh; and have thought faith and love may do and suffer all things, and nothing would injure or condemn them as long as they thus believed. Mark, ye members of God in Christ Jesus, faith in the Heavenly Father through Jesus Christ does not thus prove itself, does not work and deal in such a way as these false brethren and sisters do and teach. Take heed to yourselves; be warned of such; for they serve not our Father, but their father, the devil. But ye are not so, for they who are of Christ have crucified the flesh, with all lusts and longings. You understand me[8] well, and the brethren whom we mean. Separate yourselves from them, for they are turned away. Pray the Lord for their acknowledgment unto repentance and for our constancy to walk in the way we have entered, for the honor of God and His Christ. Amen.

¶ The articles we have discussed, and in which we are one, are these: 1. Baptism. 2. Excommunication. 3. Breaking of bread. 4. Separation from abominations. 5. Shepherds in the congregation. 6. Sword. 7. Oath.

¶ In the first place, mark this concerning baptism: Baptism should be given to all those who have learned repentance and change of life, and believe in truth that their sins have been taken away through Christ; and to all those who desire to walk in the resurrection of Jesus Christ, and to be buried with Him in death, that with Him they may rise; and to all those who with such intention themselves desire and request it of us. By this is excluded all infant baptism, the Pope's highest and first abomination. This has its foundation and witness in the Scriptures and in the usage of the Apostles—Matt. 28, Mark 16, Acts 2, 8, 16, 19. This we would with all simplicity, but firmly, hold and be assured of.

¶ In the second place, we are united concerning excommunication, as follows: Excommunication should be pronounced on all those who have given themselves to the Lord, to walk in His commandments, and on all those who have been baptized into one body of Christ, and who call themselves brothers and sisters, and yet slip away and fall into sin and are overtaken unawares. They should be warned the second time privately, and the third time publicly rebuked before the whole congregation, or be excluded according to the command of Christ, Matt. 28. But this should take place, according to the order of the Spirit of God, before the breaking of bread, that we may with one mind and with one love break and eat of one bread and drink of one cup.

¶ Thirdly, we were one and agreed concerning the breaking of bread, as follows: All who would break one bread for a memorial of the broken body of Christ, and all who would drink one draught as a memorial of the poured out blood of Christ, should beforehand be united to one body of Christ; that is, to the Church of God, of

---

[8] This change to the first person singular points to the amiable Michael Sattler, the author of the original draft.

which the head is Christ, to wit, by baptism. For, as Paul shows, we cannot at the same time be partakers of the table of the Lord and of the table of the devil; we cannot at the same time partake and drink of the cup of the Lord and of the cup of the devil; that is, all who have communion with the dead works of darkness, they have no part with the light. All who follow the devil and the world have no part with those who are called from the world to God. All who reside in the wicked [one] have no part with the good. Hence, also, it should and must be, whoso has not the call of one God to one faith, to one baptism, to one spirit, to one body, common to all the children of God, he cannot be made one bread with them, as must be if we would in the truth break bread according to the command of Christ.

¶ Fourthly, we were agreed concerning separation: This should be from the evil and wicked ones whom the devil has planted in the world, to the end alone that we should not have association with them or run with them in the multitude of their abominations. And this because all who have not entered the obedience of faith, and who have not united themselves to God to do his will, are a great abomination before God, and naught can possibly grow or issue from them but abominable things. Now, in all creatures there is either goodness or evil; they either believe or are unbelieving; they are darkness or light; of the world or out of the world; temples of God or of idols; Christ or Belial, and none may have part with the other. Now the command of God is plain to us, in which He calls us to be ever separate from evil. Thus will He ever be our God, and we shall be His sons and daughters. Further, He warns us to go out from Babylon and carnal Egypt, that we may not be partakers of their torment and sufferings, which the Lord will bring upon them.

¶ From all this we should learn that everything that is not at one with our God and Christ is nothing else than abomination, which we should avoid and flee. By this is meant all Popish and anti-Popish work and worship, assembly, church-going, wine houses, citizenship, and enjoyments of unbelief, and many other similar things which the world prizes, though they are done directly against the command of God, according to the measure of all unrighteousness, which is the world. From all this we should be separate and have no part with such, for they are clear abominations, which will make us abhorrent to our Christ Jesus, who has delivered us from the service of the flesh and filled us for the service of God by the Spirit whom He has given to us. Therefore, there will also from us undoubtedly depart unchristian and devilish weapons—sword, armor, and the like—and all use of them for friend or against enemies, through power of the word of Christ, "Resist not evil."

¶ Fifthly, we are united respecting the pastor in the congregation of God, thus: The pastor in the congregation should be one in entire accordance with the direction of Paul, who has a good report from those who are without the faith. His office should be to read, exhort, and teach; to warn, reprove, excommunicate in the congregation, and to lead in prayer for the bettering of all brethren and sisters; to take the bread, to break it, and in all things to care for the body of Christ, that it be edified and bettered, and that the mouth of the blasphemer be stopped. But he, when he is in want, must be supported by the congregation which elected him, so that he who serves the Gospel should also live from it, as the Lord has ordained.

¶ But if a pastor should do anything worthy of reproof, nothing should be undertaken with him without two or three witnesses; and if they have sinned, they shall be reproved before all the people, that the others may fear.

¶ But if the pastor is driven away, or is taken by the cross to the Lord, immediately another shall be chosen in his place, so that God's little flock may not be destroyed.

¶ Sixthly, we were united concerning the sword, thus: The sword is an ordinance of God outside of the perfection of Christ, which punishes and slays the wicked and protects and guards the good. In law the sword is ordained over the wicked for punishment and death, and the civil power is ordained to use it. But in the perfection of Christ, excommunication is pronounced only for warning and for exclusion of him who has sinned, without death of the flesh, only by warning and the command not to sin again. It is asked by many who do not know the will of Christ respecting us, whether a Christian may, or should, use the sword against the wicked in order to protect and guard the good, or for love?

¶ The answer is unanimously revealed thus: Christ teaches and commands us that we should learn from Him, for He is meek and lowly of heart, and so we will find rest for our souls. Now, Christ says to the heathen woman who was taken in adultery, not that they should stone her according to the law of his Father (yet

He also said, "as the Father gave me commandment, even so I do"), but in mercy, and forgiveness, and warning to sin no more, and says, "Go and sin no more." So we should also closely follow according to the law of excommunication. Secondly, it is asked concerning the sword, whether a Christian should pronounce judgment in worldly disputes and quarrels which unbelievers have with one another? The only answer is: Christ was not willing to decide or judge between brothers concerning inheritance, but refused to do it; so should we also do. Thirdly, it is asked concerning the sword, Should one be a magistrate if he is elected thereto? To this the answer is: It was intended to make Christ a King, and He fled and did not regard the ordinance of His Father. Thus should we do and follow Him, and we shall not walk in darkness. For He Himself says, "Whosoever will come after me, let him deny himself and take up his cross and follow me." Also, He Himself forbids the power of the sword and says, "The princes of the Gentiles exercise lordship," etc., "but it shall not be so among you." Further, Paul says, "for whom He did foreknow He also did predestinate to be conformed to the image of his son." Also, Peter says, "Christ has suffered (not ruled), leaving us an ensample that ye should follow his steps." Lastly, it is remarked that it does not become a Christian to be a magistrate for these reasons: The rule of the magistrate is according to the flesh, that of the Christian according to the Spirit; their houses and dwelling remain in this world, the Christian's is in heaven; their citizenship is in this world, the Christian's citizenship is in heaven; the weapons of their contest and war are carnal and only against the flesh, but the weapons of the Christian are spiritual, against the fortresses of the devil; the worldly are armed with steel and iron, but the Christians are armed with the armor of God, with truth, righteousness, peace, faith, salvation, and with the word of God. In short, as Christ our head was minded towards us, so should the members of the body of Christ through Him be minded, that there was no schism in the body by which it be destroyed. For every kingdom divided against its own self will be brought to destruction. Therefore, since Christ is as it stands written of Him, His members must be the same, that His body may be whole and one, to the edification of itself.

¶ Seventhly, we were united concerning oaths, thus: The oath is an assurance among those who dispute or promise, and was spoken of in the law that it should take place with the name of God, only in truth and not in falsehood. Christ, who teaches the perfection of the law, forbids to His people all swearing, whether true or false, neither by heaven nor by earth, neither by Jerusalem, nor by our head, and that for the reason which He immediately after gives, "Because thou canst not make one hair white or black." Take heed, all swearing is therefore forbidden, because we are not able to make good that which is promised in the oath, since we cannot change the least thing upon us. Now, there are some who do not believe the simple command of God, but they speak and ask thus: If God swore to Abraham by himself because He was God (when He promised him that He would do good to him and would be his God if he kept His commands), why should I not also swear if I promise a person something? Answer: Hear what the Scripture says: "God being willing more abundantly to show unto the heirs of promise the immutability of His counsel, confirmed it with an oath, that by two immutable things, in which it was impossible for God to lie, we might have a strong consolation." Mark the meaning of this Scripture: God has power to do what He forbids to you, for to Him all things are possible.

¶ "God swore an oath to Abraham," says the Scripture, "in order that He might show His counsel to be immutable;" that is, no one can withstand or hinder His will, and therefore He can keep the oath. But, as was said by Christ above, "We have no power either to hold or to give," and therefore should not swear at all.

¶ Further, some say that God has not forbidden in the New Testament to swear, that He has commanded it in the Old, and that it is only forbidden to swear by heaven, earth, Jerusalem, and by our own heads. Answer: Hear the Scriptures: "He that shall swear by heaven swears by the throne of God; and by Him that sitteth thereon." Mark, swearing by heaven is forbidden, which is only the throne of God; how much more is it forbidden to swear by God Himself! Ye fools and ye blind, which is the greater, the throne, or He who sits upon it?

¶ Still, some say, "If it is wrong to use God's name for the truth, yet the apostles, Peter and Paul, swore." Answer: Peter and Paul testify only that which God promised to Abraham by oath, and they themselves promised nothing, as the examples clearly show. But to testify and to swear are different things. When one swears he promises a thing in the future, as Christ was promised to Abraham, whom we received a long time afterwards. When one testifies he witnesses concerning that which is present, whether it be good or bad, as Simon spoke of Christ to Mary and testified, "Behold, this one is set for the fall and rising of many in Israel, and for a sign which shall be spoken against." Similarly Christ has taught us when He says, "Let your communication be yea, yea, nay, nay; for whatsoever is more than these cometh of the Evil One." He says, your speech or word shall be yea and nay, and His intention is clear.

¶ Christ is simple yea and nay, and all who seek Him simply will understand His word. Amen.

¶ Dear brethren and sisters in the Lord, these are the articles which some brethren have understood wrongly and not in accordance with the true meaning, and thereby have confused many weak consciences, so that the name of God has been grossly blasphemed; for which cause it was necessary that we should be united in the Lord, which, God be praised, has taken place.

¶ Now that ye have well understood the will of God, which has been manifested through us, it is necessary that ye from the heart and not wavering perform the known will of God. For ye well know what is the reward of that servant who sins wittingly.

¶ All that ye have done unwittingly and that ye have confessed that ye have done wrong, that is forgiven you through believing prayer, which was made by us in the assembly for the sin and guilt of us all, through the gracious pardon of God and through the blood of Jesus Christ. Amen.

¶ Mark all those who walk not according to the simplicity of divine truth, which is contained in this letter, as it was apprehended by us in the assembly, in order that each one among us be governed by the rule of discipline, and henceforth the entrance among us of false brethren and sisters be guarded against. Separate from you that which is evil and the Lord will be your God and ye shall be His sons and daughters.

¶ Dear brethren, be mindful how Paul exhorts Titus. He speaks thus: "The grace of God that brings salvation hath appeared to all men, teaching us that, denying ungodliness and worldly lusts, we should live soberly, righteously and godly in this present world, looking for that blessed hope and the glorious appearing of the great God and our Savior Jesus Christ, who gave Himself for us that He might redeem us from all iniquity and purify unto

Himself a peculiar people, zealous of good works." Think of this and practice it; so will the Lord of peace be with you.

The name of God be eternally praised and glorified. Amen.

The Lord give you His peace. Amen.

The Acts of Schleitheim on the Border on Matthias' [day], February 24, 1527.[9]

Select Bibliography for Further Reading

Bender, Harold S. "A Brief Biography of Menno Simons." In *The Complete Writings of Menno Simons*, edited by John C. Wenger and translated by Leonard Verduin, 3–29. Scottdale, PA: Herald Press, 1956.

———. *Mennonites and Their Heritage: Handbook of Mennonite History and Beliefs*. Scottdale, PA: Herald Press, 1964.

———. et al., eds. *Mennonite Encyclopedia: Comprehensive Reference Work on the Anabaptist-Mennonite Movement*. Vols. 1–4. Hillsboro, KS: Mennonite Brethren Publishing House, 1955; Cornelius J. Dyck and Dennis Martin, eds. Vol. 5. Scottdale, PA: Herald Press, 1990.

Bollinger, Dennis E. *First-Generation Anabaptist Ecclesiology, 1525–1561: A Study of Swiss, German, and Dutch Sources*. Lewiston, NY: Edwin Mellen, 2009.

Estep, William R., ed. *Anabaptist Beginnings (1523–1533): A Source Book*. Nieuwkoop, Netherlands: Bibliotheca Humanistica & Reformatorica, 1976.

Friedmann, Robert. *The Theology of Anabaptism*. Scottdale, PA: Herald Press, 1973.

George, Timothy. "No Other Foundation: Menno Simons." In *Theology of the Reformers*, 252–307. Nashville: B&H Publishing Group, 1999.

Hillerbrand, Hans Joachim. *A Bibliography of Anabaptism 1520–1630*. Elkhart, IN: Institute of Mennonite Studies, 1962.

---

[9] This translation is from Thomas Armitage, *A History of the Baptists* (New York: Bryan, Taylor, 1887), 949–52; with discussion on 340–41. Since he does not provide any translation for the last line, I have translated the line. While Armitage does not identify the document's translator, he does specify that it was translated from the original document in the archives of the Canton of Schaffhausen. The "border" mentioned in the last line of the document would have been the Canton of Schaffhausen. I have modernized some capitalization, spelling, and punctuation throughout. Armitage mistakenly refers to the document as a "Baptist" confession. It is the earliest Anabaptist confession. Ulrich Zwingli translated it from German into Latin. For comparison, there is an English translation of Zwingli's Latin in W. J. McGlothlin, *Baptist Confessions of Faith* (Philadelphia: American Baptist Publication Society, 1911), 2–9. There is also a translation in William L. Lumpkin, *Baptist Confessions of Faith*, rev. (Valley Forge, PA: Judson Press, 1969), 22–31. See also the *Global Anabaptist Mennonite Encyclopedia Online*. http://www.gameo.org/encyclopedia/contents/S345.html.

Keeney, William Echard. *The Development of Dutch Anabaptist Thought and Practice from 1539–1564*. Nieuwkoop, Netherlands: B. De Graaf, 1968.

McDill, Michael, W. "The Centrality of the Doctrine of Human Free Will in the Theology of Balthasar Hubmaier." PhD diss., Southeastern Baptist Theological Seminary, 2001.

Snyder, C. Arnold. *Anabaptist History and Theology*. Kitchener, Ontario: Pandora Press, 1997.

Springer, Nelson P., and A. J. Klassen, eds. *Mennonite Bibliography, 1631–1961*. Scottdale, PA: Herald Press, 1977.

Vedder, Henry C. *Balthasar Hubmaier: The Leader of the Anabaptists*. New York: G. P. Putnam's Sons, 1905.

Wenger, J. C. *What Mennonites Believe*. Scottdale, PA: Herald Press, 1977.

Williams, George H. *Radical Reformation*. Philadelphia: Westminster, 1962.

9

Baptist Landmarkism:
A Reappraisal of Sources

Founders, Basic Tenets, and Key Sources
of Baptist Landmarkism

The Baptist Landmark movement derives its name from the titles of two publications authored by its key leaders from the nineteenth century: (1) the work by James Madison Pendleton (1811–91) titled *An Old Landmark Re-set* (1856) and (2) the work by James Robinson Graves (1820–93) called *Old Landmarkism: What is It?* (1880). The third most influential promoter of the movement was former Presbyterian, Amos Cooper Dayton (1813–65), best known for his two-volume novel *Theodosia Ernest* (1857), a fictional pilgrimage of a young Presbyterian lady seeking for the true church among the Baptists. It was Graves, however, who essentially defined the Landmark movement, whose standard components include the following:[1]

(1) The only churches in the Bible are local churches. There is no such thing as a "universal" church.

---

[1] Unlike Graves, J. M. Pendleton conceded that, in passages such as Eph. 5:25, there is one "aggregate" church of all the redeemed. See his *Church Manual: Designed for the Use of Baptist Churches* (Philadelphia: American Baptist Publication Society, n.d.), 5–6; and his *Christian Doctrines: A Compendium of Theology* (Philadelphia: American Baptist Publication Society, 1878), 329. Dayton's work was later condensed to one volume.

(2) Jesus built the first local Baptist church and every true church since that time has been a Baptist church.

(3) The term *kingdom* in the Bible refers collectively to all of the Baptist churches.

(4) Since the only true church is a Baptist church, no other church qualifies to function in any way as a church.

(5) Jesus promised an unbroken historical succession of Baptist churches in the world until He returns for His Baptist bride.

In his famous pamphlet, *The Trail of Blood* (1931), the Landmark Baptist J. M. Carroll anachronistically equates Anabaptists with Baptists. He has Cardinal Hosius (1504–79) claiming, "Were it not that the Baptists have been grievously tormented and cut off with the knife during the past twelve hundred years, they would swarm in number greater than all the Reformers."[2] In this work, which Carroll incorrectly dates at 1524, Hosius writes of "Anabaptists [*Anabaptistarum*] who, so we read, were pronounced heretics twelve hundred years ago and deserving of capital punishment."[3] Hosius is likely referring to Donatist rebaptizers, who taught baptismal regeneration.[4] He never calls them Baptists. Landmark authors would also turn to the works of two Dutch historians to argue their case for Baptist perpetuity.

Annaeus Ypeij (Ypey) and Izaak Johannes Dermout, under commission from King William I of the Netherlands, authored the four-volume set, *History of the Dutch Reformed Church* (*Geschiedenis der Nederlandsche Hervormde Kerk*, 1819–27). For many years Landmark Baptists have circulated the following as being from Ypeij and Dermout and have claimed this as the best testimony to the apostolic origins of the Baptist denomination:

---

[2] J. M. Carroll, *The Trail of Blood* (Lexington, KY: Ashland Avenue Baptist Church, 1931), 3.

[3] Carroll offers no specific section within two huge Latin volumes and his page numbers are incorrect. I pinpoint his source as D[omini] Stanislai Hosius, *Epistle* 150, in his *Operum* (Coloniae: Apud Maternum Cholinum, 1584), 2:309. The letter is to Alberto Bavariae Duci ca. 1563.

[4] See our discussion in chapter 27 of volume 1, "A Reappraisal of the Donatist Controversy and Its Significance."

We have now seen that the Baptists who were formerly called Anabaptist, and in later times Mennonites, were the original Waldenses, and who have long in the history of the church received the honor of that origin. On this account the Baptists may be considered as the only Christian society which has stood since the days of the apostles, and as a Christian society which has preserved pure the doctrines of the Gospel through all ages. The perfectly correct external and internal economy of the Baptist denomination tends to confirm the truth, disputed by the Romish Church, that the Reformation brought about in the sixteenth century was in the highest degree necessary, and at the same time goes to refute the erroneous notion of the Catholics, that their denomination is the most ancient (Ypeij en Dermout, *Geschiedenis der Nederlandsche Hervornude Kerk*. Breda, 1819).[5]

There are serious problems with the translation and the appeal. The Dutch term for "Baptist Church" is *Baptisten Kirche*. Ypeij and Dermout never use the term. The Dutch word that the authors use for "Anabaptists" is *Wederdopers* (*weder* means "again" and *doper* means "baptize"). The authors describe these Wederdopers as having "a very harmful impact on the outer life of the Protestant community." Landmark citations omit that. Besides the word *Mennonieten* (followers of Menno Simons), the synonymous and commonly used term for "Mennonites" was *Doopsgezinden*,[6] which means "to be inclined to baptism." *Doops* is genitive of *doop* ("baptism") and *gezind* means "to favor," or "to be inclined." The *Doopsgezinden* were "inclined to baptism." Unlike their negative description of the "Anabaptists" (*Wederdopers*), Ypeij and Dermout report favorably of the *Doopsgezinden* (Mennonites), as having "a beneficial influence on the inner life of the whole community of Protestant Christians in

---

[5] John T. Christian, *A History of the Baptists* (Nashville: Broadman, 1925), 1:95–96. Volume numbers and page numbers are missing, but I pinpoint the source as being scattered phrases from volume 1, pp. 148–51, of Ypeij and Dermout. Christian offers no ellipsis points to indicate omissions of words, phrases, and paragraphs.

[6] Latourette has a valuable discussion on the *Doopsgezinden*, a term that he uses exclusively for "Mennonites." Kenneth Scott Latourette, "Nineteenth-Century Protestantism in Holland (The Kingdom of the Netherlands)," in *The Nineteenth Century in Europe: The Protestant and Eastern Churches*, vol. 2 of *Christianity in a Revolutionary Age: A History of Christianity in the Nineteenth and Twentieth Centuries* (Grand Rapids: Zondervan, 1959), 237–51.

Holland." They live "beyond reproach, as diligent and hard-working citizens, good, religious Christians, avoiding worldly attractions, and steadfastly following the best moral principles." Ypeij and Dermout lament the fact that the Mennonites were being "confused with" the Anabaptists (*Wederdopers*).[7] The Mennonites have used the name *Doopsgezind* since the seventeenth century, and it has been the official registered name of the Mennonites in the Netherlands since 1796,[8] long before Ypeij and Dermout wrote their history.

Ypeij and Dermout: Their Background and Purpose for Writing

Ypeij and Dermout were not attempting to establish any sort of Baptist history prior to the Reformation. Indeed, they never once mention the Baptists, even while specifically researching and chronicling all reputable groups outside the state church prior to the Reformation. Who were these mysterious authors whose words so often appear in English works as "proof" that the present-day Baptist movement predates the Reformation? We must begin by establishing the political landscape.

The French invasion of the Netherlands in 1795 led to a rapid series of events that transformed the Dutch Republic into a modern nation-state and began the process of separation of church and state.[9] After commanding the Dutch Army (1793–95) during the French Revolutionary wars and living in exile during the French oc-

---

[7] A. Ypeij en I. J. Dermout, *Geschiedenis der Nederlandsche Hervormde Kerk* (Breda, Netherlands: W. Van Bergen, 1819), 1:149–50. They spell it *Wederdoopers*. I have acquired the professional translation services of Marco Schuffelen, scholar of Dutch; his website: www.heardutchhere.net.

[8] Nanne van der Zijpp, "Doopsgezind," *Global Anabaptist Mennonite Encyclopedia Online*, 1956, http://www.gameo.org/encyclopedia/contents/doopsgezind.

[9] In 1848, the church became officially separated from the state. For further study, a good place to start is the helpful essay by Peter van Rooden, "History, the Nation and Religion: The Transformations of the Dutch Religious Past," in *Nation and Religion: Perspectives on Europe and Asia*, ed. Hartmut Lehmann and Peter van de Veer (Princeton, NJ: Princeton University Press, 2001), 96–111. Also valuable is Peter van Rooden, "Long-term Religious Developments in the Netherlands, c. 1750–2000," in *The Decline of Christendom in Western Europe, 1750–2000*, ed. Hugh McLeod and Werner Ustorf (Cambridge: Cambridge University Press, 2003), 113–29.

cupation (1795–1813), William (Willem), son of Prince William V of Orange, became King William I of the new United Kingdom of the Netherlands in 1815. King William appointed I. J. Dermout, D. D., as royal chaplain. It was also at this time that the University of Groningen (est. 1614) was inaugurating its school of theology. Annaeus Ypeij was on its faculty.

The Groningen School[10]

Although Groningen University's school of theology was commonly called "evangelical," this center of religious and philosophical learning was thoroughly liberal from its inception. Under the influence of German higher criticism, its faculty embraced Unitarianism, attacking such doctrines as biblical inspiration, the Trinity, the innate sinfulness of man, and the vicarious atonement of Christ. Petrus Hofstede de Groot (1802–86) and Lodewijk Louis Gerlach Pareau (1800–1866) coauthored the theological handbook defining the doctrines of the school. According to the Groningen school, Christ was only a created being who possessed a single divine-human nature and stood as the model of what every human being could achieve through education into God-likeness. It was an assortment of humanistic intellectualism blended with a strong touch of Romanticism and individualism. Such was the school that Annaeus Ypeij (1760–1837) devotedly served as theologian and church historian. Ypeij contributed a vast amount of the research and composition that went into the historical work that he coauthored with Dermout.

Their Search for Non-Calvinistic but Anti-Roman-Catholic Antecedents for the Dutch Reformed Church

King William I—strong nationalist and bureaucratic centrist—aspired to revive a national awareness and concurrently to level the religious playing field by replacing the traditional focus

---

[10] The word *Groningen* could apply to at least four entities: the province, its chief city, the city's university, and the university's school of theology. For valuable information on the Groningen School of Theology, see John F. Hurst, *History of Rationalism: Embracing a Survey of the Present State of Protestant Theology* (London: Trübner, 1867), 294–97. A helpful current view is available in Hans Schwarz, *Theology in a Global Context: The Last Two Hundred Years* (Grand Rapids: Eerdmans, 2005), 73–74.

on Reformation creedal distinctives with a new focus on pre-Reformation Dutch dissenters found outside the Roman Catholic Church. In order to promote this type of Dutch awareness, William commissioned Chaplain I. J. Dermout and Groningen historian Annaeus Ypeij to provide a *History of the Dutch Reformed Church*, with its *raison d'être* reaching slightly beyond the traditional Reformers but still outside the Roman Catholic Church. Quiet Mennonites, rather than violent Anabaptist groups, fit their need.

Viewing the Reformation as overly confessional and polemical, Ypeij and Dermout directed their research to the discovery of a new foundation of peace-loving dissenters with traits that might be construed as similar to the Groningen school and the modern Dutch Reformed Church. Carefully avoiding any appeal to violent groups or insurrectionists, they focused their research on the published resources of peaceful dissenters—but not dissent *per se*. Ypeij and Dermout were not separatists. While promoting the disestablishment of the monolithic state church, they argued that the state should support all churches. They insisted that true religion rests inwardly with intellectually enlightened individuals, rather than outwardly with ecclesiastically structured machinery.

Impelled to prove that the real groundwork for the Reformation was already in place when the traditional Reformers arrived on the scene, Ypeij and Dermout also found support in Dutch humanists such as Erasmus and the Dutch Brethren of Common Life. The authors then proceeded to echo Remonstrant voices such as Hugo de Groot (Grotius), whose Enlightenment concepts of love, toleration, and the Governmental (Moral) theory of the atonement could theoretically harmonize with the Groningen School of Theology.

Ypeij and Dermout were incredibly gifted with an elegance of style that can soar in literary beauty, though often without substance. Later historians have often looked askance at Ypeij and Dermout's history as a collection of invented traditions. Indeed, parts of their *History of the Dutch Reformed Church* appear to many as mere curiosity. While the overall work offers a scattering of helpful data,[11] the

---

[11] See the helpful study by Herman Paul, "Religious Discourse Communities: Confessional Differentiation in Nineteenth-Century Dutch Protestantism," *Swiss*

most significant impact of its authors was the popular advancement of liberal theology.

Reformed Church pastors in 1817 received political mandates from Jacobus D. Janssen, secretary of Ecclesial Affairs, on how to conduct their celebrations of the Reformation tercentenary. Consequently, even as Ypeij and Dermout were still writing the first volume of their history, their "biblical" humanism was finding circulation in their sermons and hymns, as Janssen mandated Reformed pastors to provide public readings of the poems of Ypeij and Dermout for their October 31, 1817, tercentenary celebration. However, it was not the traditional Reformers or Reformed theology that they extolled. It was Dutch nationalism, liberal theology, and Protestant ecumenism.

As for the Baptists, Ypeij and Dermout never mention even a famous name such as John Smyth, often called the Father of Modern Baptists. Because of Smyth's 1609 founding of an Amsterdam church considered by some to be the first Baptist church, large numbers of Baptists commemorated the event in 2009 with special four-hundred-year anniversary celebrations. Baptist history finds no place, however, in the work of these Dutch authors, whose innovative account spans three centuries—from the end of the fifteenth to the beginning of the nineteenth century.

Later Issues with Ypeij and Dermout

Ypeij and Dermout stood in opposition to the Secession of 1834 (*de Afscheiding*), Bible-oriented churches that departed from the liberal Dutch Reformed Church. The Secessionist churches longed for a return to a time like the Golden Age of the Dutch Republic. In the year of his death (1837), Ypeij assisted in the formation of a religious society and periodical, both called *Truth in Love*.[12] That was also the year that witnessed the decease of Queen Wilhelmina, whose funeral sermon for the occasion was delivered by I. J. Dermout.[13]

Journal of Religious and Cultural History (formerly *Schweizerische Zeitschrift für Kirchengeschichte*) 101 (2007): 107–22.

[12] Thirty years later, the periodical *Truth in Love* was renamed *Faith and Freedom*.

[13] For Dermout's funeral sermon for Queen Wilhelmina, see I. J. Dermout, "Funeral Sermon, delivered in the Cloister Church at the Hague, on Sunday, 29th October, 1837, in memory of the Queen of the Netherlands," in *The Literary*

King William's unpopular stance on various political, economic, religious, and social issues led to his abdication in 1840. He died three years later.

Select Bibliography for Further Reading

Burrage, Champlin. *The Early English Dissenters in The Light of Recent Research (1550–1641).* 2 vols. 1912. Reprint, New York: Russell and Russell, 1967.

Cook, Brenton Hunter. "Recovering the Historic View of Baptist Origins: The Seventeenth-Century Baptists' Theological Identity Interpreted Through a Progressive Illumination Paradigm." PhD diss., Bob Jones University, 2005.

Graves, J. R. *Old Landmarkism: What is It?* Memphis: Baptist Book House, Graves, Mahaffy, 1880.

Hurst, John F. *History of Rationalism: Embracing a Survey of the Present State of Protestant Theology.* London: Trübner, 1867.

McBeth, H. Leon. "The Landmark Movement." In *The Baptist Heritage: Four Centuries of Baptist Witness,* 447–61. Nashville: Broadman, 1987.

McGoldrick, James Edward. *Baptist Successionism: A Crucial Question in Baptist History.* Metuchen, NJ: Scarecrow Press, 1994.

Patterson, W. Morgan. *Baptist Successionism: A Critical View.* Valley Forge, PA: Judson Press, 1969.

Paul, Herman. "Religious Discourse Communities: Confessional Differentiation in Nineteenth-Century Dutch Protestantism." *Swiss Journal of Religious and Cultural History* (formerly *Schweizerische Zeitschrift für Kirchengeschichte*), 101 (2007): 107–22.

Pendleton, James Madison. *An Old Landmark Re-set.* 2nd ed. Nashville: Southwestern Publishing House, 1857.

Rooden, Peter van. "History, the Nation and Religion: The Transformations of the Dutch Religious Past." In *Nation and Religion: Perspectives on Europe and Asia,* edited by Hartmut Lehmann and Peter van de Veer, 96–111. Princeton, NJ: Princeton University Press, 2001.

———. "Long-term Religious Developments in the Netherlands, c. 1750–2000." In *The Decline of Christendom in Western Europe, 1750–2000,* edited by Hugh McLeod and Werner Ustorf, 113–29. Cambridge: Cambridge University Press, 2003.

Schwarz, Hans. *Theology in a Global Context: The Last Two Hundred Years.* Grand Rapids: Eerdmans, 2005.

Tull, James E. *A Study of Southern Baptist Landmarkism in the Light of Historical Baptist Ecclesiology.* New York: Columbia University Press, 1960.

Ypeij, A., en I. J. Dermout. *Geschiedenis der Nederlandsche Hervormde Kerk.* Vols. 1–2. Breda, Netherlands: W. Van Bergen, 1819 and 1822.

———. *Geschiedenis der Nederlandsche Hervormde Kerk.* Vols. 3–4. Breda, Netherlands: F. B. Hollingerus Pijpers, 1824 and 1827.

Gazette, and Journal of the Belles Lettres, Arts, Sciences, etc., no. 1093 (Saturday, December 30, 1837): 831.

10

Baptist Backgrounds, Doctrines, and Practices

There are two strands of English Baptist beginnings: General Baptists and Particular Baptists. The name *General* refers to the group's belief in Christ's general or unlimited atonement. The name *Particular* refers to that group's belief that Christ died only for the elect. The years of origin for the English General Baptists are 1611–12, while the Particular Baptists organized their first church in 1638. Baptists emerged from the English Congregationalist Separatist movement that had left the Church of England. English Separatists had continued to practice infant baptism, which became the main reason for the Baptists' departure from their ranks. From their beginnings, however, Baptists would continue to practice the Separatists' congregational type of church government.

General Baptists

The General Baptists would emerge from two major English Separatist churches: the Ancient Church and the Gainsborough Church. The "Ancient" Church began as a secret church. On October 8, 1587, John Greenwood and twenty-two other Separatists were arrested for meeting secretly for worship and thrown into the infamous Clink Prison in London's Southwark area on the south bank of the River Thames. On November 19, while visiting Greenwood in the Clink, Henry Barrowe was himself arrested and incarcerated with Greenwood. For more than five years, the two men would remain imprisoned—both in the Clink and in the nearby Fleet Prison. From their prison cells, Barrowe and Greenwood wrote numerous treatises, pamphlets, letters, and petitions, which Separatists smuggled out, a few pages at a time, and sent to Holland for printing. English Puritan Francis Johnson (1562–1618), a Cambridge graduate and chaplain to the Church of Merchant Adventurers in Middleburg (Zeeland), learned that a book by Barrowe and Greenwood was being secretly printed in the Dutch city of Dort. Authorized by the English ambassador to seize and burn all copies, Johnson spared two copies for perusal—one for a friend and one for himself. Upon studying this *Plain Refutation*, Johnson became a Separatist, returned to London, visited Barrowe and Greenwood in their cells, and soon succeeded Greenwood as ruling elder of the secret church.

In 1593, Greenwood and Barrow, along with the Welshman John Penry, were hanged by the Anglican authorities for their separatist worship. Johnson and several others were then imprisoned, and the remnant of their secret church escaped to Holland—first to Kampen, then to Naarden, and finally to Amsterdam by 1596, when Henry Ainsworth (ca. 1570–1622), a Cambridge-educated Hebrew scholar, joined them and succeeded Barrowe as teaching elder. Other English Separatist groups escaping to Amsterdam would now refer to the secret church as the "Ancient Church" since it was the first English-speaking assembly of refugees to arrive. In addition to his *Psalter* (1612), Ainsworth wrote the Ancient Church's True Confession of the Faith (1596), and Particular Baptists would later use it as a model for their own London Baptist Confession (1644). Of course, the Baptists would reject Ainsworth's article 35 on infant baptism and his article 39 that allows for the government to assist in keeping churches pure.

Following his release in 1597, Johnson joined the Ancient Church in Amsterdam. He continued as ruling elder and Ainsworth continued as teaching elder. With Johnson a Presbyterian and Ainsworth a Congregationalist, however, the church divided over church polity in 1610. Johnson and his church moved to Germany. After Johnson's death in 1618, his church members took a ship to Virginia, where Powhatan Indians destroyed their settlement near Jamestown in 1622. Meanwhile, Ainsworth served the in Ancient

Church pastorate until his death (1622). The church would maintain its existence until 1701, when the last five members closed the church and joined the English Reformed Church of Amsterdam (Presbyterian), organized in 1607 as a church for English merchants. There are plaques here commemorating the *Mayflower* Pilgrims and their associations with the Ancient Church, which itself had great influence on an eccentric preacher named John Smyth, whose story begins back in the English town of Gainsborough, on the River Trent.

Established in 1602, the Separatist church in Gainsborough of Lincolnshire called John Smyth (ca. 1570–1612), a Cambridge graduate, to become its minister. The Lord of the Manor, Sir William Hickman, befriended the group and allowed these sixty to seventy Separatists to hold their services in the great hall of the stately Old Hall Manor. Those who attended the services included Separatists such as Richard Clyfton, John Robinson, William Bradford, and William Brewster, each of whom would participate in positive ways in the long struggle for religious freedom and ecclesiastical purity. For their safety, the Gainsborough church divided in 1606, so that those who were traveling from the Scrooby area could begin worshiping at the Scrooby Manor house, home of postmaster William Brewster. Richard Clyfton served as pastor for the Scrooby church. William Bradford, future governor of Plymouth Plantation, was a member. In 1608, the Scrooby church fled to Amsterdam and attended the Ancient Church. Early the following year, under the leadership of John Robinson, the group moved down to the city of Leiden. In 1620, many of them sailed to the New World as Pilgrims on board the *Mayflower*.

Due to persecution in late 1607 or early 1608, John Smyth and at least forty members of his Gainsborough congregation had fled to Amsterdam, just before of the Scrooby church did, and they too attended services at the Ancient Church. Smyth and his group had moved into a former bakery that his group rented from the Mennonite Jan Munter. With attached buildings, the facilities provided both living quarters and a meeting hall for the Smyth congregation. Being in close contact with Mennonite influence, Smyth soon began to reveal a growing propensity to drift away from the English Separatists.

In late 1608 or early 1609, Smyth withdrew from the Ancient Church and led his followers in establishing an unaffiliated Anabaptist church that would seek official recognition from the Mennonites. With his flock gathered around a three-legged stool that held a basin of water, Smyth first rebaptized himself (se-baptism), then his congregation, by affusion (pouring). Smyth had several reasons for the proactive organization of an independent church: (1) because the Church of England was corrupt, its baptism had been worthless; (2) since believers' baptism is the only true baptism, their own pedobaptism had been antiscriptural; (3) his trust in a true successionism among the Mennonites and his hope of negotiating a union with them would be tedious and slow because of the language barrier; meanwhile, (4) the Mennonites would see their sincerity.

Smyth preached from the Greek and Hebrew and prohibited speakers from using translations or notes. His sermons often lasted for hours. Forbidden from his services were all forms of music, even the singing of psalms. The Mennonites were not impressed, and all such practices would cease among the Smyth people when they later joined with the Mennonites. Meanwhile, hoping to hasten Mennonite acceptance, Smyth disestablished his church in 1610, and his group applied to the local Waterlandian Mennonite Church for membership. They assured the Mennonites of their approval of pacifism and their refusal of oath-taking and participation in government. They also tolerated heresy lodged in the teachings of the local Dutch "Waterlanders," so called for the region in the province of North Holland. The liberal Waterlandian Mennonites had been aloof from most other Mennonite groups since about 1557. At times they had expressed various nuances of the Christological heresy of Menno Simons and Melchior Hoffman, that Jesus brought His own "heavenly flesh" into Mary's womb. Further, John Smyth and his group now embraced the dangerous Waterlandian hamartiology of Pelagianism, that is, that no one is born a sinner.

Smyth's Short Confession of Faith (1610), which he sent to the Mennonites, is Pelagian (Art. 5). The Short Confession of Faith (1610), authored by Hans de Ries and sent by the Waterlanders to Smyth, is also Pelagian (Art. 4). The Smyth group reinforces Pelagianism in its Propositions and Conclusions Concerning True

Christian Religion (1612–14)—(Arts. 17–20).[1] In 1615, three years after Smyth's death, the apostasy resulted in the desired fusion with the Mennonites.

In *The Last Booke of John Smyth Called the Retraction of His Errours and the Confirmation of the Truth*,[2] Smyth softened his stance on successionism. He had tolerated but restated the Waterlander notion of Jesus' having heavenly flesh. To Smyth, Jesus had both natural flesh and spiritual flesh, but he failed to explain what that meant. Gradually, the Waterlanders would drop their theological aberrations and amalgamate into various other Mennonite groups.

When Smyth disbanded his church in 1610, Thomas Helwys (ca. 1575–1614) led eight to ten others to break from the Smyth group. During 1611–12, Helwys's group returned to London in the face of persecution and established a church in the Newgate area. Even before Helwys's church began using the name Baptist, its critics were calling it that. Indeed, it constituted the first English Baptist church. Its Declaration of Faith was the first Baptist confession. It teaches believers' baptism (Art. 14) and denies successionism (Arts. 11–12). One of its authors' primary aims was to distinguish Baptists from Anabaptists.[3] Helwys's church became the mother of all General Baptist churches and their strong opposition to Smyth had a fourfold basis: Smyth's extreme emphasis on free will, Pelagianism, "heavenly-flesh" Christology, and successionism.

These earliest English Baptists were convinced that any church founded on the Bible had no need for any visible successionism outside the Bible. To them, visible successionism was one of the false claims of the Church of Rome. As a distinct movement, Baptists would differ from such Anabaptist tenets as pacifism, forbidding all oath-taking, and forbidding Christians from civil office-holding. Since the 1640s, beginning with the Particular Baptists, when immersion became embedded into their defining features, all Baptists

---

[1] William L. Lumpkin, *Baptist Confessions of Faith*, rev. ed. (Valley Forge, PA: Judson Press, 1969), 100, 103, and 126–27.
[2] John Smyth, *The Works of John Smyth, Fellow of Christ's College, 1594–8*, with notes and biography by W. T. Whitley for the Baptist Historical Society (Cambridge: Cambridge University Press, 1915), 2:758–59.
[3] Lumpkin, 114ff.

have differed from all major Anabaptist groups on the mode of baptism.

Thomas Helwys was incarcerated in Newgate Prison for writing a book called *A Short Declaration of the Mystery of Iniquity* (1612),[4] the first Baptist plea for full religious freedom ever published in the English language. John Morton (Murton)[5] succeeded him to the pastorate. By 1644, when the name *Baptist* became standard, there were forty-seven General Baptist churches. Some, including Helwys's church, were Arminian, believing that true believers can lose their salvation. Not all General Baptists have held to strict Arminianism. Over the years, many maintained a remarkable balance in emphasis. For instance, their Orthodox Creed (1678) asserts the perseverance of every true believer (Art. 36). In other matters, their Standard Confession (1660) prescribes baptism by "dipping" (Art. 11) and teaches premillennialism (Art. 22). Meeting in members' homes and other hiding places, these earliest Baptist churches left behind virtually no buildings or other physical monuments. London's Newgate Prison, where some died, stood as a reminder of the price they paid. Perhaps their true monuments are the eternal souls who have come to a saving knowledge of Christ through their witness.

Particular Baptists

While the General Baptists had emerged in 1611–12 in protest over John Smyth's successionist apostasy into doctrinal heresy, Particular Baptists originated as a movement in 1638 by withdrawing from an orthodox assembly called the "J-L-J" Church, so named for Jacob, Lathrop, and Jessey, its first three pastors. Henry Jacob (1563–1624), an Oxford graduate, established it in the Southwark area of London in 1616 as the first recorded independent English

---

[4] Joe Early Jr., ed., *The Life and Writings of Thomas Helwys* (Macon, GA: Mercer University Press, 2009), 155–311.

[5] John Murton, *A Description of What God Hath Predestinated Concerning Man, in His Creation, Transgression, & Regeneration: As Also an Answer to John Robinson, Touching Baptism* (n.p.: n.p., 1620); *A Humble Supplication to the King's Majesty* (1620), in vol. 2 of *The History of the English Baptists* by Thomas Crosby (London: Thomas Crosby, 1739), appendix 2:10–51; and *Persecution for Religion Judg'd and Condemn'd* (1615), in *Tracts on Liberty of Conscience and Persecution, 1614–1661*, compiled by Edward Bean Underhill (London: J. Haddon, 1846), 83–180.

church and the earliest church ever known to be designated as Congregationalist. The name indicates its way of government. In addition, the J-L-J Church was Puritan in doctrine and Separatist in practice. Henry Jacob remained with the church for only a few years before moving to Jamestown, Virginia, in 1622, where he planted a small settlement.

John Lathrop (d. 1653) then became the second J-L-J pastor. In 1632, Anglican authorities seized Lathrop with forty of his sixty members and imprisoned them—some in the infamous Clink, some in New Prison, and some in the Gatehouse—where they remained for the next two years. Their crime was refusal to support the Church of England. In 1634, Lathrop and thirty-two of his members sailed to the New World and settled at Barnstable, on Cape Cod, Massachusetts, where they maintained their church.

With Henry Jacob in Jamestown and John Lathrop in Barnstable, Henry Jessey, in 1637, became the third pastor of London's J-L-J Church. Jessey faced an unusual problem. Since 1630, many members had become Baptists and had been leaving the church. In 1638, one of these former members, John Spilsbury, became pastor of a London church that soon became recognized as the earliest Particular Baptist church. Spilsbury's church, in defense of ecclesiastical purity, insisted that infant baptism was an act of disobedience. In 1640, Spilsbury's church came to the additional conviction that immersion is the only scriptural mode of baptism. The following year, the whole church received immersion.

By 1644, when Spilsbury, along with William Kiffin, authored the London Confession, based in part upon Henry Ainsworth's True Confession, there were seven Particular Baptist churches in London. They were first called Baptists in that year, and the London Confession was the first Baptist confession to specify immersion as the proper mode of baptism (Arts. 39–40). From their beginning until 1644, Baptist churches had been called "Brethren," or "Baptized Churches," or "Churches of the Baptized Way." A twofold purpose of the 1644 London Confession was (1) to combat general accusations that all Baptists were either Arminians or Pelagians and (2) to distinguish Particular Baptists from both General Baptists and Anabaptists.

The original Spilsbury church met in secret places, including a home on Old Gravel Lane in London's Wapping section. The church later moved to Prescot Street, then to Commercial Street, and finally to Walthamstow, where it remains to this day as the historic continuation of Spilsbury's church. Today it is called the Church Hill Baptist Chapel, and it is London's oldest Baptist church. Its present building was constructed near the turn of the twenty-first century.[6]

At the J-L-J Church, Pastor Henry Jessey followed Spilsbury's example in 1645 by separating and becoming a Particular Baptist. In fact, the J-L-J Church eventually spawned several other Particular Baptist churches before discontinuing its own existence in London. All that remains today of that matrix of Particular Baptists—the original, Puritan J-L-J Church—is the Parish Church of West Barnstable, Massachusetts, perpetuated by John Lathrop. Its present building was erected in 1717. This church never became Baptist. It eventually abandoned the cardinal doctrines of its founders of 1616 and identified with the present-day apostasy. Truth germinated before it died, however, for by 1689 there were 107 separated Particular Baptist churches in the London area alone and a growing number in the American colonies. America's earliest Baptist churches, founded in Rhode Island by Roger Williams and John Clarke, were Particular in doctrine and Separatist in practice. Such are the historic roots of independent separatist Baptists. Not all Calvinistic Baptists have held to a limited atonement, or to a strict Reformed theology that rigidly equates the church with Israel. Over the years, many Calvinistic Baptists have avoided insisting on rigid systems *per se*. Williams and Clarke themselves were remarkably balanced in such matters.

Repudiation of Anabaptism

The title pages of some of the earliest Baptist confessions declare that Baptists were being "falsely called Anabaptists," as in the London Confession (1644) and the Standard Confession (1660). The earliest Baptists in America echoed the same sentiment. John Clarke

---

[6] Robert W. Oliver, *From John Spilsbury to Ernest Kevan: The Literary Contribution of London's Oldest Baptist Church* (London: Grace Publications Trust, 1985).

established the First Baptist Church in Newport, Rhode Island, around 1644. One day in 1651, Clarke, Obadiah Holmes, and another elder were visiting a sick brother near Lynn, Massachusetts. As Clarke was sharing a passage of Scripture, the men were suddenly arrested, taken to Boston, and fined by the Puritan establishment for holding an illegal church service. Holmes was beaten with thirty stripes. The main charge was that these men were "Anabaptists." The next year, while in England, John Clarke recorded the episode in his *Ill News from New-England*: "In our examination," writes Clarke, "the Governor upbraided us with the name of *Anabaptists*; to whom I answered, 'I disown the name, I am neither an Anabaptist, nor a Pedobaptist,'"[7] one who baptizes babies (*pedo* is from παιδός, "child").

When the First Baptist Church of Boston, Massachusetts, was founded in 1665, the first entry in its "Record Book" declared that this church, "commonly (though falsely) called Anabaptist," is "gathered together and entered into fellowship & communion" (1665). Baptists originated, not as Anabaptists, but as "Protestant" separatists. The Baptists' Orthodox Creed (1678), for example, explains on its title page that it is a "Protestant Confession of Faith . . . to unite and confirm all true Protestants in the Fundamental Articles of the Christian Religion against the errors and heresies of Rome."

Henry C. Vedder (1853–1935) on Baptist Beginnings

¶ The history of Baptist churches cannot be carried, by the scientific method, farther back than the year 1611, when the first Anabaptist church consisting wholly of Englishmen was founded in Amsterdam by John Smyth, the Se-Baptist. This was not, strictly speaking, a Baptist church, but it was the direct progenitor of churches in England that a few years later became Baptist, and therefore the history begins there. . . .

¶ A history of Baptist churches going farther back than the early years of the seventeenth century would, therefore, in the present

---

[7] John Clarke, *Ill News from New-England* (London: Henry Hills, 1652), 31.

state of knowledge, be in the highest degree unscientific. The very attempt to write such a history now would be a confession of crass ignorance, either of the facts as known, or of the methods of historical research and the principles of historical criticism, or of both. . . .

¶ The church that [Christ] said he would build on the rock, to which he guaranteed victory against the gates of Hades itself, is not a visible body—that is the great falsehood of Rome—but the assembly of those in all the ages who truly love God and keep the commandments of Christ. Of these there has been an unbroken line and here is the true apostolic succession—there is no other. . . . Our theory of the church as deduced from the Scriptures requires no outward and visible succession from the apostles. If every church of Christ were today to become apostate, it would be possible and right for any true believers to organize tomorrow another church on the apostolic model of faith and practice, and that church would have the only apostolic succession worth having—a succession of faith in the Lord Christ and obedience to him.[8]

The Second London Confession

For their Assembly Confession, better known as the Second London Confession (1677), revised and adopted in 1689, the Particular Baptists used the Presbyterians' Westminster Confession (1646) as their doctrinal model. As the major and most complete of all Particular Baptist confessions, the Second London was the first Baptist confession to use the word *infallible* to describe the Bible (Chap. 1). One of the confession's signatories was Benjamin Keach who, with his son Elias, condensed it into what became known as the Keach Confession, which colonial Baptists would essentially incorporate into their Philadelphia Confession of Faith (1742).

In the nineteenth century, Charles H. Spurgeon, one of a long line of famous pastoral successors of Benjamin Keach, described the Second London Confession for his New Park Street Church: "This ancient document is a most excellent epitome of the things most

---

[8] Henry C. Vedder, *Short History of the Baptists* (Valley Forge, PA: American Baptist Publication Society, 1907), 4–7. Vedder later became doctrinally liberal.

surely believed among us."[9] Later, at the 1859 dedication service of London's Metropolitan Tabernacle, Spurgeon sealed a copy of the Second London Confession, along with a copy of John Rippon's Hymn Book, inside a bottle that the church buried at the cornerstone.

The New Hampshire Confession (1833)

Baptists formed their first national organization in Philadelphia in 1814. It was called the General Missionary Convention of the Baptist Denomination in the United States of America for Foreign Missions, but more commonly known as the Triennial Convention since it met once every three years. Later they added the American Baptist Home Mission Society (1832) and the American Baptist Publication Society (1824), which published the New Hampshire Confession in 1833. While there are no known copies of its original edition, the edition that seems most likely the closest to the original is in William Crowell, *The Church Member's Hand-Book* (1850).[10] The original confession contained sixteen articles of faith and was accompanied by a church covenant. Twenty years after the original publication, J. Newton Brown, editorial secretary of the American Baptist Publication Society, revised the confession and the covenant and published them in his *Baptist Church Manual* (1853). Brown added two new articles—"Repentance and Faith" and "Sanctification." His 1853 edition of both confession and covenant quickly became the more popular *terminus a quo* for later revisions among Baptist churches. Especially welcome in the covenant (below) was Brown's addition of the promise "to abstain from the sale and use of intoxicating drinks as a beverage."

---

[9] Charles H. Spurgeon, *The Autobiography of C. H. Spurgeon 1854–1860*, compiled from his diary, letters, and records by his wife and his private secretary (London: Passmore and Alabaster, 1898), 2:160.

[10] William Crowell, *The Church Member's Hand-Book: A Guide to the Doctrines and Practice of Baptist Churches* (Boston: Gould, Kendall and Lincoln, 1850), 19–28; cf. Lumpkin, 360–67.

J. Newton Brown's 1853 Revision
of the New Hampshire Covenant[11]

¶ Having been led, as we believe, by the Spirit of God, to receive the Lord Jesus Christ as our Savior; and, on the profession of our faith, having been baptized in the name of the Father, and of the Son, and of the Holy Spirit, we do now, in the presence of God, angels, and this assembly, most solemnly and joyfully enter into covenant with one another as one body in Christ.

We engage, therefore, by the aid of the Holy Spirit, to walk together in Christian love; to strive for the advancement of this church, in knowledge, holiness, and comfort; to promote its prosperity and spirituality; to sustain its worship, ordinances, discipline, and doctrines; to contribute cheerfully and regularly to the support of the ministry, the expenses of the church; the relief of the poor, and the spread of the gospel through all nations.

¶ We also engage to maintain family and secret devotion[s]; to religiously educate our children; to seek the salvation of our kindred and acquaintances; to walk circumspectly in the world; to be just in our dealings, faithful in our engagements, and exemplary in our deportment; to avoid all tattling, backbiting, and excessive anger; to abstain from the sale and use of intoxicating drink as a beverage; and to be zealous in our efforts to advance the kingdom of our Savior.

¶ We further engage to watch over one another in brotherly love; to remember each other in prayer; to aid each other in sickness and distress; to cultivate Christian sympathy in feeling and courtesy in speech; to be slow to take offense, but always ready for reconciliation, and mindful of the rules of our Savior, to secure it without delay. We moreover engage, that when we remove from this place, we will as soon as possible unite with some other church, where we can carry out the spirit of this covenant and the principles of God's Word.

---

[11] J. Newton Brown, *The Baptist Church Manual: Containing the Declaration of Faith, Covenant, Rules of Order and Brief Forms of Church Letters* (Philadelphia: American Baptist Publication Society, 1853), 23–24. The 1833 edition is in Charles W. Deweese, *Baptist Church Covenants* (Nashville: Broadman, 1990), 157–58.

The Earliest Baptist Covenant in America

John Myles (1621–84), upon receiving his education at Oxford University, joined fellowship with London's earliest Particular Baptists. From there he went to Wales in 1649 and established the first Particular Baptist church in Ilston (near Swansea). Arriving in the New World in 1663, Myles gathered a congregation at Rehoboth in Plymouth Colony. The group soon established the nearby town of Swansea, Massachusetts, and their congregation became known as the Swansea Church. It is the oldest Baptist church in Massachusetts, and its congregation produced the earliest published Baptist covenant in Colonial America. Here is their beautiful and "Holy Covenant."[12]

The Swansea Church Covenant (1663)

The Holy Covenant the first founders of Swansea entered into at the first beginning and all the members thereof for divers years:

¶ Whereas, we poor creatures are, through the exceeding riches of God's infinite grace, mercifully snatched out of the kingdom of darkness, and by his infinite power translated into the kingdom of his dear Son, there to be partakers with all the saints of all those privileges which Christ by the shedding of his precious blood hath purchased for us, and that we do find our souls in some good measure wrought on by divine grace to desire to be conformable to Christ in all things, being also constrained by the matchless love and wonderful distinguishing mercies that we abundantly enjoy from his most free grace to serve him according to our utmost capacities, and that we also know that it is our most bounden duty to walk in visible communion with Christ and each other according to the prescript rule of his most Holy Word, and also that it is our undoubted right through Christ to enjoy all the privileges of God's house which our souls for a long time panted after, and finding no other way at present by the all-working providence of our only wise God and gracious Father to us opened for the enjoying of the same, we do therefore, after often and solemn seeking to the Lord for help and direction in the fear of his holy name, and

---

[12] Henry Melville King, *Rev. John Myles and the Founding of the First Baptist Church in Massachusetts* (Providence, RI: Preston & Rounds, 1905), 52–55.

with hands lifted up to Him, the most High God, humble and freely offer up ourselves this day a living sacrifice unto Him, who is our God in covenant through Christ our Lord and only Savior, to walk together according to his revealed Word in the visible gospel relation both to Christ, our only Head, and to each other as fellow-members and brethren of the same household of faith.

¶ And we do humbly pray that through his strength we will henceforth endeavor to perform all our respective duties towards God and each other, and to practice all the ordinances of Christ according to what is or shall be revealed to us in our respective place, to exercise, practice and submit to the government of Christ in this his church, viz: further protesting against all rending or dividing principles or practices from any of the people of God as being most abominable and loathsome to our souls and utterly inconsistent with that Christian charity which declares men to be Christ's disciples. Indeed, further declaring in that as union in Christ is the sole ground of our communion, each with other, so we are ready to accept of, receive to and hold communion with all such by judgment of charity we conceive to be fellow-members with us in our Head, Christ Jesus, though differing from us in such controversial points as are not absolutely and essentially necessary to salvation.

¶ We also hope that though of ourselves we are altogether unworthy and unfit thus to offer up ourselves to God or to do Him a [favor], or to expect any favor with, or mercy from Him, He will graciously accept of this our freewill offering in and through the merit and mediation of our dear Redeemer, and that he will employ and improve us in this service to his praise, to whom be all glory, honor, now and forever. Amen.

The Earliest Baptist Manuals

Nineteenth-century Baptists used church manuals extensively to provide guidance for the organizational life of their churches. The wide circulation of such manuals reflects their need for resources on organizational structure of local churches. Offering a basic and systematic approach to ecclesiastical order, these manuals included William Crowell's *Church Member's Manual* (1845); J. Newton Brown's *Baptist Church Manual* (1853); Edward T. Hiscox's *Baptist*

Church Directory (1859); and J. M. Pendleton's *Church Manual* (1867). By 1946, Pendleton's manual had sold at least 150,000 copies. Hiscox's work appeared well into the twentieth century under such titles as *Principles and Practices for Baptist Churches* and *The New Directory for Baptist Churches*. Providing basic introductions in Baptist history, doctrine, and practice, Hiscox also included covenants and specific instructions towards a basic orthopraxy for Baptists.

Hiscox delineated three methods in which individuals could unite with Baptist churches: (1) admission by baptism upon profession of faith, (2) admission by letter, and (3) admission by experience (or a statement of faith). The first method applied primarily to new converts. The second method required a letter from the church where the individual held membership. Such a letter "certifies to his good Christian character and regular standing, and commends him to the confidence of, and membership in, the other church." Once the church had adequately observed the individual's loyalty and commitment, a "vote of the Church" established formal admission into its membership. The third method, admission by experience, or "statement of faith," applied to candidates who "have been baptized, but by some means have lost their membership" in some church.

Hiscox explains that Baptist churches observed the Lord's Supper quarterly, bimonthly, or monthly. In many congregations, the "hand of fellowship" was offered to new members on Communion Sunday. Interestingly, Hiscox observes that some Baptists objected to "individual communion cups" and "the practice of holding the bread till all are served." They feared that such formalities would "exalt the form over the spirit and make the service ritual rather than spiritual." While some churches would continue their tradition of using wine in Communion, most shared the concerns of the temperance movement and turned to unfermented grape juice.

Fundamental Baptist Fellowship International (FBFI): Statement of Faith (2008)[13]

Section 1: The Scripture

We believe in the Scriptures of the Old and New Testaments alone as verbally, plenarily inspired of God, without error in the original writings and the sole authority of faith and practice, providentially preserved as God's eternal Word (2 Pet. 1:21; 2 Tim. 3:16, 17; 1 Pet. 1:23*b*–25). We believe in a dispensational understanding of the Bible based on the progressive unfolding of the divine mysteries from God, which result in distinguishable stewardships of God's truth (Heb. 1:1–3; Eph. 1:10; 1 Cor. 10:31).

Section 2: The Godhead

We believe in one God, an eternal Spirit existing in three distinct uncreated Persons—God the Father, God the Son, and God the Holy Spirit—yet One in essence and equal in every divine perfection and attribute (Deut. 6:4; Matt. 3:13–17; Matt. 28:19; 2 Cor. 13:14).

Section 3: Jesus Christ

We believe in the Lord Jesus Christ, God's eternal Son Who was begotten by the Holy Spirit, born of the virgin Mary, and is truly God and truly Man, one Person with two natures, divine and human (Matt. 1:18–20; John 1:1, 2, 14). We believe the Lord Jesus Christ died as a substitutionary sacrifice for the sins of all men according to the Scriptures, and all who receive Him are justified on the grounds of His shed blood (2 Cor. 15:3; 2 Cor. 5:21; Rom. 3:21–26; Heb. 2:9; 1 John 2:2). We believe in the resurrection of the crucified body of our Lord Jesus Christ, in His bodily ascension into Heaven, and in His present life there as High Priest for us (Matt. 28:1–10; Acts 1:9; Heb. 7:25–28). We believe in the imminent return of Christ prior to the inauguration of Daniel's seventieth week, at which time all believers in Christ will be caught up to meet the Lord in the air, and be kept from the promised period of divine wrath upon the Earth (Dan. 9:24–27; 1 Thess. 4:14–17; 1 Cor. 15:51–53; 1 Thess. 5:9; Rom. 5:9).

---

[13] "Statement of Faith." Article III of *Constitution*, adopted June 15, 2000, rev. June 10, 2008. Taylors, SC: Fundamental Baptist Fellowship International, http://www.fbfi.org/.

Section 4: The Holy Spirit

We believe in the eternal deity and personality of the Holy Spirit Who is one of the three Persons of the Trinity. We believe the following are among His ministries: the restraining of evil in the world to the measure of the divine will; the conviction of the world regarding sin, righteousness, and judgment; the calling and regeneration of all believers; the indwelling of those who are saved; and, the continued filling for power, teaching, and service of all among the saved who are truly yielded to Him (Rom. 8:28, 29; 1 Cor. 1:24; 2 Thess. 2:7; John 3:6; 16:7–11; Rom. 8:9; Eph. 4:30, 5:18). We believe the Holy Spirit produces His fruit in the lives of all believers (Gal. 5:22, 23; Col. 1:10, 12). We believe some gifts of the Holy Spirit were temporary. We believe that certain gifts, being miraculous in nature, were prevalent in the church in the first century. They were foundational and transitional. These gifts have ceased, being no longer needed because the Scriptures have been completed and the church has been divinely certified (Heb. 2:1–4; 1 Cor. 13:8–12; Eph. 2:20). We believe that speaking in tongues was never the common or necessary sign of the filling or baptism of the Spirit. We believe God, in accord with His own will, does hear and answer prayer for the sick and afflicted (1 Cor. 12:11, 30; 13:8; James 5:14–16).

Section 5: Man

We believe that man was created directly by God on day six of the creation week (Gen. 1:26–31), in His image (James 3:9), and in a state of sinlessness (Eph. 4:24). We believe that originally man freely chose to transgress the will of God, and thereby, incurred sin, condemnation, physical and spiritual death (Gen. 3:1–7; Rom. 5:12–19; Eph. 2:1–3) so that man is a sinner by nature and by choice, completely depraved, destitute of any moral good, and utterly unable to merit God's favor or contribute to his salvation (Rom. 3:10; Jer. 17:9; Eph. 2:9; Titus 3:5; Rom. 4:5–6).

Section 6: Salvation

We believe in the salvation of sinners through Jesus of Nazareth, the Son of God, Who is the only Savior of men by virtue of His shed blood, i.e., His substitutionary death for sinners. We believe that salvation is completely dependent on the grace of God, is a free gift of God that man cannot earn or merit in any way, and is appropriated by repentance and faith in the person and cross work of our Lord and Savior, Jesus Christ. We hold that in salvation the believer is called, regenerated, Spirit baptized into union with Christ, justified, (including the forgiveness of sin and restoration to favor with God through the merit or righteousness of Christ), adopted, sanctified, and glorified. We believe that God secures and guarantees the final salvation of every true believer, and that the genuine believer will continue in his faith and show evidence of his faith in Christ until he meets the Lord. We believe all the elect of God, once saved, are kept by God's power and are secure in Christ forever (John 14:6; Rom. 3:25; Isa. 53:4–6; Eph. 2:9; John 16:8–11; Acts 20:21; Eph. 2:8–10; John 1:13; Rom. 6:3–5; Rom. 5:1; Rom. 8:15; Heb. 10:10, 14; Rom. 8:30; John 6:39; 2 Cor. 5:17; 1 John 2:19; 1 Cor. 15:2; Rom. 8:37–39).

Section 7: Sanctification

We believe sanctification is presented in three senses in Scriptures: (1) every saved person has been sanctified through the death of Christ; (2) is being sanctified by the Holy Spirit; and, (3) will be completely sanctified at his glorification. Every believer has two natures, old and new, and the old cannot be eradicated during this life (Heb. 10:10; John 17:17; Eph. 5:25–27; 1 Thess. 4:13–18; Gal. 5:17; Rom. 7:18–25).

Section 8: Separation

We believe in the biblical doctrine of separation which encompasses: (1) separation of the local church from all affiliation and fellowship with false teachers who deny the verities of the Christian faith, and from those who are content to walk in fellowship with unbelief and inclusivism (from Christian individuals or organizations that affiliate with those who deny the faith or are content to walk with those who compromise the doctrine and practice of Scripture) (2 Thess. 3:6; 1 Cor. 5:1–11; 1 Tim. 1:18–20; Matt. 18:15–17); (2) separation of the individual believer from all worldly practices (philosophies, goals, lifestyles, amusements, habits, and practices) that dishonor the Savior; and, (3) separation of church and state (2 Tim. 3:1–5; Rom. 12:1–2; 14:13; 1 John 2:15–17; 2 John 9–11; Matt. 22:21).

Section 9: The Church

We believe in the Church—a living, spiritual body of which Christ is the Head, and of which all regenerated people in this age are a part. We believe the Church is a body peculiar to the age of grace and entirely distinct from national Israel. We believe a local church is a company of believers in Jesus Christ, immersed upon a credible confession of faith and associated for worship, work of the ministry, evangelism, observance of the ordinances (baptism and the Lord's supper), and fellowship. We believe the local church is autonomous, the center of God's program for this age, and that every Christian is bound by Scripture to give his unhindered cooperation to the ministry of his local church (Matt. 16:16–18; 1 Cor. 12:12–17; Acts 2:42–47; 1 Tim. 3:15–16; Eph. 4:11, 12; Matt. 28:19, 20; Acts 1:8). We believe that the local church is an autonomous body having the God-ordained right of self-government, free from the interference of any religious hierarchy, solely responsible to preserve its own internal integrity, maintain pure doctrine and practice, elect its own officers, ordain men to the ministry, settle its own internal affairs, and determine the method and extent of its cooperation with other churches (Jude 3; Acts 6:1–6; Acts 13:1–3; 1 Cor. 6:1–5; Acts 15). The proper form of church government is congregational (Matt. 18:15–17; Acts 6:1–6; 1 Cor. 5:4, 5). The two scriptural offices of the local church are pastor and deacon (1 Tim. 3:1, 8).

Section 10: The Ordinances

We believe there are two ordinances: baptism and the Lord's Supper. Baptism is the immersion of a believer in water and is properly called "believer's baptism." It sets forth, in a beautiful and solemn way, our identification with Christ in His death, burial, and resurrection, and the resultant responsibility to "walk in the newness of life" (Rom. 6:4). Baptism is a prerequisite to church membership. The Lord's Supper is the commemoration of the Lord's death until He comes, is a reminder of our continual fellowship with Him, and should be preceded by careful self-examination (Matt. 28:19–20; Acts 8:36–39; Rom. 6:3–5; 1 Cor. 11:23–32).

Section 11: The Great Commission

We believe the Lord Jesus Christ has commissioned us to take the Gospel to the world, and evangelism and church-planting at home and abroad should be primary in the program of the local church, which includes baptism and instruction of believers (Matt. 28:19–20; Acts 1:8).

Section 12: Last Things

We believe in the imminent rapture of the church to Heaven followed by a seven-year period of tribulation upon all the Earth. At the end of the period of tribulation, Jesus Christ shall come back to Earth in power and glory with His Church to establish the promised Davidic Kingdom. He shall reign for one thousand years during which time peace and righteousness will cover the earth, Satan shall be bound, and Israel shall be established in her own land. At the end of this glorious reign, Satan shall lead a rebellion against Christ, shall be defeated, and shall be forever banished to the Lake of Fire. The wicked dead shall be judged at the Great White Throne, and shall be condemned to everlasting conscious punishment in the Lake of Fire. The righteous shall be in eternal conscious blessedness in the presence of the Lord (John 14:3; Matt. 24:21; Rev. 19:11–16; 21:1–15; Ezek. 39:25–29; 1 Thess. 4:17).

Select Bibliography for Further Reading

Beale, David. *The Mayflower Pilgrims: Roots of Puritan, Presbyterian, Congregationalist, and Baptist Heritage.* Greenville, SC: Ambassador-Emerald International, 2000.

Burgess, Walter H. *John Smyth the Se-Baptist, Thomas Helwys, and the First Baptist Church in England, with Fresh Light upon the Pilgrim Fathers' Church.* London: James Clarke, 1911.

Coggins, James R. *John Smyth's Congregation: English Separatism, Mennonite Influence, and the Elect Nation.* Scottdale, PA: Herald Press, 1991.

Dexter, Henry Martyn. *The True Story of John Smyth: The Se-Baptist.* Boston: Lee and Shepard, 1881.

Durso, Keith E. *No Armor for the Back: Baptist Prison Writings, 1600s–1700s.* Macon, GA: Mercer University Press, 2007.

Early, Joe Jr., ed. *The Life and Writings of Thomas Helwys.* Macon, GA: Mercer University Press, 2009.

Haykin, Michael A. G., ed. *The British Particular Baptists: 1638-1910.* 3 vols. Springfield, MO: Particular Baptist Press, 1998-2003.

Jeter, Jeremiah B., et al. *Baptist Principles Reset: Consisting of a Series of Articles on Distinctive Baptist Principles.* Richmond: Religious Herald, 1901.

McGlothlin, W. J. *Baptist Confessions of Faith.* Philadelphia: American Baptist Publication Society, 1911.

Naylor, Peter. *Picking up a Pin for the Lord: English Particular Baptists from 1688 to the Early Nineteenth Century.* London: Grace Publications Trust, 1992.

Payne, Ernest A. *Thomas Helwys and the First Baptist Church in England.* 2nd ed. London: Baptist Union of Great Britain and Ireland, 1966.

Smyth, John. *The Works of John Smyth, Fellow of Christ's College, 1594-8.* Edited by W. T. Whitley. 2 vols. Cambridge: Cambridge University Press, 1915.

Wallace, O. C. S. *What Baptists Believe: The New Hampshire Confession, An Exposition.* Nashville: Sunday-School Board, Southern Baptist Convention, 1913.

White, B. R., ed. *Association Records of the Particular Baptists of England, Wales and Ireland to 1660.* 3 vols. + index vol. London: Baptist Historical Society, 1971-77.

———. *English Baptists of the Seventeenth Century.* Rev. London: Baptist Historical Society, 1996.

11

The Rise and Development of Unitarianism in America

Unitarianism is the heretical doctrine that denies the Trinity and teaches that God exists in only one person (Unipersonalism). American Unitarianism derived from England, where its earliest traces include the posthumous publication of a Latin work by John Milton (1608–74), *Angli De Doctrina Christiana* (*A Treatise on Christian Doctrine*). Not only is the work a systemization of the doctrines that Milton taught his pupils, but it is also the author's theological preparation for *Paradise Lost* and *Paradise Regained*. It serves as a virtual commentary on the esoteric language of major sections of the those works. Here are samples of Milton's aggressive arguments for an Arian subordination of Christ.

Commenting on Colossians 1:15–18 Milton avows, "When the Son is said to be *the first born of every creature*, and *the beginning of the creation of God*, nothing can be more evident than that God of his own will created, or generated, or produced the Son before all things, endued with the divine nature, as in the fullness of time he miraculously begat him in his human nature of the Virgin Mary." On Hebrews 1:1–2, Milton writes, "It must be understood from this, that God imparted to the Son as much as he pleased of the divine nature." Milton then makes it clear that he denies the Son's coessentiality with the Father.[1] On Jesus' declaration in John 10:30,

---

[1] "Of the Son of God," bk. 1, chap. 5, in *A Treatise on Christian Doctrine*, trans. Charles R. Sumner (Cambridge: Cambridge University Press, 1825), 87. Milton

"I and my Father are one," Milton asserts that Jesus "declares himself to be one with the Father in the same manner as we are one with him."[2] On Thomas's confession in John 20:28, "My Lord and my God," Milton asserts that "my Lord" is Jesus and "my God" is the Father.[3] To Milton, "The whole doctrine of the Trinity has been hastily adopted."[4] While Milton's *Areopagitica* was a brilliant defense for the freedom of the press in behalf of the Puritans, Milton was no Puritan. In like manner, Thomas Jefferson, in spite of his unorthodoxy, would advocate a broad religious freedom in America.

Thomas Jefferson (1743–1826), author of the Declaration of Independence and the third president of the United States, loathed every cardinal tenet of Christian orthodoxy, especially Calvinism. It is difficult to determine how early Jefferson began his departure from his orthodox Anglican upbringing, but it was likely during his college years at William and Mary (1760–62), where he would have heard the most radical Enlightenment ideas. The following two letters, written by Jefferson late in life, furnish something of a résumé of this man's unbelief, as well as his bitter hatred of orthodox Christianity. With the hope that every young man in America would grow up to be a Unitarian, Jefferson described Athanasius and John Calvin as "impious dogmatists":

> Verily I say these [Athanasius and Calvin] are the false shepherds foretold as to enter not by the door into the sheepfold, but to climb up some other way. They are mere usurpers of the Christian name, teaching a counter religion made up of the *deliria* of crazy imaginations, as foreign from Christianity as is that of Mahomet. Their blasphemies have driven thinking men into infidelity, who have too hastily rejected the supposed Author himself, with the horrors so falsely imputed to Him. Had the doctrines of Jesus been preached always as pure as they came from his lips, the whole

---

adamantly defends the practice of polygamy (231–32). His unhappy marriages led to his publishing *The Doctrine and Discipline of Divorce* (1644), in which he argues that mere incompatibility is legitimate grounds for a man to divorce his wife. Milton adds that the wife has no grounds for divorcing her husband!

[2] *A Treatise on Christian Doctrine*, 94–95.

[3] Ibid., 112–13.

[4] Ibid., 171; cf. John P. Rumrich, "Milton's Arianism: Why It Matters," in *Milton and Heresy*, ed. Stephen Dobranski and John P. Rumrich (Cambridge, England: Cambridge University Press, 1998), 75–92.

civilized world would now have been Christian. I rejoice that in this blessed country of free inquiry and belief, which has surrendered its creed and conscience to neither kings nor priests, the genuine doctrine of one only God is reviving, and I trust that there is not a young man now living in the United States who will not die a Unitarian.[5]

Chronology of Unitarianism
(with key events and dates for Universalism)

- 325: Nicene Creed condemns Arianism.

- 1551: Michael Servetus publishes *On the Errors of the Trinity*. In 1553 he is burned in Geneva, Switzerland as the Unitarians' "first martyr."

- 1579: Fausto Sozzini (1539–1604), perhaps better known as Faustus Socinus, arrives in Poland teaching unitarian doctrine. His followers were called Socinians. Rakow Press is established in Poland in 1585 as the first official Socinian (Unitarian) press.

- 1712: Samuel Clarke, English Unitarian, publishes his book, *The Scripture-Doctrine of the Trinity*.[6] Clarke was a master at applying the Cartesian method[7] of compiling numerous Scripture verses in such an arrangement as to make the Bible appear to contradict itself. Its intent was to raise doubt.

- 1740: Ebenezer Gay begins openly preaching Unitarianism at the Old Ship (First) Church in Hingham, Massachusetts. This church had originated as a Puritan church. The quaint building is one of the oldest in America. It later became officially Unitarian.

---

[5] Thomas Jefferson, *The Writings of Thomas Jefferson*, the memorial edition, ed. Albert E. Bergh, 20 vols. (Washington, DC: Washington Jefferson Memorial Association, 1903–04), 15:383–85; cf. 15:322–24.

[6] Samuel Clarke, *The Scripture-Doctrine of the Trinity* (London: Printed for James Knapton, at the Crown in St. Paul's Church-Yard, 1712).

[7] The philosophical system of René Descartes (*Renatus Cartesius*) 1596–1650 was popular among early Unitarians.

- 1756: A Unitarian book by Thomas Emlyn of London is reprinted in America. It is titled *An Humble Inquiry into the Scripture Account of Jesus Christ* (1702). Emlyn was said to have been the first preacher to designate himself as a Unitarian.

- 1774: Theophilus Lindsey opens Essex Street Chapel in London, marking the beginning of an official and permanent Unitarian denomination in England. Lindsey publishes a new *Book of Common Prayer Reformed according to the Plan of the Late Dr. Samuel Clarke.*[8]

- 1782: James Freeman, a Unitarian, becomes rector of King's Chapel, Boston. The church had originated in 1686 as Boston's first Anglican congregation. Freeman transforms it into America's first official Unitarian church.

- 1784: Charles Chauncy (1705–87), pastor of Boston's First Church and long-time liberal opponent of Jonathan Edwards and the Great Awakening, opens the door for Unitarianism with the publication of his full defense of Universalism, *The Mystery Hid from Ages and Generations, Made Manifest by the Gospel-Revelation: or, the Salvation of All Men* (London: Charles Dilly).[9] The ablest treatise brought out against Chauncy's work would be that of Jonathan Edwards Jr., *The Salvation of All Men Strictly Examined: and the Endless Punishment of Those Who Die Impenitent, Argued and Defended Against the Objections and Reasonings of the Late Rev. Doctor Chauncy of Boston* (New Haven, CT: A. Morse, 1790).

- 1785: King's Chapel modifies its Prayer Book to exclude references to the Trinity.

- 1785: Harvard awards an honorary DD degree to Ebenezer Gay of Old Ship Church in Hingham. Gay is often called the Father of American Unitarianism. His wife, Jerusha, was a great granddaughter of the Pilgrim Governor William Bradford. Gay's successor at the Old Ship Church was Henry Ware Sr. (1764–1845).

---

[8] Theophilus Lindsey, *Book of Common Prayer Reformed according to the Plan of the Late Dr. Samuel Clarke* (London: J. Johnson, 1774).

[9] See especially pp. 1–3 and 7–13.

- 1794: Joseph Priestley, the English scientist, comes to America and organizes two Unitarian churches in Pennsylvania.

- 1801: First Church of Plymouth, Massachusetts, calls Unitarian James Kendall as pastor. Half of the members leave and organize "Third Church," where Adoniram Judson Sr. becomes first to supply the new pulpit; he takes as his text, 2 Corinthians 6:17, "Come out from among them. . . ." (Judson Jr., later a missionary to Burma, was then fourteen years old). In 1870 the new church in Plymouth would be named the Church and Society of the Pilgrimage.

- 1803: William Ellery Channing, a Unitarian, becomes pastor of Federal St. Church, Boston.

- 1805: Hosea Ballou publishes *A Treatise on Atonement*, the first Unitarian book published in America. Ballou is also well known as a Universalist.

- 1805: Joseph Stevens Buckminster, a Unitarian, becomes pastor at Brattle Street Church, Boston.

- 1805: Of Boston's nine Congregational churches, only Old South is now orthodox.

- 1805: Henry Ware Sr. (1764–1845), a Unitarian, is appointed Hollis Professor of Divinity at Harvard (replacing the orthodox David Tappan).

- 1805: Jedidiah Morse, "Sketches of the Life and Character of Rev. David Tappan, D.D.," *Panoplist, or, the Christian's Armory* 1, no. 1 (June 1805): 1–5. This is the initial article in the high-quality Trinitarian journal established and edited by the famed geographer. He was a leading voice against Unitarianism. One of his sons was Samuel F. B. Morse, inventor of the Morse Code.[10]

- 1808: Andover Theological Seminary is founded (Trinitarian and New Divinity) as a reaction to Harvard's Unitarian takeover.

- 1809: Park Street Church in Boston is founded as Trinitarian. Its first pastor was Edward Dorr Griffin, a Hopkinsian (New

---

[10] See William B. Sprague, *The Life of Jedidiah Morse, D. D.* (New York: Anson D. F. Randolph, 1874).

Divinity). Harold Ockenga, "Father of New Evangelicalism," would begin his pastorate here in 1948.

- 1817: Henry Ware Jr. (1798–1843), a Unitarian, becomes pastor of Boston's Second Church, established in 1650 by the Mather family. In 1830, Ware would join his father on the Harvard faculty as professor of Pastoral Theology and Pulpit Eloquence.

- 1818: The First Parish Church of Dedham, Massachusetts, over the strong protest of two-thirds of its active membership, votes to ordain a Unitarian as their new pastor. The "parish" was the church's designated local community. Although most "parishioners" seldom attended church, they owned the right to vote. The Unitarians had gone out and rounded them up for this vote. The ordination council included Unitarians William E. Channing, Henry Ware, and Harvard president John Kirkland. The Trinitarians appealed to the civil court and the case reached the Massachusetts Supreme Court. See below for the 1820 outcome.

- 1819: William E. Channing preaches his famous sermon, *Unitarian Christianity*, at Jared Spark's ordination in Baltimore.[11] The sermon was later hailed as the "The Unitarian Manifesto."

- 1820: The "Dedham Decision" is rendered by the Massachusetts Supreme Court, giving the Unitarian parishes ownership of the Congregational churches whenever Trinitarians separate from them. Judge Parker who rendered the decision was a Unitarian. The result was that most of the original or "first" churches became Unitarian and kept their properties. Trinitarians called it "parish despotism."[12]

- 1825: The American Unitarian Association is founded in Boston.

- 1833: Disestablishment is finally realized in Massachusetts. Since the 1820 Dedham Decision, Unitarians had acquired ownership of about one hundred fully-furnished church buildings, as

---

[11] William E. Channing, *Discourses, Reviews, and Miscellanies* (Boston: Gray and Bowen, 1830), 289–332.

[12] Henry Ware, *Letters Addressed to Trinitarians and Calvinists* (Cambridge, MA: Hilliard and Metcalf, 1820), see especially pp. 20–21 and 23–31.

Trinitarian majorities had withdrawn. On top of that, state taxes had continued supporting Unitarian churches.[13]

- 1961: The Unitarians and Universalists merge to form the American Unitarian Universalist Association.

Transcendentalism

William Ellery Channing was the major bridge from Unitarianism to Transcendentalism. Ralph Waldo Emerson's *Nature* was published in 1836, the same year that the first Transcendentalist club was established in Boston. Emerson's 1838 *Divinity School Address* at Harvard established the movement's popularity among a number of social elites. Other Transcendentalists included Theodore Parker and Margaret Fuller. Transcendentalism finds "the voice of God in the soul of man." Emphasizing a pantheistic unity of "God" and the world, Transcendentalism argued that since each person is divine, one can, by looking inwardly, have an emotional, intuitive, communication with "deity." Such subjective experience was more authoritative to them than any mere "external object" such as the Bible. While Unitarianism looked primarily to French and German rationalism, Transcendentalism looked to the idealism of Plato's Greek philosophy and of Kant's German philosophy, as well as oriental mysticism, Hinduism, and Buddhism.

Immanuel Kant (1724–1804), especially in his *Critique of Pure Reason*, became the leading source for most Transcendentalists. Kant, whose own idol was Plato, claimed that there is a world of "things in themselves" that lies beyond the senses, and which science can never penetrate. Such a metaphysical realm formed the essence of Transcendentalist philosophy, which claimed that the visible world is only the "garment" that clothes the true, ultimate, and invisible, reality.

---

[13] Steven K. Green, *The Second Disestablishment: Church and State in Nineteenth-Century America* (Oxford: Oxford University Press, 2010), 143.

Contrasts

Unitarianism	Transcendentalism
Stagnant	Enthusiastic
Formed churches	Formed clubs
Logical	Mystical
Materialistic	Idealistic
Rationalism	Romanticism
Facts	Metaphysical inspiration
Outward	Inward
Led to skepticism	Led to sentimentalism

Summary

- Calvinism teaches that man is essentially depraved.
- Unitarianism teaches that man is essentially good.
- Transcendentalism teaches that man is essentially divine.

Select Bibliography for Further Reading

Capper, Charles, and Conrad E. Wright, eds. *Transient and Permanent: The Transcendentalist Movement and Its Contexts*. Boston: Massachusetts Historical Society, 1999.

Cassara, Ernest, ed. *Universalism in America: A Documentary History of a Liberal Faith*. Boston: Skinner House, 1997.

Cooke, George W. *Unitarianism in America: A History of Its Origin and Development*. New York: AMS Press, 1971.

Dobranski, Stephen B., and John P. Rumrich, eds. *Milton and Heresy*. Cambridge: Cambridge University Press, 1998.

Haroutunian, Joseph. *Piety versus Moralism: The Passing of the New England Theology*. 1932. Reprint, New York: Harper and Row, 1970.

Harris, Mark W. *Historical Dictionary of Unitarian Universalism*. Lanham, MD: Scarecrow Press, 2003.

Holifield, E. Brooks. *Theology in America: Christian Thought from the Age of the Puritans to the Civil War*. New Haven, CT: Yale University Press, 2003.

Miller, Perry, ed. *The American Transcendentalists: Their Prose and Poetry*. Baltimore: Johns Hopkins University Press, 1957.

———. *Transcendentalists: An Anthology*. Cambridge: Harvard University Press, 1950.

Milton, John. *A Treatise on Christian Doctrine*. Translated by Charles R. Sumner. Cambridge: Cambridge University Press, 1825.

Mott, Wesley T., ed. *Encyclopedia of Transcendentalism*. Westport, CT: Greenwood Press, 1996.

Schofield, Robert E. *The Enlightenment of Joseph Priestley: A Study of His Life and Work from 1733 to 1773*. University Park: Pennsylvania State University Press, 1997.

Scovel, Carl, and Charles C. Forman. *Journey Toward Independence: King's Chapel's Transition to Unitarianism*. Boston: Skinner House Books, 1993.

Strong, Augustus Hopkins. "Milton." In *The Great Poets and Their Theology*. 221–77. Philadelphia: American Baptist Publication Society, 1897.

Wright, Conrad E., ed. *American Unitarianism, 1805–1865*. Boston: Massachusetts Historical Society, 1999.

———. *The Unitarian Controversy: Essays on American Unitarian History*. Boston: Skinner House Books, 1994.

12

Harvard College (1636–1805): Puritanism to Unitarianism

In this chapter we will trace the spiritual, doctrinal, and moral rise and demise of Harvard College,[1] the Puritans' first school of higher learning in America. While New England's earliest nonconformist Puritans settled Salem in 1628, it was Boston with her fine harbor that soon became the focus of the Massachusetts Bay Colony. Deeply concerned for the education of their youth, the Puritans acquired a charter from the English Crown in 1636 to found a college in Cambridge, just across the Charles River. Their express purpose was to train successors for their churches. The plaque on the brick wall,[2] just outside the Johnston Gate at Harvard Yard, captures their words:

> After God had carried us safe to New England
>
> and we had builded our houses,
>
> provided necessaries for our livelihood,
>
> reared convenient places for God's worship,

---

[1] Major histories of Harvard include Samuel F. Batchelder, *Bits of Harvard History* (Cambridge: Harvard University Press, 1924); Samuel Morison, *The Founding of Harvard College* (Cambridge: Harvard University Press, 1968); Samuel Morison, *Harvard College in the Seventeenth Century*, 2 vols. (Cambridge: Harvard University Press, 1936); and Samuel Morison, *Three Centuries of Harvard 1636–1936* (Cambridge: Harvard University Press, 1964). See also Donald G. Tewksbury, *The Founding of American Colleges and Universities before the Civil War: With Particular Reference to the Religious Influences Bearing upon the College Movement* (New York: Columbia University, 1932).

[2] *New England's First Fruits* (London: Overton, 1643). The text appears also in Samuel E. Morison's *Founding of Harvard College*, appendix D.

and settled the civil government,
one of the next things we longed for
and looked after was to advance learning
and perpetuate it to posterity,
dreading to leave an illiterate ministry
to the churches when our present ministers
shall lie in the dust.

The founders named the college for John Harvard (1607–38), who having no children willed half of his estate and his entire library to the school. This contribution amounted to some four hundred books and between £700 and £850.[3] The school opened its doors in 1637 with Nathaniel Eaton as headmaster. By 1639, he was unsuccessfully defending himself against bitter charges of failing to feed the students properly and of being a tyrant. The school quickly ousted him, and the church excommunicated him. Eaton and his wife escaped to Virginia while the college closed temporarily to recover from its failed beginnings.

In 1640, Henry Dunster,[4] a Cambridge graduate, became Harvard's first president and real founder, serving until 1654. Dunster arguably was the best president ever to serve Harvard. He not only set the academic, moral, and spiritual standards that prevailed for generations, but he also established a permanent administrative and financial base for the institution:

> Dunster found Harvard College deserted by students, devoid of buildings, wanting income or endowment, and unprovided with government or statutes. He left it a flourishing university college of the arts, provided with several buildings and a settled though insufficient income, governed under the Charter of 1650 by a body of fellows and officers whose duties were regulated by statute. The Harvard College created under his presidency and largely through his efforts endured in all essential features until

---

[3] A good biography of John Harvard is Henry C. Shelley, *John Harvard and His Times* (Boston: Little, Brown, 1907).

[4] Biographies of Henry Dunster include Arseny James Melnick, *America's Oldest Corporation and First CEO: Harvard & Henry Dunster* (West Conshohocken, PA: Infinity, 2008); Samuel Dunster, *Henry Dunster and His Descendants* (Central Falls, RI: E. L. Freeman, 1876); and Jeremiah Chaplin, *Life of Henry Dunster, First President of Harvard College* (Boston: James R. Osgood, 1872).

the nineteenth century, and in some respects has persisted in the great university of today.[5]

Equally important, Dunster set respectable academic standards, not unlike the colleges of Scotland, Ireland, England, and the Continent. Entrance requirements included first, the ability to read basic classical Latin and to make practical use of it. Second, the applicant had to know the basic vocabulary and declensions of New Testament Greek. Most importantly, however, the young scholar, once enrolled, could never escape the constant reminders of the primary purpose of life, the primary purpose of his Harvard training, and the only source of all wisdom. The statement is as follows:

1. When any Scholar is able to understand Tully,[6] or such like classical Latin author extempore, and make and speak true Latin in verse and prose, *suo ut aiunt Marte*;[7] And decline perfectly the paradigms of nouns and verbs in the Greek tongue: Let him then and not before be capable of admission into the College.

2. Let every student be plainly instructed, and earnestly pressed to consider well, the main end of his life and studies is, *to know God and Jesus Christ which is eternal life*, John 17:3, and therefore to lay *Christ* in the bottom as the only foundation of all sound knowledge and learning. And seeing the Lord only giveth wisdom, let every one seriously set himself by prayer in secret to seek it of him. Prov. 2–3.[8]

Dunster combined scholarship with Christian compassion and godliness.[9] He believed that the only reason for education was the

---

[5] Morison, *Founding of Harvard College*, 246.

[6] In the 17th century, the word *Tully* referred to the Latin of Cicero (*Marcus Tullius Ciceronis*).

[7] The expression *suo (ut aiunt) Marte* was a Latin proverb, meaning "by one's own power," or "without any assistance." It was seldom translated from the Latin.

[8] *New England's First Fruits* (London: Overton, 1643).

[9] Indicative of this was his promotion of the founding of a school for American Indians at Harvard. Concerned for providing the New England Indians with a good education, Dunster took seriously the statement in the Charter of 1650 that one of the institution's purposes was "the education of the English and Indian Youth of this Country." Consequently, the Commissioners and the Corporation approved the financing of a substantial brick structure in Harvard Yard. Completed about a year after Dunster himself left the school, the building could accommodate some twenty students. Unfortunately, only about half a dozen young men attended Harvard's Indian College, and only one of these completed the four-year program (class of 1665); he died within a year of graduation. Only

cultivation of spirituality for God's glory. Spiritual and intellectual discipline was at the forefront of his curriculum, as Batchelder unsympathetically notes:

> The spiritual life of the undergraduates—the only thing that really mattered in this vale of tears—was pried into, dissected, and stimulated with relentless vigor. The scholars read the Scriptures twice a day; . . . they had to repeat or epitomize the sermons preached on Sunday, and were frequently examined as to their own religious state. . . . (At first, the sole requirement for the degree of A.B. was the ability "to read the original of the Old and New Testament into the Latin tongue and to resolve them logically.") Morning prayers were held at an hour that would have made an anchorite [monastic] blush.[10]

After fourteen years of faithful service, however, Henry Dunster became a problem to Harvard's General Court of Overseers. Dunster had become a Baptist, refusing to present his newborn fourth child, Jonathan, to the church for baptism. Dunster had come to reject infant baptism and he could not remain silent about this conviction, which he considered to be Bible-based. After public debates with notable Puritans such as John Norton and Richard Mather, Dunster would not budge on his conviction that infant baptism was unknown in the primitive church until well into the third century. Morison observes that Dunster "not only believed infant baptism to be unscriptural; he meant to testify against it upon every proper opportunity. Incidentally, Dunster was right. Infant baptism was unknown in the Christian Church until more than two centuries after the death of Christ."[11]

As a Baptist, however, Dunster had an ethical obligation to resign his position. Infant baptism was essential to the covenant theology of the legally established, tax-supported ecclesiastical "Standing Order"

---

one of them lived more than a decade after attending classes. The Indian College, however, is symbolic of a sincere Christian mission to help Native Americans. Although the school's records provide no specifics, the Puritans must have offered some concessions to assist these students in overcoming their deficiencies with the entrance requirements. The Indian College maintained its feeble existence into the next century. See Alden T. Vaughan, *New England Frontier: Puritans and Indians 1620–1675* (Boston: Little, Brown, 1965), 280–85.

[10] Batchelder, 4.

[11] *Harvard College in the Seventeenth Century*, 1:308.

of this Puritan colony. Knowing, however, that even his family's security would soon be in jeopardy outside the establishment, he felt compelled to enunciate his convictions while he still had a platform. The Court ousted Dunster and persuaded Charles Chauncy (1592–1672) to accept the call to the presidency. Dunster had contributed to the college a hundred acres of land,[12] on which he had built the president's home with his own hands. In this home, Dunster had operated the first printing press in America since 1640, turning out the first printed works in this country. Dunster, with his friend and assistant, Richard Lyon, had revised the venerable *Bay Psalm Book*. This revision, the *Dunster-Lyon Psalm Book*, first published in 1651, had become so popular by the time of Dunster's dismissal that the churches used it for more than a century after his death.[13] Now, with a sick family and winter approaching, he received an order to vacate the home, which indeed held many pleasant memories. Dunster pleaded in behalf of his beloved family, but received little sympathy:

> Apparently the Overseers were more eager to get the new president installed than to make the old president comfortable; for we find Dunster again addressing the General Court on November 16. It was a moving and pathetic appeal to their humane sentiments. Winter was coming on; he and his young family had no knowledge of the place whither they were destined; their goods and cattle could be moved at that season only with great loss; Mrs. Dunster was ill and the baby too "extremely sick" for a long journey.[14]

The General Court of Overseers allowed Dunster to remain in the house until March, but constantly hounded him with new legal proceedings over his objections to infant baptism. This continued

---

[12] Isaac Backus, *A History of New England with Particular Reference to the Denomination of Christians Called Baptists* (Boston: Edward Draper, 1777), 1:96, 227–30; and Isaac Backus, *A History of New England with Particular Reference to the Denomination of Christians Called Baptists,* 2nd ed. (Newton, MA: Backus Historical Society, 1871), 2:418.

[13] The 26th ed. of the *Dunster-Lyon Psalm Book* is titled *The Psalmes, Hymns, and Spiritual Songs of the Old and New Testament[s]: Faithfully Translated into English Metre; for the Use, Edification, and Comfort of the Saints in Publick and Private, Especially in New England* (Boston: J. Draper, 1744). It was used in New England and Scottish churches until Thomas Prince of Boston's Old South Church produced a new metrical edition in 1758.

[14] Morison, *Harvard College in the Seventeenth Century,* 1:313.

until 1655, long after the family had moved. The Court constantly deprived the Dunster family of peace and quiet. Dunster assisted in the establishment of the First Baptist Church in Boston, and then moved to Scituate, in Plymouth Colony, where he ministered until his death in 1659. In his will, he left legacies to the persons who had forced his resignation. He directed that his body be interred in Cambridge, near the school and the people that he had served. Harvard did not in any way "fall" with Dunster's dismissal in 1654. Indeed, the school would not show signs of decline until the late 1600s. Following Dunster, five presidents served during the period of 1654 to 1701: Charles Chauncy,[15] Leonard Hoar,[16] Urian Oakes, John Rogers,[17] and Increase Mather. Each of these continued to be an example of strong character, scholarship, and spiritual depth. The school began to show signs of subtle change during Increase Mather's administration, not because of Mather's presence, but because of his frequent absence and in spite of his strong Puritan character and preaching. The new changes, which tutors and administrators instigated and promoted behind Mather's back, seemed practical in nature; but they were indicators that a new generation was tired of some of the old Puritan convictions and practices.

Increase Mather was the last strong Puritan president, serving from 1685 to 1701. He was the youngest of Richard Mather's six sons, graduating from Harvard in 1656 and taking a second degree at Trinity College, Dublin. Later he became pastor of Boston's Second Church. He married Maria, the daughter of John Cotton, and ten

---

[15] Charles Chauncy, a Cambridge graduate, served as Harvard's president from 1654 to 1672. Although inconsistent with Puritan practice, Chauncy thought that baptism should be by immersion, both for adults and infants. However, he was willing, unlike Dunster, to silence such a view in order to satisfy the expected qualifications for the presidency. His scholarship was considered profound, even in the field of medicine. He was up at four in the morning in all seasons. All six of his sons became Harvard graduates.

[16] Leonard Hoar, a Harvard graduate, was also awarded an honorary degree from Cambridge University after taking a course there. Like Chauncy, he studied medicine. His presidency was only three years—1672–75.

[17] Urian Oakes served as president from 1675 to 1681. He was a Harvard graduate and was noted for his proficiency in astronomy. John Rogers served as president from 1682 to 1684. He was a Harvard graduate and a descendant of John Rogers, the martyr who was burned at Smithfield, England, during the reign of Bloody Mary.

children were born into their home. Increase Mather was one of the last of the old-line Puritans. He wrote 136 volumes, and his son Cotton wrote his life's story, which indeed is full of sadness. He witnessed the fall of the beloved Puritanism that his parents had taught him. He stood opposed to the Salem witchcraft trials of 1692–93, which only hastened Puritanism's decline and caricatured it in the popular mind. Other prominent Puritans likewise stood opposed to the trials; this, however, did not stop public condemnation of a movement that was fast becoming a thing of the past.

Mather could no more change the new generation's mindset and direction than he could change the course of the winds blowing across the Charles River. His young colleagues regarded him as too conservative, unmovable, and out of touch with their generation. It is true that he was more of a pastor than a college administrator. His attention was also drawn away from the daily affairs of the college by serious problems with the English Crown. In 1686, Harvard lost its temporary charter of 1650. For four years of his presidency (1688–92), Mather was compelled to be absent in England while attempting to secure a permanent charter. During his trips abroad, some were promoting a new spirit of innovation on the campus.

In 1699, Harvard treasurer Thomas Brattle, known as "the wealthiest man living in New England," joined with his brother William, a Harvard tutor, and John Leverett, another tutor, to establish the Brattle Street Church in Boston.[18] Known as the "Manifesto Church," Brattle Street immediately issued a manifesto[19] calling for an innovative "broad and catholic"[20] spirit of the times. Increase Mather, while mentioning no names, warned that the manifesto was liberal and destructive.[21] Persuaded that Mather's presence was an

---

[18] Samuel Kirkland Lothrop, *A History of the Church in Brattle Street, Boston* (Boston: Wm. Crosby and H. P. Nichols, 1851).

[19] *The Manifesto Church: Records of the Church in Brattle Square Boston 1699–1872* (Boston: Benevolent Fraternity of Churches, 1902).

[20] See Williston Walker, *The Creeds and Platforms of Congregationalism* (1893; repr., Boston: Pilgrim Press, 1960), 472–83.

[21] Increase Mather, *The Order of the Gospel Professed and Practiced by the Churches of Christ in New-England, Justified by the Scripture and by the Writings of Many Learned Men, Both Ancient and Modern Divines: in Answer to Questions Relating to Church Discipline* (Boston: Printed by B. Green and J. Allen for Nicholas Buttolph, 1700), 8.

obstacle, the innovators found a sympathizer in Samuel Willard, pastor of Boston's Old South Church.[22] Willard became the vice president of Harvard in 1700. Mather's friends frequently informed him of increasing campus talk of a plan to replace him as president. Mather's first love was across the Charles River at Boston's Second Church.[23] Even though his trips by horseback and ferry from Cambridge to Boston would have taken a good two hours, it was no secret to anyone that he would never move permanently from his Boston parsonage. The General Court set into motion a scheme for accomplishing Mather's removal. It was not complicated. The Court simply passed a law stating that "no man should act as president who did not reside [at the College] in Cambridge." Mather actually resided there for several weeks, but then resigned. Samuel Willard, serving as acting president from 1701 to 1707, set out to establish a Manifesto ecclesiology that would result in the repudiation of Harvard's Christian heritage. John Leverett, Harvard's president from 1708 to 1724, helped to initiate new liturgical practices that rapidly became popular in a large number of churches. The process of innovation was twofold and in this order: (1) heteropraxis (ἑτεροπρᾶξις) in liturgy, church membership, and morals; and (2) heterodoxy (ἑτεροδοξία) in fundamental theological themes. Beginning with heteropraxis, there were four primary stages.

First, *an aggressive promotion of the Half-Way Covenant ensued.* The English Reformation had turned Roman Catholic churches into Protestant churches by royal proclamation, with no requirement of personal conversion.[24] No method was in place for promoting the purity of the churches. Many early Puritans believed that conversion was a lifetime process. The earliest records of a few conversion narratives are from the 1640s. In New England during the first decade (1630s), the Puritans had only two prerequisites for Communion

---

[22] Hamilton Andrews Hill, *History of the Old South Church (Third Church) Boston 1669–1884*, 2 vols. (Boston: Houghton, Mifflin, 1890).

[23] Chandler Robbins, *A History of the Second Church, or Old North, in Boston* (Boston: John Wilson & Son, 1852).

[24] Among the most helpful discussions on this topic are Edmund S. Morgan, *The Puritan Dilemma: The Story of John Winthrop* (Boston: Little, Brown, 1958); and Edmund S. Morgan, *Visible Saints: The History of a Puritan Idea* (1963; repr., Ithaca, NY: Cornell University Press, 1965).

at the Lord's Supper and full membership: (1) infant baptism and (2) giving "consent unto the Confession of faith and the Covenant."[25] It was not until the 1640s that the ruling elders began with some consistency to examine in private those who desired Communion and full membership. The peak years of the Great Puritan migration to New England had been the 1630s, when nominal Christians had quickly taken their places within the membership of newly gathered churches. The sudden requirement of a public testimony of conversion created an enormous conflict. Would baptized parents who professed to be "Christians," but not born-again Christians, be permitted to present their newborn babies for baptism?

Puritan ministers addressed that question in 1662 and presented their decisions in a document known as the Half-Way Covenant. The Covenant stated that, by living free of scandal, all baptized professing Christians who had not yet experienced saving faith should continue in the church as half-way members and should bring their infants for baptism. Half-way members were to "own the covenant," that is, to subscribe to it, though it would not be considered as genuine. There was hope that the covenant could become a means of saving grace. Communion and full membership would require an eventual, sincere testimony of personal conversion. Thus, the churches of New England continued to receive half-way members who eventually voted themselves into full membership by virtue of their increasing majority status. Increase Mather himself came to accept the Half-Way Covenant. His own father, Richard, had drafted the document as an emergency measure of keeping order in the churches. A decade later Increase Mather wrote, "The body of the rising generation is a poor, perishing, unconverted, and (except the Lord pour down His Spirit) an undone generation."[26] The old Puritans had themselves set the table for innovation.

---

[25] Cotton Mather, "Propositions Concerning the Office of Ruling-Elders," section 6, book 5, in *Magnalia Christi Americana: Or, the Ecclesiastical History of New-England, from Its First Planting, in the Year 1620, unto the Year of Our Lord, 1698*, seven books (London: Thomas Parkhurst, 1702), 43.

[26] *Pray for the Rising Generation* (Cambridge, MA: Samuel Green, 1678); see also *The Christian History* no. 13 (May 28, 1743): 97–98.

Second, *there was an aggressive promotion of Stoddardism.* The popular Solomon Stoddard, Congregationalist pastor in Northampton, Massachusetts, insisted on admitting the moral, baptized, but unregenerate to the Lord's Supper and into full membership. (The description "unregenerate" freely occurs in the literature of the time.) His argument was that the church is Israel, baptism replaced circumcision, the whole assembly of Israel partook of the Passover meal, and the Lord's Supper is the Passover.[27] As for 1 Corinthians 11:20–34, Stoddardism taught that both the regenerates and the unregenerates should examine themselves. Any moral, sober person who would behave orderly at the Lord's Table would be deemed worthy to partake. Indeed, it was hoped that the Lord's Supper would be a means of saving grace—a "converting ordinance." Such belief was known as Stoddardism, and it became common practice across New England. Upon Stoddard's death his grandson and successor, Jonathan Edwards, would eventually abandon Stoddardism, but the church's membership already consisted of a mixed multitude. After the Awakening much of the old majority, many of whom had never experienced conversion, would succeed in voting Edwards out of the Northampton pastorate.

Third, *a shift in emphasis from preaching to ritual occurred.* The old Puritans, reacting against Anglican ceremonialism, had insisted that ministerial prayers should not be read from a "Prayer Book" and that when ministers read the Bible in public, they should expound it. Simple reading, without comment, they regarded as "dumb reading." Many ministers had not only lost their bite, but they had lost even their bark. The old Puritans insisted that preachers must have a divine call and a passion to communicate God's Word to a lost and dying people. With the popular "Manifesto" of Brattle Street calling for liturgical changes, there occurred a decided shift in emphasis from preaching to ritual.

Fourth, *there occurred the abolishing of the requirement for a personal public profession of faith.* The Manifesto Church advocated the replacement of personal testimonies with a simple congregational

---

[27] Actually, when Jesus distributed the bread and wine in the upper room, it was not the Passover "meal." It was Jesus' initiation of a simple ordinance for His people to observe from time to time "in remembrance" of Him (1 Cor. 11:25).

chant called "owning the covenant."[28] There would be no requirement for an individual public profession of faith in Christ as Lord and
Savior. This would not only keep the unregenerate in the churches,
but it would also keep them feeling good about themselves. It would
also spare the ministers the embarrassment of having so few in the
churches who could make a personal profession.[29]

The seeds of Puritanism's destruction rested in an erroneous
hermeneutical assumption that God was in federal covenant with
"New Canaan," so the next generation would turn out well. Now,
however, most of the churches were full of the unregenerates. The
new innovators were not totally to blame. They had inherited a mess.
The majority of the leaders who were departing from old Puritanism
were not theological liberals. They had no intention of promoting
error. Many of them still defended Calvinist soteriology as strongly
as their fathers had preached it. A wrong hermeneutical principle
had filled their churches with lost people, and the matter was out
of hand. Everything the innovators suggested sounded reasonable at
first sight. Their "marketing" techniques focused on the need to in-
still life in churches where people had simply "lost interest." Having
never been ordained or called to a pulpit ministry, President Leverett
put an end to the old tradition of calling Harvard the "School of the
Prophets" and its graduates the "Sons of the Prophets." Now they
were the "Sons of Harvard." Preaching no longer held the focus of
religious services.

Morison notes the wholesale departure from old Puritanism and
highlights Mather's frustration when people of the covenant seemed
so willing to abandon the orthopraxy of the original "New England
Way":

---

[28] The Puritans had founded the churches upon beautiful covenants. Here are
the first lines from a typical one: "We Covenant with the Lord, and one with
another; and we do bind ourselves in the presence of God, to walk together in all
his ways," from the "Original Covenant of the First Church in Salem," *The New
England Historical and Genealogical Register* 1, no. 3 (July 1847): 224–25.

[29] See Patricia Caldwell, *The Puritan Conversion Narrative: The Beginnings of
American Expression* (New York: Cambridge University Press, 1983). See also the
helpful definition in Daniel Reid, et al., eds., *Dictionary of Christianity in America*
(Downers Grove, IL: Intervarsity, 1990), 317.

The innovations adopted by this Brattle Street or "Manifesto" Church were all in matters of ecclesiastical polity; there was no dissent from the orthodox puritan theology professed by the New England churches. The practice of public confession of religious experiences before admission to the Lord's Supper was abandoned; the Lord's Prayer was used; the Bible was read without comment; all children of professing Christians, whether communicants or not, were admitted to baptism. These changes in "Gospel order," trivial and innocent enough as they seem to us, were really a significant challenge to the New England Way. The Mathers . . . could understand wolves trying to break down the puritan "hedge," but they had no patience with sheep trying to eat their way out.[30]

It was during this time (1721) that a generous Baptist merchant of London, Thomas Hollis (1659–1731), endowed the college with a divinity professorship, with the stipulation that the chair must be occupied by "a man of solid learning in divinity, of sound, or orthodox principles, one well gifted to teach, of a sober and pious life, and of a grave conversation."[31] The school's departure from its roots had already begun. While not all changes were wrong, some reflected an attitude of tolerance, irenicism, and a lack of spiritual perception, even in morals. During the presidency of Benjamin Wadsworth, 1725–37, restraint was unpopular and liberty was the byword, with students insisting on more freedom of expression. From the school's records, Morison describes the scene:

> It was an era of internal turbulence: for Wadsworth was no disciplinarian, and the young men resented a puritan restraint that was fast becoming obsolete. The faculty records, which begin with Wadsworth's administration, are full of "drinking frolicks," poultry-stealing, profane cursing and swearing, card-playing, live snakes in tutors' chambers, bringing "Rhum" into college rooms, and "shamefull and scandalous Routs and Noises for sundry nights in the College Yard."[32]

During Edward Holyoke's presidency (1737–69), covering the years of the Great Awakening, Harvard rejected the revival in favor

---

[30] *Harvard College in the Seventeenth Century*, 2:545.

[31] Alden Bradford, "Historical Sketch of Harvard University," *The Quarterly Register* 9, no. 4 (May 1837): 349–50, journal of the American Education Society.

[32] *Three Centuries of Harvard 1636–1936*, 78.

of academic freedom. From the time of the Brattle Manifesto, innovators had expressed extreme sympathy with latitudinarian Anglicanism, earlier known as "Cambridge Platonism," which was promoted even by the famous Whig, John Tillotson, archbishop of Canterbury, whose books Harvard tutors were highly recommending to students.[33] Conducive with Enlightenment reasoning, Cambridge Platonism led many to approach even the highest biblical truths, such as the Trinity, with enormous reliance upon human philosophies. At Harvard, signs of theological heterodoxy first appeared at this time. When George Whitefield visited the campus, he noted in his diary the careless attitudes prevalent. He complained of the anemic and dangerous doctrinal content in the popular books, such as those by Tillotson and Samuel Clarke, the English Unitarian. In 1739, three MA candidates gave the negative answer to the question as to "whether three Persons in the Godhead are revealed by the Old Testament." This is the first hint of a weak view of the Trinity at Harvard. The question was not whether the Trinity is explicitly taught in the Old Testament but whether three distinct persons of the Godhead are revealed. The candidates not only received their degrees, but also enjoyed the protection of the Overseers. Morison presents the scene:

> Harvard College and the Congregational Church were broadening down from primitive Calvinism to eighteenth-century theism or Unitarianism. This peaceful process was rudely interrupted by an evangelical revival known as the Great Awakening. The preliminary rumblings . . . did not disturb Cambridge; but in September, 1740, the whirlwind revivalist George Whitefield arrived in Boston, addressed fifteen thousand people on Boston Common, and on the twenty-fourth preached to students and townspeople in Cambridge meetinghouse. Harvard men were divided in opinion as to the wisdom and value of this first of modern revivals. . . . Conservatives who deplored the liberal tendencies of the age

---

[33] For more discussion see Charles Lyttle, "A Sketch of the Theological Development of Harvard University, 1636–1805," *Church History* 5, no. 4 (December 1936): 301–29.

were delighted at the straight hell-and-damnation Calvinism that Whitefield preached.[34]

Holyoke and his faculty immediately dubbed Whitefield "an uncharitable, censorious, and slanderous man."[35] Twenty years later, however, Whitefield would be strongly appealing in a letter to a well-to-do friend to donate "some useful puritanical books" to the college's library, which had suffered serious fire damage.[36] The gift, however, would be too late to change Harvard's direction.

Samuel Locke's presidency (1770–73) reflects yet another disappointment. He made his housemaid pregnant. The reason for his sudden resignation was not publicly known until the twentieth century. Morison reports:

> On the first of December, 1773, it was announced to an astonished public that Mr. Locke had resigned his exalted position. . . . No reason was given, and the Corporation . . . kept it a close secret. Not until the present century did it come to light, in the published Diary of President Ezra Stiles of Yale. A maidservant in the house of President Locke was great with child. Mr. Locke took the blame, retired to the country, and was promptly forgotten.[37]

Samuel Langdon, Locke's successor, served as president from 1774 to 1780 and attempted to rescue the college from apostasy. In the heat of the War for Independence, his fervent patriotism and trumpet call to battle won popular support. Following the war, however, the students rejected the preacher's voice, especially his intense expository preaching and fervent public prayers. The students humiliated Langdon with a hateful open letter that prompted his resignation, which in turn moved the students to deliver a commendation

---

[34] *Three Centuries of Harvard 1636–1936*, 84; cf. Alan Heimert and Perry Miller, eds., *The Great Awakening: Documents Illustrating the Crisis and its Consequences* (Indianapolis: Bobbs-Merrill, 1967), 340–53.

[35] *A Testimony from the President, Professors, Tutors and Hebrew Instructor of Harvard College, in Cambridge, against the Reverend Mr. George Whitefield and His Conduct* (Boston: T. Fleet, 1744), 10; Whitefield's kind response has been but seldom cited, but it is in *The Works of the Reverend George Whitefield* (London: Printed for Edward and Charles Dilly, in the Poultry; and Messrs. Kincaid and Bell, at Edinburgh, 1771–72), 4:225–26.

[36] Whitefield, *Works*, 3:307–08.

[37] *Three Centuries of Harvard 1636–1936*, 100.

and present him with a monetary farewell offering. Morison describes the scene:

> In the summer of 1780 the students drafted a petition to the Corporation for his removal. A committee of them had the boldness to inform the President what they proposed to do, and the insolence to address him in these words: "As a man of genius and knowledge we respect you; as a man of piety and virtue we venerate you; as a President we despise you." [With Langdon's resignation] the students were so sorry for the poor man that they sped his departure with a complimentary address and a subscription of money.[38]

Joseph Willard, president from 1781 to 1804, represents the last-ditch effort to rescue the school from apostasy. He once remarked that he "would sooner cut off his hand than lift it up for an Arminian professor." In the eighteenth century, the word *Arminian* was often used synonymously with *liberal*. Actually, "liberals" were pseudo-Arminians, as New Divinity men were pseudo-Calvinists. Willard, along with David Tappan, was an "Old Divinity Calvinist," a man who stood militantly and consistently against all doctrinal deviation. Tappan, the last orthodox Hollis Professor of Divinity, died in 1803 and Willard himself died the following year. The old guard had now passed off the scene. Eliphalet Pearson (acting president, 1804–06) tried to continue Willard's efforts to salvage the school. However, since the liberal board made all faculty appointments, Pearson could do nothing. When the board in 1805 replaced Tappan with a Unitarian, Henry Ware,[39] in the Hollis Chair of Divinity, Pearson immediately resigned from the presidency. The battle was over. Harvard was lost to Unitarianism. Samuel Webber immediately became the first Unitarian president (1806–10) of a Harvard whose typical student now possessed an atheistic mindset.[40]

It was also in 1805 that Brattle Street Church (est. 1699), "the Manifesto Church," became Unitarian. In 1872, its members erected

---

[38] Ibid., 162. The school changed its name to Harvard University in 1780, during Langdon's presidency.

[39] Cf. the discussion by C. C. Wright, "The Election of Henry Ware: Two Contemporary Accounts Edited with Commentary," *Harvard Library Bulletin* 17 (July 1969): 245–78.

[40] Morison, *Three Centuries of Harvard 1636–1936*, 185.

a magnificent brick building called the Brattle Square Unitarian Church, and four years later the church became extinct. First Baptist Church bought the building and continues using it to this day.[41] With Henry Ware now occupying Harvard's Hollis Chair of Divinity in violation of the Baptist donor's original intent, Congregationalist conservatives withdrew all support and established Andover Theological Seminary (1808),[42] in Andover, Massachusetts. While founded by leaders from both the Old Divinity and the New Divinity theologies,[43] Andover instantly established and defined itself as a New Divinity institution to train ministers and missionaries. Pioneer missionaries Adoniram Judson and Luther Rice soon graduated from the school and became Baptists.

Concluding Remarks

Under John T. Kirkland, president from 1810 to 1828, Harvard added a Unitarian divinity school (seminary) in 1812 while Yale was experiencing revival in the Second Great Awakening. Yale had embraced the First Great Awakening. Harvard had rejected it. While many circumstances inspired Yale's founding in 1701, there remains little doubt that one of them involved the circumstances at Harvard. Indeed, Increase Mather wrote letters strongly encouraging Yale's founders.[44]

---

[41] First Baptist Church of Boston is affiliated with the ecumenical American Baptist Churches USA.

[42] *The Constitution and Associate Statutes of the Theological Seminary in Andover: With a Sketch of Its Rise and Progress* (Boston: Farrand, Mallory, 1808). On its one-hundredth anniversary (1908) the seminary closed, and its entire library went to Harvard. Some faculty went to Newton Theological Institute, which changed its name to Andover Newton Theological School. In 2008, a new history came from the pen of Margaret Lamberts Bendroth, *A School of the Church: Andover Newton Across Two Centuries* (Grand Rapids: Eerdmans, 2008). See also Ernest Gordon, "The Looting of Andover," in *The Leaven of the Sadducees* (Chicago: Bible Institute Colportage Assoc., 1926), 138–58; David O. Beale, *In Pursuit of Purity: American Fundamentalism Since 1850* (Greenville, SC: Bob Jones University Press, 1986), 74–77; *The Andover Heresy* (Boston: Cupples, Upham, 1887); and Daniel Day Williams, *The Andover Liberals* (New York: Octagon Books, 1970).

[43] We discuss these terms in chapter 15, "The New Divinity Theology: Edwardsean Neo-Puritanism."

[44] Most of the histories of Yale mention the Mathers' dilemma with Harvard. For example, Roland H. Bainton, *Yale and the Ministry* (New York: Harper

The downgrade narrated above occurred on a small college campus that was being constantly watched by its loving sons. Harvard College, founded in 1636, had no graduating class numbering even ten until 1659. No graduating class numbered twenty until 1690 and 1695.[45] The college was over eighty years old before it graduated a class numbering forty or more, and that happened only twice up until 1762.

By 1701, when Yale College was established, Harvard was sixty-five years old. By 1725, when Harvard College was eighty-nine, its morals had begun to change, and by 1740, when the institution was just past a century old, the doctrine had begun to change. There were usually only three professors. One taught Divinity, one taught Hebrew and other oriental languages, and the other taught mathematics and natural philosophy. When the medical school was established in 1782, the administration added a fourth faculty member to teach anatomy and surgery. The fall was complete with Unitarian Henry Ware's appointment in 1805 when the school was one hundred and sixty-nine years old. Today, only the Library of Congress surpasses the school's library. Nothing surpasses the depths of its plunge from a Christian heritage.

Select Bibliography for Further Reading

Bendroth, Margaret Lamberts. *A School of the Church: Andover Newton Across Two Centuries*. Grand Rapids: Eerdmans, 2008.

Chaplin, Jeremiah. *Life of Henry Dunster, First President of Harvard College*. Boston: James R. Osgood, 1872.

Dunster, Samuel. *Henry Dunster and His Descendants*. Central Falls, RI: E. L. Freeman, 1876.

Ellis, Arthur B. *History of the First Church in Boston: 1630–1880*. Boston: Hall and Whiting, 1881.

Hill, Hamilton Andrews. *History of the Old South Church (Third Church) Boston 1669–1884*. 2 vols. Boston: Houghton, Mifflin, 1890.

Holifield, E. Brooks. *Theology in America: Christian Thought from the Age of the Puritans to the Civil War*. New Haven, CT: Yale University Press, 2003.

Lothrop, Samuel Kirkland. *A History of the Church in Brattle Street, Boston*. Boston: Wm. Crosby and H. P. Nichols, 1851.

---

and Brothers, 1957), 6; and Richard Warch, *School of the Prophets: Yale College, 1701–1740* (New Haven, CT: Yale University Press, 1973), 7–18. See also Walker, *The Creeds and Platforms of Congregationalism*, 495–97.

[45] There were twenty-two graduates in 1690 and in 1695.

The Manifesto Church: Records of the Church in Brattle Square Boston 1699–1872. Boston: Benevolent Fraternity of Churches, 1902.

Mather, Cotton. *Magnalia Christi Americana: Or, the Ecclesiastical History of New-England, from Its First Planting, in the Year 1620, unto the Year of Our Lord, 1698.* 7 bks. London: Thomas Parkhurst, 1702.

Mather, Increase. *The Order of the Gospel Professed and Practiced by the Churches of Christ in New-England, Justified by the Scripture and by the Writings of Many Learned Men, Both Ancient and Modern Divines: in Answer to Questions Relating to Church Discipline.* Boston: Printed by B. Green and J. Allen for Nicholas Buttolph, 1700.

Melnick, Arseny James. *America's Oldest Corporation and First CEO: Harvard & Henry Dunster.* West Conshohocken, PA: Infinity, 2008.

Morgan, Edmund S. *Visible Saints: The History of a Puritan Idea.* 1963. Reprint, Ithaca, NY: Cornell University Press, 1965.

Morison, Samuel Eliot. *Three Centuries of Harvard 1636–1936.* Cambridge: Harvard University Press, 1964.

Robbins, Chandler. *A History of the Second Church, or Old North, in Boston.* Boston: John Wilson & Son, 1852.

Whitefield, George. *The Works of the Reverend George Whitefield.* 6 vols. London: Printed for Edward and Charles Dilly, in the Poultry; and Messrs. Kincaid and Bell, at Edinburgh, 1771–72.

13

Yale College (1701–40): Jonathan Edwards and the Great Awakening

Political, moral, revivalistic, and philosophical dimensions provide the landscape, especially during the first two centuries of this third institution of higher learning in America, following Harvard (1636) and William and Mary (1693). From its inception, Yale has remained intrinsically woven into the fabric of New Haven, Connecticut.[1]

Soon after the Puritans arrived in Boston in 1630, they began establishing outpost settlements such as Wethersfield (1634), Saybrook (1635), and Hartford (1636), which joined to form Connecticut Colony in 1639 when freemen from several of the towns adopted the "Fundamental Orders" and elected their first governor. Meanwhile, in the spring of 1638 and in the wake of the Pequot War, John Davenport and Theophilus Eaton led in establishing New Haven Colony, which united with Connecticut Colony in the 1660s. A small group of ministers founded Yale College in 1701, and from that year until 1875, New Haven would stand with Hartford as joint capital of Connecticut. In New Haven's statutes of 1645, Davenport and others had expressed the need for a college for the "training up of youth . . . that through God's blessings they may be fitted for public

---

[1] I appreciate the generous access to Yale's Beinecke Rare Book and Manuscript Library and to the Manuscripts and Archives Department of Yale's Sterling Memorial Library.

service hereafter, either in church or commonwealth."[2] In 1700, that proposal was still unfulfilled, but additional factors were now prompting the urgency for a new college.

By the turn of the eighteenth century, Harvard College had thrown off her Puritan garments and was proudly adorning herself with more faddish robes. In 1701, the school forced out of office her last Puritan president—Increase Mather—whose son Cotton lamented, "*Religion* brought forth *Prosperity*, and the *Daughter* destroy'd the *Mother*" (*Religio peperit Divitias, & Filia devoravit Matrem*).[3] Not surprisingly, Cotton Mather would work to secure from Elihu Yale a grant for a new college. Harvard's changes were to some degree reflective of those of society at large. During the second half of the seventeenth century, morals had declined while intemperance, profanity, immorality, and desecration of the Lord's Day had increased to an alarming degree. Indeed, Puritanism as a movement had completely disappeared before the end of the seventeenth century.

During 1700 and 1701, a time when there were probably no more than thirty thousand people living in all of Connecticut,[4] the Congregational churches and clergy of the colony nominated ten of their ministers (Harvard graduates), as trustees to establish, erect, and govern a college. Representing towns along the Connecticut seaboard, the men assembled at New Haven and organized a body of ten trustees and a rector. Their second meeting convened in the parsonage of Pastor Samuel Russel (Russell) in Branford, with each man contributing whatever books he could donate towards the establishment of the Collegiate School of Connecticut (Yale's original name). These books constituted a major part of the college's original

---

[2] Franklin Bowditch Dexter, *The Removal of Yale College to New Haven in October, 1716*, a paper read October 23, 1916, in vol. 9 of the *Papers of the New Haven Colony Historical Society* (1916; repr., New Haven, CT: New Haven Colony Historical Society, 1918), 70–71.

[3] Cotton Mather, *Magnalia Christi Americana: Or, the Ecclesiastical History of New-England, from Its First Planting, in the Year 1620, unto the Year of Our Lord, 1698*, 7 bks. (London: Thomas Parkhurst, 1702), 1.3.7.

[4] See Brooks Mather Kelly, *Yale: A History* (New Haven, CT: Yale University Press, 1974), 11; and Richard Warch, *School of the Prophets: Yale College, 1701–1740* (New Haven, CT: Yale University Press, 1973), 1.

library, which President Thomas Clap later described as being "about 40 Volumes in Folio."[5] It is quite possible, too, that earlier donations of books were on hand,[6] and additional donations would soon arrive, as Pastor Russel prepared a special room for the collection and served as the first "Keeper of the Library." Forty years later, President Clap would prepare the first printed catalog of "the most valuable books in the library of Yale College," listing over twenty-six hundred volumes.[7] Most of the original volumes were of a biblical or theological nature. While the Russel house no longer stands, a room on the upstairs level of Yale's Sterling Memorial Library contains the double doors believed to be from Russel's parlor study where the men convened.[8] A two-ton monument on the green in Branford marks the site where the house stood.

---

[5] *The Annals or History of Yale-College, in New-Haven, in the Colony of Connecticut, from the First Founding Thereof, in the Year 1700, to the Year 1766* (New Haven, CT: J. Hotchkiss and B. Mecom, 1766), 3. Except for Tutor Samuel Johnson's brief *Historical Remarks Concerning the Collegiate School of Connecticut in New Haven,* recorded between the years 1717 and 1719, President Clap's work is the first history of the institution.

[6] George Wilson Pierson, *The Founding of Yale: The Legend of the Forty Folios* (New Haven, CT: Yale University Press, 1988), 247–52. Pierson presents evidence that there might well have been around one hundred books in the original library since many had been collected for an earlier college envisioned by John Davenport that never materialized. Pierson argues that such a collection likely passed on into the original Yale library.

[7] Thomas Clap, *Catalogue of the Library of Yale-College in New-Haven* (New London, CT: T[homas] Green, 1743), on microfiche at the Yale libraries. Of the original twenty-six hundred volumes in Yale's 1742 library, at least 60 to 70 percent have survived and remain in the Beinecke Rare Book and Manuscript Library collections, including much of the original 1701 library. In his introduction to the *Catalogue,* Clap reminds students of life's greatest priority: "Above all [,] have an Eye to the great End of all your Studies, which is to obtain the Clearest Conceptions of Divine Things and to lead you to a Saving Knowledge of GOD in his son JESUS CHRIST." Later acquisitions include an original Gutenberg Bible, also housed in the Beinecke.

[8] The Russel parlor doors open into the upstairs room that housed the 1742 library from the opening of Sterling Memorial Library in 1930 until the opening of the Beinecke in 1963. A special catalog for the "1742 Yale Library" allows easy access to its contents. Sterling Memorial, housing some five million volumes, remains Yale's central library. On its lower level, a large entrance hall depicts, in stone and stained glass, the history of the school's beginnings. Carved stone panels below the windows include the scene of the Branford meeting of the ministers. Above each of the ten panels is a window with stained glass panes interweaving

Following the Branford meeting, some of the trustees expressed concerns over donations. Some questioned whether they were fully vested to hold lands, or even to grant degrees since the school was without government sanction. In England, for example, colleges were simply "houses of instruction." Only the Universities of Oxford and Cambridge could actually grant degrees.[9] Never considering in that day that government aid might eventually prove only a gilded shackle for future generations, the trustees applied to the General Assembly, not only for an official charter,[10] but also for annual financial assistance. The Assembly granted both requests and completed the Collegiate School's initial organization by November 1701. The school soon moved its library to the home of its first rector, Rev. Abraham Pierson Jr. (1669–1707),[11] in Killingworth (now Clinton), Connecticut.

With one student, Pierson launched the college's first classes in 1702. A statue of Pierson stands in front of the Harkness Tower on the Yale campus, while another stands in front of the Abraham Pierson (public) School in Clinton. Just down the street, his tombstone rests in the cemetery behind Clinton's First Church, in whose pastorate Pierson once served. In front of the church, there stands a tall stone column with five folio volumes resting on its top, commemorating the legendary forty original volumes. At Rector Pierson's death, the college elected Rev. Samuel Andrew as rector, and for the next ten years the school operated in the private homes of tutors and trustees in Milford, East Guilford, Wethersfield, Saybrook, and finally New

---

the story of Yale and New Haven. One window, for example, includes Elihu Yale's portrait, while another portrays the ox carts bringing the books from Saybrook.

[9] Harvard had been granting degrees since 1642, but it had lost its charter in 1686 and had never received a permanent one from the Crown.

[10] No one at the time actually knew if the General Assembly had the power to grant such a charter for the founding of a college.

[11] Pierson's father, Abraham Pierson Sr., served the pastorate of the church at Southampton, Long Island, believed by some to be the earliest Presbyterian church in America. It was founded as a Congregationalist church. Pierson also served pastorates in Branford, CT, and Newark, NJ. A good source on both of the Piersons is William B. Sprague, *Annals of the American Pulpit; or Commemorative Notices of Distinguished American Clergymen of Various Denominations, From the Early Settlement of the Country to the Close of the Year Eighteen Hundred and Fifty-Five* (New York: Robert Carter & Brothers, 1857–69), 1:116–18 and 1:174–77.

Haven (1716)—its permanent home. Elihu Yale (1648–1721),[12] a retired officer of the British East India Company, would donate books and goods to the college on three separate occasions—the earliest donation consisting of thirty-two volumes, arriving in 1715.

In 1717, with funds approved by the Connecticut legislature, the school began work on its first building. When funds ran short, Cotton Mather of Boston wrote to Elihu Yale appealing for aid in completing the building and suggesting that perhaps the college might memorialize the Yale name:

> The Colony of Connecticut having for some years had a College of Saybrook without a collegious way of living for it, have lately begun to erect a large edifice for it in the town of New Haven. The charge of that expensive building is not yet all paid, nor are there any funds or revenues for salaries to the Professors and Instructors to the Society. Sir, though you have your felicities in your family, which I pray God continue and multiply, yet certainly, if what is forming at New Haven might wear the name of YALE COLLEGE, it would be better than the name of sons and daughters. And your munificence might easily obtain for you such a commemoration and perpetuation of your valuable name, which would indeed be much better than an Egyptian pyramid.[13]

Once again Elihu Yale came to the rescue,[14] this time with two trunks containing nine bales of fine textiles to be sold for the

---

[12] Elihu Yale was born in 1648 in Boston. His father, David Yale, was one of the original settlers of New Haven. Loyal to the Church of England and unsympathetic to Puritanism, the family returned to their home in Wales in 1651. Elihu went to India to engage in trade, about 1670, and eventually served as an officer for the East India Company. He amassed a fortune and returned to England in 1699. Although he never returned to New England, he donated books and goods to Yale College. Elihu Yale died in London in 1721 and was buried at St. Giles' Church in Wrexham, Wales, the ancient seat of the family name. A replica of the Wrexham church's beautiful tower stands on the Yale campus and has a stone from the original. Some helpful material is in T. W. Pritchard, *Elihu Yale: The Great Welsh American* (Wrexham, Wales: Wrexham Area Civic Society, 1991).

[13] Cotton Mather's letter, dated February 14, 1718, is cited in Pritchard, 24.

[14] Traditional sources usually cite £800 as the worth of Elihu Yale's gifts to the college. Pritchard, however, perhaps using 1991 rates, states that the 1718 gift alone was worth £1162, and that the third gift (1721), which included goods to be sold in behalf of the college, realized £562. In the rough draft of his will, Yale specified an additional £500 to the college; this never arrived, however, because the will was later determined to be invalid. Nevertheless, his gift of 1718 alone constituted the single largest donation made to Yale College during its first 122 years of existence.

college. The gift also included 417 books and a portrait of King George I.[15] Grateful trustees gladly named their building Yale College; although, the name would not refer to the entire institution until the Charter of 1745. That original building, finally completed in 1718, was a three-story wooden structure that stood at the corner of Chapel and College Streets.[16] On the ground floor was the great hall, or dining room. The library occupied the second floor. Some twenty-five chambers on the third floor served as a dormitory for up to seventy or eighty students. Tutors also lived in the Hall and with no plumbing each resident drew his own wash water from the well. Outhouses served as toilets. The college rector lived in a separate home, built with proceeds from a local rum tax. The students' daily schedule began with prayers at sunrise. Following prayers there were recitations, then breakfast—usually consisting of various breads and a little beer. After the final class of the day came prayer time at 4:00 p.m., followed by supper. All candles were out from 11:00 p.m. to 4:00 a.m. It was not until 1750 that the college erected its second collegiate building, a three-story brick structure, Connecticut Hall,[17] which is today the oldest building on the campus.

In the Yale Charter published in October 1701, Connecticut's governor and legislator asserted that the specific purpose for the school was "for upholding & Propagating of the Christian Protestant Religion by a succession of Learned & Orthodox men."[18] Determined to create a virtual training school in Christian man-

---

[15] The Yale University Art Gallery displays this well-preserved portrait.

[16] Located where Bingham Hall now stands, Yale's first building was 165 feet long by 21 feet wide. A 1736 description has the structure "sky color" which, along with red, was a typical color for buildings in those days. White paint was too expensive for common use until later in the century.

[17] President Thomas Clap's administration built Connecticut Hall (100 feet long by 40 feet wide) partly with funds from a lottery and partly with funds received from the government's sale of a captured French ship. Clap modeled Connecticut Hall after Harvard's Massachusetts Hall, the oldest building on Harvard's campus. Connecticut Hall was the first American collegiate building constructed with lottery money. It soon became rather commonplace even for churches to use lotteries for building purposes. Presbyterian and Congregational churches, along with the First Baptist Church in Providence, RI, would eventually utilize the practice.

[18] Franklin Bowditch Dexter, ed., *Documentary History of Yale University: Under the Original Charter of the Collegiate School of Connecticut 1701–1745* (1916; repr., New York: Arno Press, 1969), 20.

hood, the trustees met the following month and agreed on their objective that the institution's explicit purpose would be the training of ministers and magistrates. Prior to admission into the college, each applicant had to demonstrate, by special examination, his ability in Latin and Greek: "And finding them Duly prepared And Expert In Latin and Greek Authors [,] both Poetick and oratorial [,] As also ready in making Good Latin [, the rector] Shall Grant them admission Into Said School."[19] Yale's chief reason for existence would be "For the Educating and Instructing of Youth in good Literature, Arts, and Sciences; That so by the blessing of Almighty God they may be the better fitted for publick Imployment both in Church and in the Civil State." The standard theology would be the Westminster Standards,[20] and the textbook would be the *Medulla Theologiae* ("Marrow of Sacred Divinity") by the English Puritan, William Ames (1576–1633).[21] By 1714, the administration would require an additional theology text, the *Compendium Theologiae Christianae* ("Abridgement of Christian Divinity") by the Reformed theologian, Johann Wollebius (1586–1629) of Basel. These texts would be required for the next forty years. Tutors could implement additional texts according to their own discretion. Yale's founders intended that the college represent and promote the colony's Congregational churches, which were Presbyterian in doctrine but semi-Presbyterian in polity. (Their ministerial consociations, approved in the Saybrook Platform of 1708, resembled Presbyterian synods.) The original minutes of the first meeting of the board of trustees specifies explicitly their primary aim for the college:

> Whereas it was the glorious publick design of our now blessed fathers in their Removal from Europe into these parts of America, both to plant, and under the Divine blessing to propagate in this Wilderness, the blessed Reformed, Protestant Religion, in the purity of its Order, and Worship, not only to their posterity, but also to the barbarous Natives: In which great Enterprise they wanted not the Royal Commands, & favor of his Majestie Charles the Second to authorize, & invigorate them. We their unworthy

---

[19] Ibid., 30.

[20] For the text of the Westminster Standards, see Philip Schaff, *The Creeds of Christendom* (New York: Harper and Brothers, 1877), 3:600ff.

[21] Dexter, *Documentary History of Yale University*, 17–18.

posterity lamenting our past neglects of this Grand errand, & Sensible of our equal Obligations better to prosecute the Same end, are desirous in our Generation to be Serviceable thereunto— Whereunto the Liberal, & Religious Education of Suitable youth is under the blessing of God, a chief, & most probable expedient.[22]

When Timothy Cutler (1683–1765)[23] became the college's third rector in 1719, student unrest was at an alarming level, and it only increased. As a teenager, Jonathan Edwards (1703–58) witnessed the affair. At the time he enrolled, he was not quite thirteen. While living in the home of a relative, he would complete his undergraduate degree in 1720 and his masters in 1722. In a letter to his father, dated March 1, 1721, Edwards reports "the Discovery of some Monstrous impieties, and Acts of Immorality Lately Committed. In the Colledge, Particularly," Edwards had observed the "stealing of Hens, Geese, turkies, piggs, Meat, Wood &c,—Unseasonable Nightwalking, Breaking People's windows, playing at Cards, Cursing, Swearing, and Damning, and Using all manner of Ill Language, which never were at such a pitch in the Colledge as they Now are." For his father's encouragement, Edwards adds, "Through the goodness of God I am perfectly free of all their janglings."[24] Predictably, the official documents of the college during this time reveal numerous appeals to "good manners," "wholesome speech," and "respect for others."

While the misbehavior that Edwards described might seem strange or unexpected, Yale was a liberal arts college, not a seminary, and the majority of the students were training to be merchants, doctors, lawyers, and public servants. Even so, an average of forty-six percent of the graduates entered the ministry during the college's first forty years of existence.[25] In fact, colonial New England believed that "a necessary qualification of a Gospel Minister" was his training in

---

[22] Ibid., 27.

[23] A good source on Timothy Cutler is Sprague, *Annals*, 5:50–52.

[24] Cited in Ola Elizabeth Winslow, *Jonathan Edwards 1703–1758: A Biography* (New York: Macmillan, 1940), 71. Other helpful works on Edwards include George M. Marsden, *Jonathan Edwards: A Life* (New Haven, CT: Yale University Press, 2003); Conrad Cherry, *The Theology of Jonathan Edwards: A Reappraisal* (Bloomington: Indiana University Press, 1990); Perry Miller, *Jonathan Edwards* (Amherst: University of Massachusetts Press, 1949); and Iain H. Murray, *Jonathan Edwards: A New Biography* (Edinburgh: Banner of Truth Trust, 1987).

[25] Warch, 269–70.

the liberal arts.[26] On Sundays, Yale required that all students attend the Congregational church—the First (now Center) Church—on New Haven Green, where they occupied rented seats in a special section of the fore-gallery. Jonathan Edwards himself had entered the college at the age of twelve and completed his undergraduate work by the age of seventeen. His conversion seems to have occurred sometime during the final two of these years, when he became captivated by 1 Timothy 1:17, "Now unto the King eternal, immortal, invisible, the only wise God, be honour and glory for ever and ever. Amen."

It was during his two years of graduate training that Edwards wrote his book, *The Mind*, and began three additional works—*Of Being*, *Resolutions*, and *Miscellanies*, the latter consisting of theological notebooks to which he regularly added throughout his ministry. When the author was making his final entries in the last year of his life, *Miscellanies* would then consist of nine large volumes, plus a separate index, providing valuable insight into his mind and spirit. Edwards's liberal arts training had definitely had a powerful impact on his life. On January 12, 1723, at the age of nineteen, he completely yielded his life to the Lord and resolved, "that no other end but religion shall have any influence at all on any of my actions." The following year, Jonathan Edwards began a two-year tutorship at Yale College.

To help establish its library, the college had commissioned Jeremy Dummer to solicit in England for more gifts, including books. Dummer reported that when he approached Elihu Yale, the college's original benefactor, Mr. Yale rejoiced at the college's progress, but revealed his personal concern, "Whether it was well in him, being a Church man, to promote an Academy of Dissenters." After discussing it with Dummer, however, Mr. Yale "appear'd convinc't that the business of good men is to spread religion & learning among mankind," and besides, "if the Discipline of the Church of England be most agreeable to Scripture & primitive practice, there's no better

---

[26] New England preachers regularly made the case for a liberal arts education for clergymen. See, for example, Cotton Mather's *Manuductio ad Ministerium* and Samuel Willard's *Brief Directions to a Young Scholar Designing the Ministry*.

way to make men sensible of it than by giving them good reading."[27] In essence, Elihu Yale was expressing hope that his provision of books might enable the Church of England to have a major impact on this Congregationalist/Presbyterian campus. His gift of books arrived in 1721. Interestingly enough, nearly forty years later (1759), Yale College would refuse a gift offer of books from a Baptist merchant on the ground that they were unorthodox.[28] The major doctrinal menace that characterized much of Elihu Yale's contribution was what Jonathan Edwards dubbed "Arminian liberalism," with its emphasis on human ability. Edwards and other conservatives typically and freely used the term *Arminian* to include anyone, even a Universalist, who might teach that man's works can result in salvation.

The Reformed position was facing serious threats. Already, the Church of England was exerting pressure on New England ministers either to return to the Anglican fold or to pronounce themselves as separatists. Their fathers had taught them that Puritans were not separatists, only non-conformists. Puritanism was now a thing of the past. Why should they not re-enter the secure fold of the Church of England and share its secure claim of an apostolic succession? Many of these sons and grandsons of Puritans now seriously doubted the validity of their own local churches, their sacraments, and even their own ordination. With extempore pastoral prayers becoming increasingly lifeless week after week, some ministers had already succumbed to the powerful temptation of bringing the Anglican *Book of Common Prayer* to their pulpits and introducing their flocks to the beauty of its liturgy and ceremony.

Two of the most influential books from Elihu Yale's contributions were *A Defense of the Reasonableness of Conformity to the Church of England* by Benjamin Hoadley and *A Defense of Ministerial Conformity to the Church of England* by John Ollyffe. These works and similar ones encouraged what Congregationalist conservatives dubbed the "great apostasy." This historic defection from the Congregational ministry and from the Reformed faith began openly in 1722 when Rector Timothy Cutler and Tutor Daniel Brown,

---

[27] Dexter, *Documentary History of Yale University*, 193.
[28] Louis Leonard Tucker, *Puritan Protagonist: President Thomas Clap of Yale College* (Chapel Hill: University of North Carolina Press, 1962), 156–58.

along with two local ministers, Samuel Johnson of West Haven[29] and James Wetmore of North Haven, publicized their plans to travel to London for reordination in the Church of England. Following the commencement of 1722, the trustees summoned the rector and tutors to the library for inquiry. The latter presented a signed statement to the trustees: "Some of us doubt of the validity, and the rest are more fully persuaded of the invalidity, of Presbyterian ordination, in opposition to Episcopal." In October, the group met again in the college library, and a heated debate ensued. Ordering the immediate resignations of Cutler and Brown,[30] the trustees ruled that future rectors and tutors must subscribe to the Reformed creed known as the Saybrook Platform.[31] Their subscription requirement would remain in force for a century, finally suffering abolishment when the divinity school was established in 1822.

The college remained without a rector for four years; then, in 1726, Elisha Williams became its fourth. The college regulations that year reasserted that, "Every student shall consider the main end of his study to wit to know God in Jesus Christ and answerably to lead a godly sober life." To assist in this noble aim, "every student shall exercise himself in reading Holy Scriptures by himself every day [that] the word of Christ may dwell in him richly and [that] he may be filled with the knowledge of the will of God in all wisdom and spiritual understanding."[32]

In 1730, the English dissenter Isaac Watts (1674–1748), the Father of English Hymnody, sent a gift of some twenty volumes of his writings, two of which discuss the doctrine of the Trinity. One of

---

[29] Samuel Johnson had only recently resigned as tutor at Yale. His theology had become increasingly Arminian. He later founded and became the first president of King's College, later named Columbia University, in New York.

[30] Sprague, *Annals*, 5:50. At the time of the 1722 defection, there was not a single Episcopalian church in all of Connecticut. Timothy Cutler later became rector at Boston's Old North Church (Episcopalian), presently the city's oldest church building. Tutor Daniel Brown died of smallpox in England.

[31] Clap, *Annals or History of Yale-College*, 32. For the confession known as the Saybrook Platform (1708), see Williston Walker, *The Creeds and Platforms of Congregationalism* (1893; repr., Boston: Pilgrim Press, 1960), 463–523.

[32] The text is in Franklin Bowditch Dexter, *Biographical Sketches of the Graduates of Yale College with Annals of the College History* (New York: Henry Holt, 1885), 1:347. I have slightly modernized some of the spelling.

these two books was *The Christian Doctrine of the Trinity* (1722). A similar Watts title had appeared in 1724, *Three Dissertations Relating to the Christian Doctrine of the Trinity*, and its second edition, with the title shortened to *Dissertations Relating to the Christian Doctrine of the Trinity* (1726), was his other book on this topic that Watts included in his gift to Yale's library. The author, however, withheld from the gift his book titled *Four Dissertations Relating to the Christian Doctrine of the Trinity* (1725),[33] which Cotton Mather and many others had already condemned charging that it contained speculative errors. Contemporary Baptist theologian John Gill observed that Watts "is not to be reckoned a Trinitarian, being so manifestly in the Sabellian scheme, as appears by his *Dissertations* published in 1725."[34] Watts himself explained that he had withheld the volume, lest he "be charged with leading youth into heresy."[35] The college library kept even the donated 1726 edition of *Dissertations* out of circulation and out of the library's catalog for many years, lest it should influence students in an unorthodox way. When Ezra Stiles, nearly fifty years later, finally included the title in his published catalog of the library, he recorded these thoughts in his diary: "When Dr. Watts set out in Life he was clearly a Calvinist. . . . When the Arian Controversy got hold of the Dissenters . . . about 1720: Dr. Watts entered the Arian Researches, [and] *became plunged as to the real Divinity of J.C.*" While Watts sounded Sabellian to John Gill, Ezra Stiles was convinced that Watts "was an Arian on the Divinity of Christ."[36] In 1719, the same year he wrote "Joy to the World,"

---

[33] Watts's book of *Four Dissertations Relating to the Christian Doctrine of the Trinity* (1725) does not appear in the various editions of his works. The only copy of which I am aware is the one at Yale's Beinecke Rare Book and Manuscript Library, which did not acquire it until the nineteenth century. Also missing from various editions of Watts's works are his *Faithful Inquiry after the Ancient and Original Doctrine of the Trinity* (1745, repr. 1802); *Useful and Important Questions Concerning Jesus, the Son of God* (1746); and *The Glory of Christ as God-Man Display'd: in Three Discourses* (London: J. Oswald, 1746).

[34] John Gill, *Sermons and Tracts* (1814–15; repr., Streamwood, IL: Primitive Baptist Library, 1981), 3:553.

[35] Anne Stokely Pratt, *Isaac Watts and His Gift of Books to Yale College* (New Haven, CT: Yale University Press, 1938), 10–15. Pratt notes that a century passed before Yale's library acquired Watts's highly controversial *Four Dissertations Relating to the Christian Doctrine of the Trinity* (1725).

[36] Ibid., 14.

Watts had voted against requiring independent ministers to accept the doctrine of the Trinity.[37] Any degree of Unitarianism constituted far more danger than conservatives could ever possibly tolerate.

To some degree, Isaac Watts's Trinitarian aberrations resulted from untold physical and mental torments that only increased with age. Under such conditions, the gifted poet wrote majestic praises to the Holy Trinity. He was buried in London's Bunhill Fields, the cemetery of Dissenters, where lie the remains of such noble Christians as John Bunyan, Susanna Wesley, and the great theologian John Gill. One of the most insightful human appraisals of Dr. Watts is from Alfred Light in his book, *Bunhill Fields*:

> Some things believed and preached by the "seraphic doctor" are entirely opposed to the Scriptures, and invariably have been looked upon with abhorrence by all who insist on dividing the true from the false and the precious from the vile. He sought to re-adjust the doctrine of the Trinity, and fell into error with respect to the Person and work of the Lord Jesus Christ and the personality and operations of the Holy Spirit, expressing notions which the Scriptures denounce and the experiences of God's people contradict. How far his aberrations from truth may be attributed to his shattered bodily and mental faculties will probably never be known, and the matter must therefore be left. The author, however, having read carefully most of the available writings upon the subject, feels compelled to record his conviction that, whilst Watts sadly erred upon some fundamental doctrines, the claim of [the

---

[37] For Watts's vote at this "conference about the ministers at Exeter held at Salters' Hall (1719)," see *The Dictionary of National Biography*, s.v. "Watts, Isaac 1674–1748", by Henry Leigh Bennett, who observes that Watts did not think that belief in the Trinity was necessary for salvation, and that "the creed of Constantinople had become to him only a human explication of the mystery of the divine Godhead." Bennett explains that Watts's own theory "was that the human soul of Christ had been created anterior to the creation of the world, and united to the divine principle in the Godhead known as the Sophia or Logos." *The Oxford Dictionary of the Christian Church*, rev. 2nd ed., s.v. "Watts, Isaac (1674–1748)," says that "in his later years he seems to have inclined towards Unitarianism. In 1719 he opposed the imposition of the doctrine of the Trinity on dissenting ministers." See also *The New Schaff-Herzog Encyclopedia of Religious Knowledge*, s.v. "Isaac Watts."

Unitarian] Belsham and other Socinian ministers, that he died believing in their pernicious teachings, cannot be maintained.[38]

Meanwhile, Yale continued receiving additional donations of books from high church Anglicans. Rector Elisha Williams, a fervent Calvinist, serving until 1739, would see his administration constantly confronted with heavy doses of "Arminian liberalism" in these Church of England books. The well-known Anglican churchman and philosopher George Berkeley (1685–1753), for example, sent eight cases, numbering nearly a thousand volumes, in 1733. Through it all, Rector Williams preached Calvinist doctrine with renewed zeal. The following is typical of his style of preaching during this period:

> If our Salvation be wholly of Grace, how can any thing of Self come in, as a Cause or Motive thereto; or any thing we are or can do, be a ground why it is bestowed? They will Exclude one the other. If any Thing of ours be the Cause, Motive or ground of Salvation, then it is not wholly of Grace: And if it be wholly of Grace, then all of Self is wholly Excluded, As the Apostle shews, *If it be of Works, then it is not of Grace; but if it be of Grace, then it is not of Works. Otherwise Grace were no more grace.* . . . Grace, can have no Partner.[39]

As smallpox and diphtheria, especially in 1721 and 1735, along with an earthquake in 1727, brought widespread death in the area, many agreed with Jonathan Edwards that the truth, the whole truth, and nothing but the truth could bring dying individuals from darkness to light, as Edwards himself would later explain:

> It is very true, that "preaching hell cannot frighten men into religion;" but it may frighten them into serious thought, and secure to religious truth that attention, without which it cannot save the soul. After all that can be said of the power of love and of kindness, and the winning accents of mercy, and the like, it remains an awful truth, that men will not give any efficient attention to these things, till they have been first brought to see their need of them.

---

[38] Alfred W. Light, *Bunhill Fields* (London: C. J. Farncombe and Sons, 1913), 247.

[39] Cited in Warch, 165.

Till then, all that they hear about the mercy of God only gives them courage to neglect him.[40]

Chronology of the Life and Key Works of Jonathan Edwards (1703–58)

- 1703: Edwards is born October 5 at East Windsor, Connecticut.

- 1715–16: He writes his thousand-word essay, "Of Insects."

- 1716–20: During undergraduate years at Yale College (age 12 to age 17), he is captivated by 1 Timothy 1:17. Edwards's conversion seems to have occurred sometime during the final two of these Yale years.

- 1720–22: Edwards studies theology; writes *The Mind*; begins three works—*Of Being*, *Resolutions*, and *Miscellanies* (theological notebooks to which he regularly added throughout his ministry). The notebooks provide valuable insights into his mind and spirit.

- 1722: On August 22, he accepts the call to a Scotch Presbyterian church in New York City. They met in a building on William Street between Liberty and Wall. He remained at the small church for eight or nine months. He begins his Diary on December 18, the same day that he wrote Resolution #35 of 70.

- 1723: On January 12 (at age 19), Edwards completely yields his life to the Lord and resolves "that no other end but religion shall have any influence at all on any of my actions." He preaches for a church in Bolton, Connecticut, and receives an offer from Yale College. In September, he receives the Master of Arts degree from Yale.

- 1724: On May 21, he begins a two-year tutorship at Yale.

- 1726–27: He becomes co-pastor with his aging grandfather, Solomon Stoddard, at the First Church (Congregational) of Northampton, Massachusetts. Edwards is ordained in February

---

[40] Cited in Joseph Tracy, *The Great Awakening* (1842; repr., Edinburgh: Banner of Truth Trust, 1976), 220.

1727 and marries Sarah Pierrepont in July of that year. She was the seventeen-year-old great granddaughter of Thomas Hooker, the Puritan preacher and founder of the city of Hartford, Connecticut.

- 1728: On August 25, the Edwards's first child, Sarah, is born.

- 1729: On February 22, Stoddard dies. Edwards assumes full duties as pastor.

- 1731: On July 8, during Harvard's commencement week, Edwards delivers the "Great and Thursday Lecture" in Boston's First Church. Many Harvard scholars would have attended the lecture with much interest to hear this twenty-eight-year-old Yale graduate and pastor. The discourse soon appeared in print under the title *God Glorified in the Work of Redemption, by the Greatness of Man's Dependence upon Him, in the Whole of It.*

- 1733: Some stirrings of revival in Northampton. In August, Edwards preaches a sermon titled, *A Divine and Supernatural Light, Immediately Imparted to the Soul by the Spirit of God, Shown to Be both a Scriptural, and Rational Doctrine.* This would be published the following year. Perry Miller would conclude that "the whole of Edwards's system is contained in miniature within some ten or twelve of the pages of this work."[41]

- 1734: Edwards begins a series of sermons on the theme "Justification by Faith." These, along with four other revival sermons, were published in 1738 as *Discourses on Various Important Subjects, Nearly Concerning the Great Affair of the Soul's Eternal Salvation.*

- 1734–35: Outpouring of First Great Awakening occurs in Northampton with over three hundred "surprising conversions."

- 1736: Edwards publishes his *Faithful Narrative of the Surprising Work of God in the Conversion of Many Hundred Souls in Northampton, and the Neighboring Towns and Villages.* It went through three editions and twenty printings by 1739.

- 1738: Joseph Bellamy spends several months studying theology in the Edwards home.

---

[41] Perry Miller, *Jonathan Edwards* (New York: World Publishing, 1959), 44.

- 1739: Edwards begins his *Personal Narrative*. He preaches thirty sermons on "The Theology of History" (published posthumously in Edinburgh in 1774 as *A History of the Work of Redemption*).

- 1740: Edwards publishes his *Personal Narrative*. On October 17, George Whitefield arrives from Boston and spends three days in the Edwards home.

- 1741: On July 8, at Enfield, Connecticut, Edwards preaches his sermon *Sinners in the Hands of an Angry God* (ten years to the day, after the famous Boston lecture). He also publishes his *Distinguishing Marks of a Work of the Spirit of God*.

- 1742: Edwards draws up a covenant for his congregation to sign, binding the signers to live godly lives.

- 1743: Edwards publishes *Some Thoughts Concerning the Present Revival of Religion in New England, and the Way in which It ought to Be Acknowledged and Promoted*. Charles Chauncy of Boston attacks Edwards's treatise with his own *Seasonable Thoughts on the State of Religion in New England*. Samuel Hopkins spends several months studying theology in the Edwards home.

- 1744: Edwards requires verbal profession of faith as a necessary qualification for partaking of the Lord's Supper at his church.

- 1746: Edwards publishes his *Treatise Concerning Religious Affections*. This is his reply to the Charles Chauncy attack.

- 1747: Edwards publishes his *Humble Attempt to Promote Explicit Agreement and Visible Union of God's People in Extraordinary Prayer for the Revival of Religion and Advancement of Christ's Kingdom on Earth*. It is a call for Christians to devote regular hours each week in concerted prayer for revival. The work also reflects Edwards's hope for a postmillennial kingdom on earth. In May, David Brainerd comes to live in the Edwards home; he dies there on October 4.

- 1749: Edwards publishes his *Account of the Life of the Late Reverend Mr. David Brainerd, and His Humble Inquiry into the Rules of the Word of God, Concerning the Qualifications Requisite to a Complete Standing and Full Communion in the Visible Church*.

- 1750: On June 22, a council of nine churches, by a five-to-four margin, advises Edwards's dismissal. His own congregation upheld the decision. On July 2, he preached his *Farewell Sermon*, after twenty-three years of service. Edwards was forty-six years old; eight or nine of the eleven children were still at home, the youngest being two months old. The family remained in Northampton for almost a year, and Edwards still preached there on occasion.

- 1751: During the summer, Edwards becomes pastor of a small Congregational church at Stockbridge, Massachusetts, where his congregation includes Housatonic Indians. During his six years at Stockbridge, he wrote *Freedom of the Will* (1754); *Concerning the End for which God Created the World* (1765); *The Nature of True Virtue* (1765); and *Original Sin* (1758).

- 1752: Edwards publishes his *Misrepresentations Corrected, and Truth Vindicated.*

- 1757: Edwards is elected president of the College of New Jersey (at the death of President Aaron Burr, husband of Edwards's daughter Esther).

- 1758: In February, Edwards arrives at Princeton, where he receives a smallpox inoculation that proves fatal. He dies five weeks later (March 22) and is buried at Princeton.

Select Bibliography for Further Reading

Cherry, Conrad. *The Theology of Jonathan Edwards: A Reappraisal.* Bloomington: Indiana University Press, 1990.

Edwards, Jonathan. *The Works of Jonathan Edwards.* 23 vols. New Haven, CT: Yale University Press, 1970–2004.

_____. *Freedom of the Will.* Edited by Paul Ramsey. Vol. 1 of *The Works of Jonathan Edwards.* New Haven, CT: Yale University Press, 1985.

_____. *The Great Awakening.* Edited by C. C. Goen. Vol. 4 of *The Works of Jonathan Edwards.* New Haven, CT: Yale University Press, 1972.

_____. *A History of the Work of Redemption.* Edited by John F. Wilson. Vol. 9 of *The Works of Jonathan Edwards.* New Haven, CT: Yale University Press, 1989.

_____. *The Life of David Brainerd.* Edited by Norman Pettit. Vol. 7 of *The Works of Jonathan Edwards.* New Haven, CT: Yale University Press, 1985.

_____. *Original Sin*. Edited by Clyde A. Holbrook. Vol. 3 of *The Works of Jonathan Edwards*. New Haven, CT: Yale University Press, 1970.

_____. *Religious Affections*. Edited by John E. Smith. Vol. 2 of *The Works of Jonathan Edwards*. New Haven, CT: Yale University Press, 1987.

_____. *Writings on the Trinity, Grace, and Faith*. Edited by Sang Hyun Lee. Vol. 21 of *The Works of Jonathan Edwards*. New Haven, CT: Yale University Press, 2003.

Marsden, George M. *Jonathan Edwards: A Life*. New Haven, CT: Yale University Press, 2003.

Mather, Cotton. *Manuductio ad Ministerium: Directions for a Candidate of the Ministry*. Boston: Thomas Hancock, 1726.

Murray, Iain H. *Jonathan Edwards: A New Biography*. Edinburgh: Banner of Truth Trust, 1987.

Oviatt, Edwin. *The Beginnings of Yale, 1701–1726*. 1916. Reprint, New York: Arno Press, 1969.

Selesky, Harold E., ed. *A Guide to the Microfilm Edition of the Ezra Stiles Papers at Yale University*. New Haven, CT: Yale University Library, 1978.

Stiles, Ezra. *Ezra Stiles Papers at Yale University*. 22-reel microfilm. New Haven, CT: Yale University Press, 1976.

14

Revival to War (1740–77): Microcosmic Transformations inside Yale

Contending with Worldliness: The Clap Administration

Thomas Clap (1703–67)[1] was born the same year as Jonathan Edwards, and the two shared much in common. After serving for fourteen years as a much-loved pastor of the church in Windham, Clap became Yale's fifth rector in 1740 as Edwards was in the midst of revival at Northampton. Under Yale's Charter of 1745, Clap would become the first to hold the title of president, and his administration would run the entire course of the Great Awakening. Like Edwards, he was acquainted with the English evangelist George Whitefield (1715–70).

Following nearly a year's work in the south, Whitefield came to New England in September 1740. After preaching to great crowds in Boston, Northampton, Hartford, Middletown, and Wallingford, he arrived in New Haven in late October and preached several times. At the invitation of Pastor Joseph Noyes, he spoke at First Church,

---

[1] The best sources on Thomas Clap include Louis Leonard Tucker, *Puritan Protagonist: President Thomas Clap of Yale College* (Chapel Hill: University of North Carolina Press, 1962); and William B. Sprague, *Annals of the American Pulpit* (New York: Robert Carter & Brothers, 1857–69), 1:343–51.

where Yale students attended. He dined with Rector Clap and wrote in his *Journal* that the college was "about one third part as big as that of Cambridge [Harvard]. It has one Rector, three Tutors, and about a hundred Students. . . . I preached twice. . . . There were sweet Meltings. . . . I spoke closely to the Students, and showed the dreadful Ill-Consequences of an unconverted ministry."[2] Whitefield's preaching sparked an awakening among the Yale students. During the winter that followed, several revival preachers visited New Haven, and the people generally heard them gladly. Presbyterian evangelist Gilbert Tennent preached seventeen sermons, including several in the College Hall, where some of the students professed Christ. During the summer months, these students carried the revival to their own churches. At Bridgewater, for example, revival broke out under the efforts of a student who had been converted under Whitefield.

With Whitefield's departure, however, some of the itinerant New Light revival preachers failed to use caution and wisdom. They openly attacked the established Old Light clergy with such names as "hirelings," "dead dogs," and "blind leaders of the blind." There were Enlightenment rationalists who did fit such descriptions. The Old Lights retaliated by calling the New Lights "enthusiasts," "vagrants," and "wanderers." Again, there were extremists who did fit such descriptions. Generally, New Light preachers were respectable and balanced, while informal and fervent in style. Many Old Lights were faithful and conservative men, formal and subdued in style, who wished to protect the use of traditional means of grace and to avoid emotionalism. There were extremes on both sides. Among the New Lights were untrained fanatics who believed that all were hypocrites. Among the Old Lights were Universalists who believed that all were saved. Rector Clap and Pastor Noyes, as part of the established Congregational clergy, generally identified with the Old Lights. A year after Whitefield's departure, Evangelist James Davenport, a Yale graduate and great-grandson of New Haven's founder, visited New Haven. It was Davenport's practice to request from every minister a clear testimony of a personal conversion experience.

---

[2] Recorded in Franklin Bowditch Dexter, ed., *Documentary History of Yale University: Under the Original Charter of the Collegiate School of Connecticut 1701–1745* (1916; repr., New York: Arno Press, 1969), 346–47.

When displeased with a response, he would go into that minister's church and denounce him in front of his congregation. Unaware that Davenport had become a New Light fanatic, Pastor Noyes invited him to speak in the pulpit of First Church (the present Center Church UCC). Davenport then publicly proceeded to denounce his host as "an unconverted hypocrite and devil incarnate." Some months later, Davenport established a Separatist rival church in the town, named it the White Haven Church (now known as the United Church UCC),[3] and had a New Light preacher installed. Many students preferred attending the Separatist church, feeling that Pastor Noyes's preaching was dry and boring. Rector Clap felt compelled to defend Noyes since he was the college preacher. For more than a decade, these controversies would trouble Yale College. Supported by government legislation, Clap forbade the students, under heavy penalty, from attending Separatist meetings.

The year 1741 also saw the expulsion of David Brainerd (1718–47), who had experienced deep revival under Whitefield's preaching. In his diary Brainerd wrote, "Sundry passages of God's word opened to my soul with divine clearness, power and sweetness, so as to appear exceeding precious, and with clear and certain evidence of its being the word of God."[4] It was natural that he should desire to share these things with others. Older than most of his peers, Brainerd was twenty-one when he entered Yale. He was only five years younger than Whitefield and only slightly younger than his own tutors. With depth of feeling and absolute frankness, Brainerd spoke with his fellow students of the spiritual state of affairs at the college and of their own spiritual condition. The administration knew, however, that the prolonged revival emphasis was diverting students from their studies and causing severe criticism of Noyes and even of certain tutors. In a prayer meeting in College Hall, during Brainerd's second year, a tutor named Chauncey Whittelsey "prayed

---

[3] White Haven (est. 1742) and Fair Haven (est. 1769) merged to form the United Church in 1796.

[4] David Brainerd left his papers and diary with Jonathan Edwards, who edited and incorporated them into *An Account of the Life of the Late Rev. David Brainerd* (Boston: D. Henchman, 1749). See also John Thornbury, *David Brainerd: Pioneer Missionary to the American Indians* (Durham, England: Evangelical Press, 1996).

fervently for above the space of an hour." Brainerd remarked privately to a friend that Whittelsey was as "destitute of grace as this chair." A freshman overheard the remark and repeated it to a lady in town. She reported it to the rector. When the administration ordered Brainerd to make a public apology for his derogatory comment, he refused since he had made the remark in private. The administration expelled him. Brainerd denied reports that he had voiced criticism against President Clap for denying attendance at New Light meetings. During the months that followed, Brainerd continued his studies privately and received a preaching license from the Scotch Society for Promoting Christian Knowledge. They appointed him as their missionary to the Indians in the Colonies. The following May when he offered an apology for his remarks against Whittelsey, the faculty retorted that he could continue pursuing his degree only if he would complete an additional year of residence study. Already committed to the mission board, he now abandoned all hope of returning to college. Brainerd, however, had endeared himself to many of the students, and his expulsion had drawn widespread attention and controversy outside the college walls.

In May 1742, the legislature complained to Yale's administration that some of the students were publicly and rashly judging and censuring good people—tutors and magistrates alike—as being unconverted and unworthy leaders. Learning that some seniors, in rebellion against rules, had subscribed money for a special printing of John Locke's *Essay on Toleration*, the faculty quickly stepped in and put a stop to it, but not without more expulsions and widespread bitter feelings.[5] The expulsion of John and Ebenezer Cleaveland for attending a Separatist meeting and the dismissal of a trustee followed. Granted a new charter in 1745, Yale undertook a revision of the college laws the same year. These new regulations show the powerful influence of President Thomas Clap. Two samples of "The 1745 Regulations at Yale College" appear below.

From chapter 2, "Of a Religious and Virtuous Life"

7. Every student of this college shall in words and behavior show all due honor, respect and reverence towards all their superiors,

---

[5] E.g., see Dexter, *Documentary History of Yale University*, 368–72.

such as their natural parents, magistrates and ministers, and especially to the president, fellows and tutors of this college; and shall in no case use any reproachful, reviling, disrespectful or contumacious language: but on the contrary shall show them all proper tokens of reverence, obedience and respect: such as uncovering their heads, rising up, bowing and keeping silence in their presence. And particularly all undergraduates shall be [thus] uncovered in the college yard when the president or either of the fellows or tutors are there: and when they are in their sight and view in any other place: and all the bachelors of arts shall be uncovered in the college yard when the president is there; and all the scholars shall bow when he goes in or out of the college hall, or into the meeting-house, provided that the public worship is not begun. And scholars shall show due respect and distance to those who are in senior and superior classes.

From chapter 4, "Of Penal Laws"

12. That if any scholar shall write or publish any libel, or raise any false or scandalous report of the president or either of the fellows or tutors or the minister of the First Church of New Haven, or shall directly or indirectly say that either of them is a hypocrite, or carnal or unconverted, or use any such reproachful or reviling language concerning them, he shall for the first offense make a public confession in the hall; and for the second, be expelled.[6]

In the midst of such turmoil, George Whitefield had arrived back in the Colonies in October 1744. In February 1745, there appeared in print the *Declaration of the Rector and Tutors of Yale College*, endorsing a published protest of the Harvard faculty against Whitefield.[7] In spite of such increased opposition, Whitefield stopped at New Haven in 1745 for his second visit. Finding Yale's faculty, along with

---

[6] Dexter, *Biographical Sketches of the Graduates of Yale College* (New York: Henry Holt, 1896), 2:4, 8. I have slightly modernized some of the spelling. Clap also explains his conception of the college's proper demeanor in his *Religious Constitution of Colleges, Especially of Yale-College in New-Haven* (New London, CT: T. Green, 1754).

[7] A small group of New Lights set up an unlicensed seminary in New London, CT, in 1742 and called it The Shepherd's Tent. Quickly expelled from the colony, they afterwards continued for a time in Rhode Island. The persistent Old Light presence at Harvard and Yale, however, would provide momentum for the College of New Jersey (Princeton) as the leading New Light college, receiving its charter in 1746.

Pastor Noyes of First (Center) Church, hostile to him, he spoke to thousands in the open air, from a platform erected beneath two great elms on the north side of the town square.

Eight years later, in 1753, Clap had a complete change of attitude toward New Light preaching. The majority of Yale's Corporation (of which Noyes was a fellow) now noted that "the Reverend Mr. Noyes . . . has been suspected by some of the members thereof of being unsound in the Doctrine of the Trinity, the Divinity and Satisfaction of Christ, Original Sin, Election, Regeneration, and the Doctrines thereon depending."[8] Meanwhile President Clap had observed the faithful work of New Haven's Separatist Church and its New Light pastor. Disgusted with Noyes, and convinced that students needed to be in a doctrinally sound church, Clap obtained permission from the Corporation for the college to withdraw from First Church and establish its own church on the campus, with Clap serving as minister until a college pastor could be secured. To President Clap, this might also serve as an antidote to the Episcopalians, who had just founded their own Trinity Episcopal Church on New Haven Green and were already making appeals for students to attend their worship services.[9] The college soon appointed Rev. Naphtali Daggett to the professorship of divinity, which would include the duties of the college pastorate. Daggett, who had been serving the pastorate of a Presbyterian church in Smithtown, Long Island, conducted his first service in College Hall in November 1753.

When George Whitefield paid his third visit to New Haven, in December 1754, some Old Lights noted in disgust that President Clap entertained the evangelist "much like a gentleman." Moreover, the idea of a separate church within college walls met with strong local opposition. Indeed, to many, the establishment of an independent Congregational campus church, along with compulsory student attendance, constituted a virtual ecclesiastical separation. Nevertheless, the "Church of Christ in Yale College" was founded and soon "an outpouring of the Holy Spirit," under Naphtali Daggett's ministry, marked Yale's second revival. The construction of the first official

---

[8] Brooks Mather Kelly, *Yale: A History* (New Haven, CT: Yale University Press, 1974), 65; see also Tucker, 183–84.

[9] The Episcopalian pastor's two sons were students at Yale.

chapel was completed in 1763.[10] By then, however, local opposition to President Clap's unbendable leadership was provoking serious student disturbances on the campus.

When George Whitefield visited Yale for his fourth and final time in 1764, Clap received him not only with courtesy, but also with complete reconciliation. Clap would depart this life in just three more years (1767) and Whitefield would soon follow him (1770). While Clap, nineteen years earlier, had described Whitefield's preaching as "a scheme to vilify and subvert our colleges,"[11] he now welcomed the evangelist to the chapel pulpit. Whitefield preached powerfully from 1 Corinthians 3:11, "For other foundation can no man lay than that is laid, which is Jesus Christ." Recently, someone—probably a town person—had entered the college kitchen and mixed arsenic with some of the food, causing severe illness. While the students recovered with medical treatment, the contemplation of death had a powerful impact on the campus. During Whitefield's sermon many repented. When he departed from the chapel, students requested that the president go after him and beseech him for another fifteen minutes of exhortation. That last earthly meeting of the two men is a stirring scene. With George Whitefield about to depart from the campus, the venerable president, as student body representative, is standing outside the preacher's chaise, earnestly pleading for just one more "quarter of an hour's exhortation."

During some student disturbances, beginning in 1763, the General Assembly of Connecticut claimed "visitation rights," whereby they could send inspectors to observe the college. Vehemently objecting to governmental involvement, President Clap secured a statement from the students that they had been influenced by individuals not connected with the school to start "riots, rebellions and disorders [in order] to bring a scandal upon the college and the Rev. President's

---

[10] See Ralph Henry Gabriel, *Religion and Learning at Yale: The Church of Christ in the College and University, 1757–1957* (New Haven, CT: Yale University Press, 1958). The first chapel building was replaced in 1824, and this second building was replaced by the present Battell Chapel in 1876.

[11] *Declaration of the Rector and Tutors of Yale-College in New-Haven against the Reverend, Mr. Whitefield, His Principles and Designs* (Boston: T. Fleet, 1745), 10. The letter is addressed directly to Whitefield and Clap was the first to sign it.

government of it."[12] The college's original constitution had stated its purpose of preparing young men "for publick Imployment both in Church and in the Civil State." Believing that such a policy was admitting an undesirable element into the student body, President Clap attempted to establish a safeguard by revising the constitution to assert that "the principal Design of the Institution of this college was to educate persons for the Work of the Ministry." Therefore, "if any scholar shall deny the Holy Scriptures or any part of them to be the Word of God . . . after the first and second admonition, he shall be expelled."[13] Clap encountered legal skirmishes, however, when he attempted to align Yale's teachings with the Congregational ministry. Clap had continued the school's practice of permitting Episcopalian students to enroll, but he firmly insisted that they join other students in conforming to the Saybrook Platform and in attending the Congregational church services on the campus. Episcopalians constantly reminded him that the school had accepted government funds and privileges and that some of its greatest contributors were of the Church of England. A significant portion of Yale's support had come from the government. Similar to the European Reformed tradition, New England churches, schools, and governments interlaced harmoniously. Thomas Clap was determined, however, to maintain the institution's private status that he believed its founders had intended. The current crisis compelled him to do so. Indeed, since 1755, the General Assembly had withdrawn and had never renewed its annual one-hundred-pound stipend to the college. Furthermore, the college had always maintained its own self-perpetuating board of trustees.

---

[12] James B. Reynolds, Samuel H. Fisher, and Henry B. Wright, *Two Centuries of Christian Activity at Yale* (New York: G. P. Putnam's Sons, 1901), 40n2.

[13] Thomas Clap, *Religious Constitution of Colleges, Especially of Yale-College in New-Haven* (New London, CT: T. Green, 1754), on microfiche and microfilm in the Yale libraries; and Thomas Clap, *A Brief History and Vindication of the Doctrines Received and Established in the Churches of New-England, with a Specimen of the New Scheme of Religion Beginning to Prevail* (New Haven, CT: James Parker, 1755), a pamphlet of some 44 pages on microfiche and microfilm in the Yale libraries. See also Roland H. Bainton, *Yale and the Ministry: A History of Education for the Christian Ministry at Yale from the Founding in 1701* (New York: Harper and Brothers, 1957), 12.

So with Yale already separated from the established Congregational church, Clap was now attempting virtually to sever it from state control as well. In his *Annals or History of Yale-College* (1766), Clap carefully notes that the ten ministers who had gathered in the Rev. Russel's Branford home had "founded" the institution as individuals, prior to the convening of the General Court. Each of the ten men had placed his gift of books on the table in Samuel Russel's parlor and said in effect, "I give these books for the founding of a College in this Colony." Therefore, individual clergymen, not the General Court, had founded the school, according to Clap. Indeed, the legislators had passed "an act for Liberty to erect a Collegiate School,"[14] which gave the ministers carte blanche to establish their college. Oddly enough, though, there still remains no consensus among legal experts and historians on whether it was the church, the government, or merely individuals who actually founded Yale College. In reality though, the individual ministers, representing their churches, had founded the institution with the help of the government. There was but little distinction between public and private New England colleges before the middle of the nineteenth century. Besides, no matter who founded Yale, its early acceptance of government funds made it immediately liable and accountable to the government and to the citizens who paid for it. Nevertheless, in 1766, the government blinked—at least momentarily—because of Clap's insistence that, with its proposed "Commission of Visitors," the colony would be sending unnecessary inspectors to inspect the inspectors. President Clap then resigned his office "in consequence of his age and infirmities, and strong desire of private life."[15] He died early the following year, and his successors would halt the effort to liberate the college from governmental control.

---

[14] Dexter, *Documentary History of Yale University*, 20.

[15] Sprague, *Annals*, 1:347. President Clap probably suggested to the legislature that he would appeal to the Crown unless they dropped their visitation idea. In the end, though, Clap was virtually "driven from office by student riots and insurrections." See George Wilson Pierson, *The Founding of Yale: The Legend of the Forty Folios* (New Haven, CT: Yale University Press, 1988), 33; see especially Tucker, 232–62.

That year also witnessed the death of one of President Clap's major theological opponents, Jonathan Mayhew (1720–66),[16] pastor of Boston's West Meeting House. Mayhew had authored the popular sermon, *Striving to Enter in at the Strait Gate* (1761), in which he encouraged diligence in the means of grace as works of holiness unto salvation. Mayhew taught Universalism and defended it with the Governmental view of the atonement. By that time, Mayhew had already denied the deity of Christ and had embraced Unitarianism. His path to apostasy is apparent in his various works, including *On Hearing the Word* (1755), *Christian Sobriety* (1763), and *Two Sermons on the Nature, Extent, and Perfection of the Divine Goodness* (1763).

Contending with War and Infidelity: The Daggett and Stiles Administrations (1766–95)

When President Thomas Clap resigned in 1766, the college felt the loss of his firm leadership. Even in the closing years of his administration, student rebellion had begun to overthrow careful faculty supervision. The final quarter of the eighteenth century witnessed the country's philosophical pendulum swinging radically to the left in matters of academic freedom, with religious and political movements for universal rights campaigning vigorously for "free thinking." Succeeding President Clap, Rev. Naphtali Daggett, the college pastor, served as president *pro tempore* from 1766 to 1777. He was the first Yale graduate to hold the office of president, all of his predecessors being Harvard men. Daggett was a good preacher and a strong patriot during the War for Independence, but he lacked administrative and disciplinary abilities. With all attention focused on the war, the school virtually closed during this time. Tutors resigned to become army chaplains.

---

[16] This is the Mayhew who preached the sermon often called "the spark that ignited the American Revolution." See *A Discourse Concerning Unlimited Submission and Non-Resistance to the Higher Powers: With Some Reflections on the Resistance Made to King Charles I, and on the Anniversary of His Death* (Boston: D. Fowle, 1750). When the same company reprinted it in 1818, John Adams, second president of the United States, described it as having been "a great influence in the commencement of the Revolution."

While retaining the chair of divinity and his position as college pastor, Daggett resigned the presidency in 1777 in order to participate in the war. Rev. Ezra Stiles succeeded him. The British were threatening an invasion of New Haven, and Dr. Daggett was anxious to defend the town. Indeed, on the evening of July 4, 1779, a force of twenty-five hundred British troops landed just five miles from the center of New Haven. While the college quickly moved students to more secure towns,[17] about a hundred students volunteered for local military action. One of them recounted his surprise, as they were passing over West Bridge the next morning to meet the British, to see fifty-one-year-old Naphtali Daggett "riding furiously by us on his old black mare, with his long fowling-piece in his hand, ready for action."[18] The students cheered their professor on as he led the charge. Daggett set himself under cover of bushes and fired on the British until they captured him. Marched at bayonet point for some five miles in the July sun, Daggett suffered fatigue and exposure that resulted in his death the following year.

President Ezra Stiles, a highly intellectual man, had experienced tormenting personal struggles with skepticism subsequent to his 1746 graduation from Yale. "These cost me many a painful hour," said Stiles. "By this time I was so thoroughly acquainted with the scriptures, that I had no doubt whatever of the fundamental doctrines of revelation; but I had strong doubts whether the whole was not a fable and a delusion."[19] Stiles's faith in the Scriptures won out once for all, however, and he was able thereafter to give a solid and sure reason for his faith. While serving the pastorate of the Second Congregational Church of Newport, Rhode Island, for more than twenty years, Stiles had befriended the Jews, visited their synagogue,

---

[17] The freshmen went to Farmington, the sophomores and juniors to Glastonbury, and the seniors to Wethersfield.

[18] Sprague, *Annals*, 1:481.

[19] Ibid., 1:472; and *American National Biography*, s.v. "Stiles, Ezra," by Edmund S. Morgan. The most complete biography of Stiles is Edmund S. Morgan, *The Gentle Puritan: A Life of Ezra Stiles, 1727–1795* (New Haven, CT: Yale University Press, 1962). See especially the 22-reel microfilm edition of *Ezra Stiles Papers at Yale University* (New Haven, CT: Yale University Press, 1976); and Harold E. Selesky, ed., *A Guide to the Microfilm Edition of the Ezra Stiles Papers at Yale University* (New Haven, CT: Yale University Library, 1978).

and learned the Hebrew language. While Stiles entered his presidency as one of the most brilliant and capable theologians of his day, it was a time peculiarly unfavorable to ministerial training.

The war had seriously enervated the spiritual life of the colonies. While brave and noble ministers, carrying Bibles and guns, had valiantly served the patriotic cause, military service continued after the war to draw the best young men of the highest character and morals away from educational institutions, where students of the lowest character and morals were resorting to escape the draft. When President Stiles assumed the additional duties of the college pastorate, he found that, as a preacher, he was unsuccessful. He could not inspire students, and this became frustrating at times. On the Lord's Day, he would often find the need to send tutors to visit students' chambers to check up on them. As chapel speakers began their messages, President Stiles would frequently stand up and "cast his eyes, with minute attention, over all the students, first on one side of the chapel and then on the other to see that they were properly seated and decently attentive."[20] These were times that tried men's souls.

Select Bibliography for Further Reading

Acts of the General Assembly of Connecticut with Other Permanent Documents Respecting Yale University. New Haven, CT: Tuttle, Morehouse and Taylor, 1901.

Ahlstrom, Sydney E. *A Religious History of the American People*. New Haven, CT: Yale University Press, 1972.

————, ed. *Theology in America: The Major Protestant Voices from Puritanism to Neo-Orthodoxy*. Indianapolis: Bobbs-Merrill, 1967.

Baldwin, Ebenezer. *History of Yale College, from Its Foundation, A.D. 1700, to the Year 1838*. New Haven: B. and W. Noyes, 1841.

Clap, Thomas. *A Brief History and Vindication of the Doctrines Received and Established in the Churches of New-England, with a Specimen of the New Scheme of Religion Beginning to Prevail*. New Haven, CT: James Parker, 1755.

————. *Religious Constitution of Colleges, Especially of Yale-College in New-Haven*. New London, CT: T. Green, 1754.

Cowie, Alexander. *Educational Problems at Yale College in the Eighteenth Century*. New Haven, CT: Yale University Press, 1936.

Gambrell, Mary Latimer. *Ministerial Training in Eighteenth-Century New England*. 1937. Reprint, New York: AMS Press, 1967.

---

[20] Reynolds, Fisher, and Wright, 46.

Goodrich, Chauncey A. "Narrative of Revivals of Religion in Yale College, from Its Commencement to the Present Time." *The American Quarterly Register* 10, no. 3 (February 1838): 295–310, the journal of the American Education Society.

Havner, Carter Stone. "The Reaction of Yale to the Great Awakening, 1740–1766." PhD diss., University of Texas at Austin, 1977.

Heimert, Alan. *Religion and the American Mind: From the Great Awakening to the Revolution.* Cambridge, MA: Harvard University Press, 1966.

———, and Perry Miller, eds. *The Great Awakening: Documents Illustrating the Crisis and Its Consequences.* Indianapolis: Bobbs-Merrill, 1967.

Nissenbaum, Stephen. *The Great Awakening at Yale College.* Belmont, CA: Wadsworth Publishing, 1972.

Pierson, George Wilson. *The Founding of Yale: The Legend of the Forty Folios.* New Haven, CT: Yale University Press, 1988.

———. *Yale: A Short History.* New Haven, CT: Yale University Press, 1976.

Reynolds, James B., Samuel H. Fisher, and Henry B. Wright. *Two Centuries of Christian Activity at Yale.* New York: G. P. Putnam's Sons, 1901.

Tucker, Louis Leonard. *Puritan Protagonist: President Thomas Clap of Yale College.* Chapel Hill: University of North Carolina Press, 1962.

Yale College. *Declaration of the Rector and Tutors of Yale-College in New-Haven against the Reverend, Mr. Whitefield, His Principles and Designs.* Boston: T. Fleet, 1745.

15

The New Divinity Theology: Edwardsean Neo-Puritanism

Introduction to the New Divinity

Yale presidents Thomas Clap and Ezra Stiles stood at the forefront among "Old Divinity" Calvinists. Although they were not a unified movement, their key leaders also included David Tappan (d. 1803), the last orthodox Hollis Professor of Divinity at Harvard; Joseph Willard (1738–1804), the last orthodox president of Harvard (1781–1804); Edward Payson (1783–1827), one of most effective pastors in America; Asahel Nettleton (1783–1844), one of greatest evangelists in America; Bennet Tyler (1783–1858), first president of Hartford Theological Seminary (1833); Archibald Alexander (1772–1851), the first professor at Princeton Theological Seminary (est. 1812), along with his student and successor, Charles Hodge (1797–1878).

The Old Divinity men stood opposed to the innovations of an emerging movement called the "New Divinity," which gave birth to an umbrella movement that was later called the "New England Theology," also known as the "New School Theology." The umbrella movement eventually consisted of two overall categories or branches: (1) the more conservative, but innovative New Divinity theology; and (2) the more liberal, and increasingly radical "New Haven" theology.

The New Divinity theology from its inception became identified with Jonathan Edwards Sr., largely because of his two students Joseph Bellamy and Samuel Hopkins. These men were defenders of the faith but were sometimes contagiously enamored with paradox and mystery. The large systematic theology that Hopkins authored gave the additional title "Hopkinsian" to the New Divinity theology.

The New Divinity theology would fully emerge and develop among those who came after Edwards Sr., Bellamy, and Hopkins, but these three planted seed thoughts and allowed them to germinate. The theology would reach its maturity in the writings of Nathanael Emmons and Jonathan Edwards Jr. Together these two men would train or influence through their writings an entire generation of New England ministers who grew increasingly innovative, especially in issues pertaining to the imputation of sin and total depravity. The stage would be set for the radical New Haven system.

Key Features of the New Divinity Movement
(positives and negatives)

(1) Varying degrees of agreement and conviction within the camp

(2) Infralapsarian and supralapsarian advocates on the question of the primary purpose of God in permitting sin to enter the world

(3) Acceptance of the Governmental view of the atonement

(4) Mediate imputation of guilt by individual voluntary sin

(5) Abrogation of Half-Way Covenant and Stoddardism

(6) Sacraments not considered means of saving grace

(7) Increasingly optimistic views of human potential and of the ability of the unregenerate to cooperate with God in their regeneration

(8) Immediate repentance and instantaneous conversion expected

(9) Increasing reluctance towards subscribing to any creed

(10) Gradual departure in emphasis from Calvin and the Westminster Confession on imputation and depravity

(11) Revivals and revivalism under many New Divinity ministries

(12) Taking an anti-Unitarian posture while tolerating weaker views of the Trinity

---

Key Representatives of New Divinity

Jonathan Edwards Sr.

Jonathan Edwards Sr. (1703–58) graduated from Yale and became the Congregationalist pastor in Northampton, Massachusetts.[1] Through his theological and philosophical writings, he encouraged a school of followers called "Edwardseans," or the "New Divinity School," which constituted the initial stage and ultimately the more conservative of the two wings of New England Theology.[2] His own overall emphasis is Neo-Puritan, with a mix of old Puritan doctrine with philosophical idealism and evangelistic fervor. Edwards speculated at length on the idea that man has a natural ability to repent and to believe, even though he will never exercise this ability without God's grace. The New Divinity men would boldly expand upon some of the speculative seed thoughts of their venerable teacher.

Edwards held that every person is responsible for Adam's sin, not only in terms of Adam as the federal representative of the race, but by an *identity in kind*. Every person is *identical* with Adam in nature, or constitution, and therefore *identified* with him *in sin and guilt*.

---

[1] See the outline on Edwards in chapter 13, "Yale College (1701–40): Jonathan Edwards and the Great Awakening."

[2] The best works on New England Theology include Frank Hugh Foster, *A Genetic History of the New England Theology* (Chicago: University of Chicago Press, 1907); and George Nye Boardman, *A History of New England Theology* (New York: A. D. Randolph, 1899). Among more recent works on New Divinity, see Douglas A. Sweeney and Allen C. Guelzo, eds., *The New England Theology: From Jonathan Edwards to Edwards Amasa Park* (Grand Rapids: Baker, 2006); Mark Valeri, *Law and Providence in Joseph Bellamy's New England: The Origins of the New Divinity in Revolutionary America* (New York: Oxford University Press, 1994); John R. Fitzmier, *New England's Moral Legislator: Timothy Dwight, 1752–1817* (Bloomington: Indiana University Press, 1998); and Joseph A. Conforti, *Samuel Hopkins and the New Divinity Movement* (Grand Rapids: Eerdmans, 1981).

Adam was the generic type and root of humanity. Edwards depicts such vivid "*oneness* or *identity* of Adam with his posterity" that the two constitute, "as it were, *one* complex person, or *one* moral whole." As a tree, when a century old, is *one* plant with the little sprout from which it grew, as the body of a man, when forty years old, is *one* with the infant body from which it grew, and as the body and soul are *one* with each other, so there is a divine "constitution" according to which Adam and his posterity are "*looked upon as one*, and dealt with accordingly;" that in his descendants "the *first existing* of a corrupt disposition is not to be looked upon as sin belonging to them, *distinct* from their participation in Adam's first sin;" that "the *guilt* a man has upon his soul at his first existence is one and simple, viz. the guilt of the original apostasy, the guilt of the sin by which the species first rebelled against God. This, and the guilt arising from the first corruption or depraved disposition of the heart, are not to be looked upon as *two* things distinctly imputed and charged upon men in the sight of God," but are one and the same thing, according to an arbitrary constitution, like that which causes the continued identity of a river which is constantly flowing, or of an animal body which is constantly fluctuating. "When I call this an *arbitrary constitution*, I mean that it is a constitution which depends on nothing but the *divine will*, which divine will depends on nothing but the *divine wisdom*."[3]

Edwards explains that while God's permissive decree seems to make sin inevitable, the inherited sin nature makes it universally, personally, and inexplicably voluntary. Some of Edwards's students would find it difficult to evade the conclusion that God is the author of sin since He decreed to permit it into the universe. Edwards, however, argued at length from the Scriptures to demonstrate not only the sinfulness but also the guilt of infants. He refers, for example, to "the command by *Moses*, respecting the destruction of the infants of the *Midianites* (Num. 31:17) and that given to *Saul* to destroy all the infants of the *Amalekites* (1 Sam. 15:3), and what is said concerning *Edom* (Ps. 137:9), 'Happy shall he be, that taketh and dasheth thy little ones against the stones.'" To Edwards, the inclusion of infants

---

[3] Jonathan Edwards, *The Great Christian Doctrine of Original Sin Defended* (Boston: J. Johnson, 1766), 400–34.

in God's command to destroy Jerusalem in Ezekiel 9 provides absolute proof of universal guilt:

> I proceed to take notice of something remarkable concerning the destruction of *Jerusalem*, represented in Ezek. 9, when command was given to them, that had charge over the city, to destroy the inhabitants, ver. 1–8.
>
> And this reason is given for it: that their iniquity required it, and it was a just recommence of their sin, (ver. 9, 10.). . . . Command was given to the angel to go through the city, and set a mark upon their foreheads, and the destroying angel had a strict charge not to come near any man on whom was the mark; yet the infants were not marked, nor a word said of sparing them: on the contrary, infants were expressly mentioned as those that should be utterly destroyed, without pity, (ver. 5, 6.) "Go through the city and smite: let not your eye spare, neither have ye pity. Slay utterly old and *young*, both maids and *little children*: but come not near any man upon whom [there] is the mark."[4]

Conversely, however, Edwards as a philosopher makes the metaphysical and paradoxical distinction between man's "moral" (spiritual) inability and his "natural" (rational) ability, the former being lost by the fall. Edwards bases his speculations upon the theory of a twofold image of God in man. He explains,

> As there are two kinds of attributes in God, according to our way of conceiving Him, His moral attributes, which are summed up in His holiness, and His natural attributes of strength, knowledge, etc., that constitute the greatness of God; so there is a twofold image of God in man: His moral or spiritual image, which is His holiness, that is the image of God's moral Excellency (which image was lost by the fall) and God's natural image, consisting in man's reason and understanding, his natural ability, and dominion over the creatures, which is the image of God's natural attributes.[5]

Edwards's frequent mention of inherent "natural faculties" in the unregenerate opened the door for a softening of the Old Calvinist doctrine of total depravity: "Sin destroys spiritual principles, but not the natural faculties. . . . There seems to be nothing in the nature of

---

[4] Ibid., 165–66.

[5] *Treatise Concerning the Religious Affections*, 2nd ed. (Boston: J. Parker, 1768), 207 (part 3 sect. 3).

sin or moral corruption that has any tendency to destroy the natural capacity, or even to diminish it, properly speaking."[6] To Edwards this at least makes it possible to reason with an unregenerate person concerning God's existence.

Regarding the paradox between a sinner's "natural ability" to believe the gospel, and his "moral" or spiritual inability to be willing, Edwards's students, Joseph Bellamy and Samuel Hopkins, agreed with him that only the elect receive the grace to believe, that regeneration is impossible apart from the Holy Spirit, and that "natural ability is not the same as the "common grace" of Arminianism. Like Edwards, they feared any apparent agreement or possible association with "liberal" Arminianism. Like Edwards, they insisted that no "means of grace," such as sacraments, can bring regeneration. Only belief and repentance can bring salvation. They agreed with Edwards on the doctrines of God's sovereignty and unconditional election. They even agree with Edwards on immediate imputation and total depravity, but on the depravity of the will, Edwards himself made way for changes.

It was tolerance towards the Governmental theory that opened the door to compromise on volitional depravity. The fundamental purpose of the theory is to justify the Benevolent Governor of the universe in His eternal punishment of all unbelievers. The sole foundation for such justification is the inherent ability of all sinners to "hear, see, and desire" Him as Lord and Savior. In his treatise, *Freedom of the Will*, Edwards uses metaphorical terms and expressions, such as "God's government," that are compatible with the Governmental theory. He never explicitly teaches the theory, and, in his conclusion to *Freedom of the Will*, he even offers a rare affirmation of his belief in limited atonement.[7] Edwards, however, never criticizes the Governmental theory. New Divinity theologians would begin with that theory. From there they would gradually tone down and finally

---

[6] *True Grace Distinguished from the Experience of Devils* (New York: James Parker, 1753), "Improvement" 2.

[7] *A Careful and Strict Enquiry into the Modern Prevailing Notions of that Freedom of the Will, which is supposed to be Essential to Moral Agency, Virtue and Vice, Reward and Punishment, Praise and Blame*, 3rd ed. (London: J. Johnson, 1768), 28–38 (part 1 sect. 4); 407–08 (Conclusion).

discard the doctrine of the immediate imputation of Adam's guilt to his posterity. They would conclude that unregenerate humanity possesses the ability to hear the gospel, to see its beauty, and to desire to be set free in Christ. "Desire" is volitional and cooperates with the Holy Spirit in instantaneous regeneration and conversion. A Moral Governor could have had no alternative arrangement in a universe of free moral agents. At least that was the conclusion reached by the New Divinity men, especially after the passing of Bellamy and Hopkins.

Joseph Bellamy

Joseph Bellamy (1719–90), Yale graduate, studied theology in the home of Jonathan Edwards Sr. and served for half a century as the pastor in Bethlehem, Connecticut, where he built a log college and trained well over fifty pastors in the New Divinity.[8] One of his students, Chandler Robbins (1738–99), also a Yale graduate, would go on to become the last Trinitarian pastor of First Church in Plymouth, Massachusetts.

In his work, *Wisdom of God in the Permission of Sin* (1758), Bellamy argues that the existence of sin ultimately makes salvation all the more glorious.[9] Later, in *The Vindication of the Wisdom of God in the Permission of Sin, in Answer to a Pamphlet, entitled "An Attempt," &c.*, Bellamy argues from an infralapsarian perspective that God always works good out of evil and that divine providence guarantees that more good than evil will result. God permitted sin simply by not stopping it.[10] In terms of imputation, Bellamy's view is closer to Edwards Sr.'s than to that of most New Divinity innovators. Bellamy's most influential sermons included those he preached under the title, *True Religion Delineated* (1750). In spite of its clear teaching of an unlimited atonement and its metaphorical implica-

---

[8] The idea of log colleges stemmed from the Scotch-Irish Presbyterian William Tennent Sr. (1673–1746), who sailed from Northern Ireland to America about 1718 with his wife and children. As pastor of the Neshaminy Presbyterian Church in Bucks County, Pennsylvania, Tennent established a log school to educate his four sons for the ministry. Attracting many other students, Tennent's Log College became the forerunner of Princeton College.

[9] Joseph Bellamy, *The Works of Joseph Bellamy, D. D.: With a Memoir of His Life and Character* (Boston: Doctrinal Tract and Book Society, 1853), 2:1ff.

[10] Ibid., 2:97–155.

tions of a Governmental atonement, Jonathan Edwards Sr. contributes a laudatory preface.[11]

Referring to Edwards's endorsement of Bellamy's book, Allen C. Guelzo says, "Even if we disregard all the other evidence pointing to Edwards's governmentalism, and the direct implications of unlimitedness which governmentalism always carried into discussions of the extent of the atonement, it is plain that Edwards had no hesitation about putting his imprimatur upon the New Divinity doctrine of the atonement." In fact, "he pledged his own reputation on its appearance."[12]

Samuel Hopkins

Samuel Hopkins (1721–1803) graduated from Yale and then studied theology in the home of Jonathan Edwards Sr. Hopkins trained many others, especially through his books. His pastorates included the influential First Church of Newport, Rhode Island. It is unfortunate that the term *Hopkinsian* became synonymous with *New Divinity* since advocates of the latter disagreed over so many doctrinal details. Hopkins never consented to his name being used to describe any system. Whereas an element of mystical quietism often characterizes the theology of Edwards Sr., a benevolent activism most often characterizes the teachings of Hopkins. Otherwise, except for his supralapsarianism and historical premillennialism, Hopkins's two-volume *System of Doctrines* (1793) contains but little overall that is essentially different from the teachings of Jonathan Edwards Sr.[13] There is one noticeable difference in emphasis that springs from Hopkins's supralapsarianism.

When the elder Edwards speaks of God's true virtue as "disinterested" (unselfish) benevolence, or "love to Being in general," he

---

[11] Joseph Bellamy, *True Religion Delineated: as Distinguished from Formality on the One Hand, and Enthusiasm on the Other; Set in a Scriptural and Rational Light*, in 2 discourses (1750; repr., Boston: Henry P. Russell, 1804), preface by Edwards.

[12] *Edwards on the Will: A Century of Theological Debate* (Middletown, CT: Wesleyan University Press, 1989), 134–35.

[13] Samuel Hopkins, *The System of Doctrines, Contained in Divine Revelation, Explained and Defended, Showing their Consistence and Connection with Each Other, to which is added, a Treatise on the Millennium*, 2nd ed. in 2 vols. (Boston: Lincoln and Edmands, 1811). In 1:452–61 Hopkins even speaks of man as passive in the Holy Spirit's work of regeneration.

applies "Being" *first* to God, the most sacred reality, then to mankind. Hopkins, in his work *The Nature of True Virtue*, emphasizes that God's ultimate purpose for permitting sin into the world was the happiness of man. Since all sin is selfishness, a holy God could not possibly be concerned about His own glory. The cross displays the ultimate example of this. The Hopkinsian theory is that God permitted sin into the world as the necessary means to the greatest good. It is primarily for the advantage of His creatures that God overrules sin. In 1759, Hopkins preached three sermons on the theme "Sin, through Divine Interposition, an Advantage to the Universe." The sermons are (1) *Sin the Occasion of Great Good*; (2) *Sin's Being the Occasion of Great Good [Is] No Excuse for Sin, or Encouragement to [Commit] It*; and (3) *The Holiness and Wisdom of God in the Permission of Sin*.[14] While Bellamy had argued from an infralapsarian perspective that God permitted sin simply by not stopping it, Hopkins argues from a supralapsarian perspective that it was inexplicably God's will for sin to enter the universe. Christ's atoning work was the *overbalancing good*[15] since a world *redeemed* will be more glorious than a world merely *created*. The fall was the necessary prerequisite for redemption. Evil is the necessary means to a greater good. The concept rested partly upon the Augustinian oxymoron, "O blessed sin" (*O felix culpa*), which had first appeared in a fourth-century line of the Latin Easter Proclamation (*Praeconium Paschale*): "O blessed sin which received as its reward so great and so good a redeemer" (*O felix culpa quae talem et tantum meruit habere redemptorem*).[16] Samuel Hopkins was familiar with its classic expression in John Milton's poem, *Paradise Lost* (1667). In that epic portrayal of salvation history, there is a depiction of Adam just after his fall and just before his expulsion from the Garden of Eden. Michael the Archangel is hastily revealing to the guilt-ridden Adam that "King Messiah" will descend to earth,

---

[14] Samuel Hopkins, *The Works of Samuel Hopkins* (Boston: Doctrinal Tract and Book Society, 1851), 2:491–541.

[15] *System of Doctrines*, 1:414.

[16] The *Praeconium Paschale* became part of the Easter vigil in Latin churches; see *Missale Romanum* (Ratisbon, Germany: F. Pustet, 1963), 227–28. The "felix culpa" line was dropped from the western vigil years ago.

accomplish redemption for the fallen race, and defeat Satan forever-
more. "Replete with joy and wonder," Adam exclaims:

O goodness infinite, goodness immense!
That all this good of evil shall produce,
And evil turn to good; more wonderful
Than that which by creation first brought forth
Light out of darkness! Full of doubt I stand,
Whether I should repent me now of sin
By me done and occasioned, or rejoice
Much more, that much more good thereof shall spring,
To God more glory, more good-will to Men
From God—and over wrath grace shall abound.[17]

It was characteristic of Hopkins to speculate at length on mysteries, and in his writings there are times when he ventures a bit far.
In a single instance, he makes the statement for which he is best remembered. Departing from Edwards Sr., Hopkins carries the idea of
"disinterested benevolence" to an extreme by insisting that without
an unconditional willingness to be damned forever for the glory of
God, one cannot possibly love God or possess any real assurance of
salvation:

No man can know that he loves God, until he does really love him;
that is until he does seek his glory above all things, and is disposed
to say, "Let God be glorified, whatever may be necessary in order
to it," without making any exception: and this is to be willing to
be damned, if this be necessary for the glory of God. And as he
cannot know that he loves God, till he has this disposition, which
is necessarily implied in love to God, he does not know that it
is not necessary for the glory of God that he should be damned.
He therefore cannot know that he loves God, and shall be saved,
until he knows he has that disposition which implies a willingness to be damned, if it be not most for the glory of God that he
should be saved. And if anyone thinks he loves God, and shall be
saved; if he finds that his love to God does not imply, a willingness to be damned, if this were most for his glory, he has reason to
conclude that he is deceived, and that what he calls love to God
is really enmity against him. For he, who cannot love God on

---

[17] John Milton, *Paradise Lost* 12.468–78. This is from the 2nd ed. (London:
S. Simmons, 1674).

any supposition but that he will not damn but save him, is not a friend, but an enemy to God.[18]
A similar view appears in the teachings of French mystics such as Fénelon and Madame Guyon.

Nathanael Emmons

Nathanael Emmons (1745–1840) was a Yale graduate and pastor at Second Church in Wrentham (later Franklin), Massachusetts. In his home he trained as many as a hundred Christian leaders in New Divinity theology. Emmons taught an unlimited atonement, discarded the imputation of sin, and urged upon all men the obligation to practice self-regeneration through moral exercises. One of his popular sermons is titled *The Duty of Sinners to Make Themselves a New Heart* (1812). Yet he far exceeds even the supralapsarian Hopkins by insisting that God directly creates evil volition as necessary for the greater good, and that all men are obligated to be willing to be damned forever to the glory of God.[19]

Jonathan Edwards Jr.

Jonathan Edwards Jr. (1745–1801) graduated from the College of New Jersey (later Princeton), tutored there for a while, and then studied theology under Hopkins and Bellamy. He served as pastor of New Haven's White Haven Church, which James Davenport had established during the first Great Awakening. After serving in a pastorate in Colebrook, Connecticut, he became president of Union College, in Schenectady, New York. The writings of Edwards Jr. constitute the first systematic New Divinity attack against the

---

[18] Samuel Hopkins, "A Dialogue Between a Calvinist and a Semi-Calvinist," in *Sketches of the Life of the Late, Rev. Samuel Hopkins, D. D.*, ed. Stephen West (Hartford, CT: Hudson and Goodwin, 1805), 150. West extracted most of this biography from Hopkins's unpublished autobiographical material.
[19] Nathaniel Emmons, *The Works of Nathaniel Emmons*, ed. Jacob Ide (Boston: Crocker and Brewster, 1842), 2:263, 441, 683; 4:357, 373ff; 5:122–31, 277–90. Biographical material is in 1:ix–clxxv. The best reviews are Henry B. Smith, "The Theological System of Emmons," in *Faith and Philosophy: Discussions and Essays*, ed. George L. Prentiss (New York: Scribner, Armstrong, 1877); and Edwards A. Park, *Memoir of Nathaniel Emmons: With Sketches of his Friends and Pupils* (Boston: Congregational Board of Publication, 1861).

substitutionary nature of Christ's death on the cross.[20] Indeed, his elimination of the substitutionary atonement from New Divinity theology was his deadliest contribution. It was the logical outgrowth of the Governmental theory. Edwards Jr. was the individual chiefly responsible for the Plan of Union (1801),[21] the cooperative missionary and church planting endeavor between Presbyterians and Congregationalists. Besides being a prolific author,[22] Edwards Jr. personally influenced many Yale students and graduates into New Divinity theology.

Final Steps into New Haven Theology

One such graduate, Edward Dorr Griffin (1770–1837), began his many years of professional ministry as professor of Rhetoric at Andover Theological Seminary (1810–11) and concluded them as the third president of Williams College, in Williamstown, Massachusetts (1821–36). Griffin's work during the decade between those two ministries included serving as the first pastor of the Park Street Church, Boston (1811–15). The influence of Edwards Jr. and the Moral Governmental view of the atonement are apparent in Griffin's book, *The Extent of the Atonement* (1819).[23] The second pastor at Park Street would be Sereno Edwards Dwight, son of the famous Yale president, Timothy Dwight. Sereno had just professed faith in Christ in 1815, after hearing a revival sermon from Nathaniel W. Taylor,[24] pastor of New Haven's First Church and developer of the New Haven theology.

---

[20] See, e.g., Jonathan Edwards Jr., "The Necessity of the Atonement, and the Consistency between that and Free Grace, in Forgiveness," in *Theological Tracts*, ed. John Brown (1785; repr., London: A. Fullarton, 1853), 1:333–84.

[21] On the 1801 Plan of Union, see David O. Beale, *In Pursuit of Purity: American Fundamentalism Since 1850* (Greenville, SC: Bob Jones University Press, 1986), 121.

[22] *The Works of Jonathan Edwards* [Jr.], 2 vols. including a memoir of his life and character by Tryon Edwards (Andover, MA: Allen, Morrill, Wardwell, 1842).

[23] Edward Dorr Griffin, *The Extent of the Atonement* (New York: Stephen Dodge, 1819); see also his *Series of Lectures Delivered in Park Street Church, Boston, on Sabbath Evening* (Boston: Nathaniel Willis, 1813).

[24] H. Crosby Englizian, *Brimstone Corner: Park Street Church, Boston* (Chicago: Moody Press, 1968), 73; see also Harold Lindsell, *Park Street Prophet: A Life of Harold John Ockenga* (Wheaton, IL: Van Kampen Press, 1951).

Select Bibliography for Further Reading

Bellamy, Joseph. *True Religion Delineated: as Distinguished from Formality on the One Hand, and Enthusiasm on the Other; Set in a Scriptural and Rational Light.* 2 discourses. 1750. Reprint, Boston: Henry P. Russell, 1804.

———. *The Works of Joseph Bellamy, D. D.: With a Memoir of His Life and Character.* 2 vols. Boston: Doctrinal Tract and Book Society, 1850.

Boardman, George Nye. *A History of New England Theology.* New York: A. D. F. Randolph, 1899.

Conforti, Joseph A. *Samuel Hopkins and the New Divinity Movement.* Grand Rapids: Eerdmans, 1981.

Edwards, Jonathan, Jr. "The Necessity of the Atonement, and the Consistency between that and Free Grace, in Forgiveness." In *Theological Tracts,* 3 vols. edited by John Brown, 1:333–84. 1785. Reprint, London: A. Fullarton, 1853.

———. *The Works of Jonathan Edwards* [Jr.]. With "A Memoir of His Life and Character," by Tryon Edwards. 2 vols. Andover, MA: Allen, Morrill, Wardwell, 1842.

Emmons, Nathanael. *The Works of Nathanael Emmons.* 6 vols. Boston: Crocker and Brewster, 1842.

Foster, Frank Hugh. *A Genetic History of the New England Theology.* Chicago: University of Chicago Press, 1907.

Griffin, Edward Dorr. *Series of Lectures Delivered in Park Street Church, Boston, on Sabbath Evening.* Boston: Nathaniel Willis, 1813.

Guelzo, Allen C. *Edwards on the Will: A Century of Theological Debate.* Middletown, CT: Wesleyan University Press, 1989.

Haroutunian, Joseph. *Piety versus Moralism: The Passing of the New England Theology.* 1932. Reprint, New York: Harper and Row, 1970.

Holifield, E. Brooks. *Theology in America: Christian Thought from the Age of the Puritans to the Civil War.* New Haven, CT: Yale University Press, 2003.

Hopkins, Samuel. *The System of Doctrines, Contained in Divine Revelation, Explained and Defended, Showing their Consistence and Connection with Each Other, to which is added, a Treatise on the Millennium.* 2nd ed. in 2 vols. Boston: Lincoln and Edmands, 1811.

———. *The Works of Samuel Hopkins.* 3 vols. Boston: Doctrinal Tract and Book Society, 1852.

Park, Edwards A. *Memoir of Nathaniel Emmons: With Sketches of His Friends and Pupils.* Boston: Congregational Board of Publication, 1861.

Smart, Robert Davis. *Jonathan Edwards's Apologetic for the Great Awakening: With Particular Attention to Charles Chauncey's Criticisms.* Grand Rapids: Reformation Heritage Books, 2011.

Stewart, Melville. "O Felix Culpa, Redemption, and the Greater-Good Defense." *Sophia* 25, no. 3 (October 1986): 18–31.

Sweeney, Douglas A., and Allen C. Guelzo, eds. *The New England Theology: From Jonathan Edwards to Edwards Amasa Park.* Grand Rapids: Baker, 2006.

16

The New Haven Theology:
From Revival to Higher Criticism;
Timothy Dwight, Nathaniel Taylor,
and Moses Stuart

New Haven Theology, as the second branch of the New School movement, became the extremity and ruin of New England theology. It would gradually stretch speculative concepts far beyond the limits of orthodoxy even to heresy. The New Haven Theology emerged from an inner circle of Yale students whose teacher and friend was another revivalist and defender of the faith, Timothy Dwight, president and professor at Yale College. New Haven Theology is often called Taylorism since it was developed by Dwight's student Nathaniel W. Taylor. New Haven theologians became increasingly dependent on rationalism, evidentialist apologetics, and extreme conclusions drawn from the Scottish Common Sense philosophy.

Key Features of the New Haven Movement
(positives and negatives)

(1) Varying degrees of agreement and conviction within the camp

(2) Abrogation of Half-Way Covenant and Stoddardism

(3) Altars and anxious benches ultimately replacing sacraments as means of grace

(4) A Governmental theory that logically accommodates universal atonement

(5) Belief that in a truly moral universe every subject must be a free agent

(6) Belief that all are born innocent and that all actual sin is voluntary sin

(7) Belief that every person has the natural inborn ability to come to God

(8) Increasing transition from revivals to professional revivalism

(9) Taking an anti-Unitarian posture while tolerating weaker views of the Trinity

(10) Increasing resistance to subscription to creeds

(11) Later representatives finally surrendering inspiration and inerrancy while attempting to appeal to biblical authority

(12) Strained attempts at establishing an identity with Jonathan Edwards Sr.

The Dwight Administration and the Second Great Awakening (1795–1817)

The great westward movement saw some twenty thousand to fifty thousand people on the frontier without a Christian witness. Impoverished conditions followed in the wake of the War for Independence. High taxes and financial depression resulted in Daniel Shay's Rebellion in Springfield, Massachusetts (1786–87). Intemperance led to the Whiskey Rebellion of 1794 in Pennsylvania. Aggressive anti-Christian infidelity had already led the Kentucky legislature, in 1793, to dispense with its Christian chaplain as an unnecessary expense. Signs of spiritual decay were widespread. Both English and French infidelity against God and the Bible had indoctrinated many colonial soldiers. Free thinking and vice were sweeping the country. Pagan philosophy was encouraging drunkenness, fornication, dueling, and suicide. Americans had discovered that there could be a country without a king, or even a prince; that there could be a church without a pope, or even a bishop; and now, many were surmising that there could be a world without a God, or even an infallible Bible. Yale College would not escape such influences.

Yale students formed infidel clubs and scoffed at Christianity as a shackle of superstition. Lyman Beecher recalls from his student days that one evening President Stiles brought a foreign dignitary with him to the college prayers, only to find screaming students running wildly over the chapel pews. Desperately mortified, Stiles tried to quell the tumult but could not be heard. Breaking out in a rage, the president lifted his cane and struck the platform so hard that it shattered his cane to splinters.[1] Until his death in 1795, Stiles saw matters continuing to deteriorate spiritually. Attendance at the college church diminished. Many students became skeptics, kept wines and liquors in their rooms, and practiced various sorts of intemperance, profanity, gambling, and licentiousness. They adored Thomas Paine (1737–1809) and nicknamed each other by infidel heroes such as Voltaire (1694–1778) and Jean-Jacques Rousseau (1712–78). Students openly asserted that God was a mere hypothesis and that Christianity would soon disappear from the face of the earth. Even so, while the administration surely despised such attitudes, they apparently never seriously considered purging the school or even tightening its admissions policies. But such would have been impossible in 1792, with Stiles and the trustees accepting a large grant from the state and adding the governor, lieutenant governor, and six senators to the board.

Timothy Dwight (1752–1817),[2] the initial planter of New Haven Theology, was a maternal grandson of Jonathan Edwards Sr.

---

[1] Lyman Beecher, *The Autobiography of Lyman Beecher*, ed. Barbara M. Cross (Cambridge, MA: Belknap Press, 1961), 1:24.

[2] The best sources on Dwight include the "Memoir of the Life of President Dwight," in Timothy Dwight, *Theology Explained and Defended, in a Series of Sermons*, new ed. in 5 vols. (London: William Baynes and Son, 1821), 1:ix–cxx. One or more of Dwight's sons, perhaps Sereno or Benjamin, most likely wrote this valuable, though anonymous, biography. Also helpful are Charles E. Cuningham, *Timothy Dwight, 1752–1817: A Biography* (1942; repr., New York: AMS Press, 1976); Annabelle S. Wenzke, *Timothy Dwight (1752–1817)* (Lewiston, NY: E. Mellen Press, 1989); John R. Fitzmier, *New England's Moral Legislator: Timothy Dwight, 1752–1817* (Bloomington: Indiana University Press, 1998); William B. Sprague, *Annals of the American Pulpit* (New York: Robert Carter & Brothers, 1857–69), 2:152–65; and *American National Biography*, s.v. "Dwight, Timothy,"

Dwight graduated from Yale in 1769. He returned and served as a tutor under President Daggett from 1771 to 1777. When Daggett resigned in 1777, the students presented a formal petition to the Corporation requesting that they make Dwight the new president. Dwight, however, discouraged the proposition and joined an army brigade as chaplain during the War for Independence, becoming a friend of George Washington. Upon the death of his father, Dwight returned to Northampton, Massachusetts, to care for the family. From 1783 to 1795, he served the pastorate of the Congregationalist church in Greenfield, Connecticut.

In 1795, the college elected Dwight as president, and, among the one hundred ten students enrolled at Yale during 1794–95, no more than eleven professed Christianity. Deist Thomas Paine's *Age of Reason* was hot off the press. Written in a deliberately flippant and shocking style, the book was a typical affront to the Bible and Christianity. Paine condemned the Old Testament for its "obscene stories and voluptuous debaucheries." To Paine, the New Testament was inconsistent and the virgin birth only "hearsay." His *Age of Reason* received a broader circulation than the Bible. Meanwhile, the popular war hero, Ethan Allen (1738–89), a free-thinking Universalist, had published a book called *Reason: The Only Oracle of Man; or a Compendious System of Natural Religion* (1784). Allen claimed to be a Deist. His book consists of thirteen chapters divided into twenty-four short sections. Each section rants against some Christian doctrine such as creation, the Bible's inspiration, the Trinity, the depravity of man, the reality of hell, or the necessity of Christ's atonement. Timothy Dwight wrote of the book,

> When it came out, I read as much of it as I could summon patience to read. Decent nonsense may possibly amuse an idle hour: but brutal nonsense can be only read as an infliction of penal justice. The style was crude, and vulgar; and the sentiments were coarser than the style. The arguments were flimsy, and unmeaning; and the conclusions were fastened upon the premises by mere force.[3]

---

by William C. Dowling. In addition, there are important biographical chapters in Leon Howard, *The Connecticut Wits* (Chicago: University of Chicago Press, 1943); and Moses Coit Tyler, *Three Men of Letters* (New York: G. P. Putnam's Sons, 1895).

[3] Timothy Dwight, *Travels: New-England and New York* (New Haven: S. Converse, 1821), 2:407.

As president of Yale, Dwight approached every task with an enthusiasm that was both effective and contagious. His published chapel discourses demonstrate that he was one of the greatest of America's theologians, and his writings were popular both in America and in Great Britain. Lyman Beecher, who became a Christian under Dwight's ministry, describes the sentiment of many of the students towards this president: "He always met me with a smile," said Beecher, "Oh, how I loved him! I loved him as my own soul, and he loved me as a son. And once at Litchfield I told him that all I had I owed to him. . . . He was universally revered and loved."[4] Dwight delighted regularly in proclaiming Christ as "the only, the true, and the living way of access to God."[5]

Before Dwight's arrival at Yale, the tutors had persistently refused to allow students to ask critical questions. To everyone's surprise, when student infidels handed to President Dwight a list of subjects for public debate, he selected the topic, "Are the Scriptures of the Old and New Testaments the Word of God?" He encouraged them to do their best. During the debate, he respectfully heard their arguments against the Bible and then affectionately and firmly convinced them that their knowledge was superficial. In that debate, Timothy Dwight established rapport with his students. For the next six months, he preached messages emphasizing Bible truth against infidel philosophy and demonstrated a thorough knowledge in both fields. He immediately began giving talks on practical subjects such as proper habits of study. In 1796, he first preached his remarkable evangelistic sermon from Jeremiah 8:20, "The Harvest Is Past," a message that caught the attention of students and gripped them with eternal truth. This sermon would prove to be the seed of Yale's harvest time during the Second Great Awakening. Dwight essentially won the battle against infidelity and immorality when the majority

---

[4] Beecher, 1:27.

[5] See James B. Reynolds, Samuel H. Fisher, and Henry B. Wright, *Two Centuries of Christian Activity at Yale* (New York: G. P. Putnam's Sons, 1901), 52–53. For a completely unsuccessful attempt at diminishing Dwight's spiritual influence in the Awakening, see Richard D. Shiels, "The Second Great Awakening in Connecticut: Critique of the Traditional Interpretation," *Church History* 49, no. 4 (December 1980): 401–15. The author, approaching the topic from a secular viewpoint, interprets Dwight as an opportunist.

of the students began openly seeking after truth. For the graduating class of 1797, he preached two discourses on the nature and danger of infidel philosophy, and these messages left a profound impact upon chapel audiences.

The Second Great Awakening had already been spreading up and down the country for twenty-five years. As early as 1774, James Manning, pastor of the First Baptist Church and president of Brown University, in Providence, Rhode Island, had seen a deep revival in his ministry, necessitating the construction of its present majestic church building. This visitation had begun while Manning was preaching a series of sermons on justification by faith. Meanwhile, revival broke out at Dartmouth College, in Hanover, New Hampshire; the same occurred there again in 1781. Hampden-Sydney College, near Farmville, Virginia, experienced a visitation of revival in 1787. Washington College, in Lexington, Virginia, saw revival in 1790. In 1795, twenty-three New England ministers issued a "Circular Letter," calling for a nationwide "concert of prayer" for revival. By 1800, revivals had swept through many parts of western Pennsylvania, western New York, western Connecticut, western Massachusetts, and Maine. The camp meeting revivals had commenced on the frontier in 1801 and developed concurrently with the "Ivy League Revivals" in the eastern colleges. In 1802, revival came to Princeton College in New Jersey and to Williams College in Williamstown, Massachusetts, where eight additional revivals would occur during the next twenty-six years. In 1801, the Missionary Society of Connecticut (est. 1798) launched the *Connecticut Evangelical Magazine*, which became a major vehicle for the promotion of the Second Great Awakening.[6] Following the 1801 Plan of Union that essentially united Presbyterians and Congregationalists, students were now entering Yale College from the areas that had

[6] Published in Hartford, CT, the *Connecticut Evangelical Magazine* carried numerous firsthand narrative accounts of revivals during the Second Great Awakening; see especially the first eight volumes, covering the years 1801–08; see also the *Religious Intelligencer* magazine and *The Missionary Society of Connecticut Papers*, on 20 microfilm reels at the Yale libraries.

already experienced revival.[7] Four revivals would occur on the Yale campus during the Dwight administration.

In the early spring of 1802, a small group of Yale students agreed to meet daily in earnest prayer that the college might be included in the general awakening. Before long, many other students were meeting together for prayer and confession of sin. President Dwight and various faculty members were holding countless interviews with inquirers. Approximately eighty students were converted.[8] During this time, Benjamin Silliman, a tutor, made a profession of faith. To his mother, in a letter dated June 11, 1802, Silliman wrote, "Yale college is a little temple: prayer and praise seem to be the delight of the greater part of the students, while those who are still unfeeling are awed into respectful silence."[9]

Three years later, Dwight would take on the added responsibility of serving the college pastorate, which earned high admiration from students. His carefully prepared chapel sermons, *Theology Explained and Defended, in a Series of Sermons*, would constitute a multi-volume systematic theology that captured the attention of the academic world on both sides of the Atlantic. In addition, Dwight had already begun to collect and compose numerous poems and hymns for public worship, and his hymn "I Love Thy Kingdom Lord" continues to inspire Christians today.[10]

The 1808 revival came when President Dwight was under great distress over apathy that had fallen over the school. One evening at prayer, he poured out his heart so freely that the students could not

---

[7] A helpful source is Charles Roy Keller, *The Second Great Awakening in Connecticut* (1942; repr., Hamden, CT: Archon Books, 1968), 40–47 and passim.

[8] Chauncey A. Goodrich, "Narrative of Revivals of Religion in Yale College, from Its Commencement to the Present Time," *The American Quarterly Register* 10, no. 3 (February 1838): 295–96, the journal of the American Education Society. Some sources give the enrollment for 1802 as about 160, while others have it 230. All agree, however, that the number of conversions was about eighty. E.g., see Reynolds, Fisher, and Wright, 70.

[9] George P. Fisher, *Life of Benjamin Silliman . . . Chiefly from His Manuscript Reminiscences, Diaries, and Correspondence* (New York: Charles Scribner, 1866), 1:83. For another helpful work on Silliman, see Chandos Michael Brown, *Benjamin Silliman: A Life in the Young Republic* (Princeton, NJ: Princeton University Press, 1989).

[10] For a study of Dwight's poetry, see William C. Dowling, *Poetry and Ideology in Revolutionary Connecticut* (Athens: University of Georgia Press, 1990).

ignore his grief. The following Sunday, he preached on the words that Jesus had spoken to the young man of Nain, "Young man, I say unto thee, Arise" (Luke 7:14).[11] Students repented and the revival continued from April to the end of the term. The president held special weekly meetings for inquirers. All told, there were some thirty converts.

During this time, Yale experienced an unprecedented interest in foreign missions, especially in 1809, with the arrival of Henry Obookiah, a lad from Hawaii. Living for a time with President Dwight and receiving his tutoring from a student, Obookiah directly influenced Dwight to assist in the 1812 founding of the American Board of Commissioners for Foreign Missions (ABCFM), the first American mission board ever to extend its work beyond the nation's borders. In his *Memoirs* (1812), Obookiah reveals his inner struggles, victories, and profound trust in the God of heaven.[12]

The Yale revival of 1812–13 emerged directly from various student societies and activities. One convert, a senior named Elias Cornelius (1794–1832), became a special agent (later secretary) of the ABCFM (Congregationalist), traveling and preaching tirelessly to promote the gospel among the Indians. Cornelius also served as collegiate pastor of the Tabernacle Church in Salem, Massachusetts,[13] where the ABCFM had originated, and where its first missionaries— Adoniram Judson, Luther Rice, Samuel Newell, Samuel Nott, and Gordon Hall—had received their ordination on February 6, 1812, Judson and Rice soon becoming Baptists.

---

[11] The full sermon from Luke 7:11–15 appears in *Sermons by Timothy Dwight, Late President of Yale College, in two volumes* (New Haven, CT: Hezekiah Howe and Durrie & Peck, 1828), 2:186–99.

[12] *Memoirs of Henry Obookiah, a Native of Owhyhee, and a Member of the Foreign Mission School* (Elizabethtown, NJ: Edson Hart, 1819). See especially pp. 20ff. for his recollection of living in the Dwight home.

[13] Elias Cornelius served also as secretary to the American Education Society. For further study of Cornelius, see B. B. Edwards, *Memoir of the Rev. Elias Cornelius* (Boston: Perkins and Marvin, 1833); *Sketch of the Life and Character of the Rev. Elias Cornelius* (Boston: Perkins & Marvin, 1832); "Life and Character of the Late Mr. Cornelius," *The Quarterly Register* 4, no. 4 (May 1832): 249–64, journal of the American Education Society; see also Sprague, *Annals*, 2:633–43; and John McClintock and James Strong, eds., *Cyclopaedia of Biblical, Theological, and Ecclesiastical Literature*, 2:518.

In the spring of 1815, the fourth and final revival during the time of Dwight's presidency manifested itself. A group of students had been conducting secret prayer meetings early every Sunday morning. They saw their prayers answered during the first week of April, at the Sunday evening prayer meeting. It was customary in these services for some member of the senior class to read to the group a selected short sermon or devotional article. On this occasion, the reader, not a seriously inclined person, was sharing a narrative that he had never before seen. It was an account of the death of Sir Francis Newport.[14] During his recital, the narrative so gripped the young man that he could hardly complete his reading. This rush of emotion, where least expected, electrified the student audience, causing many to examine themselves and seek salvation. Some reported that "those who had been most thoughtless seemed to be most affected."[15] During these weeks, some eighty young men repented and publicly professed Christ.

Two years later, in January 1817, President Dwight died. The college enrollment had grown to 313, a large number for any college in those days. For nearly a quarter of a century, Timothy Dwight's Christian character and commanding leadership had influenced Yale students of every walk of life. During his presidency, Dwight's keen interest and encouragement in the sciences had resulted in the establishment of Yale's medical school in 1810. The Honorable Roger Sherman, judge of the Supreme Court of Connecticut, reflected in 1844 that Timothy Dwight had not only rescued the college, but he had become second only to George Washington in the impact that he left on the nation:

---

[14] Devout Christian parents had raised Sir Francis Newport, providing Christian training for the young man and making sure that he knew the fundamentals of Christianity, as well as Latin and Greek. Francis made a clear profession of faith and strongly defended the Bible. In time, he went to London and began working on a law degree. Soon, the worst sort of blaspheming students began ridiculing Newport's faith. At first, he stood strong, but as time went on, he began experiencing serious doubts concerning Christianity and the Bible. He stopped resisting the mockers and eventually joined their company as an out-and-out infidel and apostate. The moving account of Newport's death was published as "The Death-Bed of a Modern Free-Thinker," *The Connecticut Evangelical Magazine* 7, no. 1 (July 1806): 30–40.

[15] Reynolds, Fisher, and Wright, 70.

The high reputation of Dr. Dwight attracted these men . . . by sound argument and overwhelming eloquence. The effect was wonderful. The new philosophy lost its attractions. In Connecticut, it ceased to be fashionable or even reputable; and the religion of the Pilgrims, which was fearfully threatened with extermination, regained its respectability and influence. The character of the College was restored. . . . I often expressed the opinion, which length of time has continually strengthened, that no man except "the Father of his Country," had conferred greater benefits on our nation than President Dwight. Upon the subject of politics he was unreserved and decided. He always espoused the principles of the Federalists, in opposition to those of the school of Jefferson. . . . He was a strong friend of liberty; but considered law, constitutionally enacted, and justly administered, as its only preservative.[16]

New Haven Theology as the Main Wing of New England Theology

Until the establishment of divinity schools, ministerial students would complete their college training and move in with pastors for specific theological and practical studies.[17] Formal postgraduate training came into vogue with the Dutch Reformed establishing the New Brunswick Theological Seminary in 1784, the Congregationalists establishing Andover Theological Seminary in 1808, and the Presbyterians founding Princeton Seminary in 1812. Even the Unitarians at Harvard College had formed a divinity school by 1815. With disestablishment becoming official in Connecticut in 1818, a new age of collegiate competition had already begun when Yale Divinity School was established in 1822. In 1861, Yale would become the first school in the United States to grant PhD degrees. By then, however, a complete theological metamorphosis would have occurred on the Yale campus, and it all began with the emergence of what was soon to become the New Haven Theology.

---

[16] Sprague, *Annals*, 2:164–65.
[17] See Mary Latimer Gambrell, *Ministerial Training in Eighteenth-Century New England* (1937; repr., New York: AMS Press, 1967), passim; and Bainton, 49–61.

Nathaniel W. Taylor

Nathaniel W. Taylor (1786–1858), *developer* of New Haven Theology and founder of Yale Divinity School (1822), was Timothy Dwight's protégé,[18] the first Dwight Professor of Didactic Theology, serving in that position until his death. He had made a profession of faith in 1806 during a talk with Dwight. Living in the Dwight home for a while, he had also become Dwight's permanent amanuensis. Dwight had preached his ordination sermon in 1812 and installed him into the pastorate of the First (Center) Church of New Haven. A decade later, when Taylor resigned the pastorate to lead the Divinity School, his successor at First Church, Leonard Bacon Sr. (1802–81),[19] a graduate of Yale College and Andover Theological Seminary, would embrace Taylor's theological aberrations and reinforce them to students who sat under his ministry. Now located a mile off the main campus, Yale Divinity School originally stood across the street from the present Battell Chapel,[20] and it was here that Taylor took on the task of radically changing the theological tone.

Besides a handsome and imposing appearance, Taylor's brilliance in public speaking won him incredible popularity. Induction into the chair of theology required Taylor to sign a doctrinal statement that carried a solemn promise: "I hereby declare my free assent to the Confession of Faith and Ecclesiastical Discipline, agreed upon by the churches of the State, in the year 1708." The 1708 doctrinal statement was the Saybrook Platform, thoroughly Puritan in the doctrines of hamartiology and soteriology. Violating his signed

---

[18] Nathaniel W. Taylor's papers are at the Massachusetts Historical Society in Boston and at Yale University. Also valuable are the *Monthly Christian Spectator* and the *Quarterly Christian Spectator*, especially during the years 1828–38.

[19] The best sources include Theodore Davenport Bacon, *Leonard Bacon: A Statesman in the Church* (New Haven, CT: Yale University Press, 1931); and *American National Biography*, s.v. "Bacon, Leonard, Sr.," by Daniel G. Reid. Leonard Bacon's *The Genesis of the New England Churches* (New York: Harper and Brothers, 1874) is perhaps his best known work. One of his sons, Leonard Woolsey Bacon, was another well-known Congregationalist pastor and historian.

[20] Built in 1875, this is Battell Chapel's third building. The original Yale Divinity School stood across the street on the corner of College and Elm Streets, where the present Calhoun College stands. In 1932, Yale Law alumnus and benefactor John William Sterling moved the divinity school a mile up the hill to its present location on Prospect Street.

commitment to the doctrinal statement, Taylor set out at once to advance the New Haven theological system that soon became identified with his name. His insistence that the doctrine of hereditary depravity is heresy positioned the New Haven Theology to the left of even men such as Nathaniel Emmons and Jonathan Edwards Jr.[21]

In the wake of what some have dubbed a campus "revival"[22] in 1823, Taylor quickly used the occasion, when doctrine was not a focal issue, to abolish the divinity school's theological soundness test, which had required faculty members to sign the creed. Taylor wanted complete freedom to advance a system that could clear God from the charge of having originated sin. On the authority of their own reasoning, Taylor and his colleagues concluded that God would have been totally unable to prevent sin from entering a universe composed of a moral system and of free moral agents. Such a conclusion stood contrary to that of Taylor's mentor, Timothy Dwight, who had insisted that God decreed to permit sin as a means for the greatest good, thus ultimately manifesting His glory to His creatures. Dwight had agreed with Jonathan Edwards that, because God is absolutely holy, all that He determines must be good; consequently, His decisions stand above all finite investigation and scrutiny.[23]

Finally, at the 1828 Yale commencement, Taylor preached a message that became the manifesto of New Haven Theology, a sermon titled *Concio ad Clerum* ("Advice to the Clergy"), in which he

---

[21] For example, see the insightful *Letters on the Origin and Progress of the New Haven Theology: From a New England Minister to One at the South* (New York: Robert Carter and Ezra Collier, 1837), 10. Valuable discussions on New Haven Theology include Benjamin Breckinridge Warfield, "Edwards and the New England Theology," in *Encyclopedia of Religion and Ethics*, vol. 5, ed. James Hastings (Edinburgh: T. & T. Clark, 1912), 5:221–27; Frank Hugh Foster, *A Genetic History of the New England Theology*; and George Nye Boardman, *A History of New England Theology*.

[22] E.g., see Reynolds, Fisher, and Wright, 314.

[23] The best sources include Douglas A. Sweeney, *Nathaniel Taylor, New Haven Theology, and the Legacy of Jonathan Edwards* (Oxford: Oxford University Press, 2003); Walter O. Loescher, "An Analysis of the Anthropological and Soteriological Conflicts in the Theology of Timothy Dwight and His Influence on Nathaniel William Taylor" (PhD diss., Bob Jones University, 1993), 67ff.; Sidney E. Mead, *Nathaniel William Taylor 1786–1858: Connecticut Liberal* (Chicago: University of Chicago Press, 1942); and *American National Biography*, s.v. "Taylor, Nathaniel William," by Allen C. Guelzo.

defined all sin as individually voluntary—thereby attempting to protect God's integrity in the eyes of His human critics:

> God does give to each a fair trial for himself. Not a human being does or can become thus sinful or depraved but by his own choice. God does not compel him to sin by the *nature* he gives him. Nor is his sin, although a consequence of Adam's sin, in such a sense its consequence, as not to be a free voluntary act of his own. He sins freely, voluntarily. There is no other way of sinning. God (there is no irreverence in saying it) can make nothing else sin, but the sinner's act.[24]

While using the expression "universal depravity" and speaking of humanity as having inherited from Adam a propensity to sin, Taylor insists that humanity's moral depravity could not possibly "consist in a sinful nature, which they have corrupted by being *one* with Adam."[25] To the Old Calvinists, such teaching was demonic at best and foreign to the teaching of the sixteenth-century Reformer of Geneva. Acknowledging that the details of imputation are inexplicable, John Calvin had clearly expressed what he and others saw as scriptural truth, that is, "the only explanation which can be given of the expression, 'in Adam all died,' is, that he by sinning not only brought disaster and ruin upon himself, but also plunged our nature into like destruction." Calvin explained that "by the corruption into which he [Adam] himself fell, he infected his whole seed. . . . The pollution extends to all his seed. Thus, from a corrupt root [,] corrupt branches proceeding, transmit their corruption to the saplings which spring from them."[26] Both the Augustinian and the Federal-Headship insistence on the immediate imputation of guilt to humanity stood in stark contrast to a New England Taylorism that denied humanity's ontological unity in Adam.

The year following his *Concio ad Clerum*, Nathaniel Taylor demonstrated in a letter to a friend that his views were essentially the same

---

[24] *Concio ad Clerum: A Sermon Delivered in the Chapel of Yale College, September 10, 1828* (1828; repr., New Haven, CT: A. H. Maltby and Homan Hallock, 1842), 30. Taylor exhaustively expands on the above views in his *Lectures on the Moral Government of God*, 2 vols. (New York: Clark, Austin & Smith, 1859).

[25] *Concio ad Clerum*, 215.

[26] *Institutes of the Christian Religion* 2.1.

as those of Timothy Dwight.[27] Soon, other New Haven theologians, coming to the defense of the Presbyterian minister Albert Barnes, were also claiming support from Dwight and the English Baptist Andrew Fuller.[28] In his comments on Romans 5:12–19, Dwight argues that no one other than Adam can be condemned for the first sin. Like Taylor, and unlike the Old Divinity, Dwight pulls together verses such as Ezekiel 18:20, "The son shall not bear the iniquity of the father," to argue against the use of the term *impute* as a transfer of participation or guilt:

> *When I assert, that in consequence of the Apostasy of Adam all men have sinned; I do not intend, that the posterity of Adam are guilty of his transgression.* Moral actions are not, so far as I can see, transferable from one being to another. The personal act of any agent is, in its very nature, the act of that agent solely; and incapable of being participated by any other agent. Of course, the guilt of such a personal act is equally incapable of being transferred, or participated.[29]

In agreement with Dwight against imputation, Taylor identifies human reason as his co-authority. In the introduction to his article, "On the Authority of Reason in Theology," Taylor explains: "It will be our object, in the present article, to establish and briefly defend the following proposition, viz:—*that the clear, unperverted deductions of reason, are as binding in their authority, and not less truly to be relied on, than the word of God; and that the former can never contradict the latter.*"[30]

---

[27] Nathaniel W. Taylor, *An Inquiry into the Nature of Sin as Exhibited in Dr. Dwight's Theology: A Letter to a Friend, by Clericus* (New Haven, CT: Hezekiah Howe, 1829); although using the pseudonym *Clericus*, Taylor admitted to writing it; see his *Essays, Lectures, etc. upon Select Topics in Revealed Theology* (New York: Clark, Austin & Smith, 1859), 216. His assessment of Dwight's doctrine of the nature of sin is generally accurate.

[28] For example, see the "Case of the Rev. Mr. Barnes," *The Quarterly Christian Spectator* 3, no. 1 (June 1831): 292–336; and Gerald L. Priest, "Andrew Fuller's Response to the 'Modern Question'—A Reappraisal of the Gospel Worthy of all Acceptation," *Detroit Baptist Seminary Journal* 6 (Fall 2001): 45–73.

[29] Dwight, *Theology Explained and Defended*, 2:3–4 (Sermon 32).

[30] "On the Authority of Reason in Theology," *The Quarterly Christian Spectator* 9, no. 1 (March 1837): 151. The most able apologist for Taylor's views was Yale Divinity School's first professor of Church History, George Park Fisher (1827–1909); see especially Fisher's *Discussions in History and Theology* (New York: Charles Scribner's Sons, 1880), 285–354. Educated in the seminaries at

Taylor found the idea of spiritual and volitional ability so attractive that he added his own spin to it: "Man has within himself a neutral area which is able to respond to the truth."[31] Dwight rejected that idea and Lyman Beecher later recalled firsthand the obvious tension that emerged between Dwight and Taylor over the doctrines of ability and regeneration.[32] Such disagreement would always grieve Dwight, especially since his son Sereno had professed to be a Christian under Taylor's preaching. On depravity, Dwight states his position this way:

> The depravity of Man is a part of his constitution, of his nature, of himself. . . . The first great fact in the science of Man is that he is a depraved being. *This is the first and fundamental fact*, because out of it arise, and by it are characterized, all his volitions, and all his conduct. Hence everything, pertaining to Man, is colored, and qualified, by this part of his moral nature; and no description of him can be true, and no doctrine sound, or defensible, in which this consideration does not essentially enter.[33]

While Taylor equated regeneration with conversion and insisted that any person has the ability at any time to repent and believe, Dwight separated regeneration from conversion and insisted that God must always take the initiative since natural man has no spiritual ability. Nevertheless, while Dwight departed from Taylor,

---

New Haven and Andover, Fisher joined the Yale College faculty and became pastor of the college church in 1854, serving both positions until 1861, when he accepted the chair of Ecclesiastical History in the Divinity School. The most well known of his numerous works include *History of the Christian Church* (New York: Charles Scribner's Sons, 1887); *The Reformation* (New York: Scribner, Armstrong, 1873); and *History of Christian Doctrine* (New York: Charles Scribner's Sons, 1896). Fisher's successor to the chair of Church History was Williston Walker (1860–1922), whose most valuable works include *The Creeds and Platforms of Congregationalism* (1893; repr., Boston: Pilgrim Press, 1960); *A History of the Christian Church* (New York: Charles Scribner's Sons, 1918); and *A History of the Congregational Churches in the United States* (New York: Christian Literature, 1894).

[31] See Loescher, 107.

[32] Beecher, 1:241.

[33] Dwight, *Theology Explained and Defended*, 2:31–32 (Sermon 33). His coverage of the topic of depravity is in Sermons 28–33; see also Sermons 26–27, 74, 76, 80, 91, 100 passim. (Because of the age and wear of my two sets, I am referencing from two printings of Dwight's *Theology*. They are identical except for volume numbers and pagination. For each citation, I chose the set that was the more legible).

he also departed from Calvin and the Old Calvinist theologians at Princeton. With Taylor he defended the Governmental view of the atonement.[34] With Taylor he held that the atonement is unlimited and that man is active in regeneration. While Taylor's views represent a modified Arminianism, Dwight's views represent a modified Calvinism.[35] Loescher observes, "For Dwight the important issue at hand was not consistent systems of theology; rather, it was crushing infidel philosophy and equipping his students against its attacks."[36] Such "crushing" and "equipping," however, required a solid and substantive doctrine of sin, and this was lacking among Dwight's pedagogical tools. Old Divinity conservatives were convinced that with the establishment of an unorthodox hamartiology, schools such as Yale College and Divinity School, along with Andover Theological Seminary, had undoubtedly become vulnerable to arbitrary views on a host of other doctrines as well. Attention would now turn to higher criticism and the Old Testament.

Moses Stuart

Moses Stuart (1780–1852)[37] graduated from Yale in 1799 and became a tutor in 1802. Four years later he replaced the Old Calvinist pastor at the First (Center) Church of New Haven, and the church immediately saw revival, resulting in the addition of two hundred new members. Manifesting a special love for the Bible, Stuart became professor of Sacred Literature at Andover Theological Seminary in 1810, remaining there until his retirement in 1848. His influence continued at Yale through his numerous writings. His meager training in Hebrew at Yale had not prepared Stuart for Andover,

---

[34] Dwight, *Theology Explained and Defended, in a Series of Sermons*, 4th ed. in 4 vols. (London: C. Converse, 1825), 2:195 (Sermon 55); and 2:223 (Sermon 63); Dwight still maintained the propitiatory element of the atonement, but he frames it in Governmental language (2:222). For Dwight's unlimited atonement see 2:118; see also Nathaniel W. Taylor, *Lectures on the Moral Government of God*, 2 vols. (New York: Clark, Austin, and Smith, 1859).

[35] Loescher, 123–43.

[36] Ibid., 194–95; see also Fitzmier, *New England's Moral Legislator*, 105–29.

[37] The best sources on Stuart include John H. Giltner, *Moses Stuart: The Father of Biblical Science in America* (Atlanta: Scholars Press, for the Society of Biblical Literature, 1988); Sprague, *Annals*, 2:475–81; and *American National Biography*, s.v. "Stuart, Moses," by W. Andrew Hoffecker.

where he writes, "I came here with little more than a knowledge of the Hebrew alphabet" and without "the aid of any teacher."[38] Notwithstanding, he developed the first highly regarded Hebrew grammar ever produced in the English language, and he published it on a press that he built in his own home. Stuart's written works were highly esteemed around the world. He inspired students to love the study of languages, and he equipped them with the best philological methods of the day. More than one hundred of his students, including Gordon Hall, Samuel Newell, and Adoniram Judson became missionaries to foreign lands—Judson using his former teacher's methods to translate the Scriptures into Burmese.[39]

While extolling the Bible's divine inspiration and authority,[40] Stuart nevertheless allowed higher biblical criticism to find entry into Andover and Yale, largely by his avoidance of the words *infallibility* and *inerrancy*. Influenced by Johann Gottfried Eichhorn's (1752–1827) multiple-source theory of Genesis,[41] Stuart held that Moses' participation in the work included that of redactor.[42] Unlike later critics, Stuart insisted that Moses was actively involved in the production of all of the Pentateuch and that the days of creation were literal twenty-four-hour days.[43] The kind of documentary hypothesis

---

[38] A letter to the editor by Moses Stuart, "On the Study of the German Language," *The Christian Review* 6, no. 23 (September 1841): 448.

[39] Bainton, 92–93.

[40] Giltner, 47–50, 67.

[41] Eichhorn, a German Protestant orientalist of the Enlightenment, served a professorship in Jena (1775–88) and in Göttingen (1788–1827). Often called "the founder of modern Old Testament criticism," Eichhorn wrote a multivolume introduction to the Old Testament, *Einleitung in das Alte Testament* (1780–83). He held that the Pentateuch was the work of multiple authors, that Judaism evolved from paganism, and that the miracles of the Bible could best be explained in terms of natural phenomena.

[42] Jerry Wayne Brown, *The Rise of Biblical Criticism in America, 1800–1870: The New England Scholars* (Middletown, CT: Wesleyan University Press, 1969), 28, 48–59; see also pp. 45–59, 94–110, and passim; and Giltner, 29–44. Stuart's position often seems closer to that of the French professor of medicine, Jean Astruc (1684–1766), who in 1753 published anonymously a work containing his "conjectures on the original documents that Moses appears to have used in composing the Book of Genesis."

[43] Giltner, 68–69. Stuart insisted that Paul wrote the book of Hebrews; see the introduction to his two-volume *Commentary on Hebrews* (1827–28).

that Moses Stuart used was a precursor of the so-called modern science of biblical theology.

Stuart's debt to Eichhorn actually began at the auction of the library of the late Unitarian Joseph Stevens Buckminster (1784–1812).[44] This used-book sale would change Moses Stuart's life forever. John Giltner, Stuart's biographer, relates what happened:

> At the sale Stuart purchased for himself and the Andover Library a number of important items. And prize books were there to be had, for Buckminster had collected some 2,300 works while in Europe in 1806 and 1807, many of which were on biblical subjects, and some of which he had introduced to America. The jewel for Stuart was Johann Gottfried Eichhorn's *Einleitung in das Alte Testament*, published in Jena in 1780–1783. We need to pause for a moment here, for with the procurement of this book Stuart was about to enter a new world. It is now generally conceded that Eichhorn's was the first truly comprehensive, modern introduction to Old Testament "higher" criticism. (The term itself was Eichhorn's creation.) It is impossible to overstress the importance of the work for Stuart's subsequent career as teacher and writer. Its pages were to excite him at almost every turn, and to open windows upon broad vistas of biblical learning totally new to his experience.[45]

At the auction Stuart soon found himself in one-on-one competition with his liberal friend, Edward Everett, Buckminster's successor at Boston's Brattle Street Church. Stuart himself describes the scene and the aftermath:

> I remember, with lively and pleasant emotion, the contest between him and me at the sale for Eichhorn's *Introduction to the Old Testament*. . . . We bid upon the volumes (there were four) until we rose above six dollars apiece, (for a moderate octavo on coarse hemp-paper); and finally I won the prize by bidding six dollars and a quarter for each volume. I have since purchased all four for as many dollars. Yet the acquisition of that book has spread its influence over my whole subsequent life.[46]

---

[44] Joseph Stevens Buckminster was the pastor of Boston's Brattle Street Church and turned it into a Unitarian church in 1805. He soon became the first Dexter Lecturer in Biblical Criticism at Harvard.

[45] Giltner, 8–9.

[46] Moses Stuart, "On the Study of the German Language," *The Christian Review* 6, no. 23 (September 1841): 457.

While Stuart opposed the Unitarian movement of his day, he translated and published one of Friedrich Schleiermacher's essays on the Trinity.[47] With this liberal theologian of the University of Berlin, Stuart scorned the doctrine of the eternal sonship of Christ. Schleiermacher (1768–1834) speculated that the classic Trinitarian formula could not apply to God's ultimate being since God is so intertwined with the material world. This line of reasoning, developed further by Albrecht Ritschl (1822–89), would conclude that whatever does not have immediate practical value is without any real value at all. It was for this reason that, with Schleiermacher, Moses Stuart disdainfully described the classical creeds of Christendom as having little if any value. While Stuart was less radical than Schleiermacher, in his introduction to Schleiermacher's work, he eulogizes the liberal as a model Christian and eagerly introduces him to evangelical conservatives.[48] Charles Hodge at Princeton saw Schleiermacher's teachings as pantheistic.[49] It is undeniable that Stuart's work contributed to the decline of the importance of the doctrine of the Trinity in nineteenth-century New England theology.

During Stuart's entire forty years at Andover, his colleague Leonard Woods (1774–1854), a Harvard graduate, was serving as professor of Theology. Woods was an evangelical Calvinist and a founder of the American Tract Society and of the American Board of Commissioners for Foreign Missions, but he raised no significant voice of opposition to Stuart. In his *History of Andover Seminary*, Woods frequently hints at the tension that existed among his colleagues, especially on the matter of subscribing to the creed.[50] But while opposing Unitarianism, Woods defends Stuart.

---

[47] Moses Stuart, *Letters on the Eternal Generation of the Son of God, addressed to the Rev. Samuel Miller* (Andover, MA: Flagg and Gould, 1822); and Frederic Schleiermacher, "On the Discrepancy between the Sabellian and Athanasian Method of Representing the Doctrine of a Trinity in the Godhead," trans. with notes and illustrations by Moses Stuart, in *Biblical Repository and Quarterly Observer* 5, no. 18 (April 1835): 265–353; and 6, no. 19 (July 1835): 1–116.

[48] See Stuart's introduction to Schleiermacher, "On the Discrepancy between the Sabellian and Athanasian Method," 60–65.

[49] Charles Hodge, *Systematic Theology* (New York: Scribner, Armstrong, 1877), 2:138–40.

[50] Leonard Woods, *History of Andover Seminary* (Boston: James R. Osgood, 1885).

Moses Stuart brutally attacks the Old Calvinist doctrine of the imputation of Adam's guilt to the human race. With the supposition that each person becomes a sinner whenever he becomes account-able, Stuart asserts that in the Bible there is absolutely no doctrine of imputation, either of Adam's sin or of Christ's righteousness.[51] During Stuart's final twelve years at Andover, one of his closest col-leagues was Edwards A. Park (1808–1900), the man who would de-fine the New Haven Theology. While serving at Andover (1836–81), Park founded the journal *Bibliotheca Sacra* (1844) and edited it for decades. Park taught Dynamic (partial) Inspiration of the Bible, claimed to be Edwardsean, professed to be a five-point Calvinist, and wrote a major defense for the New England Theology.[52]

Final Preparations for Bushnellianism

In 1824, Yale College hired Josiah Willard Gibbs (1790–1861)[53] as librarian and lecturer of Biblical Literature. Two years later, Nathaniel W. Taylor brought Gibbs into the Divinity School to teach Greek and Hebrew. A Yale College graduate (1809), Gibbs had re-ceived his seminary training at Andover, while residing in the home of Professor Moses Stuart. Like Stuart, Gibbs accepted a German docu-mentary hypothesis of the Pentateuch and adamantly defended it: "Our theologians, English and American [,] have been very reluctant to admit this theory. But we do not see how the truth of it can well be denied. . . . It is not a question to be decided by appeals to popular impressions, but by a candid examination of all the facts."[54] Applying multiple-source theories to New Testament books as well, Gibbs drew

---

[51] Moses Stuart, "Have the Sacred Writers Any Where Asserted that the Sin or Righteousness of One is Imputed to Another?" *American Biblical Repository* 7, no. 22 (April 1836): 241–330; and Moses Stuart, *Commentary on the Epistle to the Romans* (New York: J. Leavitt, 1832), 200–243, 533–53, in his comments on Rom. 5:12–19.

[52] Edwards Amasa Park, "New England Theology," *Bibliotheca Sacra* 9, no. 33 (January 1852): 170–220.

[53] Gibbs's papers are housed in Yale's Sterling Memorial Library. His son wrote the family history—Josiah Willard Gibbs, *Memoir of the Gibbs Family of Warwickshire, England and United States of America* (Philadelphia: Lewis and Greene, 1879); see also *American National Biography*, s.v. "Gibbs, Josiah Willard," by Benjamin R. Foster.

[54] Cited in Bainton, 106.

similar conclusions, such as his proposition that Matthew might have taken his first chapter from some other document.[55] Specializing in the study of philology, Gibbs went to great extremes in attempting to demonstrate the evolution of Bible words, many of which he often stripped of any concrete meaning. Such ideas would form the basis of the liberal theology of Gibbs's student, Horace Bushnell.[56]

Select Bibliography for Further Reading

Beecher, Lyman. *The Autobiography of Lyman Beecher*. Edited by Barbara M. Cross. Cambridge, MA: Belknap Press, 1961.

Brown, Jerry Wayne. *The Rise of Biblical Criticism in America, 1800–1870: The New England Scholars*. Middletown, CT: Wesleyan University Press, 1969.

Dwight, Timothy. *The Nature, and Danger, of Infidel Philosophy: Exhibited in Two Discourses, Addressed to the Candidates for the Baccalaureate, in Yale College / by the Rev. Timothy Dwight, D.D., President of Yale College; September 9th, 1797*. New Haven, CT: George Bunce, 1798.

———. *Sermons by Timothy Dwight, Late President of Yale College*. 2 vols. New Haven, CT: Hezekiah Howe and Durrie & Peck, 1828.

———. *Theology Explained and Defended, in a Series of Sermons*. New ed. 5 vols. London: William Baynes and Son, 1821.

Loescher, Walter O. "An Analysis of the Anthropological and Soteriological Conflicts in the Theology of Timothy Dwight and His Influence on Nathaniel William Taylor." PhD diss., Bob Jones University, 1993.

Priest, Gerald L. "Revival and Revivalism: A Historical and Doctrinal Evaluation." *Detroit Baptist Seminary Journal* 1 (Fall 1996): 223–52.

———. "Andrew Fuller's Response to the 'Modern Question'—A Reappraisal of the Gospel Worthy of all Acceptation." *Detroit Baptist Seminary Journal* 6 (Fall 2001): 45–73.

Reynolds, James B., Samuel H. Fisher, and Henry B. Wright. *Two Centuries of Christian Activity at Yale*. New York: G. P. Putnam's Sons, 1901.

Sweeney, Douglas A. *Nathaniel Taylor, New Haven Theology, and the Legacy of Jonathan Edwards*. Oxford: Oxford University Press, 2003.

Taylor, Nathaniel W. "On the Authority of Reason in Theology." *The Quarterly Christian Spectator* 9, no. 1 (March, 1837): 151–62.

———. *Concio ad Clerum: A Sermon Delivered in the Chapel of Yale College, September 10, 1828*. New Haven: Hezekiah Howe, 1828.

Wayland, John Terrill. "The Theological Department in Yale College, 1822–1858." PhD diss., Yale University, 1933. This was also reprinted under the same title, New York: Garland Publishing, 1987, as part of the series American Religious Thought of the 18th and 19th Centuries.

---

[55] Brown, *Rise of Biblical Criticism in America*, 171–75.

[56] Bainton, 120–21. Bushnell expresses appreciation for the influence of Gibbs in his theology.

17

Horace Bushnell, Charles Finney, D. L. Moody, and Beyond

Horace Bushnell

Horace Bushnell (1802–76)[1] graduated from Yale in 1827. He returned as a tutor in 1829 to enter law school, and, upon completion of his studies in 1831, he was pressured into making a decision during what some have called a revival[2] preached by Yale College professor Chauncey A. Goodrich (1790–1860),[3] who had been teaching extreme New Haven views on original sin as early as 1821.[4]

---

[1] The bulk of the Bushnell papers are housed in the library of Yale Divinity School and in Yale University's Sterling and Beinecke Libraries. In addition, miscellaneous papers are in Harvard University's Houghton Library. The oldest standard biography of Bushnell was compiled by his daughter, Mary A. Cheney (Bushnell), ed., *Life and Letters of Horace Bushnell* (New York: Charles Scribner's Sons, 1903). Bushnell's works were published in 12 volumes in 1903. He continues to draw wide attention; e.g., see James O. Duke, *Horace Bushnell on the Vitality of Biblical Language* (Chico, CA: Scholars Press, 1984); Robert Lansing Edwards, *Of Singular Genius, of Singular Grace: A Biography of Horace Bushnell* (Cleveland, OH: Pilgrim Press, 1992); Lee J. Makowski, *Horace Bushnell on Christian Character Development* (Lanham, MD: University Press of America, 1999); and *American National Biography*, s.v. "Bushnell, Horace," by E. Brooks Holifield.

[2] It is described as a "Great Revival" in James B. Reynolds, Samuel H. Fisher, and Henry B. Wright, *Two Centuries of Christian Activity at Yale* (New York: G. P. Putnam's Sons, 1901), 314.

[3] *American National Biography*, s.v. "Goodrich, Chauncey Allen," by Allen C. Guelzo.

[4] *Letters on the Origin and Progress of the New Haven Theology. From a New England Minister to One at the South*, 7–11.

Not a gifted speaker, Goodrich had the unpleasant task of teaching homiletics in Yale Divinity School.[5] As for Bushnell's "profession," one of his early biographers described it as a "conversion to duty."[6] Bushnell's doubts concerning the Trinity would eventually help to earn him an honorary degree from Harvard. Meanwhile, he began two years of study in Yale Divinity School, where Nathaniel W. Taylor molded his theology and Josiah Willard Gibbs shaped his philology. Building on the ideas of Taylor and Gibbs, Bushnell concluded that since truth is abstract, words are incapable of communicating it. Bushnell would turn to human experience for his authority.

Graduating in 1833, he became pastor of the North (now Park) Congregational Church in Hartford, Connecticut, where he remained until 1859. That was the same year that Yale College officially abolished its evening prayer time. Ironically, this was the year that prayer meeting revivals were sweeping much of the country. For years, Bushnell preached repeatedly in the Yale chapel. Insisting that words can have no absolute meaning, Bushnell questioned the value of creeds and "frankly consigned Genesis to mythology."[7] Yale soon eliminated its long-standing Sunday afternoon preaching service. After all, why listen to so many words when words have no real meaning except that which each hearer ascribes to them? Roland Bainton notes that from Hartford, Horace Bushnell "was to exert a greater influence over the mind of the Yale Divinity School than that of any formal member of the faculty."[8]

Influenced by the Romantic Movement, Bushnell looked more to nature than to the Bible for truth and believed with Schleiermacher that true religion always focuses on human feeling. Such ideas

---

[5] Chauncey A. Goodrich bought and edited the *Monthly Christian Spectator* newspaper in 1828 to spread Taylor's views. He eventually transformed the paper into the *Quarterly Christian Spectator*, and it continued until 1838. These papers are a prime source for researching the essence of the New Haven Theology. Goodrich would later serve as editor of the third and fourth editions of the *American Dictionary of the English Language*, produced by his father-in-law, Noah Webster, who had graduated from Yale in 1778.

[6] Theodore T. Munger, *Horace Bushnell: Preacher and Theologian* (Boston: Houghton, Mifflin, 1899), 23–29.

[7] See Roland H. Bainton, *Yale and the Ministry* (New York: Harper and Brothers, 1957), 119.

[8] Ibid., 114.

find expression in Bushnell's *Nature and Supernatural Together Constituting the One System of God* (1858). His *God in Christ* (1849) is a Modalistic denial of Christ's distinct personality. The various editions of his book *Christian Nurture* reveal the development of his basic ideas, which deny the necessity of instantaneous regeneration.[9] He asserts that a child born of Christian parents enters the world as a Christian. The parental responsibility is to nurture the child's inherent regeneration. The child should grow up with the assumption that he has been a Christian from the day that he was born. The book's title prompted the creation of the Horace Bushnell Chair of Christian Nurture in the Yale Divinity School.[10] In his book, *The Vicarious Sacrifice* (1866), he prefers the moral influence view of the atonement to any doctrine of vicarious propitiation of God's holiness. Bushnell insists that Jesus did nothing more for us than what God expects us to do for others. His books continue to provide encouragement to liberal theological aberrations such as Christological Modalism and the Social Gospel. With the rapid leftward turn of New Haven theologians, the New England Theology was in a tailspin by the mid-nineteenth century.

The Plan of Union: Old School versus New School

In the earliest years of the nineteenth century, the New School men had hardly considered themselves liberals in the modern sense of the term. Most never questioned the Bible's authority; in fact, they embraced its inspiration. Indeed, in 1801 an agreement called the Plan of Union was established to provide for close cooperation between the Presbyterians and the Congregationalists in forming new churches in the rapidly expanding American West, which meant western New York and Ohio at the time. For thirty-five years, great numbers of churches were founded under the Plan of Union, but basic differences in theology and polity within the Presbyterian Church would lead to the Schism of 1836–37, when the denomination divided into the Old School and New School branches.

---

[9] See especially editions 1847, 1861, 1867, 1872, and 1876.
[10] Bainton, 124.

The Old School had already sounded the alarm. As early as 1830, for instance, Archibald Alexander, father of the Old Princeton Theology, had cautioned, "If the doctrine of imputation be given up, the whole doctrine of original sin must be abandoned. And if this doctrine be relinquished, then the whole doctrine of redemption must fall, and . . . what remains will not be worth a serious struggle." Pointing to Scripture such as Ephesians 2:3, which describes all people as "by nature the children of wrath," Alexander adds, "The cardinal point of the Pelagian system was the denial of original sin" and this was "their radical error, from which all the rest naturally germinated."[11]

The Old School party, as the name implies, insisted on maintaining the denomination's distinctive traits: strict Presbyterian church government; benevolent and evangelistic work carried out by Presbyterian agencies or boards; Reformed theology as it has been historically understood; and traditional methods of evangelism, in contrast to the emerging "new measures" as practiced by Charles Finney, the popular evangelist of the New Haven theology.

The Old School had succeeded in bringing Albert Barnes (1798–1870) and Lyman Beecher (1775–1863) to trial in the 1830s. Barnes, pastor of First Presbyterian Church in Philadelphia, is best remembered today for his *Notes on the Old and New Testaments*. Beecher, president of Lane Theological Seminary, appeared more inclined than Barnes towards extreme New Haven Theology.[12] Although the church acquitted these men of all charges of heresy in 1835 and 1836 respectively, the trials themselves and especially Barnes's "provisional censure" in 1831 reflected the increasing tension between the Old and New Schools—tension that would lead to the Great Schism of 1837–69. In 1837, the Old School conservatives controlling the General Assembly abrogated the 1801 Plan of Union, officially separating the already divided parties.

It was during the Great Schism that Andover Seminary professor Edwards A. Park, in the *Bibliotheca Sacra*, served as historian

---

[11] "Early History of Pelagianism," *The Biblical Repertory and Theological Review* 2, no. 1 (January 1830): 93, 112.

[12] Milton Rugoff, *The Beechers: An American Family in the Nineteenth Century* (New York: Harper and Row, 1981), 152–70.

and apologist for the New England Theology.[13] His discourse "The Theology of the Intellect and of the Feelings"[14] led to a major controversy with Charles Hodge of Princeton Theological Seminary.[15] In addition, the schism would eventually sever Charles Finney, with his new measures and new doctrines, along with Oberlin College, from any working relationship with Presbyterian churches.

Charles G. Finney and Oberlin Theology

Charles G. Finney (1792–1875)[16] was born in Warren, Connecticut. While studying law in Adams, New York, in 1821, he experienced what he describes as a conversion and a baptism of the Holy Spirit. Two years later the Presbyterian churches commissioned him to preach. Receiving Presbyterian ordination in 1824, he worked as a revivalist in upstate New York for the next five years. In New York City he served as pastor of Second Presbyterian Church (1832–36) and Broadway Tabernacle (1836–37). Now, with the great Schism about to erupt and his New Haven aberrations already under scrutiny from the Presbyterians, Finney and Broadway Tabernacle became Congregationalist in 1834.

Meanwhile, in 1832, Lyman Beecher (1775–1863), the famous New England preacher, and father of Henry Ward Beecher and Harriet Beecher Stowe, had become president of Lane Theological Seminary in Cincinnati, Ohio, a school recently established (1829) under the Plan of Union. Beecher had studied theology

---

[13] "New England Theology," *Bibliotheca Sacra* 9, no. 33 (January 1852): 170–220.

[14] "The Theology of the Intellect and of the Feelings," *Bibliotheca Sacra* 7, no. 27 (July 1850): 533–69. This was "a discourse delivered before the Convention of the Congregational Ministers of Massachusetts, in the Brattle Street Meetinghouse, Boston, May 30, 1850."

[15] Charles Hodge, "Professor Park's Sermon," *Biblical Repertory and Princeton Review* 22, no. 4 (October 1850): 642–74; Charles Hodge, "Prof. Park's Remarks on the Princeton Review," *Biblical Repertory and Princeton Review* 23, no. 2 (April 1851): 306–47; and Charles Hodge, "Professor Park and the Princeton Review," *Princeton Review* 23, no. 4 (October 1851): 674–95.

[16] The prime source is Garth M. Rosell and Richard A. G. Dupuis, eds., *The Memoirs of Charles G. Finney: The Complete Restored Text* (Grand Rapids: Zondervan, 1989); see also Keith J. Hardman, *Charles Grandison Finney 1792–1875: Revivalist and Reformer* (Syracuse: Syracuse University Press, 1987).

under Timothy Dwight and served as pastor of several prominent churches. Although his early ministry was characterized by conservative Calvinism, by the 1830s he had become a popularizer of New Haven Theology.

In 1834, over the opposition of fiery abolitionists such as Theodore D. Weld, Beecher refused to offer courses to African Americans.[17] When tensions climaxed between abolitionist students and the board of trustees, Professor John Morgan (1802–84) and board member Asa Mahan (1799–1889), along with some fifty students, left the Cincinnati school. In the fall of 1835, the group accepted an invitation to help establish a theological department at Oberlin Collegiate Institute, an Ohio school that had just been established in 1833 under the Plan of Union. Asa Mahan became Oberlin's president and Charles Finney became professor of Theology. The 1844 catalog refers to the Theology Department as "Oberlin Theological Seminary" for the first time. In 1850, Oberlin Collegiate Institute became Oberlin College, and in 1851, Finney became its second president. It was here that Asa Mahan and Charles Finney originated a scheme of sanctification that received the label of "Oberlin Perfectionism."

Finney's emphasis had shifted from mere conversion to perfectionism,[18] a "second experience," called entire sanctification, but not identical with the Wesleyan and Methodist doctrine of sanctification. While Finney remained without theological training, he wrote his own books, including a *Systematic Theology*, based upon his classroom lectures at Oberlin.

Two Contrasting Emphases that Emerged from the Oberlin Theology

A Twofold Pragmatism	A Twofold Perfectionism
utilitarian in the outward life	deeper (or higher) inward life
new measures for evangelism	mysticism and quietism

---

[17] Lyman Beecher's tomb is in Grove Street Cemetery in New Haven.

[18] Prime sources for Oberlin's views, as promoted by Asa Mahan and Charles G. Finney, include the college's periodicals, *The Oberlin Evangelist* (24 vols. 1839–62) and *The Oberlin Quarterly Review* (4 vols. 1845–49).

While Charles Finney's style of writing includes enormous contradiction, the following statements are predominant key themes that stand out as repetitious and characteristic features of his theology. Every person is born with a bad nature, but not a depraved one: "We deny that the human constitution is morally depraved."[19] Adam's sin did not result in the imputation of guilt to anyone. God is just and justice demands that neither sin nor holiness can be transmitted, inherited, or imputed from one person's account to another person's account. Hence, the atonement cannot involve the transfer of our guilt to Christ or of His righteousness to us. Finney explains: "The doctrine of an imputed righteousness, or that Christ's obedience to the law was accounted as our obedience, is founded on a most false and nonsensical assumption; to wit, that Christ owed no obedience to the law in His own person." In Finney's view, Christ "for himself" alone, was "bound to love God with all his heart, and soul, and mind, and strength, and his neighbor as Himself. He did no more than this. He could do no more. It was naturally impossible, then, for Him to obey in our behalf."[20]

On the basis of the Governmental theory of the atonement, Finney again insists that under a system of justice there can be no imputation of anyone's sin or righteousness to anyone else. Instead, the agonizing death of His innocent Son on the cross was the Father's public demonstration of His "Moral Government," an illustration of punishment, and a deterrent to sin, in order that He as "Benevolent" Governor might be able to extend mercy to anyone He wished without raising doubts about His evenhandedness. Christ's death was not an expiatory payment to any offended party. The cross was an exhibition of disinterested benevolence and loving punishment to deter sin and to make forgiveness and punishment fair in the case of any sinner. Rather than being a satisfaction for man's sin debt, Christ's atonement was a "Moral Influence," an example for all mankind to follow. Finney explains,

In the atonement, God has given us the influence of his own example, has exhibited his own love, his own compassion, his own

---

[19] Charles G. Finney, *Lectures on Systematic Theology* (London: William Tegg, 1851), 391.

[20] Ibid., 548–49.

self-denial, his own patience, his own long-suffering, under abuse from enemies. . . . This is the highest possible moral influence. . . . The influence of the atonement, when apprehended by the mind, will accomplish whatever is within the compass of moral power to effect.[21]

According to Finney, election is based upon foreseen sanctification and perseverance.[22] All of the sanctified elect will ultimately persevere.[23] Regeneration is the initial and volitional change of mind, character, and direction towards sanctification.[24] He also calls this initial experience "conversion." While Finney often mentions God as being actively involved in man's regeneration, the emphasis remains on man's ability.[25] When entire sanctification is attained, the converted Christian becomes a justified Christian. Rather than being a forensic act of God, justification is the attainment of entire sanctification. A key condition of justification is entire surrender and full sanctification.[26]

Finney says that a truly repentant sinner yields his will to God and turns from his sin for the time being, but the old sinful inner man remains as part of the double personality of the new convert.[27] Since sanctification can be lost, justification must be reattained whenever necessary, and this requires a "fresh baptism of the Holy Spirit." Rejecting the traditional Protestant view that a Christian is a saint and sinner at the same time (*simul iustus et peccator*), Finney developed a gospel that included a second stage intended to eliminate the old man and to give exclusive residence to the new man. The second stage is a special experience that lifts the Christian from partial to complete sanctification. The attainment of this experience is always possible and obligatory to the Christian, just as the initial regeneration is always possible and obligatory to the sinner. The only stumbling block is imperfect faith, which constantly divides Christians into two classes—the simply converted and the entirely

---

[21] Ibid., 338.
[22] Ibid., 768.
[23] Ibid., 836ff.
[24] Ibid., 410.
[25] Ibid., 479–521.
[26] Ibid., 555.
[27] Ibid., 523.

sanctified. While Finney never knows precisely how to categorize those who are merely converted, he insists that man is able perfectly to keep all the law of God. He views the man in Romans 7 as still struggling under the law and the man in Romans 8 as the apostle Paul, who has finally attained unto entire sanctification.[28]

While elements of Finney's rationalism, moral atonement, human ability, and benevolence passed into the liberal social gospel, elements of his natural theology, human ability, regeneration, conversion, and sanctification found lodging among many conservatives within the broad spectrum of evangelicalism.[29] Far-reaching aspects of Finney's theology made rapid inroads into Yale College and Divinity School.

Yale and Theology to the Early Twentieth Century

The remainder of the nineteenth century witnessed enormous doctrinal change on the Yale campus. It was an era of great personalities, and Yale saw her share—students, professors, and guest speakers. Baptist theologian August H. Strong (1836–1921), for example, was converted under Charles Finney and educated under Nathaniel Taylor at Yale. Episcopalian bishop Phillips Brooks (1835–93), who composed the Christmas carol "O Little Town of Bethlehem" for Sunday school children during the Civil War, annually addressed Yale's Berkeley Association of Episcopalian students, advancing the tenets of the Protestant Episcopal Church. Then the popular Lyman Beecher Lectures brought a wide spectrum of speakers to the campus. One student during these years, Reuben Archer

---

[28] Ibid., 584ff.; 598ff.; 735–66.

[29] Melvin Vulgamore, "Social Reform in the Theology of Charles Grandison Finney" (PhD diss., Boston University, 1963); Leonard I. Sweet, "The View of Man Inherent in New Measures Revivalism," *Church History* 45, no. 2 (June 1976): 206–21; Charles Hodge's review of "Finney's Lectures on Systematic Theology," *Biblical Repertory and Princeton Review* 19, no. 2 (April 1847): 237–77; Benjamin Breckinridge Warfield, *Perfectionism* (New York: Oxford University Press, 1931), 2:3–215; Gerald L. Priest, "Revival and Revivalism: A Historical and Doctrinal Evaluation," *Detroit Baptist Seminary Journal* 1 (Fall 1996): 223–52; and Whitney R. Cross, *Burned-Over District: The Social and Intellectual History of Enthusiastic Religion in Western New York, 1800–1850* (Ithaca, NY: Cornell University Press, 1981).

Torrey (1856–1928),[30] would become one of America's best-known Congregational evangelists, teachers, and authors, receiving his education at Yale University (1871–75) and Yale Divinity School (1875–78). During his training at Yale and later at the German Universities of Leipzig and Erlangen, Torrey would experience profound torment with skepticism, finally emerging as an apologist for the Christian faith, editing *The Fundamentals* (1910–15), and contributing three articles to the set.

At the Moody Church in Chicago, a young boy listened attentively to Torrey preach. At the end of the service, he stood to his feet and accepted Christ as his Lord and Savior. That boy was William Whiting Borden (1887–1913), who would eventually inherit his father's multimillion dollar estate. While on a world tour, ten years following his conversion, Borden heard R. A. Torrey preach again, this time in London. Borden surrendered his life to serve God on the mission field. He enrolled at Yale and became actively involved with the Student Volunteer Movement (SVM) in reaching people for Christ. He founded the Yale Hope Mission to reach the "down and outers." Attending an SVM conference in Nashville, Tennessee, Borden listened to guest speaker Samuel Zwemer, missionary to the Muslims. Here, Bill Borden knew that he had found his calling to reach the Muslims of northwest China. Graduating with honors from Yale in 1909, then Princeton Seminary in 1912, Borden joined the China Inland Mission and sailed for Egypt to study Arabic. Ministering among the poor in Cairo, he contracted cerebro-spinal meningitis. Bill Borden died at the age of twenty-six on April 9, 1913. Mrs. Howard Taylor preserved his story in *Borden of Yale '09: The Life that Counts* (1926). Near the end of that memorable year

---

[30] See Roger Martin, *R. A. Torrey: Apostle of Certainty* (Murfreesboro, TN: Sword of the Lord Publishers, 1976); see especially the two works by Reuben Archer Torrey, *The Higher Criticism and the New Theology* (Montrose, PA: Montrose Christian Literature Society, 1911); and *The Fundamental Doctrines of the Christian Faith* (New York: George H. Doran, 1918). In 1889, D. L. Moody invited Torrey to become the superintendent of his new school in Chicago (now the Moody Bible Institute.) Torrey would also serve the pastorate of the Chicago Avenue Church, now the Moody Church. He and Charles Alexander conducted evangelistic meetings together in many parts of the world. From the years 1912 to 1919, he also served as dean of the Bible Institute of Los Angeles and pastor of the Church of the Open Door.

of 1909, Borden would likely have heard Walter Rauschenbusch explaining the social gospel to students in the college chapel. Unlike Bill Borden, Yale would increasingly fall under the influence of theological liberals who steadily filled every available teaching position in both the college and divinity school.

William Rainey Harper (1856–1906), a higher critic, had already taught Hebrew at Yale from 1886 to 1891, when he left to become the first president of the University of Chicago, where he also taught Hebrew and Old Testament.[31] Harper's successor at Yale, Edward L. Curtis (1853–1911), another higher critic, was a contributing author of the *International Critical Commentary*, in which he asserts that the books of Chronicles as history are essentially worthless.[32] George Barker Stevens (1854–1906) came to Yale in 1886 as professor of New Testament. He had embraced theological liberalism in German schools and now openly taught higher criticism at Yale, advancing it in his *Theology of the New Testament* (1899) and *The Pauline Theology* (1892).[33]

Meanwhile, Evangelist Dwight Lyman Moody (1837–99) was promoting Yale. While theologically conservative in his preaching, Moody often appeared oblivious to serious doctrinal deviation. Such an attitude confused many, including one of his sons,[34] to the point of embracing theological liberalism. Moody had first visited Yale as a speaker in 1878 and returned to speak over the next twenty years. During the year of his death (1899), Moody shared the Yale platform

---

[31] For samples of William Rainey Harper's liberalism, see his *History of Old Testament Prophecy: Syllabus* (Chicago: University of Chicago Press, 1896); and *A Critical and Exegetical Commentary on Amos and Hosea* (New York: Scribner's Sons, 1905). See also Thomas Wakefield Goodspeed, *William Rainey Harper: First President of the University of Chicago* (Chicago: University of Chicago Press, 1928).

[32] Edward Lewis Curtis and Albert Alonzo Madsen, *A Critical and Exegetical Commentary on the Books of Chronicles* (New York: Charles Scribner's Sons, 1910), 6–16 and passim. See also Bainton, 179; and 212–13.

[33] George Barker Stevens, *The Theology of the New Testament* (New York: Charles Scribner's Sons, 1899); and *The Pauline Theology: A Study of the Origin and Correlation of the Doctrinal Teachings of the Apostle Paul* (New York: Scribner, 1892); see Bainton, 179–81.

[34] See Paul Moody's letter to the *Christian Century* (August 2, 1923), which prompted a spirited response from R. A. Torrey, "Mr. Paul D. Moody's Gross Calumny of His Honored Father, D. L. Moody," *Moody Bible Institute Monthly* 24, no. 2 (October 1923): 51–52.

with George Adam Smith,[35] a higher critic of the Bible. To his audience, Moody insisted, "I have been pretty well acquainted with Yale for twenty years, and I have never seen the University in so good a condition religiously as it is now." The evangelist then added, "My oldest son graduated here, and if my other son, who is now in the Freshman class, gets as much good out of Yale as his brother did, I shall have reason to thank God through time and eternity." When asked later how he and George Adam Smith, with such divergent views on the Bible's inspiration and inerrancy, could appear on the same platform, Moody replied, "Perhaps in God's sight we are not so far apart as we appear to be to man."[36]

Yale, however, would celebrate its imminent bicentennial of 1901 by reorganizing the college church, removing all doctrinal statements for membership, and extending a welcome to some of the most liberal theologians in the world. Just weeks after Moody's appearance, Francis Greenwood Peabody (1847–1936), the Harvard Unitarian, would be speaking from the same pulpit in Battell Chapel, encouraging the Unitarian students already enrolled at Yale. One of Moody's closest friends, Scottish evangelist and evolutionist,[37] Henry Drummond (1851–97), had ten years earlier (1889) already established Yale's Catholic Club, encouraging more Roman Catholics to enroll.[38] The Catholic Club would soon merge into a resident organization, under the leadership of the Dominican Fathers. The bicentennial year also saw the retirement of church historian George P. Fisher, the last of the old faculty members.

---

[35] Heavily weighted with higher criticism, the eight lectures that Smith delivered at Yale in 1899 became a sensation, soon appearing in print both in New York and in London; see George Adam Smith, *Modern Criticism and the Preaching of the Old Testament: Eight Lectures on the Lyman Beecher Foundation, Yale University*, 2nd ed. (New York: A. C. Armstrong and Son, 1901).

[36] Reynolds, Fisher, and Wright, 107–15; see especially 111 and 115.

[37] See Henry Drummond, *The Lowell Lectures on the Ascent of Man* (New York: James Pott, 1894).

[38] Ibid., 241ff.; Moody himself invited to his Northfield Conferences some of the most outspoken liberal speakers, including William Rainey Harper and Drummond's biographer, George Adam Smith—authored *Life of Henry Drummond* (New York: Doubleday & McClure, 1898).

Conclusion: The Aftermath

Yale's external campus would begin to take its present form during the 1920s and 30s, when Edward S. Harkness[39] offered to rebuild the institution after the "college model" of England's Oxford and Cambridge universities. The first six colleges formally opened in 1933. Since then, with additional gifts, six more have opened.[40] As a microcosm of the university, each college has its own courtyard, dining hall, common room, and library. Each has a resident master and dean, along with a fellowship of faculty members and outside advisers.

During the college's first century, some forty percent of its graduates entered the Christian ministry. The first half of the 1800s saw the numbers decline to ten percent. During the second half of that century, the figures dropped to between six and seven percent.[41] New faculty would continue bringing new theology. Charles C. Torrey (1863–1956), a higher critic, came to Yale in 1900 as professor of Semitic Languages.[42] Benjamin Wisner Bacon (1860–1932), grandson of Leonard Bacon Sr., was another Yale higher critic who denied the historicity of much of Genesis and denied the miracles of Christ. Bacon also served the college pastorate.[43] Frank Chamberlin Porter

---

[39] Completed in 1921, the 221-foot Harkness Tower—Yale's landmark—holds the statues of Elihu Yale, Jonathan Edwards, Nathan Hale, Noah Webster, James Fenimore Cooper, John C. Calhoun, S. F. B. Morse, and Eli Whitney. Above them, another tier depicts female representations of four basic areas of study—medicine, business, law, and the church. In the corners of the buttresses on either side are representations of twelve forces of life—ranging from Order, Effort, and Prosperity, to War, Death, and Peace. One would need binoculars to capture adequately the treasures of Harkness Tower, with its numerous figures, symbols, and gargoyles.

[40] The twelve colleges are Berkeley; Branford; Calhoun; Davenport; Ezra Stiles; Jonathan Edwards; Morse; Pierson; Saybrook; Silliman; Timothy Dwight; and Trumbull. Davenport College was home to President George W. Bush ('68) during his college days.

[41] Reynolds, Fisher, and Wright, iii–iv.

[42] See Charles C. Torrey, *The Second Isaiah: A New Interpretation* (New York: Charles Scribner's Sons, 1928); also by Torrey, *The Chronicler's History of Israel: Chronicles-Ezra-Nehemiah Restored to Its Original Form* (New Haven, CT: Yale University Press, 1954). See also Bainton, 179 and 212–13.

[43] Samples of Benjamin W. Bacon's liberal works include, *The Genesis of Genesis: A Study of the Documentary Sources of the First Book of Moses in Accordance with the Results of Critical Science* (Hartford, CT: Student Publishing, 1892); and *The*

(1859–1946), holding the chair of Biblical Theology during the early 1900s, was constantly preoccupied with demythologizing the Gospels, vilifying Paul for his Christology, and questioning the major prophetic books of the Bible.[44] The theological liberal, Douglas C. Macintosh (1877–1948),[45] descendent of the Puritan John Cotton, was professor of Theology at Yale from 1909 to 1948. There would be no turning back from the school's embrace of theological liberalism. The story continues, with only the names changing. Even Roman Catholic journalist William F. Buckley Jr., upon graduating in 1950, wrote *God and Man at Yale*, a book describing the school as essentially anti-Christian.[46]

Yale's founders created their official seal depicting an open book with the Hebrew words for *Urim and Thummim* ("lights and perfections"), based upon the breastplate of judgment in Exodus 28:30 and used for guidance in times of crisis during Israel's earliest history.[47]

Story of Jesus and the Beginnings of the Church: A Valuation of the Synoptic Record for History and for Religion (New York: Century, 1927); see also Bainton, 213–19.

[44] See Frank Chamberlin Porter, *The Mind of Christ in Paul: Light From Paul on Present Problems of Christian Thinking* (New York: Charles Scribner's Sons, 1930); see also Porter's *Messages of the Apocalyptical Writers: The Books of Daniel and Revelation and Some Uncanonical Apocalypses, with Historical Introductions and a Free Rendering in Paraphrase* (New York: Charles Scribner's Sons, 1905). For a helpful discussion, see Bainton, 219–26; and Roy A. Harrisville, *Frank Chamberlain Porter: Pioneer in American Biblical Interpretation* (Missoula, MT: Scholars Press for the Society of Biblical Literature, 1976).

[45] See especially Macintosh's, *Theology as an Empirical Science* (New York: Macmillan, 1919); and *The Problem of Knowledge* (New York: Macmillan, 1915). Valuable studies on Macintosh include Kenneth Cauthen, *The Impact of American Religious Liberalism* (New York: Harper and Row, 1962), 169–87; Preston Warren, *Out of the Wilderness: Douglas Clyde Macintosh's Journeys through the Grounds and Claims of Modern Thought* (New York: Peter Lang, 1989); and S. Mark Heim, "The Path of a Liberal Pilgrim: A Theological Biography of Douglas Clyde Macintosh," part 1, *American Baptist Quarterly* 2, no. 3 (September 1983): 236–55; see also part 2, *American Baptist Quarterly* 4, no. 3 (September 1985): 300–20; see also Bainton, 227–33.

[46] *God and Man at Yale: The Superstitions of Academic Freedom* (Chicago: Regnery, 1951), 5, 13, 16–17, 34–35, 53, and passim.

[47] A valuable discussion on the origin and significance of the seal, especially its inclusion of Hebrew in a day when so few could read it, appears in Dan A. Oren, *Joining the Club: A History of Jews and Yale* (New Haven, CT: Yale University Press, 1985), 305–14. Like other published attempts at finding the origin of the seal, Oren's work overlooks the fact that both Timothy Cutler and Samuel Johnson were accomplished Hebraists (especially Cutler) and could have designed the seal

The Latin translation, *Lux et Veritas* ("light and truth"), also appears on the seal. The postmodern worldview concludes that each has his own "light and truth" and thus absolute truth does not exist. Isaiah 8:20 says, "If they speak not according to this word, it is because there is no light in them."

Select Bibliography for Further Reading

Bainton, Roland H. *Yale and the Ministry: A History of Education for the Christian Ministry at Yale from the Founding in 1701.* New York: Harper and Brothers, 1957.

Beale, David. *In Pursuit of Purity: American Fundamentalism Since 1850.* Greenville, SC: Bob Jones University Press, 1986.

Buckley, William F. *God and Man at Yale: The Superstitions of Academic Freedom.* Chicago: Regnery, 1951.

Cross, Whitney R. *Burned-Over District: The Social and Intellectual History of Enthusiastic Religion in Western New York, 1800–1850.* Ithaca, NY: Cornell University Press, 1981.

Dorrien, Gary. *The Making of American Liberal Theology: Imaging Progressive Religion 1805–1900.* Louisville: Westminster John Knox, 2001.

Edwards, Robert Lansing. *Of Singular Genius, of Singular Grace: A Biography of Horace Bushnell.* Cleveland, OH: Pilgrim Press, 1992.

Evans, Christopher H. *The Kingdom Is Always but Coming: A Life of Walter Rauschenbusch.* Grand Rapids: Eerdmans, 2004.

Finney, Charles G. *Lectures on Systematic Theology.* London: William Tegg, 1851.

Hardman, Keith J. *Charles Grandison Finney 1792–1875: Revivalist and Reformer.* Syracuse: Syracuse University Press, 1987.

Hodge, Charles. "Finney's Lectures on Systematic Theology." *Biblical Repertory and Princeton Review* 19, no. 2 (April 1847): 237–77 (a review of Finney's book).

Martin, Roger. *R. A. Torrey: Apostle of Certainty.* Murfreesboro, TN: Sword of the Lord Publishers, 1976.

Park, Edwards Amasa. "New England Theology." *Bibliotheca Sacra* 9, no. 33 (January 1852): 170–220.

Rosell, Garth M., and Richard A. G. Dupuis, eds. *The Memoirs of Charles G. Finney: The Complete Restored Text.* Grand Rapids: Zondervan, 1989.

Sweet, Leonard I. "The View of Man Inherent in New Measures Revivalism." *Church History* 45, no. 2 (June 1976): 206–21.

Vulgamore, Melvin. "Social Reform in the Theology of Charles Grandison Finney." PhD diss., Boston University, 1963.

---

just before joining the Anglican fold. During 1722, there was discussion on the topic of acquiring a collegiate seal and, in October, the General Assembly granted to the college trustees the right to have someone design one. That was the same month that the trustees forced the resignations of Cutler and Johnson. If the seal were their handiwork, this would also explain why the earliest use of it does not appear until 1736.

Wacker, Grant. *Augustus H. Strong and the Dilemma of Historical Consciousness.* Macon, GA: Mercer University Press, 1985.

Warfield, Benjamin Breckinridge. *Perfectionism.* 2 vols. New York: Oxford University Press, 1931.

18

Evangelicalism and the Bible: Apologetics and Philosophy since 1800

Christian apologetics is the science of defending the Christian faith against false doctrine and unbelief. First Peter 3:15 says, "But sanctify the Lord God in your hearts: and be ready always to give an answer to every man that asketh you a reason of the hope that is in you with meekness and fear." The expression, "to give an answer" (ἀπολογίαν), is from the word ἀπολογία (*apologia*), which means "speaking in defense." Our word *apologetics* finds its source in this word. The practice of apologetics is commanded in Scripture for all believers. It reflects the truth of Isaiah 1:18*a*: "Come now, and let us reason together, saith the Lord." The apostle Paul illustrated this when he stood up to address a hostile crowd in Jerusalem. Paul began with the words, "Men, brethren, and fathers, hear ye my defence (ἀπολογίας, *apology*)" (Acts 22:1).

The Basic Debate over Apologetics

First, the debate concerns epistemology (from ἐπιστήμη, "knowledge" + λόγος, "study of"), specifically the origin and nature of knowledge. Second, the debate concerns hamartiology (from ἁμαρτία, "sin" + λόγος, "study of"), specifically the ability or inability of fallen, unregenerate man to translate extra-biblical evidence into a true comprehension and acceptance of God and His inscripturated Word. In fundamentalist-evangelical Christianity, various features often overlap among the three most common schools of apologetics: classical, evidential, and presuppositional.

Classical, or traditional, apologetics begins with a threefold assumption: the validity of the law of noncontradiction, the validity of the law of causality, and the basic reliability of sense perception. As their starting point, classical apologists seek to establish the truth of a theistic universe. To do so they employ the traditional philosophical-rational arguments (proofs) for the existence of God, especially the cosmological and teleological arguments. There are variations of emphasis in the manner in which they use such arguments. From theistic arguments, they proceed to ancient manuscripts, patristic literature, and ecclesiastical tradition to substantiate Christian claims. Classical apologists have included Roman Catholics ranging from Anselm and Thomas Aquinas to Peter Kreeft. There is also a broad range of classical apologetic literature among Protestants, including works from Enlightenment liberals John Locke and William Paley and from such diverse evangelical conservatives as C. S. Lewis, Norman Geisler, and R. C. Sproul.

When appealing to evidences, one must avoid the potential danger of being unduly influenced by empiricism (from ἐμπειρικός, "experienced"), the theory that, in its classical sense, attributes the source of all knowledge to human experience.[1] Aristotle was dominated by the motive that the only essential and true method of rational inquiry is empirical observation, classification, and logic, based upon syllogistic reasoning—the principles of which he discovered. In strict Aristotelianism, experience is the basis of all science—even all reality. British empiricist John Locke (1632–1704) amplified Aristotle's proposition that humans possess no innate or inborn knowledge. According to Locke the mind at birth is a blank tablet (*tabula rasa*) on which the experiences gained from sense impressions are recorded

---

[1] Fundamentalist evidentialist, J. Oliver Buswell, in *A Christian View of Being and Knowing* (Grand Rapids: Zondervan, 1960), advocated what some called "pure empiricism." Some caution against empiricism appears in R. C. Sproul, John Gerstner, and Arthur Lindsley, *Classical Apologetics: A Rational Defense of the Christian Faith and a Critique of Presuppositional Apologetics* (Grand Rapids: Zondervan, 1984), 271–72.

throughout one's life. The Christian must always be aware of such potential pitfalls. Most evidentialist apologists succeed in doing that.

Evidential apologists use the classical arguments for God's existence, but normally not as their starting point since they believe that mankind has innate knowledge of God's existence and the natural revelation of His creative handiwork. Like classical apologists, they use ancient literature, but they generally draw from a wider range of evidence. British philosopher Francis Bacon (1561–1626) is remembered for refining and popularizing the "inductive" method, which is to "induce" or sway conclusions on the basis of evidences. Evidentialism has appeared in a variety of sources, ranging from the *Systematic Theology* of Charles Hodge to Josh McDowell's *Evidence that Demands a Verdict*.

Since all Scripture presupposes our knowledge of God, John Calvin speaks correctly of the "sense of the Deity" endued in every soul as a "natural instinct."[2] This innate or antecedent knowledge of God enables man to interpret the world around him. Indeed, such knowledge makes *all* rational thinking to some degree presuppositional. The distinguishing characteristic of "presuppositional apologetics" is the presentation of axiomatic presuppositions *from the Bible*, followed by the demonstration of the truth of such propositions from within the corpus of canonical Scripture. As with other approaches, presuppositionalism includes its own subcategories, such as "Kuyperian," "revelational," and "rational." Its most prolific authors have included Abraham Kuyper, Cornelius Van Til, and Gordon H. Clark. We will discuss both evidentialism and presuppositionalism in more detail below.

The Essentials of Evidentialist Apologetics and Scottish Common Sense Realism

Common sense realism originated in the works of three major Scottish authors and defenders of evidentialist apologetics: Thomas Reid (1710–96), *Inquiry into the Human Mind on the Principles of Common Sense*; James Oswald (d. 1793), *An Appeal to Common Sense in Behalf of Religion*; and James Beattie (1735–1802), *An Essay on*

---

[2] *Institutes* 1.3.1.

the Nature and Immutability of Truth in Opposition to Sophistry and Skepticism; and *Evidences of the Christian Religion Briefly and Plainly Stated* (1786).

In the juxtaposition of the terms *common sense* and *realism*, *common sense* means "intuition," and *realism* is the belief that, by man's intuition, real knowledge can be directly and immediately apprehended, independently of either experience or reason. We might illustrate the definition this way: since man has the intuition to smell a flower, experience a pleasant sensation, and thereby reach a reliable conclusion regarding some property of that flower, man also has an intuition (common sense) about right and wrong, or truth and error. The popular evangelist Reuben A. Torrey was known for describing his Scottish common sense philosophy this way: "In ninety-nine out of a hundred cases the meaning that the plain man gets out of the Bible is the correct one." This became the mantra of evidential apologetics among evangelicals and fundamentalists: "When the plain sense of Scripture makes common sense, seek no other sense."

A Christian evidentialist is one who seeks by the inductive method to argue the trustworthiness of Christian beliefs, by using particular evidences to "induce," or incite general conclusions. Inductive reasoning proceeds from particular evidences to *a posteriori* ("resulting") general conclusions.

The earliest major opponent of common sense realism was Immanuel Kant (1724–1804), whose philosophy is a corruption of Plato's idealism. The basis of Plato's idealism, or *universals as real existences*, is that *idea* is the original pattern of reality. *Ideal* describes its perfection. To Plato, reason is the ultimate basis of reality, but it is more than that. Reason is essential goodness. It is universal and transcendent. Human reason is derived. Conversely, Kantian idealism supposes that all truth originates in the human mind. Therefore, every moral dilemma must be solved by rational rather than intuitive solutions. To Plato's philosophy, Kant added a strong dosage of skepticism regarding the ability of knowing anything absolutely. It is not surprising therefore that conservative Christians of the common sense school were suspicious of any philosopher who employed rationalism to furnish conclusions contrary to common sense.

The Essentials of Presuppositional Apologetics

A presuppositionalist, using deductive reasoning, starts with general premises (presuppositions) and proceeds to deduce (infer) particular truths *a priori* ("from the former"). A major difference between deduction and induction is that induction goes outside the data at hand while deduction remains within the data. As a simple illustration, suppose that all you knew about horses came from your observations of six horses: horse 1 is white; horse 2 is white; horse 3 is white—all six horses turn out to be white. The evidentialist, using the inductive method and perhaps intuition, might be prone to conclude, "Horse seven will be white," or, "All horses are white." The presuppositionalist, using the deductive method and the data at hand, would conclude, "There are at least six white horses."

Verbal Inspiration, Inerrancy, and Apologetical Methods

Since the early nineteenth century, the major conservative criticism against evidentialism has been that the testimony of the Holy Spirit is undermined by preoccupation with evidences for the truth of Scripture. For instance, some think that the discovery of Noah's ark could cause multitudes to accept Christianity. I am not suggesting that evidences are unimportant. Indeed, Beattie wrote his *Evidences* in order to combat effectively the skeptical empiricism of the Scottish naturalist David Hume (1711–76). Common sense apologists also used evidences as antidotal to the skepticism engendered by Kant's rationalistic idealism.

Some evidences are discovered while others are self-evident in God's creation, or "natural" revelation: "For the invisible things of him from the creation of the world are clearly seen, being understood by the things that are made, even his eternal power and Godhead; so that they are without excuse" (Rom. 1:20). Christian evidential apologists, often assuming that there can be some neutral starting-point, claim that many biblical truths can be knowable to any person *a posteriori*, that is, on the basis of evidences from the phenomenal world, or the world of observable existence.[3] For example, the use of the "intelligent design" argument for the proposition, "God created

---

[3] The word *phenomenal* is φαινόμενον, from φαίειν, "to show."

the world," could help persuade *a posteriori* that the proposition is true.

A proposition that is knowable *a priori*, though, can be known independently of any external evidence or experience, except the experience of learning the language from which the proposition derived. For Christians this source is the Bible. Christian presuppositionalists, assuming the nonexistence of neutrality regarding the fundamentals, claim that the unregenerate man can be exposed to the truth but that he can only corrupt the truth. The natural man cannot become a regenerate man by observing nature. While not ignoring the value of legitimate external evidences, Christian presuppositionalists believe that the natural man only suppresses natural revelation. Therefore, these apologists *begin* with presuppositions such as the following, derived from Scripture: "God exists," "The Scriptures are God's inspired and inerrant Word," "God created the cosmos," "All have sinned," and "Jesus died for our sins." Christian presuppositionalists normally state their presuppositions in terms of *propositions* and then attempt to demonstrate their verity from within the biblical data at hand. For the sake of argument, some present their presuppositions in terms of *hypotheses* and then seek to verify them by scriptural persuasion. The Holy Spirit works special illumination through His Word. We will proceed chronologically, beginning with Robert Haldane, his apologetics, and the Bible.

Robert Haldane and Merle d'Aubigné

The well-known Scotsman Robert Haldane (1764–1842) is perhaps best remembered for his *Exposition of the Epistle to the Romans* (London, 1835–39). He began with the presupposition of the Bible's verbal inspiration and inerrancy, then freely utilized elements of evidentialism as defenses. These appear in his work *The Evidence and Authority of Divine Revelation* (London, 1816) and in *The Books of the Old and New Testaments Proved to Be Canonical* (1830), a complement to Alexander Carson's *The Inspiration of the Scriptures* (1830).

Having separated from the Presbyterian Church in Scotland, Haldane was in Geneva, Switzerland, in 1816–17, where the famed Academy, established in 1559 by John Calvin, was now in a state of apostasy.[4] The teachings of Unitarianism, higher criticism, and Romanticism had reduced the Scripture's inspiration to the level of secular poetry. Using rented rooms in Geneva, Haldane began holding Bible studies on Paul's epistle to the Romans with groups of young theological students enrolled in the Academy. Among those who were converted in Haldane's Bible studies was future historian Merle d'Aubigné (1794–1872). Converted after hearing for the first time in his life Paul's doctrine of total depravity, Merle would later refer to Haldane's "parlor studies" as the "cradle of the Second Reformation of Geneva," known as the *Réveil* ("Awakening").[5] Another convert from those studies was the Geneva-born, Swiss student, F. S. R. Louis Gaussen (1790–1863), who would describe Haldane as the "second father of the Geneva Church."[6]

F. S. R. Louis Gaussen

For twelve years (1816–28), Gaussen labored from within, trying to turn the Church of Geneva from Unitarianism back to orthodox Calvinism. During these years, while serving a pastorate in Satigny in the canton of Geneva, Gaussen's greatest achievement was the founding of the Evangelical Society of Geneva (1831), with the support of various international *Réveil* groups. This prompted the established Unitarian-dominated Church of Geneva to dismiss Gaussen from the pastorate. In 1832, the Evangelical Society, under the direction of Gaussen and Merle d'Aubigné, established in Geneva the Evangelical School of Theology (*École de Théologie Evangélique*), where Gaussen spent the last three decades of his life teaching and writing his books that became so popular in the English-speaking world. Gaussen's apologetical approach would provide an admirable

---

[4] See John B. Roney and Martin I. Klauber, eds., *The Identity of Geneva: The Christian Commonwealth, 1564–1864* (Westport, CT: Greenwood Publishing Group, 1998).

[5] Alexander Haldane, *Memoirs of the Lives of Robert Haldane of Airthrey, and of His Brother, James Alexander Haldane* (New York: Robert Carter & Brothers, 1853), 409; and John B. Roney, *The Inside of History: Jean Henri Merle d'Aubigné and Romantic Historiography* (Westport, CT: Greenwood Publishing Group, 1996).

[6] Alexander Haldane, *Memoirs*, 403; see also Kenneth J. Stewart, *Restoring the Reformation: British Evangelicalism and the Francophone 'Réveil' 1816–1849* (Milton Keynes, England: Paternoster, 2006), 95–107.

model for future generations, especially in the defense of the plenary inspiration of all canonical Scripture.

Famous among Gaussen's literary achievements was the well-beloved, *Theopneustia: The Plenary Inspiration of the Holy Scriptures.* His title is from 2 Timothy 3:16, "All [πᾶσα] scripture [γραφὴ] is given by inspiration of God [θεόπνευστος, *theopneustos*]," or "God-breathed." In the early pages, as Gaussen sets out to demonstrate that all Scripture is God-breathed, he explains his method in presuppositional terms. Promising to remain within the data at hand, Gaussen's deductive defense will be "by the Scriptures, and by the Scriptures alone. Having once admitted the Scriptures to be true, it is for themselves to inform us what they are," and "how they are inspired, and to what extent. . . . It is, therefore, solely on the declarations of Holy Scripture that we are bound to stand. We have no other authority for the doctrines of our faith; and *Theopneustia* is one of those doctrines."[7] Gaussen speaks often of the regenerating and illuminating work of the Holy Spirit as the convincing agent. At other times, Gaussen would employ a more evidentialist apologetic, as in his work *The Canon of the Holy Scriptures from the Double Point of View of Science and of Faith* (1863).[8]

The Princeton Tradition

Two Scottish presidents of the College of New Jersey (renamed Princeton University in 1886) would play major roles in bringing elements of common sense moral philosophy to America. The first was a signer of the Declaration of Independence, John Witherspoon (1723–94),[9] an orthodox Calvinist and direct descendent of John Knox. The second was James McCosh (1811–94), who desired a revision of the Westminster Standards and preferred not even to be

---

[7] F. S. R. Louis Gaussen, *Theopneustia: The Plenary Inspiration of the Holy Scriptures* (London: Samuel Bagster and Sons, 1841), 38. The work was written in French in 1840 and translated into English the following year.

[8] F. S. R. Louis Gaussen, *The Canon of the Holy Scriptures from the Double Point of View of Science and of Faith* (London: James Nisbet, 1863).

[9] John Witherspoon, *Works*, 4 vols., 2nd ed. rev. (Philadelphia: William W. Woodward, 1802). The set is prefaced with valuable biographical material.

called a Calvinist.[10] In Princeton Theological Seminary (est. 1812),[11] scholars Archibald Alexander, Charles Hodge, Benjamin B. Warfield, and J. Gresham Machen would utilize elements of common sense philosophy to defend the perspicuity of Scripture against higher criticism and rationalistic approaches of interpretation coming from Germany. Unlike James McCosh, they were thoroughly orthodox Calvinists. To them, the common sense approach would illustrate that the Bible is not merely a book of concepts, but literal events—a welcome antidote to Kantian idealism.

Archibald Alexander (1772–1851), first professor of Princeton Seminary, employed Scottish common sense evidentialism from the first day of class. In his opening lecture, on the "Nature and Evidence of Truth" (1812), Alexander insists, "The greatest possible assurance which we can have of any truth is that the constitution of our nature obliges us to assent to it."[12] His son James W. Alexander defined the work of theologians as arriving at truth by investigating propositions of Scripture as one would investigate science.

In like manner Charles Hodge (1797–1878), in his *Systematic Theology* (1871–73; 3 vols.), applies the inductive Baconian method to theology, a science based on biblical data. Hodge explains, "If natural science be concerned with the facts and laws of nature, theology is concerned with the facts and the principles of the Bible. . . . The object . . . is to systematize the facts of the Bible, and ascertain the principles or general rules which those facts involve."[13] In his opening section, titled "The Knowledge of God is Innate," Hodge

---

[10] William Milligan Sloane, ed., *The Life of James McCosh* (New York: Charles Scribner's Sons, 1896), 173, 252–53. The work derives largely from autobiographical material. McCosh said, "I deny that Charles Hodge or Alexander Hodge has departed from the Confession of Faith" (253). He had actually hoped that they would depart from its limited atonement. McCosh claimed that the Westminster Standards could not address the new issues of the nineteenth century.

[11] David B. Calhoun, *Princeton Seminary: Faith and Learning 1812–1868*, vol. 1 (Edinburgh: Banner of Truth Trust, 1994); and David B. Calhoun, *Princeton Seminary: The Majestic Testimony 1868–1920*, vol. 2 (Edinburgh: Banner of Truth Trust, 1996).

[12] "Nature and Evidence of Truth," in *The Princeton Theologians 1812–1921: Scripture, Science and Theological Method from Archibald Alexander to Benjamin Warfield*, ed. Mark A. Noll (Grand Rapids: Baker, 2001), 65.

[13] *Systematic Theology* (New York: Scribner, Armstrong, 1873), 1:18.

describes sense perceptions and moral truths as intuitive axioms "assumed in all reasoning." He reminds his readers that Reformed theology teaches from Romans 1 that the knowledge of God is "innate and intuitive, founded on the very constitution of our nature."[14] It is clear that Hodge is avoiding the full package of Lockean empiricism. Like Gaussen, Hodge never hesitates to ground inerrancy in inspiration.

John H. Gerstner says, "Among the Old Princetonians none has contributed more than the big three of Charles Hodge, B. B. Warfield, and J. Gresham Machen, with Warfield being the unequalled leader."[15] Their insistence on the rational apprehension of faith, even the reasonableness of faith, often invited the charge of "rationalism." In a chapter of *The Fundamentals*, Warfield elevates subjective experience above all else. He claims, "The supreme proof to every Christian of the deity of his Lord is then his own inner experience of the transforming power of his Lord upon the heart and life."[16] The Old Princeton theologians insisted, however, that feelings do not guide understanding. Rather, feelings are tested by understanding. While such verbiage seems to give the Bible a backseat, each of these men embraced biblical inerrancy and depended ultimately upon biblical authority. The Old Princeton theologians never lost the element of piety in scholarship.

The theological journal *Presbyterian Review* began to appear in 1880, under the joint editorship of the liberal Charles A. Briggs of Union Theological Seminary (NY) and, successively, A. A. Hodge, Francis L. Patton, and B. B. Warfield—Old Princeton conservatives. During 1881–83, the journal published a series of eight articles on the critical study of the Bible. The Old Princetonians were confident that inductive evidence for inerrancy is possible in manuscript comparisons available through the work of lower textual criticism. The eight articles alternated between liberal and conservative editors.

---

[14] Ibid., 1:191–94.

[15] Cited in Gordon R. Lewis and Bruce Demarest, *Challenges to Inerrancy: A Theological Response* (Chicago: Moody Press, 1984), 347; see also John H. Gerstner, *Reasons for Faith* (New York: Harper and Brothers, 1960).

[16] "The Deity of Christ," in *The Fundamentals: A Testimony to the Truth*, ed. A. C. Dixon (Chicago: Testimony Publishing, 1910), 1:27.

The first article in the series was titled "Inspiration" and it was co-authored by A. A. Hodge (1823–86), professor of Theology at Princeton Seminary, and Benjamin B. Warfield (1851–1921), professor of New Testament at Western Theological Seminary in Pittsburgh. Warfield would move to Princeton in 1887. In this first article, the following passage has drawn conservative criticism:

> Very many religious and historical truths must be established before we come to the question of Inspiration; as, for instance, the being and moral government of God, the fallen condition of man, the fact of a redemptive scheme, the general historical truth of the Scriptures, and the validity and authority of the revelation of God's will, which they contain—*i.e.*, the general truth of Christianity and its doctrines. Hence it follows that, while the Inspiration of the Scriptures is true, and being true is a principle fundamental to the adequate interpretation of Scripture, it nevertheless is not in the first instance a principle fundamental to the truth of the Christian religion. In dealing with skeptics it is not proper to begin with the evidence which immediately establishes Inspiration, but we should first establish Theism, then the historical credibility of the Scriptures, and then the divine origin of Christianity. Nor should we ever allow it to be believed that the truth of Christianity depends upon any doctrine of Inspiration whatever. Revelation came in large part before the record of it, and the Christian Church before the New Testament Scriptures. Inspiration can have no meaning if Christianity is not true, but Christianity would be true and divine, and being so, would stand, even if God had not been pleased to give us, in addition to His revelation of saving truth, an infallible record of that revelation absolutely errorless, by means of Inspiration.[17]

Once more, the major charge against evidentialism was that the testimony of the Holy Spirit seemed undermined by such strong demands for evidences. Warfield insisted that we must first prove "the authenticity, credibility and general trustworthiness of the New Testament writings before we prove their inspiration." In an 1893 article, Warfield continued:

---

[17] Archibald A. Hodge and Benjamin B. Warfield, "Inspiration," *Presbyterian Review* 2, no. 6 (April 1881): 225ff.

Inspiration is not the most fundamental of Christian doctrines, nor even the first thing we prove about the Scriptures. It is the last and crowning fact as to the Scriptures. These we first prove authentic, historically credible, generally trustworthy, before we prove them inspired. And the proof of their authenticity, credibility, general trustworthiness would give us a firm basis for Christianity prior to any knowledge on our part of their inspiration, and apart indeed from the existence of inspiration.[18]

Warfield based his ideas on this assumption: "Sinful and sinless men are, after all, both men; and being both men, are fundamentally alike and know fundamentally alike."[19] He believed that, while only the Holy Spirit can regenerate a soul, external evidences have their part to play in the conversion of a soul:

> We are not absurdly arguing that Apologetics has in itself the power to make a man a Christian or to conquer the world to Christ. Only the Spirit of Life can communicate life to a dead soul, or can convict the world in respect of sin, and of righteousness, and of judgment. But we are arguing that faith is, in all its exercises alike, a form of conviction, and is, therefore, necessarily grounded in evidence. And we are arguing that evidence accordingly has its part to play in the conversion of the soul; and that the systematically organized evidence which we call Apologetics similarly has its part to play in the Christianizing of the world.[20]

While one might justly criticize some of his apologetical nuances, Warfield stood as a champion in the defense of the fundamentals of the Christian faith.[21] He increasingly sharpened his arguments

---

[18] "The Real Problem of Inspiration," *Presbyterian and Reformed Review* 4, no. 14 (April 1893): 209–10; cf. Warfield's book, *The Inspiration and Authority of the Bible* (Philadelphia: Presbyterian and Reformed, 1948), 160–226.

[19] Benjamin B. Warfield, "Introductory Note," in *Apologetics: Or the Rational Vindication of Christianity* by Francis R. Beattie (Richmond: Presbyterian Committee of Publication, 1903), 1:28. Beattie (1848–1906) is also known for his work *The Presbyterian Standards: An Exposition of the Westminster Confession of Faith and Catechisms* (Richmond: Presbyterian Committee of Publication, 1896).

[20] Warfield, "Introductory Note," in Beattie's *Apologetics*, 1:25–26.

[21] For more discussion, see Moisés Silva, "Old Princeton, Westminster, and Inerrancy," in *B. B. Warfield: Essays on His Life and Thought*, ed. Gary L. W. Johnson (Phillipsburg, NJ: P&R Publishing, 2007), 76–91.

and guarded his nuances. This would later become evident in the deliberations between the Warfieldians and Kuyperians.

The Neo-Calvinist Dutch School of Apologetics

Abraham Kuyper (1837–1920),[22] the firstborn son of a Reformed minister of a Dutch state church, graduated in 1858 from the University of Leiden and decided to enter the ministry. Since it was expected that ministers of Reformed churches receive their training in the state schools, Kuyper remained at the official University of Leiden and received his training from modernists and theological liberals. Completing his graduate work in 1861, he entered the ministry as an unbeliever. While struggling to minister to his first church, a small Reformed church in Beesd, Kuyper came under the godly influence of a few lowly members and converted to conservative Reformed Christianity.

Grieved over the infestation of doctrinal and moral apostasy within the official Dutch Reformed Church (*Hervormde Kerk*), Kuyper determined to permeate church and state with Reformed Christianity. He called for a return to the doctrines of the Canons of Dort, the Belgic Confession, and the Heidelberg Catechism. With a brilliant mind, enormous gifts as a public speaker, and popularity among the working classes, he became an ardent defender of the Reformed faith. When in 1867 he began ministering to a state-controlled church of 35,000 members in Utrecht, the common people gravitated to his sermons.

In 1870, he accepted the call to the national church of the Netherlands, *Nieuwe Kerk* (New Church), with its 140,000 members, the largest church in the country, and situated next to the Amsterdam's Royal Palace at Dam Square. Kuyper's preaching drew great crowds. Inside the church, liberal opposition would constantly rage against Kuyper. His well-prepared sermons were masterpieces of oratorical delivery. One professor recalled "that hearing Kuyper read,

---

[22] See James E. McGoldrick, *Abraham Kuyper: God's Renaissance Man* (Darlington, UK: Evangelical Press, 2000); and Frank Vandenberg, *Abraham Kuyper: A Biography* (Grand Rapids: Eerdmans, 1960).

just read, Psalm 148 was clearer exposition of that Psalm than most sermons preached on it and brought tears to his eyes."[23]

Being elected to Parliament in 1874, Kuyper resigned from the ministry. The state would not permit him to take his seat in Parliament without leaving the ministry. Re-elected the following year, Kuyper took a heavy work load that resulted in nervous exhaustion, incapacitating him for fifteen months, most of which he spent in Italy and Switzerland. By 1878, the Dutch government forbade all state churches from refusing membership to anyone for doctrinal reasons. Kuyper would never return to the pastorate. As part of his vision to fill every realm of society with Reformed Christianity, he founded the Free University of Amsterdam (FUA) in 1880. It was independent and free from both ecclesiastical and state control. As the founder and first *rector magnificus* of FUA, Kuyper was also professor of Theology and professor of Literature. This included writing and Kuyper's literary style reflects his forceful personality. A primary purpose of FUA was the defense of the faith.

While Kuyper expressed a dislike for apologetics *per se*, he was presuppositional in his approach. He explains both his epistemological method and his theology in his *Encyclopedia of Sacred Theology* (1898). During his term as prime minister of the Netherlands (1901–5), Kuyper urged Christians to participate at every level of society. He explains this appeal in his book, *De Gemeene Gratie* ("The Common Grace").[24] While he uses the term *antithesis* to describe the spiritual gulf that exists between Christians and non-Christians,[25] Kuyper insists that the "bridge" by which God connects the two

---

[23] Herman C. Hanko, "Abraham Kuyper: Dutch Calvinist," *The Standard Bearer* 73, no. 10 (February 15, 1997): n.p., electronic ed., http://sb.rfpa.org/index2.cfm?mode=wide.

[24] Originally published in 3 vols. in 1902–4, Kuyper's *De Gemeene Gratie* is currently being translated into English for publication by the Acton Institute in Grand Rapids, MI. His basic teachings on common grace are also in Abraham Kuyper, *A Centennial Reader*, ed. James D. Bratt (Grand Rapids: Eerdmans, 1998). The year of publication marked the centenary of Kuyper's 1898 celebrated Stone Lectures delivered at Princeton Seminary.

[25] Van Til would make use of Kuyper's idea of *antithesis*, but would be uncomfortable with the Kuyperian *common grace*.

groups is "common grace" (*gemeene gratie*), administered to the wicked as a sort of "antitoxin," to restrain the full effects of sin.[26]

In the Kuyperian system, known as Neo-Calvinism, common grace creates in society an "organic church," working outside the walls of organized churches. The organic church becomes a "neutrality" zone, in which the righteous and the unrighteous can coalesce in works of common interest, such as in labor unions and voting booths,[27] making the world a better place and at the same time spreading the Reformed faith throughout the world. In the Kuyperian system, this societal activity becomes the "cultural mandate" to all Christians. While in Parliament, Kuyper formed coalitions with Roman Catholics in order to break the hold of liberal parties over educational issues. He believed that divine justice demands protection for the welfare of unbelievers, regardless of their unbelief since every person is created in the image of God.[28] This was not a postmillennial social gospel such as that of Walter Rauschenbusch in America.

Kuyper claimed that his cultural mandate was grounded in Reformed covenant theology. He was totally committed to the traditional amillennial theology of the Dutch Reformed tradition. He exhorted Christians to "live out" the Word of God in every sphere of their lives—science, politics, the arts, etc. In the climax to his inaugural address at the dedication of the FUA, Kuyper famously thundered, "Oh, no single piece of our mental world is to be hermetically sealed off from the rest, and there is not a square inch in the whole

---

[26] In America the Protestant Reformed Church (PRC) emerged in 1924 as a split from the Christian Reformed Church (CRC) during a heated "Common Grace Controversy." The CRC blamed the PRC for hyper-Calvinism and for being anti-missionary. The PRC blamed the CRC for changing Kuyperian common grace into Arminianism general grace. Rejecting any form of common grace, the PRC established the Protestant Reformed Theological Seminary in Grandville, Michigan. See Herman Hoeksema, *The Protestant Reformed Churches in America: Their Origin, Early History and Doctrine* (Grand Rapids: First Protestant Reformed Church, 1936); and Herman C. Hanko, *The History of the Free Offer* (Grandville, MI: Reformed Free Publishing Association, 1989).

[27] Abraham Kuyper, *The Problem of Poverty*, trans. James W. Skillen (Grand Rapids: Baker, 1991). This is the speech that opened the first Christian Social Congress in the Netherlands in 1891.

[28] George Harinck, "Abraham Kuyper, South Africa, and Apartheid," in *The Princeton Seminary Bulletin* 23, no. 2 (Spring 2002): 184–87.

domain of our human existence over which Christ, who is Sovereign over all, does not cry: 'Mine!'"[29]

To Kuyper, there is a basic difference as well as an essential connectivity between philosophy and science. The philosopher sees the forest. The scientist sees a tree. One must be outside an object in order to see it wholly. Philosophy is a foundational study that examines totalities. Science abstracts and analyzes an individual aspect of reality. This produces contradiction since all aspects of reality are interrelated. Kuyper refers to the *Paradoxes* of Zeno, fifth-century BC Greek philosopher, to illustrate his point. Zeno makes this assertion: "That which is in locomotion must arrive at the half-way stage before it arrives at the goal."[30] For proof, Zeno offers the paradox of a race between a fleet-footed athlete, Achilles, and a plodding tortoise. The former can never catch the later if the latter is given a head start. This is because in the time it takes Achilles to make up half the distance, the tortoise has moved ahead some distance. Achilles then covers half that distance, but the tortoise has again moved forward. Achilles must once again cover half that distance. Theoretically, if the tortoise keeps moving, Achilles will never catch up, for he will have to travel an infinite number of finite distances. With such antinomy, one might be tempted to doubt all theoretical thought. Such a paradox is created mentally by confusing the spatial sphere and the sphere of motion. Space and motion must not be confounded since each sphere is autonomous in its own right, and each has its own laws. This autonomy was given by God in creation and Kuyper urged that a proper understanding of "sphere sovereignty" will eliminate contradictions commonly found in false philosophies. God's sovereignty extends to every sphere. As God is one, truth is one. Truth is all-pervasive. Each sphere of the cosmos must be understood in light of the whole cosmos.

Kuyper insisted that all theoretical thought is dominated by presuppositions, and one who is unaware of his own false presuppositions will be enslaved by them. "In Adam," the natural man can neither philosophize nor theologize but, in Christ, "in whom are

---

[29] Abraham Kuyper, "Sphere Sovereignty," in *Centennial Reader*, 488.
[30] The notion is cited and rebutted in Aristotle, *Physics* 6.9.

hid all the treasures of wisdom and knowledge," the regenerate can do both (Col. 2:3). The philosophy that the apostle Paul condemns is that which is "after the tradition of men, after the rudiments of the world, and not after Christ" (Col. 2:8). In Neo-Calvinism the primary presuppositions include creation, fall, and redemption.[31] All men are born with the knowledge of God the Creator. Since the fall, man has suppressed that knowledge. Redeemed men acknowledge the Creator. Only redemption can lead to true philosophy. False presuppositions arise from unregenerate hearts that deny the Creator. Only the Christian is able to synthesize immanent, theoretical thought with the transcendental presuppositions of "creation-fall-redemption." While Kuyper's political activities did not bring enormous positive results, his prolific writings, with their broad assortment of topics, reflect his genius. His strong convictions reflect his character.

With the Dutch government's suspending Kuyper's standing within the church and forbidding FUA graduates from ministering in state churches, two hundred congregations (150,000 people) joined him in 1886, as he separated from the national Dutch Reformed Church (*Hervormde Kerk*). The churches identifying with Kuyper were called the *Doleantie* ("Grievers"), sorrowfully leaving in grief over the apostasy of church and state. In 1892, Kuyper's *Doleantie* would merge with a separatist group known as the Secession of 1834 (*de Afscheiding*), also called the Christian Reformed Church. Its counterpart in America also became known as the Christian Reformed Church (est. 1857),[32] whose schools are Calvin College and Calvin Theological Seminary in Grand Rapids, Michigan.

---

[31] The exact expression may have originated from Herman Dooyeweerd.

[32] Peter DeKlerk and Richard R. De Ridder, eds., *Perspectives on the Christian Reformed Church: Studies in Its History, Theology, and Ecumenicity* (Grand Rapids: Baker, 1983), in honor of John Henry Kromminga at his retirement as president of Calvin Theological Seminary. The Christian Reformed Church (CRC) emerged in 1857 as a split from the Reformed Protestant Dutch Church in North America, renamed in 1867 as the Reformed Church in America (RCA). The latter movement had originated in 1628 in New Amsterdam (later named New York). Reasons for the CRC's separation from the RCA included decline in strict Dutch Calvinism, acceptance of freemasonry, laxity in discipline, open communion, and the use of hymns. The CRC used Psalms only.

De Afscheiding had emerged as primarily a movement of the common folk.[33] They were spiritual heirs of the *Nadere Reformatie* ("Dutch Further Reformation"),[34] and they had left the *Hervormde Kerk* over apostasy and government intrusion. The spiritual piety of *de Afscheiding* made it similar to the *Réveil*. During the period between the Secession of 1834 and its merger with Kuyper's *Doleantie* in 1892, key doctrinal issues over Kuyper's Neo-Calvinist teachings had prevented any formal union. Under the mediating influence of Herman Bavinck, from a Secessionist family, a degree of tolerance seemed possible and, in their 1892 merger, the combined groups became known as the *Gereformeerde Kerken in Nederland* (GKN), or Reformed Churches in the Netherlands. From four hundred Secession churches and three hundred *Doleantie* churches, its total membership was three hundred thousand. In spite of this, persistent doctrinal controversies over Neo-Calvinism led to the Synod of Utrecht in 1905 which, after heated debate, issued a sort of "pacification formula" designed to appease both sides. The synod concluded that both sides should tolerate each other as standing within the boundaries of the Reformed confessions. For many, the issues were never resolved. We will identify and consider the nature of these controversies.

Kuyper's Neo-Calvinist system includes two distinct doctrines that reside inseparably in eternity past: the *covenant of redemption* and the *decree of election*. To Kuyper, God's covenant of redemption is the decree to redeem His people and to redeem them collectively. The focus is not on the individual. Such a fusion of the covenant with election constitutes a Kuyperian supralapsarianism (hyper-Calvinism).[35] It provided a speculative basis for two additional

---

[33] See Peter Y. De Young and Nelson Kloosterman, eds., *The Reformation of 1834: Essays in Commemoration of the Act of Secession and Return* (Orange City, IA: Mid-America Reformed Seminary, 1984).

[34] Also called the Dutch Second Reformation, this movement (ca. 1600–1750) was similar to the English Separatists and Puritans. They translated much Puritan literature into Dutch; see Maurice Eugene Osterhaven, *The Spirit of the Reformed Tradition: The Reformed Church Must Always Be Reforming* (Grand Rapids: Eerdmans, 1971); and Scott Maze, *Theodorus Frelinghuysen's Evangelism: Catalyst to the First Great Awakening* (Grand Rapids: Reformation Heritage Books, 2011).

[35] Supralapsarianism places God's decree of election before, or above (supra), His decree to permit the fall. The infralapsarian Seceders placed the decree of election after or below (infra) His decree to permit the fall.

Kuyperian claims: (1) God's pre-Adamic *collective justification* of all His elect and (2) a *presumed regeneration* in the sacrament of baptism. Kuyper went beyond the Synod of Dort (1619) by teaching a collective "birth" into the "covenant of grace" and a collective "incorporation into Christ." All of this plays out genealogically through the seed of covenant families.[36] For many concerned Christians, the emphasis of Kuyper's system essentially displaced the Reformation focus on personal justification "by faith." Modern aberrations concerning justification, baptism, and regeneration would eventually expand such elements far beyond Kuyper's original system.

The Later Kuyperian (or Neo-Calvinist) Tradition

When Kuyper retired from the FUA on January 1, 1908, his formal ties with the university ceased. He devoted the remainder of his life to his writing. In late 1902, due to Kuyper's duties as prime minister, Herman Bavinck (1854–1921)[37] had succeeded him as professor of Theology at FUA where he would remain for this rest of his life. Bavinck's father had been among the first ministers of the Secession of 1834. Although Herman had spent his six years as a student at the liberal University of Leiden, where his faith was seriously challenged, he had identified with the *Réveil*. Upon graduation in 1881, he had served a one-year pastorate at a Secession church in Franeker, then as professor of Theology at the Theological School of *de Afscheiding* in Kampen (1883–1901).

Now, at the FUA, students generally described Bavinck as a superb professor. While he exceeded Kuyper in refined scholarship,[38] Kuyper's powerful presence and assertiveness exceeded that of the

---

[36] Kuyper, "Common Grace," in *Centennial Reader*, 165–201. For a particularly concise statement, see p. 188.

[37] See Ron Gleason, *Herman Bavinck: Pastor, Churchman, Statesman, and Theologian* (Phillipsburg, NJ: P&R Publishing, 2010); Eric D. Bristley, *A Guide to the Writings of Herman Bavinck* (1854–1921) (Grand Rapids: Reformation Heritage Books, 2008); and Cornelius Jaarsma, *The Educational Philosophy of Herman Bavinck: A Textbook in Education* (Grand Rapids: Eerdmans, 1935).

[38] For more, see Joel R. Beeke, "The Atonement in Herman Bavinck's Theology," in *The Glory of the Atonement: Biblical, Theological, and Practical Perspectives*, ed. Charles E. Hill and Frank A. James III (Downers Grove, IL: InterVarsity, 2004), 324–45.

more irenic Bavinck.[39] Some have compared the two with Luther and Melanchthon. One was passionate and the other was pacifistic. Both left lasting impressions upon Christians around the globe. To Kuyper and Bavinck, *special grace* is saving grace. It is supernatural and spiritual. It removes the guilt and pollution of sin and lifts the sentence of condemnation. God's decree of election determines the extent of special grace. At another level, both men also taught that *special revelation* is Christ's incarnation.

During his earliest years at FUA, Bavinck set forth his theology in *Gereformeerde Dogmatiek* (1906–11), translated as *Reformed Dogmatics*.[40] Dutch (and German) theologians use the word *dogmatics* in the same way that English theologians use the word *theology*. While accepting the essentials of Kuyper's doctrine of "the common grace" (*de gemeene gratie*), that is, the societal "bridge" that unites Christians and non-Christians, Bavinck typically describes it in terms of *general grace* (*algemeene genade*) and joins it directly with *general revelation* (natural revelation). Bavinck defines their function as analogous to the mutual function between special revelation (incarnation) and special grace (salvation).[41] Christ's incarnation acts as the "bridge" that unites God and man. Not only is this approach similar to that of Thomas Aquinas, but Cornelius Van Til also charges that Bavinck employed secular reasoning to identify the source of his presuppositions.[42]

---

[39] See Gleason, "On Border Terrain: Did Bavinck Change Theologically Later in Life?" in *Herman Bavinck*, 398–419; cf. Abraham Kuyper, "Modernism: A Fata Morgana in the Christian Domain," *Centennial Reader*, 87–124; on 97–98 he dares to speak of "heresy."

[40] Herman Bavinck, *Reformed Dogmatics*, 4 vols. trans. John Vriend and ed. by John Bolt (Grand Rapids: Baker, 2003–8).

[41] To Bavinck, "It is common grace which makes special grace possible, prepares the way for it, and later supports it; and special grace, in its turn, leads common grace up to its own level and puts it into its service." Herman Bavinck, *Our Reasonable Faith*, trans. Henry Zylstra (Grand Rapids: Eerdmans, 1956), 38. This elevation of common grace would distance Bavinck from the strictest Secessionists, who already resented his affiliation with the FUA.

[42] Herman Bavinck, *De Algemeene Genade* (Kampen: Zalsman, 1894); and Cornelius Van Til, "Christian Epistemology: The Positions of Herman Bavinck and Valentine Hepp," in *An Introduction to Systematic Theology: Prolegomena and the Doctrines of Revelation, Scripture, and God*, 2nd ed., ed. William Edgar

In the broader scope of the Kuyperian-Bavinck view, special revelation begins with creation and encompasses all of God's providential works leading up to its central (incarnation) moment of history. The incarnation is "special" revelation because it is the climactic event in the revelation of "special" (saving) grace. Scripture is not "revelation." Scripture "contains" the revelation. Scripture is the "inspired record" of God's revelation. Comparing the inscripturated word with Christ's incarnation, Bavinck concludes that the human quality of Scripture, as weak and feeble as it may be, must also be a true record of God's revelation.[43] After Kuyper and Bavinck passed off the scene, liberals took their seats in the FUA and essentially transformed the whole system. As we have seen, though, speculative theology was present from the beginning.

In its fully developed form, the Neo-Calvinist system diminished any antithesis between converting grace and common grace, between belief and unbelief—between Christianity and the world. "Common grace" was posited within an eschatological and covenant framework. The church continued to be viewed as Israel and the term *kingdom-work* took on a radical meaning. There emerged the bold assertion that God does not normally save souls individually or at random. Rather, He perpetuates His covenant from generation to generation through families. A major factor in the death of the movement was its covenant-based doctrine of "presumptive regeneration." Children born and baptized into Reformed families were treated as regenerate, covenant members of God's family, at least until the fruit of their mature lives later indicated an unregenerate condition. Such teachings, including "eternal justification," have in recent years encouraged "New Perspectives" on Paul's doctrine of justification by faith alone.[44]

(Phillipsburg, NJ: P&R Publishing, 2007), 89–116. Van Til shows how Hepp increased the emphasis on natural revelation.

[43] Bavinck, *Reformed Dogmatics*, 1:432–35 and passim; Bavinck, *Our Reasonable Faith*, 95–115; and Abraham Kuyper, *Encyclopedia of Sacred Theology: Its Principles*, trans. J. Hendrik De Vries (New York: Charles Scribner's Sons, 1898), 428–73.

[44] Defenses of presumptive regeneration include Douglas Wilson, *Standing on the Promises: A Handbook of Biblical Childrearing* (Moscow, ID: Canon Press, 1997); and Lewis Bevens Schenck, *The Presbyterian Doctrine of Children in the Covenant: an Historical Study of the Significance of Infant Baptism in the Presbyterian*

The Issue of Inerrancy in Apologetics

The mission of the organic, covenant church became the renewing of a fallen cosmos by seeking to atone for the ills of society. Though Kuyper and Bavinck had expected a visitation of revival in Amsterdam, modernists would welcome the covenant-kingdom mandate as a fresh philosophical rationale for a socially and culturally engaged church. In practice the developed system ignored sin's effect on the human mind as it continued to identify the Great Commission with the Cultural Mandate. Nature and natural law were placed on par with the Scriptures. The written Word became a mere application of natural law, and a sharp dichotomy was posited between a mundane Scripture text and a supra-temporal Word of God. The system extended the character of "invisibility" from the true and perfect body of Christ to the true and perfect Word of God. As visible churches reflect the cosmic body, the Bible reflects cosmic truth. Like the local churches, the recorded books of Scripture were assumed to have been less than perfect even from their origin.

Such an assumption was a lethal departure not only from Reformed doctrine but from historic Christianity. Both conservatives and liberals on both sides of the Atlantic have firmly established the fact that the Old Princeton theologians did not invent the doctrine of the inerrant autographa of Scripture.[45] The teaching of biblical inerrancy begins with the Jews and continues in Jesus' training of His disciples. From the earliest patristic era it was already an established doctrine.[46] In circa 405, Augustine assured Jerome,

---

Church (Phillipsburg, NJ: P&R Publishing, 1940). For a critical review of the latter work, see Maurice J. Roberts, "Children in the Covenant: A Review Article," *Banner of Truth* (June 2005): 20–24.

[45] For an impressive compilation of pre-Warfieldian advocates of inerrant autographa, see Randall H. Balmer, "The Princetonians and Scripture: A Reconsideration," *Westminster Theological Journal* 44, no. 2 (Fall 1982): 352–65.

[46] Ronald F. Satta, *The Sacred Text: Biblical Authority in Nineteenth-Century America* (Eugene: Pickwick Publications, 2007); Harold Lindsell, "Infallibility in the Church," in *The Battle for the Bible* (Grand Rapids: Zondervan, 1976), 41–71; cf. George Duncan Barry, *The Inspiration and Authority of Holy Scripture: A Study in the Literature of the First Five Centuries* (London: Society for Promoting Christian Knowledge, 1919). Barry was looking for inspiration sources, but his broad coverage includes inerrancy.

I have learned to yield this respect and honor only to the canonical books of Scripture: of these alone do I most firmly believe that the authors were completely free from error. And if in these writings I am perplexed by anything which appears to me opposed to truth, I do not hesitate to suppose that either the Ms. is faulty, or the translator has not caught the meaning of what was said, or I myself have failed to understand it.[47]

Nineteenth-century liberals readily conceded that their own higher criticism of the text was an affront against the convictions of historic Christianity. For example, the liberal Yale professor, George Trumbull Ladd (1842–1921), in his massive two-volume work, *The Doctrine of Sacred Scripture* (1893), begins with Jewish scholarship, continues through the patristic era, and on to his own day in a continual attack against advocates of biblical inerrancy.[48] Later attempts to sequester Old Princeton as the derivation of the doctrine of inerrancy were naïve at best. In fact, when Charles Briggs proposed such a notion as a major defense in his 1893 trial for mocking biblical inerrancy, he was found guilty of heresy and suspended from the Presbyterian ministry.[49] The continuing onslaught has been overwhelming, however, for some evangelicals.[50] When historic Christian institutions grew weary of defending the biblical text, they at last threw down their weapons and walked off the field of battle. In Europe, the Free University of Amsterdam led this trend away from the biblical text.

Following the death of Kuyper in 1920 and the death of Bavinck in 1921, Valentine Hepp (1879–1950) became professor

---

[47] Augustine, *Letter* 82.1.3, to Jerome, in NPNF 1 (1:350), written ca. 405. Augustine desired an Old Testament "canon" of 44 books, with the same apocryphal books of the present RCC Bible. The RCC would not add those books until the Council of Trent (16th c.). Augustine, *On Christian Doctrine* 2.8.12–13; 2.15.22, a sect. written ca. 396; and *City of God* 18.42–43, a sect. written ca. 425–27. Jerome rejected the Apocrypha's canonicity.

[48] George T. Ladd, *The Doctrine of Sacred Scripture: A Critical, Historical and Dogmatic Inquiry into the Origin and Nature of the Old and New Testaments* (Edinburgh: T. & T. Clark, 1883), 1:9; 2:54–98; and passim.

[49] Satta, *The Sacred Text*, 75–96; and Beale, *In Pursuit of Purity*, 144–47.

[50] Ronald F. Satta, "Fundamentalism and Inerrancy: A Response to the Sandeen Challenge," *Evangelical Journal* 21, no. 2 (Fall 2003): 66–80; and Ronald F. Satta, "Inerrancy: The Prevailing Orthodox Opinion of the Nineteenth-Century Theological Elite," *Faith and Mission Journal* 24, no. 1 (Fall 2006): 79–96.

of Theology at FUA and lived to conduct a proverbial swan song for a dying Kuyperian conservatism.[51] Following the 1929 conservative exodus from the liberal Princeton Seminary, Hepp gave Princeton's 1930 Stone Lectures. He stood against J. Gresham Machen and other separatists who had left Princeton, and he opposed the founding of Westminster Seminary. Back at FUA, Herman Dooyeweerd (1894–1977)[52] in 1926 became professor of the Philosophy of Law and began to systematize Neo-Calvinism.[53] The developing theology at FUA allowed no place for biblical inerrancy and relegated biblical "infallibility" to the realm of *message*.

With no absolute foundation, the whole Kuyperian paradigm would implode. If the *a priori* paradigm of creation-fall-redemption is validly presuppositional, it must rest upon an absolute source. Kuyper and Bavinck were devout and godly scholars who had influenced a generation with their system. They had believed and taught the verbal inspiration and "perfection" of all Scripture. But their use of *perfection* was commonly perceived as compatible with the English idea of *infallible*. Higher critics were insisting that the "message" of Scripture could remain infallible within an errant text.

Kuyper and Bavinck were aware of attacks from higher criticism but failed to confront such critics with any explicit use of a proper word equivalent with *inerrant*. Words such as *perfect* and *infallible* no

---

[51] Bearing allegiance to key social and cultural elements of the older Kuyperian hermeneutics, a right-wing group called the Theonomic Reconstructionist movement attempted to keep Neo-Calvinism alive. The Reconstructionists developed rival bases in Vallecito, CA, and Tyler, TX, under the respective leadership of R. J. Rushdoony and his son-in-law Gary North. Rushdoony worked primarily in law, and his *Institutes of Biblical Law* (1973) was the initiating text of the movement's law program. Gary North specialized in economics. Other spokesmen have included Greg Bahnsen, Gary DeMar, Kenneth Gentry, and David Chilton.

[52] See William Young, "Herman Dooyeweerd," in *Creative Minds in Contemporary Theology*, ed. Philip Edgcumbe Hughes, 2nd ed. revised (Grand Rapids: Eerdmans, 1973), 270–305; and L. Kalsbeek, *Contours of a Christian Philosophy: An Introduction to Herman Dooyeweerd's Thought* (Toronto: Wedge Publishing Foundation, 1975).

[53] David VanDrunen, *Natural Law and the Two Kingdoms: A Study in the Development of Reformed Social Thought* (Grand Rapids: Eerdmans, 2010); and H. A. Dooyeweerd, *A New Critique of Theoretical Thought*, 4 vols. (Philadelphia: Presbyterian and Reformed, 1953–58); *Transcendental Problems of Philosophic Thought* (Grand Rapids: Eerdmans, 1948); and *The Twilight of Western Thought* (Nutley, NJ: Craig Press, 1960).

longer had the cutting edge. The field of battle was the text. While Kuyper and Bavinck had not openly opposed autographic inerrancy, they were conceptual idealists who displayed but little interest at this level. In many circles, such neglect tended to neutralize Christianity's foundation of biblical inerrancy. The Old Princeton theologians would properly refocus to the true field of battle in America, but, without that same foundational focus, Dutch Neo-Calvinists would continue dwelling on multiple levels or realms of divine revelation.

Karl Barth and Neo-Orthodoxy

Such language would increasingly resemble the esoteric language of Neo-Orthodoxy, crafted and systematized by the Swiss theologian, Karl Barth (1886–1968).[54] Born in Basel, Switzerland, Barth was the son and grandson of Swiss Reformed ministers. He received a liberal education at the Universities of Bern, Berlin, Tübingen, and Marburg. After serving as an apprentice pastor in Geneva (1909–11), he held the pastorate of the Reformed church in Safenwil, Switzerland, until 1921. At the outbreak of the Great War in 1914, Barth's theology was shaken to its foundation. He became completely disillusioned with liberal Protestant theology as ninety-three German intellectuals, including most of his former professors, signed a manifesto supporting the war policies of Kaiser Wilhelm II.

The post-war publication of Barth's commentary, *Der Römerbrief* (*The Epistle to the Romans*, 1919),[55] led to his appointment to the chair of Reformed Theology at the University of Göttingen in 1921. In 1925, he became professor of Dogmatics and New Testament Exegesis at the University of Münster. In 1930, he joined the staff of the University of Bonn as professor of Systematic Theology. In 1934, he was the principal author of the famous "Theological Declaration of Barmen," a document opposing the encroachments of Hitler's National Socialism on German churches. The Barmen Declaration called for obedience to Christ as the only *Führer* of the church. In

---

[54] For a basic overview of Barth's life and a summary of his views, see G. W. Bromiley, "Karl Barth," in *Creative Minds in Contemporary Theology*, ed. Philip Edgcumbe Hughes, 2nd ed. rev. (Grand Rapids: Eerdmans, 1973), 27–62.

[55] See Karl Barth, *The Epistle to the Romans*, trans. from the 6th ed. by Edwyn Hoskyns (Oxford: Oxford University Press, 1933).

the following year, the University of Bonn dismissed Barth, and the National Socialist Party deported him back to Switzerland for refusing to take the oath of allegiance to Hitler. Barth then became professor of Systematic Theology at the University of Basel, where he remained until retirement in 1962.[56] As for his own political philosophy, Barth was a lifelong socialist of the Marxist class, and he refused to lift voice or pen against it. To Barth, capitalism was equal to Hitler's war in elevating human depravity.

Barth's major work was his *Church Dogmatics* (*Kirchliche Dogmatik*, 1932–67),[57] divided into four general topics: Revelation, God, Creation, and Reconciliation. He promises that his system will serve as an antidote to Kant's denial of man's cognitive knowledge of God, a view that old liberals such as Friedrich Schleiermacher and Albrecht Ritschl had continued to propagate. Barth promises a fresh approach to preaching. His system is to free pastors from the shackles of a fallible text and to open new heights for creative preaching (1.2.531–32).[58] However, like the liberals, Barth rejects any possibility of essential knowledge of God. He criticizes the old liberal theologians for minimizing three things: transcendence of God, the dominance of global sin, and the distinction and distance between God and man. On the one hand, he attacks those who emphasize natural revelation as a means of attaining knowledge of God. On the other hand, he attacks those who point to the text of Scripture as the essential source of divine knowledge. To Barth, both are hopelessly fallible. There is no absolute knowledge of God within human grasp (1.1.187ff.). Neo-Orthodoxy is a system of nonstop contradictories.

---

[56] The most valuable and thorough studies of Barth's theology include Gordon H. Clark, *Karl Barth's Theological Method* (Philadelphia: Presbyterian and Reformed, 1963); Cornelius Van Til, *Barth's Christology* (Philadelphia: Presbyterian and Reformed, 1962); *Christianity and Barthianism* (Philadelphia: Presbyterian and Reformed, 1965); and *The New Modernism: An Appraisal of the Theology of Barth and Brunner*, 3rd ed. (Philadelphia: Presbyterian and Reformed, 1973).

[57] For this writing I am using Karl Barth, *Church Dogmatics*, trans. by a team of scholars and ed. G. W. Bromiley and T. F. Torrance, 13 vols. (1936–77; repr., Peabody, MA: Hendrickson, 2010). This set adds an index vol. 14.

[58] Ibid. All of the Barth references in parentheses within the text are to Barth, *Church Dogmatics*. The last part of the reference is pagination. E.g., in 1.2.531–32, the 1.2 is the volume number and the *531–32* indicates page numbers.

The following concepts constitute the essential bond between the method and the corpus of Barthian theology. Barth's theology is "dialectical" because of its method of juxtaposing interacting oppositions (paradoxes). His is a theology of "crisis" because of its ongoing struggle to resolve one paradox after another. These include an absolutely transcendent God disclosing Himself in a lowly Jesus, the infinite becoming finite, the eternal becoming temporal, and the elect as already justified but not yet holy. The only hope that Barthianism offers is "faith in itself" (*fideism*), apart from reason, evidence, or inerrant Scripture. Contrary to the common assertion that Barth accepted Christ's literal resurrection, Barth's extended discussions on the resurrection narratives allow only for the possibility of a "tiny margin" of historicity (3.2.446; 4.1.333–36).[59] He then reduces the tiny margin to zero in the sixth edition of his commentary on Romans, where he concludes that Christ's resurrection was "non-historical."[60]

Looking beyond *Historie*, which is the stuff that historians write in books, Barth points to a trans-history, or meta-history, that is, ultimate "Revelation" (*Geschichte*), which he identifies with Christ Himself (4.3.1.3ff.). Barth denies the historicity of much of the Bible, including the account of the creation and of Adam's fall. There is no imputation of sin, but everyone sins (4.1.492). "Original sin" is merely the first sin committed by each individual (1.2.155ff.). The Bible's vulnerability extends to its theology. Evolution happened. Both the "saga" of sin and the "rhyme" of redemption in biblical narrative are errant and fallible (1.2.509). Bible content can only reflect the higher, non-historic *Geschichte*. No one can know what parts of the Bible might be historical. Barth posited "salvation-history" (*Heilsgeschichte*) into *Geschichte* and scorned the sixteenth-century Reformers for viewing it as *Historie*.

Barth insists that Christ's entry into a temporal body was the "Christ-event," the "'Moment'—which is no moment *in* time."[61] At this moment, time (the tangent line) touched eternity. The event

---

[59] This is discussed with additional sources in Gordon H. Clark, *Historiography: Secular and Religious*, 2nd ed. (Jefferson, MD: Trinity Foundation, 1994), 270–77.

[60] Karl Barth, *Epistle to the Romans* (1933; repr., Oxford: Oxford University Press, 1968), 195 and passim.

[61] Ibid., 108–9; 116.

united all humanity into Christ who *is Geschichte* ("Revelation"). Christ had now assumed humanity's fallen state, the very "flesh of sin."[62] God in Christ became temporal and humanity in Christ became God-like. This union of God and humanity makes incarnation an ongoing reality (1.2.45ff.).

Barth's neo-Reformed theology rejects two traditional Reformed covenants: the "covenant of redemption," between the Father and Christ, and the "covenant of works," between God and Adam. Barth's system teaches one covenant and one decree—both residing in eternity past and both merged into one: the *covenant of grace* and the *decree of election*. The covenant of grace is the basis for the decree of election. Covenant and decree are one eternal reality (3.1.228ff.). Christ was the electing God and Christ was the elected man (2.2.94ff.). Christ is the only person elected. All humanity is in Him, and being in Christ, all humanity is collectively elected (2.2.313).

This fusion of the covenant with election constitutes what Barth considers a purified supralapsarianism (2.2.127–45).[63] It also provides for the Barthian doctrine of *collective justification* "supra-temporal" of all humanity (4.1.514–28). This minimizes sacramental grace in the Barthian system. Election has two sides. Negatively, Christ ascribed all reprobation, perdition, and death to Himself. Positively, Christ ascribed salvation and life to mankind. As federal head and substitute for the human race, Christ has already completed everything necessary for man's salvation, without man's cooperation or consent (2.2.162–74).

Christ's humiliation was the humiliation of God, and Christ's exaltation was the exaltation of man (4.1.358–779). The purpose and work of the atonement were to unite humanity with God. While Barth avoids the word *universalism*, he is unable to deny it. His emphasis is that all humanity is "in Christ" and in possession of spiritual benefits (2.2.742–63). The "good news" is to inform them. Barth's

---

[62] *Church Dogmatics* 1.2.147-59 and 2.1.397-98. For a rebuttal see Oliver Crisp, "Did Christ Have a Fallen Human Nature?" *International Journal for Systematic Theology* 6, no. 3 (2004): 270-88.

[63] See also 2.2.509ff. Supralapsarianism places God's decree of election before or above (supra) His decree to permit the fall. Infralapsarianism places the decree of election after or below (infra) His decree to permit the fall.

Christocentric theology, or Christomonism, portrays an asymmetrical "Trinity" (2.2.3ff.). He speaks of the Father as the mysterious, "Wholly-Other," who is hidden from human knowledge (2.1.179ff.).

We should pause here to consider, "What is the biblical concept of Christocentric theology?" We know from the Bible that in all His glorious work in the unfolding drama of redemption, Christ is pre-eminent above all of His creation. His work is the Christocentric theme of Scripture, and it is the very essence of the gospel. Our preaching must be Christocentric in the same soteriological way. To avoid the unbiblical concept of an asymmetrical Trinity, we should never lose sight of this fact: the three distinct *persons* of the one Holy Trinity are ontologically consubstantial. They are equally and eternally one-in-three. With Barth, it is impossible really to know much of anything of consequence from the Bible.

Barth positions the "Word of God" at multiple levels: (1) the perfect, nonhistorical realm of *Geschichte* (Christ); (2) the fallible written word; and (3) its proclamation (preaching). He teaches that God mysteriously speaks, when or if He wishes, through the proclamation, or Kerygma (Κήρυγμα) (1.2.743–884). Whatever God speaks through becomes a Word of God. Typically, when commenting on specific passages of Scripture, Barth speculates, reflects, and often applies his thoughts to the real world. Conversely, however, the equivocal historicity that he assigns to the text of Scripture leaves nothing that is truly exegetical. With nothing more than a trans-historical, or meta-historical creation, fall, and redemption, Barth can offer nothing texturally meaningful to anyone. He has removed the text from its historical center—its field of battle—and posited it within a realm created within a figment of his own imagination. Barth's removal of history from theology is tantamount to a destruction of theology and a transformation of the gospel of Christ into another gospel.[64]

---

[64] Other valuable sources that elaborate on the key threads of the fabric of Barthian theology include Norman Geisler, "Barth, Karl," in *Baker Encyclopedia of Christian Apologetics* (Grand Rapids: Baker, 1999), 69–71; Robert L. Reymond, *Barth's Soteriology* (Philadelphia: Presbyterian and Reformed, 1967); Fred Klooster, *The Significance of Barth's Theology* (Grand Rapids: Baker, 1961); Phillip R. Thorne, *Evangelicalism and Karl Barth: His Reception and Influence in North American Evangelical Theology* (Allison Park, PA: Pickwick Publications, 1995); John

Contrary to the deluge of evangelical voices encouraging a return to Barth's works, no individual has done more to close God's Word, camouflage the historical gospel, and create dead churches than Karl Barth. Among the appeals for a reconsideration of Barth, only rarely does one find a clear and specific warning. Instead, there is the recurring call for "common ground."[65] To elevate Barth to a position in any way comparable with John Calvin is to risk leading people into a theological abyss. Barthianism was disseminated by a loosely aligned movement called post-liberalism, or neo-liberalism. From its earliest stage, it found its place within the halls of the Free University of Amsterdam.

The Kuyperian (or Neo-Calvinist) Tradition to the Present

Gerrit Cornelis (G. C.) Berkouwer (1903–96), who in 1945 succeeded Valentine Hepp to the professorship of Theology at FUA, sounded conservative in his lectures, especially the earlier ones, often praising and citing Bavinck. From 1950 to 1975, as Berkouwer was producing his fourteen-volume *Studies in Dogmatics*, he was also shaping a pro-Barthian outlook.[66] Like Barth, he could sound conservative by attacking liberal higher criticism of the Bible; like Barth, he rejected biblical inerrancy as earnestly as the higher critics; and like Barth, he tried to convince textual critics that they too should quit wasting time over textual minutia and move "revelation" to a conceptual level.

Warwick Montgomery, "Karl Barth and Contemporary Theology of History," *Bulletin of the Evangelical Theological Society* 6, no. 2 (May 1963): 39–49; and McGrath, *Iustitia Dei: A History of the Christian Doctrine of Justification*, 3rd ed. (Cambridge: Cambridge University Press, 2005), 392–406.

[65] As seen in such diverse works as Craig G. Bartholomew, "Calvin, Barth, and Theological Interpretation," in *Calvin, Barth, and Reformed Theology*, ed. Neil B. MacDonald and Carl R. Truman (Eugene, OR: Wipf and Stock, 2008), 163–77; Donald K. McKim, ed., *How Karl Barth Changed My Mind* (Grand Rapids: Eerdmans, 1986); and George Hunsinger, ed., *For the Sake of the World: Karl Barth and the Future of Ecclesial Theology* (Grand Rapids: Eerdmans, 2004).

[66] This is especially noticeable in G. C. Berkouwer, *Holy Scripture*, trans. Jack B. Rogers, vol. 13 in the series Studies in Dogmatics (Grand Rapids: Eerdmans, 1975). This is a book of doubt concerning the divine source and character of the Scriptures.

Barthian approval of his *Dogmatics* led Berkouwer into an alliance with Hendrikus Berkhof (1914–95),[67] professor of Systematic Theology in the University of Leiden, the principal left-wing institution of the Dutch Reformed Church from which Kuyper had separated. Berkouwer was now the leading professor of Theology at the FUA.[68] In his book, *The Triumph of Grace in the Theology of Karl Barth* (1954),[69] described by Barth as a "great book,"[70] Berkouwer expresses admiration for the Swiss theologian, criticizes only minor details, and accepts the key elements of Barthianism.[71]

Distancing themselves from Kuyper's conservatism, Berkouwer and Berkhof became the Dutch founders of a so-called "middle orthodoxy," essentially Neo-Orthodoxy, whose speculative theology served as the bridge to some of the most radical theological liberals in Europe. It spread rapidly to American seminaries. In essence Berkouwer replaced Kuyper's perspicuity of Scripture with a "mysteriousness of scripture," or theological paradox. To a Reformed Church Synod, Berkouwer publicly admitted serious personal reservation about the historicity of Adam.[72] As promoter of the World Council of Churches, Berkouwer became the leading ecumenist of his day. In spite of his earlier criticism of the Roman Catholic Church, Berkouwer, as an invited observer at the opening of the Second Vatican Council, took the occasion to celebrate the release of his optimistic book *The Second Vatican Council and the New Catholicism* (1962). The book received high praise from Catholic leadership.

---

[67] Not to be confused with Louis Berkhof (1873–1957), the conservative author of *The History of Christian Doctrines* and *Systematic Theology* (*Reformed Dogmatics*). In 1906, he became professor of Theology at Calvin Theological Seminary, and in 1931, he also assumed the presidency and continued until his retirement in 1944.

[68] See Hendrikus Berkhof, *Christian Faith: An Introduction Study of the Faith*, trans. and rev. Sierd Woudstra (Grand Rapids: Eerdmans, 1986); *Two Hundred Years of Theology: Report of a Personal Journey* (Grand Rapid: Eerdmans, 1989); and *Introduction to the Study of Dogmatics* (Grand Rapids: Eerdmans, 1985).

[69] Trans. Harry R. Boer and published by Eerdmans in 1956.

[70] Barth, *Church Dogmatics*, 4.2.xii. He calls opponents "butchers and cannibals."

[71] This is also summarized in G. C. Berkouwer, *A Half Century of Theology: Movements and Motives* (Grand Rapids: Eerdmans, 1977), 39–74.

[72] RES *News Exchange*, January 19, 1971. The group is now the Reformed Ecumenical Council, and its publication is the REC *News Exchange*.

In 1967, Harry Martinus Kuitert (b. 1924), a radical unbeliever, succeeded his mentor Berkouwer to the chair of Systematic Theology at FUA. His book *Jesus, the Inheritance of Christianity* (1998) is an assault on the deity of Christ and all Trinitarian doctrine. Kuitert's popular curiosity titled *I Have My Doubts: How to Become a Christian without Being a Fundamentalist*[73] received international attention. It failed to fulfill the promise in its subtitle. In 2005, Kuyper's Reformed Churches in the Netherlands, along with the liberal Dutch Reformed Church, joined a multi-ecumenical merger to form the Protestant Church in the Netherlands. This was a gargantuan departure from Kuyper and Bavinck.

Like Calvin, Kuyper had emphasized the *testimonium Spiritus Sancti*. For it is the work of the Spirit, not the force of Christian evidences, that leads one to certainty. "Except a man be born again, he *cannot see* the kingdom of God" (John 3:3). While returning mild criticism towards Kuyper's presuppositionalism, B. B. Warfield carefully described their divergences as differences "of degree, not of kind." In fact, Warfield wrote the introduction to the English edition of Kuyper's *Encyclopedia of Sacred Theology*.[74] At Warfield's invitation in 1898, Kuyper had delivered the Stone Lectures at Princeton Seminary.[75] The occasion had provided Kuyper with his first widespread exposure to a North American audience, and Princeton used the opportunity to confer on him an honorary doctorate in law.

J. Gresham Machen and His Influence

The year after Kuyper's decease in 1920, Warfield also passed into eternity leaving his friend and colleague, J. Gresham Machen, to face the most intense decade of theological battles in American

---

[73] Harry Martinus Kuitert, *I Have My Doubts: How to Become a Christian without Being a Fundamentalist*, trans. John Bowden (Valley Forge, PA: Trinity Press International, 1993). This was originally published under the title *Het algemeen betwijfeld christelijk geloof* (1992).

[74] Abraham Kuyper, *Encyclopedia of Sacred Theology*, xi–xix.

[75] Abraham Kuyper, *Lectures on Calvinism* (Grand Rapids: Eerdmans, 1931). A decade later, Herman Bavinck would deliver the Stone Lectures, published under the title, *The Philosophy of Revelation* (1908). The Stone Lectureship had been created in 1871 with funds provided by Princeton Seminary director and trustee Levi P. Stone.

history. While Kuyper was passionate, visionary in statesmanship, and focused on societal reform, Machen was controlled, refined in scholarship, and focused on academic reform.

J. Gresham Machen (1881–1937)[76] was the greatest intellectual spokesman for fundamentalist conservative evangelicalism during the 1920s and 30s.[77] As a popular speaker within coalitions of diversity, such as the Winona Lake Bible Conference, Machen found an unusual set of allies in such men as William Jennings Bryan, Billy Sunday, and James M. Gray (dean of the dispensationalist Moody Bible Institute). Gray at one point suggested that Machen succeed him at Moody Bible Institute. Of course, Machen could never do that. He was thoroughly Reformed. He encouraged these associations for the sake of the war against infidelity.[78] In 1926, Machen answered criticism emerging from his own colleagues:

> Do you suppose, gentlemen, that I do not detect faults in many popular defenders of supernatural Christianity? Do you suppose that I do not regret my being called, by a term that I greatly dislike, a "Fundamentalist"? Most certainly I do. But in the presence of a great common foe, I have little time to be attacking my brethren who stand with me in defense of the Word of God. I must continue to support an unpopular cause.[79]

As professor of New Testament, Machen separated from Princeton Seminary in 1929, together with Old Testament scholars Robert Dick Wilson and Oswald T. Allis, and professor of Apologetics Cornelius Van Til. That year they founded Westminster Theological Seminary in Philadelphia. The issue concerned theological liberalism in the Presbyterian Church, USA, and the denomination's

---

[76] See D. G. Hart, *Defending the Faith: J. Gresham Machen and the Crisis of Conservative Protestantism in Modern America* (Grand Rapids: Baker, 1995); and Ned B. Stonehouse, *J. Gresham Machen: A Biographical Memoir* (Grand Rapids: Eerdmans, 1954).

[77] See, e.g., Machen's *The Origin of Paul's Religion* (1921); *Christianity and Liberalism* (1923); *What is Faith?* (1925); *New Testament Greek for Beginners* (3rd printing 1925); *The Virgin Birth of Christ* (1930); and *The Christian Faith in the Modern World* (1936).

[78] For prime examples of such associations, see Mark Edward Sidwell, "The History of the Winona Lake Bible Conference," (PhD diss., Bob Jones University, 1988).

[79] Stonehouse, *J. Gresham Machen*, 337–38.

restructured and unprecedented liberal control over Princeton Seminary. Being expelled from the Northern Presbyterian Church in 1936, Machen established the Presbyterian Church in America, renamed the Orthodox Presbyterian Church (OPC) in 1938.

Among those who joined with Machen were J. Oliver Buswell, then president of Wheaton College, and Carl McIntire, who was becoming a leading separatist fundamentalist. After Machen's death in 1937, McIntire founded the Bible Presbyterian denomination. Westminster Theological Seminary also suffered division that year, as some of its faculty and administration joined McIntire in the founding of Faith Theological Seminary in Philadelphia, with Allan A. MacRae soon becoming president. Buswell and MacRae were not only supporters of McIntire but also strong proponents of common sense evidentialism. As the last of a long line of Old Princeton evidentialists, J. Gresham Machen would pass into eternity on January 1, 1937. Even during the final stage of his active ministry, the faithful professor was still reminding his Philadelphia radio audience, "The Bible is quite useless unless it is a record of facts." And he quickly added, "Thank God, it is a record of facts."[80]

Cornelius Van Til and Presuppositionalism

Cornelius Van Til (1895–1987),[81] born in the Netherlands, immigrated to the United States with his family in 1905. He was a member of the Christian Reformed Church and studied at Calvin College, Princeton University, and Princeton Seminary. Van Til taught for a year at Princeton but resigned when the Seminary was reorganized in 1929. At Machen's request, he joined the OPC and became professor of Apologetics at Westminster where he remained until his death.

---

[80] J. Gresham Machen, "Do We Believe in Verbal Inspiration?" A 1935 series of radio addresses, published as *The Christian Faith in the Modern World* (New York: Macmillan, 1936), 57–58.

[81] See John R. Muether, *Cornelius Van Til: Reformed Apologist and Churchman* (Phillipsburg, NJ: P&R Publishing, 2008); James Emery White, *What is Truth? A Comparative Study of the Positions of Cornelius Van Til, Francis Schaeffer, Carl F. H. Henry, Donald Bloesch, and Millard Erickson* (Nashville: B&H Publishing Group, 1994); and Eric D. Bristley, *A Guide to the Writings of Cornelius Van Til: 1895–1987* (Chicago: Olive Tree Communications, 1995).

Although Van Til seldom referred to himself as a presupposition-alist, his name has become virtually synonymous with the method. While sharing the Old Princeton commitment to the authority and inerrancy of Scripture, Van Til viewed the evidential approach to apologetics, as taught by Charles Hodge and B. B. Warfield, as a dependence upon human autonomy. The Christian faith should utilize evidences but not evidences interpreted autonomously. To Van Til there are ultimate presuppositions that must form the basis of all theistic proof. The God of the Bible is the supreme presupposition, rather than one rational conclusion among many. The one true God is the necessary starting place for all rational thought and order in the universe.

Since their conclusions are normally the same as their premises, presuppositionalists often face the charge of "circular reasoning." To the charge of circularity, however, Van Til replied that the non-Christian's argument, too, is circular: "All reasoning is, in the nature of the case, *circular reasoning*. The starting point, the method, and the conclusion are always involved in one another." The unbeliever's depraved unbelief *is* his presupposition, which in turn governs his conclusion. Since all positions partake equally of circularity at this level, it should not be a point of criticism against any position.[82] Van Til held Hodge and Warfield at fault for attributing to human reason the ability to judge God's written revelation.[83] He viewed their Baconian method as inconsistent with the foundational concepts of Christian theology, especially Warfield's notion that the claims of Christianity must be established by evidences and natural revelation prior to God's written Word.

While evidentialists claimed "neutral" assumptions, Van Til countered that there is no neutral ground. Man cannot serve two masters. All truth is God's truth. Unbelief distorts and changes the truth into a lie. The only God-honoring apologetic is that which

---

[82] Cornelius Van Til, *The Defense of the Faith*, 3rd ed. (Nutley, NJ: Presbyterian and Reformed, 1967), 101; and Cornelius Van Til, *Christian Apologetics* (Nutley, NJ: Presbyterian and Reformed, 1976), 130; see also 5ff.

[83] "Christian Epistemology: The Position of Charles Hodge," in *An Introduction to Systematic Theology: Prolegomena and the Doctrines of Revelation, Scripture, and God*, 2nd ed. (Phillipsburg, NJ: P&R Publishing, 2007), 71–88.

presupposes the truth of God's Word. In a nutshell, a presuppositionalist is one who claims no neutrality. He brings premises into every intellectual inquiry, and such premises include the supernatural inspiration and inerrancy of Scripture. Non-Christians cannot share such presuppositions. Indeed, as antithetical to Christianity, they presuppose the contrary. The task of the Christian apologist is to proclaim the written Word and trust the Holy Spirit to regenerate non-Christians.

While he questioned claims of common truth between believers and non-believers and challenged the empiricism of the Old Princeton tradition, Van Til avoided social applications of presuppositionalism. His discomfort with the Neo-Calvinist term *common grace* prompted him to warn, "When men dream dreams of a paradise regained by means of common grace, they only manifest the 'strong delusion' that falls as punishment of God upon those who abuse his natural revelation."[84] Van Til's nephew added that the term should be used in quotation marks to distinguish it from saving grace.[85]

Van Til's Critics and Defenders

With his emphasis on God's incomprehensibility and man's inability of really knowing the mind of God, Van Til drew a qualitative difference between divine and human knowledge. These two could never coincide. Man's knowledge is always analogical to God's knowledge.[86] Gordon H. Clark (1902–85)[87] countered that if only God has truth and man possesses only analogy, then man does not possess truth at all. In contrast to Van Til's revelational presupposi-

---

[84] *Christian Apologetics*, 71.

[85] Henry R. Van Til, *The Calvinistic Concept of Culture* (Grand Rapids: Baker, 1959), 244.

[86] Cornelius Van Til, "The Incomprehensibility of God" and "The Apologetic Import of the Incomprehensibility of God," in *Introduction to Systematic Theology*, 260–309. Also reflective of Van Til's position is Fred H. Klooster, *The Incomprehensibility of God in the Orthodox Presbyterian Conflict* (Franeker, Netherlands: T. Wever, 1951). Critical articles against Van Til's position, along with Van Til's responses, are compiled in E. R. Geehan, ed., *Jerusalem and Athens: Critical Discourses on the Philosophy and Apologetics of Cornelius Van Til* (Phillipsburg, NJ: Presbyterian and Reformed, 1971).

[87] Clark taught at the University of Pennsylvania, Wheaton College, Butler University, and Covenant College (Lookout Mountain, GA).

tionalism, Clark's rational presuppositionalism concluded that the fall of man did not destroy the divinely implanted *a priori* rationality that enables all humanity to know and to harmonize God's natural laws, including the law of non-contradiction. Clark saw this as a connecting point between the regenerate and the unregenerate. He claimed that Van Til's approach would lead to despair. Those were the essential issues surrounding the "Clark-Van Til controversy," lasting from 1944 to 1948.[88]

Upon Clark's ordination in 1945 by the Philadelphia presbytery of the Orthodox Presbyterian Church (OPC), Van Til and some colleagues at Westminster charged that Clark's ordination procedure had been irregular and that his beliefs contradicted Reformed views on God's incomprehensibility and man's noetic depravity. Even though the OPC ruled in 1948 that Clark's ordination was valid, he left the OPC and joined the United Presbyterian Church, now the Presbyterian Church (USA). In 1958, he united with the Reformed Presbyterian Church in North America, General Synod, which eventually merged into the Presbyterian Church in America (PCA).[89]

Van Til's emphasis had originated in opposition to an "Arminian" (actually Pelagian) exaggeration of man's ability into a sort of autonomous humanity. Clark's position had originated in opposition to an exaggeration of God's transcendence into a sort of "Wholly Other" unknowable Being. Clark's students included Edward J. Carnell and Carl F. H. Henry. Van Til's students included John M.

[88] Herman Hoeksema, *The Clark-Van Til Controversy*, miscellaneous articles originating from the 1940s in *The Standard Bearer* (Unicoi, TN: Trinity Foundation, 2005). *The Standard Bearer* is the denominational magazine of the Protestant Reformed Church, well-known for hyper-Calvinist and anti-missionary emphases.

[89] In 1948, Clark left the OPC. After that he was in the United Presbyterian Church until its 1958 merger with the Presbyterian Church, USA, which created the United Presbyterian Church in the USA. The latter merged in 1983 with the Presbyterian Church in the US to form the Presbyterian Church (USA). In 1958, Clark joined the Reformed Presbyterian Church in North America, General Synod, which merged in 1965 with the Evangelical Presbyterian Church (a split from the Bible Presbyterians) to become the Reformed Presbyterian Church, Evangelical Synod. The latter merged in 1982 into the Presbyterian Church in America (PCA). For a simple chart see David Beale, *In Pursuit of Purity: American Fundamentalism Since 1850* (Greenville, SC: Bob Jones University Press, 1986), 123.

Frame,[90] Greg L. Bahnsen, and Francis Schaeffer. Both Van Til and Clark would write numerous valuable books, and Clark would become especially popular as a professor at Covenant College, Lookout Mountain (1974–83). His effective arguments against any reliance upon empiricism led some to describe his presuppositional approach as "scripturalism."[91] Over the years, both Clark and Van Til refined their arguments, but the controversy had created two camps that outlived both men.

In contrast to Barth, who denied all natural knowledge of God, Van Til clearly affirmed that the natural man, "in spite of himself," knows and recognizes God, and even performs moral deeds. As Van Til explains, this is possible by virtue of three things: (1) the creation of man in the image of God; (2) the ineradicable sense of deity indelibly engraved upon man; and (3) the restraining influence of "general grace."[92] Van Til stood firmly upon his conviction that there remains a sharp antithesis between the regenerate and the unregenerate consciousness. Van Til identified the authority of Scripture with the authority of God. The existence of God and the inerrancy of His inscripturated Word were for Van Til the basic presuppositions. Those debates continue to stimulate Christian thinking towards a more biblical balance. It is important that seminary students learn from the pitfalls of the past. The minister of God is called to become a specialist in the Word of God. He must carefully and reverently exegete its text, and he must proclaim its propositions with humility and boldness and with the convicting power of the Holy Spirit.

Van Til explains that there must be both an *a priori* and an *a posteriori* aspect in the work of systematic theology. Theologians such as Charles Hodge perform the *a posteriori* aspect of collecting and systematizing the facts of Scripture. The *a priori* aspect appears when we *interpret* (draw conclusions about) those facts through the

---

[90] John M. Frame, "Presuppositional Apologetics," in *Five Views on Apologetics*, ed. Steven N. Cowan (Grand Rapids: Zondervan, 2000), 207–48; and John M. Frame, *Cornelius Van Til: An Analysis of His Thought* (Phillipsburg, NJ: Presbyterian and Reformed, 1995). After Van Til retired, Frame began teaching apologetics courses at Westminster.

[91] W. Gary Crampton, *The Scripturalism of Gordon H. Clark* (n.p.: Trinity Foundation, 1999).

[92] *An Introduction to Systematic Theology*, 63–66.

light of Scripture.[93] The route from revelation to theology is interpretation. Van Til emphasizes that when God existed alone, there was no *a posteriori* aspect of knowledge. Time did not exist. The *a posteriori* element of knowledge applies only to human knowledge. God is incomprehensible, but not to Himself. Due to man's finiteness and fallen condition, human knowledge must be analogical to God's knowledge. Contrary to evidentialism, and due to the noetic effects of sin, Van Til warns that man possesses insufficient knowledge, both qualitatively and quantitatively, to argue on the basis of the law of noncontradiction. Yet, those who are regenerated, and only those, are able correctly to interpret *a priori* knowledge and to bring a biblical worldview into any conversation.

In spite of heated battles among Reformed conservatives, with presuppositionalists such as Van Til on one side, and evidentialists such as Hodge and Warfield on the other, they still recognized and respected their common heritage. They remained committed to the essential system and hermeneutical method of Reformed theology. In spite of extreme speech, hubris, and at times error, most of the heat was over methods of defense and forms of expression. They were still bonded in personal piety. As one, they defended biblical inspiration and inerrancy and militated against the liberal unbelief of their day.[94]

Like each of us, Warfield and Van Til were prone to speculation and misplaced emphasis within a system. But both depended upon the Holy Spirit. Van Til accepted Warfield's evidences, but he conceived of them as the defensive second army behind a bold

---

[93] Ibid., 26ff.

[94] For further discussion see Paul C. Gutjahr, *Charles Hodge: Guardian of American Orthodoxy* (Oxford: Oxford University Press, 2011); Paul Kjoss Helseth, *"Right Reason" and the Princeton Mind: An Unorthodox Proposal* (Phillipsburg, NJ: P&R Publishing, 2010), 128–31; W. Andrew Hoffecker, *Piety and the Princeton Theologians: Archibald Alexander, Charles Hodge, and Benjamin Warfield* (Grand Rapids: Baker, 1981); Owen Anderson, *Benjamin B. Warfield and Right Reason: The Clarity of General Revelation and Function of Apologetics* (Lanham, MD: University Press of America, 2005); John W. Stewart, *Mediating the Center: Charles Hodge on American Science, Language, Literature, and Politics* (Princeton, NJ: Princeton Theological Seminary, 1995); John W. Stewart and James H. Moorhead, eds., *Charles Hodge Revisited: A Critical Appraisal of His Life and Work* (Grand Rapids: Eerdmans, 2002); and Fred G. Zaspel, *The Theology of B. B. Warfield: A Systematic Summary* (Wheaton, IL: Crossway, 2010), 77–80, 574.

presuppositional offense. Both believed and implemented the Bible and the Reformed standards. Both believed that Adam's race is totally depraved. The two men were not worlds apart. Sharing the same Reformed heritage that united Old Princeton with Kuyper and Bavinck, Van Til contributed a complimentary introduction to Warfield's *Inspiration and Authority of the Bible* (1948), as Warfield had contributed the gracious introduction to Kuyper's *Encyclopedia of Sacred Theology* (1898).

Francis Schaeffer and Evangelical Apologetics

Francis Schaeffer (1912–84)[95] studied at Westminster under the influence of Machen and Van Til and then became the first student to enroll at Carl McIntire's Faith Theological Seminary and the first to be ordained by the Bible Presbyterian Church. In 1948, Schaeffer was in Amsterdam for the initial meeting of McIntire's International Council of Christian Churches, a conservative voice of opposition to the liberal World Council of Churches. During that meeting Schaeffer met the Dutchman Hans Rookmaaker (1922–77),[96] who was to illuminate and expand Schaeffer's vision for the broader culture.

Rookmaaker's own worldview had been impacted by Neo-Calvinist philosophy but under the tutelage of J. P. A. Mekkes in a Nazi prisoner-of-war camp in Poland. After World War II, Rookmaaker answered the FUA call for Christian workers. He studied art history, which was unusual in Reformed circles. Rookmaaker went on to become professor of the History of Art at the FUA and his book *Modern Art and the Death of a Culture* (1970) became a popular text in evangelical circles. Few individuals ever left a deeper impression upon Francis Schaeffer, and a lifelong friendship developed.

After serving on the faculty at Faith Theological Seminary (1953–54), Schaeffer moved to Europe. In 1955, the Schaeffer family opened their home in the Swiss Alps as a center, named L'Abri

---

[95] Bryan A. Follis, *Truth with Love: The Apologetics of Francis Schaeffer* (Wheaton, IL: Crossway, 2006); Colin Duriez, *Francis Schaeffer: An Authentic Life* (Wheaton, IL: Crossway, 2008); and Barry Hankins, *Francis Schaeffer and the Shaping of Evangelical America* (Grand Rapids: Eerdmans, 2008).

[96] Laurel Gasque, *Art and the Christian Mind: The Life and Work of H. R. Rookmaaker* (Wheaton, IL: Crossway, 2005).

("Shelter") Fellowship, where people could come to find honest answers to difficult questions about God, man, and the world around us. For this ministry Schaeffer became known throughout Europe. Even in America, *Time* magazine described him as the "apostle to the intellectuals." Beginning in 1965, he taught module courses in apologetics every other year in St. Louis, Missouri, at Covenant Seminary, whose founders had broken from Carl McIntire and Faith Theological Seminary in 1954–56.

As a strong advocate of evidentialism, J. Oliver Buswell, professor of Systematic Theology at Covenant Seminary, may have had some influence upon Schaeffer's approach to apologetics. Of course, Schaeffer had studied in Van Til's stronghold at Westminster, and he had also used the word *presuppositional* a few times to describe his own apologetics.[97] Schaeffer, however, was neither a precise Van Tillian presuppositionalist nor a precise evidentialist. While Van Til had impacted his assertive style and Rookmaaker inspired his worldview, it was Machen's common sense realism that laid the groundwork for Schaeffer's "apologetic of verification." Schaeffer essentially replaced Van Til's unmovable presuppositional axioms with tentative presuppositional "hypotheses," which he subjected to the test of verification by evidences shown during his presentations. The use of "hypothesis" was only for the sake of argument. During a typical lecture, it would soon become obvious to listeners that Schaeffer was already personally certain of all "hypothetical" proposals regarding any cardinal doctrine of Christianity. It was also obvious not only that Schaeffer loved the Bible, but also that he loved people. In such a setting Francis Schaeffer was effective.

Using the term *space-time history* to argue against the Neo-Orthodox escape into a non-literal realm, Schaeffer defended biblical inerrancy. He argued that the source of saving faith rests outside of man. It is the gift of God. True faith directs the believing sinner to God. Faith is no blind leap in the dark. It looks outward to the Christ who died upon the cross, finished the work of atonement, and rose on the third day—all within space-time history. Saving faith is

---

[97] For a helpful discussion, see William Edgar, "Two Christian Warriors: Cornelius Van Til and Francis Schaeffer Compared," in *Westminster Theological Journal* 57, no. 1 (Spring 1995): 57–80.

not faith in itself (Barthian fideism), but faith in the person of Christ and in the work that He has historically finished with His ascension. The proper ground of salvation is the work of Christ in space and time. Such is the essence of Schaeffer's teaching. True Christian faith turns by sovereign grace towards an objective person and His objective work, as seen in Paul's description of the gospel as "the power of God unto salvation to everyone that believeth" (Rom. 1:16). "Believe on the Lord Jesus Christ, and thou shalt be saved" (Acts 16:31).

As most in the public view, Schaeffer did not escape criticism,[98] but his positive influence as author, evangelist, and film-maker continues to be effective and widespread.[99] Schaeffer died in 1984, but reprints of his books and new biographies continue. Throughout his ministry, Schaeffer described his work as chiefly evangelistic. Against the teachings of Barthianism, he embraced and gave heed to Cornelius Van Til's urgent warning:

> What Barth considers to be the objective basis for the faith is found in *his* Christ, and in the resurrection of *his* Christ. And *this* resurrection of *this* Christ does not follow upon his death as one event in time follows another. . . . On Barth's view, there would be no true objectivity for the gospel message if the resurrection were directly identified with a fact of history following upon the death of Christ as another fact of history, for then the revelation of God in the resurrection would no longer be divine revelation. Then revelation no longer would be *hidden* as well as revealed. Therewith all the evils of a natural theology and of a self-enclosed anthropology would have returned. If Barth's idea of the objectivity of the gospel is to be maintained, then, on his own view, that of the Reformation must be rejected. Barth answers Bultmann,[100] as he

---

[98] See the articles in Ronald W. Ruegsegger, ed., *Reflections on Francis Schaeffer* (Grand Rapids: Zondervan, 1986). I find no lasting value in the words of his son, Frank Schaeffer, *Crazy for God: How I Grew Up as One of the Elect, Helped Found the Religious Right, and Lived to Take All (or Almost All) of It Back* (New York: Carroll & Graf, 2007).

[99] Francis Schaeffer's major works include *Art and the Bible* (1973); *A Christian Manifesto* (1981); *The God Who Is There* (1968); *The Great Evangelical Disaster* (1984); *How Should We Then Live?* (1976); *Escape from Reason* (1968); and *No Final Conflict: The Bible Without Error in All that It Affirms* (1975).

[100] See Rudolf Bultmann (1884–1976), *Jesus Christ and Mythology* (New York: Charles Scribner's Sons, 1958); and its rebuttal by Robert L. Reymond, *Bultmann's Demythologized Kerygma* (Philadelphia: Presbyterian and Reformed, 1967).

answered Romanism and all others, in terms of his Christ-Event, and this answer is based on a purely subjective foundation. We cannot walk down this incline of subjectivism for some distance and then arbitrarily stop. Bultmann and Barth stand together in their common opposition to the gospel of grace as founded on the Christ of the Scriptures. We dare not follow Barth any more than we dare follow Bultmann.[101]

Post-Conservative Evangelicalism and Apologetics

Edward J. Carnell (1919–67) of Fuller Theological Seminary was "utterly ashamed" at such criticism of Barth. Carnell declared that he "felt actual physical pain when I read in *Time* magazine that Cornelius Van Til, one of my former professors, had said that Barthianism is more hostile to the Reformers than is Roman Catholicism." Carnell accepted Barth as an "inconsistent evangelical" and scorned Van Til as one who should "ask God to forgive him for such an irresponsible judgment."[102] Likewise, Bernard L. Ramm (1916–92), known for his *Protestant Christian Evidences*, joined with those who moved into the ranks of Barthian hermeneutics and theology.[103]

As a conservative evidentialist, Clark H. Pinnock (1937–2010) authored *A Defense of Biblical Infallibility* (1967), followed by *Set Forth Your Case* (1968), in which he proclaimed, "It is high time for us to restock the arsenal of Christian evidences and confront

---

[101] Van Til, *Christianity and Barthianism*, 444–45.

[102] "Barth as Inconsistent Evangelical," *Christian Century* (June 6, 1962): 713–14; see also Rudolph Nelson, *The Making and Unmaking of an Evangelical Mind: The Case of Edward Carnell* (Cambridge: Cambridge University Press, 1987).

[103] Bernard Ramm, *Protestant Christian Evidences* (Chicago: Moody Press, 1953); and Bernard Ramm, "Helps from Karl Barth," in *How Karl Barth Changed My Mind*, ed. Donald K. McKim (Grand Rapids: Eerdmans, 1986), 121–26. Following his embrace of Barth's theology, Ramm wrote *After Fundamentalism: The Future of Evangelical Theology* (San Francisco: Harper and Row, 1983). Kevin J. Vanhoozer then described Ramm as a "John the Baptist" who "pointed to Christ and prepared a way for evangelical theology to go forward," in "Bernard Ramm," in *Handbook of Evangelical Theologians*, ed. Walter A. Elwell (Grand Rapids: Baker, 1993), 306. Contrary assessments include Robert Lee Jones, *Scripture and Theology: An Analysis of Bernard Ramm's Proposal to Adopt Karl Barth's Methodology* (Portland, OR: Western Conservative Baptist Seminary, 1985); and Phillip R. Thorne, *Evangelicalism and Karl Barth*.

our contemporaries with a solid message."[104] Afterwards, however, Pinnock ceased his defense of biblical inerrancy, departed from conservative evangelicalism,[105] and penned an overall negative critique of Francis Schaeffer's worldview.[106] Pinnock's latest works defend and promote the theology of Neotheism, or Open Theism, teaching that much of the future is still open or unknown to God. The system presents a low view of God's omniscience and ability to control the universe.[107] Regarding Neo-Orthodoxy, Pinnock had long concluded that Karl Barth "is no new modernist, but rather a new ally in the orthodox tradition." Pinnock "warmly" welcomed Barth "into the ranks of evangelical theologians" and thanked him for "enriching" his own thinking.[108]

Since the doctrines of biblical inspiration, inerrancy, and preservation are vitally related to the discussions above, there is provided below a list of helpful works on these topics as well as valuable works on the canon of Scripture.

---

[104] *Set Forth Your Case: Studies in Christian Apologetics* (Nutley, NJ: Craig Press, 1967), 126.

[105] See the Pinnock story, "I Was a Teenage Fundamentalist," *The Wittenburg Door*, no. 70 (December 1982/January 1983): 18.

[106] "Schaeffer on Modern Theology," in *Reflections on Francis Schaeffer*, ed. Ronald W. Ruegsegger (Grand Rapids: Zondervan, 1986), 173–93.

[107] Clark H. Pinnock, *Most Moved Mover: A Theology of God's Openness* (Grand Rapids: Baker, 2001); and Clark Pinnock, et al., *The Openness of God: A Biblical Challenge to the Traditional Understanding of God* (Downers Grove, IL: InterVarsity Press, 1994). The earliest such work was by Richard Rice, *The Openness of God* (Minneapolis: Bethany, 1980). The best rebuttals of Open Theism include Bruce A. Ware, *God's Lesser Glory: The Diminished God of Open Theism* (Wheaton, IL: Crossway, 2000); and Norman L. Geisler and H. Wayne House, *The Battle for God: Responding to the Challenge of Neotheism* (Grand Rapids: Kregel Publications, 2001).

[108] "Assessing Barth for Apologetics," in *How Karl Barth Changed My Mind*, ed. Donald M. McKim (Grand Rapids: Eerdmans, 1986), 162. A work of parallel significance is Andreas Pangritz, *Karl Barth in the Theology of Dietrich Bonhoeffer*, trans. Barbara and Martin Rumscheidt (Grand Rapids: Eerdmans, 2000). Other sympathetic accounts revealing the extent of Barthian influence include Gary Dorrien, *The Barthian Revolt in Modern Theology: Theology without Weapons* (Louisville, KY: Westminster John Knox, 2001) and *The Word as True Myth: Interpreting Modern Theology* (Louisville, KY: Westminster John Knox, 1997).

Select Bibliography for Further Reading

Works Defending Biblical Inerrancy

The Chicago Statement on Biblical Inerrancy. Chicago: International Council on Biblical Inerrancy, 1978.

Custer, Stewart. *Does Inspiration Demand Inerrancy? A Study of the Biblical Doctrine of Inspiration in the Light of Inerrancy*. Nutley, NJ: Craig Press, 1968.

Gaussen, F. S. R. Louis. *Theopneustia: The Plenary Inspiration of the Holy Scriptures*. London: Samuel Bagster and Sons, 1841.

Geisler, Norman L., ed. *Inerrancy*. Grand Rapids: Zondervan, 1980.

————, and William E. Nix. *From God to Us: How We Got Our Bible*. Chicago: Moody Press, 1986.

Hannah, John D., ed. *Inerrancy and the Church*. Chicago: Moody Press, 1984.

Lewis, Gordon R., and Bruce Demarest. *Challenges to Inerrancy: A Theological Response*. Chicago: Moody Press, 1984.

Lightner, Robert P. *A Biblical Case for Total Inerrancy: How Jesus Viewed the Old Testament*. Grand Rapids: Kregel, 1978.

Lindsell, Harold. *The Battle for the Bible*. Grand Rapids: Zondervan, 1976.

————. *The Bible in the Balance*. Grand Rapids: Zondervan, 1976.

Satta, Ronald F. *The Sacred Text: Biblical Authority in Nineteenth-Century America*. Eugene, OR: Pickwick Publications, 2007.

Schnaiter, Sam, and Ron Tagliapietra. *Bible Preservation and the Providence of God*. N.p.: Xlibris Corporation, 2002.

Woodbridge, John D. *Biblical Authority: A Critique of the Rogers/McKim Proposal*. Grand Rapids: Zondervan, 1982.

Young, Edward J. *Thy Word Is Truth: Some Thoughts on the Biblical Doctrine of Inspiration*. Grand Rapids: Eerdmans, 1957.

Conservative Works on the Canon of Scripture

Beckwith, Roger. *The Old Testament Canon of the New Testament Church and Its Background in Early Judaism*. Grand Rapids: Eerdmans, 1985.

Fisher, Milton C. "The Canon of the Old Testament." In The Expositor's Bible Commentary, 12 vols. edited by Frank E. Gaebelein, 1:385–405. Grand Rapids: Zondervan, 1979.

Guthrie, Donald. "The Canon of the New Testament." In *The Zondervan Pictorial Encyclopedia of the Bible*, 5 vols. edited by Merrill C. Tenney, 1:731–45. Grand Rapids: Zondervan, 1975–76.

General Works

Beacham, Roy E., and Kevin T. Bauder, eds. *One Bible Only? Examining Exclusive Claims for the King James Bible*. Grand Rapids: Kregel, 2001.

Beale, David. *A Pictorial History of Our English Bible*. Greenville, SC: Bob Jones University Press, 1982.

————. *In Pursuit of Purity: American Fundamentalism Since 1850*. Greenville, SC: Bob Jones University Press, 1986.

Dorrien, Gary. *The Remaking of Evangelical Theology*. Louisville, KY: Westminster John Knox, 1998.

Elliott, Paul M. *Christianity and Neo-Liberalism: The Spiritual Crisis in the Orthodox Presbyterian Church and Beyond.* Unicoi, TN: Trinity Foundation, 2005.

Gatewood, Willard B., Jr., ed. *Controversy in the Twenties: Fundamentalism, Modernism, and Evolution.* Nashville: Vanderbilt University Press, 1969.

Hoffmeier, James K., and Dennis R. Magary, eds. *Do Historical Matters Matter to Faith: A Critical Appraisal of Modern and Postmodern Approaches to Scripture.* Wheaton, IL: Crossway, 2012.

Loetscher, Lefferts A. *Facing the Enlightenment and Pietism: Archibald Alexander and the Founding of Princeton Theological Seminary.* Westport, CT: Greenwood Press, 1983.

Noll, Mark A., and David N. Livingstone, eds. *B. B. Warfield, Evolution, Science, and Scripture: Selected Writings.* Grand Rapids: Baker, 2000.

Rhoads, Gladys Titzck, and Nancy Titzck Anderson. *McIntire: Defender of Faith and Freedom.* N.p.: Xulon Press, 2012.

Schaeffer, Francis A. *The Complete Works of Francis A. Schaeffer.* 5 vols. 2nd ed. Wheaton, IL: Crossway, 1985.

_____. *Letters of Francis A. Schaeffer: Spiritual Reality in the Personal Christian Life.* Edited with introductions by Lane T. Dennis. Westchester, IL: Crossway, 1985.

Schenck, Lewis Bevens. *The Presbyterian Doctrine of Children in the Covenant: An Historical Study of the Significance of Infant Baptism in the Presbyterian Church.* Phillipsburg, NJ: P&R Publishing, 1940.

Stewart, John W., and James H. Moorhead, eds. *Charles Hodge Revisited: A Critical Appraisal of His Life and Work.* Grand Rapids: Eerdmans, 2002.

Warfield, Benjamin Breckinridge. *The Works of Benjamin B. Warfield.* 10 vols. New York: Oxford University Press, 1930. Reprint, Grand Rapids: Baker, 2003.

Wells, David F. *Above All Earthly Pow'rs: Christ in a Postmodern World.* Grand Rapids: Eerdmans, 2005.

19

Pagan, Jewish, and Christian
Attitudes towards Abortion

Since the 1973 pro-abortion ruling by the United States Supreme Court, the abortion problem has confronted Christianity more than it has at any other time in modern history. Now Bible believers must face this controversial issue and take a biblical stand. Thoughtful glimpses into the past can not only instruct but also challenge and inspire the twenty-first-century Christian who feels intimidated by a hostile and humanistic society. We will begin with precise definitions of a few technical terms that frequently appear in the discussion.

In medical terms, an unborn child is an *embryo* from his conception through his first eight weeks, at which time most of his internal organs have formed, all of his external features are present, he is about an inch long, and his heart has been beating for two weeks. From the end of the eighth week until birth he is a *fetus*. A *miscarriage* is the loss of a pregnancy before the child has developed enough to survive outside the uterus, or prior to about twenty weeks of the pregnancy. In the United States, most states require a death certificate when such fetal death occurs after twenty weeks of pregnancy. A normal pregnancy is about forty weeks in duration. A *premature birth* is the delivery of a baby before or during the thirty-seventh week of pregnancy, and, according to the American Medical Association, "most

premature babies grow up to be normal and healthy."[1] These definitions should be helpful for our discussions throughout the chapter.

Translating and Interpreting Exodus 21:22–23

(22) If men strive, and hurt a woman with child, so that her *fruit
depart* from her, and yet no *mischief* follow: he shall be surely
punished, according as the woman's husband will lay upon him;
and he shall pay as the judges determine. (23) And if any *mischief*
follow, then thou shalt give life for life. (italics added)

Liberal interpreters have made three basic assertions from the
Exodus passage:
(1) God does not regard the unborn as a person.
(2) God penalizes the liable man with only a fine when the
woman miscarries and her unborn dies.
(3) God gives the death sentence if the mother herself dies.

According to that view, the unborn do not come under the protection of the sixth commandment. Conservatives have countered
with three major observations from the same passage.

First, the Hebrew word for "depart" (יָצָא, "to come out") most
likely refers to a premature birth,[2] rather than to a miscarriage,[3] and
normally refers to a child who is sufficiently healthy. The word is
used twelve times in the Old Testament to describe children coming

---

[1] *American Medical Association: Complete Medical Encyclopedia* (New York:
Random House, 2003), 1014; see 502, 558, 850, and 1011–15.

[2] The NIV (1984), e.g., renders Exod. 21:22, "she gives birth prematurely," indi-
cating that the child is alive. In this case, if there is no injury to the child or to the
mother, a fine is paid. In the case of injury, to the child or the mother, the penalty
is "life for life," etc. The 1963 ed. of the NASB rendered Exod. 21:22, "she has a
miscarriage," but later editions changed it to "she gives birth prematurely."

[3] Evangelicals taking a liberal position on the issue have preferred "miscar-
riage," implying that the mother's life is of more importance than that of the fetus.
Kenneth Kantzer, for instance, insisted that the passage "explicitly distinguishes the
killing of a fetus from murder on the ground that the fetus is not a human life."
To Kantzer, the unborn is only "potentially" human. See his article, "The Origin of
the Soul as Related to the Abortion Question," in *Birth Control and the Christian:
A Protestant Symposium on the Control of Human Reproduction*, ed. Walter O.
Spitzer and Carlyle L. Salor (Wheaton: Tyndale House, 1969), 553. Likewise,
Nancy Hardesty argued that the Exodus 21 passage "explicitly distinguishes
between destruction of a fetus and the killing of a person." See her article, "Where
Does Life Begin?" *Eternity* (February 1971): 43.

out of the mother's womb. In ten of these twelve references, the birth described is a normal birth. (The two exceptions are Num. 12:12, where it refers to a stillborn child, and Job 3:11 where it refers to one who died during delivery.) Most typically, the word refers to the birth of one who is healthy enough to grow up as completely normal. Had Moses meant to convey the idea of "miscarriage," he would likely have used some form of the Hebrew word for miscarriage, as he does in Genesis 31:38 and Exodus 23:26a ("cast," שָׁכַל). Hosea does likewise in 9:14, where he speaks of "a miscarrying" (מַשְׁכִּיל), as does Job 21:10.

Second, the Hebrew word for "fruit" (yeled, יֶלֶד) occurs eighty-eight times in the Old Testament and means "young child" or "youth." One should assign the same meaning to the "fruit" of Exodus 21:22 as to the "child" (yeled) of Isaiah 9:6a: "For unto us a child is born, unto us a son is given." The word yeled also occurs in Job 38:41; 39:3; Isaiah 11:7; Ruth 1:5; and Exodus 1:17–18. Unless Exodus 21:22 is the only exception, yeled always refers to a live youth, which clearly advances the idea that the Exodus passage has reference to a premature birth.[4]

Third, the word for "mischief" ('ason, אָסוֹן, actually meaning "harm" or "injury") does not necessarily refer only to the woman. It could just as well refer both to the mother and to the child. In this case, the passage concerns a struggle in which one man accidentally strikes a woman with child and causes her to give birth prematurely. If there is no harm or injury either to the mother or to the child, the man must pay the fine that the woman's husband determines and that the judges agree to be fair. If harm does occur either to the mother or to the child, the man must pay according to the law of retribution (lex talionis), that is, "life for life, eye for eye." Meredith Kline adds that "this law, found in Exodus 21:22–25, turns out to be perhaps the most decisive positive evidence in the Scripture that the fetus is to be regarded as a living person."[5]

---

[4] This is developed more fully by Todd S. Beall, "The Abortion Issue and Exodus 21:22," *Reflections* (Spring 1984): 5–6.

[5] "*Lex Talionis* and the Human Fetus," *JETS* 20 (September 1977): 193.

The Ancient Greek World

The earliest known record of an abortive technique goes back to the ancient Chinese during the reign of Emperor Shen Nung almost three millennia before Christ. A medical document from this period prescribes the use of mercury to induce an abortion. An Egyptian medical papyrus of 1550 BC describes similar techniques. Most of the surviving literature on the subject, however, comes from the Greeks and Romans. Among the classical Greeks, Hippocrates (ca. 460–357 BC)—Father of Medicine—describes carefully fashioned medical instruments designed for abortion at that time. The spirit of his famous Oath, however, suggests an essentially antiabortion attitude:

> I swear by Apollo, the healer, Asclepius, Hygieia, and Panacea, and I take to witness all the gods, all the goddesses, to keep according to my ability and my judgment, the following Oath. . . . I will give no deadly medicine to anyone if asked, nor suggest any such counsel; and in like manner I will not give to a woman a pessary[6] to produce abortion.

Both Plato and Aristotle favored abortion on social and economic grounds. In Plato's philosophy, the soul pre-exists the body. Each soul consists of reason, spirit, and desire. It unites with the body at birth. Plato usually associates life with breath. To him the child is not humanly alive until it begins to breathe. Moreover, Plato asserts in his *Republic* that the wishes of the state must determine all matters regarding child planning since the state must create conditions necessary for producing the highest quality of human being. A woman, therefore, may bear children only while she is between twenty and forty years of age. After that, any offspring must be aborted. A man may beget offspring only while he is between twenty-five and fifty-five:

> A woman, I said, at twenty years of age may begin to bear children to the State, and continue to bear them until forty; a man may begin at five-and-twenty, when he has passed the point at which the pulse of life beats quickest, and continue to beget children until he be fifty-five. . . . And we grant all this, accompanying

---

[6] Ancient physicians used the pessary as a vaginal suppository to induce abortions.

the permission with strict orders to prevent any embryo which may come into being from seeing the light; and if any force a way to the birth, the parents must understand that the offspring of such an union cannot be maintained, and arrange accordingly. (Book V)

Widely differing from his teacher Plato, Aristotle insists that the soul is never a separate immaterial agent acting upon a material body. Soul and body can never be distinct. There is a tri-fold hierarchy of souls: plants consist of *vegetative souls*, with powers of growth and re-production. Animals, in addition, possess *sensitive souls*, with powers of perception and motion. Each animal has at least one sense faculty, touch being the most universal. With touch, one learns pleasure, and to know pleasure is to have the sense of desire. Humans, in addition, have *rational souls*, with powers of reason and thought. The process occurs this way: at conception the unborn human is a vegetative soul. By the time of its "formation," it has also gained a sensitive (animal) soul. At the point of its birth, the human baby has, in addition, a rational soul. "Formation" of limbs begins to occur forty days after conception for the male and ninety days after conception for the female.[7] When formation begins, sensation begins; therefore, animal life begins at formation. For Aristotle, the expression "life and sensation" is synonymous with "formation."

As with Plato's view, the state must always be the final judge since every person is the property of the state, and every decision must be made in the interest of the state's welfare. State regulation is necessary for producing the proper conditions for bringing the high-est quality of human beings into the world. Thus, Aristotle insists on infanticide for any "deformed" child:

> As to the exposure and rearing of children, let there be a law that no deformed child shall live, but that on the ground of an excess in the number of children, if the established customs of the state forbid this (for in our state, population has a limit), no child is to be exposed, but when couples have children in excess, let abortion be procured before sense and life have begun; what may or may

---

[7] *Historia Animalium* (*History of Animals*) 7.3.

not be lawfully done in these cases depends on the question of life and sensation.[8]

Aristotelian philosophers, therefore, considered the unborn as an incomplete person; and this pagan philosophy had a significant influence upon the third-century BC Jews who translated the Hebrew Old Testament into Greek.

The Ancient Jewish World

Here again is the Exodus 21 passage:

(22) If men strive, and hurt a woman with child, so that her fruit [*yeled*, יֶלֶד, "young child"] depart [יָצָא, "comes out"] from her, and yet no mischief ['*ason*, אָסוֹן, "harm" or "injury"] follow: he shall be surely punished, according as the woman's husband will lay upon him; and he shall pay as the judges determine. (23) And if any mischief ['*ason*] follow, then thou shalt give life for life.

The Jews in Alexandria, Egypt, who began translating the Septuagint (LXX) during the late third century BC, read Aristotle extensively; consequently, Aristotelian philosophy influenced their translation of Exodus 21:22–23. As pagan philosophy has sometimes influenced Bible translators in more modern times, so humanistic philosophy sometimes influenced the Alexandrian translators of the LXX, including this passage. Aristotle had been the first to make a distinction between the unborn who are "formed" and those who are "unformed," and the Jewish translators transferred his philosophy directly into this key passage. Following the philosophy of Aristotle, they rendered the Hebrew word '*ason* (אָסוֹן, which means "harm" or "injury") as "formed" (ἐξεικονισμένον),[9] making it thus: (22) καὶ ἐξέλθῃ τὸ παιδίον αὐτῆς μὴ ἐξεικονισμένον ἐπιζήμιον ζημιωθήσεται· καθότι ἂν ἐπιβάλῃ ὁ ἀνὴρ τῆς γυναικὸς δώσει μετὰ ἀξιώματος. (23) Ἐὰν δὲ ἐξεικονισμένον ᾖ δώσει ψυχὴν ἀντὶ ψυχῆς. In English, verse 22 translates in part, "and [if] the child should come out of her not having been fully formed . . . he shall

---

[8] *Politics* 7.16.

[9] See, e.g., Henry George Liddell and Robert Scott, *A Greek-English Lexicon* (New York: Harper and Brothers, 1846), 400, 475, where ἐξεικονίζω, (ἐκ εἰκονίζω), is shown to be from εἰκών, which means to "mold" or "fashion."

be fined." Verse 23 translates, "But if it had been fully formed, then he shall give life for life." Thus, while extending the "life for life" clause to the unborn, they made the arbitrary Aristotelian distinction between the status of an unborn child who is formed and one who is unformed.

The Alexandrian Jew Philo (ca. 30 BC–AD 50), following the LXX influence on Exodus 21, expresses his view that if one has a conflict with a woman with child and strikes her, causing a miscarriage, he shall pay a fine if the child is still "unformed." However, adds Philo, if the child is "formed," the man shall die. Philo compares the unborn in the womb with a statue lying in the "sculptor's workshop," waiting only to be released into the world:

> If anyone has a contest with a woman who is pregnant, and strike her a blow on her belly, and she miscarry, if the child which was conceived within her is still unfashioned and unformed, he shall be punished by a fine, both for the assault which he committed and also because he has prevented nature, who was fashioning and preparing that most excellent of all creatures, a human being, from bringing him into existence. But if the child which was conceived had assumed a distinct Shape in all its parts, having received all its proper connective and distinctive qualities, he shall die; for such a creature as that is a man, whom he has slain while still in the workshop of nature, who had not thought it as yet a proper time to produce him to the light, but had kept him like a statue lying in a sculptor's workshop, requiring nothing more than to be released and sent out into the world.[10]

Josephus (ca. AD 37–100), Jewish priest and historian, discusses the Exodus 21 passage in his *Antiquities of the Jews*. In this work, his understanding of the passage is inferior to Philo's. Likely representative of the thinking among the Pharisees of his day, Josephus's advice is that one who kicks a woman with child and causes a miscarriage should pay a fine, as the judges decide, but if the woman dies, he should also die:

> If men strive together, and there be no instrument of iron, let him that is smitten be avenged immediately, by inflicting the same punishment on him that smote him: but if when he is carried

---

[10] Philo, *De Specialibus Legibus* (*The Special Laws*) 3.19.108–109, On Laws Concerning Murderers.

home he lie sick many days, and then die, let him that smote him not escape punishment; but if he that is smitten escape death, and yet be at great expense for his cure, the smiter shall pay for all that has been expended during the time of his sickness, and for all that he has paid the physician. He that kicks a woman with child, so that the woman miscarry, let him pay a fine in money, as the judges shall determine, as having diminished the multitude by the destruction of what was in her womb; and let money also be given the woman's husband by him that kicked her; but if she die of the stroke, let him also be put to death, the law judging it equitable that life should go for life. (4.8.33, or 4.278 in some translations)

In his *Contra Apionem*, however, written near the end of his life,[11] Josephus calls both abortion and infanticide "murder." A woman who commits either "will be a murderer of her child, by destroying a living creature, and diminishing human kind" (2.25, or 2.202 in some translations).

The Ancient Roman World

The Romans, like the ancient Greeks, approached abortion with an entirely humanistic attitude. Current social and economic conditions dictated policy. If the state wanted births, it made abortion a crime. If the state had no desire for an increase in population, it permitted and even encouraged not only abortion but infanticide. Toward the end of the Roman Republic and the beginning of the Empire, both abortion and infanticide were virtually commonplace in this pagan society. In the first century, the Stoics were among the most highly esteemed philosophers. Nero's tutor and advisor, Seneca, the Stoic philosopher, boasts in his treatise, *On Anger*, "We destroy our monstrous children, and also, drown our children if they are weak or unnaturally formed; it is not anger but reason to separate the useless from the sound."[12] In a letter Seneca does thank his mother for not aborting him![13]

---

[11] Desmond Seward, *Jerusalem's Traitor: Josephus, Masada, and the Fall of Judea* (Cambridge, MA: Da Capo Press, 2009), 269.

[12] *Portentosos fetus extinguimus, liberos quoque, si debiles monstrosique editi sunt, mergimus; nec ira sed ratio est a sanis inutilia secernere* (*De Ira* 1.15.1).

[13] *To Helvia on Consolation* 16.3.

The Ancient Christian World

Records from primitive Christianity reveal a clear denunciation of *all kinds* of abortion and infanticide.[14] The earliest church fathers frequently emphasize the sanctity of human life, and with few exceptions their constant condemnation of abortion depends in no way upon philosophical theories regarding the soul's origin or when human life begins. From the second century comes the cry, "Thou shalt not murder a child by abortion, nor again shalt thou kill it when it is born" (*Epistle of Barnabas* 19; *The Teaching of the Twelve Apostles* 2). Echoing the same message is the apologist Athenagoras of Athens, in his *Plea for the Christians* (35), as he defends believers against the false pagan charge of cannibalism and argues that Christians not only regard the unborn child as a created being in God's image, but they also condemn both infanticide and abortion as homicide.

In his *Instructor* for new converts, Clement of Alexandria (ca. 150–215) likewise emphasizes the dehumanizing effect of destroying one's offspring. He explains that women who have recourse to lethal drugs to conceal fornication destroy not only the unborn within them, but their own humanity as well (2.10).

Tertullian of Carthage (ca. 160–220), the scholar, lawyer, presbyter, preacher, and apologist, defends Christians against the false accusation that they sacrifice children: "In our case, murder being once for all forbidden, we may not destroy even the fetus in the womb. . . . To hinder a birth is merely a speedier man-killing." The early Christians closely associated abortion with infanticide. Tertullian mentions ritualistic pagan sacrifices of children. He describes the cruel drowning and the exposing of infants to cold, hunger, and wild dogs (*Apology* 9). Attacking Plato and the Stoics, who said that the child does not receive its soul until it breathes, Tertullian, a bold advocate of traducianism, argues in his *Treatise on the Soul* that the soul begins to exist simultaneously with the body. The seed of the soul is planted with the seed of the body, and "the embryo becomes a

---

[14] Early Christians repeatedly emphasize their conviction that God places great value on human life. They point to such passages as these: Gen. 30:22–23; Ps. 139:13–15; Jer. 1:5; and Isa. 49:5.

human being . . . from the moment that its form is completed" (36–37). On the basis of Exodus 21:22–23, he charges that anyone who causes abortion is liable to the law of retribution. Tertullian does not speculate concerning the time of the formation. In his *Exhortation to Chastity* (12), he preaches against the practice of dissolving conceptions with abortifacient drugs. "To us," explains this Christian attorney, "it is no more lawful to hurt [a child] in process of birth, than one [already] born." Tertullian speaks of a crude abortion instrument that was "in the shape of a copper [or bronze] needle or spike." He also describes the method of using an "embryo-knife":

> Among surgeons' tools there is a certain instrument, which is formed with a nicely-adjusted flexible frame for opening the *uterus* first of all, and keeping it open; it is further furnished with an annular blade, by means of which the limbs within the womb are dissected with anxious but unfaltering care; its last appendage being a blunted or covered hook, wherewith the entire *foetus* is extracted by a violent delivery.[15]

Defending third-century Christianity against the absurd pagan charge of infant slaughter, the North African apologist, Minucius Felix of Cirta (in modern Algeria) retorts that the Romans are the ones guilty of this wicked crime. The pagans were exposing their children to wild birds and beasts and even strangling them to death. In the Roman world, the term used to describe the killing of a close relative was *parricide*. Some women were committing parricide by taking drugs to destroy the nascent life within their wombs. Even worse they were learning such practices from the myths surrounding their own pagan gods. Saturn, for instance, was said to have devoured his children, and humans sacrificed their infants to him (*Octavius* 30).

Hippolytus of Rome (ca. 170–236), one of the most eminent Christian scholars and prolific writers of the third century, attacks the practice of abortion within the church at Rome. Before the discovery of Hippolytus's works, the Roman Catholic Church had canonized him as a saint. This became an embarrassment when the true Hippolytus came to light in 1842, with the discovery at Mount Athos of his *Refutation of All Heresies*, also called *Philosophumena*

---

[15] *Treatise on the Soul* 25.

(Φιλοσοφούμενα, or *Philosophical Teachings*). The work reveals Hippolytus as an accuser of the church of Rome. He had castigated certain Roman bishops for doctrinal heresy and disciplinary laxity. According to Hippolytus, Bishop Callistus had established a school that had become popular for its lack of morality. Some "reputed believers," women of the church, were "choosing their bedfellows" from among the lowest ranks of society and were resorting to drugs to cause sterility. Some were tightly binding their stomachs to force abortions and to prevent embarrassment to their wealthy families. Bishop Callistus was allowing such unrepentant women to partake of communion, and Hippolytus accuses them all of "inculcating adultery and murder at the same time" (9.7).

Cyprian of Carthage (ca. 200–258), in a letter to Cornelius, bishop of Rome, complains of an African priest who had joined the Novatians, a group that strongly opposed receiving back into the church those who under persecution offered sacrifices to idols. Cyprian reports that this African priest kicked his own wife, causing her to lose her child. "The womb of his wife was smitten by a blow of his heel," and the dead child is "the fruit of a father's murder [parricide]," explains Cyprian. Does this man "dare to condemn the hands of those who sacrifice [to idols, under severe persecution], when he himself is more guilty in his feet," by which his own son was slain (*Epistle* 48.2–3)?

In the fourth century, the anonymous and highly esteemed *Constitutions of the Holy Apostles* (or *Apostolic Constitutions*) echoes a pro-life theme that has been influenced by Aristotle's emphasis on "shape" or "formation" of the unborn: "Thou shalt not slay a child by causing abortion, nor kill that which is begotten; for everything that is shaped, and has received a soul from God, if it be slain, shall be avenged, as being unjustly destroyed" (7.1.3).

Lactantius (ca. 250–325), the "Christian Cicero" of Nicomedia (in Asia Minor), in his treatise *On the Workmanship of God*, continues the Christian assault against the old Stoic view that infants become human only when they begin to breathe. Lactantius explains that on the fortieth day after conception, God "forms the offspring" in the womb, then creates and infuses the soul within the body (12, 17, 19). His view reflects the influence of Aristotle and of the Septuagint translation of Exodus 21:22–23. While the writer has nothing directly to say about abortion, he does cry out against infanticide and uses the word *parricide* to describe those who with wicked hands "mar the work of God" (*The Divine Institutes* 6.20).

A local church council, which met at Elvira, Spain, in 305, decreed to excommunicate for life any woman who committed abortion after adultery. In 314, a provincial council, meeting in Ancyra, the capital of Galatia in Asia Minor, decreed ten years' penance for adulterous women who took drugs (*pharmakeia*, φαρμακεία) for abortion. Two and a half centuries earlier, the apostle Paul had condemned the Galatian pagans for their practice of the same—φαρμακεία— translated "witchcraft" in the KJV (Gal. 5:20). The Ancyra Council condemned even those who manufacture such drugs.

Basil of Caesarea (ca. 329–79) scoffs at alleged hair-splitting differences between formed and unformed babies. In a canonical (official) letter (ca. 347) to Bishop Amphilochius of Iconium, Basil condemns abortion at any stage as murder, concurs with the ten-year penalty set in 314 at Ancyra, and keeps alive the Christian message that God is the Giver of life and that both life and death belong to His Providence:

> The woman who purposely destroys her unborn child is guilty of murder. With us there is no nice enquiry as to its being formed or unformed. In this case it is not only the being about to be born who is vindicated, but the woman in her attack upon herself; because in most cases women who make such attempts die. The destruction of the embryo is an additional crime, a second murder, at all events if we regard it as done with intent. The punishment, however, of these women should not be for life, but for the term of ten years. And let their treatment depend not on mere lapse of time, but on the character of their repentance. (*Epistle* 188:2)[16]

Chrysostom of Constantinople (ca. 344/354–407) rebukes men who cause harlots to become murderers in resorting to abortion:

> Why sow where the ground makes it its care to destroy the fruit? where there are many efforts at abortion? where there is murder before the birth? for even the harlot thou dost not let continue a

---

[16] Cf. *Epistle* 188:8, where Basil adds, "Women also who administer drugs to cause abortion, as well as those who take poisons to destroy unborn children are murderesses."

mere harlot, but makest her a murderess also. You see how drunkenness leads to whoredom, whoredom to adultery, adultery to murder; or rather to a something even worse than murder. For I have no name to give it, since it does not take off the thing born, but prevent its being born. Why then dost thou abuse the gift of God, and fight with His laws, and follow after what is a curse as if a blessing, and make the chamber of procreation a chamber for murder, and arm the woman that was given for childbearing unto slaughter? For with a view to drawing more money by being agreeable and an object of longing to her lovers, even this she is not backward to do, so heaping upon thy head a great pile of fire. For even if the daring deed be hers, yet the causing of it is thine. Hence too come idolatries, since many, with a view to become acceptable, devise incantations, and libations, and love-potions, and countless other plans. Yet still after such great unseemliness, after slaughters, after idolatries, the thing seems to many to belong to things indifferent, aye, and to many that have wives too. (*Homily* 24, on Romans 13)

Ambrose of Milan (ca. 339–97) preached nine homilies on the six days of creation (*Hexaemeron*). His "fifth-day" sermon, on the creation of the birds, rebukes certain females by contrasting them with crows and other winged fowl that take the greatest of care with their young. Man is the only part of God's creation that studies ways to destroy his own children:

> Even the wealthy, in order that their inheritance may not be divided among several, deny in the very womb their own progeny. By the use of parricidal mixtures they snuff out the fruit of their wombs in the genital organs themselves. In this way life is taken away before it is given. Who except man himself has taught us ways of repudiating children? (*Hexaemeron* 5.18.58)

Jerome (ca. 347–420), writing from Rome in 384, addresses one of his most well-known letters, to a young and well-educated friend named Eustochium, who has just dedicated her life to perpetual virginity. Jerome describes the ubiquitous and lustful temptations of a Roman society that had prompted many sincere believers to seek escape by means of monasteries and convents. Even as a powerful advocate of monasticism, Jerome is compelled to address the widespread hypocrisy among those who had dedicated their lives to virginity and chastity. This letter offers first-hand insight of fourth-century monasticism. Jerome is seeking to encourage his young friend by including his own testimony of the struggles that he encountered with his thought life even as a monk living in the desert outside Rome. He discovers the most dangerous of all "scorpions and wild beasts" to be those that lurk deep within his own breast. Such is the condition of each individual, male and female, from birth. In the following citation, Jerome is explaining the temptations that come even to individuals who retreat from the world. He explains his great grief over the sin of adultery and the practice of abortion, even within monastic cells and wilderness retreats. To Jerome victory can come only through the cleansing of God's Word:

> How often, when I was living in the desert, in the vast solitude which gives to hermits a savage dwelling-place, parched by a burning sun, how often did I fancy myself among the pleasures of Rome! I used to sit alone because I was filled with bitterness. Sackcloth disfigured my unshapely limbs and my skin from long neglect had become as black as an Ethiopian's. Tears and groans were every day my portion; and if drowsiness chanced to overcome my struggles against it, my bare bones, which hardly held together, clashed against the ground. Of my food and drink I say nothing: for, even in sickness, the solitaries have nothing but cold water, and to eat one's food cooked is looked upon as self-indulgence. Now, although in my fear of hell I had consigned myself to this prison, where I had no companions but scorpions and wild beasts, I often found myself amid bevies of girls. My face was pale and my frame chilled with fasting; yet my mind was burning with desire, and the fires of lust kept bubbling up before me when my flesh was as good as dead. Helpless, I cast myself at the feet of Jesus, I watered them with my tears, I wiped them with my hair: and then I subdued my rebellious body with weeks of abstinence. I do not blush to avow my abject misery; rather I lament that I am not now what once I was. I remember how I often cried aloud all night till the break of day and ceased not from beating my breast till tranquility returned at the chiding of the Lord. I used to dread my very cell as though it knew my thoughts; and, stern and angry with myself, I used to make my way alone into the desert. Wherever I saw hollow valleys, craggy mountains, steep cliffs, there I made my oratory, there the house of correction for my unhappy flesh. There, also—the Lord Himself is my witness—when

> I had shed copious tears and had strained my eyes towards heaven,
> I sometimes felt myself among angelic hosts, and for joy and glad-
> ness sang: "because of the savor of thy good ointments we will run
> after thee" [Song of Sol. 1:3–4]. (*Letter* 22.7)

Continuing the same letter to this daughter of Paula, the saintly widow who established convents and learned Greek and Hebrew, Jerome laments that the "mother church" has already lost many of its "virgins" to paganism, through the incredible and insatiable temptations that led them to kill their babies:

> I cannot bring myself to speak of the many virgins who daily fall
> and are lost to the bosom of the church, their mother: stars over
> which the proud foe sets up his throne. . . . Some go so far as to
> take potions, that they may insure barrenness, and thus murder
> human beings almost before their conception. Some, when they
> find themselves with child through their sin, use drugs to procure
> abortion, and when (as often happens) they die with their off-
> spring, they enter the lower world laden with the guilt not only
> of adultery against Christ but also of suicide and child murder.
> (*Letter* 22.13)

Augustine of Hippo (354–430) reveals an Aristotelian influence via the LXX. Discussing the question of whether aborted babies will be included in the resurrection, he believes it only natural "to think that unformed abortions perish, like seeds that have never fructified." Instantly though, he has second thoughts:

> But who will dare to deny, though he may not dare to affirm, that
> at the resurrection every defect in the form shall be supplied, and
> that thus the perfection which time would have brought shall not
> be wanting, any more than the blemishes which time did bring
> shall be present: so that the nature shall neither want anything
> suitable and in harmony with it that length of days would have
> added, nor be debased by the presence of anything of an opposite
> kind that length of days has added; but that what is not yet com-
> plete shall be completed, just as what has been injured shall be
> renewed. (*Enchiridion* 85)

Augustine adds, "To deny that fetuses ever lived at all who are cut out limb by limb from the womb, lest the mothers die also if the fetuses were left dead, would seem too audacious" (86).

The above statement affords an opportunity for some analysis concerning Augustine's thinking on the origin of the soul.

He sometimes wavers between creationism and traducianism. Creationism, sometimes called "concreationism," affirms that God creates the soul *ex nihilo* and unites it with the body either at conception or at some later point up to birth. Generally, creationists have held that the union occurs at conception.

There are two types of traducianism. (1) Physical traducianism is expressed in either of two ways: (a) the soul develops concurrently from inanimate matter with the body; or (b) the soul is actually in the sperm and is conveyed by organic generation. (2) Spiritual traducianism, sometimes called generationism, holds simply that each soul derives from the soul of the parents.

Traducianism by definition includes the belief that the unborn child receives a soul at conception. Augustine sometimes leans towards generationism but never seems sure enough to decide on the meaning of the Exodus 21 passage. He would not have recommended abortion at any stage of development or under any circumstances. His conviction was that even in marriage all sex that is not for the specific purpose of procreation is venial sin, and he condemns married couples whose "lustful cruelty" prompts them to commit infanticide, to abort babies whether formed or unformed, or even to use contraception.[17]

In a sort of cautious agnosticism, Augustine leaves us with ambivalence concerning his view of when human ensoulment occurs, that is, the time when the unborn body receives its soul from God.[18] He depicts the soul's entry into the body, whenever that may occur, as the moment of "quickening," but he also insists that a human soul cannot live in an unformed body. An unborn cannot be a person until formation occurs. Augustine equates "formation" with sensation. While he affirms his belief that the abortion of one who is formed is murder, his idea of a "delayed ensoulment" leads him to believe that abortion is not murder if the unborn is

---

[17] Augustine, *On Marriage and Concupiscence* 1.17 (xv); and *On the Good of Marriage* 1–35.

[18] See especially Augustine, *The Soul and Its Origin* 4.4. This view is similar to that of Jerome, *Commentarius in Ecclesiasten* 2.5 (Migne *PL* 23.1076–86). See also John T. Noonan Jr., "An Almost Absolute Value in History," in *The Morality of Abortion: Legal and Historical Perspectives*, ed. John T. Noonan Jr. (Cambridge: Harvard University Press, 1970), 15.

without formation (sensation). Commenting on Exodus 21:22–25, Augustine answers his own great "question of the soul," or ensoulment, with an unequivocal Aristotelian distinction between unborn who are formed and those who are unformed. Apparently attempting as much euphemism as possible, Augustine finally proposes from Exodus 21:22–25 that God's law simply does not treat the abortion of an unformed baby as homicide:

> Here the question of the soul is prone to incite, whether what is not formed can indeed be understood as not ensouled, and therefore that it is not homicide, because it can be said not yet to have been determined whether it did not have a soul yet. Following that, it says: *But if it was formed, he will give life for life.* . . . If, therefore, this child was still formless as yet, but already ensouled in a formless way (because the great question of the soul is not to be decided by un-argued and rash opinion), therefore the Law does not provide that it [abortion] pertains to homicide, because a live soul cannot yet be said to be in a body that lacks feeling, when such is not yet formed in flesh, and therefore not yet endowed with senses.[19]

The Quinisext Council (692), often called the Council in Trullo, established a canon of ecclesiastical law against abortion. The word *quinisext* is from the Latin *quinque* ("five") + *sextus* ("sixth"). Thus, the Council was "quinisext" because its purpose was to supplement decisions of the fifth and sixth Ecumenical Councils held earlier in 553 and 680–81. The word *Trullo* refers, not to a place, but to a dome. The Quinisext Council (692) was the second of two "Trullan" Councils, named such because they met in the hall (or

---

[19] S. Aurelii Augustini, *Liber Secundus: Quaestiones in Exodum* LXXX (Exod. 21:22–25), *In Heptateuchum Locutionum Libri Septem.* To my knowledge no English translation has ever been published. Italics are retained from Migne: "Hic de anima quaestio solet agitari, utrum quod formatum non est, ne animatum quidem possit intelligi, et ideo non sit homicidium, quia nec examinatum dici potest, si adhuc animam non habebat. Sequitur enim et dicit: *Si autem formatum fuerit, dabit animam pro anima.* . . . Si ergo illud informe puerperium jam quidem fuerit, sed adhuc quodammodo informiter animatum (quoniam magna de anima quaestio non est praecipitanda indiscussae temeritate sententiae), ideo Lex noluit ad homicidium pertinere, quia nondum dici potest anima viva in eo corpore quod sensu caret, si talis est in carne nondum formata, et ideo nondum sensibus praedita" (Migne *PL* 34.626). Augustine did not retract the statement.

chapel) underneath the great dome (*Trullus*) of the imperial palace in Constantinople.

Canon XCI of the Quinisext Council establishes this law: "Those who give drugs for procuring abortion, and those who receive poisons to kill the fetus, are subjected to the penalty of murder." The eastern churches regard this as a "general" council, but the Roman Catholic Church ranks it as being local since it did not participate.

Thomas Aquinas (1224–74), upholding and advancing Augustine's views, held that if an unformed fetus were inadvertently killed by striking the mother, the person responsible for the incident would not be guilty of homicide. In reference to Exodus 21:22–23, Thomas writes: "He that strikes a woman with child does something unlawful: wherefore if there results the death either of the woman or of the animated [humanly ensouled] fetus, he will not be excused from homicide, especially seeing that death is the natural result of such a blow."[20] Thomas held to the Aristotelian tri-fold development of the human soul:

(1) that plants consist of *nutritive* or *vegetative souls*, with powers of growth and reproduction;

(2) that animals, in addition, possess *sensitive souls*, with powers of perception and motion; and

(3) that humans, in addition, have *rational souls*, with powers of reason and thought.

Thomas expressed the Aristotelian development in these terms:

(1) the *nutritive* soul (received at conception);

(2) the *sensitive* soul (received at the beginning of the formation of limbs); and

(3) the *intellectual* soul (received at birth as a direct creation of God).

Thomas clearly held to the creationist view on the origin of the intellectual soul:

Consequently it must be said that the soul is in the embryo; the nutritive soul from the beginning, then the sensitive, lastly the

---

[20] *Summa Theologica*, Secunda Secundae Partis, Question 64 (on Murder), Article 8, reply to objection 2. All *Summa* references are from *The "Summa Theologica" of St. Thomas Aquinas*, trans. Fathers of the English Dominican Province, 22 vols., 2nd rev. ed. (London: Burns Oates & Washbourne, 1912–36).

intellectual soul. . . . We conclude therefore that the intellectual soul is created by God at the end of human generation, and this soul is at the same time sensitive and nutritive, the pre-existing forms being corrupted.[21]

Thomas understood Augustine to have taught that God created Adam's animal soul at the same time that He created the angels, prior to the creation of earth[22] and that Adam received his intellectual soul at the physical formation of his body. But Thomas never encouraged abortion. Indeed, like Augustine, he stood opposed to abortion at any stage of prenatal development, even the so-called "unanimated" period of human gestation. Abortion is never right for any reason. It is always wrong. His rationale was that only God can infuse a soul. To kill an unborn that God had intended to infuse with a rational soul is to come between God and God's unborn, created by Him and for His own purposes.

Pope Pius IX stated the church's official position in a papal bull of 1869: no distinction would be made between *"fetus animatus"* (ensouled) and *"fetus inanimatus"* (non-ensouled) in future ecclesiastical decisions. The term *fetus* would be used without any such distinctions. The soul unites with the body at conception.

Conclusion

Most importantly, the Bible teaches that all life is in God's hands: "God remembered Rachel, and God hearkened to her, and opened her womb. And she conceived, and bare a son; and said, God hath taken away my reproach" (Gen. 30:22–23). God knows us from eternity, and He forms us in the womb for His own purposes: "Before I formed thee in the belly I knew thee; and before thou camest forth out of the womb I sanctified thee, and I ordained thee a prophet unto the nations" (Jer. 1:5). "And now, saith the Lord that formed me from the womb to be his servant, to bring Jacob again to him, Though Israel be not gathered, yet shall I be glorious in the eyes of the Lord, and my God shall be my strength" (Isa. 49:5).

---

[21] Ibid., Prima Pars, Question 118 (The Production of Man from Man as to the Soul), Article 2, reply to objection 2.

[22] Ibid., Prima Pars, Question 91 (The Production of the First Man's Body), Article 4, reply to objection 5.

Our response must be one of praise to our sovereign and all-wise God: "For thou hast possessed my reins: thou hast covered me in my mother's womb. I will praise thee; for I am fearfully and wonderfully made: marvelous are thy works; and that my soul knoweth right well" (Ps. 139:13–14).

Pro-life conservatives of the twenty-first century stand in the mainstream of historic Christianity and need not capitulate to liberalization movements. In the final analysis, Bible believers appeal not to the ancient Fathers, but to the true and living God of the Fathers. Abortion occurs far more frequently in our present society than it did in the Roman world. Modern medical techniques encourage its practice. The early church responded with no encouragement from the state; twenty-first-century Christianity must follow such noble examples. The sands of time blow over the ruins of ancient civilizations that refused to heed the Christian message.

Select Bibliography for Further Reading

Anderson, Norman. *Issues of Life and Death.* Downers Grove, IL: InterVarsity, 1977.

Ashley, B. M., and K. D. O'Rourke. *Health Care Ethics.* St. Louis: Catholic Health Association of the States, 1982.

Beall, Todd S. "The Abortion Issue and Exodus 21:22." *Reflections* (Spring 1984): 5–6.

Beauchamp, Tom L., and James F. Childress. *Principles of Biomedical Ethics.* 2nd ed. Oxford: Oxford University Press, 1983.

Beckwith, Francis. *Defending Life: A Moral and Legal Case against Abortion Choice.* New York: Cambridge University Press, 2007.

Burtchaell, James Tunstead. *Rachel Weeping: The Case against Abortion.* San Francisco: Harper and Row, 1984.

Foreman, Mark. *Christianity and Bioethics: Confronting Clinical Issues.* Joplin, MO: College Press, 1999.

Geisler, Norman L. *Christian Ethics.* 2nd ed. Grand Rapids: Baker, 2010.

Kline, Meredith. "Lex Talionis and the Human Fetus." *Journal of the Evangelical Theological Society* 20 (September 1977): 193–201.

Koop, C. Everett. *The Right to Live; the Right to Die.* Wheaton: Tyndale House, 1976.

Krason, Stephen M. *Abortion: Politics, Morality, and the Constitution.* New York: University Press of America, 1984.

Lammers, Stephen, and Allen Verhey, eds. *On Moral Medicine.* Grand Rapids: Eerdmans, 1987.

Leikin, Jerrold B., and Martin S. Lipsky, eds. *American Medical Association: Complete Medical Encyclopedia.* New York: Random House, 2003.

Mappes, Thomas A., and Jane S. Zembaty. *Biomedical Ethics*. 2nd ed. New York: McGraw-Hill, 1986.

Miller, Roman J., and Beryl H. Brubaker, eds. *Bioethics and the Beginning of Life: An Anabaptist Perspective*. Scottdale, PA: Herald Press, 1990.

Monagle, John F., and David C. Thomasma. *Medical Ethics: A Guide for Health Professionals*. Rockville, MD: Aspen, 1977.

Moreland, J. P., and Norman L. Geisler. *The Life and Death Debate*. New York: Praeger, 1990.

Noonan, John T., Jr. "An Almost Absolute Value in History." In *The Morality of Abortion: Legal and Historical Perspectives*, edited by John T. Noonan Jr., 1–59. Cambridge: Harvard University Press, 1970.

20

Conclusion: Observations and Applications

Assessing What We Have Learned

"I took that course and even enjoyed much of it; but I don't remember much about it." Have you heard that comment or said it yourself? Certainly, it is better to remember more than to remember less. However, you should never attempt to measure the value of a literary education on the basis of how many facts you remember. Far more important than what one remembers is what one becomes. Memory allows the ghosts of Baptists and Anabaptists, Pilgrims and Puritans, Quakers and Amish, Calvinists and Arminians to visit together with the elusive characters of Helen of ancient Troy and Captain Ahab in the novel *Moby Dick*. God wonderfully created us this way. In the mind, characters meander among themselves, and ideas merge freely, losing their identity, like summer clouds merging into beautiful patterns above a lake. This is God's own design.

You might not remember the date, names, or even the exact cause of some deep experience of joy or sorrow. The experience, however, remains far more significant than the details. You may forget the name of a person who lived next door or down the hall, but that person never moved out of your life. It is far more important to have known than to remember. Quite frequently, it is only after knowledge has receded from the conscious memory that it becomes significant.

391

Likewise, there is no way to measure what you "got" from a friendship, a sermon, a book, or even a semester of history. The mind has a fascinating filing mechanism of its own for thoughts, principles—ideas. As Elizabeth Barrett Browning once wrote, "Whatever acts upon you, becomes *you*." Browning was right. We are what we will be five years from now, except for the people we meet and the books we read. I remember one particular college professor primarily for the way he introduced us to great books. I do not recall a significant percentage of what he actually said, but I will be forever grateful to him for acquainting us with the *sources*—those wonderful tools that enable us to do our own research and discover the facts for ourselves—*when we need them*.

Keep ongoing files containing sources of information, such as bibliographies and book lists, for reading and researching for the rest of your life. Meanwhile, give your mind and your all to God, and make the most of every moment. You have learned far more than you might think you have! Make it your goal to master the Scriptures as much as you can with the aid of the Holy Spirit.

Recognizing Progressive Illumination

Carved in huge Latin letters across the Reformation Wall in Geneva, Switzerland, is the motto: *POST TENEBRAS LUX* ("after darkness, light"). The Reformation had been the burst of sunlight that ended a millennium of darkness. The Roman Church had kept the Bible from the people. The Reformation had opened the Bible to the people, even the common man. God's work of illuminating His Word to His elect is a continual process. It did not end with the Reformation.

In the years leading up to the Synod of Dort (1618–19), separatist pastor John Robinson debated key proponents of Arminianism at the University of Leiden. Afterwards he wrote *A Defense of the Doctrine Propounded by the Synod at Dort*.[1] In an eyewitness account of Robinson's farewell address to the *Mayflower* Pilgrims of his con-

---

[1] John Robinson, *A Defense of the Doctrine Propounded by the Synod at Dort* (Amsterdam: Successors of G. Thorpe, 1624). I slightly modernized original spelling.

gregation, one member, Edward Winslow, recalled how Robinson "was very confident [that] the Lord had more truth and light yet to break forth out of his holy word." Robinson took the occasion "to bewail the state and condition of the Reformed Churches, who were come to a period in religion, and would go no further than the instruments of their Reformation: As for example, the *Lutherans* they could not be drawn to go beyond what Luther saw." He goes on:

> [As for] the *Calvinists*, they stick where he left them: a misery much to be lamented; for though they were precious shining lights in their times, yet God had not revealed his whole will to them: And were they now living, saith he, they would be as ready and willing to embrace further light, as that they had received. Here also he put us in mind of our Church-Covenant (at least that part of it) whereby we promise with one another, to receive whatsoever light or truth shall be made known to us from his written Word: but withal exhorted us to take heed what we received for truth, and well to examine and compare, and weigh it with other Scriptures of truth, before we received it; For, saith he, "It is not possible [that] the Christian world should come so lately out of such thick antichristian darkness, and that full perfection of knowledge should break forth at once."[2]

God's written revelation is complete. The Lord's "breaking forth of truth and light from His Holy Word" is progressive illumination. It is the perpetual unfolding of the history of theology. From the creation to the consummation, vital doctrines are interwoven. The man of God who opens his Bible to preach "thus saith the Lord" must be adequately prepared to fulfill that obligation.

The great evangelical bishop of Liverpool, J. C. Ryle (1816–1900) advised,

> Cultivate the habit of reading prophecy with a single eye to the literal meaning of its proper names. Cast aside the old traditional idea that Jacob, and Israel, and Judah, and Jerusalem, and Zion, must always mean the Gentile Church, and that predictions about the second Advent are to be taken spiritually, and first Advent predictions literally. Be just, and honest, and fair. If you expect the Jews to take the 53rd of Isaiah literally, be sure you take the 54th

---

[2] Edward Winslow, *Hypocrisy Unmasked* (London: Richard Cotes for John Bellamy, 1646), 97–98. I slightly modernized the original spelling.

and 60th and 62nd literally also. The Protestant Reformers were not perfect. On no point, I venture to say, were they so much in the wrong as in the interpretation of Old Testament prophecy.[3]

Every Christian in modern society has at his disposal far more Bible study tools than sixteenth-century believers possessed. Such a luxury brings responsibility.

"From the beginning" (*ab initio*) of patristic literature, the science of historical theology moves through the ages, investigates doctrinal development, and makes its results available as profitable tools of inquiry. Even so, for our absolute standard, we must be drawn beyond the temporal "unto the fountains" (*ad fontes*) of inerrant Scripture, whose reservoir quenches our thirst, cleanses our hearts and minds, and progressively elucidates the past, present, and future of Israel and Christ's church. Psalm 42:1 says, "As the hart *panteth after the water brooks*, so panteth my soul after thee, O God." The Vulgate renders it *ad fontes*, "drawn unto the fountains," as the psalmist pleads, "In the same way that the stag is drawn unto the fountains of water, so is my soul drawn unto you, O God."[4]

Taking Heed and Giving Warning

Take heed therefore unto yourselves, and to all the flock, over the which the Holy Ghost hath made you overseers, to feed the church of God, which he hath purchased with his own blood. For I know this, that after my departing shall grievous wolves enter in among you, not sparing the flock. Also of your own selves shall men arise, speaking perverse things, to draw away disciples after them. (Acts 20:28–31)

There shall be false teachers among you, who privily shall bring in damnable heresies, even denying the Lord that bought them, and bring upon themselves swift destruction. . . . many shall follow their pernicious ways; . . . the way of truth shall be evil spoken of. (2 Pet. 2:1*b*–2*a*)

---

[3] *Coming Events and Present Duties: Being Miscellaneous Sermons on Prophetical Subjects*, 2nd ed. (London: William Hunt, 1879), 195–96.

[4] *quemadmodum desiderat cervus ad fontes aquarum ita desiderat anima mea ad te Deus.* Unlike our English Bibles, the Vulgate numbers the chapter and verse as Ps. 41:1.

> Beloved, . . . it was needful for me to write unto you, and exhort you that ye should earnestly contend for the faith which was once delivered unto the saints. For there are certain men crept in unawares. (Jude 3–4*a*)
>
> Look to yourselves, that we lose not those things which we have wrought, but that we receive a full reward. . . . If there come any unto you, and bring not this doctrine, receive him not into your house, neither bid him God speed: for he that biddeth him God speed is partaker of his evil deeds. (2 John 8, 10–11)

We must never entangle the message of the gospel with a manmade organization or institution that harbors a false gospel. "For we must all appear before the judgment seat of Christ; that every one may receive the things done in his body, according to that he hath done, whether it be good or bad. Knowing therefore the terror of the Lord, we persuade men" (2 Cor. 5:10–11*a*).

> Wherefore Jesus . . . with his own blood, suffered without the gate. Let us go forth therefore unto him without the camp, bearing his reproach. (Heb. 13:12–13)

Avoiding a Dangerous and Subtle Step towards Apostasy

It was Thomas Aquinas who coined the term "contrived ignorance" (*ignorantia affectata*) to describe a false teaching that can be deemed so useful that one protects it and withholds it from the light, in order to continue using it. In times like these, "the act of the will is brought to bear on the ignorance, as when a man wills not to know, that he may have an excuse for sin, or that he may not be withheld from sin; according to *Job* xxi.14: *We desire not the knowledge of Thy ways*. And this is called *affected ignorance*."[5] Thomas labeled this kind of ignorance, not exculpatory but inculpatory, or willful, sinful ignorance. God requires intellectual honesty whenever we articulate

---

[5] Thomas Aquinas, *Summa Theologica*, Prima Secundae Partis, Question 6 (The Voluntary and the Involuntary), Article 8, answer to objection 3, from *The "Summa Theologica" of St. Thomas Aquinas*, trans. Fathers of the English Dominican Province, 22 vols., 2nd rev. ed. (London: Burns Oates & Washbourne, 1912–36).

anything, especially His Word. In fact, willful ignorance is often one of the earliest steps to apostasy, from which there is no turning back.

The one who departs from the faith in unbelief is like the unclean raven that went forth from the hand of Noah. Flying with weary wings, he never finds a clean resting place for his feet. He goes to and fro, returning to the ark but never entering into its rest. He must feed upon dead carcasses floating in waters of judgment.

Brief Recap of the Seven Principles of Historical Theology

1. *Doctrinal truth and doctrinal error have coexisted since humanity's fall and will continue to coexist until God removes the curse from creation.* The Bible rests supremely upon the character of its Source, the truthfulness of its content, and continuing witness of its Author. Historical theology reveals satanic challenges to truth and Christian responses to error down through the ages. The study of historical theology helps us to understand who we are and what is important to God, as He transforms our lives by His Spirit, through His Word, and for His glory.

2. *The contrasts between God and man dictate the inevitable presence of theological mystery.* The essence of truth reflects the nature of the triune God—the source of all truth. We must receive it with reverence and diligence. The battle remains all about hermeneutics. There are mysteries that we cannot comprehend. God is incomprehensible, but He is not unknowable. His Word is not a book of secret codes and hidden allegories. The Author of the words "whosoever will save his life shall lose it: but whosoever will lose his life for my sake, the same shall save it" (Luke 9:24) was not a teacher of mysticism.

3. *There is a vital necessity for properly distinguishing between human and divine elements of doctrine and practice.* Into systems of theology, men import the baggage of human authority, finite logic, oral traditions, and metaphysical eccentricities. The only absolute and infallible standard is God's Word, which is always consistent with infinite logic. At best, a confession or creed is still a *norma normata*, "a rule that is ruled." Only the Bible is the *norma normans*, "the rule that rules or judges."

4. *Christians must distinguish between essentials and nonessentials.* Every part of God's Word is inspired, inerrant, and important, but some parts are of greater significance than other parts. In thoughtful minds, there will always be differing depths of conviction regarding emphasis and application. There are *adiaphora* (ἀδιάφορα), or nonessentials, and there are fundamentals, and we must always know the difference.

5. *Historical theology illustrates the true meaning and importance of balance.* We must discover both the heartache and the joy of preaching the whole counsel of God without apology. His thoughts are higher than our thoughts (Isa. 55:8–9). We must seek His mind and wisdom for true balance.

6. *A special relationship connects every believer with an innumerable company of individuals whose lives, doctrines, and practices have influenced each of us.* Many who ignore and turn away from these priceless connections with the past often retreat into an atmosphere of isolation and pride.

7. *The awareness of God's sovereign providence provides immovable confidence and stability, even in the midst of perpetual attack upon Christ's church.* There is no power in existence that is capable of frustrating God's purposes. Our sovereign God turns the works of wicked hands into the fulfillment of His eternal purposes and righteous decrees (Acts 3:18; Acts 4:26–28; Isa. 53:4). Providence is not simply an occasional act of God whereby He steps into the historical process in behalf of His people. Providence encompasses all of history,[6] "according to the purpose of him who worketh all things after the counsel of his own will: that we should be to the praise of his glory, who first trusted in Christ" (Eph. 1:11*b*–12).

Concluding Principles and Observations
concerning Prophetic Scripture

The cross was not an interruption of the inauguration of Christ's millennial kingdom. Jesus came to die for our sins. The Old Testament prophets foretold Israel's rejection of the Messiah, and Jesus Himself

---

[6] See Edward M. Panosian, David A. Fisher, and Mark Sidwell, *The Providence of God in History* (Greenville, SC: Bob Jones University Press, 1996).

repeated the prophecy. Bible prophecies regarding Christ's second coming and related events await future fulfillment. The present age of the church is the unfolding of a span of time determined in the eternal councils of God. The span occurs between the sixty-ninth and seventieth weeks of Daniel 9:24–27, and God has not revealed the length of its duration.

Contrary to some current opinions, there is nothing in Scripture to warrant an AD 70 fulfillment of our Lord's second coming. Christ compassionately prophesied the soon-coming destruction of Jerusalem. In Luke 19:43–44, He says, "The days shall come upon thee, that thine enemies shall cast a trench about thee, and compass thee round, and keep thee in on every side, and shall lay thee even with the ground, and thy children within thee; and they shall not leave in thee one stone upon another; because thou knewest not the time of thy visitation." The visitation occurred when "He came unto his own, and his own received him not" (John 1:11). After the nation's rejection of Messiah, God sent temporary spiritual blindness upon Israel (Rom. 11:25).

In Luke 21:6, Jesus said, "The days will come, in the which there shall not be left one stone upon another, that shall not be thrown down." His disciples then ask, "When shall these things be?" (Luke 21:7). Our Lord's answer spans from that moment, just prior to His cross, to His second advent. His answer includes warnings both to those who heard His words and to those who will be on earth at the consummation of the Times of the Gentiles. As did the Old Testament prophets, Jesus uses the artistic Middle Eastern teaching technique of compacting distantly-related events into a single landscape. For instance, Isaiah 61:1–2a describes Jesus' first advent: "The Spirit of the Lord God is upon me; because the Lord hath anointed me to preach good tidings unto the meek; he hath sent me to bind up the brokenhearted, to proclaim liberty to the captives, and the opening of the prison to them that are bound; to proclaim the acceptable year of the Lord. . . ." In Luke 4:16–22, Jesus entered the synagogue in Nazareth and read aloud that exact first-advent passage from Isaiah. He then "closed the book, and gave it again to the minister, and sat down. And the eyes of all them that were in the synagogue were fastened on him. And he began to say unto them,

This day is this scripture fulfilled in your ears" (20–21). Immediately following the point where Jesus had stopped reading, Isaiah describes events related to Christ's second advent. Thus, Jesus has provided a perfect illustration of "rightly dividing the word of truth" (2 Tim. 2:15). In Luke 21, Jesus again uses a compacted landscape, just as God had often inspired His Old Testament prophets to record the prophetic Word.

Jesus warns of the soon-coming destruction of Jerusalem: "And when ye shall see Jerusalem compassed with armies, then know that the desolation thereof is nigh" (Luke 21:20). "And they shall fall by the edge of the sword, and shall be led away captive into all nations: and Jerusalem shall be trodden down of the Gentiles, until the times of the Gentiles be fulfilled" (Luke 21:24). Our Lord's description then reaches immediately to the consummation of the times of the Gentiles, which will end as they began, with Gentile armies surrounding Jerusalem. At that time, Christ will return to crush the powers of the antichrist. He explains, "And there shall be signs in the sun, and in the moon, and in the stars. . . . For the powers of heaven shall be shaken. And then shall they see the Son of man coming in a cloud with power and great glory" (Luke 21:25–27).

In Matthew 16:27, Jesus describes His second coming: "For the Son of man shall come in the glory of his Father with his angels; and then he shall reward every man according to his works." Then, in verse 28, He adds that, before that takes place, some who are hearing His words will witness a foregleam of His second coming: "Verily I say unto you, There be some standing here, which shall not taste of death, till they see the Son of man coming in his kingdom." The next verse (17:1) has them at the Mount of Transfiguration. The transfiguration was the mountaintop glimpse of the glory of Christ's coming kingdom:

> After six days Jesus taketh Peter, James, and John his brother, and
> bringeth them up into an high mountain apart, and was trans-
> figured before them: and his face did shine as the sun, and his
> raiment was white as the light. And, behold, there appeared unto
> them Moses and Elias talking with him. . . . While he yet spake,
> behold, a bright cloud overshadowed them: and behold a voice

out of the cloud, which said, This is my beloved Son, in whom I am well pleased; hear ye him. (Matt. 17:1–5)

As an eyewitness of the transfiguration, Peter later describes it as a foregleam of the powerful coming of Christ in honor and glory: "We made known unto you the *power* and *coming* of our Lord Jesus Christ" as "eyewitnesses of his *majesty*. For he received from God the Father *honour* and *glory*, when there came such a voice to him from the excellent glory, This is my beloved Son, in whom I am well pleased. . . . this voice which came from heaven we heard, when we were with him in the holy mount. We have . . . a more sure word of prophecy; whereunto ye do well that ye take heed" (2 Pet. 1:16–19). Jesus had revealed His "power," "majesty," "honor," and "glory," to fortify His disciples for trials, persecution, and death. This was "a more sure word of prophecy," for they had now witnessed a preview of His coming.

Matthew 24:34 says, "This generation shall not pass, till all these things be fulfilled." The word *generation* is not limited to a time frame. Standard lexicons, Bible dictionaries, and concordances consistently show that the word translated "generation" refers not only to contemporaries, but most frequently to "clan, race, or kind." In prophetic Scripture it refers to Israel. The root of *generation* is *genos*, meaning "descendants, nation, or class." The word *genealogy* has its root in the same word. It refers to ancestry and lineage. In Matthew 23:33–36, Jesus speaks of "this generation" of His day as existing from the earliest times. He speaks of a crime committed by "this generation" that had actually occurred in the record of 2 Chronicles 24:20–21. In Matthew 23:35, He says, "ye slew" the prophet (Zacharias). Isaiah 6:9–12 prophesies to the generation of Isaiah's day, and in Matthew 13:14, Jesus identifies that same generation as the Jewish leaders among His own audience, "a generation of vipers." Paul spoke in Acts 28:25–27 to the same generation (Israel), and they will be here when Jesus returns. Indeed, "this generation shall not pass, till all these things be fulfilled" (Matt. 24:34).

In Acts 1:6, the disciples asked Jesus, "Wilt thou at this time restore again the kingdom to Israel?" They knew that Jesus and the Old Testament had promised that this event would occur. Contrary, however, to the notion that in the church God will restore the kingdom to spiritual Israel, Jesus answers, "It is not for you to know the times or the seasons" (Acts 1:7). His answer makes it clear that the restoration of the kingdom to Israel was a future event. Moreover, there is not a shred of evidence in Scripture that the restoration occurred in AD 70, or that the church will ever bring it to fruition.

The church is never called "spiritual Israel" or "new Israel." In the New Testament the term *Israel* is not used of the church in general or of Gentile believers in particular. The term *Israel* occurs about seventy-five times in the New Testament, and, with only one exception, it refers to the nation of Israel or to the Jewish people as a whole. The exception is Galatians 6:16, where it refers to a Jewish remnant of believers within the local church. Here, Paul is encouraging Jewish Christians in the Galatian church that they, not the Jewish legalists, are the true "Israel of God." The legalists were attempting to persuade Jewish believers that they must place themselves back under the law. Paul makes it plain that, in the spiritual sense, Christian Jews are the only complete Jews. Galatians 3:29 adds that to be in Christ is to be of the spiritual seed of Abraham.

This spiritual oneness of all believers, however, does not equate the church with Israel. The term *Israel* includes the land that God promises to Abraham's offspring in such passages as Genesis 12:1–3; 13:14–17; 17:8; and Romans 11:25–32. The term also encompasses Christ's literal restoration of David's throne that God promises in such passages as 2 Samuel 7:13–16, Psalm 89:3–4, Luke 1:32, and Acts 2:30. At a time when many will least expect it, Christ will return to fulfill the prophetic Scriptures. He will establish His literal kingdom and rule from the throne of David. Meanwhile, we will do well to remember Peter's warning: "Wherefore, beloved, seeing that ye look for such things, be diligent that ye may be found of him in peace, without spot, and blameless" (2 Pet. 3:14).

Select Bibliography for Further Reading
on Eschatology and Hermeneutics

Barndollar, W. W. *Jesus' Title to the Throne of David*. Findlay, OH: Dunham Publishing, 1963.

———. *The Validity of Dispensationalism*. Des Plaines, IL: Regular Baptist Press, 1964.

Baron, David. *Zechariah: A Commentary on His Visions and Prophecies.* 1918. Reprint, Grand Rapids: Kregel, n.d.

Beale, David. "Ante-Nicene Eschatology: An Historical and Theological Analysis." PhD diss., Bob Jones University, 1980.

Benware, Paul N. *Understanding End Times Prophecy: A Comprehensive Approach.* Chicago: Moody, 2006.

Bigalke, Ron J., Jr., ed. *Progressive Dispensationalism: An Analysis of the Movement and Defense of Traditional Dispensationalism.* Lanham, MD: University Press of America, 2005.

Custer, Stewart. *From Patmos to Paradise: A Commentary on Revelation.* Greenville, SC: BJU Press, 2004.

Ehlert, Arnold D. *A Bibliographic History of Dispensationalism.* Grand Rapids: Baker, 1965.

Horner, Barry E. *Future Israel: Why Christian Anti-Judaism Must be Challenged.* NCA Studies in Bible and Theology. Nashville: B&H Academic, 2007.

Houghton, Myron. *Law and Grace.* Schaumburg, IL: Regular Baptist Books, 2011.

Johnson, S. Lewis Jr. "Paul and the 'The Israel of God': An Exegetical and Eschatological Case-Study." In *Essays in Honor of J. Dwight Pentecost,* edited by Stanley D. Toussaint and Charles H. Dyer, 181–96. Chicago: Moody, 1986.

Thomas, Robert L. *Evangelical Hermeneutics: The New Versus the Old.* Grand Rapids: Kregel, 2002.

Varner, William. *Jacob's Dozen: A Prophetic Look at the Tribes of Israel.* Bellmawr, NJ: Friends of Israel Gospel Ministry, 1987.

Vlach, Michael J. "The Church as a Replacement of Israel: An Analysis of Supersessionism." PhD diss., Southeastern Baptist Theological Seminary, 2004.

———. *Dispensationalism: Essential Beliefs and Common Myths.* Los Angeles: Theological Studies Press, 2008.

———. *Has the Church Replaced Israel?: A Theological Evaluation.* Nashville: B&H Publishing Group, 2010.

Walvoord, John F. *Daniel: The Key to Prophetic Revelation: A Commentary.* Chicago: Moody, 1971.

———. *The Revelation of Jesus Christ: A Commentary.* Chicago: Moody, 1966.

Appendix 1

Antipodes and the Shape of the Earth: A History of Christian Views

Historians usually credit the Greeks with being the first to suggest a spherical earth. References to a spherical earth appear as early as the late sixth and early fifth centuries BC, with Pythagoras and his school, eventually followed by Aristotle, Euclid, and Aristarchus. By the third and second centuries, Greek astronomers Eratosthenes and Hipparchus had calculated the circumference of the earth to within a few percentage points of our modern measurements. Round-earth teachings continue to appear in works by Strabo and Crates in the second century, followed by Ptolemy and others during the early Christian centuries, when the sphericity of the earth was widely accepted by the educated Greek-speaking world and even by the Roman world. This is not to suggest that there were no exceptions. Among pagan writers there were still those who held to the notion of a flat earth.[1]

Key Biblical Passages

The Old Testament is the oldest record, however, and it testified to the sphericity of the earth before most of the Greeks wrote of it. Proverbs 8:27 suggests a round earth by use of the word *circle* (e.g., ESV, NKJV, and NASB). Today, of course, man can view the

---

[1] For full discussions, with references and citations, see D. R. Dicks, *Early Greek Astronomy to Aristotle* (Ithaca, NY: Cornell University Press, 1970), 23ff., 49ff., 72ff., 92ff., 197, and passim.

earth from space and observe for himself that the planet is spherical. Thought by many to be the oldest book of the Bible, Job explains that the earth is suspended in space: "He stretches out the north over the void and hangs the earth on nothing" (26:7, ESV). Job 26:10 indicates that where light terminates, darkness begins, and this suggests day and night on a spherical globe: "He has inscribed a circle on the face of the waters at the boundary between light and darkness" (ESV). The psalmist, in Psalm 103:12, speaks of the earth as having no end: "As far as the east is from the west, so far hath he removed our transgressions from us." This expression is similar to those such as "the rising" and "the setting," which are related to our terms *sunrise* and *sunset*. The circle of the globe continues infinitely. The spherical earth is also described in Isaiah 40:21–22 as "the circle of the earth." Psalm 103:11 says, "For as the heaven is high above the earth, so great is his mercy toward them that fear him." Like God's infinite mercy, the circle of the earth knows no end.

The implication of a round earth is depicted as well in Luke 17, where Jesus is describing His return to this earth. In verses 30 and 31, He says that His return will be "in that day." In verse 34, He says that it will be "in that night." This is an allusion to light on one side of the globe and simultaneous darkness on the other side.

Contrary to some critics of Scripture, the Old Testament is not teaching a flat-earth view when it speaks of the "four corners of earth." In Hebrew the word translated "corners" is *kanaph* (כָּנָף). While the word can be translated in a variety of ways, it generally means "extremity." It is translated "borders" in Numbers 15:38. In Ezekiel 7:2, it is translated "four corners" and again in Isaiah 11:12 "four corners." In Job 37:3 and 38:13, it means "ends." The Greek equivalent to *kanaph* (Rev. 7:1; 20:8) is *gonia* (γωνία). The Greek meaning is perhaps more closely related to our modern divisions known as quadrants. So literally, *gonia* means "angles" or "divisions." It is customary to divide a map into quadrants as shown by the four directions. When the Bible, as in the book of Revelation, refers to angels standing at the "four corners" of the earth, *gonia* obviously has reference to the compass points, the cardinal directions: north, south, east, and west. Similar terminology is often used today when we speak of the sun's rising and setting, even though the earth, not the sun, is doing the moving. Bible writers used the "language of appearance," just as people have always done. Regardless of the various ways that we might find *kanaph* translated, it simply refers to *extremities*. It is doubtful that any religious Jew would ever misunderstand the true meaning of *kanaph*. Isaiah 11:10–12, for instance, describes how the Messiah, the Root of Jesse, will regather His people from the "four corners of the earth," obviously meaning that the Jewish people will come from every extremity, or obscure corner of the globe, to be gathered again into Israel:

> And in that day there shall be a Root of Jesse, Who shall stand as a banner to the people; for the Gentiles shall seek Him, and His resting place shall be glorious. It shall come to pass in that day that the Lord shall set His hand again the second time to recover the remnant of His people who are left, from Assyria and Egypt, from Pathros and Cush, from Elam and Shinar, from Hamath and the islands of the sea. He will set up a banner for the nations, and will assemble the outcasts of Israel, and gather together the dispersed of Judah from the four corners of the earth. (Isa. 11:10–12, NKJV)

The Five Patristic Authors Who Rejected the Existence of Antipodes

Although there was no scientific study of cosmography during the patristic period of church history, the overall corpus of patristic teaching on the subject is consistent with belief in the spherical shape of the earth. Some used the various biblical arguments presented above. Five Christian writers rejected it, as did some pagans who drew the earth as a flat disk with oceans around it. Naturally, those who held to a flat earth rejected the existence of "antipodes," from *anti*, αντί ("against") and *podes*, ποδός ("feet"), referring to people opposite our feet, or on the other side of the planet.

405

Theophilus of Antioch (ca. 115–80)

Theophilus writes despairingly against the idea of the earth being spherical. He insists that the earth is a flat surface covered by the heavens as by a dome-shaped lid.[2]

Lactantius of Nicomedia (ca. 250–325)

Lactantius was an eminent North African apologist who witnessed both the agony of persecution and the alliance of Christianity with imperial patronage. Appointed by Emperor Diocletian as an instructor of Latin rhetoric in Nicomedia, Lactantius lost his post when he converted from paganism to Christianity. His fame reached the ears of Constantine, who brought him to his courts in Gaul and committed to him the tutelage of his son Crispus. The primary literary work of Lactantius is his *Divine Institutes*, whose Latin was so nearly perfect that he would later be hailed as the "Christian Cicero." While he wrote much that is valuable and edifying, Lactantius not only ridiculed the idea of antipodes but also mocked all who held to the sphericity of the earth—including the best of secular thought and virtually the whole corpus of patristic literature. In the face of the best scholarship of the day—secular and biblical—Lactantius dogmatically insists that the earth is flat and that those who disagree with him have fallen into "ridiculous fictions." In the end, he has no substantive answers to their arguments:

> How is it with those who imagine that there are antipodes opposite to our footsteps? . . . Is there any who are so senseless as to believe that there are men whose footsteps are higher than their heads? or that the things which with us are in a recumbent position, with them hang in an inverted direction? that the crops and trees grow downwards? that the rains, and snow, and hail fall upwards to the earth? . . . What course of argument, therefore, led them to the idea of the antipodes? . . . They thought that the world is round like a ball, and they fancied that the heaven revolves in accordance with the motion of the heavenly bodies. . . . I should be able to prove by many arguments that it is impossible for the

---

[2] *To Autolycus* 2.32; and 2.13. Unless otherwise noted, all patristic references are from the ANF and the NPNF.

heaven to be lower than the earth, were it not that this book must now be concluded. (*The Divine Institutes* 3.24)[3]

While Lactantius expands his *Divine Institutes* into four additional books, he never again addresses the topic of antipodes or the earth's shape. He is the single prominent patristic author to teach clearly that the earth is flat, and, as we will discuss below, modern evolutionists have used him to generalize and to caricature the whole corpus of patristic literature as "flat earth preachers." Lactantius does, however, get in his blows against pagan dreamers who imagined Adam's offspring as unsophisticated wanderers who lived in caves and graves, slept on beds of leaves, and by nodding and grunting, eventually managed to communicate with each other:

> Some relate that those men who were first born from the earth, when they passed a wandering life among the woods and plains, and were not united by any mutual bond of speech or justice, but had leaves and grass for their beds, and caves and grottos for their dwellings, were a prey to the beasts and stronger animals. Then, that those who had either escaped, having been torn, or had seen their neighbors torn, being admonished of their own danger, had recourse to other men, implored protection, and at first made their wishes known by nods; then that they tried the beginnings of conversation, and by attaching names to each object, by degrees completed the system of speech. (*The Divine Institutes* 6.10)

Severian (Severianus) of Gabala (late 4th–early 5th c.)

Syria's major port city, Gabala (modern Jeble), lies some fourteen miles south of Laodicea (modern Latakia). Widely-known as the bishop of Gabala, Severian received an invitation to preach in Constantinople for the Greek Orthodox patriarch John Chrysostom, known as the "Golden Mouth" preacher. As "an ambitious social climber," Severian in about 400 decided to "try his fortune" and move to Constantinople,[4] where Chrysostom unsuspectingly entrusted him with important leadership roles. Severian's preaching in this renowned Greek city was orthodox, but some of his Greek pronunciations in a Syrian accent came under local criticism. A

---

[3] Cf. *The Divine Institutes* 3.3.
[4] J. N. D. Kelly, *Golden Mouth: The Story of John Chrysostom; Ascetic, Preacher, Bishop* (Grand Rapids: Baker, 1995), 173.

competitive spirit of hubris would soon hold sway. When a deacon refused to rise as Severian was passing by, Severian became infuriated, and a church conflict broke out. Two ancient historians report that the deacon was Chrysostom's right-hand man in the church.[5]

Severian soon made himself a political favorite at the imperial palace, and his rhetoric became increasingly vitriolic towards Chrysostom. Reportedly, he participated in or promoted some malicious whispering to Empress Eudoxia that Chrysostom had made misogynic remarks from the pulpit. Chrysostom was well aware that Eudoxia was using her family's wealth to gain control over her husband, Emperor Arcadius.[6] In his sermons, the patriarch apparently made remarks that his enemies were eagerly waiting to report. Eudoxia became enraged and determined to have her revenge. So Severian and others assisted Eudoxia in a contrived plot that resulted in the condemnation and deposition of John Chrysostom from his pulpit and his exile to Asia Minor. That decision was made at the infamous Synod of the Oak (403), a site located in the suburbs of Chalcedon, just across the Bosphorus Strait.

Infuriated at the casuistry and mistreatment of their beloved pastor, the people of Constantinople demanded the return of the banished servant of God. Their words were heeded, and the people soon welcomed their pastor back with the singing of psalms. As they escorted Chrysostom back into his famous pulpit, Severian fled the city. The next year (404), Severian, with a coalition of Chrysostom's enemies, arranged a second trial that succeeded in the permanent exile of Chrysostom, who died in 407. Accordingly, Severian's reputation and popularity were perpetually degraded to the extent that he would never be regarded as a representative of any segment of Christianity. Chrysostom, on the other hand, remains one of Christianity's most recognized names among patristic pastors, authors, and rhetoricians. He is one of the most oft-cited church fathers.

Most of Severian's written works remain without a critical edition or an English translation. An anti-Semitic homily has received

---

[5] Socrates Scholasticus, *Ecclesiastical History* 6.11–16; and Sozomen, *Ecclesiastical History* 8.10–19.

[6] Emperor Arcadius was the eldest son and successor of Theodosius I. The son and successor of Arcadius was Theodosius II.

but slight notice.[7] Best known are the *Homilies on the Creation* (*de Creatione Mundi*), in which Severian argues for a flat earth.[8] Lack of scholarly interest has been attributed to the man's reputed lack of orthopraxy and his unpopular exegetical methods. Severian thought, for example, that the head of the race was named Adam because the letters of his name are the first letters of four Greek words used for the four corners of the earth: ἀνατολή (east); δύσις (west); ἄρκτος (north); and μεσημβρία (south). His sermons were ignored by scholars until 2010 when InterVarsity Press published the first English translation of the creation homilies. Contrary to modern-day assertions, discussed later, Severian is hardly representative of any patristic consensus on the shape of the earth.

Cosmas of Alexandria (6th c.)

Cosmas, surnamed Indicopleustes (navigator of India), was a trader who lived during the time of the Emperor Justinian I. He traveled the Mediterranean Sea, the Red Sea, and the Persian Gulf, visiting such sites as Ceylon and India several times. Later in life, having finally become weary of the world and its gains, Cosmas left his merchant work and embraced an ascetic lifestyle, devoting his time to writing about the countries he had visited and adding spiritual application. Of his several works, the only one that has survived is his *Christian Topography*, written in Greek in twelve books. He begins the first book with the specific purpose of being "against those who, while wishing to profess Christianity, think and imagine like the pagans that the heaven is spherical." He promises a refutation of "the theory of the sphere and the antipodes."[9] Cosmas claims that the earth was not only flat but shaped like a rectangular vaulted arch

---

[7] See Migne *PG* 61.793–802, hidden at the end of a volume by Chrysostom.

[8] Severian of Gabala, Homily 3, in *Homilies on Creation and Fall*, trans. Robert C. Hill, in a volume of the series, *Ancient Christian Texts: Commentaries on Genesis 1–3*, ed. Thomas C. Oden and Gerald L. Bray (Downers Grove, IL: InterVarsity Press, 2010). In his notes, Hill takes the higher critical approach to Genesis and implies that Severian's flat-earth nonsense is consistent with the teachings of Scripture. The work includes seven of Severian's homilies, the first six of which generally fall under the rubric *In Cosmogoniam*. For the oldest text of Severian's homilies on creation and fall, see Migne *PG* 56.429ff.

[9] *Christian Topography*, trans. and ed. J. W. McCrindle (London: Hakluyt Society, 1897), 7ff.

lying beneath the heavens. He has a specific cosmic shape in mind: "The Tabernacle prepared by Moses in the wilderness . . . was a type and copy of the whole world."[10] Quite the contrast to the highly educated Lactantius, Cosmas, in the same paragraph, describes himself as destitute of literary training, having devoted his whole life to mercantile pursuits. His entanglement in business has incapacitated him from diligent studies. He bemoans extremely poor health and weak eyesight. He pleads that he is "deficient in the school-learning of the Pagans, without any knowledge of the rhetorical art, ignorant how to compose a discourse in a fluent and embellished style, and . . . occupied with the complicated affairs of everyday life."[11]

Cosmas was unschooled in theological studies as well. The church fathers ignore him altogether and never acknowledge him as a Christian leader. His book was not known until its discovery in the latter half of the seventeenth century. Nevertheless, some have still claimed his view as the typical patristic position. The overwhelming patristic consensus, however, was that the earth is spherical, which Greek scholars had generally maintained for several centuries. Likewise, the spherical view of the earth has always been the norm for Christians of all walks of life.

Augustine of Hippo (354–430)

Augustine thinks there is neither scientific nor biblical proof of antipodes and far too little evidence for determining the definite shape of the earth. He once refers to the earth as a "globe"[12] but insists that a journey to the other side, even if it had dry land, would have proved too great for any of Adam's descendants:

> But as to the fable that there are Antipodes, that is to say, men on the opposite side of the earth, where the sun rises when it sets to us, men who walk with their feet opposite ours, that is on no ground credible. And, indeed, it is not affirmed that this has been

---

[10] Ibid., 138ff.

[11] Ibid., 23–24.

[12] *Literal Meaning of Genesis* 2.13.27 in John Hammond Taylor's translation; in Edmund Hill's translation, the reference would be cited as 2.27. For a careful argument that Augustine held to an "essentially flat earth," see Leo C. Ferrari, "Augustine's Cosmography," *Augustinian Studies* 27, no. 2 (1996): 129–77; and Leo C. Ferrari, "Cosmography" in *Augustine through the Ages: An Encyclopedia*, ed. Allan D. Fitzgerald (Grand Rapids: Eerdmans, 1999), 246.

learned by historical knowledge, but by scientific conjecture, on the ground that the earth is suspended within the concavity of the sky, and that it has as much room on the one side of it as on the other: hence they say that the part which is beneath must also be inhabited. But they do not remark that, although it be supposed or scientifically demonstrated that the world is of a round and spherical form, yet it does not follow that the other side of the earth is bare of water; nor even, though it be bare, does it immediately follow that it is peopled. For Scripture, which proves the truth of its historical statements by the accomplishment of its prophecies, gives no false information; and it is too absurd to say, that some men might have taken ship and traversed the whole wide ocean, and crossed from this side of the world to the other, and that thus even the inhabitants of that distant region are descended from that one first man. (*City of God* 16.9)

In summary, from the vast amount of data, we know that from the first century to the middle of the eighth century only five professing Christians deny the existence of antipodes. Of the five, two of them, Severian, and Cosmas, were never claimed or cited as spokesmen for Christians. Theophilus was probably better known than those two, but he was never cited for anything. Of the two remaining, Lactantius was virtually ignored, even forgotten, until medieval scholastics discovered his skillful Latin compositions. What they held up to their students was his perfect Latin, not his cosmography. As for Augustine, he argues at length against antipodes and probably believes that the earth is flat. On the other hand, he seems to refer to the earth on one occasion as a "globe," and he always avoids focusing any discussion directly against the possibility of the earth's circularity. In no way can a belief in flat-earth cosmography define the consensus of patristic Christianity. Such a view is totally at variance with biblical teachings and anomalous to Christian dogma.

The Shape of the Earth according to Remaining Patristic Sources

Clement of Rome (fl. in first c.) appears to believe that antipodes exist, but he does not use the word. He calls them men (ἄνθρωποι) and marvels that there is a "world beyond the impassable ocean" that is "regulated by the same enactments [standards] of the Lord"[13] that we have.

Tertullian of Carthage (ca. 160–220) describes the earth as an "orb" that was once completely covered with water even to the heights of its mountains.[14]

Basil of Caesarea (ca. 329–79), in his *Hexaemeron*, regards the earth's precise shape to be of small importance compared with other things that he considers more clearly revealed in Scripture.[15] Heavily influenced by Neo-Platonism, Basil follows Plato, Philo, and Origen in referring to the fashioner (shaper) of universe as "demiurge" (δηυιουργός).[16] Like Origen he applies the title to Christ as the "good creator." He seems to lean cautiously towards the widely held view in his day, that the universe consists of a series of concentric circles, with the earth, whatever its shape, in its center.[17] His younger brother, Gregory of Nyssa, however, wrote and published a defense of Basil's *Hexaemeron* and confidently includes references to a spherical earth.[18] Thomas Aquinas also understands Basil to be teaching a spherical earth.[19]

While John of Damascus (ca. 665–749) is vague concerning the shape of earth and its position in the heavens, he is clearly willing to accept any view that can be confirmed by Scripture. He mentions both sphericity and cone-shape as possibilities of the earth's shape. After citing poetic Scriptures that speak figuratively of the earth's "foundations" and "pillars," John concludes that it is "suspended" in the midst of the heavens, referring in part to Job 26:7:

> The earth is one of the four elements, dry, cold, heavy, motionless, brought into being by God, out of nothing on the first day. *For in the beginning,* he said, *God created the heaven and the earth*: but the seat and foundation of the earth no man has been able to declare. Some, indeed, hold that its seat is the waters: thus the

---

[13] *Epistle of Clement to the Corinthians* 20.
[14] *On the Pallium* 2.
[15] *The Hexaemeron* Homily 9.1.
[16] Ibid., Homily 1.5 and Homily 2.2.
[17] Ibid., Homily 1.9–10 and Homily 3.3–4.
[18] *In Hexaemeron Explicatio Apologetica* (Migne *PG* 44.61–124, passim). Gregory says that when the earth was without form and void, it had no shape. Gregory says that God then formed it into a circular shape (Migne *PG* 44.77).
[19] *Summa Theologica*, Prima Pars, Question 66, Article 3.

divine David says, *To Him who established the earth on the waters.* Others place it in the air. Again some other says, *He who hangeth the earth on nothing* [Job 26:7]. And, again, David, the singer of God, says, as though the representative of God, *I bear up the pillars of it* [Ps. 75:3], meaning by "pillars" the force that sustains it. Further, the expression, *He hath founded it upon the seas* [Ps. 24:2], shows clearly that the earth is on all hands surrounded with water. But whether we grant that it is established on itself, or on air or on water, or on nothing, we must not turn aside from reverent thought, but must admit that all things are sustained and preserved by the power of the Creator. "In the beginning," then, as the Holy Scripture says, it was hidden beneath the waters. . . . Some hold that the earth is in the form of a sphere, others that it is in that of a cone. At all events it is much smaller than the heaven, and suspended almost like a point in its midst. (*Exposition of the Orthodox Faith* 2.10)

Why So Many Still Believe that Most Early Christians Viewed the Earth as Flat

Until the modern evolution debates of the nineteenth century, western centers of learning generously recognized the intellectual and cultural contributions of Christianity. In defense of Darwin, however, newspapers, educators, and popular authors would create the "flat-earth myth" that Christianity and the Bible are bigoted, superstitious, and intolerant in a modern world of secular enlightenment. Contrariwise, Lactantius plus three obscure men are the only clear sources for a flat earth in the patristic period of the Christian church, a period reaching nearly to the ninth century. Ironically, Lactantius may actually have been "the one church father who clearly rejected sphericity," says J. B. Russell.[20] Patristic and biblical Christianity should never be defined by the anomalous notion of a flat earth.

---

[20] *Inventing the Flat Earth: Columbus and Modern Historians* (Westport, CT: Praeger Publishers, 1991), 70. While Russell does not write as a creationist, his careful research has documented the secular humanist invention and propagation of the flat-earth myth as a promotion of the evolutionary hypothesis and as a direct attack against God, the Bible, the church, and history. His work provides important help on the nineteenth century, especially on authors such as Irving, Draper, and White.

Up until around 1830, it was a commonly known fact that mainline Christianity has from its earliest times consistently held to the sphericity of the earth. Then three key authors invented a myth and convinced most of America that it was fact. In 1828, the popular American storyteller Washington Irving (1783–1859) decided that he would set the record straight with the publication of *A History of the Life and Voyages of Christopher Columbus*.[21] This book, hailed by liberal media and public educators to this day as scholarly and authoritative, created the flat-earth myth of Christianity and set in motion the process of caricaturing all of Christianity and the Bible as being filled with superstition, ignorance, and intolerance. The historical context of Irving's myth was the Roman Catholic Church, but conservative Protestant Christians have also been targets of the attack. Secular animosity against creationist Christianity would increase intensely after Irving's time. Irving was a superb composer of legend, but his imagination sometimes produced "history" as well. In parts of his book, Irving writes historical fiction under the guise of history. The non-specialist reader has no way of knowing this. Even so, the entire book is popularly accepted as fact even to this day!

The most significant myth-making scene in Irving's book is a 1486 Council of Salamanca, with young Columbus, the "simple mariner"—lone defender of a spherical earth—appearing before bigoted inquisitors, ignorant monks, and stubborn theologians wearing black hoods—all insisting from the authority of the Bible and the church fathers that the earth was as flat as a pancake. Actually, however, the fifteenth-century debate with Columbus was not at all over the shape of the earth. It was over the width of the ocean. Harvard Professor, Samuel Eliot Morison, in his *Admiral of the Ocean Sea*, assesses Washington Irving's description as "pure moonshine." Morrison's conclusion is that, "Washington Irving, scenting his opportunity for a picturesque and moving scene, took a fictitious account of this

---

[21] Washington Irving, *A History of the Life and Voyages of Christopher Columbus* (New York: G. & C. Carvill, 1828), 1:13–81. Irving is popular for his *Sketch Book* (1820), which includes such great classic stories as "The Legend of Sleepy Hollow" ("The Headless Horseman") and "Rip Van Winkle."

nonexistent university council published 130 years after the event, elaborated on it, and let his imagination go completely."[22]

A British-born chemistry professor at the University of New York, John William Draper (1811–82), further popularized the flat-earth myth with his 1874 *History of the Conflict between Religion and Science*.[23] Since much of his material pertains to pre-Reformation history, the bulk of Draper's attack points to the Roman Catholic Church. His careless generalizations, though, reach far beyond Catholics to anyone at any time who believes all that the Bible proclaims. Draper passionately claims that, at the downfall of the Roman Empire, the "affairs of men fell into the hands of ignorant and infuriated ecclesiastics, parasites, eunuchs and slaves."[24] This antichurch diatribe asserts that the Bible and Christianity in general are filled with flat-earth dogma. Apparently parroting Washington Irving, Draper claims that ecclesiastics at the Council of Salamanca "condemned" Columbus's idea of a "globular earth" by their use of arguments "from the Pentateuch, the Psalms, the Prophecies, the Gospels, the Epistles, and the writings of the Fathers—St. Chrysostom, St. Augustine, St. Jerome, St. Gregory, St. Basil, St. Ambrose."[25] The patristic literature that he actually cites, however, is noticeably limited to the standard three culprits—Cosmas, Lactantius, and Augustine. He quickly narrows that down to Augustine as the most influential enemy of truth: "Considering the eminent authority which has been attributed to the writings of St. Augustine by the religious world for nearly fifteen centuries . . . it was mainly he who diverted the Bible from its true office."[26] Draper's book was a best seller. Some of the ecclesiastical corruption that Draper mentions was indeed true, and his criticism of Pope Pius IX and his *Syllabus of Errors* is based upon fact. Ironically, though, the overgeneralized flat-earth myth would continue pouring into the mainstream of America and the British Isles from the very institutions that were claiming the highest scholarship.

---

[22] *Admiral of the Ocean Sea: A Life of Christopher Columbus* (Boston: Little, Brown, 1942), 89.
[23] John William Draper, *History of the Conflict between Religion and Science*, vol. 12 of the International Scientific Series (New York: D. Appleton, 1874).
[24] Ibid., vii.
[25] Ibid., 160–61.
[26] Ibid., 62.

In 1865, Andrew Dickson White (1832–1918) and Ezra Cornell became the co-founders of Cornell University in Ithaca, New York. Both men publicly positioned themselves on the radical left and waged all-out war against Christian creationists in the battle over origins. Indeed, they established Cornell University for that purpose. From its founding, the school had the reputation of being the most secular-oriented university in America. In 1896, Cornell's president and professor of History, Andrew Dickson White, published his *History of the Warfare of Science with Theology in Christendom.*[27] In his preface White describes the book as an endorsement and further development of the earlier work by John William Draper. He then proceeds with unprecedented militancy to attribute to the Bible, as well as to Christianity at large, the "flat-earth" references from a minuscule number of church fathers. Atheist booksellers soon began adding White's book to their recommendation lists. Pathetically lacking in sources for charges nuanced in overgeneralization, White is repeatedly obliged to call up the few well-worn citations from Cosmas, Lactantius, and Augustine. The Draper-White myth remains popular among anti-Christian institutions of learning.

Select Bibliography for Further Reading

Anastos, Milton V. "The Alexandrian Origin of the 'Christian Topography' of Cosmas Indicopleustes." *Dumbarton Oaks Papers* 3 (1946): 73–80.

Barnes, Timothy D. "Lactantius and Constantine." *Journal of Roman Studies* 63 (1973): 29–46.

Butler, James Davie. "Life of John Chrysostom." *Bibliotheca Sacra* 1, no. 4 (1844): 669–702.

Cosmas. *Christian Topography.* Translated and edited by J. W. McCrindle. London: Hakluyt Society, 1897.

Dicks, D. R. *Early Greek Astronomy to Aristotle.* Ithaca, NY: Cornell University Press, 1970.

Ehrhardt, Arnold. *The Beginning: A Study in the Greek Philosophical Approach to the Concept of Creation from Anaximander to St. John.* Manchester: Manchester University Press, 1968.

Ferrari, Leo C. "Augustine's Cosmography." *Augustinian Studies* 27, no. 2 (1996): 129–77.

---

[27] Andrew Dickson White, *History of the Warfare of Science with Theology in Christendom,* 2 vols. (New York: D. Appleton, 1896). He repeats the same few patristic references throughout; for our discussion, see esp. his chapter on geography (1:89–113).

_____. "Cosmography." In *Augustine through the Ages: An Encyclopedia*, edited by Allan D. Fitzgerald, 246. Grand Rapids: Eerdmans, 1999.

Kelly, J. N. D. *Golden Mouth: The Story of John Chrysostom; Ascetic, Preacher, Bishop*. Grand Rapids: Baker, 1995.

Lactantius, Lucius Coelius Firmianus. *Divinarum Institutionum*. Basileae: Andream Cratan Drum, 1532.

Russell, Jeffrey Burton. *Inventing the Flat Earth: Columbus and Modern Historians*. Westport, CT: Praeger Publishers, 1991.

Severian of Gabala. *Homilies on Creation and Fall*. Translated by Robert C. Hill. A volume in the series Ancient Christian Texts: Commentaries on Genesis 1–3, edited by Thomas C. Oden and Gerald L. Bray. Downers Grove, IL: InterVarsity, 2010.

Stephens, W. R. W. *Saint John Chrysostom: His Life and Times; A Sketch of the Church and the Empire in the Fourth Century*. London: John Murray. 1880.

Appendix 2

The Age of the Earth:
A History of Christian Views

Some of the earliest patristic writers teach that since a day is as a thousand years and God created the earth in six literal days, then the earth will last for six thousand literal years, followed by a literal millennium of rest that is typified by the seventh day of creation. The teaching originated from popular Jewish sources emphasizing that the letter *aleph*, the Hebrew arithmetical character for 1,000, appears six times in the first chapter of Genesis. This was thought to be a foregleam of the length of world history, followed by one thousand years of Sabbath rest.[1] For the church, the major negative impact of the concept was that it negated the Christian expectation of an imminent return of Christ.

We will now list and discuss the church fathers who taught that view. Even though they did not know the Hebrew language, these Fathers were aware of Hellenistic Jewish sources and nuances surrounding the teaching. Indeed, the viewpoint had become very popular—even in oral tradition—and not one of the church fathers expresses any concern that it might be dangerous. Indeed, some of the choicest patristic defenders of the faith embrace it, virtually all of the Fathers see it as innocuous, and most apply it in imaginative ways. Eusebius of Caesarea thought that the six days typified

---

[1] D. T. Taylor, *The Voice of the Church on the Coming and Kingdom of the Redeemer; or, a History of the Doctrine of the Reign of Christ on Earth*, 3rd ed. (Philadelphia: Lindsay & Blakiston, 1856), 26.

six world ages of varying spans of time. He made it so popular that when the Venerable Bede imagined a revision, he was temporarily suspected of heresy. Augustine liked the idea of applying typology to the six days, but his amillennialism forced him to spiritualize the seventh day. He finally settled with his own analogy between six ages of the world and six stages of human life.

The earliest Fathers who clearly and consistently teach the literal seven-millenary schema include the following:[2] Barnabas, Irenaeus of Lyon, Hippolytus of Rome, Cyprian of Carthage, Victorinus of Pettau, Methodius of Olympus and Patara, and Lactantius.

They base this seven-millenary view of world history primarily on two verses:

Psalm 90:4: For a thousand years in thy sight are but as yesterday when it is past, and as a watch in the night.

2 Peter 3:8: But, beloved, be not ignorant of this one thing, that one day is with the Lord as a thousand years, and a thousand years as one day.

An Examination of Current Claims of an Old Earth in Patristic Literature

The church fathers taught that, in the septenary week of creation, each twenty-four-hour day typifies a period of one thousand literal years of world history, which includes the millennium of rest. Hugh Ross, one of the most prominent evangelical advocates of long days and an old earth, claims that he has an abundance of patristic support for his view.[3] According to Ross, when the church fathers ex-

---

[2] Justin Martyr would be included here if he had provided a little more explicit detail. From the content of all his works, however, we do know that there is absolutely no basis for any assertion that Justin held to any long-day view of creation.

[3] *Creation and Time: A Biblical and Scientific Perspective on the Creation-Date Controversy* (Colorado Springs, CO: NavPress, 1994), 17–18; and *The Fingerprint of God* (New Kensington, PA: Whitaker House, 1989). Another defender of progressive creation and an old earth is Vern S. Poythress, in "A Christian-Theistic View of the Age of the Universe," *The Bulletin of Westminster Theological Seminary* 29, no. 6 (1990): 3, 6; and *Redeeming Science* (Wheaton: Crossway, 2006). He also tries to persuade the reader that no one can know if the biblical flood of Noah's day was anything more than a merely local incident. Then he seeks to defend the notion of a local occurrence.

press the seven-millenary view of world history, they mean that each creation-day of Genesis is a thousand years in length.[4] Is this assumption a *non sequitur*? Traditional creationists believe that it is. None of these church fathers say that the days of creation are anything other than twenty-four-hour days. The church fathers who embrace the seven-millenary view usually cite or make reference to Psalm 90:4, and they often add 2 Peter 3:8. These verses are not addressing the length of the creation days. It will be helpful to understand precisely what these verses in context are teaching.

Psalm 90 is contrasting man's time with God's infinity, and 2 Peter 3 is contrasting man's impatience with God's immutability. In Psalm 90, man is as grass that quickly withers. The psalm showcases the antithesis between man's measured days and God's fathomless Being and eternal presence: "The days of our years are threescore years and ten; and if by reason of strength they be fourscore years, yet is their strength labor and sorrow; for it is soon cut off, and we fly away" (Ps. 90:10). For the Lord of eternity, any expanse of time, even a thousand years, is as a nanosecond. "Before the mountains were brought forth, or ever thou hadst formed the earth and the world, even from everlasting to everlasting, thou art God" (Ps. 90:2). In summary, while Psalm 90 reminds us that our eternal God created time for the governance of man's ephemeral existence on earth, 2 Peter 3:1–18 "stirs up" our minds with absolute certainty of a divinely predestined point of consummation for all history and time itself.

Below are the two patristic passages to which Ross appeals from Justin Martyr and Irenaeus of Lyons. We will examine the passages in light of their contextual and literary setting.

Justin Martyr (ca. 100–167):

> Now we have understood that the expression used among these words, "According to the days of the tree [of life] shall be the days of my people; the works of their toil shall abound," obscurely predicts a thousand years. For as Adam was told that in the day he

---

[4] For a more complete refutation of Ross's theory of "progressive creationism," see Jonathan Sarfati, *Refuting Compromise: A Biblical and Scientific Refutation of Progressive Creationism (Billions of Years), As Popularized by Astronomer Hugh Ross* (Green Forest, AR: Master Books, 2004).

ate of the tree he would die, we know that he did not complete a thousand years. We have perceived, moreover, that the expression, "The day of the Lord is as a thousand years," is connected with this subject. (*Dialogue with Trypho* 81)

Irenaeus of Lyon (fl. late 2nd c.):

And there are some again, who relegate the death of Adam to the thousandth year; for since "a day of the Lord is as a thousand years," he did not overstep the thousand years, but died within them, thus bearing out the sentence of his sin. Whether, therefore, with respect to disobedience, which is death; whether [we consider] that, on account of that, they were delivered over to death, and made debtors to it; whether with respect to [the fact that on] one and the same day on which they ate they also died (for it is one day of the creation); whether [we regard this point] that with respect to this cycle of days, they died on the day in which they did also eat, that is, the day of the preparation, which is termed "the pure supper," that is, the sixth day of the feast, which the Lord also exhibited when He suffered on that day; or whether [we reflect] that he (Adam) did not overstep the thousand years, but died within their limit—it follows that, in regard to all these significations, God is indeed true. (*Against Heresies* 5.23.2)

The tradition that surrounds the above citations makes them significant, both hermeneutically and historically. Both citations refer to Genesis 2:17, where God says to Adam and Eve, "But of the tree of the knowledge of good and evil, thou shalt not eat of it: for in the day that thou eatest thereof thou shalt surely die." So the question is asked, "Did Adam and Eve die on the same day that they sinned?" The most natural and common meaning is that the instant Adam and Eve sinned they became totally dead spiritually, their bodies became suddenly mortal, and they began the physical process of aging and dying. Justin Martyr and Irenaeus, however, are implementing a popular rabbinical interpretation that "the day" spoken of in Genesis 2:17 was one thousand years in length. When Adam died after 930 years, there were still seventy years left in "the day," according the old Jewish allegory. But the day in Genesis 2:17 is subsequent to the creation week. Church fathers such as Justin and Irenaeus connect the day in Genesis 2:17 with the six creation days only because, in Jewish apocalyptic literature, each twenty-four-hour creation day *typifies* one thousand years. The Fathers are not *interpreting* the creation days as one-thousand-year days.

Justin Martyr, Irenaeus, and other church fathers often reveal their awareness of the popular Jewish sources that interpret the "day" of Adam's death in Genesis 2:17 as one thousand years in length. A look at such sources will shed light on the interpretation of the verse as the Jewish interpreters themselves explain it and as the church fathers apply it. We will begin with the oldest commentary in the world on the book of Genesis. It was written in Hebrew in the second century BC by an anonymous Pharisee. The book is called the *Book of Jubilees*, and it distinguishes between man's earthly time and the "testimony of the heavens." Here is the passage:

> And at the close of the nineteenth jubilee, in the seventh week in the sixth year 930 A.M. thereof, Adam died, and all his sons buried him in the land of his creation, and he was the first to be buried in the earth. And he lacked seventy years of one thousand years; for one thousand years are as one day in the testimony of the heavens and therefore was it written concerning the tree of knowledge: "On the day that ye eat thereof ye will die." For this reason he did not complete the years of this day; for he died during it.[5]

Further, in the section on Genesis 2:17 of the *Midrash Rabbah*, an important Hebrew exposition of Genesis, God separates "man's day" from "Mine." Clearly, the word *day* has a two-fold application in the verse: "man's day" and "the day of the Lord." The church fathers understood this distinction, both from the Hellenistic Jewish literature and from the context of Psalm 90:4. Here is the passage from *Midrash Rabbah*:

> For thus spoke I to him: "For in the day that thou eatest thereof thou shall surely die" (Gen. 2:17). Now ye do not know whether that means one day of Mine or one day of yours. But behold! I will grant him one day of Mine, which is a thousand years, and he will live nine hundred and thirty years and leave seventy for his

---

[5] *The Book of Jubilees: or the Little Genesis* (4:29–30), trans. R. H. Charles (London: Adam and Charles Black, 1902), 41. In his notes, Charles observes, "This interpretation of a day as a thousand years was current among the Jews." He brings into his analytical notes a large amount of similar literature, such as Babylonian Talmud, *Sanhedrin* 97a; and Mishnah, *Tamid* 7.4. See also D. S. Russell, *Method and Message of Jewish Apocalyptic* (Philadelphia: Westminster Press, 1964).

children, as it is written, "The days of our years are threescore years and ten" (Ps. 90:10).[6]

A few pages later, we see again the distinction between man's days and "one day of Thine," depicting the familiar two-fold application of "day":

> Remember, O Lord, Thy compassions and Thy mercies, for they have been from of old (Ps. 25:6) . . . wherewith Thou didst treat Adam, for thus saidst Thou to him, "For in the day that thou eatest thereof thou shalt surely die" . . . and hadst Thou not given him one day of Thine, which is a thousand years.[7]

So there is a clear distinction made between the day of the Lord and man's days. Justin, Irenaeus, and other church fathers follow the same line of thought in Genesis 2:17: Adam lived 930 years, which is seventy years short of a full "day of the Lord." Irenaeus, who was arguably the most careful premillennialist among the early Fathers, took a literal approach to both the prophetic days and the creative days of Scripture. In the context of book 5 in *Against Heresies* (cited above), Irenaeus repeatedly speaks in literal terms of such phenomena as the years of the tribulation period, the number 666, two resurrections, and a one-thousand-year reign of Christ. Ross ignores Irenaeus's context, which teaches that six literal days of creation typify six thousand literal years of world history. Irenaeus concludes that the seventh day typifies the millennial-Sabbath reign of our Lord:

> For in as many days as this world was made, in so many thousand years shall it be concluded. And for this reason the Scripture says: "Thus the heavens and the earth were finished, and all their adornment. And God brought to a conclusion upon the sixth day the works that He had made; and God rested upon the seventh day from all his works." This is an account of the things formerly created, as also it is a prophecy of the things to come. For the day of the Lord is as a thousand years; and in six days created things were completed: it is evident, therefore, that they will come to an end at the sixth thousand year. (*Against Heresies* 5.28.3)

---

6 *Midrash Rabbah: Genesis*, trans. H. Freedman in 2 vols. (London: Soncino Press, 1939), vol. 1, 19.8 Midrash Kabbah. While its final edition would evolve over a much longer period, the origins of the *Midrash Rabbah: Genesis* find their roots in the Hellenistic period, and the work draws material from Philo and Josephus.

7 Ibid., vol. 1, 22.1 Bereshith.

Justin Martyr links the expression, "one day is with the Lord as a thousand years," with a literal future millennium, suggestive of the seven-millenary schema of world history. It is more than likely, therefore, that he followed the accepted practice of taking the creation days literally as well. In fact, in the context of the passage to which Ross alludes (without citing), Justin is actually making the case to a Jew named Trypho that "right-minded Christians" believe that the Bible promises a literal regathering of Jews to the real city of Jerusalem, in geographical Israel, for Messiah's reign of one thousand years. Like the Jewish sources, Justin is using typology in this case. Six literal creation days typify six thousand literal years, followed by a literal millennial reign of Messiah. If the Jewish authors and the church fathers had held that each day of the creation week was one thousand years in length, then strangely, they would be saying that God rested for a one thousand year period! That would not only be foreign to Exodus 20:11 but uncharacteristic of the Jewish sources and the church fathers, including Justin. Such a view is simply absent from biblical, rabbinic, and patristic literature.

Justin insists, "I and others, who are right-minded Christians on all points, are assured that there will be a resurrection of the dead, and a thousand years in Jerusalem, which will then be built, adorned, and enlarged, [as] the prophets Ezekiel and Isaiah and others declare." One of Justin's favorite Scripture books is Revelation, whose authorship he attributes to "a certain man with us, whose name was John, one of the apostles of Christ, who prophesied, by a revelation that was made to him, that those who believed in our Christ would dwell a thousand years in Jerusalem, which will then be built, adorned, and enlarged, [as] the prophets Ezekiel and Isaiah and others declare" (*Dialogue with Trypho* 80–81).

The above analysis brings us to a three-fold conclusion: (1) there is no evidence from Irenaeus to support Ross's claim for one-thousand-year days; (2) Justin Martyr provides insufficient evidence for dogmatically stating his view on the length of the creation days; and (3) the twenty-four-hour day remains the most consistent view within the text and context of Justin's overall discussions.

Ross promotes the idea of the earth's being billions of years old. He attacks the position that the creation days are twenty-four-hour days, and he ridicules the concept of a young earth of only a few thousand years. Ross claims that "a majority" of the church fathers "who wrote on the subject" rejected the interpretation of the creation days as twenty-four-hour periods.[8] Moreover, according to Ross, it is rare to find a church father entertaining any serious interest at all in the age of the earth. Ross's treatment of patristic sources fails to establish any of those claims.

First, he appeals to a work called *Preparation for the Gospel*, by Eusebius, bishop of Caesarea, and applauds Eusebius for never once mentioning the date for the creation.[9] But Ross seems unaware of Eusebius's *Chronicle*,[10] where the author not only mentions a date for the creation but advocates a young earth. Eusebius calculates that Christ was born in AA (*Anno Adam*) 5199 and that there were 5228 years from Adam to the crucifixion in the fifteenth year of Emperor Tiberius.

Second, Ross appeals again to Eusebius's *Preparation for the Gospel* and claims that the ancient historian nowhere addresses the length of the creation days. Conversely, one could hardly ask for a better description of seven literal creation days than the following from *Preparation for the Gospel*. Eusebius is explaining the literal significance of God's arrangement of six days plus one day:

> In six days He made the heaven and the earth and all things that are therein, to distinguish the times, and predict the order in which one thing comes before another: for after arranging their order, He keeps them so, and makes no change. He has also plainly declared that the seventh day is ordained for us by the Law, to be a sign of that which is our seventh faculty, namely reason, whereby we have knowledge of things human and divine. Also the whole world of living creatures, and of all plants that grow, revolves in sevens.[11]

---

[8] Ross, *Creation and Time*, 24.

[9] Ibid., 20.

[10] Eusebius, *Chronicle* Part 2, in Migne *PL* 27.441–508, trans. from the Greek into Latin by Jerome. Eusebius calculates that there were 5,579 years from Adam until the fourteenth year of Emperor Valens. See Migne *PL* 27.507–8; and Eusebius, *Chronicorum*, editit, Alfred Schoene, libri duo (Berolini: Apud Weidmannos, 1866–75), 1:129–32.

[11] Eusebius, *Praeparatio Evangelica* 13.12, trans. E. H. Gifford (Oxford: Oxford University Press, 1903), 3:2.663ff. Volume 3 is bound in two separate books.

In his search for patristic support for the long-day view, Ross claims that Lactantius, Victorinus of Pettau, and Methodius of Olympus "all concurred" that the creation days are "thousand-year epochs."[12] To the contrary, not one of those church fathers expresses such a view. After clearly enunciating literal days of the creation and a literal millennium, Lactantius concluded that the earth was fewer than six thousand years old: "For six thousand years have not yet been completed, and when this number shall be made up, then at length all evil will be taken away, that justice may reign."[13] Victorinus, who wrote the oldest extant *Commentary on the Apocalypse of the Blessed John* as well as a treatise *On the Creation of the World*, expresses the conviction that he is living near the end of the six-thousand-year mark of world history, prior to a literal millennium. We will examine his exact remarks below in a separate section. As for Methodius, he believes that the earth is fewer than six thousand years old. "In the seventh thousand [millennium] of years," he explains in *Banquet of the Ten Virgins*, "we shall celebrate the great feast of true tabernacles" (Discourse 9.1). His works fully and consistently advance a young earth, literal days of creation, and a literal millennium. In conclusion, the patristic sources provide no support for the old-earth viewpoint advocated by Hugh Ross and others.

Key Post-Reformation Teachings on the Age of the Earth

Well into the eighteenth century there existed a scholarly consensus that the creation took place around 4000 BC. Consider, for instance, the creation dates given by this cluster of geniuses—all living within a few decades of one another: Johannes Kepler (3993 BC);[14] Christen Longomontanus (3964 BC);[15] John Lightfoot (3928

---

[12] Ross, *Creation and Time*, 19; cf. 102.

[13] Lactantius, *Epitome of the Divine Institutes* 80.

[14] German scholar, Johannes Kepler (1571–1630), *Mysterium Cosmographicum* (*Secret of the Universe*), chap. 23, note 4, 2nd ed., Frankfort, 1621, trans. A. M. Duncan (New York: Abaris Books, 1981), 223. Kepler invented mathematical astrophysics and wrote numerous works expressing its laws.

[15] Danish scholar Christen Longomontanus (1562–1647) wrote *De Chronoiabio Historico* (1627).

BC);[16] James Ussher (4004 BC);[17] and Isaac Newton (3998 BC).[18] Newton's calculations of the precession rate of the equinoxes gave him the date of 3998 for the creation of world[19]—only six years different from Ussher's date.

John Lightfoot, in his treatise, *A Few and New Observations upon the Book of Genesis*, speculated from Genesis 1:26 that the Trinity created Adam at nine o'clock in the morning. Andrew White of Cornell University created the popular myth that James Ussher made that statement. In his *History of the Warfare of Science with Theology in Christendom* (1896), White merges Ussher's "4004" with Lightfoot's "nine o' clock in the morning." White then chides the young-earth view for his own fabricated statement that "man was created by the Trinity on the twenty-third of October, 4004 B.C., at nine o'clock in the morning."[20] From our discussion of Columbus and the flat-earth myth, we know that this was not the only blunder that White made in a book that helped to turn the tide of popular opinion away from

---

[16] John Lightfoot (1602–75) was a biblical scholar and vice-chancellor of the University of Cambridge. Significant to our study is his work, *The Harmony of the Four Evangelists, Among Themselves, and with the Old Testament*, Part 1, Prolegomena 1, sect. 8 (London: W. R. for Robert Scott, Thomas Basset, John Wright, and Richard Chriswell, 1682), 390. In 1684, the same publisher reprinted this title in *The Works of the Reverend and Learned John Lightfoot* 1:379ff.

[17] James Ussher (1581–1656) was vice-chancellor of Trinity College, Dublin. See his *Annales Veteris Testamenti: A Prima Mundi Origine Deducti* (1650), which translates as "Annals of the Old Testament: Deduced from the First Origins of the World." The work spans from the creation to the Maccabees. In 1654, Ussher published his *Annalium pars Posterior*, expanding the former work to the Emperor Vespasian (AD 73). Ussher's complete work first appeared in English in 1658 as *The Annals of the World* (London: F. Crook and G. Bedell, 1658). For a modern English edition, see James Ussher, *The Annals of the World*, revised and updated by Larry and Marion Pierce (Green Forest, AR: Master Books, 2009).

[18] Isaac Newton (1643–1727) co-invented calculus and discovered the first quantitatively successful law of gravity. Significant to our study is *The Chronology of Ancient Kingdoms Amended: A Short Chronicle from the First Memory of Things in Europe, to the Conquest of Persia by Alexander the Great* (London: Printed for J. Tonson in the Strand, and J. Osborn and T. Longman in Paternoster Row, 1728); see also *Newton's Revised History of Ancient Kingdoms—A Complete Chronology*, ed. Larry and Marion Pierce (Green Forest, AR: Master Books, 2009).

[19] This date is accurately provided by David A. Weintraub, *How Old Is the Universe?* (Princeton, NJ: Princeton University Press, 2011), 14. This is especially significant since Weintraub himself believes that the earth is billions of years old.

[20] Andrew Dickson White, *History of the Warfare of Science with Theology in Christendom* (New York: D. Appleton, 1896), 1:256.

Christianity and towards secularism. Since that time, the ancient idea of a young earth has been ridiculed in secular and even evangelical circles. Such derision, though, has not influenced the Hebrew calendar.

Highly-esteemed in Jewish history, a second-century chronicle known as the *Seder Olam Rabbah* ("Book of the Order of the World")[21] is believed to have been largely written by Rabbi Yose ben Halafta (d. AD 160). Chronicling the age of the earth, the author uses biblical data from the creation to Alexander's conquest of Persia. He then brings it down to his own day. From the creation of Adam, he calculates the creation at 3761 BC. It was Rabbi Yose who also invented the Hebrew calendar that is in use to this day. On the Hebrew calendar, the year 2000 was AM (*Anno Mundi*, or Year of the World) 5760.

Concluding Observation

A modern departure from the teachings of the *Seder Olam Rabbah* is a new theory advanced by Israeli physicist Gerald Schroeder, who proposes a new big-bang theory for the origin of the earth. To support his view, Schroeder appeals to such authorities as the Kabala and the Jewish Kabalistic scholar, Nachmanides (1194–1270), chief rabbi of Catalonia, Spain. His Spanish name was Bonastrug da Porta, and he spent the last years of his life in Israel. Often called "Ramban," an acronym for Rabbi Moshe Ben Nachman, he became known as a philosopher, poet, and biblical exegete, writing a *Commentary on Torah*. Schroeder argues that his own theory is not contradictory to Nachmanides's comments on Genesis 1:1.

Schroeder theorizes that the original creation was nothing more than "a speck of light energy." He surmises that "the universe started as a minuscule speck, perhaps not larger than a grain of mustard

---

[21] *Seder Olam*, trans. Heinrich W. Guggenheimer (Northvale, NJ: Jason Aronson, 1998). Creationists, both Jew and Gentile, recognize mistakes in *Seder Olam* but, like all such calculations, the mistakes involve tens and hundreds but not thousands of years. Indeed, Jewish authors readily take the Gen. 2:4 occurrence of "in the day that" as the normal Hebrew idiom for "at the time when" (cf. Num. 3:1; 2 Sam. 22:1).

and stretched out from there."[22] This energy, shooting forth at the modern reckoning of the speed of light, caused a "big bang" from which the universe came into existence some fifteen billion years ago, which in actual earth-time contracts to six twenty-four-hour days. Contrary to the big bang theory, traditional creationists believe that God created the sun with its light already extended to earth. God did not require the earth to wait for sunlight to arrive. Just as He spoke mature birds, fish, animals, and trees into existence, God also spoke the full expansion of sunlight into existence.

Select Bibliography for Further Reading

The Book of Jubilees: or the Little Genesis. Translated by R. H. Charles. London: Adam and Charles Black, 1902.

Eusebius of Caesarea. *Chronicorum.* Editit by Alfred Schoene. Libri duo. Berolini: Apud Weidmannos, 1866–75.

———. *Praeparatio Evangelica.* Translated by E. H. Gifford. 5 vols. Oxford: Oxford University Press, 1903. Vol. 3 of the 4-vol. set is bound into two vols.

Kepler, Johannes. "On the Astronomical Beginning and End of the Universe and the Platonic Year." In *Mysterium Cosmographicum (The Secret of the Universe),* translated by A. M. Duncan, 221–25. New York: Abaris Books, 1981.

Lightfoot, John. *A Few and New Observations upon the Book of Genesis.* In *The Whole Works of the Rev. John Lightfoot, D.D.,* edited by John Rogers Pitman, 2:329-49. London: J. F. Dove, 1822.

———. *A Harmony of the Four Evangelists, Among Themselves, and with the Old Testament.* London: W. R. for Robert Scot, Thomas Basset, John Wright, and Richard Chriswell, 1682.

Midrash Rabbah: Genesis. Translated by H. Freedman. 2 vols. London: Soncino Press, 1939.

Mortenson, Terry. "Jesus, Evangelical Scholars, and the Age of the Earth." *The Master's Seminary Journal* 18, no. 1 (Spring 2007): 69–98.

Newton, Isaac. *The Chronology of Ancient Kingdoms Amended: A Short Chronicle from the First Memory of Things in Europe, to the Conquest of Persia by Alexandria the Great.* London: J. Tonson in the Strand, and J. Osborn and T. Longman in Paternoster Row, 1728.

———. *Newton's Revised History of Ancient Kingdoms—A Complete Chronology.* Edited by Larry and Marion Pierce. Green Forest, AR: Master Books, 2009.

Sarfati, Jonathan. *Refuting Compromise: A Biblical and Scientific Refutation of Progressive Creationism (Billions of Years), As Popularized by Astronomer Hugh Ross.* Green Forest, AR: Master Books, 2004.

---

[22] "The Age of the Universe," http://www.geraldschroeder.com/AgeUniverse. aspx; and *The Science of God* (New York: Simon and Schuster, 1997). See also Schroeder's DVD, "Evidence of God" (Dallas: Zola Levitt Ministries, 2007).

Seder Olam. Translated by Heinrich W. Guggenheimer. Northvale, NJ: Jason
    Aronson, 1998. Authorship is attributed in part to Rabbi Yose ben Halafta.
Ussher, James. *The Annals of the World*. London: F. Crook and G. Bedell, 1658.
————. *The Annals of the World*. Revised and updated by Larry and Marion
    Pierce. Green Forest, AR: Master Books, 2009.

Appendix 3

The Doctrine of Creation:
Barnabas to Ambrose

While much of the material in this chapter includes the Noahic flood, most of my comments will relate more specifically to the controversies revolving around creation and age of the earth. The whole corpus of patristic literature consistently defends a global flood, and there are excellent works[1] that refute the current denials of a universal flood.

Barnabas (mid-2nd c.)

Barnabas is the earliest to set forth the seven-millenary schema of world history, claiming that each of the six literal creation days typifies a thousand years of world history. Generally, those who embraced this view were premillennialists, adding that the Sabbath day typifies the future millennium. While Barnabas never specifically reveals his millennial view, he consistently sets forth literal days for man's time, with a typological span of world history:

---

[1] For bibliographies and in-depth coverage of the biblical record of the flood, see Terry Mortenson and Thane H. Ury, eds., *Coming to Grips with Genesis: Biblical Authority and the Age of the Earth* (Green Forest, AR: Master Books, 2009); Andrew A. Snelling, *Earth's Catastrophic Past: Geology, Creation, and the Flood*, 2 vols. (Dallas: Institute for Creation Research, 2009); Jack P. Lewis, *A Study of the Interpretation of Noah and the Flood in Jewish and Christian Literature* (1968; repr., Leiden: E. J. Brill, 1978), 101–20; and Henry M. Morris and John C. Whitcomb, *The Genesis Flood: The Biblical Record and Its Scientific Implications* (Philadelphia: Presbyterian and Reformed, 1961).

¶ The Sabbath is mentioned at the beginning of the creation: "And God made in six days the works of His hands, and made an end on the seventh day, and rested on it, and sanctified it." Attend, my children, to the meaning of this expression, "He finished in six days." This implieth that the Lord will finish all things in six thousand years, for a day is with Him a thousand years. And He Himself testifieth, saying, "Behold, today will be as a thousand years." Therefore, my children, in six days, that is, in six thousand years, all things will be finished. (*Epistle of Barnabas* 15)[2]

The seventh millennium will be followed by the "beginning of another world,"—ὅ ἐστιν ἄλλου κόσμου ἀρχήν—and this new creation is cryptically referred to as the eighth day, which is also the first. Unlike most patristic authors, Barnabas seems to regard the seventh millennium as the new heaven and new earth—Christ will "change [ἀλλάξει] the sun, and the moon, and the stars" at the time when He destroys "the time of the wicked man" (ἀνόμου) (15).

Hermas of Rome (first half of 2nd c.)

Setting forth what he considers the first mandate or fundamental of the faith, Hermas begins with the one true God who created all things *ex nihilo*. It is the earliest extra-biblical expression of creation "out of nothing," and Hermas adds that we are to believe, fear, and obey Him for victory over evil:

¶ First of all, believe that there is one God who created and finished all things, and made all things out of nothing. He alone is able to contain the whole, but He Himself cannot be contained. Have faith therefore in Him, and fear Him; and fearing Him, exercise self-control. Keep these commands, and you will cast away from you all wickedness, and put on the strength of righteousness, and live to God, if you keep this commandment. (*Pastor*, Mandate 1)

Justin Martyr (ca. 100–167) and Theophilus of Antioch (ca. 115–80)

The ante-Nicene fathers believed that in Genesis 1:1–2 God created the earth *ex nihilo*. Enveloped in deep water and darkness, the

---

[2] Except where otherwise noted, patristic citations and references are from ANF, NPNF 1, and NPNF 2.

earth was unformed, empty, uninhabited, and ready for its six-day preparation for habitation. God "created it not in vain," but "formed it to be inhabited" (Isa. 45:18). The Spirit of God "moved" (brooded) over the face of the waters. On the first day, God created light and separated it from the darkness. Alister McGrath teaches that Justin Martyr and Theophilus of Antioch followed the Gnostics in embracing the Platonist notions that God did not create anything *ex nihilo* and that He simply shaped preexistent matter.[3] To the contrary, here is Theophilus in his own words: "God made all things out of nothing; for nothing is coeval with God." Theophilus argues his view at length, insisting that "sacred scripture" shows from the beginning that the matter itself, from which God fashioned the world, was first of all created by Him.[4] To Theophilus, "The power of God is seen in this, that, first of all, He creates out of nothing, according to His will, the things that are made."[5] The apologist explains that in the beginning God created the earth *ex nihilo*—out of nothing—unformed and empty. The remainder of the creation account narrates the six literal days in which God made living things—vegetation, animals, and Adam—out of His original *ex nihilo* creation. That is precisely the position of the church fathers and of traditional creationists to this day. It is the key to a proper understanding of patristic descriptions of the six-day creation. We will expand upon Theophilus's view after we allow Justin to state his affirmation of an *ex nihilo* creation.

In his *First Apology* (10), Justin explains that God does not need material offerings since He is the Creator of every physical thing, "as in the beginning He created us when we were not." Justin depicts God as conducting a workshop, so to speak, on the ethic of work

---

[3] *Christian Theology: An Introduction*, 5th ed. (Oxford: Wiley-Blackwell, 2011), 219. McGrath offers no evidence or qualifier for such an assertion. Cf. the liberal view of Gerhard May, *Creatio Ex Nihilo: The Doctrine of "Creation out of Nothing" in Early Christian Thought*, trans. A. S. Worrall (Edinburgh: T. & T. Clark, 1994), 17–18, originally published as *Schöpfung aus dem Nichts* (Berlin: Walter de Gruyter, 1978). In part, May proposes that there is even insufficient biblical evidence for *ex nihilo* creation and that the doctrine was devised by Christian apologists in reaction to Gnostic tenets that matter is evil and an evil god created it.

[4] Theophilus, *To Autolycus* 2.10. Athenagoras of Athens, in his argument against pantheism, also argues against the eternality of matter (*A Plea for the Christians* 15).

[5] Theophilus, *To Autolycus* 2.13.

and rest. In a nutshell, here is Justin's sermon: God began by instantaneously creating *ex nihilo* all of the unformed material necessary for His six-day project. He could have made the earth of Genesis 1:1 completely formed and filled, but He chose to use six normal work days to illustrate for man the wisdom of acquiring the necessary materials and regulating his life with work and rest. Justin explains that, in the beginning, for His glory and for man's benefit, "God created all things out of unformed matter."[6] Unlike our Creator, we cannot bring our resources into existence *ex nihilo*. We must trust Him alone for all of our resources.

Some have referenced Justin's *First Apology* (59) as asserting that God did not create the heavens and earth *ex nihilo* but used pre-existing material that ancient Greek poets personified as "Erebus."[7] It is assumed that since Plato supposedly held to such a view and since Justin sometimes appeals to Plato, he must have embraced the same view. There is simply no evidence that Justin ever teaches that God shaped uncreated matter. It was "unformed matter,"[8] not uncreated matter, that God used in His creation week of preparing the earth for man, who would be the crown of creation. Justin never even hints that the creation of matter is not *ex nihilo*. A fuller description of his view will follow this brief elucidation of *Erebus*, a term frequently used but seldom explained.

The story of Erebus originated not from Plato but from the eighth-century BC Greek poet Hesiod in his *Theogony* (θεογονία), meaning "birth of the gods" (from θεός, "God" + γίγνεσθαι, "to be born"). In Greek creation mythology, as taught by Hesiod, Darkness existed first; Chaos, known as The Gap, sprang from Darkness. The

---

[6] Justin, *First Apology* 10. His train of thought on the topic begins in chapter 9.

[7] There is some good material in defense of *ex nihilo* in Paul Copan, "Is *Creatio Ex Nihilo* a Post-Biblical Invention? An Examination of Gerhard May's Proposal," *Trinity Journal* 17.1 (Spring 1996): 77–93. This is a conservative critique of the liberal work by Gerhard May, *Creatio ex Nihilo*. While offering good arguments and evidence against May's proposal, Copan continues on too far when he attributes pagan ideas to Basil of Caesarea. His evidence consists of alleged quotations from Basil where Basil is actually quoting from pagans in order to refute them. Copan depends too heavily upon secondary sources, he repeats the mistaken idea that Justin Martyr did not teach an *ex nihilo* creation, and he gives the wrong reference to the Justin passage.

[8] *First Apology* 10.

underworld god, Erebus, was born from Chaos and Darkness and was known as Tartarus. Erebus was the embodiment of primordial darkness and was considered the void from which the earth and all other things developed.[9]

It is imperative to view Justin as writing his *Apology* to cultured classes of Greek-speaking pagans. Such is typically his method. Justin is building bridges by referencing his arguments with pagan literary terms with which his readers are familiar. He uses *Erebus* as a familiar term to transition the minds of his pagan readers to biblical truths such as the fire of Deuteronomy 32:22 and particularly to the truth of the early verses of Genesis 1, where God creates earth's matter from nothing as "without form, and void" and with "darkness upon the face of the deep." Pagan creation myths had their own crude and corrupt parallels to the scene presented in the Genesis account. For instance, Erebus marries his sister, Nox (Nyx), the goddess of night, and their offspring were named Hemera (Day) and Aether (Sky). Justin often connects with such literature, but without proper explanation, and at times it encumbers truth with confusion. The "substance" to which Justin refers is the original earth that God created *ex nihilo* in Genesis 1:1–2, ready in the ensuing verses to be formed in six days for habitation. Here is the passage:

> ¶ And that you may learn that it was from our teachers—we mean the account given through the prophets—that Plato borrowed his statement that God, having altered matter which was shapeless, made the world, hear the very words spoken through Moses, who, as above shown, was the first prophet, and of greater antiquity than the Greek writers; and through whom the Spirit of prophecy, signifying how and from what materials God at first formed the world, spake thus: "In the beginning God created the heaven and the earth. And the earth was invisible and unfurnished, and darkness was upon the face of the deep; and the Spirit of God moved over the waters. And God said, Let there be light; and it was so." So that both Plato and they who agree with him, and we ourselves, have learned, and you also can be convinced, that by the word of God the whole world was made out of the substance spoken of

---

[9] Hesiod, *Theogony* 123, trans. M. L. West (Oxford: Oxford University Press, 1999), 6ff. See also Patricia Turner and Charles Russell Coulter, *Dictionary of Ancient Deities* (New York: Oxford University Press, 2000), 122, 170.

before by Moses. And that which the poets call Erebus, we know was spoken of formerly by Moses. (*First Apology* 59)

In the following citation, Justin asserts that Plato had been influenced by the Old Testament but had chosen to conceal his source:

¶ And from what source did Plato draw the information that time was created along with the heavens? For he wrote thus: "Time, accordingly, was created along with the heavens; in order that, coming into being together, they might also be together dissolved, if ever their dissolution should take place." Had he not learned this from the divine history of Moses? For he knew that the creation of time had received its original constitution from days and months and years. Since, then, the first day which was created along with the heavens constituted the beginning of all time (for thus Moses wrote, "In the beginning God created the heavens and the earth," and then immediately subjoins, "And one day was made," as if he would designate the whole of time by one part of it), Plato names the day "time," lest, if he mentioned the "day," he should seem to lay himself open to the accusation of the Athenians, that he was completely adopting the expressions of Moses. And from what source did he derive what he has written regarding the dissolution of the heavens? Had he not learned this, too, from the sacred prophets, and did he not think that this was their doctrine? (*Hortatory Address to the Greeks* 33)

Theophilus of Antioch (cont'd.)

We have seen in his apology *To Autolycus* (2.10; 2.13) that Theophilus sets forth his belief that God created the heavens and the earth *ex nihilo*. In an entire chapter (2.11), he rehearses the biblical account of creation and affirms his belief in six literal twenty-four-hour days. Next, he seeks profusely to honor the great God of creation (2.12). Here are significant parts of his narrative:

¶ Of this six days' work no man can give a worthy explanation and description of all its parts, not though he had ten thousand tongues and ten thousand mouths; nay, though he were to live ten thousand years, sojourning in this life, not even so could he utter anything worthy of these things, on account of the exceeding greatness and riches of the wisdom of God which there is in the six days' work above narrated. (*To Autolycus* 2.12)

¶ On the fourth day the luminaries were made; because God, who possesses foreknowledge, knew the follies of the vain philosophers, and that they were going to say that the things which grow on the earth are produced from the heavenly bodies, so as to exclude God. In order, therefore, that the truth might be obvious, the plants and seeds were produced prior to the heavenly bodies, for what is posterior cannot produce that which is prior. (*To Autolycus* 2.15)

¶ And on the sixth day, God having made the quadrupeds, and wild beasts, and the land reptiles, pronounced no blessing upon them, reserving His blessing for man, whom He was about to create on the sixth day. (*To Autolycus* 2.17)

We have already learned that Theophilus opposed the idea of the earth being spherical and that he described the earth as a flat surface covered by the heavens as by a dome-shaped lid (2.32 and 2.13). He does demonstrate a profound interest in philosophy, Jewish history, secular history, and even the Hebrew language. He loves to defend a literal and universal flood of Noah's day, and he defends a young earth. Calculating the biblical genealogies and counting from the creation to the emperor Aurelius Verus (d. 169), he believes the earth to be only 5698 years old at the time of his writing:

¶ And from the foundation of the world the whole time is thus traced, so far as its main epochs are concerned. From the creation of the world to the deluge were 2242 years. And from the deluge to the time when Abraham our forefather begat a son, 1036 years. And from Isaac, Abraham's son, to the time when the people dwelt with Moses in the desert, 660 years. And from the death of Moses and the rule of Joshua the son of Nun, to the death of the patriarch David, 498 years. And from the death of David and the reign of Solomon to the sojourning of the people in the land of Babylon, 518 years 6 months 10 days. And from the government of Cyrus to the death of the Emperor Aurelius Verus, 744 years. All the years from the creation of the world amount to a total of 5698 years, and the odd months and days. (*To Autolycus* 3.28)[10]

---

[10] See also *To Autolycus* 3.17–19; and 3.26.

Irenaeus of Lyon (fl. late 2nd c.)

Having previously introduced Irenaeus's view, we will now present his essential position within the chronology of patristic authors. In the first citation below, Irenaeus is asserting his belief in the doctrine of creation *ex nihilo*. In the next one, he is in agreement with most other ante-Nicene fathers that each of the six creation days is a literal twenty-four-hour day and that it typifies one thousand years of the earth's existence. The curse will be removed after six thousand years and the millennium will follow:

¶ While men, indeed, cannot make anything out of nothing, but only out of matter already existing, yet God is in this point preeminently superior to men, in that He Himself called into being the substance of His creation, when previously it had no existence. (*Against Heresies* 2.10.4)

¶ For in as many days as this world was made, in so many thousand years shall it be concluded. And for this reason the Scripture says: "Thus the heaven and the earth were finished, and all their adornment. And God brought to a conclusion upon the sixth day the works that He had made; and God rested upon the seventh day from all His works." This is an account of the things formerly created, as also it is a prophecy of what is to come. For the day of the Lord is as a thousand years; and in six days created things were completed: it is evident, therefore, that they will come to an end at the sixth thousand year. And therefore throughout all time, man, having been molded at the beginning by the hands of God, that is, of the Son and of the Spirit. (*Against Heresies* 5.28.3–4)

Tatian of Assyria (ca. 110–72)

Tatian teaches the doctrine of creation *ex nihilo*: "For matter is not, like God, without a beginning . . . but brought into existence by the Framer of all things alone" (*Address to the Greeks* 5).

Tertullian of Carthage (ca. 160–220)

In his work, *Against Hermogenes*,[11] a polemic against the pagan idea of the eternality of matter, Tertullian argues for creation *ex*

---

[11] *Against Hermogenes* 1–2.

nihilo. In another work he describes the earth as an "orb" that was once completely covered with water even to the heights of its mountains.[12]

Clement of Alexandria (ca. 150–215)

In *Stromata* 1.21, Clement holds to a young earth and calculates that Adam was created about 5592 BC. Although the Greek philosopher Plato is sometimes contradictory in expressing his own belief regarding the eternality of matter, Clement praises him for believing Moses' account of a personal God creating the earth *ex nihilo*:

¶ The philosophers, having so heard from Moses, taught that the world was created [γενητόν]. And so Plato expressly said, "Whether was it that the world had no beginning of its existence, or derived its beginning from some beginning? For being visible, it is tangible; and being tangible, it has a body." Again, when he says, "It is a difficult task to find the Maker and Father of this universe," he not only showed that the universe was created, but points out that it was generated by him as a son, and that he is called its father, as deriving its being from him alone, and springing from non-existence. (*Stromata* 5.14)[13]

Clement then interprets the act of creation as taking place outside of time and the days of creation as having allegorical meanings:

¶ That, then, we may be taught that the world was originated, and not suppose that God made it in time, prophecy adds: "This is the book of the generation: also of the things in them, when they were created in the day that God made heaven and earth." (*Stromata* 6.16)

Clement suggests that the "seven days" could figuratively symbolize seven heavens, one above the other, as an octave of seven spheres having seven inner spheres, which are the seven planets. The fixed stars are all within an eighth sphere, which completes the octave and "borders on the intellectual world" of spirits, where angels

---

[12] *On the Pallium* 2.

[13] In addition to the clear citations provided here, Henry Chadwick mentions three other places where Clement declares that the world is made out of nothing. See his discussion in *Early Christian Thought and the Classical Tradition: Studies in Justin, Clement, and Origen* (Oxford: Oxford University Press, 1966), 46.

abide. He adds that the seven days could even typify seven periods of earth history, followed by an eighth, which is the eternal rest.[14]

Origen of Alexandria (ca. 185–254)

It is vital to keep in view the basics of Origen's inseparably connected philosophical speculations and interpretational methods. To avoid repetition of material discussed in other sections, we begin with a package summary of Origen's worldview.

This world is one of an endless cycle of worlds that have existed one at a time. There is no beginning to the cycle since any concept of "beginning" must be outside of time. Each world exists as part of an eternal generation of worlds. Matter is not eternal *in its present state*. At the end of each world, there occurs a transmutation of form and a transformation of appearance, as God creates the next world. This present world is likely not the last. Each world is created as a literal event. Adam and Eve were real people, but the six-day account should also be interpreted figuratively. God created the earth *ex nihilo* in Genesis 1:1 and formed it in a short amount of time. It did not evolve. God created earth-time when He created the earth. The earth is relatively young—being far below ten thousand years old. The flood was a literal and universal event.

While Origen's *Homilies on Genesis*[15] are useful as samples of his preaching, they are mostly symbolic or figurative applications with virtually no real exegesis. Equally speculative are the short fragments remaining from his *Commentary on Genesis*. For instance, when God says in Genesis 1:14, "Let there be lights in the firmament of the heaven to divide the day from the night; and let them be for signs," Origen explains the "signs" as the twelve signs of the zodiac, created by God as a secret language that only the angels can read. This is God's way of sending special instructions to the angels. Origen does use the occasion to condemn horoscopes and all human attempts at reading the future from the stars. He urges that the stars have no

---

[14] *Stromata* 4.25.

[15] Origen, *Homilies on Genesis and Exodus*, vol. 71 of *The Fathers of the Church*, trans. Ronald E. Heine (Washington, DC: Catholic University of America Press, 1982). Homily 1 of Genesis covers the creation week and Homily 2 covers Noah's flood.

power to determine human character or human destiny. God alone created the universe, and the will of man alone determines human destiny.[16] The following readings, from a variety of sources, provide some of the best samples of Origen's style, method, and doctrine:

> ¶ But if any one disbelieves the swiftness of the power of God in regard to these matters, he has not yet had a true conception of the God who made the universe, who did not require times to make the vast creation of heaven and earth and the things in them; for, though He may seem to have made these things in six days, there is need of understanding to comprehend in what sense the words "in six days" are said, on account of this, "This is the book of the generation of heaven and earth," etc. Therefore it may be boldly affirmed that the season of the expected judgment does not require times, but as the resurrection is said to take place "in a moment, in the twinkling of an eye," so I think will the judgment also be. (*Commentary on Matthew* book 14.9)
> ¶ That all things were created by God, and that there is no creature which exists but has derived from Him its being, is established from many declarations of Scripture; those assertions being refuted and rejected which are falsely alleged by some respecting the existence either of a matter co-eternal with God, or of unbegotten souls. (*De Principiis* 1.3.3)

Origen also teaches in *De Principiis* (1.7.1; 2.2) that God created the earth out of nothing. In the following citation, he argues that he can find some literal truth in the creation account:

> ¶ Concerning, then, the creation of the world, what portion of Scripture can give us more information regarding it, than the account which Moses has transmitted respecting its origin? And although it comprehends matters of profounder significance than the mere historical narrative appears to indicate, and contains very many things that are to be spiritually understood, and employs the letter, as a kind of veil, in treating of profound and mystical subjects; nevertheless the language of the narrator shows that all visible things were created at a certain time. . . . The world is both said to have a beginning and to hope for an end. (*De Principiis* 3.5.1)

---

[16] Origen, *Commentary on Genesis*, fragment from book 3, trans. in Joseph W. Trigg, *Origen* (New York: Routledge, 1998), 86–102. The short fragment is the longest one from this commentary.

¶ But this is the objection which they generally raise: they say, "If the world had its beginning in time, what was God doing before the world began? . . . Such is the objection which they are accustomed to make to our statement that this world had its beginning at a certain time, and that, agreeably to our belief in Scripture, we can calculate the years of its past duration. To these propositions I consider that none of the heretics can easily return an answer that will be in conformity with the nature of their opinions. But . . . not then for the first time did God begin to work when He made this visible world; but as, after its destruction, there will be another world, so also we believe that others existed before the present came into being. And both of these positions will be confirmed by the authority of Holy Scripture. For that there will be another world after this is taught by Isaiah, who says, "There will be new heavens, and a new earth. . . ." It is not, however, to be supposed that several worlds existed at once, but that, after the end of this present world, others will take their beginning. (*De Principiis* 3.5.3)

Referring to the Old and New Testaments, Origen says that literal history is the exception rather than the rule. One should look primarily for mystical meanings. Earlier, in *De Principiis* (4.1.11), he has emphasized hidden mystical codes that he sees in the number *six*, and he believes this to be one of the most important things to discover in Genesis 1–3:

¶ [As to the Scriptures,] these do not contain throughout a pure history of events, which are interwoven indeed according to the letter, but which did not actually occur. Nor even do the law and the commandments wholly convey what is agreeable to reason. For who that has understanding will suppose that the first, and second, and third day, and the evening and the morning, existed without a sun, and moon, and stars? and that the first day was, as it were, also without a sky? And who is so foolish as to suppose that God, after the manner of a husbandman, planted a paradise in Eden, towards the east, and placed in it a tree of life, visible and palpable, so that one tasting of the fruit by the bodily teeth obtained life? and again, that one was a partaker of good and evil by masticating what was taken from the tree? And if God is said to walk in the paradise in the evening, and Adam to hide himself under a tree, I do not suppose that anyone doubts that these things figuratively indicate certain mysteries, the history having taken place in appearance, and not literally. Cain also, when going forth from the presence of God, certainly appears to thoughtful men as likely to lead the reader to inquire what the presence of God is, and what the meaning of going out from Him is. And what need is there to say more, since those who are not altogether blind can collect countless instances of a similar kind recorded as having occurred, but which did not literally take place? (*De Principiis* 4.1.16)

As Origen combats Celsus's belief in the eternality of earth and matter, he reveals his own young-earth conviction. To Origen, the earth is very much younger than ten thousand years old; although, to him, the idea of literal days is "silly." They must be interpreted figuratively:

¶ After these statements, Celsus, from a secret desire to cast discredit upon the Mosaic account of the creation, which teaches that the world is not yet ten thousand years old, but very much under that, while concealing his wish, intimates his agreement with those who hold that the world is uncreated. For, maintaining that there have been, from all eternity, many conflagrations and many deluges, and that the flood which lately took place in the time of Deucalion is comparatively modern, he clearly demonstrates to those who are able to understand him that, in his opinion, the world was uncreated. But let this assailant of the Christian faith tell us by what arguments he was compelled to accept the statement that there have been many conflagrations and many cataclysms, and that the flood which occurred in the time of Deucalion, and the conflagration in that of Phaethon, were more recent than any others. (*Contra Celsum* 1.19)

¶ But after this investigation of his [Celsus's] assertions, as if his object were to swell his book by many words, he repeats, in different language, the same charges which we have examined a little ago, saying: "By far the most silly thing is the distribution of the creation of the world over certain days, before days existed: for, as the heaven was not yet created, nor the foundation of the earth yet laid, nor the sun yet revolving, how could there be days?" Now, what difference is there between these words and the following: "Moreover, taking and looking at these things from the beginning, would it not be absurd in the first and greatest God to issue the command, Let this (first thing) come into existence, and this second thing, and this (third); and after accomplishing so much on the first day, to do so much more again on the second, and third, and fourth, and fifth, and sixth?" We answered to the best of our ability this objection to God's "commanding this first, second, and third thing to be created," when we quoted the words, "He said, and it was done; He commanded, and all things stood fast;" remarking that the immediate Creator, and, as it were, very Maker of the world was the Word, the Son of God; while the Father of the Word, by commanding His own Son—the Word—to create the world, is primarily Creator. And with regard to the creation of the light upon the first day, and of the firmament upon the second, and of the gathering together of the waters that are under the heaven into their several reservoirs on the third (the earth thus causing to sprout forth those (fruits) which are under the control of nature alone, and of the (great) lights and stars upon the fourth, and of aquatic animals upon the fifth, and of land animals and man upon the sixth, we have treated to the best of our ability in our notes upon Genesis, as well as in the foregoing pages, when we found fault with those who, taking the words in their apparent signification, said that the time of six days was occupied in the creation of the world, and quoted the words: "These are the generations of the heavens and of the earth when they were created, in the day that the Lord God made the earth and the heavens." (*Contra Celsum* 6.60)

Hippolytus of Rome (ca. 170–236)

Hippolytus goes to great length to demonstrate the seven-thousand-year scheme of world history. In his intricate explanation for the reason that there are 150 Psalms, Hippolytus thinks that "the number fifty is sacred," a fact which can be seen in "the celebrated festival of Pentecost." The number *fifty* "contains seven sevens, or a Sabbath of Sabbaths," explains Hippolytus, "and above these full Sabbaths, a new beginning, in the eight, of a really new rest that remains above the Sabbaths."[17] It is curious that D. H. Kromminga would assert that "of a distinct millennial kingdom Hippolytus makes no explicit mention" and that "Hippolytus' prospectus of the coming events again looks more like the current

---

[17] Hippolytus, fragments from *Commentary on the Psalms* i.3–4; ANF (5:199–200).

amillennial scheme of the last things than like any chiliastic scheme."[18] There is no basis for such an assertion; in fact, just the opposite can easily be demonstrated: "The first appearance of our Lord in the flesh took place in Bethlehem, under Augustus, in the year 5500," remarks Hippolytus, "and He suffered in the thirty-third year." Furthermore, "6,000 years must needs be accomplished, in order that the Sabbath may come." And immediately the ancient author adds that "the Sabbath is the type and emblem of the future kingdom of the saints, when they 'shall reign with Christ.'" Hippolytus cites 2 Peter 3:8, "A day with the Lord is as a thousand years," and concludes that since "in six days God made all things, it follows that 6,000 years must be fulfilled." To further demonstrate his assertion, Hippolytus employs a unique exegesis of Revelation 17:10; he explains that the six thousand years "are not yet fulfilled, as John says: 'five are fallen; one is,' that is, the sixth; 'the other is not yet come.'"[19]

While current premillennialists would not follow him meticulously, there is sufficient evidence to conclude that, contrary to Kromminga's assertions, Hippolytus was definitely a chiliast and that every basic element of premillennial eschatology is present in his works. Clearly adducing that Christ's first advent had occurred in the Year of the World 5500, Hippolytus affirms his conviction that the six literal days of creation typify six thousand years of world history,[20] followed by a literal millennium. Hippolytus, therefore, affirms his belief in a young earth created *ex nihilo* and formed by the Lord for His own pleasure:

¶ Genesis 1:5 "And it was evening, and it was morning, one day."

---

[18] *The Millennium in the Church* (Grand Rapids: Eerdmans, 1945), 60–61; likewise, A. J. Visser wrongly concludes that Hippolytus "gives no hint as to his notion of Millennium." See A. J. Visser, "A Bird's-Eye View of Ancient Christian Eschatology," *Numen* 14, fasc. 1 (March 1967): 14. Similarly, Ned B. Stonehouse mistakenly remarks that "the most natural conclusion is that this seventh day does not signify a thousand years, but is taken spiritually as typical of the eternal rest of the righteous." See his work, *The Apocalypse in the Ancient Church* (Goes, Netherlands: Oosterbaan and Le Cointre, 1929), 104.

[19] Fragments from *Commentary on Daniel* 2.4. Later Hippolytus concludes, "From the birth of Christ, then, we must reckon the 500 years that remain to make up the 6000, and thus the end shall be" (2.6). ANF (5:179).

[20] Ibid.

¶ He did not say "night and day," but "one day," with reference to the name of the light. He did not say the "first day;" for if he had said the "first" day, he would also have had to say that the "second" day was made. But it was right to speak not of the "first day," but of "one day," in order that by saying "one," he might show that it returns on its orbit and, while it remains one, makes up the week.

¶ Genesis 1: 6 "And God said, Let there be a firmament in the midst of the water."

¶ On the first day God made what He made out of nothing. But on the other days He did not make out of nothing, but out of what He had made on the first day, by molding it according to His pleasure. (*Commentary on Genesis*, fragments on 1:5–6 in ANF 5:163)

Julius Africanus of Palestine (ca. 170–240)

Julius Africanus—traveler, historian, prolific writer, and Christian philosopher—wrote a *Chronology*, which begins with the cosmogony of Moses, continues to the advent of Christ, and then summarizes the events from Christ to Emperor Macrinus. He places the birth of Christ at AA 5500. Africanus affirms his belief in a young earth:

¶ The Jews, deriving their origin from them as descendants of Abraham, having been taught a modest mind, and one such as becomes men, together with the truth by the spirit of Moses, have handed down to us, by their extant Hebrew histories, the number of 5500 years as the period up to the advent of the Word of salvation, that was announced to the world in the time of the sway of the Caesars. (Fragment 1 of the Five Books of the *Chronology of Julius Africanus*)

Cyprian of Carthage (ca. 200–258)

Cyprian was a young-earth creationist believing the earth to be under six thousand years old. While he is generally acknowledged as a moderate millenarian,[21] Le Roy E. Froom correctly and more precisely

---

[21] E.g., even amillennial writers concede this; see J. A. Brown "The Second Advent and the Creeds of Christendom," *Bibliotheca Sacra* 24, no. 96 (October 1867): 638; and William G. T. Shedd, *A History of Christian Doctrine* (Minneapolis: Klock & Klock, 1978), 2:394.

describes him as a premillenarian.[22] Cyprian believes that the antichrist is at hand but that Christ's advent is also at hand. The Lord will return at the end of the tribulation period to destroy the adversary of the church, to judge the nations, and to reward the resurrected saints by giving them a place in His kingdom.[23] Cyprian speaks of "the first seven days in the divine arrangement containing seven thousand years."[24] He had earlier elucidated his conviction that six thousand years of human history had almost passed: "It is an ancient adversary and an old enemy with whom we wage our battle," remarks Cyprian. "Six thousand years are now nearly completed since the devil first attacked man."[25]

Archelaus of Lycopolis in Mesopotamia (ca. 300)

Archelaus describes creation as being accomplished in "the space of six days":

¶ Thus, to take an example, after God had made the world, and all things that are in it, in the space of six days, He rested on the seventh day from all His works by which statement I do not mean to affirm that He rested because He was fatigued, but that He did so as having brought to its perfection every creature which He had resolved to introduce. And yet in the sequel it, the new law, says: "My Father worketh hitherto, and I work." Does that mean, then, that He is still making heaven, or sun, or man, or animals, or trees, or any such thing? Nay; but the meaning is that when these visible objects were perfectly finished, He rested from that kind of work; while, however, He still continues to work at objects invisible with an inward mode of action, and saves men. (*The Acts of the Disputation with the Heresiarch Manes* 31)

---

[22] *The Prophetic Faith of Our Fathers* (Washington, DC: Review and Herald Publishing Association, 1950), 1:331.

[23] Cyprian's beliefs concerning the events related to the second advent are treated in David Beale, "Ante-Nicene Eschatology: An Historical and Theological Analysis" (PhD diss., Bob Jones University Seminary, 1980), 222–24.

[24] Treatise 11, *Exhortation to Martyrdom*, addressed to Fortunatus 11.

[25] Ibid., preface 2.

Peter of Alexandria (ca. 300)

Peter of Alexandria teaches an instantaneous creation from nothing:

¶ For if, according to the Word of salvation, He who made what is without, made also that which is within, He certainly, by one operation, and at the same time, made both, on that day, indeed, on which God said, "Let us make man in our image, after our likeness;" whence it is manifest that man was not formed by a conjunction of the body with a certain preexistent type. For if the earth, at the bidding of the Creator, brought forth the other animals endowed with life, much rather did the dust which God took from the earth receive a vital energy from the will and operation of God. (Fragment 6, *Of the Soul and Body*)

Victorinus of Pettau (d. ca. 300)

Setting forth his defense of a premillennial return of Christ, Victorinus, in his *Commentary on the Apocalypse of the Blessed John*, adduces that "in Judea, all the saints shall assemble together, and will worship the Lord" (comment on Rev. 1:15). This "worship" will be the millennial rest. In his treatise *On the Creation of the World*, Victorinus reflects, "As I meditate and consider in my mind concerning the creation of this world in which we are kept enclosed, even such is the rapidity of that creation." He avers that God rapidly and *ex nihilo* "produced that entire mass for the adornment of His majesty in six days; on the seventh to which He consecrated it." To him the six literal days of creation are representative of six thousand years of world history. According to this divine "sevenfold arrangement," the "true Sabbath will be in the seventh millenary of years, when Christ with His elect shall reign."

Arnobius of Sicca, North Africa (d. ca. 303)

The apologist Arnobius, in his work *Against the Heathen* 1.31, tells of third-century pagan dreamers who imagined a fallacious "big bang," whereby the universe came into existence by concourses of multi-shaped atoms joined by chance collisions in space:

¶ Of those who have given themselves to philosophizing, we have heard that some deny the existence of any divine power, that others inquire daily whether there be or not; that others construct the whole fabric of the universe by chance accidents and by random collision, and fashion it by the concourse of atoms of different shapes.

Methodius, Bishop of Olympus, then of Patara, both in the Province of Lycia in Asia Minor (ca. 260–311)

In his works *Concerning Free Will* and in fragments of extracts from his work *On Things Created*, Methodius clearly affirms his strong belief in a Genesis 1:1 creation *ex nihilo*. In the following, from his *Banquet of the Ten Virgins*, he expresses his belief in six literal twenty-four-hour days of creation and the significance of the number *six*:

> ¶ Moreover, it is evident that the creation of the world was accomplished in harmony with this number, God having made heaven and earth, and the things which are in them, in six days; the word of creative power containing the number six, in accordance with which the Trinity is the maker of bodies. For length, and breadth, and depth make up a body. And the number six is composed of triangles. (*The Banquet of the Ten Virgins*, Discourse 8.11)

Zechariah prophesied that the seven-day Feast of Tabernacles will be observed in the millennium. Methodius considers the possibility of a relationship between the septenary of days appointed for celebrating the Feast of Tabernacles and the seven-millenary schema of world history. Methodius cautions that this is as uncertain as the time of the consummation of the world. Even so, in the creation week, we might find a hint that God wonderfully completed the fabric of world history in the number *six* of the days of His creation week. Even though, at times equating the future millennium with the new heavens and new earth, Methodius thinks these events could generally begin six thousand years after creation:

> ¶ In the seventh thousand of years, resuming again immortal, we shall celebrate the great feast of true tabernacles in the new and indissoluble creation, the fruits of the earth having been gathered in, and men no longer begetting and begotten, but God resting from the works of creation. For since in six days God made the heaven and the earth, and finished the whole world, and rested on the seventh day from all His works which He had made, and

blessed the seventh day and sanctified it, so by a figure in the seventh month, when the fruits of the earth have been gathered in, we are commanded to keep the feast to the Lord, which signifies that, when this world shall be terminated at the seventh thousand years, when God shall have completed the world, He shall rejoice in us. (*The Banquet of the Ten Virgins*, Discourse 9.1)

Lactantius of Nicomedia (ca. 250–325)

Despite his flat-earth aberration, which we have discussed, Lactantius remains in full agreement with the rest of patristic literature in teaching that the earth is young—less than six thousand years. In *The Epitome of the Divine Institutes*, he concludes, "For six thousand years have not yet been completed, and when this number shall be made up, then at length all evil will be taken away, that justice may reign."[26] He believed that God created the heavens and the earth *ex nihilo*,[27] and he is in agreement with the vast majority of patristic literature in maintaining that God formed all living things in six literal twenty-four-hour days, representing a literal seven-thousand-year schema of world history. Lactantius explains:

¶ Therefore let the philosophers, who enumerate thousands of ages from the beginning of the world, know that the six thousandth year is not yet completed, and that when this number is completed the consummation must take place, and the condition of human affairs be remodeled for the better, the proof of which must first be related, that the matter itself may be plain. God completed the world and this admirable work of nature in the space of six days, as is contained in the secrets of Holy Scripture, and consecrated the seventh day, on which He had rested from His works. But this is the Sabbath-day, which in the language of the Hebrews received its name from the number, whence the seventh is the legitimate and complete number. For there are seven days, by the revolutions of which in order the circles of years are made up; and there are seven stars which do not set, and seven luminaries which are called planets, whose differing and unequal movements are believed to cause the varieties of circumstances and times. Therefore, since all the works of God were completed in six days, the world must

---

[26] *Epitome of the Divine Institutes* 80.
[27] *Divine Institutes* 1.3.

continue in its present state through six ages, that is, six thousand years. For the great day of God is limited by a circle of a thousand years, as the prophet shows, who says "In Thy sight, O Lord, a thousand years are as one day." And as God labored during those six days in creating such great works, so His religion and truth must labor during these six thousand years, while wickedness prevails and bears rule. And again, since God, having finished His works, rested the seventh day and blessed it, at the end of the six thousandth year all wickedness must be abolished from the earth, and righteousness reign for a thousand years; and there must be tranquility and rest from the labors which the world now has long endured. (*The Divine Institutes* 7.14)

Eusebius of Caesarea (ca. 260–340)

Eusebius, in his *Chronicle*, advocates a young earth. He places the birth of Christ at AA 5199 and calculates that there were 5,579 years from Adam until the fourteenth year of Emperor Valens.[28]

Hilary of Poitiers (d. ca. 367)

Setting forth a literal *ex nihilo*[29] creation, Hilary asserts that the earth will last six thousand years, and then Christ will return. Among Hilary's typological illustrations is the account of Joshua's marching the Hebrews around Jericho for six days. Each day represents a thousand years of earth history, and Rahab's deliverance portrays the millennium.[30] Like Augustine, Hilary returns often to the eternal reality of creation in the mind of God, with seminal seeds, each generating rapidly at God's command:

¶ For although, as Moses teaches, each act of creation had its proper order—the making of the firmament solid, the laying bare of the dry land, the gathering together of the sea, the ordering of the stars, the generation by the waters and the earth when they brought forth living creatures out of themselves; yet the creation of the

---

[28] Eusebius, *Chronicle* Part 2, in Migne *PL* 27.441–508, trans. from the Greek into Latin by Jerome. See Migne *PL* 27.507–508; and Eusebius, *Chronicorum*, editit, Alfred Schoene, libri duo (Berolini: Apud Weidmannos, 1866–75), 1:129–32.

[29] *On the Trinity* 4.16.

[30] *Traité des Mystères*, trans. Jean-Paul Brisson (Paris: Les Éditions du Cerf, 1947), 157ff.; cf. 139ff.

heaven and earth and other elements is not separated by the slightest interval in God's working, since their preparation had been completed in like infinity of eternity in the counsel of God. (*On the Trinity* 12.40)

John Chrysostom of Constantinople (ca. 344/354–407)

Chrysostom was of the school of Antioch in his literal approach to Scripture. He had ministered in Antioch before going to Constantinople, and people thronged to his churches. Most of his homilies reveal a straightforward and practical approach to preaching. These sermons include his teaching that the creation was *ex nihilo* in a literal twenty-four-hour, six-day week. Especially helpful are the following: *Homilies on Genesis 1–17*;[31] *Homilies on John* (Homily 5: John 1:3); *Homilies on Romans* (Homily 3: Rom. 1:18); *Homilies on First Corinthians* (Homily 17: 1 Cor. 6:12); and *Homilies on Hebrews* (Homily 22: Heb. 11:3–4).

In this sample from one of Chrysostom's sermons, the preacher describes the universe of Genesis 1:1 as created unformed, in a moment, and out of nothing. His portrait in words could almost suggest that the earth is suspended in space by this omnipotent God who is incomprehensible though not unknowable by faith:

¶ For with God nothing is difficult: but as the painter who has made one likeness will make ten thousand with ease, so also with God it is easy to make worlds without number and end. Rather, as it is easy for you to conceive a city and worlds without bound, so unto God is it easy to make them; or rather again it is easier by far. For thou consumest time, brief though it be, in thy conception; but God not even this, but as much as stones are heavier than any of the lightest things, yea even than our minds; so much is our mind surpassed by the rapidity of God's work of creation. Do you marvel at His power on the earth? Think again how the heaven was made, not yet being; how the innumerable stars, how the sun, how the moon; and all these things not yet being. Again, tell me

---

[31] John Chrysostom, *Homilies on Genesis 1–17*, trans. Robert C. Hill, in vol. 74 of *The Fathers of the Church*, ed. Thomas P. Halton (Washington, DC: Catholic University of America Press, 1986).

how after they were made they stood fast, and upon what? What foundation have they? and what the earth? What comes next to the earth? and again, what after that which came next to the earth? Do you see into what an eddy the eye of your mind is plunged, unless you quickly take refuge in faith and the incomprehensible power of the Maker? (*On First Corinthians Homily* 17.3, 1 Cor. 6:12, in NPNF 1 [12:98])

Ephrem the Syrian (306–73)

Ephrem, in his *Commentary on Genesis*, clearly affirms a Genesis 1:1 creation *ex nihilo*, six literal twenty-four-hour days of formation, and a young earth. His only aberration is his unique position among patristic authors in claiming that it was a wind rather than the Spirit of God hovering over the face of the waters in Genesis 1:2. Not surprisingly, in his hymns, Ephrem is far more poetic and less literal.

Cyril of Jerusalem (315–86)

Cyril, in his *Catechetical Lectures* (11–12), sets forth the things that one must believe in order to remain a member of his church. These include belief in a literal creation account in Genesis.

Athanasius of Alexandria (ca. 298–373)

Against pagan philosophies, Athanasius, in the first citation below, defends the Genesis 1:1 creation as *ex nihilo*. He not only appeals to the biblical record, but also to the *Shepherd* of Hermas, who had set forth the earliest extra-biblical defense of *ex nihilo* creation. In the second citation, Athanasius describes the six days of creation as literal days:

¶ They vainly speculate. But the godly teaching and the faith according to Christ brands their foolish language as godlessness. For it knows that it was not spontaneously, because forethought is not absent; nor of existing matter, because God is not weak; but that out of nothing, and without its having any previous existence, God made the universe to exist through His word, as He says firstly through Moses: "In the beginning God created the heaven and the earth;" secondly, in the most edifying book of the *Shepherd*, "First of all believe that God is one, which created and framed all things, and made them to exist out of nothing." (*On the Incarnation of the Word* 3.1)

¶ And all the visible creation was made in six days—in the first, the light which He called day; in the second the firmament; in the third, gathering together the waters, He bared the dry land, and brought out the various fruits that are in it; and in the fourth, He made the sun and the moon and all the host of the stars; and on the fifth, He created the race of living things in the sea, and of birds in the air; and on the sixth, He made the quadrupeds on the earth, and at length man. (*Against the Arians Discourse* 2.16.19)

Basil of Caesarea (ca. 329–79)

One of the most valuable patristic works on creation is Basil's *Hexaemeron* (ἑξαήμερος, from ἕξ, "six" + ἡμέρα, "day"), a series of nine sermons on the six days of creation. His focus is on Genesis 1:1–2:3.[32] Basil affirms the Mosaic authorship of Genesis and clearly avers that the creation account of Genesis 1:1–2 is *ex nihilo*, followed by six literal twenty-four-hour days of formation. Each part of creation has a divine purpose. Basil speaks at times of the conceptual or spiritual world that existed only in the mind of God from eternity, but his overall focus is on the literal record. Basil's sermons are full of practical application as he stands convinced that creation's marvelous design constantly displays God's wisdom, power, gentle care, and judgment. Here are sample readings:

¶ Genesis 1:5 *And God called the light Day and the darkness He called Night.* Since the birth of the sun, the light that it diffuses in the air, when shining on our hemisphere, is day; and the shadow produced by its disappearance is night. But at that time it was not after the movement of the sun, but following this primitive light spread abroad in the air or withdrawn in a measure determined by God, that day came and was followed by night.

---

[32] Basil's brother, Gregory of Nyssa, would write a defense of the *Hexaemeron* and include an extended coverage to the end of Genesis 2. Its title is *Explicatio Apologetica in Hexaemeron*, and at present there is no published translation. Gregory repeats significant parts of it, however, in his treatise, *De Opificio Hominis* (*On the Creation of Man*), which is addressed to his other brother, Peter, who had requested it.

¶ *And the evening and the morning were the first day.* Evening is then the boundary common to day and night; and in the same way morning constitutes the approach of night to day. It was to give day the privileges of seniority that Scripture put the end of the first day before that of the first night, because night follows day: for, before the creation of light, the world was not in night, but in darkness. It is the opposite of day which was called night, and it did not receive its name until after day. Thus were created the evening and the morning. Scripture means the space of a day and a night, and afterwards no more says day and night, but calls them both under the name of the more important: a custom which you will find throughout Scripture. Everywhere the measure of time is counted by days, without mention of nights. "The days of our years," says the Psalmist [90:10]. "Few and evil have the days of the years of my life been," [Gen. 47:9] said Jacob, and elsewhere "all the days of my life" [Ps. 23:6]. Thus under the form of history the law is laid down for what is to follow.

¶ *And the evening and the morning were one day.* Why does Scripture say "one day" not "first day"? Before speaking to us of the second, the third, and the fourth days, would it not have been more natural to call that one the first which began the series? If it therefore says "one day," it is from a wish to determine the measure of day and night, and to combine the time that they contain. Now twenty-four hours fill up the space of one day—we mean of a day and of a night; and if, at the time of the solstices, they have not both an equal length, the time marked by Scripture does not the less circumscribe their duration. It is as though it said: twenty-four hours measure the space of a day, or that, in reality a day is the time that the heavens starting from one point take to return there. Thus, every time that, in the revolution of the sun, evening and morning occupy the world, their periodical succession never exceeds the space of one day.

¶ But must we believe in a mysterious reason for this? God who made the nature of time measured it out and determined it by intervals of days; and, wishing to give it a week as a measure, he ordered the week to revolve from period to period upon itself, to count the movement of time, forming the week of one day revolving seven times upon itself: a proper circle begins and ends with itself. Such is also the character of eternity, to revolve upon itself and to end nowhere. If then the beginning of time is called "one day" rather than "the first day," it is because Scripture wishes to establish its relationship with eternity. It was, in reality, fit and natural to call "one" the day whose character is to be one wholly separated and isolated from all the others. If Scripture speaks to us of many ages, saying everywhere, "age of age, and ages of ages," we do not see it enumerate them as first, second, and third. It follows that we are hereby shown not so much limits, ends and succession of ages, as distinctions between various states and modes of action. "The day of the Lord," Scripture says, "is great and very terrible," and elsewhere "Woe unto you that desire the day of the Lord: to what end is it for you? The day of the Lord is darkness and not light." A day of darkness for those who are worthy of darkness. No; this day without evening, without succession and without end is not unknown to Scripture, and it is the day that the Psalmist calls the eighth day, because it is outside this time of weeks. Thus whether you call it day, or whether you call it eternity, you express the same idea. Give this state the name of day; there are not several, but only one. If you call it eternity still it is unique and not manifold. Thus it is in order that you may carry your thoughts forward towards a future life, that Scripture marks by the word "one" the day which is the type of eternity, the first fruits of days, the contemporary of light, the holy Lord's Day honored by the Resurrection of our Lord. "*And the evening and the morning were one day.*" (*The Hexaemeron* Homily 2.8)

In the following, Basil delights in reminding his readers that God dried the waters from the earth and adorned the planet with life and order before He made the sun. Yet men have worshiped the sun rather than its maker. "At the same time, lest we should attribute the drying of the earth to the sun, the Creator shows it to us dried before the creation of the sun" (*The Hexaemeron* Homily 4.5).

❡ Some consider the sun as the source of all productiveness on the earth. It is, they say, the action of the sun's heat which attracts the vital force from the centre of the earth to the surface. The reason why the adornment of the earth was before the sun is the following: that those who worship the sun, as the source of life, may renounce their error. If they be well persuaded that the earth was adorned before the genesis of the sun, they will retract their unbounded admiration for it, because they see grass and plants vegetate before it rose. (*The Hexaemeron* Homily 5.1)

¶ "Let the earth bring forth grass." In a moment earth began by germination to obey the laws of the Creator, completed every stage of growth, and brought germs to perfection. The meadows were covered with deep grass, the fertile plains quivered with harvests, and the movement of the corn was like the waving of the sea. Every plant, every herb, the smallest shrub, the least vegetable, arose from the earth in all its luxuriance. (*The Hexaemeron* Homily 5.5)

¶ Heaven and earth were the first; after them was created light; the day had been distinguished from the night, then had appeared the firmament and the dry element. The water had been gathered into the reservoir assigned to it, the earth displayed its productions, it had caused many kinds of herbs to germinate and it was adorned with all kinds of plants. However, the sun and the moon did not yet exist, in order that those who live in ignorance of God may not consider the sun as the origin and the father of light, or as the maker of all that grows out of the earth. That is why there was a fourth day, and then God said: "Let there be lights in the firmament of the heaven." (*The Hexaemeron* Homily 6.2)

After carefully studying the doctrines and hermeneutics of Origen of Alexandria and even embracing significant features, Basil clearly rejects Origen's allegorizing of the Genesis account of creation:

¶ I know the laws of allegory, though less by myself than from the works of others. There are those truly, who do not admit the common sense of the Scriptures, for whom water is not water, but some other nature, who see in a plant, in a fish, what their fancy wishes, who change the nature of reptiles and of wild beasts to suit their allegories, like the interpreters of dreams who explain visions in sleep to make them serve their own ends. For me grass is grass; plant, fish, wild beast, domestic animal, I take all in the literal sense. "For I am not ashamed of the gospel" [Rom. 1:16*a*]. (*The Hexaemeron* Homily 9.1)[33]

Gregory of Nazianzus (ca. 326–90)

Gregory speaks often of the conceptual, or intellectual, world of eternity. He longs to see the renewal of this "second" or present world to its pristine condition. He frequently marvels at the unique creation of the first man. Having instantly spoken other things into

---

[33] For additional criticism of creation allegory, see *The Hexaemeron* Homily 3.9.

existence, God made Adam in a special way. God lovingly formed a single human being into His image and breathed into his nostrils His own breath. Gregory then portrays the whole physical world as being like a wonderfully designed lute. Everything about the lute speaks to the beholder of an unseen lute-maker and lute-player. In like manner, the earth reminds rational creatures of the true God who designed, created, and continues to work with His masterpiece:

¶ Now our very eyes and the Law of Nature teach us that God exists and that He is the Efficient and Maintaining Cause of all things: our eyes, because they fall on visible objects, and see them in beautiful stability and progress, immovably moving and revolving if I may so say; natural Law, because through these visible things and their order, it reasons back to their Author. For how could this Universe have come into being or been put together, unless God had called it into existence, and held it together? For every one who sees a beautifully made lute, and considers the skill with which it has been fitted together and arranged, or who hears its melody, would think of none but the lute-maker, or the lute-player, and would recur to him in mind, though he might not know him by sight. And thus to us also is manifested Him who made and moves and preserves all created things, even though He is not comprehended by the mind. And very wanting in sense is he who will not willingly go thus far in following natural proofs. (*The Second Theological Oration* 28.6)

Sulpitius (Sulpicius) Severus of Aquitania (ca. 363–420)

Sulpitius was a Latin historian from Aquitania, in present-day southwest France. He was a contemporary of Augustine, and his major literary work is a *Chronicle or Sacred History* (*Chronicorum Libri duo or Historia Sacra*), written around 403. His chronicle begins with Adam and Eve and ends with events during his own lifetime. Following the longer Septuagint dates for the patriarchal period, Sulpitius still believed that the earth was fewer than six thousand years old:

¶ The world was created by God nearly six thousand years ago, as we shall set forth in the course of this book; although those who have entered upon and published a calculation of the dates, but little agree among themselves. As, however, this disagreement is due either to the will of God or to the fault of antiquity, it ought not to be a matter of censure. After the formation of the world man was created, the male being named Adam, and the female Eve. (*The Sacred History* 1.2)

Ambrose of Milan (ca. 339–97)

Ambrose preached and published nine homilies, called *The Hexaemeron*, on the six days of creation. He clearly affirms belief in creation *ex nihilo* [34] and draws upon the work of Basil of Caesarea, teaching six literal twenty-four-hour days.

Conclusion

Thus far in our study, there is no evidence that any patristic writer ever denies God's creation of the earth *ex nihilo*. Not one church father denies a young earth, including the two who hold to allegorical days—Clement and Origen of Alexandria. In addition, not a single church father denies the universality of the flood of Noah's day. When the Fathers speak of the extent of the flood, they clearly and even enthusiastically describe it as global.

Select Bibliography for Further Reading

Ambrose. *Hexaemeron, Paradise, and Cain and Abel.* Translated by John J. Savage. Vol. 42 in the series, *The Fathers of the Church*, edited by Roy Joseph Deferrari, et al. New York: Fathers of the Church, 1961.

Chadwick, Henry. *Early Christian Thought and the Classical Tradition: Studies in Justin, Clement, and Origen.* Oxford: Oxford University Press, 1966.

Chrysostom, John. *Homilies on Genesis 1–17.* Translated by Robert C. Hill. Vol. 74 of *The Fathers of the Church*, edited by Thomas P. Halton. Washington, DC: Catholic University of America Press, 1986.

Dembski, William A., Wayne J. Downs, and Justin B. A. Frederick, eds. *The Patristic Understanding of Creation: An Anthology of Writings from the Church Fathers on Creation and Design.* Riesel, TX: Erasmus Press, 2008.

Eusebius of Caesarea. *Chronicorum.* Editit by Alfred Schoene. Libri duo. Berolini, Germania: Apud Weidmannos, 1866–75.

---

[34] Ambrose, *Hexaemeron*, First Homily 1.16, trans. John J. Savage, in vol. 42 of *The Fathers of the Church* (New York: Fathers of the Church, 1961), 15–16. See also Ambrose, *On Belief in the Resurrection* 2.64 in *The Two Books on the Decease of his Brother Satyrus*.

Lactantius, Lucius Coelius Firmianus. *Divinarum Institutionum*. Basileae: Andream Cratan Drum, 1532.

Lewis, Jack P. "Noah and the Flood: In Jewish, Christian, and Muslim Tradition." *The Biblical Archaeologist* 47, no. 4 (December 1984): 224–39.

———. *A Study of the Interpretation of Noah and the Flood in Jewish and Christian Literature*. 1968. Reprint, Leiden: E. J. Brill, 1978.

Pelikan, Jaroslav. "Creation and Causality in the History of Christian Thought." *The Journal of Religion* 40, no. 4 (October 1960): 246–55.

Robbins, Frank Egleston, *The Hexaemeral Literature: A Study of Greek and Latin Commentaries on Genesis*. Chicago: University of Chicago Press, 1912.

Smulders, Pieter Frans. *Hilary of Poitiers' Preface to His Opus Historicum: Translation and Commentary*. Leiden: E. J. Brill, 1995.

Theophilus of Antioch. *Ad Autolycum*. Translated by Robert M. Grant. Oxford: Clarendon Press, 1970.

Van Winden, J. C. M. "In the Beginning: Some Observations on the Patristic Interpretation of Genesis 1:1." *Vigiliae Christianae* 17, no. 2 (June 1963): 105–21.

Wolfson, Harry A. "Patristic Arguments against the Eternity of the World." *The Harvard Theological Review* 59, no. 4 (October 1966): 351–67.

Appendix 4

The Doctrine of Creation: Augustine to the Modern Era

While advocates of almost every theory concerning origins have claimed Augustine for support, one of the most common interpretations of his view goes something like this: God created all things literally, completely, simultaneously, and instantaneously—in less than a nanosecond—and the six days are an allegorical story of what happened in that instant. While much of that statement is indeed what the bishop believed, his concepts are usually not anywhere near that simple or literal. Since Augustine's full and complex view unfolds in segments, we will chronologically set forth his key statements and consider not only his overall theory, but also his philosophical background, his hermeneutical procedures, and his far-reaching influence. For proper comprehension, as we begin our journey, it will be helpful to have a copy of the book of Genesis close at hand.

Augustine was never satisfied with his two earliest attempts at explaining the creation account: *On Genesis: A Refutation of the Manichees* (written ca. 388–89) and *Unfinished Literal Commentary on Genesis* (written ca. 393–95). He is far more successful in the last three books (11–13) of his *Confessions* (written ca. 397–401), which constitute a virtual commentary on Genesis 1. Immediately following the completion of his *Confessions*, he focused on what became his major and best work on Genesis, and he titled it *The Literal Meaning of Genesis* (written ca. 400–15).

In that book, however, Augustine does not present the literal meaning of Genesis, at least, not in the usual sense of the term. To

461

him the literal meaning is whatever he thinks God intended to convey. Also, Augustine's approach is a great departure from all that he had read, learned, and taught in some of the highest caliber classical schools of his day. The normal literary style of the day was allegorical, fanciful, and often mythical. Authors expected their readers to interpret their literature to their own individual fancy. Beyond nonliteral methods, there were no consistent standards of biblical hermeneutics, not even in the Jewish commentaries. By his definition, Augustine considered himself as having presented the literal meaning as much as possible. The title that he gave to his book was not intended to deceive the reader. In fact, his exegesis seemed to him more painstakingly literal (in his sense of the term) than any biblical exposition he had ever seen.

Augustine's initial purpose had been "to talk about the Scriptures according to their proper meaning of what actually happened, not according to riddling, enigmatic reference to future events." He soon decides, however, that God could not have been restricted to time, as we know it, during the days of creation.[1] He assumes of the creation days that "no Christian will have the nerve to say that they should not be taken in a figurative sense."[2] Finally, he crafts his own sentiment in the form of a question, as he rhetorically wonders of Genesis 1:1, "What is meant, apart from its allegorical significance, by 'In the beginning God made heaven and earth?'"[3]

Throughout his coverage of the creation days, Augustine agonizes in speculation over imagined epistemological and figurative meanings of numerous words in the biblical text. He utilizes an elaborate numerological theory on numbers, especially the number *six*, and he seems perplexed at some of his own minutiae. In his *Retractions*,

---

[1] Augustine, *Literal Meaning of Genesis* 1.34, trans. Edmond Hill, ed. John E. Rotelle, I/13 of *The Works of Saint Augustine* (Hyde Park, NY: New City Press, 2002). For another good translation, see *Literal Meaning of Genesis*, vol. 1, books 1–6, trans. John Hammond Taylor, vol. 41 of *Ancient Christian Writers*, ed. Johannes Quasten, et al. (New York: Paulist Press, 1982); and *Literal Meaning of Genesis*, vol. 2, books 7–12, trans. John Hammond Taylor, vol. 42 of *Ancient Christian Writers*, ed. Johannes Quasten, et al. (New York: Newman Press, 1982). Except where indicated otherwise, references to *The Literal Meaning of Genesis* are from Edmond Hill's translation.

[2] *Literal Meaning of Genesis* 1.1.

[3] Ibid., 1.2.

written at the end of his life, he includes none of that, but he does describe his book, on the *Literal Meaning of Genesis*: "In this work, many questions have been asked rather than solved, and of those which have been solved, fewer have been answered."[4]

At the start of *Literal Meaning of Genesis*, over which he labored for more than fourteen years, Augustine is totally baffled about how to find a suitable arrangement for the first two chapters of the Bible. He notices, for instance, that Genesis 2:2 says that God completed His creative work and rested, yet the passage continues recording more creative work. Genesis 2:5 records that there were as yet no plants in the earth, even though Genesis 1:12 had said that the earth brought forth all kinds of vegetation. Genesis 2:7, 21–22 records the creation of Adam and Eve, even though they had been created in Genesis 1:26–27. Determined at least to avoid a state of nonplus, Augustine decides to unravel his dilemma by dividing Genesis 1 and 2 into two separate creation accounts: 1:1–2:3 and 2:4–25. A key to understanding his exegesis is this: even though Augustine must present his two accounts separately, one at a time, they are inseparably related. The context of the first account is outside of time, and the context of the second is diachronic. *Literal Meaning of Genesis* contains twelve books, the first four of which unfold Augustine's exegesis of the first creation account.

In this first account (1:1–2:3), which unfolds completely outside of space and time, God simultaneously and instantaneously brings all things into a conceptually "real" existence *in God*. Such is the essence of the "six days" of the first creation and the "seventh day" on which God ceased from the work. That was not literal. In fact everything occurred in the eternal Mind. Time did not exist. The word *day* is used only as an allegorical tool for describing a creation that was nonliteral, invisible "reality," existing only in God (as God conceived it). It was ultimate reality, as Plato would insist. The allegorical story begins in Genesis 1:1 with "In the beginning God created the heaven and the earth." It ends in 2:3 with the work completed and God blessing the seventh day.

---

[4] Augustine, *The Retractions* [2.50], trans. Mary Inez Bogan, vol. 60 of *The Fathers of the Church*, ed. Roy Joseph Deferrari, et al. (Washington, DC: Catholic University of America Press, 1968), 169.

Book 5 of *Literal Meaning of Genesis* begins Augustine's exegesis of the second creation account, which starts with Genesis 2:4, "These are the generations of the heavens and of the earth when they were created, in the day that the Lord God made the earth and the heavens." In that verse, light and space are created, as God suddenly makes the heavens—sun, moon, and stars—and earth *ex nihilo* to become physical realities. In that moment light instantly *appears* on earth as a corporeal reality. (Einstein adds that even if the original light had *traveled* to earth, it still could not be measured in terms of light years.)[5] In that moment life begins corporeally to exist, without individual development, [6] but within divine laws or *causales*, called "seminal designs, or reasons" (*rationes seminales*), analogous to the seeds of a tree,[7] and in sync with a predetermined schedule[8] to become "formed and distinguished from one another,"[9] in God's time.

Everything that we just read about Genesis 2:4 occurred in "one day." That was the only day that God made, and it was made outside of time. It was the second creation moment. *Augustine's two creation moments are inseparable.* The first creation moment had been revealed in a step-by-step seven-day allegorical story of seven separate and interrelated stories, all of which had occurred conceptually, simultaneously, and instantly—outside of space and time. Now, in the second creation moment, God turns it all—simultaneously and instantly—into physical matter, occupying real space, in one day— "in *the day* that the Lord God made the earth and the heavens." Augustine explains, "This is the one and only day that God made, and it was by repetition of that day that the second and third and the

---

[5] Einstein believed that distance and time-durations are relative to velocity. An instant appearance of light traveling from any distance in one direction is not contrary to science. On the basis of Einstein's theory of relativity, it is arguable that only reflected (two-way) light is constantly measurable. The article listed here is not about Augustine or patrology, but it well illustrates the concept that when God created light it instantly appeared on earth: Jason Lisle, "Distant Starlight—the Anisotropic Synchrony Convention," *Answers* 6, no. 1 (January–March 2011): 68–71, a publication of Answers in Genesis, which produces high-quality materials. Lisle holds a PhD in astrophysics from the University of Colorado at Boulder.

[6] *Literal Meaning of Genesis* 5.8; 5.13; and 6.25.

[7] *City of God* 11.6 and *Literal Meaning of Genesis* 5.33.

[8] *Literal Meaning of Genesis* 1.17; 1.34; 4.33; 4.51; 6.11; and 6.18.

[9] Ibid., 5.1.

rest were made, up to the seventh day."[10] Like the first creation moment, this second "moment" occurs outside of time!

Believing that time began with movement, Augustine does not name the movement of light as the beginning of time, which adumbrates that he thought of light as instantly appearing in space rather than traveling through space.[11] He suggests that the clock (course) of time may have begun with the movement of the springs (mist) beginning to come up from out of the earth in Genesis 2:6,[12] at which time the context of the biblical narrative becomes diachronic. Now, living things begin to spring from their elemental and inchoative state into independent existences.[13] Unlike the instant of the first creation moment, this one will unfold "over intervals of time"[14] as the species develop, each in its own time—vegetation, birds, fish, animals—even Adam who would come "from mud," and Eve, from his "rib."

Even though Adam was designed spiritually to develop into God's image, his body would develop no differently from the bodies of the animals. Indeed, the very idea of God's actually molding a man with His hands in Genesis 2:7 is "an excessively childish notion."[15] The description of Adam naming the animals probably has a mystical but as yet unknown significance.[16] Similarly, God is not literally forming Eve with His hands from Adam's rib in Genesis 2:21–22. Augustine does not explain, but he leaves the reader wondering—did God plant a unique seed principle in Adam's flesh for this one-of-a-kind creation? Like Origen, Augustine can be highly speculative in his books and mundanely practical in his pulpit. Thus, for him, the mystery of Adam's rib seems homiletically applicable while mystically dormant for some future illumination.[17] Adam's body "most

---

10 Ibid., 5.3.
11 See footnote 713 in Lisle, "Distant Starlight."
12 *Literal Meaning of Genesis* 5.20. See also *Confessions* 11.10–31.
13 *Literal Meaning of Genesis* 6.8–11, 19.
14 Ibid., 5.20 and 6.4.
15 Ibid., 6.20–23.
16 Ibid., 9.20–22.
17 Ibid., 9.23.

likely" formed directly into "perfect manhood."[18] In fact, all original species developed directly into various stages of maturity, according to God's will for each one of them. Augustine believes that the souls of Adam and Eve were created in the first creation moment, with each one ready "to be sent into the body" at its proper time by God's command. "At a signal from God," the souls of Adam and Eve came to them at the proper moment of bodily development.[19]

Augustine's *Literal Meaning of Genesis* has a chapter called, "God created all things simultaneously," in which he summarizes the two creation moments—one conceptual, the other physical. Unwrapped here is the key to his cosmogonal thinking. Since God is eternally *omniscient*, the first creation moment is outside of time and simultaneous—not appearing in "stages" or "steps." Since God is eternally *omnipotent*, the second creation moment is also outside of time and simultaneous—the mass of matter instantly appearing in space, initiating the motion of time, with individual development beginning to spring out at intervals—according to causal seeds and embedded laws:

> The motion we now see in creatures, measured by the lapse of time, as each one fulfills its proper function, comes to creatures from those causal reasons [*rationes seminales*] implanted in them, which God scattered as seeds at the moment of creation when *He spoke and they were made, He commanded and they created.* . . . Time brings about development of these creatures according to the laws of their numbers, but there was no passage of time when they received these laws at creation.[20]

Augustine does not tell us precisely how long it might have taken for man and other kinds of life to appear,[21] but being a divinely predetermined work, the initial process was likely far shorter

---

[18] Ibid., 6.29; this is Augustine's conclusion to a discussion he initiated in 6.23–25.

[19] Ibid., 7.35–38. Thomas Aquinas understood Augustine as teaching that God created Adam's animal soul at the same time that He created the angels in Gen. 1:1 and that Adam received his intellectual soul at the physical formation of his body. See Thomas Aquinas, *Summa Theologica*, Prima Pars, Question 91 (The Production of the First Man's Body), Article 4, reply to objection 5.

[20] *Literal Meaning of Genesis* 4.33.51–52 in John Hammond Taylor's translation; in Edmund Hill's translation, the reference would be cited as 4.51–52.

[21] Ibid., 5.23.

in time than one might imagine. Indeed, Augustine's concept of initial development is clearly not in terms of aeons, or billions, or thousands—perhaps not even hundreds of years. In fact, Augustine's description of Adam's "coming from the slime" seems to be a rapid "springing forth," like a spontaneous generation. This was not a new theory!

There were already two church fathers, Origen of Alexandria and Basil of Caesarea, who had utilized in their writings the phenomenon of the spontaneous generation of creatures such as bees, flies, and wasps. Such was generally accepted by secular writers such as Pliny the Elder (1st c. AD) and Ovid (late 1st. c. BC–early 1st c. AD).[22] Origen explains his conviction that "from the beginning of the world," such "laws were established" that "at the present time a snake should be formed out of a dead man, growing . . . out of the marrow of the back, and that a bee should spring out of an ox, and a wasp from a horse, and a beetle from an ass, and, generally, worms from the most of bodies."[23] While Origen never connects spontaneous generation directly with creation, Basil does take it to that level. Basil equates ongoing spontaneous generation with God's *modus operandi* in the original creation of the Genesis record:

> The command was given, and immediately the rivers and lakes becoming fruitful brought forth their natural broods; the sea travailed with all kinds of swimming creatures; not even in mud and marshes did the water remain idle; it took its part in creation. Everywhere from its ebullition frogs, gnats and flies came forth. For that which we see today is the sign of the past. (*The Hexaemeron* Homily 7.1)[24]

---

[22] Pliny the Elder, in his *Natural History* 10.86, speaks of snakes spontaneously generating from the spinal marrow of a human corpse. Ovid, in his *Metamorphoses*, speaks of phenomena such as sexless bees spontaneously generating from the carcasses of bulls. Such was seen as common knowledge. See Pliny the Elder, *The Natural History*, trans. John Bostock and Henry Thomas Riley (London: Taylor and Francis, 1855); and Ovid, *The Metamorphoses*, trans. Henry T. M. A. Riley (London: George Bell and Sons, 1898).

[23] Origen, *Against Celsus* 4.57. Except where otherwise noted, patristic citations and references are from ANF, NPNF 1, and NPNF 2.

[24] Cf. *Hexaemeron* Homily 9.2. Some of Augustine's material that sounds most unique is actually not original with him. For example, Basil's younger brother, Gregory of Nyssa, wrote a defense of his *Hexaemeron* in which, prior to Augustine, he speaks of God's instantaneously creating all things with seminal seeds. For the

It is true that Augustine was not able to read the Greek fathers very well in the original language, at least not until much later in life. Yet, Augustine had access to Latin translations of two Greek fathers—Origen and Basil. Rufinus had translated Origen's works, even his *Homilies on Genesis* (*In Genesim Homilae*), and Eustathius had translated Basil's *Hexaemeron*. It is virtually certain that Augustine had read them. His library was enormous, and he was an avid reader, especially of anything pertaining to the creation account. Augustine embraced and advanced the thought of Origen and Basil. To him, "some animals are born out of corruption;" some, "like bees, have no sex."[25] The *rationes seminales* of plants or animals that spring from dead corpses or vegetation were timed by "the immutable creator" to bring them forth after sin and death entered.[26] Still, when asked how huge beasts, "such as wolves and animals of that kind," could have been found on remote islands soon after the universal flood of Noah's day, Augustine explains that these animals came quickly into existence by a spontaneous generation from the earth, just as during the rapid unfolding of the original creation: they "were produced out of the earth *as at their first creation*, when God said, 'Let the earth bring forth the living creature.'"[27] Augustine is clearly equating this sort of spontaneous generation with God's mode of operation in the rapid appearance of living species in the Genesis account. This is in perfect accordance with Augustine's idea of timed *rationes seminales*, "predispositions," implanted from the beginning. But how could a fully-formed adult suddenly come forth from a "seed-principle" without first going through a normal growth process? Augustine had thought about that, and he has his answer. Seed-principles have *double* potentiality: (1) causing natural or gradual growth whenever the conditions in the earth are favorable, which is the normal way; and (2) providing for miraculous instant production into maturity whenever God wishes to intervene in such a way, as indeed He did in

---

Greek text see Gregorius Nyssenus, *In Hexaemeron Explicatio Apologetica* (Migne *PG* 44.61–124). Basil's nine *Hexaemeron* homilies are in Migne *PG* 29.4ff.

[25] *City of God* 15.27.

[26] *Literal Meaning of Genesis* 3.22–23.

[27] *City of God* 16.7, italics mine. Augustine believed that the first living creatures such as creeping things, birds, etc., were produced from water (*Literal Meaning of Genesis* 3.1–3).

the original creation. So these causes have the power of providing for those rare occasions, even in the future, that call for the miraculous production of new creatures:

> We must conclude, then, that these reasons were created to exercise their causality in either one way or the other: by providing for the ordinary development of new creatures in appropriate periods of time, or by providing for the rare occurrence of a miraculous production of a creature, in accordance with what God wills as proper for the occasion.[28]

Augustine explains that God ordained the use of seed-principles even in rapid and miraculous production of life; after all, Adam came forth instantly even from dust or natural elements of the earth. In other words, the *rationes seminales* are intrinsically ready for imminent fast-forward action at God's intervention and command. Thus, Adam and all living creatures sprang forth quickly at God's command in God's timing.

Any assumption, therefore, that these church fathers held to modern evolutionary views is totally unwarranted. Not only was creation naturally spontaneous, it was supernaturally spontaneous— truly a miraculous event. The church fathers sometimes err but never are they even remotely Darwinian. Nor did the pagan authors, such as Pliny the Elder and Ovid, display any concepts resembling modern evolution. Instead, they depict popular pagan gods making and giving things good and things bad. Even when the pagan philosophers such as Empedocles (5th c. BC) or Aristotle (4th c. BC) on rare occasions express some vague *idea* of gradualism, they never once express any *theory* of evolution. In fact, Aristotle defended the earth's eternality, but he expressed no evolutionary theory of gradualism. As to the church fathers, not one denies creation *ex nihilo*, and their cosmogony consistently requires a young earth.

Augustine believed the span of recorded human history to be fewer than six thousand years. Like Eusebius, Augustine is aware of the Hebrew text, but he generally follows the chronology of the Septuagint for the patriarchal ages. The LXX chronology begins with Adam at the age of 130 begetting his son Seth (Genesis 5). Augustine

---

[28] *Literal Meaning of Genesis* 6.14.25 in John Hammond Taylor's translation; in Edmund Hill's translation, the reference would be cited as 6.25.

states that he is following the LXX reckoning, and he correctly observes that LXX deviations from the Hebrew texts had added 586 years to the span of time from the birth of Seth to the flood.[29] The number of years that had transpired before the flood was, "according to our copies of the Scripture, 2262 years,[30] and according to the Hebrew text, 1656 years."[31]

Such a concept allows no place for billions of years. Augustine's *City of God* (written ca. 412–27) is a theological philosophy of history. In the conclusion of a section containing a sharp polemic against pantheism and other pagan philosophies that taught the eternality of matter, Augustine argues that the earth was divinely created with a specific "beginning," a minute guidance, and a predetermined time clock for everything occurring within it. He believes that a creation so designed and so providentially governed from a specific beginning to a predetermined completion must be young in comparison with pagan concepts of countless ages or even "many thousands" of years of chance and chaos. He concludes:

¶ They are deceived, too, by those highly mendacious documents which profess to give the history of many thousand years, though, reckoning by the sacred writings, we find that not 6000 years have yet passed. (*City of God* 12.10)

¶ As to those who are always asking why man was not created during these countless ages of the infinitely extended past, and came into being so lately that, according to Scripture, less than 6000 years have elapsed since He began to be, I would reply to them regarding the creation of man, just as I replied regarding the origin of the world to those who will not believe that it is not eternal, but had a beginning, which even Plato himself most plainly declares, though some think his statement was not consistent with his real opinion. If it offends them that the time that has elapsed since the creation of man is so short, and his years so few according to our authorities, let them take this into consideration, that nothing that has a limit is long, and that all the ages of time being finite,

---

[29] C. F. Keil and F. Delitzsch, *Commentary on the Old Testament* (1865; repr., Grand Rapids: Eerdmans, 1973), 1:122.

[30] Augustine most likely made a simple copying error when he wrote "2262." He no doubt meant to write "2242," as do the other patristic writers, such as Eusebius and Jerome, who followed the LXX.

[31] *City of God* 15.20.

are very little, or indeed nothing at all, when compared to the interminable eternity. (*City of God* 12.12)

As we have now seen, while Augustine's view of creation is peculiar at times, he never approaches anything even remotely resembling Darwinian evolution. However, a process of caricaturing Augustine and other church fathers as pro-evolutionists began in 1896 with the publication of *Evolution and Dogma*, written by John Augustine Zahm, a Roman Catholic professor of Physics at the University of Notre Dame.[32] His views became especially popular among American readers with little if any knowledge of the Fathers. Zahm falsely claims there is nothing in modern evolution that is contrary to the teachings of Augustine and Aquinas, and that the fathers of the church actually contributed to the rise of the theory of evolution. Zahm and his followers falsely and arbitrarily equate any patristic use of such things as seed-principles and spontaneous generation with an embrace of evolutionary ideas. They make multiple blanket statements accompanied with no legitimate documentation. Many took them at their word.

The Roman Catholic controversy over evolution became so heated that the 1920s saw the beginning of an onslaught of works claiming Augustine as an evolutionist. The most significant of these included Henry de Dorlodot's *Darwinism and Catholic Thought* (1922),[33] E. C. Messenger's *Evolution and Theology: The Problem of Man's Origin* (1932), and Michael J. McKeough's *The Meaning of the Rationes Seminales in St. Augustine* (1926). McKeough, a Roman Catholic philosopher, makes the ludicrous claim that Augustine's notion of "the gradual appearance of living things upon the earth through the operation of natural laws and secondary causes

---

[32] John Augustine Zahm, *Evolution and Dogma* (Chicago: D. H. McBride, 1896). When Zahm's book was translated into Italian, it came under condemnation by the Congregation of the Index in Rome. This controversy immediately gave it more publicity and popularity in the United States, as documented in Zahm's biography by Ralph Weber, *Notre Dame's John Zahm* (Notre Dame, IN: University of Notre Dame, 1961).

[33] Henry de Dorlodot, *Darwinism and Catholic Thought*, trans. Ernest C. Messenger (New York: Benziger, 1922). The original title is *Le Darwinisme au point de vue de l'orthodoxie catholique* (Brussels: Lovanium, 1921). The same theme is echoed in the discussion of the controversy by E. C. Messenger, *Evolution and Theology: The Problem of Man's Origin* (New York: Macmillan, 1932).

constitutes a satisfactory philosophical basis for evolution, and merits for him the title of Father of Evolution."[34]

To the contrary, while his view of creation is sometimes novel and at times even hermeneutically absurd, Augustine stands far aloof from any naturalistic evolutionary hypotheses or old-earth theories. This is absolutely certain for at least three sound reasons. (1) Augustine holds to a young earth that was created instantly. In the second creation moment, God *suddenly* made the heaven and the earth *ex nihilo* into physical matter, with seeds of life immediately beginning to burst forth.[35] (2) There was no place for chaos or chance. Augustine insists that the God of order and design was and remains personally at work in every minute detail, even the timing, of His providential and foreordained work.[36] (3) The *rationes seminales* are incapable of producing any new "kinds," or families since, in Augustine's view, God from the beginning created every "kind" that will ever exist.[37]

In spite of modern attempts to use Augustine's nonliteral days as grounds that he held to a sort of evolutionary old-earth gradualism, such a premise cannot be sustained. Only three church fathers explicitly teach that the creative days of Genesis are allegorical: Clement and Origen of Alexandria and Augustine of Hippo. All three believe in a young earth. Clement has the earth less than six thousand years old;[38] Origen well under ten thousand years;[39] and Augustine under

---

[34] *The Meaning of the Rationes Seminales in St. Augustine* (Washington, DC: Catholic University of America Press, 1926), 109–10. Likewise, Howard J. Van Till, "Basil, Augustine, and the Doctrine of Creation's Functional Integrity," *Science and Christian Belief* 8 (1996): 21–38.

[35] E.g., *Literal Meaning of Genesis* 5.8; 5.13; and 6.25; *Confessions* 12.29.40; and his work against the Manichee Felix, *De Actis Cum Felice Manichaeo* 2.18 (Migne *PL* 42.547–48). The complete work is in Migne *PL* 42.519–52.

[36] E.g., *Literal Meaning of Genesis* 5.27–28; and *Confessions* 7.13; 12.29; 13.5. This is a recurring theme throughout Augustine's works. It flows naturally from his worship and praise to God.

[37] E.g., see *Literal Meaning of Genesis* 4.22; cf. 5.46 and 6.19. For further study on this point, I recommend Henry Woods, *Augustine and Evolution: A Study in the Saint's De Genesi ad Litteram and De Trinitate* (1924; repr., Eugene, OR: Wipf and Stock Publishers, n.d.). When Augustine speaks of "kinds" he is referring to families, not species, and likely not even genera.

[38] *Stromata* 1.21.

[39] *Contra Celsum* 1.19.

six thousand years.[40] Their hermeneutical method was dangerously wrong and continues to lead many astray in some other areas, but not one of these three allegorists was an "evolutionist." Besides, that would be an anachronistic use of the term.

For Augustine, there are basic philosophical reasons that necessitate allegorical days. He illustrates this way: matter is as the sound of the speaker's voice. Form is his spoken word. The sound of the voice is the basic material of words. The speaker does not begin with an unformed voice to create words. Matter and form then are simultaneous.[41] The creation account is written in a way that adapts to the limited capacity of angelic and human minds to comprehend eternal events in categories of space and time. Thus, when Genesis 1:2 speaks of the original creation as being "without form," it must simply mean that it was in darkness. There was no light. Otherwise, to have been "without form" would philosophically mean to have been without any sort of existence. Every reality always exists in concept![42] When Augustine speaks of "matter" and "form," he is thinking of them conceptually as existing simultaneously, although we are unable to state them simultaneously. Finite minds simply cannot understand the meaning of the Scripture unless the narrative proceeds "slowly, step by step."[43] So the Bible must be interpreted this way, for these concepts can be understood in no other way. Therefore, just "what kind of days these were it is extremely difficult, or perhaps impossible for us to conceive, and how much more to say!"[44] Louis Berkhof is correct when he says that Augustine "was evidently inclined to think God created all things in *a moment of time*, and that the thought of days was simply introduced to aid the finite intelligence."[45]

Augustine's philosophical theories are at times strikingly original, and his conclusions are often spectacularly novel. When compelled to seek more biblical support for his approach to simultaneous creation, he finally settled for an apocryphal proof text. Accepting the

---

[40] *City of God* 12.10, 12.
[41] *Literal Meaning of Genesis* 1.29.
[42] *Confessions* 12.3–6.
[43] *Literal Meaning of Genesis* 4.52 and passim.
[44] *City of God* 11.6 (written 413–26).
[45] Louis Berkhof, *Systematic Theology* (1938; repr., Grand Rapids: Eerdmans, 1972), 127.

Apocrypha as canonical,[46] Augustine utilized the Old Latin translation of the Sirach (Ecclesiasticus) 18:1 as "scripture" to support his
notion of simultaneous creation.[47] The original Hebrew text of the
Sirach (Ecclesiasticus), "The Wisdom of Jesus the Son of Sirach," had
been lost by Augustine's day. But it did exist in two translations—
Greek and Latin—with the Greek being the older. The second-
century BC Greek translation of Sirach, along with the other apocryphal books, had eventually been attached to the Septuagint (LXX)
in an effort to preserve such non-inspired, but historically valuable,
writings. The LXX rendering of Sirach (Ecclesiasticus) 18:1 is, Ὁ
ζῶν εἰς τὸν αἰῶνα ἔκτισε τὰ πάντα κοινῇ, "He who lives forever
created all things in common (κοινῇ)." This text is referring to God's
creating the whole universe with each life form "in common," that
is, within its own kind.

Augustine was restricted to the familiar Latin. He knew no
Hebrew and had but little working knowledge of Greek. The Old
Latin translation of Sirach had likely originated in North Africa during the early Christian era, hence much later than the Greek LXX,
and Augustine insisted that the Old Latin of Sirach (Ecclesiasticus)
18:1 provided the inspired support that he needed for his view of the
origin of the universe. The Old Latin has it, *Qui vivit in aeternum
creavit omnia simul*, that is, "He who lives forever created all things
simultaneously." So Augustine, for reasons he never clearly reveals,
ignores the older Greek that derives directly from the Hebrew with
God's creating "all things in common [κοινῇ]." Instead, he strangely
embraces the Latin with God creating "all things [*omnia*] simultaneously [*simul*]." While Augustine argues on the basis of *simul*, the
wider context and usage of the word in Sirach (Ecclesiasticus) 18:1
itself do not necessarily accent his point of view. The focus appears
simply to be that God alone—righteous and merciful—created the
"whole universe." This appears clear in the Revised Standard Version
for Catholics:

> He who lives forever created the *whole universe*; the Lord alone will
> be declared righteous. To none has he given power to proclaim his

---

[46] See *On Christian Doctrine* 2.8.12–13; and 2.15.22; see also *City of God*
18.42–43.

[47] E.g., see *Literal Meaning of Genesis* 5.35; 6.4; and 6.11.

works; and who can search out his mighty deeds? Who can measure his majestic power? And who can fully recount his mercies? It is not possible to diminish or increase them, nor is it possible to trace the wonders of the Lord. (vv. 1–6; italics mine)

Traditional creationists have generally agreed with Augustine that Genesis 1:1 means that God spoke all matter into existence prior to the first day. Augustine departs, though, from the traditional creationist position that God formed His created matter in six literal twenty-four-hour days. Using allegorical hermeneutics, Augustine presents the six days of the Genesis account as nonliteral narrative.

A primary reason for Augustine's perceived ambivalence in terms of "days" in the "first" creation account (1:1–2:3) is his self-imposed desire to find a place for the creation of angels. Struggling to understand how angels could have been rejoicing at the beginning of the creation (Job 38:7), he decides that the angels must have been created prior to anything else and that their origin is not recorded in the creation account. He believes that the number *six* must have a mystical significance relative to angelic contemplation of the creation week.

Augustine finds that *six* "is the first perfect number," because it is the sum of its parts. These parts, one, two, and three, when added together make six. Believing it to be inspired, Augustine becomes enamored with the apocryphal Book of Wisdom 11:20*b*, where he makes another discovery: there is a three-fold arrangement in the works of creation, according to which, God "ordered all things in measure, number and weight." Just so, the number *six* "parallels" that very "order of the works of creation" since it rises in three steps into a triangle, without the possibility of any other number being inserted: six is composed of *one* (being a sixth), *two* (being a third), and *three* (being a half).[48] The chart below depicts Augustine's threefold categorical arrangement of the "six" creative days, depicting the harmony with which God providentially ordered all things in measure, number, and weight.

---

[48] *Literal Meaning of Genesis* 4.2–14.

I	Day 1: light	Angelic enlighten-ment	Measure applies to the limits God set upon creation.
II	Day 2: firmament Day 3: earth and sea	Completion of upper universe Completion of lower universe	Number applies to the harmony of God's creation.
III	Day 4: sun, moon, & stars Day 5: water and sky life Day 6: land life	Completion of all individual things contained within the universe of heavens and earth	Weight applies to the allocation of distinctive parts of creation to specific places.

Amazingly similar to the allegory of Philo, the first-century Jew,[49] Augustine's arrangement of days, as seen above, is categorical, not chronological. Those are not literal days. Also, parallel to Plotinus's speculations on the threefold knowledge of the *nous*,[50] Augustine accordingly sets forth three types of angelic knowledge, represented by day, evening, and morning. *Day* signifies the intuitive enlightenment of angels. *Evening* typifies angelic knowledge derived from natural sense or ability, while *morning* represents angelic knowledge derived from God's visionary revelation.[51] Everything occurs simultaneously. In all of it, however, God is still sovereign and totally in control.

A primary reason for Augustine's perceived ambivalence in terms of "days" in the "second" creation moment, starting with Genesis 2:4, is his perplexity over the phrase "in the day." The verse says, "These are the generations of the heavens and of the earth when they were created, in the day that the Lord God made the earth and

---

[49] Speaking of Moses and the six creation days, Philo says, "The world was not created in time. . . . We must understand that he [Moses] is speaking not of a number of days, but that he takes six as a perfect number. Since it is the first number which is equal in its parts, in the half, and the third and sixth parts, and since it is produced by the multiplication of two unequal factors, two and three." Philo, *The First Book of the Treatise on the Allegories of the Sacred Laws, After the Work of the Six Days of Creation*, sect. 2, trans. C. D. Yonge, in *The Works of Philo Judaeus*, 2 vols. (London: Henry G. Bohn, 1854). Philo also taught that God created all things simultaneously, as seen in his work, *On the Creation of the World* 3, trans. C. D. Yonge in the same work.

[50] Plotinus, *Enneads* 5. Tractate 1.1–12.

[51] *Literal Meaning of Genesis* 4.41, 46–47.

the heavens." Even though the expression "in the day" was a normal Hebrew idiom for "at the time when,"[52] Augustine, as Philo before him, took it to mean instantaneous creation of all things. Further, Augustine saw such an allegorical approach as a key toward answering Manichaean questions that had troubled his mind since earlier years: "What was God doing before He created anything?" "Did the Creator need the aid of time to create the world?" Augustine carefully explains that all of God's thoughts and actions are eternal thoughts and actions. Creation resides in eternity prior to residing in time. Time follows creation. Time is tangent to the circle of eternity. It spins off from creation. Therefore, time begins from creation rather than creation from time. Time could not exist without creation's motion, and the creation could not move without first existing.[53] The sovereign and majestic Trinity rules all of these things eternally.

Earlier patristic writers generally express no real concern over the origin or contemplations of angels, and they evidently assumed that the Creator of time could have chosen to work within time as He continues to do since He is both immanent and transcendent. Augustine anticipates some disagreement, and he acknowledges that his view of allegorical days is a departure from traditional views.[54]

In the final three books (11–13) of Augustine's *Confessions* (written 397–401), the great bishop of Hippo makes his conviction clear that all of creation came inexplicably and directly from the sovereign and providential hand of God:

> But how didst Thou make the heaven and the earth, and what was the instrument of Thy so mighty work? For it was not as a human worker fashioning body from body, according to the fancy of his mind, in some wise able to assign a form which it perceives in itself by its inner eye. And whence should he be able to do this, hadst not Thou made that mind? And he assigns to it already existing, and as it were having a being, a form, as clay, or stone, or wood, or gold, or such like. And whence should these things be, hadst not Thou appointed them? Thou didst make for the workman his body,—Thou the mind commanding the limbs,—Thou the

---

[52] See, e.g., Num. 3:1 and 2 Sam. 22:1.
[53] *Literal Meaning of Genesis* 5.12.
[54] Ibid., 4.45.

matter whereof he makes anything,—Thou the capacity whereby he may apprehend his art, and see within what he may do without,—Thou the sense of his body, by which, as by an interpreter, he may from mind unto matter convey that which he doeth, and report to his mind what may have been done, that it within may consult the truth, presiding over itself, whether it be well done. All these things praise Thee, the Creator of all. But how dost Thou make them? How, O God, didst Thou make heaven and earth? Truly, neither in the heaven nor in the earth didst Thou make heaven and earth; nor in the air, nor in the waters, since these also belong to the heaven and the earth; nor in the whole world didst Thou make the whole world; because there was no place wherein it could be made before it was made, that it might be; nor didst Thou hold anything in Thy hand wherewith to make heaven and earth. For whence couldest Thou have what Thou hadst not made, whereof to make anything? For what is, save because Thou art? Therefore Thou didst speak and they were made, and in Thy Word Thou madest these things. (*Confessions* 11.5)

Leo I of Rome (d. 461)

¶ But what is the sun or what is the moon but elements of visible creation and material light: one of which is of greater brightness and the other of lesser light? For as it is now day time and now night time, so the Creator has constituted divers kinds of luminaries, although even before they were made there had been days without the sun and nights without the moon. (Sermon 27.5)

John of Damascus (ca. 665–749)

We saw earlier that the well-known Damascene was hesitant concerning the specific shape of the earth. To John, it could be spherical or cone shaped. It was not that important since it was not clear to him in the pages of Scripture.[55] However, he does clearly affirm his belief in the creation of the heavens and the earth *ex nihilo* and six literal twenty-four-hour days of making the earth inhabitable and filling it with living things:

---

[55] *Exposition of the Orthodox Faith* 2.10.

¶ The earth is one of the four elements, dry, cold, heavy, motionless, brought into being by God, out of nothing on the first day. *For in the beginning*, he said, *God created the heaven and the earth.* (*Exposition of the Orthodox Faith* 2.10)

¶ Our God Himself, Whom we glorify as Three in One, *created the heaven and the earth and all that they contain*, and brought all things out of nothing into being: some He made out of no pre-existing basis of matter, such as heaven, earth, air, fire, water: and the rest out of these elements that He had created, such as living creatures, plants, seeds. For these are made up of earth, and water, and air, and fire, at the bidding of the Creator. (*Exposition of the Orthodox Faith* 2.5)

¶ Fire is one of the four elements, light and with a greater tendency to ascend than the others. It has the power of burning and also of giving light, and it was made by the Creator on the first day. For the divine Scripture says, *And God said, Let there be light, and there was light.* Fire is not a different thing from what light is, as some maintain. Others again hold that this fire of the universe is above the air and call it ether. In the beginning, then, that is to say on the first day, God created light, the ornament and glory of the whole visible creation. For take away light and all things remain in undistinguishable darkness, incapable of displaying their native beauty. *And God called the light day, but the darkness He called night.* Further, darkness is not any essence, but an accident: for it is simply absence of light. The air, indeed, has not light in its essence. It was, then, this very absence of light from the air that God called darkness: and it is not the essence of air that is darkness, but the absence of light which clearly is rather an accident than an essence. And, indeed, it was not night, but day, that was first named, so that day is first and after that comes night. Night, therefore, follows day. And from the beginning of day till the next day is one complete period of day and night. For the Scripture says, *And the evening and the morning were one day.*

¶ When, therefore, in the first three days the light was poured forth and reduced at the divine command, both day and night came to pass. But on the fourth day God created the great luminary, that is, the sun, to have rule and authority over the day: for it is by it that day is made: for it is day when the sun is above the earth, and the duration of a day is the course of the sun over the earth from its rising till its setting. And He also created the lesser luminaries, that is, the moon and the stars, to have rule and authority over the night, and to give light by night. (*Exposition of the Orthodox Faith* 2.7)

Bede the Venerable (ca. 672–735)

Bede spent his life in the northeast corner of Britain. He was born in Wearmouth and moved to nearby Jarrow as a young man. The local monasteries, by continually adding manuscripts to their libraries, provided the best education, and Bede's greatest love was the Bible. From his biblical studies there emerged profound interest in multiple fields of study.[56] Best known for his *Ecclesiastical History of the English People*, which gained for him the title Father of English History, he also labored as a monk, priest, musician, scientist, and theologian. Bede wrote much in defense of advanced cosmology, and his scholarship stood among the best of his day. His appellation *Venerable* was first used at the Council of Aachen in 835—a century after his death. At the end of the nineteenth century, his name was added to the list of *doctores ecclesiae*.

His work *De Temporum Ratione* (*On the Reckoning of Time*)[57] advanced the construction of the Christian calendar, adjusted the dating of Easter, and calculated the date of the earth's creation at 3952 BC. In these literary works, the young-earth scholar popularized and standardized the use of AD (*Anno Domini*) that Dionysius Exiguus had invented in 525 for referencing the dates for the Christian era. It is possible that Bede was referring not to the birth but to the conception of Christ: *anno ab incarnatione Domine* or *anno incarnationis dominicae* ("in the year of the incarnation of the Lord"). Although Bede would not have had any working knowledge of Hebrew, he cites a remarkable number of church fathers, as well as Greek and Roman classics. His own numerous works, written in Latin, include commentaries on well over half of the Bible.

---

[56] A helpful source is A. Hamilton Thompson, *Bede: His Life, Times and Writing* (Oxford: Clarendon Press, 1935).

[57] Bede, *The Reckoning of Time*, trans. Faith Wallis, in Translated Texts for Historians 29 (Liverpool: Liverpool University Press, 1999). Wallis's introduction, notes, and commentary are quite helpful.

His *Commentary on Genesis* (*In Genesim*)[58] is divided into four books, with the first covering the first three chapters, including a *hexaemeron*. On Genesis 1:6–8, Bede describes the earth as a sphere and, citing Job 26:7, adds that it "hangs upon nothing." At 1:5, he says, "At this point one day is completed, namely, twenty-four hours." When he reaches 2:4, "In the day that the Lord God made the earth and the heavens," Bede admirably explains the other application of the word *day*:

> ¶ This verse should not seem to contradict the previously mentioned word of God, but it ought to be clearly understood that this Scripture uses the word *day* to mean all that time when the primordial creation was formed. . . . In its customary fashion Scripture used the word *day* for time, as the apostle did when he said, "Behold, now is the day of salvation." . . . And the prophet [Isa. 29:18] did not speak about one day specifically but about the very great season of divine grace: "In that day the deaf shall hear the words of this book."

On 2:8 (the Garden of Eden), Bede explains that some typology could be applied, but "it still must be understood in a literal sense." Later in that section, he adds, "The waters of the flood . . . covered deeply the entire surface of our world."

Thomas Aquinas (1224–74)

As a model scholastic, Aquinas labors to bridge the philosophical gap between Augustine and Aristotle. The thirteenth-century rediscovery of Aristotle's works on natural history had resulted in a flood of commentaries on the philosopher's works. There was not only the widespread acceptance of his ideas but also the growing temptation to reach first for Aristotle rather than Moses. As for Aquinas, however, on the topic of creation, rather than citing the biological opinions of Aristotle,[59] he attempts to achieve balance by citing the

---

[58] Bede, *Commentary on Genesis*: Book I, trans. Carmen S. Hardin, in a volume of the series, *Ancient Christian Texts: Commentaries on Genesis 1–3*, ed. Thomas C. Oden and Gerald L. Bray (Downers Grove, IL: InterVarsity Press, 2010). Hardin includes a valuable introduction and notes on Bede's life and work.

[59] Aquinas does not ignore Aristotle on creation. He drops in an occasional reference to the philosopher, but with little or no comment. This is not because he does not find agreement with him. Aquinas is simply trying to keep the focus on

Bible and the Fathers. Aquinas's approach is to demonstrate as much agreement as possible between Augustine's figurative days and the patristic consensus of twenty-four-hour days. Aquinas was foremost a peacemaker. It is not unusual to find him advising that both sides have the "same end results."

Neo-Platonism had supplied Augustine with his view of ultimate reality and had led him first and foremost to a conceptual and simultaneous creation. While utilizing as much as he can of Augustine's thought, even to the point of referencing Sirach (Ecclesiasticus) 18:1, Aquinas typically equivocates, always balancing the arguments on both sides in order, as he explains, to be "impartial."[60] He always protects Augustine, sometimes even obfuscating significant deviations. Medieval scholastics simply feared the appearance of any major deviation from the "master" from Hippo. It is significant that Aquinas substantiates virtually every major point with references to early patristic authors, and he especially likes the *Hexaemeron* of Basil of Caesarea. Nevertheless, Aquinas does have his own opinions, and eventually he makes it clear not only that he believes in creation *ex nihilo*,[61] as Augustine had taught, but also that he joins the patristic consensus in defending a creation week of twenty-four-hour days.

Aquinas postulates that for the initial creation day, the Genesis account uses the expression "one day" rather than "first day" in order "to denote that one day is made up of twenty-four hours. Hence, by mentioning 'one,' the measure of a natural day is fixed." There is, therefore, a succession of time and of the various things created. When asked if it were true, as Augustine had taught, that there was only one creation day, Aquinas replies that it was not one but six distinct days—twenty-four-hour days. He is careful and correct to

---

the early Fathers. On certain other topics he does not hesitate to lean heavily upon Aristotle.

[60] Thomas Aquinas, *Summa Theologica*, Prima Pars, Question 74, Article 2; cf. Question 66, Articles 1 and 2. Even though he tries to be impartial, Aquinas is consistent with traditional creationism. He speaks in a general way of a "simultaneous" creation in Gen. 1:1, but eventually explains that it was followed by six twenty-four-hour days of formation. He never applies "simultaneous" in the Augustinian fashion. All *Summa* references are from *The "Summa Theologica" of St. Thomas Aquinas*, trans. Fathers of the English Dominican Province, 22 vols. 2nd rev. ed. (London: Burns Oates & Washbourne, 1912–36).

[61] Ibid., Prima Pars, Question 46, Article 2.

attribute the idea to Basil of Caesarea, and he lends support by reinforcing Basil's explanation that from the very beginning God established the natural order of things. God created the sun to regulate an absolute standard of time for man. The movements of the heavens are designed for specific purposes in regulating the earth:

⁋ The words *one day* are used when day is first instituted, to denote that one day is made up of twenty-four hours. Hence, by mentioning *one*, the measure of a natural day is fixed. Another reason may be to signify that a day is completed by the return of the sun to the point from which it commenced its course. And yet another, because at the completion of a week of seven days, the first day returns which is one with the eighth day. The three reasons assigned above are those given by Basil. (*Hom.* ii in *Hexam.*)[62]

⁋ The general division of time into day and night took place on the first day, as regards the diurnal movement, which is common to the whole heaven and may be understood to have begun on that first day. But the particular distinctions of days and seasons and years, according as one day is hotter than another, one season than another, and one year than another, are due to certain particular movements of the stars: which movements may have had their beginning on the fourth day.[63]

⁋ We hold, then, that the movement of the heavens is twofold. Of these movements, one is common to the entire heaven, and is the cause of day and night. This, as it seems, had its beginning on the first day. The other varies in proportion as it affects various bodies, and by its variations is the cause of the succession of days, months, and years. Thus it is, that in the account of the first day the distinction between day and night alone is mentioned; this distinction being brought about by the common movement of the heavens. The further distinction into successive days, seasons, and years recorded as begun on the fourth day, in the words, *let them be for seasons, and for days, and years* is due to proper movements.[64]

---

[62] Ibid., Prima Pars, Question 74, Article 3, reply to objection 7.
[63] Ibid., Prima Pars, Question 70, Article 2, reply to objection 3.
[64] Ibid., Prima Pars, Question 67, Article 4, reply to objection 3.

An Overview of the Reformation
to the Nineteenth Century

In agreement with the patristic consensus of a young earth, Martin Luther (1483–1564) affirms that "the world was not in existence before 6,000 years ago."[65] Contrary to Augustine's view of nonliteral days, the Reformers "regarded the days of creation as six literal days."[66] Luther sharply criticizes Augustine's idea "that the world was created instantaneously and all at the same time, not successively in the course of six days. Moreover, Augustine resorts to extraordinary trifling in his treatment of the six days."[67] To Luther, each day of creation was twenty-four hours, with "evening and morning," which is "speaking of the natural day that revolves from east to west."[68] John Calvin (1509–64), attacking Augustine's "unskillful" reliance on the Latin translation of Sirach (Ecclesiasticus) 18, wrote a scathing critique of the bishop of Hippo's view:

> Here the error of those is manifestly refuted, who maintain that the world was made in a moment. For it is too violent a cavil to contend that Moses distributes the work which God perfected at once into six days, for the mere purpose of conveying instruction. Let us rather conclude that God himself took the space of six days, for the purpose of accommodating his works to the capacity of men. . . . For the confirmation of the gloss above alluded to, a passage from Ecclesiasticus is unskillfully cited. "He who liveth for ever created all things at once," (Ecclus. xviii.1.) For the Greek adverb κοινῇ, which the writer uses, means no such thing, nor does it refer to time, but to all things universally.[69]

The Irish Articles (1615)

The Irish Articles set forth a literal creation out of nothing:
> In the beginning of time, when no creature had any being, God, by his word alone, in the space of six days, created all things, and

---

[65] Martin Luther, *Lectures on Genesis, Chapters 1–5*, vol. 1 of *Luther's Works*, ed. Jaroslav Pelikan (St. Louis: Concordia, 1958), 1:3. Hereafter I will refer to this set as LW.

[66] Berkhof, 127.

[67] Martin Luther, *Lectures on Genesis, Chapters 1–5*, in LW 1:4–5.

[68] Ibid., 1:48.

[69] John Calvin, *Commentaries on the First Book of Moses Called Genesis*, vol. 1, trans. John King (Edinburgh: Calvin Translation Society, 1847–50), on 1:5.

afterwards, by his providence, doth continue, propagate, and order them according to his own will. (Article 18)

The Westminster Confession (1647)

The Westminster Confession follows the sixteenth-century Reformers in expressing creation out of nothing in the space of six days:

> It pleased God the Father, Son, and Holy Ghost, for the manifestation of the glory of his eternal power, wisdom, and goodness, in the beginning, to create, or make of nothing [*ex nihilo*] the world, and all things therein, whether visible or invisible, in the space of six days [*intra sex dierum spatium*], and all very good. After God had made all other creatures, he created man, male and female.[70]

Many others followed by repeating the same position in their own confessions, including the Baptist London Confession of 1677 (1688).[71] Similarly, the teachings of Francis Turretin (1623–87) supported six literal days, while disapproving of Augustine's nonliteral days:

> Augustine thought that creation took place not during an interval of six days, but in a single moment. . . . But there are the following objections to this opinion: (1) the simple and historical Mosaic narration, which mentions six days and ascribes a particular work to each day; (2) the earth is said to have been without form and void and darkness rested upon the face of the deep (which could not have been said if all things had been created in one moment); (3) in the fourth commandment . . . God is said to have been engaged in creation six days and to have rested on the seventh. . . . This reason would have had no weight if God had created all things in a single moment.[72]

---

[70] Westminster Confession, chapter 4, sections 1–2.

[71] London Confession of 1677 (1688), chapter 4, sections 1–2. This confession omits Westminster's *ex nihilo*, "of nothing." Perhaps the omission was because God created some things from previously created matter. For example, man was made from the dust. Evolution was not an issue. The Baptist Orthodox Creed of 1678 does include Westminster's *ex nihilo* in its article 11.

[72] Francis Turretin, *Institutes of Elenctic Theology*, trans. George Musgrave Giger and ed. James T. Dennison Jr. (Phillipsburg, NJ: P&R Publishing, 1992–97), 1:444–45.

An Overview of the Nineteenth Century to the Present

Some conservatives appealed to Augustine's idea of nonliteral days to support an accommodation to the evolutionists' long ages for the earth's existence.[73] The Scotsman James McCosh (1811–94), who became president of the College of New Jersey (Princeton) in 1868, attempted to reconcile Darwin's theories with the Bible, accepted theistic evolution, and influenced many conservative theologians.[74] At Princeton Seminary, Charles Hodge (1797–1878) made an appeal to Augustine for support in his defense of progressive creationism. Hodge had once embraced the Gap Theory but later changed to Augustine's notion of nonliteral days.[75] Misreading Augustine's teaching on creation, Hodge wrote, "There is, therefore, according to the Scriptures, not only an immediate, instantaneous creation *ex nihilo* by the simple word of God, but a mediate, progressive creation; the power of God working in union with second causes. Augustine clearly recognizes this idea." Hodge then cites a passage from Augustine's commentary on Genesis, appealing to his usage of Sirach (Ecclesiasticus) 18:1. Hodge had departed from the Reformers' teachings on the creation days,[76] but his strong opposition to raw Darwinism never ceased, as clearly demonstrated in his

---

[73] David N. Livingstone, *Darwin's Forgotten Defenders: The Encounter between Evangelical Theology and Evolutionary Thought* (Vancouver, BC: Regent College, 1984), 100–145.

[74] James McCosh, *The Religious Aspect of Evolution*, rev. ed. (New York: Charles Scribner's Sons, 1890); see also William Milligan Sloane, ed., *The Life of James McCosh* (New York: Charles Scribner's Sons, 1896), 122–24, 234. The work derives largely from autobiographical material. See also James McCosh, *Christianity and Positivism: A Series of Lectures to the Times on Natural Theology and Christian Apologetics* (London: Macmillan, 1875). McCosh gave these lectures in 1871 at Union Theological Seminary in New York.

[75] John Corrigan Wells, "Charles Hodge's Critique of Darwinism: The Argument to Design" (PhD diss., Yale University, 1986), 57–60; Wells had it published with a new subtitle and under his other first name, Jonathan Wells, *Charles Hodge's Critique of Darwinism: An Historical-Critical Analysis of Concepts Basic to the 19th Century Debate* (Lewiston, NY: Edwin Mellen, 1988).

[76] John W. Stewart, *Mediating the Center: Charles Hodge on American Science, Language, Literature, and Politics* (Princeton, NJ: Princeton Theological Seminary, 1995); and John W. Stewart and James H. Moorhead, eds., *Charles Hodge Revisited: A Critical Appraisal of His Life and Work* (Grand Rapids: Eerdmans, 2002).

answer to the question, *What Is Darwinism?* (1874). "It is atheism," concluded Hodge.[77] Other Old Princeton theologians agreed.

Benjamin B. Warfield (1851–1921), in his articles "On the Antiquity and the Unity of the Human Race" and "The Manner and Time of Man's Origin," opts to draw no chronological inferences from the genealogies of the fifth and eleventh chapters of Genesis and defends an old earth. His argument for the unity of the human race is a valuable exposure of racial pride in the institution of slavery. Warfield argues that the entire biblical structure of creation, fall, and redemption is solidly grounded in the assumption that "the race of man is one organic whole."[78] It was not his biblical position on the unity of the human race that offended many conservatives; it was his defense of an old earth.[79] For similar reasons, J. Gresham Machen (1881–1937) declined from engaging in major evolution debates of his day.[80] Unlike James McCosh, who characteristically hesitated to draw any conclusion inconsistent with theistic evolution, Hodge, Warfield, and Machen maintained that man was created—body and soul—by the special, immediate, and direct act of God.

Although their commitment to external "evidences" often resulted in contradictory and erroneous forms of expression, Hodge, Warfield, and Machen maintained their personal Reformed faith and piety, defended the inspiration and inerrancy of the original manuscripts of the Bible, and militated against the liberal unbelief of their

---

[77] Charles Hodge, *What Is Darwinism?* (New York: Scribner, Armstrong, 1874), 176–77; see also Charles Hodge, *Systematic Theology* (New York: Scribner, Armstrong, 1877), 1:557.

[78] "On the Antiquity and the Unity of the Human Race," *The Princeton Theological Review* 9, no. 1 (January 1911): 18.

[79] Ibid., 1–25; and Warfield, "The Manner and Time of Man's Origin," *The Bible Student* 8, no. 5 (November 1903): 241–52. On Gen. 5 and 11, Warfield prematurely refers the reader to his colleague, William Henry Green, "Primeval Chronology," *Bibliotheca Sacra* 47 (April 1890): 285–303. Green (1825–1900) taught Oriental and Old Testament Literature for half a century at Princeton Seminary. For a valuable compilation of sources, see Mark A. Noll and David N. Livingstone, eds., *B. B. Warfield, Evolution, Science, and Scripture: Selected Writings* (Grand Rapids: Baker, 2000).

[80] Ned B. Stonehouse, *J. Gresham Machen: A Biographical Memoir* (Grand Rapids: Eerdmans, 1954), 401–2.

day.[81] The Old Princeton men always tempered Enlightenment science with doxological science. They neither invented the doctrine of inerrancy nor gazed condescendingly upon the generations who by faith had grounded inerrancy *a priori* in Scripture alone. They believed that the Holy Spirit would work upon the minds as well as the hearts of unregenerate men. It was their trust in Scripture, not Enlightenment rationalism, that most highly motivated them. Conversely, there were evangelicals who rejected inerrancy and accepted evolutionary concepts. An early proponent of this attitude was James Orr.

The Scottish evangelical theologian and apologist James Orr (1844–1913) gave up on the inerrancy of Scripture, denied the Mosaic authorship of the Pentateuch, and closely identified with theistic evolutionists such as George Frederick Wright at Oberlin College.[82] Writing in *The Fundamentals* at the turn of the twentieth century, Orr erroneously appeals to Augustine: "One may well ask, as was done by Augustine long before geology was thought of, what kind of 'days' these were. . . . There is no violence done to the narrative in substituting in thought 'aeonic' days—vast cosmic periods—for 'days' in our narrower, sun-measured scale."[83] A decade

---

[81] For further study see Paul C. Gutjahr, *Charles Hodge: Guardian of American Orthodoxy* (Oxford: Oxford University Press, 2011); Paul Kjoss Helseth, *"Right Reason" and the Princeton Mind: An Unorthodox Proposal* (Phillipsburg, NJ: P&R Publishing, 2010); and W. Andrew Hoffecker, *Piety and the Princeton Theologians: Archibald Alexander, Charles Hodge, and Benjamin Warfield* (Grand Rapids: Baker, 1981); Owen Anderson, *Benjamin B. Warfield and Right Reason: The Clarity of General Revelation and Function of Apologetics* (Lanham, MD: University Press of America, 2005); John W. Stewart, *Mediating the Center: Charles Hodge on American Science, Language, Literature, and Politics* (Princeton, NJ: Princeton Theological Seminary, 1995); John W. Stewart and James H. Moorhead, eds., *Charles Hodge Revisited: A Critical Appraisal of His Life and Work* (Grand Rapids: Eerdmans, 2002); and Fred G. Zaspel, *The Theology of B. B. Warfield: A Systematic Summary* (Wheaton: Crossway, 2010), 369–94.

[82] See Glen G. Scorgie, *A Call for Continuity: The Theological Contribution of James Orr* (Macon, GA: Mercer University Press, 1988), 79–120 and passim.

[83] James Orr, "Science and Christian Faith," in *The Fundamentals: A Testimony to the Truth*, ed. A. C. Dixon and R. A. Torrey (Chicago: Testimony Publishing, 1910–15), 4:101. Some contributors to the set were not "fundamentalists," a designation that would not be coined until 1920. Orr had already advocated theistic evolution in his book, *The Progress of Dogma* (London: Hodder and Stoughton, 1901), 327–30. Orr had also made the appeal to Augustine in his book, *The*

later, John T. Scopes's attorney would show that William Jennings Bryan's nonliteral interpretation of the six days of Genesis 1–2 as long periods departed from the Bible as much as Scope's nonliteral teaching of evolution.[84]

The Gap Theory

The gap theory is so-called because it places a gap of time between the first two verses of Genesis:

(1) "In the beginning God created the heavens and the earth."
(2) "And the earth was without form, and void; and the darkness was upon the face of the deep. And the Spirit of God moved upon the face of the waters."

The standard version of the gap theory is also called the "Ruin-Reconstruction" theory and maintains the following: (1) Genesis 1:1 records the creation of an original earth with a pre-Adamic race. (2) There is a gap between the first two verses of Genesis that is sufficiently long to account for a pre-Adamic race and its fall, a catastrophic destruction in judgment, billions of fossils, and millions of years of geologic time. (3) Genesis 1:2 is the beginning of the account of six literal twenty-four-hour days of the re-creation of the earth including Adam and Eve. Framers of the theory were attempting to reconcile the Bible with popular claims of an old earth.

A widely used critique of the gap theory, including its history, varieties, beliefs, and personalities, is the work by Weston Fields, *Unformed and Unfilled: A Critique of the Gap Theory*. While recognizing its variety of nuances, Fields accurately summarizes the overall theory this way:

> In the far distant dateless past, God created a perfect heaven and perfect earth. Satan was ruler of the earth which was peopled by a race of "men" without any souls. Eventually, Satan, who dwelled in a Garden of Eden composed of minerals (Ezek. 28), rebelled by desiring to become like God (Isa. 14). Because of Satan's fall, sin entered the universe and brought on the earth God's judgment

---

Christian View of God and the World: As Centering in the Incarnation, 8th ed. (New York: Charles Scribner's Sons, 1907), 421.

[84] Ray Ginger, *Six Days or Forever?* (Oxford: Oxford University Press, 1958), 171–73.

in the form of a flood (indicated by the water of 1:2), and then a global ice age when the light and heat from the sun were somehow removed. All the plant, animal, and human fossils upon the earth today date from this "Lucifer's flood" and do not bear any genetic relationship with the plants, animals, and fossils living upon the earth today.[85]

While a few traces of the gap theory appear in the seventeenth and eighteenth centuries, it was G. H. Pember (1836–1910) who fully developed the view and popularized it, in his book *Earth's Earliest Ages*, first published in 1884. By 1942, it was in its fifteenth edition. Pember received the BA and MA degrees from Cambridge University. Being well read in the classics, he freely utilizes Greek mythology in his work. For instance, in his response to the traditional view that in Genesis 1:1–2 God first created the earth without its final form, being as yet unpopulated and in darkness, Pember charges that the traditional view emerged from the influence of ancient Greek mythology on the church, beginning with the earliest church fathers and continuing to the present. In Greek creation mythology, as taught by Hesiod, everything originated in primordial darkness and without form. Pember insists that Genesis 1:1 describes a complete and perfect creation and verse 2 describes the beginning of a re-creation with the Spirit of God moving upon the face of the waters. Millions of years and a great catastrophic judgment occurred between those two verses, and in the gap are the answers to all "geological difficulties."[86]

The publication of *The Scofield Reference Bible* by Oxford University Press in 1909 (rev. 1917)[87] led the way in disseminating the gap theory. Between the first two verses of Genesis, C. I. Scofield (1843–1921) inserted his note: *Earth made waste and empty by judgment (Jer. 4:23–26)*. His note on verse 2 explains:

---

[85] Weston Fields, *Unformed and Unfilled: A Critique of the Gap Theory* (1976; repr., Green Forest, AR: Master Books, 2005), 13.

[86] G. H. Pember, *Earth's Earliest Ages and Their Connection with the Modern Spiritualism and Theosophy* (London: Hodder and Stoughton, 1884), 19–21.

[87] Oxford University Press continues to publish the 1917 edition of Scofield's notes without changes other than the new titles, *The Scofield Study Bible* and *The Old Scofield Study Bible*. Oxford also continues to publish the 1967 *New Scofield Study Bible*.

Jer. 4:23–26, Isa. 24:1 and 45:18 clearly indicate that the earth had undergone a cataclysmic change as the result of a divine judgment. The face of the earth bears everywhere the marks of such a catastrophe. There are not wanting intimations which connect it with a previous testing and fall of angels. See Ezk. 28:12–15 and Isa. 14:9–14, which certainly go beyond the kings of Tyre and Babylon.

Scofield's note on verse 11 aims to sever all doubt: "Relegate fossils to the primitive creation, and no conflict of science with the Genesis cosmogony remains."

In 1967, Oxford University Press published *The New Scofield Study Bible*. Its notes on Genesis 1 scarcely mention the gap theory, but the view is clearly expressed in the notes for Isaiah 45:18. The editors refer to the gap theory as the "Divine Judgment interpretation." E. Schuyler English chaired the editorial committee, whose eight additional men included Alva J. McClain of Grace Theological Seminary and John F. Walvoord of Dallas Theological Seminary. The chairman, however, in his short *Companion to the New Scofield Reference Bible* (1972), reveals a positive attitude towards the long-day view and an old earth: "The days of creation might have been days of twenty-four hours each or they could have been aeons in duration. (Among earnest Christians both views are held.)"[88] Evangelist Harry Rimmer (1890–1952), in his work, *Modern Science and the Genesis Record* (1937), defended the gap theory. Ronald Numbers has shown that Rimmer was equally certain that the flood in Noah's day was just a local affair.[89] Canadian physiologist, Arthur C. Custance (1910–85), in his work *Without Form and Void: A Study of the Meaning of Genesis 1:2*,[90] represents the most exhaustive defense of the gap theory. The most reckless defense is from the controversial Pentecostal evangelist Finis Jennings Dake (1902–87). The Assemblies of God

---

[88] E. Schuyler English, *Companion to the New Scofield Reference Bible* (Oxford University Press, 1972), 50.

[89] *The Creationists* (Berkeley: University of California Press, 1993), 67–68. Rimmer said that he had taught the day-age theory before embracing the gap theory. Apparently he never changed his mind on the extent of the flood. Rimmer could entertain the crowds, and he never turned down a debate, but the former prizefighter was not the best among biblical scholars.

[90] A. C. Custance, *Without Form and Void* (Brookville, Canada: published by the author, 1970).

ordained Dake but later revoked the ordination due to controversies over various moral issues. He joined the Church of God (Cleveland, Tennessee), but at the time of his death he was denominationally unaffiliated. *Dake's Annotated Reference Bible* defends the gap theory and claims that "when men finally agree on the age of the earth, then place the many years (over the historical 6,000) between Genesis 1:1 and 1:2, there will be no conflict between the Book of Genesis and science."[91]

Critics of the gap theory argue that it is contradictory to other Scripture to place the fall of Satan into the supposed gap. They see Exodus 20:11 as including all the angels in the original creation and Colossians 1 as supportive. In Genesis 1:31, God declares "everything" that He had created as "very good." There could have been no rebellion before this time. Satan and the angels that followed him must have fallen sometime after day seven but prior to the fall of Adam and Eve.[92] The Bible does not record the time or precise sequence of the angelic apostasy. In addition to scientific reasons, the strongest arguments against the gap theory are textual, and they appear in works whose authors include Weston Fields, Henry Morris, John Morris, and Paul F. Taylor.[93]

Conclusion

It is not until the nineteenth century that we find departures from the conviction that God created *ex nihilo* the heavens and the

---

[91] Finis Jennings Dake, *Dake's Annotated Reference Bible*, (Lawrenceville, GA: Dake Bible Sales, 1961), 51. This reference Bible is sometimes mistakenly marketed as "fundamentalist" in its "theological perspective." To the contrary, the reckless notes and extreme Arminianism do not represent fundamentalism as a movement. Indeed, it would be quite unusual to find a *Dake Annotated Reference Bible* in any typical fundamentalist gathering.

[92] See http://www.answersingenesis.org/articles/nab/gap-ruin-reconstruction-theories.

[93] Fields, *Unformed and Unfilled*; Paul F. Taylor, *The Six Days of Genesis: A Scientific Appreciation of Chapters 1–11* (Green Forest, AR: Master Books, 2007); John Morris, *The Young Earth: The Real History of the Earth—Past, Present, and Future*, rev. and expanded (Green Forest, AR: Master Books, 2008); P. J. Wiseman, *Creation Revealed in Six Days* (London: Marshall, Morgan and Scott, 1948), 23–27; O. T. Allis, *God Spake by Moses* (1951; repr., Philadelphia: Presbyterian Reformed, 1979), 153–59; and Henry Morris, *The Genesis Record* (Grand Rapids: Baker, 1987).

earth. Only three church fathers—Clement and Origen of Alexandria and Augustine of Hippo—held to allegorical days of creation, and all three insisted on a young earth. No church father denies a young earth, and many of them provide specific years or spans of time to demonstrate the earth's young age. The same conviction continues through the Reformation era and into the modern era. In the wake of the publication of Darwin's evolutionary hypothesis, aberrant systems such as long-day creation, the gap theory, and progressive or theistic creation began making inroads into Christian schools and churches.

Exodus 20:10–11 says, "The seventh day is the sabbath of the Lord thy God: in it thou shalt not do any work, . . . for in six days the Lord made heaven and earth, the sea, and all that in them is, and rested the seventh day: wherefore the Lord blessed the sabbath day, and hallowed it." To conservatives today, this means that God created the earth and everything in it in six literal days and rested on the seventh day.

Select Bibliography for Further Reading

Defenses of Creationism

Brown, Walt. *In the Beginning: Compelling Evidence for Creation and the Flood*. 8th ed. Phoenix: Center for Scientific Creation, 2008.

Ham, Ken, et al. *Already Compromised*. Green Forest, AR: Master Books, 2011.

Kelly, Douglas F. *Creation and Change: Genesis 1.1–2.4 in the Light of Changing Scientific Paradigms*. Geanies House, Fearn, Ross-shire, Scotland, UK: Mentor, 1997.

Lisle, Jason. "Distant Starlight—the Anisotropic Synchrony Convention." *Answers* 6, no. 1 (January–March 2011): 68–71. This is a publication of Answers in Genesis.

McCabe, Robert V. "A Defense of Literal Days in the Creation Week." *Detroit Baptist Seminary Journal* 5 (Fall 2000): 97–123.

MacArthur, John. *The Battle for the Beginning: Creation, Evolution, and the Bible*. Nashville: Thomas Nelson, 2001.

Morris, Henry M. *The Biblical Basis for Modern Science*. Green Forest, AR: Master Books, 2002.

———. *Biblical Creationism*. Green Forest, AR: Master Books, 2000.

———. *The Long War against God*. Green Forest, AR: Master Books, 2000.

———, and John C. Whitcomb. *The Genesis Flood: The Biblical Record and Its Scientific Implications*. Philadelphia: Presbyterian and Reformed, 1961.

Morris, John. *The Young Earth: The Real History of the Earth—Past, Present, and Future*. Rev. ed. Green Forest, AR: Master Books, 2008.

Mortenson, Terry. *The Great Turning Point: The Church's Catastrophic Mistake on Geology—After Darwin.* Green Forest, AR: Master Books, 2004.

———. "Jesus, Evangelical Scholars, and the Age of the Earth." *The Master's Seminary Journal* 18, no. 1 (Spring 2007): 69–98.

———, and Thane H. Ury, eds. *Coming to Grips with Genesis: Biblical Authority and the Age of the Earth.* Green Forest, AR: Master Books, 2009.

Pipa, Joseph A., Jr., and David W. Hall, eds. *Did God Create in Six Days?* Taylors, SC: Southern Presbyterian Press, 1999.

Sarfati, Jonathan. *Refuting Compromise: A Biblical and Scientific Refutation of Progressive Creationism (Billions of Years), as Popularized by Astronomer Hugh Ross.* Green Forest, AR: Master Books, 2004.

Snelling, Andrew A. *Earth's Catastrophic Past: Geology, Creation, and the Flood.* 2 vols. Dallas: Institute for Creation Research, 2009.

Taylor, Paul F. *The Six Days of Genesis: A Scientific Appreciation of Chapters 1–11.* Green Forest, AR: Master Books, 2007.

General Works

Augustine. *On Genesis: A Refutation of the Manichees; Unfinished Literal Commentary on Genesis; and The Literal Meaning of Genesis.* Translated by Edmond Hill and edited by John E. Rotelle. I/13 of *The Works of Saint Augustine.* Hyde Park, NY: New City Press, 2002.

———. *The Literal Meaning of Genesis.* Vol. 1: Books 1–6. Translated by John Hammond Taylor. Vol. 41 of *Ancient Christian Writers*, edited by Johannes Quasten, et al. New York: Paulist Press, 1982.

———. *The Literal Meaning of Genesis.* Vol. 2: Books 7–12. Translated by John Hammond Taylor. Vol. 42 of *Ancient Christian Writers*, edited by Johannes Quasten, et al. New York: Newman Press, 1982.

Bede the Venerable. *Commentary on Genesis: Book I.* Translated by Carmen S. Hardin. A volume in the series, *Ancient Christian Texts: Commentaries in Genesis 1–3*, edited by Thomas C. Oden and Gerald L. Bray. Downers Grove, IL: InterVarsity, 2010.

———. *The Reckoning of Time.* Translated by Faith Wallis. In Translated Texts for Historians 29. Liverpool: Liverpool University Press, 1999.

Ehrhardt, Arnold. *The Beginning: A Study in the Greek Philosophical Approach to the Concept of Creation from Anaximander to St. John.* Manchester: Manchester University Press, 1968.

Goudge, Thomas A. "Evolutionism." In *Dictionary of the History of Ideas: Studies in Selected Pivotal Ideas*, 5 vols. edited by Philip P. Weiner, 2:174–89. New York: Charles Scribner's Sons, 1973–74.

Lewis, Jack P. "The Days of Creation: An Historical Survey of Interpretation." *Journal of the Evangelical Theological Society* 32, no. 4 (December 1989): 433–55.

———. "Noah and the Flood: In Jewish, Christian, and Muslim Tradition." *The Biblical Archaeologist* 47, no. 4 (December 1984): 224–39.

———. *A Study of the Interpretation of Noah and the Flood in Jewish and Christian Literature.* 1968. Reprint, Leiden: E. J. Brill, 1978.

Livingstone, David N. *Darwin's Forgotten Defenders: The Encounter between Evangelical Theology and Evolutionary Thought.* Vancouver, BC: Regent College, 1984.

Thompson, A. Hamilton. *Bede: His Life, Times and Writing.* Oxford: Clarendon Press, 1935.

Van Till, Howard J. "Basil, Augustine, and the Doctrine of Creation's Functional Integrity." *Science and Christian Belief* 8 (1996): 21–38.

Wolfson, Harry A. "Patristic Arguments against the Eternity of the World." *The Harvard Theological Review* 59, no. 4 (October 1966): 351–67.

Index